# Research and Development in Intelligent Systems XIX

Springer
*London*
*Berlin*
*Heidelberg*
*New York*
*Hong Kong*
*Milan*
*Paris*
*Tokyo*

Max Bramer, Alun Preece and Frans Coenen (Eds)

# Research and Development in Intelligent Systems XIX

## Proceedings of ES2002, the Twenty-second SGAI International Conference on Knowledge Based Systems and Applied Artificial Intelligence

Professor Max Bramer, BSc, PhD, CEng, FBCS, FIEE, FRSA
Faculty of Technology, University of Portsmouth, Portsmouth, UK

Alun Preece
University of Aberdeen, Dept of Computer Science, Aberdeen, UK

Dr Frans Coenen
Department of Computer Science, University of Liverpool, Liverpool, UK

British Library Cataloguing in Publication Data
SGAI International Conference on Knowledge Based Systems
and Applied Artificial Intelligence (22nd)
Research and development in intelligent systems XIX :
Proceedings of ES2002, the twenty-second SGAI International
Conference on Knowledge Based Systems and Applied
Artificial Intelligence. - (BCS conference series)
1.Expert systems (Computer science) - Congresses
2.Intelligent control systems - Congresses
I.Title II.Bramer, M. A. (Max A.), 1948- III.Preece, Alun,
1968- IV.Coenen, Frans V.British Computer Society.
Specialist Group on Expert Systems
006.3'3
ISBN 1852336749

Library of Congress Cataloging-in-Publication Data
A catalog record for this book is available from the Library of Congress



ISBN 1-85233-674-9 Springer-Verlag London Berlin Heidelberg
a member of BertelsmannSpringer Science+Business Media GmbH
http://www.springer.co.uk


Printed in Great Britain



Typesetting: Camera-ready by editors
Printed and bound at the Athenæum Press Ltd., Gateshead, Tyne & Wear
34/3830-543210 Printed on acid-free paper SPIN 10886204

# TECHNICAL PROGRAMME CHAIRMAN'S INTRODUCTION

**M.A.BRAMER**
University of Portsmouth, UK

This volume comprises the refereed technical papers presented at ES2002, the Twenty-second SGAI International Conference on Knowledge Based Systems and Applied Artificial Intelligence, held in Cambridge in December 2002. The conference was organised by SGAI, the British Computer Society Specialist Group on Artificial Intelligence (previously known as SGES).

The papers in this volume present new and innovative developments in the field, divided into sections on Machine Learning, Knowledge Representation and Reasoning, Knowledge Acquisition, Constraint Satisfaction, Scheduling and Natural Language Processing.

This year's prize for the best refereed technical paper was won by a paper entitled *Covering the Path Space: A Casebase Analysis for Mobile Robot Path Planning* by M Kruusmaa (Department of Mechatronics, Tallinn Technical University, Estonia) and J Willemson (Department of Computer Science, Tartu University, Estonia). SGAI gratefully acknowledges the long-term sponsorship of Hewlett-Packard Laboratories (Bristol) for this prize, which goes back to the 1980s.

This is the nineteenth volume in the *Research and Development* series. The Application Stream papers are published as a companion volume under the title *Applications and Innovations in Intelligent Systems X*.

On behalf of the conference organising committee I should like to thank all those who contributed to the organisation of this year's technical programme, in particular the programme committee members, the referees and our administrators Linsay Turbert and Helen Forster.

Max Bramer
Technical Programme Chairman, ES2002

# ACKNOWLEDGEMENTS

### ES2002 CONFERENCE COMMITTEE

Dr Frans Coenen, University of Liverpool (Conference Chairman)
Dr Robert Milne, Sermatech Intelligent Applications Ltd (Deputy Conference Chairman, Finance and Publicity)
Dr Nirmalie Wiratunga (Deputy Conference Chair, Poster Session)
Prof. Adrian Hopgood, Nottingham Trent University (Tutorial Organiser)
Ann Macintosh, Napier University (Application Programme Chair)
Richard Ellis, Stratum Management Ltd (Deputy Application Programme Chair and Exhibition Organiser)
Professor Max Bramer, University of Portsmouth (Technical Programme Chair)
Dr. Alun Preece, University of Aberdeen (Deputy Technical Programme Chair)

### TECHNICAL PROGRAMME COMMITTEE

Prof. Max Bramer, University of Portsmouth (Chair)
Dr. Alun Preece, University of Aberdeen (Vice-Chair)
Dr. Frans Coenen, University of Liverpool
Prof. Adrian Hopgood, Nottingham Trent University
Mr. John Kingston, University of Edinburgh
Dr. Nirmalie Wiratunga, Robert Gordon University, Aberdeen

### TECHNICAL PROGRAMME REFEREES

Belen Diaz Agudo (Complutense University of Madrid)
Samir Aknine (University of Paris 6)
Andreas Albrecht (University of Hertfordshire)
Daniel Allsopp (Cranfield University)
Yaxin Bi (University of Edinburgh)
Arkady Borisov (Riga Technical University)
Max Bramer (University of Portsmouth)
Frans Coenen (University of Liverpool)
Bruno Cremilleux (University of Caen)
John Debenham (University of Technology, Sydney)
Mercedes Gomez-Albarran ( University Complutense, Madrid)
Anne Håkansson (Sweden)
Mark Hall (University of Waikato)
Eveline M. Helsper (Utrecht University, The Netherlands)
Ray Hickey (University of Ulster)
Adrian Hopgood (Nottingham Trent University)
John Kingston (University of Edinburgh)
Thorsten Kurz (University of Neuchâtel, Switzerland)
Peter Lane (University of Nottingham)

Brian Lees (University of Paisley)
Hui Liu (Brunel University)
Peter Lucas (University of Aberdeen)
David McSherry (University of Ulster)
Daniel Manrique (Campus de Montegancedo, Madrid)
Robert Milne (Sermatech Intelligent Applications, Scotland)
Lars Nolle (Nottingham Trent University)
Alun Preece (University of Aberdeen)
Paul Roach (University of Glamorgan)
María Dolores Rodríguez-Moreno (Universidad de Alcalá, Madrid)
Damian Ryan (Queen Mary, University of London)
Miguel A. Salido ( Universidad Politecnica de Valencia, Spain)
Barry Smyth (University College, Dublin)
Kilian Stoffel (University of Neuchatel)
Jonathan Timmis (University of Kent)
Kai Ming Ting (Monash University, Australia)
Ian Watson (University of Auckland, New Zealand)
Nirmalie Wiratunga (Robert Gordon University, Aberdeen)
John Yearwood (University of Ballarat)

# CONTENTS

## BEST REFEREED TECHNICAL PAPER



## SESSION 1A: MACHINE LEARNING 1



## SESSION 1B: KNOWLEDGE REPRESENTATION AND REASONING 1



## SESSION 2A: MACHINE LEARNING 2

## SESSION 2B: KNOWLEDGE REPRESENTATION AND REASONING 2



## SESSION 3A: KNOWLEDGE ACQUISITION

## SESSION 3B: KNOWLEDGE REPRESENTATION AND REASONING 3



## SESSION 4: CONSTRAINT SATISFACTION AND SCHEDULING



## SESSION 5: NATURAL LANGUAGE PROCESSING

# BEST REFEREED TECHINCAL PAPER

# Covering the Path Space: A Casebase Analysis for Mobile Robot Path Planning

Maarja Kruusmaa
Tallinn Technical University
Dept. of Mechatronics
Ehitajate tee 5, Tallinn, Estonia

Jan Willemson
Tartu University
Dept. of Computer Science
Liivi 2, Tartu, Estonia

**Abstract**

This paper presents a theoretical analysis of a casebase used for mobile robot path planning in dynamic environments. Unlike other case-based path planning approaches, we use a grid map to represent the environment that permits the robot to operate in unstructured environments. The objective of the mobile robot is to learn to choose paths that are less risky to follow. Our experiments with real robots have shown the efficiency of our concept. In this paper, we replace a heuristic path planning algorithm of the mobile robot with a seed casebase and prove the upper and lower bounds for the cardinality of the casebase. The proofs indicate that it is realistic to seed the casebase with some solutions to a path-finding problem so that no possible solution differs too much from some path in the casebase. This guarantees that the robot would theoretically find all paths from start to goal. The proof of the upper bound of the casebase cardinality shows that the casebase would in a long run grow too large and all possible solutions cannot be stored. In order to keep only the most efficient solutions the casebase has to be revised at run-time or some other measure of path difference has to be considered.

**Keywords.** Case-based reasoning, path planning, covering in metric spaces

## 1 Introduction

The work presented in this paper is a theoretical extension of a research in mobile robotics. We investigate the problem of generating a seed casebase to cover the solution space of a mobile robot. In our earlier work we have implemented a case-based reasoning approach to mobile robot path planning and tested it on real robots [1]. In this work we prove the theoretical upper and lower bound of the casebase to show the feasibility and limitations of our approach.

The rest of this paper is organised as follows. In the next subsection we give an insight to the field of robot navigation and explain the relevance of the problem. Section 2 describes our approach and reviews our previous experimental results. In Section 3 we give the basic definitions and state the main robot path space covering problem in Section 4. Sections 5 and 6 prove (exact) lower and upper bounds, respectively, for the stated covering problem. Section 7 compares the old heuristic approach to the new one presented in the current paper. Section 8 draws some conclusions and discusses the future work.

### Motivation

Our work is motivated by the fact that most of mobile robot applications imply repeated traversal in a changing environment between predefined start and goal points. For example, a mobile robot could be used to transport details and sub-assemblies between a store and production lines. This task implies repeated traversal between the store and the production cells. A mobile robot can also be used for surveillance. This task implies visiting certain checkpoints on a closed territory in a predefined order.

Real environments where these kind of mobile robots have to operate are dynamic by nature. From the point of view of mobile robot navigation, it means that unexpected obstacles can appear and disappear. The nature and density of the obstacles is usually unknown or too difficult to model.

At the same time a mobile robot in a dynamic environment has to fulfill its assignment as fast and safely as possible. This means choosing paths between target points that are most likely unblocked and where the robot does not spend too much time maneuvering between obstacles.

Very few research studies reported so far consider this problem of path selection [2, 3]. Unlike these approaches, we do not assume that the structure of the environment is known a priori. Therefore our approach is applicable also in cases where very little is known about the environment and where the structure of the environment may change.

## 2 System Description

Our approach to mobile robot path selection consists of a general world model and of a memory that stores the path traveling experiences for later use. The memory is a casebase. The casebase stores the paths traversed in the past in a form of cases.

The world model is a map that permits path planning. Since in a dynamic environment the robot is not able to model all the aspects of its surrounding, the map is always more or less imprecise.

Figure 1 captures the bottom line of this approach. The global planner receives tasks from the user. The tasks are requests to move to a specific point from its present location. The global planner has a map of the environment that represents only the very general geometry of the environment and the locations of the target points. The presence and location of dynamic obstacles in the environment are unknown. Given a new task, the global planner can either find a new solution by using a map-based path planner or re-use one of the earlier found paths from the casebase. The path planned by the global planner is presented to the low-level planning and execution unit that is responsible for task decomposition (if necessary), replanning, localisation, sensor data processing and actuator control.

The objective of the global planner is to choose the best travel path according to some criterion (e.g. time, distance, safety). Case-based reasoning permits the robot to remember and learn from its past experiences. The robot will adapt to the changes in the dynamic environment and learn to use paths that are better.

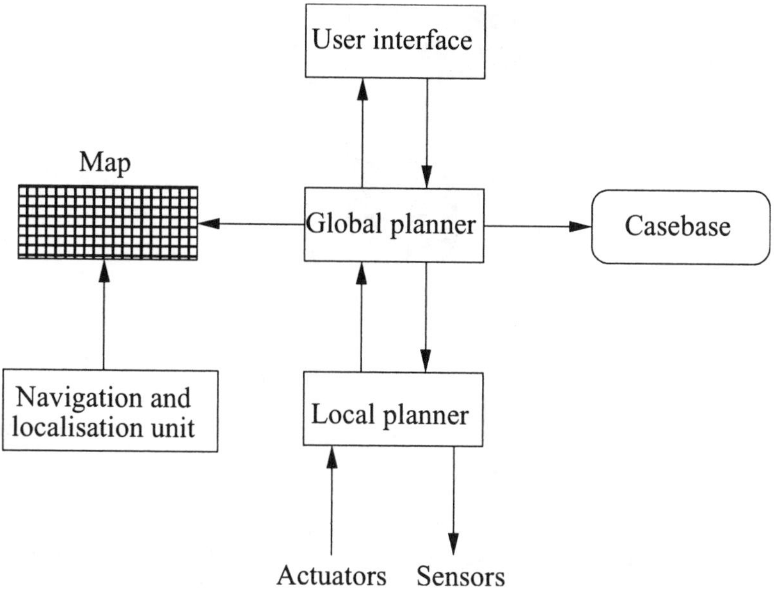


Figure 1: General overview of path planning

## 2.1 Case-based Reasoning

Case-based reasoning (CBR) solves new problems by adapting previously successful solutions to similar problems. The past experiences are stored in a casebase which is managed by applying database techniques. To facilitate the case retrieval the cases in a casebase are indexed. When a new problem occurs, the indices are extracted from its features and used to find matching cases in a casebase. If more than one matching case is found the candidate cases are evaluated to find the most suitable one.

Unless the retrieved case is a close match, the solution will probably have to be modified before using it for problem solving. If the modified case is found to be successful, it produces a new case which is stored in a casebase. Thus, in case-based reasoning, learning is through accumulation of new cases.

In the approach described in this paper, the problem is to find the best path from a given starting point to a given goal. The solution to the problem is a path to that goal. The outcome of the solution is the cost of the path that reflects how easy it was to follow that path. If the robot traverses a path repeatedly, the cost of the path is updated after every traversal. The cost will then reflect the average characteristics of that path. By choosing the path with the lowest cost, the robot can reduce collision risk and minimise travel distance.

Path planning by means of CBR is described in [4, 5, 6, 7]. These approaches are used for planning in static environments. PRODIGY/ANALOGY uses CBR for dynamic path planning in the city of Pittsburgh [8]. Unlike these studies our study

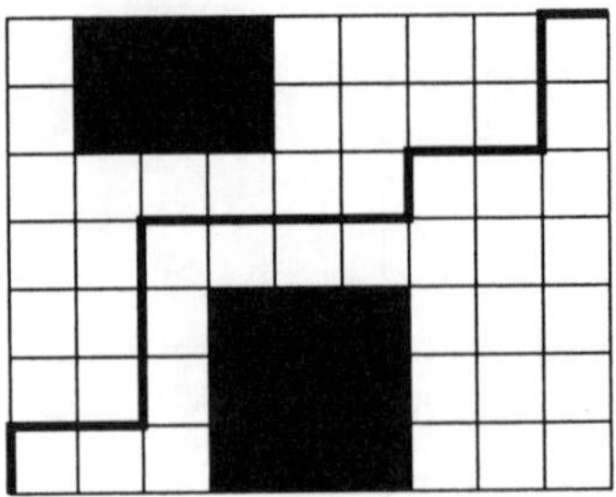

Figure 2: A grid map

does not use a graph-based map for path planning but a grid map that permits more detailed path planning, offers more alternatives to path-find problems and does not presume a rigid structure of the environment.

Since there can be several alternative paths between given target points, every problem in the casebase can have several solutions. To find the most similar problem from the casebase we use the nearest neighbor retrieval. i.e. the robot will look for a case where the start and goal points are as close as possible to the current problem.

However, to analyse our casebase, we assume that our casebase consists of only one problem having many solutions. This will be the problem having the greatest number of possible solutions, namely, the problem of traversing between the diagonally opposite corners. It follows from our problem formalisation that all other path planning problems are subproblems of this most general one. Our objective is to seed the casebase with all different solutions to the current problem according to our similarity measure.

## 2.2 Path Planning

In the context of mobile robotics, path planning means finding a collision-free path from start to goal. The method of path planning depends on the world model of the robot (see e.g. [9] for an overview of intelligent robotics and path planning techniques).

In this work we use a common world representation in mobile robotics – a grid map. A grid map represents the world as a grid of small cells. Some cells that are known to contain static obstacles can be marked as occupied. In our previous work we have developed a modification of a heuristic algorithm that due to random perturbations on the map generates many alternative solutions to a single find-path problem.

Figure 2 shows a grid map. Black cells on the map represent static obstacles. The paths form start to goal are generated with our heuristic algorithm.

There are two problems associated with our method of path generation. First, it cannot be guaranteed that it would theoretically find all the possible paths from the given start to the given goal.

Second, even on a relatively small grid the amount of different paths between specified target points is overwhelming. At the same time most of the paths differ form each other only by a very small amount. To overcome this problem, we have defined a similarity metrics (see Section 3). With the help of similarity metrics we can treat paths that differ very little to be the same.

The paths that the robot has followed are stored in the casebase. We here take an advantage of our similarity metrics and store only cases (e.g. paths) that are different from each other. This remarkably reduces the size of the casebase.

In our experiments we have started with an empty casebase. If a necessary solution is not in the casebase or its quality is not good enough, a new solution can be generated using map-based path planning. We have tested our approach intensively both in simulated environments and with real robots. The tests show that the robot is very quickly able to adapt to the changes in the environment and learn to use less risky paths. All the tests indicate that the size of the casebase is very small even if the environment is large.

However, the tests also point to the shortcomings of our approach. Our path planning algorithm modifies the map to generate new random solutions. During the tests it was observed that many paths that the algorithm generates are very similar to each other. The robot spent much time waiting for a different solution to be found. It also appeared that sometimes the robot got trapped to the local minima – some paths that would have been easy to follow where never generated.

## 2.3 Seeding the Casebase

To overcome these disadvantages of our current implementation we investigate the possibility to seed the robot's casebase with all possible solutions to the current problem. Theoretically, the amount of possible paths from a given start to a given goal is enormous. Many of them differ from each other only by a very small amount and most of them are infeasible from the point of view of path following (i.e. unnecessarily crooked or long). We therefore have constrained the set of paths that are used in the casebase.

To justify our constraints we have to explain some details of robot path following. In a real life, a robot is never able to follow precisely the path that it has planned. It will always drift away form its course because of localisation errors, sensor noise and imprecision of mechanical linkages. In dynamic environments, it also has to drive around unexpected obstacles. The latter can significantly deviate the robot from its course. Therefore our similarity metrics is based on the deviation of paths. We consider paths that deviate much from each other to be different. On the contrary, paths that lead through the approximately same regions of the map are similar. Our similarity metrics is defined in the next section.

Mobile robots use obstacle avoidance routines and run-time re-planning to negotiate dynamic obstacles. In our experiments with real robots we have observed that the planned path and the eventually followed path often differ significantly because re-planning around obstacles and localisation errors sometimes lead the robot in a completely other direction than it was heading first. We therefore found that the most practical measure of the traversability of a path is the similarity between the planned and the actually followed path. The better the robot was able to follow the path that it planned the better the path is. The secondary measure that we have used to evaluate paths is the time of path following. This measure is also very practical because mobile robots are normally expected to fulfill their assignment as fast as possible.

It therefore seems to be feasible to seed the casebase with paths that are rather short and straight. These paths are most likely to satisfy our criteria of good traversability. Short paths are most likely to lead the robot faster to the goal. Too curved paths are technically too hard to follow (and therefore it also takes longer time to reach the goal). We have therefore constrained our set of paths to those allowing only right and up moves. It will exclude all the unnecessarily long and complex paths (actually all paths having back turns).

The drawback of this condition is that the robot would not operate efficiently in a maze-like environment. However, most of real environments are not mazes. Another shortcoming, though not so severe, is the occurrence of the zigzagged paths since we allow only up and right moves. This is typical to all grid-based path planning methods and mobile robots usually use path relaxation techniques to smoothen the path at run-time.

In the rest of the paper we address two problems of casebase management. The first question is whether it is possible to seed the casebase with a relatively low number of different cases so that the whole solution space will be covered. The answer to this question is affirmative.

The second question is whether it is possible to run the system without managing the casebase. For instance, the robot may generate the potential solutions randomly with the only condition that the paths in the casebase should not be too similar. The answer to this question is negative. The maximal number of different solutions may become too high, the casebase grows too large and the robot looses its ability to manage the whole base. Therefore, less useful solutions have to be forgotten. In the next sections we will formalise the problem, define a similarity metrics and prove lower and upper bounds for the cardinality of the casebase.

## 3 Basic Definitions

Let $[a, b]$, $a \leq b \in \mathbb{Z}$ denote the set $\{a, a+1, \ldots, b\}$. We will consider a robot moving on a rectangular grid $[0, m] \times [0, n]$ allowing only right and up moves. The robot starts from the point $(0, 0)$ (which we consider to be the lower left corner of the grid) and it must reach the point $(m, n)$.

**Definition 1** *By a* path *on the grid* $[0, m] \times [0, n]$ *we mean a sequence of grid points*

$$((x_0, y_0), (x_1, y_1), \ldots, (x_{m+n}, y_{m+n}))$$

*such that*

1. $x_0 = y_0 = 0$, $x_{m+n} = m$, $y_{m+n} = n$;

2. *for each* $i \in [0, m+n-1]$, *the condition*

$$(x_i = x_{i+1} \;\&\; y_i + 1 = y_{i+1}) \vee (x_i + 1 = x_{i+1} \;\&\; y_i = y_{i+1})$$

*holds.*

*The set of all paths on the grid is denoted by* $\mathcal{P}_{m,n}$

Next we define a notion of similarity between the paths. Intuitively speaking, we say that two paths taken by a robot are similar if they do not diverge from each other too much. In order to express this idea, we need to define an appropriate distance measure first. There are several possibilities for such a definition, in this paper we use the following one.

**Definition 2** *We say that the* grid distance *between a point* $c_1 \in [0,m] \times [0,n]$ *and a path* $P_2 \in \mathcal{P}_{m,n}$ *is the quantity*

$$d_g(c_1, P_2) = \min_{c_2 \in P_2} \{d(c_1, c_2)\}$$

*where* $d(c_1, c_2)$ *denotes the* $\mathbb{R}^2_\infty$*-distance between the points* $c_1$ *and* $c_2$*, i.e.* $d(c_1, c_2) = \max\{|x_1 - x_2|, |y_1 - y_2|\}$*, where* $c_1 = (x_1, y_1)$ *and* $c_2 = (x_2, y_2)$*.*

*By* grid distance *of the paths* $P_1, P_2 \in \mathcal{P}_{m,n}$ *we mean the quantity*

$$d_g(P_1, P_2) = \max_{c_1 \in P_1} \{d_g(c_1, P_2)\}.$$

The maxmin construction of $d_g$ is generally known as *directed Hausdorff distance* (see e.g. [10]). It is not the case that for any inner metrics $d$ the directed Hausdorff distance is a real distance since it mostly fails to be symmetric; such a problem occurs, for instance, if $d$ is the Euclidean distance. Several approaches can be taken in order to fix the problem, most commonly one replaces the directed distance by $\max\{d_g(P_1, P_2), d_g(P_2, P_1)\}$ [10] or even $d_g(P_1, P_2) + d_g(P_2, P_1)$ [11].

In this paper, however, we show that for our very special choice of base set and inner metrics, the directed Hausdorff distance gives rise to a real distance.[1]

**Lemma 1** *The pair* $(\mathcal{P}_{m,n}, d_g)$ *is a metric space.*

Proof. First we note that $d_g(P_1, P_2)$ is always a non-negative integer. The identity and triangle inequality axioms of metric space are easy to check (in fact, they hold for every directed Hausdorff distance).

In order to prove symmetry, we first prove that the following assertion holds true for every two paths $P_1, P_2 \in \mathcal{P}_{m,n}$:

$$\forall c_1 \in P_1 \, \exists c_2 \in P_2 \, [d_g(c_1, P_2) = d_g(c_2, P_1)]. \tag{1}$$

Take a point $c_1 \in P_1$. Note first that if $c_1 \in P_2$, then we have $d_g(c_1, P_2) = 0$ and we can take $c_2 = c_1$ to satisfy (1).

If $c_1 \notin P_2$, then assume w.l.o.g. that the path $P_2$ runs above the the point $c_1$. Take the closed ball $B$ with center $c_1$ and radius $d_g(c_1, P_2)$ in metric space $([0,m] \times [0,n], d)$ where $d$ is the $\mathbb{R}^2_\infty$-distance as in Definition 2. (Note that this

[1] One may argue that the Euclidean $\mathbb{R}^2$ metric is better suited for practical purposes than the $\mathbb{R}^2_\infty$ metric. On the other hand, we feel that working on the (in fact discrete) grid, the $\mathbb{R}^2_\infty$ metric is actually more natural. Besides that, the norms corresponding to the two distance measures are equivalent and do not differ more than $\sqrt{2}$ times.

ball actually looks like a square with edge length $2d_g(c_1, P_2)$ and center $c_1$.) We see from Definition 2 that no interior point of $B$ belongs to the path $P_2$, but some of the boundary points do. In particular, the upper left corner of $B$ must always belong to $P_2$. Now taking this point as $c_2$ we see that no point of $P_1$ can be closer to $c_2$ than $c_1$ is, hence $d_g(c_1, P_2) = d_g(c_2, P_1)$ as was required to prove (1).

Now let $\bar{c}_1 \in P_1$ be such a point that $d_g(\bar{c}_1, P_2) = \max_{c_1 \in P_1} \{d_g(c_1, P_2)\}$. Then by (1) we can choose a point $\bar{c}_2 \in P_2$ such that $d_g(\bar{c}_1, P_2) = d_g(\bar{c}_2, P_1)$. Thus

$$d_g(P_1, P_2) = d_g(\bar{c}_1, P_2) = d_g(\bar{c}_2, P_1) \leq \max_{c_2 \in P_2} \{d_g(c_2, P_1)\} = d_g(P_2, P_1).$$

Similarly we prove that $d_g(P_2, P_1) \leq d_g(P_1, P_2)$ and hence $d_g(P_1, P_2) = d_g(P_2, P_1)$. □

In the light of Lemma 1, the next definition is just a utilisation of a standard definition of a (closed) ball in metric space.

**Definition 3** *By a* ball *with center $P$ and radius $\delta$ in the space $(\mathcal{P}_{m,n}, d_g)$ we mean the set*

$$B(P, \delta) = \{P' \in \mathcal{P}_{m,n} : \ d_g(P, P') \leq \delta\}.$$

Denoting $\pi(m, n) := |\mathcal{P}_{m,n}|$, we have the following standard result with the standard one-line proof.

**Lemma 2** $\pi(m, n) = \binom{m+n}{m}$.

Proof. Each path contains $m + n$ steps, out of which $m$ are made rightwards. □

# 4 Problem Statement

We will be looking at the following covering problem in the metric space $(\mathcal{P}_{m,n}, d_g)$.

**Problem.** For a given integer $\delta$ and grid dimensions $m$ and $n$, find a lower and upper estimate to the cardinality of a subset $S \subseteq \mathcal{P}_{m,n}$ such that the following conditions hold.

$$\bigcup_{P \in S} B(P, \delta) = \mathcal{P}_{m,n} \tag{2}$$

$$\forall P' \in S \left[ P' \notin \bigcup_{P \in S \setminus \{P'\}} B(P, \delta) \right] \tag{3}$$

The lower estimate corresponds to the question about efficient covering. In this setting we ask what is the minimal number of pre-planned paths required in the casebase in order embrace all the possible paths with deviation not exceeding the threshold $\delta$.

The upper estimate, on the contrary, deals with the worst case. In this case we consider a process of random path generation and ask what is the largest path set that can occur if we every time only include new paths that deviate more than by $\delta$ from all the previously recorded paths.

# 5 Lower Bound

**Theorem 1** *For every $\delta \in \mathbb{N}$ and every subset $S \subseteq \mathcal{P}_{m,n}$ satisfying the properties (2) and (3), the inequality*

$$|S| \geq \pi\left(\left\lfloor \frac{m}{2\delta+1} \right\rfloor, \left\lfloor \frac{n}{2\delta+1} \right\rfloor\right) \tag{4}$$

*holds. Evenmore, there exists such a set $S$ that the properties (2) and (3) are satisfied and equality holds in inequality (4).*

Proof. First we consider a special case when $m, n \vdots 2\delta + 1$ and a subset $T \subseteq \mathcal{P}_{m,n}$ defined by the following condition:

$$T = \{((x_0, y_0), \ldots, (x_{m+n}, y_{m+n})) \in \mathcal{P}_{m,n} : \forall i \in [0, m+n]\ x_i \vdots 2\delta+1 \vee y_i \vdots 2\delta+1\}.$$

We note that for $P_1 \neq P_2 \in T$ the inequality $d_g(P_1, P_2) \geq 2\delta + 1$ holds. Hence, no two different elements of the set $T$ can be contained in the same ball of radius $\delta$. Consequently, when covering the space $\mathcal{P}_{m,n}$ with balls of radius $\delta$ and with centers in the elements of $S$ (as required by condition (2)), there must be at least the same number of balls as there are elements in the set $T$. But the paths of $T$ are essentially grid paths on a grid with dimensions $\frac{m}{2\delta+1} \times \frac{n}{2\delta+1}$ (and grid squares of dimensions $(2\delta + 1) \times (2\delta + 1)$), hence

$$|T| = \pi\left(\frac{m}{2\delta+1}, \frac{n}{2\delta+1}\right)$$

and the inequality stated in the theorem is proven for this special case.

In order to prove the inequality in the case $m, n \not\vdots 2\delta + 1$, simply note that it is always possible to consider a subgrid of dimensions

$$(2\delta+1)\left\lfloor \frac{m}{2\delta+1} \right\rfloor \times (2\delta+1)\left\lfloor \frac{n}{2\delta+1} \right\rfloor$$

and a set of (partial) paths defined in a similar manner as in the case of the set $T$. The argument presented above can then be easily adopted to this case as well.

The existence of a set $S$ providing equality will also be proven for the case $m, n \vdots 2\delta+1$ first. We will prove that we can take $S = T$ where $T$ is the set defined above. It has the right cardinality and the condition (3) is obvious. It remains to prove that the condition (2) also holds. In order to do so, we have to show that every possible path from the set $\mathcal{P}_{m,n}$ belongs to some ball $B(P', \delta)$, where $P' \in T$.

Let $P \in \mathcal{P}_{m,n}$ be any path in the grid. We divide the grid to $(2\delta + 1) \times (2\delta + 1)$ squares and construct a new path $P'$ so that

1. it goes along the edges of the big squares (then $P' \in T$); and

2. for every point $c_1$ on the path $P$ there exists a point $c_2$ on the path $P'$ such that $d(c_1, c_2) \leq \delta$ (then $d_g(P, P') \leq \delta$).

We will follow the path $P$ through big squares and show for each case which edges or vertices of the big squares must be taken into the path $P'$. We distinguish the cases by location of start- and endpoints of the path $P$ in a big square. There are four possible regions for start- and endpoints, each containing two segments of length $\delta$ and they are situated in four corners of a big square. There are 8 possible cases and the corresponding parts of the path $P'$ are for all the cases shown in Figure 3.

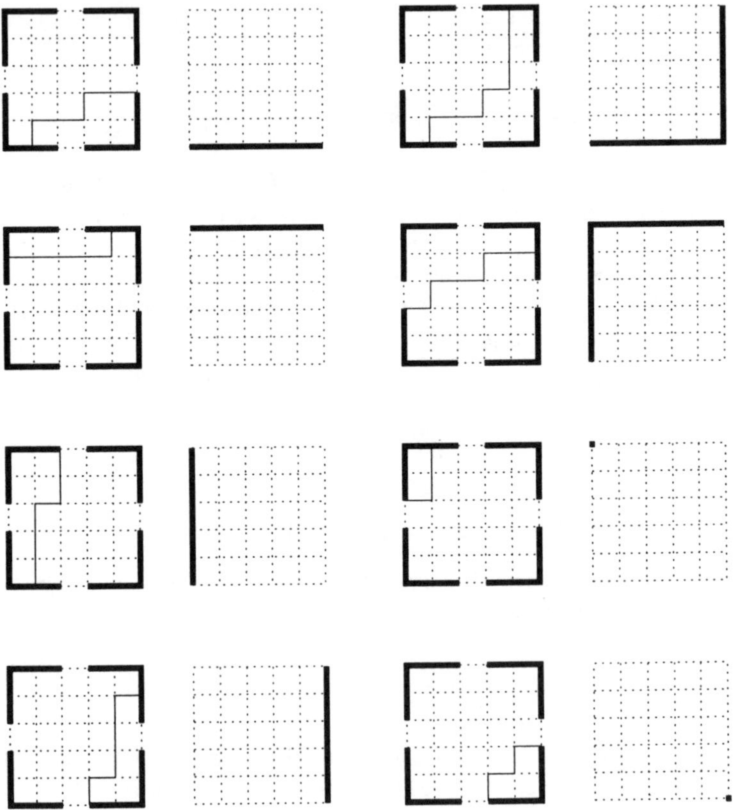

Figure 3: Construction of path $P'$ from path $P$

Generalising this existence proof to the case $m, n \not| \, 2\delta + 1$ is once again easy. As done above, we choose a subgrid with dimensions

$$(2\delta + 1) \left\lfloor \frac{m}{2\delta + 1} \right\rfloor \times (2\delta + 1) \left\lfloor \frac{n}{2\delta + 1} \right\rfloor,$$

but we have to be a bit more careful. Namely, the subgrid must be located so that no distance between an edge of the subgrid and the corresponding edge of the whole grid is not bigger than $\delta$ in order to embrace all the possible paths in the grid. Since the largest remainder of $m$ and $n$ when divided by $2\delta + 1$ is $2\delta$ this locating can be done. It only remains to pad the paths given by the set $T$ in the subgrid with any subpath joining the lower left corner of the whole grid with the lower left corner of the subgrid; and similarly for the upper right corners. □

# 6 Upper Bound

**Theorem 2** *For every $\delta \in \mathbb{N}$ and every subset $S \subseteq \mathcal{P}_{m,n}$ satisfying the properties (2) and (3), the inequality*

$$|S| \leq \begin{cases} \pi\left(\left\lfloor \frac{m}{\delta} \right\rfloor, \left\lfloor \frac{n}{\delta} \right\rfloor\right), & \text{if } \delta \text{ is odd} \\ \pi\left(\left\lfloor \frac{m}{\delta+1} \right\rfloor, \left\lfloor \frac{n}{\delta+1} \right\rfloor\right), & \text{if } \delta \text{ is even} \end{cases}$$

*holds. Evenmore, there exists such a set $S$ that the properties (2), (3) and*

$$|S| = \pi\left(\left\lfloor \frac{m}{\delta+1} \right\rfloor, \left\lfloor \frac{n}{\delta+1} \right\rfloor\right)$$

*are satisfied.*

Proof. The proof of this theorem is very similar to the proof of Theorem 1. First we consider the case when $\delta$ is even and $m, n \vdots \delta$. We define the set $T$ as follows:

$$T = \{((x_0, y_0), \ldots, (x_{m+n}, y_{m+n})) \in \mathcal{P}_{m,n} : \forall i \in [0, m+n]\ x_i \vdots \delta+1 \vee y_i \vdots \delta+1\}.$$

Assume that we also have a set $S$ corresponding to the conditions (2) and (3).

Similarly to the proof of Theorem 1, one can show that for every path $P \in S$ there exists a path $P' \in T$ such that $d_g(P, P') \leq \frac{\delta}{2}$. If for two different paths $P_1, P_2 \in S$ the corresponding path $P' \in T$ is the same, we have

$$d_g(P_1, P_2) \leq d_g(P_1, P') + d_g(P', P_2) \leq \frac{\delta}{2} + \frac{\delta}{2} = \delta,$$

a contradiction with the condition (3). Hence, the set $S$ cannot have more elements than the set $T$ does. As in Theorem 1, we have

$$|T| = \pi\left(\frac{m}{\delta+1}, \frac{n}{\delta+1}\right)$$

and the inequality stated in the theorem is proven in this case.

In order to generalise the result for the case $m, n \nmid \delta + 1$ as well, we once again consider a subgrid of dimensions

$$(\delta + 1)\left\lfloor \frac{m}{\delta + 1} \right\rfloor \times (\delta + 1)\left\lfloor \frac{n}{\delta + 1} \right\rfloor$$

situated in the center of the $m \times n$ grid. We also note that choosing $S = T$ gives the required set to achieve equality in the theorem's inequality.

The proof for the case when $\delta$ is odd is completely analogous. The only difference arises from the fact that in this case we can not require any path $P$ to have a path in the (appropriately chosen) set $T$ at most of distance $\frac{\delta}{2}$ away, but we have to use the value $\frac{\delta - 1}{2}$ instead. □

# 7 Comparison of Approaches

To demonstrate the advantage of the current approach compared to our previous heuristic one we use parameters from one of our previous real-world experiments. For a grid of $51 \times 67$ cells and with the similarity measure $\delta = 5$ the size of the seed casebase would be

$$\pi\left(\left\lfloor \frac{51}{2 \cdot 5 + 1} \right\rfloor, \left\lfloor \frac{67}{2 \cdot 5 + 1} \right\rfloor\right) = \binom{4 + 6}{4} = 210$$

cases.

At the same time, if the heuristic path generation algorithm was used, the new generated paths never covered the solution space although the experiments consisted of more than 500 runs. Another set of our previous experiments, 20 000 runs in a simulated environment, gave a similar result. Moreover, the heuristic algorithm often generated random paths that were similar to old paths already stored in the casebase. Roughly quarter of the new generated paths were innovative ones, i.e. dissimilar to all paths in the casebase.

The advantage of the new approach is thus twofold:

1. It generates the seed casebase that is guaranteed to cover the paths space of the robot while the previous heuristic approach did not give such a guarantee.

2. It speeds up learning because all paths are stored in the seed casebase. Unlike the heuristic approach, the robot does not spend time on looking for new innovative solutions.

However, if $\delta$ is reduced, the size of the seed casebase increases rapidly. For $\delta = 2$ the seed casebase would have to contain over a million cases already.

In practice, a robot would never try all the possible solutions. When it has found a solution that is good enough, it reduces exploration. When the cost of the current path increases, it starts exploring new possibilities again. The seed casebase gives a theoretical guarantee that none of the possible solutions remains undiscovered.

The idea of proving the upper bound was to check if we could show the maximum number of possible cases in the casebase. It would give a confidence to the casebase designer that the casebase would not grow bigger than a certain feasible amount. Unfortunately, the upper bound of the casebase is too high. For an example given above ($m = 51$, $n = 67$, $\delta = 5$), the casebase would contain

$$\pi\left(\left\lfloor \frac{51}{5} \right\rfloor, \left\lfloor \frac{67}{5} \right\rfloor\right) = \binom{10+13}{10} = 1144066$$

cases.

Thus, a casebase maintenance strategy that keeps the size of the casebase under control is still needed. In our previous work, we have used forgetting strategies based on the quality of a solution. For example, when the learning process is success-driven the robot remembers only best solutions. When learning is failure-driven, the robot remembers the worst solutions. The casebase is then only used to verify whether a new solution generated from scratch is good enough. Our experiments have not shown the superiority of one of the forgetting strategies. It rather seems that the casebase management technique strongly depends on the characteristics of the environment and the problem at hand.

# 8 Conclusions and Future Work

Our work was motivated by the fact that our previous heuristic technique was not able to generate all possible different solutions to the current findpath problem. We therefore investigated the possibility to create a seed casebase that covers the whole solution space of the robot.

In this paper, we have proven the lower and upper bound of the solution space. The proof of the lower bound shows that it is realistic to seed the casebase with a solution set that contains a close match to every possible solution path. This would give a guarantee that none of the paths theoretically remains undiscovered.

At the same time, the proof of the upper bound indicates that it is unrealistic to save all possible different solutions to the casebase. In order to keep the casebase constrained, it has to be revised at runtime.

One of the possible solutions to the casebase explosion can be based on the following observation. Although our casebase contains paths distant from each other in the sense of grid distance, many paths still overlap significantly. It would make the casebase much smaller, if we only would try to cover all the fragments of the grid with the paths instead of traversing all the paths themselves. The question how well this can be done is a subject for future research.

It is also important to emphasize that the examples above represent the number of solutions to only one problem. This problem is the most general one – traversing between the diagonally opposite corners. Other problems will be subproblems of this one and will require a smaller number of solutions to cover their solutions spaces. In practical mobile robot applications there are usually rather few target points (unless it is a mapping or exploration problem). In our future research we also intend to analyse the dependency between the number of solutions and the size of the casebase.

We also intend to investigate some different similarity measures to reduce the size of the solutions space even more. One possibility is to define similarity as the size of the area surrounded by the paths.

## References

[1] M.Kruusmaa. Repeated Path Planning for Mobile Robots in Dynamic Environments. Ph.D.Thesis. Chalmes Univeristy of Technology, Gothenburg, Sweden, 2002.

[2] H.Hu, M.Brady. Dynamic Global Path Planning with Uncertainty for Mobile Robots in Manufacturing. *IEEE Transactions on Robotics and Automation.* Vol.13, No.5, October 1997, pp.760-767. 1997.

[3] K.Z.Haigh. M.M.Veloso. Planning, Execution and Learning in a Robotic Agent. *AIPS-98* pp.120–127, June 1998.

[4] C.Vasudevan, K.Ganesan. Case-based Path Planning for Autonomous Underwater Vehicles. *Proc. of 1994 IEEE Int. Symposium on Intelligent Control,* pp.160–165, August 16-18, 1994.

[5] A.K.Goel, K.S.Ali, M.W.Donnellan, A.Gomex de Silva Garza, T.J.Callantine. Multistrategy Adaptive Path Planning. *IEEE Expert*, Vol.9, No.6, Dec.1994, pp.57–65. 1994.

[6] S.Fox, D.B.Leake. Combining Case-based Planning and Introspective Reasoning. *Proc. of the Sixth Midwest Artificial Intelligence and Cognitive Science Society Conference,* Carbondale, IL, April 1995.

[7] L.K.Branting, D.W.Aha. Stratified Case-based Reasoning: Reusing Hierarchical Problem Solving Episodes. *Proc. of the Fourteenth International Joint Conference on Artificial Intelligence,* Montreal, Canada, August 20–25, 1995.

[8] K.Z.Haigh, M.Veloso, Route Planning by Analogy. *Case-Based Reasoning Research and Development, Proc. of ICCBR-95,* pp.169–180. Springer-Verlag, 1995.

[9] R.R.Murphy. Introduction to AI Robotics. The MIT Press, 2000.

[10] D. Huttenlocher, D. Klanderman and A. Rucklige. Comparing images using the Hausdorff distance. In *IEEE Transactions on Pattern Analysis and Machine Intelligence*, Vol.15, No.9, pp.850–863, September 1993.

[11] E. Belogay, C. Cabrelli, U. Molter, and R. Shonkwiler. Calculating the Hausdorff distance between curves. *Information Processing Letters*, 64(1):17–22, 14 October 1997.

# SESSION 1A:

# MACHINE LEARNING 1

# A Rough Set Model with Ontological Information for Discovering Maximal Association Rules in Document Collections

Yaxin Bi, Terry Anderson and Sally McClean
Faculty of Informatics, University of Ulster at Jordanstown,
Newtownabbey, Co. Antrim, BT37 0QB, N. Ireland, UK
{y.bi, tj.anderson, si.mcclean}@ulster.ac.uk

Abstract

In this paper we investigate the applicability of a Rough Set model and method to discover maximal associations from a collection of text documents, and compare its applicability with that of the maximal association method. Both methods are based on computing co-occurrences of various sets of keywords, but it has been shown that by using the Rough Set method, rules discovered are similar to maximal association rules, and it is much simpler than the maximal association method. In addition, we also present an alternative strategy to taxonomies required in the above methods, instead of building taxonomies based on labelled document collections themselves. This is to effectively utilise ontologies which will increasingly be deployed on the Internet.

## 1. Introduction

Associations in complex data objects, such as tuples or documents, occur when one set of attributes is likely to co-occur with another set. The prototypical application is the analysis of supermarket transactions where associations like "68% of all customers who buy fish also buy white wine" may be found in a transaction database. For knowledge discovery – data mining – in databases, an association is a rule to be mined from databases which infers an attribute set from another. In connection with knowledge discovery – text mining – in document collections, an association between two keyword sets is their co-occurrence to be discovered in a document collection. Currently, association rules have demonstrated their value in discovering interesting correlations between sets of attributes in databases. This approach is potentially very useful for detecting interesting associations in the huge volume of online text documents on the Internet.

The algorithm for mining association rules – regular association rules – from large databases containing supermarket transactions was first introduced by Agrawal [1]. A number of its derivatives have subsequently been developed to enhance its exploitation in distinct application domains. One of them which is applied to discover association rules from text document collections was proposed by Feldman [2], which is mainly used to mine maximal association rules by computing co-occurrence frequencies of the various keywords labelling the documents. There are two advantages of the maximal associations over the regular associations: first it can significantly reduce the number of associations generated and secondly it is capable of capturing associations otherwise lost by using regular associations. Conventionally, regular association rules are based on the notion of frequent sets of attributes which occur in many documents [1, 3, 4], whereas maximal association rules are based on frequent maximal sets of attributes which appear maximally in many documents. Like the regular association rules, maximal association rules are rules of the form X → Y with attribute sets X and Y. However, while a regular association rule X → Y means that if X then Y (with some confidence), a maximal association rule X → Y says that if X maximally then Y maximally.

The primary difficulty associated with the maximal association approach is that the generation of frequent maximal set is based on an underlying assumption – a taxonomy existing for the document collections. However this assumption may be only feasible for collections of labelled documents with keywords which are mainly for training text classifiers and very expensive to construct, therefore limiting the general applicability of this approach. This paper presents an alternative strategy to taxonomies. It aims to effectively utilise ontologies which are increasingly being deployed on the Internet, instead of building taxonomies based on labelled document collections themselves. In addition, we investigate also the applicability of Rough Set theory to detecting maximal associations, and compare this to the maximal association method [2]. The work reported in this paper shows that by using Rough Set theory, rules discovered are similar to maximal association rules, and the rough set approach is much simpler than the maximal association method in discovering maximal association rules.

## 2. Problem Statement

In this section, we first illustrate a major problem in relation to the regular association method through a simple example derived from the widely used Reuters-21578 [5], a labelled document collection, i.e. a benchmark for text categorisation, as follows:

Assume that there are 10 articles regarding "*corn*" which relate to the *USA* and *Canada* and 20 other articles concerning "*fish*" and the countries *USA*, *Canada* and *France* [2]. Then the following regular association rules can be obtained by the regular rule method as described in the later sections:

Association rule 1: {USA, Canada} → {fish} with confidence 66%
Association rule 2: {USA, Canada, France} → {fish} with confidence 100%
Association rule 3: {USA, Canada} → {corn} with confidence 33%

Figure 1: A set of regular association rules

The confidence of Rule 3 in Figure 1 is too low to represent a strong connection between *USA-Canada* and "*corn*". In essence, failure to capture the relation between *USA-Canada* and "*corn*" is because the whole collection of articles is treated as a search space for the association rules regardless of the context information of co-occurrence of *USA-Canada* and "*corn*". As a result, such an association can not be captured by the regular association algorithms if a confidence threshold over 33% is specified. However, by using the method of maximal association rules, Rule 3 in Figure 1 has a confidence of 100%.

# 3. Reuse of Ontologies for a Taxonomy

Given a collection of unlabeled documents in a raw form, assigning the documents to a set of topics to construct a training data set for text categorization must be done by hand. It is therefore very expensive to build, particularly, for large document collections. A similar challenge is faced by those constructing a corresponding taxonomy for such a collection, a step required in discovering maximal association rules by using the maximal association method [2]. Unfortunately, the earlier work assumes that such a taxonomy exists for a given collection of documents. In [6], Feldman presents a further development of the previous work, introducing a semi-automatic approach for constructing taxonomies from unlabeled document collections. This approach is closely similar to work of ontology construction in many organisations or different enterprises. In this work, we introduce an alternative strategy to the taxonomies – the incorporation of ontologies into maximal association rules.

An ontology is defined as a shared formal conceptualization of a particular domain [7], which can be used to specify what concepts represent and how they are related. In practice, an ontology can be regarded as a controlled vocabulary providing a concrete specification of term names and term meanings. Currently, many simple ontologies are available in many forms – many exist as freeware on the web today and also many exist as internal information organization structures within companies, universities, etc. such as, WordNet, providing a thesaurus for 100,000 terms explained in natural language [8]; UN Classifications Registry a classification scheme for universal products and services, keeping updated information on statistical classifications maintained by the United Nations Statistics Division [9]; and RAMON, holding international statistical classifications by EUROSTAT [10], and so forth. Basically, these simple ontologies can be characterized as follow [11]:

- Finite controlled (extensible) vocabulary
- Unambiguous interpretation of classes and term relationships
- Explicit hierarchical subclass relationships between classes

In fact, such simple ontologies are easily accessible today. As an example, we look at "Status in the Family of International Classifications: Reference Classification" [9], to examine how it can be reused for constructing a taxonomy required as above. The Reference Classification consists of 9 categories, Figure 2 shows one of the categories, i.e. Category 0, representing "Agriculture, forestry and fishery products". This category is further broken down into 4 subclasses, for example, one of the subclasses 01 called "Products of agriculture", where the category (subclass) 01 in turn contains a subclass 011 – "Cereals" which in turn has a subclass 0112 – Maize (corn) as illustrated in Figure 3. Obviously, Figure 2 and 3 provide a concrete specification of the concept of *agriculture, forestry and fishery products* and explicit hierarchical relationships between the concept and relevant terms, which can be used to constitute a taxonomy for classifying products or other purposes. For our purpose, we take a simple strategy regardless of the hierarchy of controlled words, i.e. transforming the controlled words from a hierarchy into an unordered set of controlled words, in order to ensure consistency with the taxonomy in this context, e.g. *products of agriculture* = {*products*, *agriculture*, *cereals*, *corn*}.

**CPC Ver.1.1 (Draft)**

Click on any code to see more detail. Click here for top level only.

- 0 - Agriculture, forestry and fishery products
  - 01 - Products of agriculture, horticulture and market gardening
  - 02 - Live animals and animal products
  - 03 - Forestry and logging products
  - 04 - Fish and other fishing products

Figure 2: A simple ontology (Status in the Family of International Classifications): top level

This Division is divided into the following Groups:

- 011 - Cereals
- 012 - Vegetables
- 013 - Fruit and nuts
- 014 - Oil seeds and oleaginous fruit
- 015 - Living plants; cut flowers and flower buds; flower seeds and fruit seeds; vegetable seeds
- 016 - Beverages and spice crops
- 017 - Unmanufactured tobacco
- 018 - Plants used for sugar manufacturing
- 019 - Raw vegetable materials n.e.c.

Figure 3: A simple ontology (Status in the Family of International Classifications): second level

## 4. The Data Model and Definition

First we introduce a data model of an information system (also called an attribute-value system) [12], which is able to represent textual information in a collection of documents, and facilitate the process of computing maximal association rules based on a rough set approach.

Let $S = \langle U, A, V, f \rangle$ be an information system, where $U = \{u_1, \ldots, u_{|U|}\}$ is a finite set of objects, and $A = \{a_1, \ldots, a_{|A|}\}$ is a finite attribute set; $V = \{V_{a1}, \ldots, V_{a|A|}\}$ is a set of attribute values where $V_{a_i} = \{V_{a_{i1}}, \ldots, V_{a_{ik}}\}$ is the domain of attribute $a_i$; $V_{a_{ij}}$ is a categorical value and there is a mapping $f(u, a)$: $U \times A \rightarrow V_a$ which assigns the particular values from the domain of attributes to objects such that $f(u, a) \in V_a$, for all $u \in U$ and $a \in A$.

| U/A | USA | Canada | France | *corn* | *fish* |
|---|---|---|---|---|---|
| $u_1$ | 1 | 1 | 0 | 1 | 0 |
| … | … | … | … | … | … |
| $u_{10}$ | 1 | 1 | 0 | 1 | 0 |
| $u_{11}$ | 1 | 1 | 1 | 0 | 1 |
| … | … | … | … | … | … |
| $u_{30}$ | 1 | 1 | 1 | 0 | 1 |

Table 1: An information table

Using this data model, each document is regarded as an object of an information system – a vector of attribute values. Each attribute represents a term (keyword) in a document, and attribute values – term weights – are computed using either the weighting formula TF-IDF [13] or a Boolean formula as is used in this paper.

An information system for the example in Section 2 can be expressed intuitively in terms of an *information table* as shown in Table 1.

Now we start with some formal definitions of relevant terms based on an information system and then derive some results that are needed to compute maximal association rules.

## 4.1 The Support Documents of a Keyword Set

In an information table, each row $u$ corresponds to a set of attributes, a keyword co-occurrence set in $u$ can be defined as $Coo(u)=\{a \in A \mid f(u, a)=1\}$. For example, keyword co-occurrence sets in Table 1 are below:

$Coo(u_1)=Coo(u_2)=\ldots= Coo(u_{10})=$\{USA, Canada, corn\}

$Coo(u_{11})=Coo(u_{12})=\ldots= Coo(u_{30})=$\{USA, Canada, France, fish\}

Figure 4: Co-occurrence sets

We now say that a document $u$ supports a given set of attributes $X$ if $X \subseteq Coo(u)$. The strength of $X$ in the information table, denoted by $stg(X)$, is the number of documents $u$ supporting $X$, formally that is, $stg(X) = |\{u \mid X \subseteq Coo(u)\}|$.

An *association* between $X$ and $Y$ is a relation representing how they are correlated with each other. It can be regarded as an expression of the form $X \leftrightarrow Y$, where $X$ and $Y$ are subsets of the attribute set $A$. Similarly, the *strength* of the association $stg(X \leftrightarrow Y)$ is based on the strength of $X \cup Y$ as well, i.e., the number of documents supporting $X \cup Y$. A formal definition of the *strength* is $stg(X \leftrightarrow Y) = stg(X \cup Y) = |\{u \mid X \cup Y \subseteq Coo(u)\}|$, and the *confidence* of an association, denoted by $cfi(X \leftrightarrow Y)$, is given as follows:

$$stg(X \cup Y)/\max(stg(X), stg(Y)) = \frac{|\{u \mid X \cup Y \subseteq Coo(u)\}|}{\max(|\{u \mid X \subseteq Coo(u)\}|, |\{u \mid Y \subseteq Coo(u)\}|)} \quad (1)$$

Having defined associations, we look at an association rule. An *association rule* is an implication of the form $X \rightarrow Y$, where $X$ and $Y$ are the subsets of the attribute set $A$, and called *antecedent* and *consequent*, respectively. The *strength* of the *association rule* is $stg(X \rightarrow Y) = stg(X \cup Y) = |\{u \mid X \cup Y \subseteq Coo(u)\}|$ and the *confidence* of the rule $cfi(X \rightarrow Y)$ is defined as:

$$stg(X \cup Y) / stg(X) = \frac{|\{u \mid X \cup Y \subseteq Coo(u)\}|}{|\{u \mid X \subseteq Coo(u)|} \qquad (2)$$

It is important that an association reflects a mutual relation between two sets of attributes as described in the above definitions. The confidence of an association such as $X \leftrightarrow Y$ is the same with that of the association $Y \leftrightarrow X$, thus it does not matter which of them is placed before or after. However, once an association is transformed to an association rule, an inference implication from one antecedent to a consequent is established with a certain confidence. To illustrate the process of computing associations and association rules, the following examples demonstrate what associations and corresponding rules are found from Table 1.

The associations found are as follows

$\{USA, Canada\} \leftrightarrow \{fish\}$ with confidence

$$\frac{|\{u \mid \{USA, Canada\} \cup \{fish\} \subseteq Coo(u)\}|}{\max(|\{u \mid \{USA, Canada\} \subseteq Coo(u)\}|, |\{u \mid \{fish\}\} \subseteq Coo(u)\}|)}$$

$$= \frac{|\{u_{11}, \ldots, u_{30}\}|}{\max(|\{u_1, \ldots u_{10}, \ldots, u_{30}\}|, |\{u_{11}, \ldots, u_{30}\}|)} = 20 / \max(30,20) = 66\%$$

$\{USA, Canada, France\} \leftrightarrow \{fish\}$ with confidence

$$\frac{|\{u \mid \{USA, Canada, France\} \cup \{fish\} \subseteq Coo(u)\}|}{\max(|\{u \mid \{USA, Canada, France\} \subseteq Coo(u)\}|, |\{u \mid \{fish\}\} \subseteq Coo(u)\}|)}$$

$$= \frac{|\{u_{11}, \ldots, u_{30}\}|}{\max(|\{u_{11}, \ldots, u_{30}\}|, |\{u_{11}, \ldots, u_{30}\}|)} = 20 / \max(20,20) = 100\%$$

$\{USA, Canada\} \leftrightarrow \{corn\}$ with confidence

$$\frac{|\{u \mid \{USA, Canada\} \cup \{corn\} \subseteq Coo(u)\}|}{\max(|\{u \mid \{USA, Canada\} \subseteq Coo(u)\}|, |\{u \mid \{corn\}\} \subseteq Coo(u)\}|)}$$

$$= \frac{|\{u_1, \ldots, u_{10}\}|}{\max(|\{u_1, \ldots u_{10}, \ldots, u_{30}\}|, |\{u_1, \ldots, u_{10}\}|)} = 10 / \max(30,10) = 33\%$$

Also, the corresponding association rules found are presented Figure 5.

$\{USA, Canada\} \rightarrow \{fish\}$ with confidence 66%
$\{USA, Canada, France\} \rightarrow \{fish\}$ with confidence 100%
$\{USA, Canada\} \rightarrow \{corn\}$ with confidence 33%

Figure 5: Corresponding association rules

As seen in the above figure that the last confidence value is too low to represent a strong connection between *USA-Canada* and "*corn*". In consequence, such rules can not be effectively captured by using the regular associations. The major reason for this limitation is that most algorithms for mining regular association rules consider all attributes as a rule search space, regardless the local context information such as co-occurrence of *USA-Canada* and "*corn*". However, according to the definition of maximality in the next section, we can see that the maximal association rule, {*USA*, *Canada*}→{*corn*}, has a confidence of 10/10=100% since whenever *USA-Canada* occur *maximally* without any other country (in and only in documents $u_1$-$u_{10}$ as shown in Table 1), "*corn*" also appears *maximally* without any other goods (also in and only in documents $u_1$-$u_{10}$ as shown in Table 1).

In the next section, we introduce a definition of maximality between two keyword sets. This involves partitioning the vocabulary of index terms.

# 5. Partitioning the Vocabulary of Index Terms and the Definition of Maximality

For the definition of maximality, we employ an underlying taxonomy $\tau$ of attributes which is derived from labeled document collections or ontologies. With the taxonomy $\tau$ , an interesting correlation between attributes from different categories can be obtained.

## 5.1 Partitioning the Indexing Vocabulary of Terms

Let $A$ be an attribute set, which is partitioned to classes $T_1$, $T_2$,...,$T_S$. We denote the partition by $A/\tau$ : $T_1$, $T_2$, ..., $T_S$; alternatively rewritten as: $A/\tau=\{T_1, T_2, ..., T_S\}$, where $\tau$ is the corresponding equivalence relation of the partition such that $a\tau b$ for $a, b \in A$ if and only if $a$ and $b$ are in the same class, and $T_s\in 2^A$; $T_s \neq \varnothing$; $T_i \cap T_j = \varnothing$; $A=\cup_{s=1}^{S} T_s$. Such a partition is called a *taxonomy*, and each class is called a category.

Consider Table 1, the set of terms $A$ = {*USA*, *Canada*, *France*, *corn*, *fish*} can be partitioned into two categories, this is, $A/\tau=\{T_1, T_2\}$, where $T_1$ = *countries* ={*USA*, *Canada*, *France*}, and $T_2$ = *products** = {*corn*, *fish*}. The taxonomy is {*countries*, *products*}, in which *countries* and *products* are categories.

## 5.2 The Definition of Maximality

Based on an underlying taxonomy $\tau$ of attributes, the definition of maximality can be further introduced, and the interesting correlation between sets of attributes from different categories can be obtained.

---

* *products here means products of agriculture and fishery*

For a given subset of attributes $X \subseteq A$, we can find a unique decomposition $X = X_1 \cup X_2 \cup \ldots \cup X_k$ such that $X_1 \subseteq T_1^i$, $X_2 \subseteq T_2^i$, ..., $X_k \subseteq T_k^i$, where $T_j^i$ ($j = 1, 2, \ldots, k$) are categories of $\tau$. Here, we define $T_j^i$ as the *maximal category* of $X_j$, and denote $T_j^i$ as $T_j^i = T_{Xj}$.

### 5.2.1 Maximally Supported Sets of Terms

Using the above relevant terms, here we extend the notions of *support* and *strength* for maximal associations. Given a subset of attributes $X_j \subseteq T_j^i$ and a row $u$ in the context of regular associations, as defined previously that $u$ supports $X_j$ if $X_j \subseteq Coo(u) \cap T_{Xj}$. The strength of $X_j$ in an information table, denoted by $stg(X_j)$, is the number of documents supporting $X_j$, such that $stg(X_j) = |\{u \mid X_j \subseteq Coo(u) \cap T_{Xj}\}|$. In addition, this supported set $X_j$ of attributes can also be denoted by a *taxonomy pair*, i.e. $\{X_j : T_{Xj}\}$ with the strength $stg(X_j)$.

Now for an $X_j \subseteq T_j^i$ and a row $u$, we say that *u maximally supports* $X_j$ if $X_j = Coo(u) \cap T_{Xj}$. The max-strength of $X_j$ in an information table, denoted by $msg(X_j)$, is the number of documents maximally supporting $X_j$, that is $msg(X_j) = |\{u \mid X_j = Coo(u) \cap T_{Xj}\}|$. This maximally supported set $X_j$ of terms is denoted by a taxonomy pair $\{X_j : T_{Xj}\}$ with max-strength $msg(X_j)$. To interpret these definitions, Figure 6 and 7 give two examples of the supported sets and maximally supported sets found from Table 1.

$\{\{Canada,France,USA\}: countries\}$ with $stg = |\{u_{11}\text{-}u_{30}\}| = 20$
$\{\{Canada,USA\}: countries\}$ with $stg = |\{u_1\text{-}u_{10}, u_{11}\text{-}u_{30}\}| = 30$
$\{\{France,USA\}: countries\}$with $stg = |\{u_{11}\text{-}u_{30}\}| = 20$
$\{\{Canada,France\}: countries\}$ with $stg = |\{u_{11}\text{-}u_{30}\}| = 20$
$\{\{Canada\}: countries\}$ with $stg = |\{u_1\text{-}u_{10}, u_{11}\text{-}u_{30}\}| = 30$
$\{\{USA\}: countries\}$with $stg = |\{u_1\text{-}u_{10}\}, u_{11}\text{-}u_{30}\}| = 30$
$\{\{France\}: countries\}$ with $stg = |\{u_{11}\text{-}u_{30}\}| = 20$
$\{\{corn\}: products\}$ with $stg = |\{u_1\text{-}u_{10}\}| = 10$
$\{\{fish\}: products$ with $stg = |\{u_{11}\text{-}u_{30}\}| = 20$

Figure 6: Supported sets

$\{\{Canada,France,USA\}: countries\}$with $msg = |\{u_{11}\text{-}u_{30}\}| = 20$
$\{\{\text{Canada},USA\}: countries\}$ with $msg = |\{u_1\text{-}u_{10}\}| = 10$
$\{\{corn\}: products\}$ with $msg = |\{u_1\text{-}u_{10}\}| = 10$
$\{\{fish\}: products\}$ with $msg = |\{u_{11}\text{-}u_{30}\}| = 20$

Figure 7: Maximally supported sets

### 5.2.2 Maximally Supported Sets of Terms in the General Case

Assume that a set of attribute terms $X = X_1 \cup X_2 \cup \ldots \cup X_k$ ($X \neq \emptyset$; $Xi \subseteq Ti$ for $i=1, 2, \ldots, k$) and a row $u$, in the regular case, we say that $u$ supports $X$ if $X_k \subseteq Coo(u) \cap T_{Xk}$ for all $k$. The strength of $X$ in the information table, denoted by $stg(X)$, is the number of documents supporting $X$: $stg(X) = |\{u \mid X_i \subseteq Coo(u) \cap X_i;\ i=1, 2, \ldots, k\}|$.

This *supported set* $X$ of terms is denoted by $k$ taxonomy pairs $\{X_1{:}T_{X1}, X_2{:}T_{X2}, ..., X_k{:}T_{Xk}\}$ with strength $stg(X)$.

As opposed to the supported set for regular associations, now given a set of terms $X = X_1 \cup X_2 \cup \dots \cup X_k$ ($X \neq \emptyset$; $X_i \subseteq T_i$ for $i=1, 2, ..., k$) and a row $u$, we say that $u$ *maximally* supports $X$ if $X_k = Coo(u) \cap T_{Xk}$ for all $k$. The max-strength of $X$ in the information table, denoted by $msg(X)$, is the number of documents maximally supporting $X$: $msg(X) = |\{u \mid Xi = Coo(u) \cap T_{Xi};\ i=1, 2, ...,k\}|$. This *maximally supported set* $X$ of terms is denoted by $k$ taxonomy pairs: $\{X_1{:}T_{X1}, X_2{:}T_{X2},..., X_k{:}T_{Xk}\}$ with max-strength $msg(X)$. Figure 8 shows maximally supported sets found from Table 1.

{{*Canada, France, USA*}: *countries*, {*fish*}: *products*} with $msg = |\{u_{11}\text{-}u_{30}\}| = 20$
{{*Canada,USA*}: *countries*,{*corn*}: *products*}with $msg = |\{u_1\text{-}u_{10}\}| = 10$

Figure 8: Maximally supported set

### 5.2.3 Maximal Associations and Maximal Association Rules

Having defined the maximality and maximally supported set, in this section, we concentrate on maximal associations and maximal association rules. In contrast to the regular associations, a *maximal association* between $X$ and $Y$ is also an expression of the form $X \leftrightarrow Y$, but where $X$ and $Y$ are maximally supported sets. The *strength* of the association is specified as $msg(X \cup Y)$, and confidence of the association is computed by the formula $msg(X \cup Y)$ / max($msg(X)$, msg($Y$)). Figure 9 provides an example of the maximal associations derived from Table 1.

**Maximal association 1**: {*Canada, France, USA*}: *countries* ↔ {*fish*}: *topics* with strength $msg = |\{d_{11}\text{-}d_{30}\}| = 20$ and confidence 20 / max(20,20) = 1 = 100%.
**Maximal association 2**: {*Canada, USA*}: countries ↔ {*corn*}: *products* with strength $msg = |\{d_1\text{-}d_{10}\}| = 10$ and confidence10 / max(10,10) = 1 = 100%.

Figure 9: Maximal association discovered from Table 1

Similarly, a *maximal association rule* is an expression of the form $X \rightarrow Y$, where $X$ and $Y$ are maximally supported sets. The *strength* of the association rule is denoted as $msg(X \cup Y)$, and confidence of the association is computed by the formula of $msg(X \cup Y)$ / $msg(X)$. The following figure shows an example of maximal association rules detected from Table 1.

**Maximal association rule 1**: {Canada, France, USA}: *countries* → {*fish*}: *products* with strength $msg = |\{d_{11}\text{-}d_{30}\}| = 20$ and confidence 20/20 = 1 = 100%.
**Maximal association rule 2**: {*Canada, France, USA*}: *countries* ←{*fish*}: *products* with strength $msg = |\{d_{11}\text{-}d_{30}\}| = 20$ and confidence 20/20 = 1 = 100%.
**Maximal association rule 3**: {*Canada, USA*}: *countries* → {*corn*}: *products* with strength $msg = |\{d1\text{-}d10\}| = 10$ and confidence 10/10 = 1 = 100%.
**Maximal association rule 4**: {*Canada, USA*}: *countries* ← {*corn*}: *products* with strength $msg = |\{d_1\text{-}d_{10}\}| = 10$ and confidence 10/10=1=100%.

Figure 10: Maximal association rules discovered from Table 1

### 5.3 General Taxonomy and Ontologies

Generally, a *taxonomy* $T$ of $A$ is a collection of attribute subsets $\{T_1, T_2, ..., T_k\}$, where $T_i \subseteq A$, $T_i \neq \varnothing$; for all $i$; and $\cup_{i=1}^{k} T_i = A$; i.e., these subsets $T_i$ together cover $A$. However, in practice, it is not necessary that these subsets $T_k$ are disjoint from each other, it is possible that $T_i \cap T_j \neq \varnothing$ for some $i, j = 1, 2, ..., k$, $i \neq j$, and particularly $A \subseteq \cup_{i=1}^{k} T_i$.

To consider the construction of a taxonomy $T$ from domain-specific ontologies, we will look at the fragments of the simple ontology of "Status in the Family of International Classifications: Reference Classification" as shown in Figure 2 and 3. The major difference between an ontology and taxonomy is that an ontology has an inherent hierarchical structure, as opposed to the flat structure of a taxonomy $T$, but it is feasible to transform a hierarchical structure to a flat structure to construct a taxonomy $T$ as shown above. To formally represent a simple ontology with a flat structure, we first define some terminology to be used in the next section.

Let an *ontology* $O = \{O_1, O_2, \ldots, O_k\}$ be a set of mutually exclusive concepts, where $O_i$ may consist of a set of base values or/and a set of sub-concepts. Assume $O^g$ is a directed acyclic graph on the concepts, an edge in $O^g$ represents an *is-a* relationship. Consequently, $O^g$ represents a set of nodes and relationships among nodes. If there is an edge from the node $p$ to the node $c$ in $O^g$, we call $p$ is a parent of $c$ and $c$ a child of $p$. Thus we model an ontology as a graph $O^g$. For example, suppose the taxonomy as described in Section 5.1 be derived from an ontology $O^g$, a node *country* is then a node which has possible base values of *USA*, *Canada*, *France*, and a node *agriculture-forestry-fishery-products* consists of a set of sub-nodes of *products-agriculture*, *live-animals-animal-products*, *fish-fishing-products* as illustrated in Figure 2 and 3. The implementation of transforming ontologies to a taxonomy is a straightforward task which remains to be implemented in further work.

## 6. Rough Set Approach for Maximal Association Rules

Using the rough set method, we can quite easily discover knowledge that is similar with maximal association rules. In fact we only use the lower approximation of the rough set method to attribute subsets (i.e., supported subsets). We introduce below the several rough set essential concepts based on the data model described in Section 4 [12], and present a brief description of the rough set brief approach for computing association rules.

### 6.1 Rough Set Basics

With attribute $a \in A$, two objects $u, v \in U$ are defined as *equivalence relation* over $U$ if and only if $f(u, a) = f(v, a)$. An *equivalence relation* gives a group of partitions over $U$ with respect to attribute $a$, denoted by $U / a$, and $U / a = \{W_1, \ldots, W_r\}$ such that any two objects $u$ and $v$ are in the same *equivalence class* $X_i$ if and only if they have the same attribute value derived from $V_a$. Particularly, when $a = d$, the *equivalence class* also is called *decision class*. For $X_i$, there are the following properties: $W_i \subseteq U$, $W_i \neq \emptyset$, $W_i \cap W_j = \emptyset$ for $i \neq j$, $i, j = 1, \ldots, r$ and $\cup W_i = U$.

An *indiscernibility relation* is associated with every subset of attributes $B \subseteq A$ and is defined as $IR(B) = \{(u, v) \in U^2 \mid \forall a \in B, f(u, a) = f(v, a)\}$. Obviously, $IR(B)$ is an *equivalence relation* and is regarded as the intersection of all equivalence relations belonging to $B$. For $IR(B)$, it is alternatively written as $IR\{a_1, \ldots, a_k\}$, and for partitions over $U$ with respect to attribute $a$, denoted by $U / a$, also $U / IR\{a\}$.

Given a subset of attributes, $B \subseteq A$, if there is $Q \subseteq B$, $U / IR(B) = U / IR(Q)$, and $Q$ is minimal among all subsets of $B$, then we say $IR(Q)$ is a *reduct* of $B$, and the attributes within a reduct are significant so that none of them can be omitted. Note that $B$ may have a group of reducts.

Finally, based on the above definitions, for each subset $W \subseteq U$ with respect to decision attribute $D$, there is an *equivalence relation* $R \subseteq IR(B)$ with respect to condition attribute $C$. We call two subsets $\underline{R}\,W = \cup \{Y \mid Y \in U / R \wedge Y \subseteq W\}$ and $\overline{R}\,W = \cup \{Y \mid Y \in U / R \wedge Y \cap W \neq \emptyset\}$ the *lower* and *upper approximation* of $W$ respectively. In order to measure the accuracy of lower approximation, we use the formula $cfi_R = |\underline{R}W| / |U|$ [12].

## 6.2 Rough Set for Discovering Maximal Association Rules

A pre-requisite of using the rough set approach is a transformation from Table 1 to Table 2. To this end, we need techniques to partition a given set of attributes to a set of concepts against a taxonomy, in other words, for a given document collection, to map terms from the document collection to a set of concepts within a taxonomy. Figure 11 shows an algorithm for achieving such a transformation.

```
Let O = {O_1, O_2, ..., O_k} be an ontology, which is composed of subsets of concepts
Let S = <U, A, V, f> be an information system as defined in Section 4,
Let W be a set buffer
Let M be a matrix representing an information table
for ( i = 0, i < |U|, i ++ ) do begin
    for (h, j = 0, j < |O|, j ++) do begin
        for (k = 0, k < |A|, k++ ) do begin
            If (f(u_i, a_k) = 1 ∧ a_k ∈ O_j ) then
                W := W ∪ a_k
            end
        end
        if W ≠ ∅ then
        comment: M (h, 0) is the top row of the matrix, and Q'_j is a name of concept
                 which is regarded an attribute
          M (h, 0) := Q'_j ; M (i, h) := W; W := ∅; h++
        end
    end
end
```

Figure 11: An algorithm for transformation

To demonstrate our approach for computing association rules, here we briefly describe a simple process of rule reduction by using the rough set method, more details of the rough set algorithms and their implementation have been described in our previous work [13].

| **U/C** | *Countries* | *Products* |
|---|---|---|
| $U_1$ | {*Canada, USA*} | {*corn*} |
| … | … | … |
| $u_{10}$ | {*Canada, USA*} | {*corn*} |
| $u_{11}$ | {*Canada, France, USA*} | {*fish*} |
| … | … | … |
| $u_{30}$ | {*Canada, France, USA*} | {*fish*} |

Table 2: A transformed information table

Given an information table like Table 2, the idea of the algorithms comes from computing lower approximations of any pairs of attributes. The algorithms first start with partitioning on each attribute; and then mutually computing lower approximations to find supported sets of attributes, denoted by *Spt*, until the end of exhausting all combinations of every pairs of attributes; finally transforming each pair of attributes to a rule with a confidence value.

To compare confidence values obtained using both methods of the maximal association rule method and rough set, here we use the same measuring method with the maximal association method as described in Section 5.2.3, rather than the conventional formula of the rough set method, i.e. $cfi_R = |\underline{R}W| / |U|$.

Looking at Table 2, it easy to see that for the attributes $x$ = *countries* and $y$ = *products*, the partition $U / x = U$ / *countries* is composed of $W_1$, $W_2$ where $W_1 = \{u_1\text{-}u_{10}\}$, and $W_2 = \{u_{11}\text{-}u_{30}\}$; the partition $U / y = U$ / *products* is $Z_1 = W_1$, and $Z_2 = W_2$ too. As defined in Section 6.1, the supported sets from the attribute *countries* to $Z_1$ and $Z_2$ are obtained by computing the lower approximation as $Spt_{countries}(Z_1) = \cup_{i=1,2;W_i \subseteq Z_1} W_i = W_1 = \{u_1\text{-}u_{10}\}$ and thus Figure 12 shows the following rule discovered:

> **Rule 1:** *countries* = {*Canada, USA*}→ *products* ={*corn*} with confidence $\frac{|spt_{countries}(Z_1)|}{|W_1|} = \frac{|\{u_1 : u_{10}\}|}{|\{u_1 : u_{10}\}|} = \frac{10}{10} = 100\%$ according to *countries* $(W_1)$={*Canada, USA*}.

Figure 12: Association rules discovered from Table 2

and the supported set to $Z_2$ is $Spt_{countries}(Z_2) = \cup_{i=1,2;W_i \subseteq Z_2} W_i = W_2 = \{u_{11}\text{-}u_{30}\}$ and the following rule is discovered as illustrated in Figure 13:

> **Rule 2:** *countries* = {*Canada, USA*}→ *products* ={*fish*} with confidence $\frac{|spt_{countries}(Z_2)|}{|W_2|} = \frac{|\{u_{11} : u_{30}\}|}{|\{u_{11} : u_{30}\}|} = \frac{20}{20} = 100\%$ according to *countries* $(W_2)$ = {*Canada, France, USA*}.

Figure 13: Association rules discovered from Table 2

Conversely, we consider the association rule from the attributes *products* to *countries*, it can be found that $Spt_{products}(W_1) = \cup_{i=1,2;Z_i \subseteq W_1} Zi = Z_1 = \{u1\text{-}u10\}$ and the following rule is discovered as represented in Figure 14:

**Rule 3:** *products* =$\{corn\}$ → *countries* = $\{Canada, USA\}$ with confidence $\frac{|spt_{countries}(W_1)|}{|Z_1|} = \frac{|\{u_1 : u_{10}\}|}{|\{u_1 : u_{10}\}|} = \frac{10}{10} = 100\%$ according to *products* $(Z_1)=\{corn\}$.

Figure 14: Association rules discovered from Table 2

and as the same with the above, we have $Spt_{products}(Z_1) = \cup_{i=1,2;Z_i \subseteq W_2} Zi = Z_2 = \{u_{11}\text{-}u_{30}\}$ and the following rule is discovered:

**Rule 4:** *products* =$\{fish\}$ → *countries* = $\{Canada, France, USA\}$ with confidence $\frac{|spt_{countries}(W_2)|}{|Z_2|} = \frac{|\{u_{11} : u_{30}\}|}{|\{u_{11} : u_{30}\}|} = \frac{20}{20} = 100\%$ according to *products* $(Z_2)=\{fish\}$.

Figure 15: Association rules discovered from Table 2

These rules are the same as those maximal association rules discovered from Table 1 as shown in Figure 10. However, this example demonstrates that the rough set approach to discovering knowledge is much simpler than the maximal association method.

# 7. Summary and further work

In this paper, we investigate how to discover maximal association rules from text document collections by using rough set theory. This work is aiming at theoretical aspects and has shown that Rough Set approach is conceptually and computationally more elegant and efficient than the established the maximal association rule methods, and the further results such as efficiently and accurately to identify supported sets could be achieved through incorporating a mechanism for handling vagueness and uncertainty into computing lower and higher approximations.

In addition, we also address the possible reuse of simple ontologies which increasingly evolve on the Internet, with the emergence of classification repositories holding a variety of simple and sophisticated domain-specific ontologies. We believe that it will become crucial important to support reuse of such ontologies for knowledge discovery and automated inference in the near future. Clearly, given a document collection, an issue of how to determine which ontology will be used to construct a taxonomy remains further more investigations, and one strategy to achieve this end is an interest-oriented (supervised) approach. Moreover, some investigation work on implementation aspects is underway.

## Acknowledgement

The authors are indebted to Professor Jiwen Guan for his valuable help on this work. Also we would thank Dr Joanne Lamb for her support on the work when the first author worked at CES, the University of Edinburgh.

### References

1. Agrawal R, Imielinski T and Swami A. Mining Association Rules between Sets of Items in Large Databases. Proceedings of the ACM SIGMOD conference, pp207-216, Washington D.C., 1993.
2. Feldman, R., Aumann, Y., Amir, A., Zilberstein, A., Klösgen, W.: Maximal Association Rules: A New Tool for Mining for Keyword Co-Occurrences in Document Collections. pp167-170, 1997.
3. Srikant, R. and Agrawal, R. Mining Generalized Association Rules. Proc. of the 21st Int'l Conference on Very Large Databases, Zurich, Switzerland, Sep. 1995.
4. John D. Holt, Soon Myoung Chung: Multipass Algorithms for Mining Association Rules in Text Databases. Knowledge and Information Systems 3(2): pp168-183, 2001.
5. Reuters-21578, http://www.research.att.com/~lewis/reuters21578.html, (April 2002).
6. Feldman, R., Fresko, M., Kinar, Y., Lindell, Y., Liphstat, O., Rajman, M., Schler, Y., Zamir, O.: Text Mining at the Term Level. pp65-73, 1998.
7. Gruber, T. A translation Approach to Portable Ontology Specifications. *Knowledge Acquisition.* Vol 5, 1993.
8. WordNet, www.cogsci.princeton.edu/~wn, (April 2002).
9. UN Classifications Registry, esa.un.org/unsd/cr/registry, (April 2002).
10. RAMON, europa.eu.int/comm/eurostat/ramon, (April 2002).
11. McGuinness, D. L. Ontologies Come of Age. To appear in Dieter Fensel, Jim Hendler, Henry Lieberman, and Wolfgang Wahlster, editors. The Semantic Web: Why, What, and How, MIT Press, 2002.
12. Pawlak Z. Rough Set: Theoretical Aspects of Reasoning About Data. Kluwer Academic, 1991.
13. Bi, Y., Anderson, T. and McClean, S. Rule Generation Based on Rough Set Theory for Text Classification. Twentieth SGES International Conference on KBS and Applied AI. pp101-112, 2000.
14. Ahonen-Myka, H. Finding All Frequent Maximal Sequences in Text. Proceedings of the 16th International Conference on Machine Learning ICML-99 Workshop on Machine Learning in Text Data Analysis, eds. D. Mladenic and M. Grobelnik, pp. 11-17, J. Stefan Institute, Ljubljana, 1999.
15. Hotho, A., Mädche, A., Staab, S.: Ontology-based Text Clustering, Workshop "Text Learning: Beyond Supervision",IJCAI 2001.

# Simplest Rules Characterizing Classes Generated by $\delta$-Free Sets

Bruno Crémilleux
GREYC CNRS-UMR 6072, University of Caen
F-14032 Caen Cedex, France

Jean-François Boulicaut
Laboratoire d'Ingénierie des Systèmes d'Information
INSA Lyon
F-69621 Villeurbanne Cedex, France

**Abstract**

We present a new approach that provides the simplest rules characterizing classes with respect to their left-hand sides. This approach is based on a condensed representation ($\delta$-free sets) of data which is efficiently computed. Produced rules have a minimal body (i.e. any subset of the left-hand side of a rule does not enable to conclude on the same class value). We show a sensible sufficient condition that avoids important classification conflicts. Experiments show that the number of rules characterizing classes drastically decreases. The technique is operational for large data sets and can be used even in the difficult context of highly-correlated data where other algorithms fail.

**Keywords:** characterization of classes, rule conflicts, $\delta$-free sets, association rules, classification rules.

## 1 Introduction

*Context and motivations.* Frequent association rules is one popular data mining technique. This kind of process has been studied a lot of times since the definition of the mining task in [1]. Association rules can tell something like "It is frequent that when properties $A_1$ and $A_2$ are true within an example, then property $A_3$ tends to be true". We provide a simple formalization of this task in Section 2.1. Finding rules that characterize classes and classification rules are important research topics as well. Starting from a collection of examples associated with a known class value, classification concerns the design of models that enable to predict accurate class values for unseen examples. The set of examples for which the class value is given is the so-called learning set. Various knowledge representation formalisms have been used for designing classifiers. Classification rules (which are rules that conclude on one class value) are quite popular for that purpose and the literature is abundant (see for example [12]). Mining rules that characterize classes can be viewed as a special form of association rule mining where conclusions of rules are pre-specified.

However, known techniques are not able to handle dense and highly-correlated data (i.e., problems for rule mining) and the large number of produced rules leads to rule conflicts and over-fitting (i.e., rules may be over-specified and miss-classification arise when using them for classifying unseen examples). To cope with these drawbacks, we consider the efficient extraction of the set of the simplest rules characterizing classes w.r.t. their left-hand sides. Furthermore, we found a property that avoids classification conflicts. Such results form a sound basis for the selection of classification rules and the design of a classifier.

*Related work.* Until recently, extracting rules characterizing classes used to undergo two steps: first, association rules were mined from the learning set and then the identification of the classification rules was performed mainly as a post-processing step ([2, 13]). CBA system (Classification Based on Association) is presented in [13]. The selection of a subset of classification rules is done in two steps: first, all rule concluding on the class are produced, some of them are pruned using the pessimistic error rate [20]. Second, a classifier builder selects the final set of rules according to the numbers of well-classified and miss-classified examples of the training set. Besides a high computational cost, Freitas [9] has shown the limitations of such an approach, emphasizing the differences between classification rules and association rules. Furthermore, the huge number of potential interesting classification rules makes this approach difficult (indeed, how to identify the most relevant rule to classify a new case might be quite difficult). Bayardo [3] suggests to add pruning strategies to control combinatorial explosion in the number of candidates. Target-constraint association rules [4] can be used, but rule sets contain many redundant rules useless for prediction. In [15], Liu et al. add two improvements on their CBA system. On one side, to deal with unbalanced class distribution, they use multiple class minimum frequencies in rule generation. On the other side, to tackle large data sets, they propose a technique to combine CBA with the decision tree method and the Naïve-Bayes method. Recent works revisit these questions and bring improvements. In [11], memory consumption and time complexity have been decreased by features selection and, in a post-processing stage, rules covering most examples are selected. CMAR [14] uses statistical techniques to avoid bias and improve efficiency by relevant data structures. The minimum subset of classification rules having the same prediction power (defined by statistical measures or the confidence) as the complete class rule set is computed in [16].

*Contributions.* The contribution of this paper is twofold. First, we provide the simplest rules that characterize classes w.r.t. their left-hand sides, i.e., a key point in classification. Given a rule characterizing a class, one wants that any own and proper subset of its left-hand side does not enable to conclude on the same class value. It is possible to work on difficult contexts such as dense and highly-correlated learning sets. Second, we highlight a property to avoid important classification conflicts for unseen examples. This allows to use such rules to design a classifier. Furthermore, we think that this work proposes an original use of frequent sets (frequent $\delta$-free sets are a generalization of frequent sets) and condensed representations [18].

*Organization of the paper.* The next section defines the concept of $\delta$-strong rule for class characterization. It shows how the simplest rules characterizing classes are derived. We present in Section 3 a property that avoids classification conflicts. Experimental results are given in Section 4.

# 2 Mining the $\delta$-strong rules characterizing classes

Let us provide a simple formalization of $\delta$-strong rule mining task. We start to recall standard definitions.

## 2.1 Association Rule Mining

**Definition 1 (item, itemset, example)** *Assume* $\mathbf{R} = \{A_1, \ldots, A_n\}$*, is a schema of boolean attributes. One attribute from* $\mathbf{R}$ *is called an* item *and a subset of* $\mathbf{R}$ *is called an* itemset. $\mathbf{r}$*, an instance of* $\mathbf{R}$*, is a multi-set of* examples. *Thus,* $\mathbf{r}$ *can be considered as a boolean matrix.*

For instance, these attributes can identify molecule properties. In practice, one can have hundreds of thousands of examples and hundreds of attributes. In our experiments (see section 4) data have 6,150 fragments. This is obviously a difficult mining context.

**Definition 2 (association rule)** *Given* $\mathbf{r}$*, an instance of* $\mathbf{R}$*, an* association rule *on* $\mathbf{r}$ *is an expression* $X \Rightarrow B$*, where the itemset* $X \subseteq \mathbf{R}$ *and* $B \in \mathbf{R} \setminus X$.

The intuitive meaning of a potentially interesting association rule $X \Rightarrow B$ is that all the items in $X \cup \{B\}$ are true (value 1) for enough examples and that when an example contains true for each item of $X$, then this example tends to contain true for item $B$ too. This semantics is captured by the classical measures of *frequency* and *confidence* [1].

**Definition 3 (frequency, confidence)** *Given* $W \subseteq \mathbf{R}$, $\mathcal{F}(W, \mathbf{r})$ *(or frequency of* $W$*) is the number of examples in* $\mathbf{r}$ *that contain* 1 *for each item in* $W$*. The frequency of* $X \Rightarrow B$ *in* $\mathbf{r}$ *is defined as* $\mathcal{F}(X \cup \{B\}, \mathbf{r})$ *and its confidence is* $\mathcal{F}(X \cup \{B\}, \mathbf{r}) / \mathcal{F}(X, \mathbf{r})$*. We define an absolute frequency (a number of examples* $\leq |\mathbf{r}|$*). We also use the relative frequency* $\mathcal{F}(X \cup \{B\}, \mathbf{r}) / |\mathbf{r}|$*, i.e., a value in* $[0, 1]$.

The standard association rule mining task concerns the discovery of *every* rule whose frequency and confidence are greater than user-specified thresholds. In other words, one wants rules that are frequent "enough" and valid. The main algorithmic issue concerns the computation of every frequent set.

**Definition 4 (frequent itemset)** *Given* $\gamma$ *a frequency threshold* $\leq |\mathbf{r}|$*. An itemset* $X$ *is said* frequent *or* $\gamma$*-frequent if* $\mathcal{F}(X, \mathbf{r}) \geq \gamma$.

The complexity of frequent itemset mining is exponential with the number of attributes. Many research works (e.g. [22, 19, 6]) concern the contexts for which such a discovery remains tractable, even though a trade-off is needed with the exact knowledge of the frequencies and/or the completeness of the extractions.

## 2.2 $\delta$-strong rules

A rule characterizing classes must conclude on class values with a rather high confidence. $\delta$-strong rules introduced in [6] satisfy such a constraint.

**Definition 5 ($\delta$-strong rules)** *Given* $\mathbf{R}$, *a matrix* $\mathbf{r}$, *a frequency threshold* $\gamma$, *and an integer* $\delta$, *a* $\delta$-strong rule *on* $\mathbf{r}$ *is an association rule* $X \Rightarrow B$, *where* $\mathcal{F}(X \cup \{B\}, \mathbf{r}) \geq \gamma$, $\mathcal{F}(X, \mathbf{r}) - \mathcal{F}(X \cup \{B\}, \mathbf{r}) \leq \delta$, $X \subseteq \mathbf{R}$, *and* $B \in \mathbf{R} \setminus X$.

A $\delta$-strong rule is violated by at most $\delta$ examples. In other words, its confidence is at least equal to $1 - (\delta/\gamma)$. From a technical perspective, $\delta$-strong rules can be built from $\delta$-free sets that constitute their left-hand sides [6]. Let us provide the key intuition for the concept of $\delta$-free set. An itemset $X$ is called $\delta$-free if there is no $\delta$-strong rule that holds between two of its own and proper subsets. We illustrate this notion with Table 1 (this table consists of 8 examples, each one identified by its Id, and there are 4 items denoted $A_1 \dots A_4$).

| Id | Items | | | |
|---|---|---|---|---|
| | $A_1$ | $A_2$ | $A_3$ | $A_4$ |
| 1 | 1 | 1 | 1 | 1 |
| 2 | 1 | 1 | 1 | 1 |
| 3 | 1 | 1 | 1 | 1 |
| 4 | 1 | | 1 | |
| 5 | | 1 | 1 | |
| 6 | | | 1 | |
| 7 | 1 | | 1 | 1 |
| 8 | 1 | 1 | | 1 |

Table 1: A set of 8 examples described by 4 items

The case $\delta = 0$ (corresponding to 0-free-sets) is important: no rule with confidence equal to 1 holds between proper subsets of $X$. For instance, $A_1A_2$ is a 0-free set because all rules constructed from proper subsets of $A_1A_2$ have at least one exception: examples numbers 4 and 7 for the rule $A_1 \Rightarrow A_2$ and example number 5 for the rule $A_2 \Rightarrow A_1$. If $\delta = 1$, $A_1A_2$ is not a 1-free set owing to the rule $A_2 \Rightarrow A_1$ which has only one exception. On the contrary, $A_1$ and $A_2$, for instance, are 1-free sets.

$\delta$-free sets are related to the concepts of closed itemsets in [19] and almost-closures in [5]. In the case $\delta = 0$, let us provide the relationship with the *closure* operator.

**Definition 6 (closure)** *Given an itemset $X$, the* closure *of $X$ is the maximal superset (w.r.t. set inclusion) of $X$ that has the same frequency than $X$.*

For instance in Table 1, with $X = A_1A_2$, $A_4$ belongs to the closure of $X$ (i.e. $A_4$ is always true when $A_1$ and $A_2$ are true). In that case, frequencies of $A_1A_2$ and $A_1A_2A_4$ are the same. The closure of $X$ can be computed efficiently during the computation of the frequency of $X$ and, in our example, one avoids to count the frequencies of $A_1A_2A_4$. In highly-correlated data, it reduces drastically the extraction time [19, 5]. Frequent closed itemsets are the closures of 0-free sets.

When $\delta > 0$, we are interested in the *almost-closures* of a frequent $\delta$-free set $X$: $B$ belongs to the almost-closure of $X$ if $\mathcal{F}(X, \mathbf{r}) - \mathcal{F}(X \cup \{B\}, \mathbf{r}) \leq \delta$. It is easy to provide $\delta$-strong rules from the $\gamma$-frequent $\delta$-free sets and their almost-closures: in this case, we have the rule $X \Rightarrow B$ with at most $\delta$ exceptions. Following our example given in Table 1, $A_4$ belongs to the almost-closure of $A_1$ with $\delta = 1$ (there is only one exception, example number 4).

A collection of frequent $\delta$-free sets is a condensed representation of the collection of frequent itemsets. If $\delta = 0$, one can compute the frequency of every frequent itemset. If $\delta > 0$, one can approximate the frequency of every frequent itemset $X$ with a bounded error: when an itemset $X$ is not $\delta$-free, its frequency is approximated from the frequency of the largest $\delta$-free set included in $X$ [6]. In [6], it is shown that the error is very low in practice.

One interesting property of *freeness* is its anti-monotonicity w.r.t. itemset inclusion (a property $\rho$ is *anti-monotone* iff for all itemsets $X$ and $Y$, $\rho(X)$ and $Y \subseteq X$ implies $\rho(Y)$). It gives a safe pruning criterion for level-wise search in the itemset lattice [17, 6]. Accordingly, it is possible to design efficient algorithms for frequent $\delta$-free set discovery and have tractable extractions for practical mining tasks that are intractable with `apriori`-like algorithms (see Section 4).

## 2.3 $\delta$-strong rules and minimal body

We have seen that $\delta$-strong rules have a number of exceptions bounded by $\delta$ and can be efficiently extracted from large sets of highly-correlated data. Furthermore, this formalism offers a property of minimal body which is a key point for a classification purpose.

**Definition 7 (rule with a minimal body)** *Given a frequency threshold $\gamma$ and an integer $\delta$, a rule $X \Rightarrow B$ has a* minimal body *if there is no frequent rule $Y \Rightarrow B$ with $Y \subset X$ and a confidence greater or equal to $1 - (\delta/\gamma)$.*

This definition means that we consider only minimum sets of items to end up on $B$, the uncertainty being controlled by $\delta$. In practical applications, more specified rules concluding on $B$ can exist. Nevertheless, Section 3 gives a property showing that, under a sensible assumption, any specified rule $R$ characterizes the same class as the rule with a minimal body which is included in $R$.

**Property 1 (minimal body)** *Given a frequency threshold $\gamma$, an integer $\delta$ and $X \Rightarrow B$ a rule with a minimal body, then $X$ is a $\delta$-free set.*

This result comes from properties of $\delta$-free sets [6]. The key intuition of this result is that a $\delta$-free set $X$ is a minimal conjunction of items to know the frequencies of a set of items $\mathcal{C}$ ($\mathcal{C}$ is bounded by the closed itemset defined by $X$ and its closure). As all itemsets of $\mathcal{C}$ have the same frequency, $X$ is a minimal conjunction of items which has to be used to produce all rules having their left-hand sides stemming from $\mathcal{C}$. The whole collection of $\delta$-free sets ensures to produce all rules with minimal body.

Nevertheless, let us note that it can happen that a $\delta$-strong rule has not a minimal body. For instance, in Table 1, $A_1A_2A_3$ is a 0-free set having $A_4$ in its closure. It means that the rule $A_1A_2A_3 \Rightarrow A_4$ exists (with a frequency value of 3). We have seen in the previous section that there is also the rule $A_1A_2 \Rightarrow A_4$ (with a frequency value of 4) which is the simplest rule to conclude on $A_4$ with $\delta = 0$. Our prototype can be seen as an instance of the level-wise search algorithm presented in [17] which allows to recognize a minimal conjunction of items concluding on $B$. Let us consider $X$ a $\delta$-free set with $k$ items (i.e. a $k$-$\delta$-free set produced at level $k$). When the almost-closure of $X$ is computed, we start to merge the almost-closures of all $(k-1)$-$\delta$-free sets included in $X$. $\delta$-strong rules with a minimal body will be infer only from new items added in the almost-closure of $X$ (i.e. items which do not belonging to the set of the almost-closures of all $(k-1)$-$\delta$-free sets included in $X$).

We argue that this property of minimal body is a fundamental issue for class characterization. Not only it prevents from over-fitting [21] (i.e. over-specified rules acquired on the learning set and leading to miss-classified unseen examples) but also it makes the characterization of an example easier to explain. It provides a feedback on the application domain expertise that can be reused for further analysis.

## 2.4 $\delta$-strong rules characterizing classes

Let us consider a classification task with $k$ class values. Assuming $C_1, \ldots, C_k$ are the $k$ items that denote class values.

**Definition 8 ($\delta$-strong rule characterizing classes)** *A* $\delta$-strong rule characterizing classes *is a $\delta$-strong rule with a minimal body that concludes on one class value (i.e., $C_i$).*

Hereafter, we consider the typical case where each example is associated to a unique class value. Thus, we have the following equality (see equation 1). Let us notice that when it is clear from the context, $\mathbf{r}$ is omitted:

$$\sum_{i=1}^{k} \mathcal{F}(C_i) = |\mathbf{r}| \qquad (1)$$

The value of $\delta$ is fundamental to obtain relevant rules. Let us recall that when $\delta = 0$, every extracted rule has a confidence value of 1. This is a problem for the practical impact. Indeed, it is rare that rules characterizing classes with confidence 1 hold in real data. In many application domains, such as biology or medicine, where the same cause does not always produce the same effect and/or where parameter values that are used for decision making are unknown, we must accept exceptions for rules. Experts are trained to cope with some bounded uncertainty.

The more $\delta$ raises, the more the confidence decreases. Intuitively, we feel that when the confidence decreases (i.e. the uncertainty increases), it can give rise to more and more classification conflicts. In order to characterize classes, it is useful to verify whether this formalism enables to point out situations (and under which assumptions) where rule conflicts can be avoided. The next section studies the relationship between the values for $\delta$ and $\gamma$ and classification conflicts. We show that with respect to a simple property, we can avoid some types of classification conflicts.

# 3 Avoid rule conflicts

Let us consider now a systematic study of three pairs of rules that lead to classification conflicts.

## 3.1 Identical body conflicts

An identical body conflict is characterized by a pair of rules that have the same body but conclude on different class values. It means that a same $\delta$-free set gives rise to at least two $\delta$-strong rules characterizing classes. For example :

$$R_1 : X \Rightarrow C_1 \qquad R_2 : X \Rightarrow C_2$$

The pair $\{R_1, R_2\}$ does not characterize properly classes and leads to a conflict when an example to be classified contains $X$. Obviously, the more $\delta$ is large w.r.t. $\gamma$, the more that identical body conflicts can appear.

Let us now consider a sufficient condition on $\delta$ and $\gamma$ values such that identical body conflicts are impossible. Assume that we have the $\delta$-strong rule characterizing classes $R_1 : X \Rightarrow C_1 \ \{\delta_1\}$ with frequency $\gamma_1$ and $\delta_1$ exceptions (figure between braces indicated the exact number of exceptions). Note that the choice of $C_1$ for the class value is arbitrary. Given that $R_1$ is a $\delta$-strong rule, we get:

$$\gamma_1 = \mathcal{F}(X \cup \{C_1\}) \geq \gamma$$
$$\delta_1 = \mathcal{F}(X) - \mathcal{F}(X \cup \{C_1\}) \leq \delta$$

Let us look now for conditions on $\gamma$ and $\delta$ values that prevent the existence of a $\delta$-strong rule characterizing classes $R_2 : X \Rightarrow C_2 \ \{\delta_2\}$ with frequency $\gamma_2$ and $\delta_2$ exceptions such that $C_2$ is a class value different from $C_1$. As each example is associated to a unique class value, we have from the Equation 1 (the inequality becomes an equality if the class has just the two values $C_1$ and $C_2$):

$$\mathcal{F}(X \cup \{C_1\}) + \mathcal{F}(X \cup \{C_2\}) \leq \mathcal{F}(X)$$

It points out a lower bound for $\delta$ w.r.t. $\gamma_2$:

$$\gamma_2 = \mathcal{F}(X \cup \{C_2\}) \leq (\mathcal{F}(X) - \mathcal{F}(X \cup \{C_1\}) \leq \delta \tag{2}$$

If $R_2$ is a $\delta$-strong rule, we have $\gamma_2 \geq \gamma$. This inequality combined with inequality 2 enables to compare $\gamma$ and $\delta$:

$$\gamma \leq \gamma_2 \leq \delta \tag{3}$$

The inequality 3 shows that it is sufficient to take $\delta < \gamma$ to enforce that $R_2$ is not a $\delta$-strong rule characterizing classes.

**Property 2** *If $\delta < \gamma$, there is no identical body conflict.*

## 3.2 Included bodies conflicts

Given the pair $\{R_1, R_2\}$, there is an included bodies conflict if the left-hand side of $R_1$ is included in the left-hand side of $R_2$ (or vice-versa) and if $R_1$ and $R_2$ have different right-hand sides. For instance:

$$R_1 : X \Rightarrow C_1 \qquad R_2 : X \cup Y \Rightarrow C_2$$

It means that the $\delta$-free set that produces one of the rules is included in the $\delta$-free set from which the other rule is derived. The pair $\{R_1, R_2\}$ is not a reliable characterization of classes since it leads to a conflict as soon as an example supports $X$ (however, this pair suggests that when $Y$ is added to $X$ there may be an interesting exceptional situation if the frequency of the rule $X \cup Y \Rightarrow C_2$ is small w.r.t. the frequency of the rule $X \Rightarrow C_1$).

Let us now discuss about a sufficient condition on $\delta$ and $\gamma$ such that there is no included bodies conflict. Assume that there is a $\delta$-strong rule characterizing classes $X \Rightarrow C_1$ $\{\delta_1\}$ with frequency $\gamma_1$ and $\delta_1$ exceptions. Let us look now for conditions on $\gamma$ and $\delta$ values that prevent the existence of a $\delta$-strong rule characterizing classes $R_2$ $X \cup Y \Rightarrow C_2$ $\{\delta_2\}$ with frequency $\gamma_2$ and $\delta_2$ exceptions with $Y \subseteq \mathbf{R} \setminus X$. As previously, the following inequality holds:

$$\mathcal{F}(X \cup \{C_1\}) + \mathcal{F}(X \cup \{C_2\}) \leq \mathcal{F}(X)$$

and thus: $\mathcal{F}(X \cup \{C_2\}) \leq \mathcal{F}(X) - \mathcal{F}(X \cup \{C_1\}) \leq \delta$
and we have: $\gamma_2 = \mathcal{F}(X \cup Y \cup \{C_2\}) \leq \mathcal{F}(X \cup \{C_2\})$

As for the first kind of conflict, we can get a lower bound for $\delta$ w.r.t. $\gamma_2$:

$$\gamma_2 = \mathcal{F}(X \cup Y \cup \{C_2\}) \leq \mathcal{F}(X \cup \{C_2\} \leq \delta \tag{4}$$

To enforce that $R_2$ is $\delta$-strong, we must have $\gamma_2 \geq \gamma$. This bound, combined with the one from inequality 4 enables to compare $\gamma$ and $\delta$:

$$\gamma \leq \gamma_2 \leq \delta \tag{5}$$

Inequality 5 shows that it is a sufficient condition to take $\delta < \gamma$ to enforce that $R_2$ cannot be a $\delta$-strong rule characterizing classes.

**Property 3** *If $\delta < \gamma$, there is no included bodies conflict.*

### 3.3 Distinct bodies conflicts

A distinct bodies conflict can not be foreseen: it occurs only when an unseen example is to be classified. Assume an example is supported by a pair of rules (that have distinct but not included bodies) concluding on two different class values. For instance, the pair:

$$R_1 : X \Rightarrow C_1 \qquad R_2 : Y \Rightarrow C_2$$

leads to a conflict when the unseen example satisfies $X \cup Y$. Note that we can have $X \cap Y \neq \emptyset$.

It is not possible to avoid such a conflict when producing the rules. On the other hand, interestingly, one can see that if $\delta < \gamma$, there is no distinct bodies conflict within the pair $\{R_1, R_2\}$ if there is a $\delta$-strong rule characterizing classes $X \cup Y \Rightarrow C_i$. Indeed, we saw that if $\delta < \gamma$, the existence of a $\delta$-strong rule $X \cup Y \Rightarrow C_i$ avoids the existence of simpler rules (with bodies that are subsets of $X \cup Y$, like $R_1$ and $R_2$) that conclude on classes.

The property $\delta < \gamma$ enforces no identical body conflict and no included bodies conflict. It also enforces no distinct bodies conflict for pairs of rules that are such that the union of their left-hand sides gives rise to a $\delta$-strong rule characterizing classes. If there is not such a $\delta$-strong rule, that means that the learning set does not contain enough examples, according to the thresholds, in order to solve the ambiguity on the relationship between the union of the left-hand sides of the rules and classes.

## 4 Experiments

The purpose of the first experiment is to compare the number of all classification rules versus the number of $\delta$-strong rules characterizing classes. Data come from the discovery challenge on thrombosis data (see `http://lisp.vse.cz/challenge/pkdd2001/`), classes are collagen diseases. After a data preparation work [8], the resulting file gathers 721 tuples described by 56 binary items. As this training set is small, we were able to run an `apriori`-based algorithm even with a low frequency threshold ($\gamma = 3$, i.e., 0.5%).

We performed three experiments (see Table 2) with different values of $\gamma$ and $\delta$. On the one hand, we mined $\delta$-strong rules characterizing classes. On the other hand, we extracted with the same value of $\gamma$ with an `apriori`-based algorithm all classification rules with a single item in their right-hand side and with a confidence threshold equals the lowest confidence value possible for a $\delta$-strong rule characterizing classes (this value, denoted *minconf.*, depends on $\delta$ and $\gamma$: see Table 2). In this table, each percentage is the number of $\delta$-strong rules characterizing classes divided by the number of classification rules. We see that mining the $\delta$-strong rules characterizing classes strongly reduces the number of rules.

| | No. of rules | |
|---|---|---|
| | $\delta$-strong rules characterizing classes | classification rules |
| $\gamma = 3$ $\delta = 2$ $(minconf. = 33\%)$ | 1,342 (1.77%) | 76,004 |
| $\gamma = 6$ $\delta = 3$ $(minconf. = 50\%)$ | 526 (4.25%) | 12,366 |
| $\gamma = 6$ $\delta = 5$ $(minconf. = 16\%)$ | 801 (2.65%) | 30,260 |

Table 2: Comparison of numbers of rules

The goal of the second experiment is to show that $\delta$-strong rules characterizing classes can be extracted efficiently from large data sets and we give a first approach to design a classifier stemming from these rules. Data are those used in the Predictive Toxicology Challenge (PTC) for 2000-2001 (see `http://www.informatik.uni-freiburg.de/~ml/ptc/`). The aim is to predict chemical carcinogens (i.e. the class) on several rodents populations (each file contains about 350 examples). Each molecule is represented by 6,150 binary attributes (i.e. chemical fragment). It is a hard context for association rule mining since we have a huge number of attributes. On these data, with most values of $\gamma$ indicated in Table 3, `apriori`-like algorithms fail due to an excessive memory requirement (we used a PC with 768 MB of memory and a 500 MHz Pentium III processor with Linux operating system). For different values of $\delta$ and $\gamma$ (but always with $\delta < \gamma$), Table 3 gives the extraction time, the number of $\delta$-free sets and almost-closures that contain a class value on male rats. This last number can be seen as the number of potential $\delta$-strong rule characterizing classes (i.e., with any frequency and confidence values). Results on other populations are given in [7].

As expected, the more we increase the value of $\delta$, the more we can have tractable extractions for lower frequency thresholds. Note that with $\delta = 0$, there is no rule characterizing classes for the frequency threshold we can use. It illustrates the added-value of the relaxed constraint on $\delta$.

It is not sensible to use the whole collection of $\delta$-strong rules characterizing classes to classify unseen examples because some rules can have low frequency (and/or confidence if $\delta$ is large w.r.t. $\gamma$). These rules with a poor quality may introduce errors and have to be deleted. We are giving now a first approach to design a classifier stemming from the $\delta$-strong rules characterizing classes. This approach has techniques in common with the method used by the classifier

| $\gamma/\lvert\mathbf{r}\rvert$ | $\delta$ | Time (sec.) | No. of $\delta$-free sets | No. of almost-closures with a class value |
|---|---|---|---|---|
| 0.15 | 15 | intractable | - | - |
| 0.15 | 17 | 3814 | 24671 | 2835 |
| 0.15 | 20 | 1563 | 17173 | 4529 |
| 0.20 | 10 | 3300 | 26377 | 0 |
| 0.20 | 15 | 850 | 12071 | 8 |
| 0.20 | 20 | 323 | 7109 | 305 |
| 0.30 | 10 | 69 | 3473 | 0 |
| 0.40 | 0 | intractable | - | - |
| 0.40 | 10 | 36 | 922 | 0 |
| 0.50 | 0 | 201 | 56775 | 0 |

Table 3: Time, $\delta$-free sets and almost-closures w.r.t. $\delta$ and $\gamma$

builder of CBA [13] that we have mentioned in Section 1, except that we use a test file to select rules (and we think that this point is important). Data are split into a training file (4/5 of data) and a test file (1/5 of data). Class has the same frequency distribution in each file and in the whole data. For each rule, we compute a score (denoted $\Delta$) which is the difference between the well-classified and the miss-classified examples of the test file. Then rules are sorted w.r.t. $\Delta$ and, by varying $\Delta$, we define a family of nested sets of rules by the following way: for a value $\Delta_1$ of $\Delta$, we kept rules having $\Delta$ higher or equal to $\Delta_1$. All rules belonging to the set defined by $\Delta_1$ belong to sets defined by $\Delta_2$ with $\Delta_2 < \Delta_1$. Then, we use a set of rules with a high value of $\Delta$ to classify unseen examples.

We tested this approach on a validation file (185 new chemicals not used to build and select the $\delta$-strong rules characterizing classes) provided by the organizers of the ECML-PKDD 2001 Predictive Toxicology Challenge. When there is a distinct bodies conflict, the class value which maximizes the amount of products of the frequency by the confidence of triggered rules is predicted. According to the population of rodents, the used sets of rules to predict have between 9 and 76 rules. The rate of well-classified chemicals varies between 61.1% and 76.8% with an average of 70.55% Note that predict chemical carcinogens has been identified as a difficult classification task (the correct classification score for experts in the domain ranges from 28% to 78% [10]). We also used the learning classification rules software `C4.5` [20]. Decision trees are built from the same training sets and also tested with the validation file. With 5 as the minimum value of examples for subtrees, trees have around 50 nodes and rates of well-classified 60%. This approach achieved good results against decision trees.

# 5 Conclusion

We have developed an original technique based on $\delta$-free sets to mine the simplest rules characterizing classes w.r.t. their left-hand sides. We claim that extracting such a set of rules brings several advantages. As the number of rules decreases and as rules are simpler, sets of rules characterizing classes are more understandable. Secondly, it prevents from over-fitting which is fundamental in real-world domains for classes characterization. Experiments show a significant reduction of the number of rules. This approach is effective even in the case of huge, dense and/or highly correlated learning data sets.

A straightforward use of such rules is the characterization of classes. Then, we have shown a sensible sufficient condition that avoids important classification conflicts. Such results form a sound basis for the selection of classification rules and the design of a classifier.

## Acknowledgements

The authors thank Christophe Rigotti for his contribution to this research and his constructive comments on the paper.

# References

1. Agrawal, R. and Imielinski, T. and Swami, A. Mining association rules between sets of items in large databases, In *Proceedings SIGMOD'93*, ACM Press, pp. 207-216, 1993.

2. Ali, K. and Manganaris, S. and Srikant, R. Partial classification using association rules, In *Proceedings of the Third International Conference on Knowledge Discovery and Data Mining, KDD'97*, AAAI Press, pp. 115-118, 1997.

3. Bayardo, R. J., Brute-force mining of high-confidence classification rules, In *Proceedings of the Third International Conference on Knowledge Discovery and Data Mining, KDD'97*, AAAI Press, pp. 123-126, 1997.

4. Bayardo, R. J. and Agrawal, R. and Gunopulos, D. Constraint-based rule mining in large, dense database, In *Proceedings ICDE'99*, pp. 188-197, 1999.

5. Boulicaut, J. F. and Bykowski, A. Frequent closures as a concise representation for binary data mining, In *Proceedings of the Fourth Pacific-Asia Conference on Knowledge Discovery and Data Mining, PAKDD'00*, LNAI 1805, Springer-Verlag, pp. 62-73, Kyoto, Japan, 2000.

6. Boulicaut, J. F. and Bykowski, A. and Rigotti, C. Approximation of frequency queries by means of free-sets, In *Proceedings of the Fourth European Conference on Principles and Practice of Knowledge Discovery in Databases, PKDD'00*, LNAI 1910, Springer-Verlag, pp. 75-85, Lyon, France, 2000.

7. Boulicaut, J. F. and Crémilleux, B. Delta-strong classification rules for characterizing chemical carcinogens, In *Proceedings of the Predictive Toxicology Challenge for 2000-2001 co-located with PKDD'01*, Freiburg, Germany, 2001.

8. Boulicaut, J. F. and Crémilleux, B. Delta-strong classification rules for predicting collagen diseases, In *Discovery Challenge on Thrombosis Data for 2000-2001 co-located with PKDD'01*, pp. 29-38, Freiburg, Germany, 2001.

9. Freitas, A. A. Understanding the crucial differences between classification and discovery of association rules - a position paper, In *SIGKDD Explorations*, Vol. 2(1), pp. 65-69, 2000.

10. Helma, C. and Gottmann, E. and Kramer, S. Knowledge Discovery and data mining in toxicology Technical Report, University of Freiburg, 2000.

11. Jovanoski, V. and Lavrac, N. Classification Rule with Apriori-C, In *Proceedings of the Integrating Aspects of Data Mining, Decision Support and Meta Learning workshop, co-located with PKDD'01*, 81-92, Freiburg, Germany, 2001.

12. King, R.D. and Feng, C. and Sutherland, A. Statlog: Comparison of classification algorithms on large real-world problems, In *Applied Artificial Intelligence*, 1995.

13. Liu, B. and Hsu, W. and Ma, Y. Integrating classification and association rules mining, In *Proceedings of the Fourth International Conference on Knowledge Discovery & Data Mining, KKDD'98*, AAAI Press, pp. 80-86, 1998.

14. Li, W. and Han, J. and Pei, J. CMAR: Accurate and Efficient Classification Based on Multiple Class-Association Rules, In *Proceedings of the IEEE International Conference on Data Mining, ICDM'01*, San Jose, California, 2001.

15. Liu, B. and Ma, Y. and Wong, C. K. Classification using association rules: weaknesses and enhancements, In *Data mining for scientific applications*, Kumar, V. et al (eds), pp. 1-11, 2001.

16. Li, J. and Shen, H. and Topor, R. Mining the Smallest Association Rule Set for Predictions, In *Proceedings of the IEEE International Conference on Data Mining, ICDM'01*, San Jose, California, 2001.

17. Mannila, H. and Toivonen, H. Levelwise search and borders of theories in knowledge discovery In *Data Mining and Knowledge Discovery*, vol. 3(1), pp. 241-258, 1997.

18. Mannila, H. and Toivonen, H. Multiple uses of frequent sets and condensed representations, In *Proceedings of the Second International Conference on Knowledge Discovery and Data Mining, KDD'96*, pp. 189-194, Portland, Oregon, 1996.

19. Pasquier, N. and Bastide, Y. and Taouil, R and Lakhal, L. Efficient mining of association rules using closed itemset lattices. In *Information Systems* 24(1), pp. 25-46. 1999.

20. Quinlan, J. R. C4.5 Programs for machine learning Morgan Kaufmann, San Mateo, Californie, 1993.

21. Schaffer, C. Overfitting avoidance as bias, In *Machine Learning*, vol. 10, pp. 153-178, 1993.

22. Toivonen, H. Sampling large databases for association rules, In *Proceedings of the 22nd International Conference on Very Large Databases, VLDB'96*, Morgan Kaufmann, pp. 134-145, 1996.

# Epicurean-style Learning Applied to the Classification of Gene-Expression Data*

Andreas A. Albrecht
Dept. of Computer Science, Univ. of Hertfordshire
Hatfield, Herts AL10 9AB, UK

Staal A. Vinterbo
Harvard Medical School, Decision Systems Group
Boston, MA 02115, USA

Lucila Ohno-Machado
Harvard Medical School, Decision Systems Group
Boston, MA 02115, USA, and
MIT, Division of Health Sciences and Technology
Cambridge, MA 02139, USA

**Abstract**

We investigate the use of perceptrons for classification of microarray data where we use two datasets that were published in Khan et al., *Nature* [Medicine],vol.7, 2001, and Golub et al., *Science*, vol. 286, 1999. The classification problem studied by Khan et al. is related to the diagnosis of small round blue cell tumours of childhood (SRBCT) which are difficult to classify both clinically and via routine histology. Golub et al. study acute myeloid leukemia (AML) and acute lymphoblastic leukemia (ALL). We used a simulated annealing-based method in learning a system of perceptrons, each obtained by resampling of the training set. Our results are comparable to those of Khan et al. and Golub et al., indicating that there is a role for perceptrons in the classification of tumours based on gene expression data. We also show that it is critical to perform feature selection in this type of models, i.e., we propose a method for identifying genes that might be significant for the particular tumour types. For SRBCTs, zero error on test data has been obtained for only 10 out of 2308 genes; for the ALL/AML problem, our results are competitive to the best results published in the literature, and we obtain 6 genes out of 7129 genes that are used for the classification procedure. Furthermore, we provide evidence that Epicurean-style learning is essential for obtaining the best classification results.

## 1 Introduction

Measuring gene expression levels is important for understanding the genetic basis of diseases. The simultaneous measurement of gene expression levels for

*Research partially supported by EPSRC Grant GR/R72938/01 and by the Taplin award from the Harvard/MIT Health Sciences and Technology Division.

thousands of genes is now possible due to microarray technology [17, 18]. Data derived from microarrays are difficult to analyze without the help of computers, as keeping track of thousands of measurements and their relationships is overwhelmingly complicated. Several authors have utilized unsupervised learning algorithms to cluster gene expression data [6]. In those applications, the goal is to find genes that have correlated patterns of expression, in order to facilitate the discovery of regulatory networks. Recent publications have begun to deal with supervised classification for gene expression derived from microarrays [7]. The goal in these applications is usually to classify cases into diagnostic or prognostic categories that are verifiable by a "gold-standard". Additionally, researchers try to determine which genes are most significantly related to the category of interest. Since the number of measurements is very large compared to the number of arrays, there is tremendous potential for overfitting in models that do not utilize a pre-processing step for feature selection. The feature selection process itself is of interest, as it helps to determine the relative importance of a gene in the classification. Approaches for feature selection in the context of gene expression analysis are currently being investigated. Developing a strategy for selecting genes that are important in a classification model, regardless of their absolute expression levels, is important in this context. Determining whether simple learning models can be successfully applied to this type of problem is also important. In this paper, we propose an algorithm for learning perceptrons based on simulated annealing and a resampling strategy and show that it can be successfully applied to the analysis of gene-expression data. One of the key features of our approach is training perceptrons [16, 19] on randomly selected subsets of the entire sample set. In the present application, it turns out that the learning procedure is finished in almost all cases with zero error, which might be caused by the small amount of samples available (although the size of each sample is quite large, e.g., 7129 gene data in the ALL/AML problem). However, even in the case of image classification considered in [2], the same effect has been observed on subsets of about 160 samples, each of them with 14161 inputs. Thus, in almost all cases the perceptron computed on a subset represents a true hypothesis on a part of the entire sample set. The different hypotheses are then taken together by a voting procedure to form the final hypothesis. This approach goes along the lines of a learning method which has been called Epicurean learning by Cleary et al. in [5] (with reference to [21]), motivated by Epicurus' paradigm that all hypotheses fitting the known data should be retained [8]. Furey et al. [7] used a similar method when they compared SVM classifications of gene-expression data to a perceptron-based learning algorithm (referring to the approach of taking linear combinations of decision rules obtained at each iteration step as described in [12]). We provide results from computational experiments showing that the classification rate becomes worse if the size of randomly chosen subsets becomes close to the entire sample set, although different hypotheses are calculated by the underlying stochastic local search.

# 2 Methods

Let $D \subseteq Q^n$ be our input data table where each of the columns corresponds to expression measurements for a particular gene over the tissues investigated. Further let $Q^n \to \{1, 2, \ldots, m\}$ be a partial function that for $D$ returns the tumor class associated with each row.

We would like to find a realization of a function $F : Q^n \to 2^{\{1,2,\ldots,m\}}$ that represents an extension of $c$ that we can use to classify new, unseen expression measurement vectors.

We do this as follows. For each class $i \in \{1, 2, \ldots, m\}$, we construct a classifier $F_i : Q^n \to [0, 1]$. These $F_i$ are then combined to form $F$ as:

$$F(x) = \{j | F_j(x) = \max_i F_i(x)\}.$$

The number $|F(x)|$ gives us an indication of how uniquely we were able to classify $x$. We choose to discard the classification if $|F(x)| > 1$.

We now turn to the construction of the functions $F_i$. A *perceptron* $p$ is a function $p : R^n \times R^n \times R \to \{0, 1\}$ such that

$$p(x, w, \vartheta) = p_{w,\vartheta}(x) = \tau_\vartheta(wx),$$

where $\tau$ is the unit step function at threshold $\vartheta$ defined as

$$\tau_\vartheta(y) = \begin{cases} 0 & \text{if } y < \vartheta, \\ 1 & \text{otherwise.} \end{cases}$$

Given $k_i$ perceptrons, we define $F_i$ to be

$$F_i(x) = \frac{1}{k_i} \sum_{j=1}^{k_i} p_{w,0}^{ij}(x).$$

where the $w$'s are restricted to be rational (for simpler notations, we assume $\vartheta = 0$ and always $x_n = 1$, i.e., $w_n$ represents the threshold). There are two problems that need to be solved:

1. Finding the $w_j^i$'s, i.e., training the perceptrons;
2. Finding $k_i$ for each class $i$.

The parameter $k_i$ is chosen empirically. We will discuss how this is done in Section 4. In the remainder of this section we address the training of the perceptrons, and pragmatics regarding reduction of the input dimensionality.

## 2.1 Perceptron Training

Let $T = T^+ \cup T^-$ be a training set composed of positive and negative examples, respectively. We want to find the parameters $w$ of the perceptron $p$ that maximize the separation of the positive and negative examples in $T$.

Höffgen and Sin on [13] have shown that finding a linear threshold function that minimizes the number of misclassified vectors is NP-hard in general. Hence we need to apply heuristics to the problem of training a perceptron.

Simulated annealing has been proven to be a versatile tool in combinatorial optimisation [1, 15], and is our choice of optimization strategy. In [3], we have demonstrated on randomly generated disjunctive normal forms that the classification rate improves if the perceptron algorithm is combined with logarithmic simulated annealing. An application to real world data has been provided in [2].

Given a search space $W$ in which we want to find an element that minimizes an objective function $o : W \to N$, an initial "current location" $w_s \in W$, a function $s : W \to W$ that in a stochastic fashion proposes a next "current location" that we hope will lead to the wanted optimum, a function $a : N \times W \times W \to \{0, 1\}$ that accepts or reject the proposed next current location, and finally a stopping criterion. We can illustrate the strategy by the following simple pseudo-code skeleton:

```
w ← w_s; k ← 0
while not stop(k, w)
    k ← k + 1; w_n ← s(w)
    if a_k(w, w_n) = 1
        w ← w_n
```

The idea of the algorithm is to, while initially allowing locally suboptimal steps, become more restrictive in allowing locally sub-optimal steps to be taken over time. The hope is to avoid premature convergence to local minima. In our case we define our objective function to be the number of misclassified elements in $T$. Let

$$M_T(w) = \{x \in T^+ | p_{w,0}(x) < 1\} \cup \{x \in T^- | p_{w,0}(x) > 0\},$$

then we can define our objective function as $o(w) = |M_T(w)|$. The set $M_T(w)$ can be viewed as a neighborhood of $w$ containing all the possible next steps we can take from $w$. As a *first key feature* of our heuristic, we now construct a probability mass function $u$ over $M_T(w)$ as

$$q(x) = |xw| / \sum_{y \in M_T(w)} |yw|.$$

Elements that are "further away" from being classified correctly by $p_{w,0}$ are assigned higher values by $q$. We now define

$$s(w) = w - \chi(x) \cdot \mathrm{sample(M_T(w), q)/\sqrt{ww}},$$

where sample stochastically selects one element from the set $M_T(w)$ with the probability given by $q$, and $\chi(x) = 1$ for $x \in T^-$, $\chi(x) = -1$ for $x \in T^+$. The acceptance function at step $k$ (the $k$'th time through the while-loop) is defined as

$$a(w_{k-1}, w_k) = \begin{cases} 1 & \text{if } \pi(w_{k-1}, w_k) > \rho, \\ 0 & \text{otherwise,} \end{cases}$$

where

$$\pi(w_{k-1}, w_k) = \begin{cases} 1 & \text{if } o(w_k) - o(w_{k-1}) \leq 0, \\ e^{-(o(w_k)-o(w_{k-1}))/t(k)} & \text{otherwise,} \end{cases}$$

and $\rho \in [0,1]$ is uniformly randomly sampled at each step $k$. The function $t$, motivated by Hajek's Theorem[11] on convergence of inhomogenous Markov chains for big enough constants $\Gamma$, is defined as

$$t(k) = \Gamma / \ln(k+2), \quad k \in \{0, 1, \ldots\},$$

and represents the "annealing" temperature (*second key feature*). As $t$ decreases, the probability of accepting a $w$ that does not decrease the objective function decreases. We empirically chose $\Gamma$ in the range of $(|T^+| + |T^-|)/5$ up to $(|T^+| + |T^-|)/3$, essentially using the same method as in [2].

Finally our stopping criterion is given by a pre-determined number of iterations through the while-loop.

## 2.2 Perceptron Training Set Sampling

In order to generate (a large number of) different hypotheses as well as to achieve zero learning error in a short time, the following sampling scheme for training sets is applied (*third key feature*):

Let $C_i^+ = \{x \in D | c(x) = i\}$, be the positive examples for class $i$ in $D$, and let $C_i^- = D - C_i^+$, be the negative examples of class $i$ in $D$. Further, let for two parameters $\alpha, \beta \in (0,1]$, $s_i^+ = \lfloor \alpha |C_i^+| \rfloor$, and let $s_i^- = \lfloor \beta |C_i^-| \rfloor$. For each $j$ in $\{1, 2, \ldots, k_i\}$ we randomly sample $T_{i,j}^+ \subseteq C_i^+$ and $T_{i,j}^- \subseteq C_i^-$such that $|T_{i,j}^+| = s_i^+$, and $|T_{i,j}^-| = s_i^-$. The set $T_{i,j} = T_{i,j}^+ \cup T_{i,j}^-$ is then the training set used to train perceptron $p_j$ in $F_i$.

The Boosting Method (cf. [20, 21]) tries to reduce the training error by assigning higher probabilities to "difficult" samples in a recursive learning procedure. In our approach, we observed that almost all subsets are learned with zero error even for relatively large fractions of the entire sample set (about 0.5 in [2] and 0.75 in the present study). Thus, according to the procedure described in the previous section, the method we are using belongs to the class of voting predictions. Recent research has shown that classification performance can be significantly improved by voting on multiple hypotheses [21]; for a more detailed discussion cf. [5]. We note that the particular examples are trained multiple times, e.g., for the ALL/AML data set, the average occurrence of an ALL sample in randomly chosen subsets is about 220 in trials with the best classification rate.

## 2.3 Dimensionality Reduction

In our case where the data $D$ presents a massively underdetermined system, i.e., there are many more gene expression measurements than there are tissue samples, experiments have shown that reducing the dimensionality of the data is beneficial [14]. The scheme we applied is based on selecting the genes that incur the coefficients with the biggest absolute values in the perceptrons after having completed training on all dimensions in the data (*fourth key feature*). Let $g(w,q)$ be the set of $q$ positions that produce the $q$ biggest values $|w_l|$ in $w = (w_1, w_2, \ldots, w_n)$ (ties are ordered arbitrarily). Let $G_i = \cap_{j=1}^{p} g(w_j^i, q)$ be the set of dimensions selected for class $i$, i.e., here we have $k_i = p$ for all $i = 1, \ldots, m$. Each $G_i$ is truncated to $\kappa := \min_{i \in \{1,\ldots,m\}} |G_i|$ positions with the largest associated values (called priority genes). Training each $F_i$ is then repeated with the data $D$ projected onto the dimensions in $G_i$ for $k_i = K$ perceptrons, $i = 1, \ldots, m$. The importance of weight size in learning procedures has been emphasised by P. Bartlett in [4].

# 3 Data Sets

Improvements in cancer classification have been central to advances in cancer treatment [9]. Usually, cancer classification has been based primarily on the morphological appearance of the tumour which has serious limitations: Tumours with similar appearance can follow significantly different clinical courses and show different responses to therapy. In a few cases, such clinical heterogeneity has been explained by dividing morphologically similar tumours into subtypes. Key examples include the subdivision of small round blue cell tumours and acute leukemias. Both tumour classes are considered in the present section.

## 3.1 SRBCT Data

For the first series of computational experiments, the data used in this paper are provided by Khan et al. in [14]. Given are gene-expression data from cDNA microarrays containing 2308 genes for four types of small, round blue cell tumours (SRBCTs) of childhood, which include neuroblastoma (NB), rhabdomyosarcoma (RMS), Burkitt lymphoma (BL) and the Ewing family of tumours (EWS), i.e., here we have $m = 4$. The number of training samples is as follows: 23 for EWS, 8 for BL, 12 for NB, and 20 for RMS. The test set consists of 25 samples: 6 for EWS, 3 for BL, 6 for NB, 5 for RMS, and 5 "others". The split of the data into training and test sets was the same as in the paper by Khan et al., where it has been shown that a system of artificial neural networks can utilize gene expression measurements from microarrays and classify these tumours into four different categories. In [14], 3750 ANNs are calculated to obtain 96 genes for training the final ANN which is able to classify correctly the 20+5 test data.

## 3.2 AML/ALL Data

The data are taken from Golub et al. [9]. The training set consists of 7129 gene-expression data for 11 samples of acute myeloid leukemia (AML) and 27 samples of acute lymphoblastic leukemia (ALL), respectively (i.e., $m = 2$ in this case). For the test, 14 AML samples and 20 ALL samples are used (again, each of them is represented by 7129 gene-expression data). Current clinical practice involves an experienced specialist's interpretation of the tumour's morphology, histochemistry, immunophenotyping, and cytogenetic analysis, each performed in a separate, highly specialised laboratory. Golub et al. analysed various aspects of cancer classification in [9]. In particular, by using the model of self-organising maps, Golub et al. obtained a strong prediction for 18 out of the 20 ALL test samples and 10 out of the 14 AML samples (i.e., a total of six misclassifications).

In [10], the same data have been analysed by Support Vector Machines using a recursive feature elimination method. On 8 and 16 genes, the classification error is zero with a minimum margin of 0.05 and 0.03 (medium margin 0.49 and 0.38, respectively).

# 4 Results

The algorithm described in Section 2 has been implemented in $C^{++}$ and we performed computational experiments for the data sets from Section 3 on SUN Ultra 5/333 workstation with 128 MB RAM. For both data sets, we present three types of results from computational experiments.

## 4.1 SRBCT Data

In Table 1, computations include all 2308 input variables (gene-expression data). The parameter settings are $\alpha = 0.75$ and $\beta = 0.25$ for balanced but still sufficiently large numbers of positive and negative examples. The entries in the table are the errors on classes in the order [EWS,BL,NB,RMS]. We recall that the number $K$ of threshold functions (perceptrons) is the same for all four classes, i.e., $K = k_i$, $i = 1, \ldots, 4$. The values are typical results from three to five runs for each parameter setting; the deviation is very small and therefore average values are not calculated.

| $K$ | 11 | 33 | 99 | 297 | 891 |
|---|---|---|---|---|---|
| Error Distr. | [1,1,5,0] | [1,1,5,0] | [0,1,5,0] | [0,1,5,0] | [0,1,5,0] |
| Total errors | 35% | 35% | 30% | 30% | 30% |

**Table 1**

In Table 2, the training procedure has been performed on priority genes only, i.e., on $\kappa$ genes that are determined by the intersection of $p$ sets (derived from $p$ perceptrons) consisting of $q$ most significant weights.

The parameters are $p = 5$, 9, 11 and $q = 250$ ($q$ is large enough to have non-empty intersections), and the numbers of priority genes are $\kappa = 23$, 10, 8. The results are stable for values close to $p = 9$ and larger $K \geq 300$, i.e., the error is equal to zero if $p \in \{8, 9, 10\}$ and $K >> 300$. While the top rating for each example is in general at least twice as large as the second largest one (for most cases much higher), the rating for the test example No. 20 is only marginally better than the second best rating. This example causes the misclassification on EWS for $p = 11$ and for the first three entries of $p = 9$. On this example, Kahn et al. report a vote of 0.40 [14], and our ratings are in the same range between 0.41 to 0.45. The rating of the five "other" examples is below 0.25.

| $p$ / $K$ | 11 | 33 | 99 | 297 | 891 |
|---|---|---|---|---|---|
| 5 ($\kappa = 23$) | [1,0,4,0] | [1,0,4,0] | [0,0,4,0] | [0,0,4,0] | [0,0,4,0] |
| Total errors | 25% | 25% | 20% | 20% | 20% |
| 9 ($\kappa = 10$) | [1,0,2,0] | [1,0,2,0] | [1,0,0,0] | [0,0,0,0] | [0,0,0,0] |
| Total errors | 15% | 15% | 5% | 0% | 0% |
| 11 ($\kappa = 8$) | [1,0,1,0] | [1,0,1,0] | [1,0,0,0] | [1,0,0,0] | [1,0,0,0] |
| Total errors | 10% | 10% | 5% | 5% | 5% |

**Table 2**

Thus, our method is sensitive to the right choice of $p$. We obtain zero classification error on 10 genes only, whereas in [14] 96 genes are used for classification (which are derived from 3750 ANNs; the ANNs are trained and evaluated on different selections out of the sample set). The run-time ranges from 1 *min* (for $p = 5$ and $K = 11$) up to 113 *min* (for $p = 11$ and $K = 891$).

Since we are using $|w_l|$ for the selection of priority genes, it is interesting to know whether the largest absolute values of weights correspond to the most significant average values of gene-expression data. Table 3 provides the rank of the average value for priority genes calculated for $K = 297$ and the EWS cancer type. In this run, we have $p = 9$ and $\kappa = 10$ (cf. Table 2). We recall that $q = 250$; for the largest average values of gene-expression data this means the range of ranks 2059, ..., 2308. In Table 3, 40% of the genes to not belong to

| | Ranking of Priority Genes for SRBCT Data | | | | |
|---|---|---|---|---|---|
| Gene number | 246 | 469 | 509 | 545 | 1708 |
| Rank number | 2280 | 2290 | 1580 | 2284 | 2186 |
| Gene number | 1781 | 1834 | 1841 | 1961 | 2223 |
| Rank number | 2306 | 2166 | 1770 | 1544 | 2049 |

**Table 3**

this range; thus, there seems to be no direct correspondence between the rank of the average value of gene-expression data and the absolute value of weights in classifying threshold functions from the first layer of the depth-three circuit, although all ten ranks belong to the upper halve of rank values.

For $p = 9$ ($\kappa = 10$) and $K = 297$ we investigated the impact of the random choice of subsets from the entire sample set. Since the sample sets are relatively small, the parameter settings $\alpha = 0.75$ and $\beta = 0.25$ were chosen in our basic experiments displayed in Table 2. We performed experiments for $\alpha = 0.85, ..., 1.0$ and $\beta = 0.35, ..., 0.5$. The results are shown in Table 4.

Our algorithm represents a stochastic search procedure, and therefore it produces (in general) different hypotheses even for the case $\alpha = \beta = 1.0$. To have a balanced number of positive and negative examples, we chose $\alpha = 1.0$, $\beta = 0.5$ as maximum values.

| $p$ / $[\alpha, \beta]$ | [0.80,0.30] | [0.85,0.35] | [0.90,0.40] | [0.90,0.40] | [1.0,0.5] |
|---|---|---|---|---|---|
| 9 ($\kappa = 10$)<br>Total errors | [0,0,0,0]<br>0% | [0,0,2,0]<br>10% | [0,0,3,0]<br>15% | [0,0,3,0]<br>15% | [0,0,3,0]<br>15% |

**Table 4**

Table 4 clearly demonstrates the effect of Epicurean learning: The classification results become worse if the number of potential training subsets becomes smaller.

## 4.2 AML/ALL Data

In this case, we have a binary classification problem. We used a normalisation of input values where for each sample the mean of gene-expression values is subtracted and then divided by the standard deviation.

In Table 5, the training has been performed on all 7129 input variables (gene-expression data). The entries in the table are the errors in the order [ALL,AML]. The values are typical results from several runs for each parameter setting.

| $K$ | 33 | 99 | 297 | 891 | 2673 |
|---|---|---|---|---|---|
| Error Distr. | [0,3] | [1,2] | [1,2] | [2,2] | [2,1] |
| Total errors | 8.8% | 8.8% | 8.8% | 11.8% | 8.8% |

**Table 5**

The classification improves on the results published in [9]. The run-time is between 1 *min* and 44 *min*. The problem is whether the same or even better results are possible on significantly smaller numbers of gene data inputs.

For the computation on priority genes, two depth-three circuits are computed for $\beta = 0.5$ with the same number of training samples from ALL which implies $\alpha = 0.25$. The parameters are $p = 7$, 11, 15 for the same $q = 250$ as for SRBCT data. In Table 6, some typical results are presented:

| $p$ | 7 | 11 | 15 |
|---|---|---|---|
| Error Distr. | [1,2] | [1,0] | [1,1] |
| Total errors | 8.8% | 2.9% | 5.9% |
| $\kappa$ | 27 | 6 | 4 |
| K | 273 | 297 | 315 |

**Table 6**

The corresponding number of priority genes are given by $\kappa$. The run-time ranges from 41 *min* (for $p = 7$ and $K = 273$) up to 454 *min* (for $p = 15$ and $K = 315$).

Compared to the results from [10], we have a single misclassification on ALL test samples, but the average margin is 0.51 and the minimum margin is 0.1.

| | Ranking of Priority Genes for ALL/AML | | | | | |
|---|---|---|---|---|---|---|
| Gene number | 5562 | 5710 | 6179 | 6181 | 6201 | 6345 |
| Rank number | 7101 | 7046 | 6984 | 7079 | 6287 | 6693 |

**Table 7**

In Table 7, we provide the rank of the average value for priority genes calculated for $K = 297$ and $p = 11$ ($\kappa = 6$). Due to the stochastic nature of our procedure, the set of priority genes usually differs slightly in different runs. Since we have $q = 250$ again, the largest average values of gene-expression data correspond to the rank numbers 6880, ..., 7129. In Table 7, 33% of the genes do not belong to this range.

| $p$ / $\beta$ | [0.50] | [0.625] | [0.75] | [0.825] | [1.0] |
|---|---|---|---|---|---|
| 11 ($\kappa = 6$) | [1,0] | [1,1] | [1,1] | [1,1] | [1,2] |
| Total errors | 2.9% | 5.9% | 5.9% | 5.9% | 8.8% |

**Table 8**

As for SRBCT data, we analysed the impact of an increasing size of randomly chosen subsets of the entire sample set. For $p = 11$ and $K = 297$, we performed computational experiments for $\beta = 0.5, ..., 1.0$ with the same number of samples from ALL. As can be seen from Table 8, the classification becomes worse as the number of potential training subsets decreases, if compared to the results from Table 6.

# 5 Discussion

Initial reports on the analysis of gene expression data derived from microarrays concentrated on unsupervised learning, in which the main objective was to determine which genes tend to have correlated patterns of expression. In early experiments, the number of actual arrays was usually small, especially when compared to the number of measurements per case, which is generally in the order of thousands. As microarray technology evolves and becomes less expensive, the number of arrays tends to grow, allowing for the construction of supervised learning models. Supervised learning models are increasingly being used, and classification of cases into diagnostic or prognostic categories has been attempted. Besides classification performance, an important goal of these models is to determine whether a few genes can be considered good markers for disease. It is important to investigate whether simple learning models can be successfully used for this purpose. In this paper, we showed an algorithm based on simulated annealing that is used to train a system of perceptrons, each obtained by resampling of the training set. The model was able to successfully classify previously unseen cases of SBRCTs and AML/ALL data using a small number of genes. Furthermore, we provided experimental evidence that Epicurean-style learning might be essential to obtain satisfactory classification results.

## Acknowledgments

The authors would like to thank the anonumous referees for their careful reading of the paper and helpful suggestions.

# References

[1] E.H.L. Aarts. *Local Search in Combinatorial Optimization.* Wiley & Sons, 1998.

[2] A. Albrecht, M.J. Loomes, K. Steinhöfel, and M. Taupitz. A Modified Perceptron Algorithm for Computer-Assisted Diagnosis. In: M. Bramer, A. Preece, and F. Coenen, eds., *Research and Development in Intelligent Systems XVII*, pp. 199–211, BCS Series, Springer-Verlag, 2000.

[3] A. Albrecht and C.K. Wong. Combining the Perceptron Algorithm with Logarithmic Simulated Annealing. *Neural Processing Letters*, 14(1):75-83, 2001.

[4] P. Bartlett. The Sample Complexity of Pattern Classification with Neural Networks: The Size of Weights is more Important than the Size of the Network. *IEEE Tansactions on Information Theory*, 44(2):525-536, 1998.

[5] J.G. Cleary, L.E. Trigg, G. Holmes, and M.A. Hall. Experiences with a Weighted Decision Tree Learner. In: M Bramer, A Preece, and F Coenen, eds., *Research and Development in Intelligent Systems XVII*, pp. 35–47, BCS Series, Springer-Verlag, 2000.

[6] M.B. Eisen, P.T. Spellman, P.O. Brown, D. Botstein. Cluster Analysis and Display of Genome-wide Expression Patterns. *Proc. Natl. Acad. Sci. USA*, 95(25):14863-8, 1998.

[7] T.S. Furey, N. Cristianini, N. Duffy, D.W. Bednarski, M. Schummer, and D. Haussler. Support Vector Machine Classification and Validation of Cancer Tissue Samples Using Microarray Expression Data. *Bioinformatics*, 16:906-914, 2000.

[8] C.-F. Geyer. *Epikur*. Junius-Verlag, Hamburg, 2000.

[9] T.R. Golub, D.K. Slonim, P. Tamayo, C. Huard, M. Gaasenbeek, J.P. Mesirov, H. Coller, M.L. Loh, J.R. Downing, M.A. Caligiuri, C.D. Bloomfield, and E.S. Lander. Molecular Classification of Cancer: Class Discovery and Class Prediction by Gene Expression Monitoring. *Science*, 286:531–537, 1999.

[10] I. Guyon, J. Weston, St. Barnhill, and V. Vapnik. Gene Selection for Cancer Classification using Support Vector Machines. *Machine Learning*, 46(1-3):389-422, 2002.

[11] B. Hajek. Cooling Schedules for Optimal Annealing. *Mathem. of Operations Research*, 13:311 – 329, 1988.

[12] D. Helmbold and M.K. Warmuth. On Weak Learning. *J. of Computer and System Sciences*, 50:551-573, 1995.

[13] K.-U. Höffgen, H.-U. Simon, and K.S. van Horn. Robust Trainability of Single Neurons. *J. of Computer System Sciences*, 50:114–125, 1995.

[14] J. Khan, J.S. Wei, M. Ringner, L.H. Saal, M. Ladanyi, F. Westermann, F. Berthold, M. Schwab, C.R. Antonescu, C. Peterson, and P.S. Meltzer. Classification and Diagnostic Prediction of Cancers Using Gene Expression Profiling and Artificial Neural Networks. *Nature* [Medicine], 7(6):673-679, 2001.

[15] S. Kirkpatrick, C.D. Gelatt, Jr., and M.P. Vecchi. Optimization by Simulated Annealing. *Science*, 220:671 – 680, 1983.

[16] M.L. Minsky and S.A. Papert. *Perceptrons*. MIT Press, Cambridge, Mass., 1969.

[17] N.J. Maughan, F.A. Lewis, and V. Smith. An Introduction to Arrays. *J. of Pathology*, 195:3-6, 2001.

[18] J. Quackenbush. Computational Analysis of Microarray Data. *Nature Reviews* [Genetics], 2(6):418-427, 2001.

[19] F. Rosenblatt. *Principles of Neurodynamics.* Spartan Books, New York, 1962.

[20] R.E. Schapire. The Strength of Weak Learnability. *Machine Learning*, 5(2):197-227, 1990.

[21] R.E. Schapire, Y. Freund, P. Bartlett, and W.S. Lee. Boosting the Margin: A New Explanation for the Effectiveness of Voting Methods. *The Annals of Statistics*, 26(5):1651-1686, 1998.

[22] V. Vapnik. *Statistical Learning Theory*, Wiley&Sons, 1998.

# Case and Feature Subset Selection in Case-Based Software Project Effort Prediction

Colin Kirsopp and Martin Shepperd
Empirical Software Engineering Research Group
School of Design, Engineering and Computing
Bournemouth University
Royal London House,
Bournemouth, BH1 3LT, United Kingdom
{ckirsopp, mshepper}@bmth.ac.uk
http://dec.bournemouth.ac.uk/ESERG

Abstract

Prediction systems adopting a case-based reasoning (CBR) approach have been widely advocated. However, as with most machine learning techniques, feature and case subset selection can be extremely influential on the quality of the predictions generated. Unfortunately, both are NP-hard search problems which are intractable for non-trivial data sets. Using all features frequently leads to poor prediction accuracy and pre-processing methods (filters) have not generally been effective. In this paper we consider two different real world project effort data sets. We describe how using simple search techniques, such as hill climbing and sequential selection, can achieve major improvements in accuracy. We conclude that, for our data sets, forward sequential selection, for features, followed by backward sequential selection, for cases, is the most effective approach when exhaustive searching is not possible.

## 1. Introduction

It is generally accepted that early, accurate estimates of development effort are important to the success of most software projects. Estimates are required when tendering bids, for evaluating risk, scheduling resources and monitoring progress. Inaccurate estimates have implications upon all these activities, and so, ultimately, impact the final project outcome. Consequently there has been significant research into prediction systems by the software engineering community over the years.

Despite this activity, results — at least in terms of accuracy — have been quite mixed. There are a number of reasons why the project effort prediction problem is proving to be quite challenging. First, the data is frequently complex with many features, both continuous and categorical, and exhibiting strong tendencies for multi-collinearity, but nevertheless with many underlying dimensions. Second, the relationships between the predicted features, in our case effort, and the independent features are not well understood. Third, the data is often subject to considerable measurement error. For example, even defining what constitutes project effort in a large organisation is a challenging problem. Moreover, there are often reasons such as politics why the resultant data may only bear an approximate resemblance to reality. Lastly, there are significant problems of heterogeneity both within datasets and certainly between different measurement environments. For this reason it has seldom been efficacious to merge training sets to build larger data sets [1]. Unfortunately, as a result of the above problems, no prediction technique has proved consistently accurate, even when we relax the accuracy criterion to merely require that a technique generates useful predictions.

A variety of techniques have been proposed to help solve the problem of making accurate, yet timely, software project predictions. Early examples included COCOMO [2], and proprietary methods such as SLIM [3]. More recently there has been a tendency to focus on the development of local models, for instance, by means of statistical regression [4] or machine learning methods such as rule induction [5], neural networks [6], genetic programming [7,8] and CBR [9].

Our research group has been active over a number of years applying CBR techniques to the domain of software project effort estimation. This paper deals with our approach to using of case-based reasoning (CBR) for prediction purposes and the use of search techniques for feature and case subset selection.

This paper focuses on making more effective use of CBR techniques for building prediction systems in the problem domain of software project effort, although it is hoped that some of the issues will be pertinent to a wider class of prediction problem. We can characterise the problem domain as one in which predictions are infrequent, but of high value and where the problem domain is not well understood, since we do not (yet!) have a deep theory of software engineering.

The next section describes the use of CBR in software effort prediction systems. This is followed by a review of the work on feature and case selection. An empirical study of the effectiveness of various feature and case selection techniques is then introduced including more background on the problem domain and our two data sets. The results from this study and some final conclusions are then presented.

# 2. Case-Based Prediction

CBR is an approach that has originated from analogical reasoning, dynamic memory and the role of previous situations in learning and problem solving. In recent years it has received considerable attention. Cases can be thought of as abstractions of events (solved or unsolved problems) that are limited in time and space, for example in our problem domain each software project will form an individual case.

CBR basically comprises four stages [10]:

- the *retrieval* of similar cases
- *reuse* of the retrieved cases to find a solution to the problem
- where necessary, *revision* of the proposed solution
- and *retention* of the solution to form a new case

When a new problem arises, a possible solution can be sought by retrieving similar cases from the case repository or case base. The solution may be revised based upon experience of reusing previous cases and the outcome retained to supplement the case repository. Consequently, issues concerning case characterisation, similarity [11,12], and solution revision must be addressed prior to

CBR system deployment. For a more extensive review of CBR the reader is referred to [12].

The Empirical Software Engineering Research Group at Bournemouth have been involved in the development of CBR techniques and tools to build software effort prediction systems since the mid 1990s. Our basic approach to case-based prediction is embodied in a CBR shell entitled ArchANGEL[1] that allows cases, usually projects for effort prediction, to be characterised by an arbitrary set of $n$ features. These may be continuous (e.g. expected level of code reuse) or categorical (e.g. development method). Obviously, it is a constraint that these features must be known (or reliably estimated) at the time of prediction. A new project, for which a prediction is required (known as the target case), is also characterised by the same feature set and plotted in standardised $n$-dimensional feature space. Euclidean distance is used to identify the most similar cases to the target and these, since they have known values for effort, are used as the basis of the prediction. ArchANGEL allows adaptation strategies to be applied to the set of analogies to produce the prediction. Currently, variations of $k$ nearest neighbour ($k$NN) methods are available. Selecting all cases within a given distance has also been tried but didn't give any clear advantages over the simpler $k$NN approach. For the study described in this paper the prediction is calculated as the inverse distance weighted average of the effort values from the nearest 2 cases[2].

Rule-based adaptation strategies would also be possible within the ArchANGEL framework but it is hard to see how these could be applied in an automated manner, particularly in conjunction with feature selection. Rules are generally based on the value of particular features. This means that either, features used in rules couldn't be removed by selection, or rules would need to be modified if features they used were removed. Another alternative would be that rules were added after feature selection, in which case the feature selection is done with a prediction function that is different from the final prediction function and so the feature set would not be properly optimised.

We believe that using CBR for prediction purposes can offer a number of benefits.

- It can bypass some of the problems associated with knowledge elicitation together with extracting and codifying that knowledge.
- CBR systems can also handle failed cases (i.e. those cases for which an accurate prediction was not made). This is useful as it enables users to identify potentially high risk situations when predictions may not be trustworthy.
- Analogy is able to deal with poorly understood domains (such as software projects) since solutions are based upon what has actually happened as opposed to chains of rules created by rule induction systems.
- Users may be more willing to accept solutions from analogy based systems since they are derived from a form of reasoning more akin to human problem solving, as opposed to the somewhat arcane chains of rules or

[1]ArchANGEL is the most recent version of the ANGEL software tool for project prediction. It may be downloaded from dec.bmth.ac.uk/ESERG/ANGEL/

[2] $k = 2$ was found to be the optimum value for both of these datasets in a previous study [13]

neural nets. This can be particularly important if prediction systems are to be not only deployed but also have reliance placed upon them.

It is not, therefore, surprising that a number of researchers have worked with case-based prediction systems for various software project characteristics such as effort and duration. In general results have been encouraging although not consistently good. One major challenge is that of feature and case selection which is the main theme of this paper.

# 3. Feature and Case Subset Selection

Our research group have had some success in producing more accurate results than traditional regression based techniques [14]. Subsequently, other research groups have reported more mixed experiences. Niessink and van Vliet [15] and Mendes *et al.* [16] also reported that CBR out-performed other techniques, but Briand *et al.* [17] obtained poor levels of accuracy. We believe that the reasons for this are at least twofold. First, effectiveness of any prediction technique depends upon characteristics of the dataset. For example, regression will do well if the majority of observations fall close to some hyperplane. Conversely, CBR will tend to be more effective when discontinuities exist in underlying relationships between effort and the independent variables. Second, CBR (along with any machine learning technique) is vulnerable to features that are irrelevant, or even misleading, for the particular prediction task.

Typically data sets are not collected with a particular prediction task in mind. In any case, it can still be challenging to identify the optimal feature subset since we are not necessarily looking for the most strongly correlated features. This is known as the feature subset selection problem. Likewise, not all cases are necessarily useful sources of analogy. In general there exists some subset of cases that will lead to optimal predictions. This is known as case subset selection. These are both combinatorial and therefore hard search problems. In practice the problem is even more complex since the choice of cases may interact with the choice of features and *vice versa*. For smaller data sets our approach has been to conduct an exhaustive search using a jack knifing procedure. This is not possible for larger data sets such as that used by Briand *et al.* so the researchers were forced to use a simple statistical procedure to identify features strongly associated with project effort. All cases were included. It is our opinion that this is likely to have a very negative impact upon the accuracy of CBR prediction systems.

In general approaches to feature and case selection can be characterised as filters or wrappers [18]. Filters work independently of the machine learning algorithm and typically use some statistical procedure. They are computationally more tractable but at the expense of accuracy (this was the approach adopted by Briand *et al.*). Wrappers work by applying the machine learning algorithm itself on some sample of the data set in order to determine the fitness of the subset. This tends to be computationally far more intensive, but can find better subsets than the filter methods. Wrapper approaches have included different variants of hill climbing algorithms [19], simulated annealing algorithms [20], forward and backward sequential selection algorithms [11]. These have generally been reported to lead to improvements in accuracy without the prohibitive computational cost of an exhaustive search although with less efficiency than the filters.

# 4. The Empirical Study

In this work we used two software project effort data sets (see Table 1) to examine the effectiveness and efficiency of different algorithms in the search for optimised feature and case subsets. An optimised case or feature set is one that leads to more accurate predictions.

Table 1. Data Set Characteristics

| Characteristic | Desharnais | Finnish |
|---|---|---|
| No. of cases | 77 | 407 |
| No. of features | 9 | 43 |
| No. of categorical features | 1 | 5 |

The smaller data set (Desharnais) was selected because the size permitted an exhaustive search of all possible combinations of features (though not of cases). The Finnish data set was chosen since the search space was considerably larger[3] and therefore more representative of larger software engineering data sets.

Previously we have experimented with hill climbing algorithms for feature subset selection along with random search and forward sequential selection [21]. We found all techniques offered improvements over the naïve strategy of using all features. However, taking into account computational efficiency as well as accuracy forward sequential selection was the most effective algorithm. In this work we apply these techniques (as well as backward sequential selection and random mutation hill climbing) to both feature and case selection.

First, however, we consider in more detail how feature and case selection can be viewed and tackled as search problems. Since both searches are combinatorial they are likely to be NP-hard. Representation is straightforward as a string of $n$ bits where $n$ is the number of features or cases and the bits are toggled to depict inclusion or exclusion. Since a number of the search algorithms rely on the notion of neighbourhood this is defined as any move that is possible by toggling any single bit. This means that the neighbourhood for case selection for the Finnish data set is relatively large with 407 possible moves. This leads to some performance issues that we will return to later. The fitness function — strictly speaking cost — is the sum of the absolute residuals derived from jack knifing across the entire data set. We use absolute residuals since for the purposes of this analysis we are indifferent to under and over estimates. We now consider each search technique in more detail.

Most of the tables in the paper show results for 'no optimisation'. This is the result produced by using all available features or cases. It is included in the main result tables for comparison against the results from the search algorithms.

The random search repeatedly selects and evaluates random bit strings as the selected features or cases. This is equivalent to sampling the fitness landscape. Elsewhere [21] we have used this data to help us better understand the fitness landscape.

The next two search techniques are variations of hill climbing. The steepest ascent hill climber has a randomly generated initial start position. The algorithm then evaluates each possible move in the neighbourhood and selects the best

[3] There are $2^{407}$-1 combinations of case subsets alone!

available move. This process is repeated until none of the moves in the neighbourhood are better than the current position. The search is then restarted at a new random position.

The random mutation hill climbing (RMHC) algorithm differs from steepest ascent hill climbing (SAHC) in that in does not need to explore the entire neighbourhood before making a move. It moves to a new position as soon as a better position is found. However, if the neighbourhood were searched systematically (as in steepest ascent) this would bias the search toward those features or cases that are tested first. The solution to this is to test the positions in the neighbourhood in a random order. Positions are not revisited within a step. If none of the moves in the neighbourhood are better than the current position the climb ends.

Sequential selection algorithms are a variation on steepest ascent hill climbing [11]. They use a heuristic to set the start position (rather than use random start position) and no backtracking is allowed. The fixed starting point means that only a single search is possible rather than the multi-start, which is possible with the conventional hill climbing algorithms. The forward sequential selection (FSS) variation starts from an empty set of features (or cases) and adds one feature at each step of the climb. Once a feature has been added it may not be removed. Backward sequential selection (BSS) starts from the complete set of features (or cases) and removes one feature at each step of the climb. Once a feature has been removed it may not be replaced.

# 5. Results

In this section we consider the results we obtained from the two project effort data sets when we applied various feature and case selection algorithms to the case base. Results will be presented for feature subset selection, case subset selection, case subset selection *given* an already optimised feature set and finally feature subset selection *given* an already optimised case set. Each of the tables shows the accuracy as the sum of absolute residuals so lower values are to be preferred. We also give some idea of computational performance as the number of subsets (either of cases or features) that are evaluated. Each row provides the results for a different search algorithm starting with no optimisation as a form of benchmark.

## 5.1 Feature Subset Selection

This section shows the results for optimising the feature subset but using all available cases for the training set.

From Table 2 we see that the poorest results are obtained from the unoptimised CBR system. In other words, if all features are used we get the least accurate predictions. This is to be expected since it is generally accepted that feature and case selection are important aspects of machine learning. The next row shows the results of randomly sampling the search space 500 times. Interestingly even a simple procedure such as this yields some benefit with between 20 and 30% reduction in the error of predictions. The reader should note that 500 evaluations is almost equivalent to the size of the feature search space (511) for the Desharnais dataset.

Next we consider forward and backward sequential selection. The forward search efficiently finds what is in fact the optimum value[4] for the Desharnais dataset with only 35 evaluations and a good value for the Finnish data set with only 160 evaluations. In general we find forward searching to work well for features since most good subsets include relatively few features (perhaps due to the presence of collinearity). The backward search is less effective for feature selection again due to the sparse nature of the selected subsets.

Results from the two hill climbing variants are given in the next two rows. Both successfully find the optimum for Desharnais and yield good results for the Finnish dataset. In terms of accuracy there is little to distinguish the two algorithms, however, the random mutation hill climber is 4 to 5 times more computationally efficient for the Finnish dataset. Again this is not unexpected since the large neighbourhood must be exhaustively evaluated by the steepest ascent algorithm. Finally, an exhaustive search with the 44 features of the Finnish dataset is not feasible.

Table 2. Results for feature subset selection

| Search Algorithm | Desharnais | Finnish |
|---|---|---|
| No Optimisation | 177694 | 88208 |
| Random | 142016<br>(500 evals) | 60174<br>(500 evals) |
| FSS | 138125<br>(35 evals) | 31823<br>(160 evals) |
| BSS | 154209<br>(42 evals) | 56251<br>(429 evals) |
| RMHC | 138125<br>(8 climbs)<br>(204 evals) | 29697<br>(100 climbs)<br>(24,000 evals) |
| SAHC | 138125<br>(1 climb)<br>(45 evals) | 29901<br>(100 climbs)<br>(120,000 evals) |
| Exhaustive | 138125<br>(511 evals) | N/C |

## 5.2 Case Subset Selection

This section shows the results for optimising the cases used for the training set but using all available features.

From Table 3 we see, as for the feature selection, that the poorest result is obtained from the unoptimised CBR system. Interestingly there is a much reduced (negligible for the Finnish dataset) improvement for random selection of case subsets. We believe this is for two reasons. First, the inclusion/exclusion of individual cases has far less impact than features since theoretically an individual case may be seldom, or even never, used whilst a feature is used for all predictions.

[4] The optimum is known from the exhaustive search results

Second, the case subset search space is very much larger and so a smaller fraction of the available combinations will have been sampled.

Next we consider forward and backward sequential selection. A forward search is not possible for selecting cases since to evaluate a case subset, a prediction system must be built based on this subset. A prediction is based upon the $k$ nearest neighbours and so a minimum of $k$ cases must be present to evaluate a particular case subset. Forward sequential selection starts by evaluating each case subset with only 1 case. This means the forward searching would only be possible with $k = 1$ (remember $k = 2$ was used in this study). The backward search yields improved results and is computationally quite efficient, though the results here aren't nearly as close to the hill climbing results as the FSS results were for the feature selection.

Table 3. Results for case subset selection

| Search Algorithm | Desharnais | Finnish |
|---|---|---|
| No Optimisation | 177694 | 88208 |
| Random | 146142<br>(500 evals) | 87737<br>(500 evals) |
| FSS | N/A | N/A |
| BSS | 122206<br>(1292 evals) | 69004<br>(37000 evals) |
| RMHC | 109984<br>(100 climbs)<br>(43000 evals) | N/C |
| SAHC | 107077<br>(100 climbs)<br>(196000evals) | N/C |
| Exhaustive | N/C | N/C |

For the Desharnais dataset the hill climbing algorithms once again produced the best results. Again, however, these algorithms were expensive in computation time. The problem of computability becomes even more acute for the Finnish dataset because of the larger search space involved. We estimated that the random mutation hill climber would take around 2 months to complete a run of 100 hill climbs. The steepest ascent would take several times longer! Clearly, exhaustive searches are non-computable.

## 5.3 Case Subset Selection given Optimised Feature Set

This section shows the results for optimising the cases used for the training set but capitalising upon a previously optimised feature subset. The feature subset used was the best available subset from any search algorithm from the feature subset search results.

The first interesting point from table 4 is the random sampling results for the Finnish dataset. While in case only optimisation random searching made little difference, here the results are significantly worse than the starting point (feature optimised but using all cases). This is likely to be due to the feature set being optimised in the presence of the full case-base. In the presence of the features chosen using all cases the residuals result for the full case-base is likely to be very much better than the mean of the fitness landscape. This, along with the size of the landscape means that it would be very unlikely to find a better result randomly.

Table 4. Results for case subset selection given optimised features

| Search Algorithm | Desharnais | Finnish |
|---|---|---|
| No Optimisation | 138125 | 29697 |
| Random | 122395<br>(500 evals) | 36937<br>(500 evals) |
| FSS | N/A | N/A |
| BSS | 101783<br>(1827 evals) | 23304<br>(33000 evals) |
| RMHC | 97136<br>(100 climbs)<br>(41,000 evals) | 24177<br>(100 climbs)<br>(320,000 evals) |
| SAHC | 96323<br>(100 climbs)<br>(247,000 evals) | N/C |
| Exhaustive | N/C | N/C |

As previously discussed, FSS is not possible for case selection. The BSS results for both data sets produce significant gains over the feature only and case only optimisation. The hill climbing algorithms for Desharnais again produce slightly better results than the BSS but at greater computational cost. The random mutation hill climber is on this occasion six times more efficient than the steepest ascent hill climber. The RMHC result for the Finnish dataset is for the first time worse than a sequential search algorithm. It is, however, unclear why BSS produced better results for this search. The RMHC climb run for the Finnish dataset was also the longest run performed[5] (around 2 weeks). The steepest ascent hill climber (for the Finnsh dataset) and the exhaustive search (for both datasets) were not considered computationally viable.

## 5.4 Feature Subset Selection given Optimised Case Set

This section shows the results for optimising the feature subset after optimising the cases used in the training set. The cases used in the training set were the best available subset from any search algorithm from the case subset search results.

The results shown in Table 5 contrast with those shown in the previous section (Table 4). Whereas running case selection after features selection is clearly advantageous, case selection then feature selection produces poor results. For the Desharnais dataset the case optimisation has run in such a way that no further optimisation is possible by feature selection, i.e., including all features is the

---

[5] Note that the size of the dataset (features and cases) also impacts on the time for the evaluation of each case subset. This means that the evaluation of case subsets for the Finnish dataset took around 8 times longer than for Desharnais (and 30 times as long where the full feature set was used).

optimum result. The Finnish results show some improvement in the FSS and hill climbing results but not nearly as good as the feature then case results and not even as good as the feature only results. The BSS result is interesting in that it was unable to make any improvement even though the other search methods did. It would appear that doing the case selection in the presence of all features has created a local minimum at this point which trapped the BSS algorithm.

Table 5. Results for feature subset selection given optimised cases

| Search Algorithm | Desharnais | Finnish |
|---|---|---|
| No Optimisation | 107077 | 69004 |
| Random | 107077<br>(500 evals) | 66994<br>(500 evals) |
| FSS | 144925<br>(35 evals) | 33087<br>(277 evals) |
| BSS | 107077<br>(10 evals) | 69004<br>(44 evals) |
| RMHC | 107077<br>(1 climb)<br>(27 evals) | 32560<br>(100 climbs)<br>(24000 evals) |
| SAHC | 107077<br>(1 climb)<br>(49 evals) | 32720<br>(100 climbs)<br>(63000 evals) |
| Exhaustive | 107077<br>(511 evals) | N/C |

## 5.5 Summary of Accuracy Results

Table 6 shows the relative reduction in error for both datasets across all 4 permutations of feature and case selection. Feature then case selection produces the best results for both datasets. It can be seen that for the Desharnais dataset the prediction errors have been almost halved and for the Finnish dataset they are less that a quarter of the original value. The greater improvement seen in the Finnish dataset is probably due to the greater scope for optimisation in this larger dataset, particularly in the reduction of the very large feature set (as demonstrated by the good feature only results).

Table 6. Performance improvements after optimisation

| | Feature only | Case Only | Feature then Case | Case then Feature |
|---|---|---|---|---|
| Desharais | 22% | 40% | 46% | 40% |
| Finnish | 66% | 22% | 76% | 63% |

## 5.6 Numbers of Feature and Cases Removed

It is interesting to examine the numbers of cases and feature that are removed from the optimised datasets. Table 7 shows a comparison of the original size of the datasets and their size after optimisation. The figures shown for the optimised datasets are for the best results found by any search method. The data clearly shows that the optimised feature sets are far more sparse than the optimised case sets, i.e., the percentage reduction in the number of features is much greater than the percentage reduction in the number of cases. The differences in the percentage of removed cases between Desharnais and Finnish datasets is likely to be due to the different search algorithms that found the best results in these instances. The Desharnais result was produced by RMHC and the Finnish result by BSS. The best hill climbing result for the Finnish dataset removed around 50% of the cases as with the Desharnais dataset and the best BSS result for the Desharnais dataset removed a much lower 36%.

Table 7. Size of optimised datasets

| | Desharnais | | Finnish | |
|---|---|---|---|---|
| | No. of features | No.of cases | No. of features | No.of cases |
| No Optimisation | 9 | 77 | 43 | 407 |
| Feature & Case Optimisation | 3 | 38 | 9 | 316 |
| Fractional Reduction | 67% | 51% | 79% | 22% |

## 5.7 Individual Case Usage

To begin to investigate which features or cases were thought useful, a count was made of the number of times a particular case or feature was used in the sets of 100 hill climbs. These results show patterns in feature and case selection with some cases almost always included in the selected subset and others almost always absent. There are far more of these outliers (and they are more extreme) than could be explained by the Poisson distribution that might be expected if they were randomly selected.

Table 8 shows the Spearman rank correlations between these counts for the four hill climbing runs involving case selection for the Desharnais dataset. The table shows the results for SA and RM hill climbing for both case only optimisation and also feature then case optimisation. The high correlation between SA and RM hill climbing performing the same type of optimisation shows that the 'usefulness' of cases is independent of the hill climbing algorithm used. The correlations between the case only and the feature then case optimisations are, however, very low. In other words a useful case with the unoptimised feature set is no more likely to be useful with the optimised feature set than any other case. This indicates that the cases selected are highly dependent on the feature subset used.

Table 8. Correlations for case usage in the Desharnais case selection hill climbing results

| | SA case only | RM case only | SA feature then case | RM feature then case |
|---|---|---|---|---|
| SA case only | 1.000 | | | |
| RM case only | 0.943 | 1.000 | | |
| SA feature then case | 0.110 | 0.140 | 1.000 | |
| RM feature then case | 0.136 | 0.157 | 0.986 | 1.000 |

If a similar analysis is done for the feature selection results for the Finnish dataset we see a high correlation between the RMHC for feature only and the RMHC for case then feature (0.961)[6]. This means that, although the cases selected during optimisation are highly dependent on the features used, features selected seem largely independent of the cases used. This clearly suggests (as do the main results) that feature selection should be done before case selection. It also suggests that there may be no benefit in trying to simultaneously optimise cases and features as a single extremely large search problem.

# 6. Comparison with other work

It is difficult to compare these results with previous work as most work on subset selection for ML deals with classification problems rather than prediction problems and so the measures of accuracy used are different. However, some comparison of the general effects found by others can be made.

Skalak [19] gives results for classification problems on four different datasets including the use of RM hill climbing and Monte Carlo methods (random sampling). The focus of the work appears to be mostly on reduction of storage rather than optimisation of accuracy. His results show that, in his datasets, around 50% of the features were selected and between 0.6% and 3.9% of the cases. These reductions in storage accompanied slight improvement in accuracy. The feature usage here is slightly higher than in our datasets but not significantly so. A major difference is the case usage where typically 1% of cases were used in comparison to 49% and 78% in our datasets. This difference is likely to be due to coarseness of the result that is required[7]. In classification tasks one prototype per class may be all that is required to give good predictive accuracy, but when a continuous result is needed it would appear that many more cases are required.

Aha and Bankert [11] found that FSS outperformed BSS when the optimal number of selections is small while BSS is preferred otherwise. Our results agree with these findings. The optimal feature subsets in our study include small numbers

---

[6] The full table of results isn't repeated here as the RM and SA hill climbing results were previously demonstrated to be equivalent.

[7] Skalak's datasets were of a comparable size (47 to 303 cases) so this cannot be used to explain the differences.

of features and FSS clearly outperforms BSS. The case subsets contain a larger proportion of the full set and BSS performs well.

# 7. Conclusions

Based on the results from this study we would cautiously make the following recommendations.

- Feature and case subset selection should be used to improve accuracy.
- Where the number of features or cases is small, use exhaustive searching. This will always produce the optimum result. For our system the upper limit of exhaustive computability lies between 15 and 20 features or cases.
- When datasets are too large for exhaustive searching, use FSS for feature selection and *then* BSS for case selection. This provides a good compromise between degree of optimisation and computational efficiency.
- When datasets are too large for exhaustive searching and accuracy and confidence are more important than computation time, use random mutation hill climbing. However, large numbers of repeated climbs may not be possible for very large datasets.
- Always prefer random mutation hill climbing to steepest ascent hill climbing. SAHC produces equivalent accuracy to RMHC but with greater computational cost. The efficiency gains of RMHC over SAHC seem likely to increase as the size of the neighbourhood increases.

To summarise, in this paper we have considered the use of CBR as part of a prediction system for project managers who need to estimate the amount of effort required at an early stage during the software development. We have shown for two different data sets that techniques such as feature and case subset selection have a very marked impact upon the quality of predictions. We have also shown that simple search heuristics such as hill climbing and sequential selection techniques can yield very useful results even when the search space is very large. The results from these datasets also suggest that the results of feature subset selection are largely independent of the case subset used, whilst case selection is highly dependent on the feature subset used. If this is true there will be little to gain from trying to simultaneously optimise cases and features. It suggests that a 'divide and conquer' strategy searching features then cases will be as effective and more efficient that the far larger and less tractable combined search.

This paper presents only the initial results from this study and further work is necessary to gain increased confidence in the above recommendations and to gain a better understanding of the mechanisms affecting search performance. The following objectives for future work are being considered:

- Applying other search techniques to the same problem, e.g., genetic algorithms, simulated annealing;
- Repeating the analysis with a wider range of datasets to see if the results generalise;
- Investigating why particular cases and features are selected or rejected.

## Acknowledgements

The authors are indebted to Jean-Marc Desharnais and STTF Ltd for making their data sets available.

## References


1. Jeffery R, Ruhe M, Wieczorek I. Using public domain metrics to estimate software development effort, presented at 7th IEEE Intl. Metrics Symp., London, 2001.
2. Boehm BW. Software engineering economics, IEEE Transactions on Software Engineering, vol. 10, pp. 4-21, 1984.
3. Putnam LH. A general empirical solution to the macro software sizing and estimating problem, IEEE Transactions on Software Engineering, vol. 4, pp. 345-361, 1978.
4. Kok P, Kitchenham BA, Kirakowski J. The MERMAID approach to software cost estimation, presented at Esprit Technical Week, 1990.
5. Selby RW & Porter AA. Learning from examples: generation and evaluation of decision trees for software resource analysis, IEEE Transactions on Software Engineering, vol. 14, pp. 743-757, 1988.
6. Finnie GR, Wittig GE, Desharnais J-M. A comparison of software effort estimation techniques using function points with neural networks, case based reasoning and regression models, J. of Systems Software, vol. 39, pp. 281-289, 1997.
7. Burgess CJ & Lefley M. Can genetic programming improve software effort estimation? A comparative evaluation, Information & Software Technology, vol. 43, pp. 863-873, 2001.
8. Dolado JJ. On the problem of the software cost function, Information & Software Technology, vol. 43, pp. 61-72, 2001.
9. Shepperd MJ & Schofield C. Effort estimation by analogy: a case study, presented at 7th European Software Control and Metrics Conference, Wilmslow, UK, 1996.
10. Aamodt A & Plaza E. Case-based reasoning: foundational issues, methodical variations and system approaches, AI Communications, vol. 7, 1994.
11. Aha DW & Bankert RL. A comparative evaluation of sequential feature selection algorithms, in Artificial Intelligence and Statistics V., D. Fisher and J-H. Lenz, Eds. New York: Springer-Verlag, 1996.
12. Kolodner JL. Case-Based Reasoning: Morgan-Kaufmann, 1993.
13. Kirsopp C & Shepperd MJ. Making inferences with small numbers of training sets, presented at Intl. Conf. on Empirical Assessment of Software Engineering, Keele Univ, UK, 2002.
14. Shepperd MJ & Schofield C. Estimating software project effort using analogies, IEEE Transactions on Software Engineering, vol. 23, pp. 736-743, 1997.
15. Niessink F & van Vliet H. Predicting maintenance effort with function points, presented at Intl. Conf. on Softw. Maint, Bari, Italy, 1997.
16. Mendes E, Counsell S, Mosley N. Measurement and effort prediction of web applications, presented at 2nd ICSE Workshop on Web Engineering, Limerick, Ireland, 2000.
17. Briand L, Langley T, Wieczorek I. Using the European Space Agency data set: a replicated assessment and comparison of common software cost modeling techniques, presented at 22nd IEEE Intl. Conf. on Softw. Eng., Limerick, Ireland, 2000.
18. Kohavi R & John GH. Wrappers for feature selection for machine learning, Artificial Intelligence, vol. 97, pp. 273-324, 1997.
19. Skalak DB. Prototype and feature selection by sampling and random mutation hill climbing algorithms, presented at 11th Intl. Machine Learning Conf. (ICML-94), 1994.
20. Debuse JCW & Rayward-Smith VJ. Feature subset selection within a simulated annealing data mining algorithm, J. of Intelligent Information Systems, vol. 9, pp. 57-81, 1997.
21. Kirsopp C, Shepperd MJ, Hart J. Search heuristics, case-based reasoning and software project effort prediction, presented at GECCO 2002: Genetic and Evolutionary Computation Conf., New York, 2002.

# SESSION 1B:

# KNOWLEDGE REPRESENTATION AND REASONING 1

# Generating Context-Based Explanations

Anneli Edman
Department of Information Science, Computer Science Division,
Uppsala University, Sweden

Abstract

Explanations are vital in knowledge-based systems. One problem, however, is that they ought to describe the domain context, not only the formal part utilised in the reasoning. A solution is thus to reproduce informal knowledge relating and complementing the formal one. The term "context-based explanations" is used for explanations based on formal and informal domain knowledge. An architecture generating such context-based explanations is described and appropriate knowledge to be presented is investigated.

## 1 Introduction

Explanations are vital in knowledge-based systems (KBS). The user's confidence in the system's conclusions enhances if explanations present the system's domain knowledge in an appropriate way. Moreover, the user's participation in the system's reasoning, e.g. giving correct input, is facilitated through explanations. Explanations can even be as important as the conclusions themselves [1].

The user's contribution may play a more important role than just inserting data. A knowledge-based system cannot initially include all knowledge that will be needed to mirror a domain [2], which implies that knowledge must be acquired incrementally from the user when required. The reason for the incompleteness may be that it is hard to cover the knowledge, there are gaps in the completeness of the knowledge, such as missing constraints, and the knowledge is changing [3]. A solution to the problem is that the user and the system co-operate in the problem solving and that the system is augmented with the user's contributions. The focus may not even be to fully automate the problem solving, but to optimise the combination of user and knowledge-based system [4].

Domain knowledge is formally reproduced in the system's knowledge base. Except from the problem that a system from the start may not include all necessary knowledge, there is the problem that the domain context cannot formally be captured. The reason is, of course, that the various forms of knowledge communicated by human beings are richer than formal representations. The question arises, therefore, how these forms could best be exploited in a knowledge-based system. A formalisation of domain knowledge in a system can be supplemented with informal descriptions of the domain context. This informal knowledge would relate to and complement the knowledge in the formalisation and thereby extend the knowledge in the system. Moreover, since a formalisation is unable to reproduce all knowledge in the formal theory a formalisation is, in general, only partial with respect to the domain context. Therefore, a well functioning system requires that knowledge be furnished from the outside, in principle from the user. Therefore, the system must be capable of adequately presenting both the informal and formal knowledge in explanations to the user.

Utilising both the formal and informal domain knowledge when generating explanations is in line with Chandrasekaran's and Swartout's research. Their general idea is that the more explicitly the knowledge underlying a system's design is represented the better explanations the system can give [1]. More of the domain knowledge can be captured if different reproduction forms are used. Hence, a combination of informal and formal domain knowledge may mirror the context of a domain. The explanations can therefore be seen as context-based.

In this paper an architecture is presented that co-operates with the user in the reasoning and generates explanations based on formal and informal domain knowledge. This kind of explanations will be called context-based. Regarding the content in the explanations the notions of conceptual context and inferential context are introduced. The conceptual context is presented through different kind of figures showing relations between objects and conclusions and conceptualisations of the domain. The inferential context mirrors the problem solving. Knowledge types to be presented as the inferential context are elaborated in the paper.

The paper is organised as follows: In section 2 is context-based explanations discussed and then is a classification of knowledge in such explanations presented. In section 3 formal and informal knowledge are investigated and the concepts inferential and conceptual context are introduced. A real knowledge-based system is used for the examples. In section 4 the architecture is described. Then follows conclusions and further work in section 5.

# 2 Context-Based Explanations and Knowledge Types

The notion "context-based explanations" is described and a categorisation of knowledge within this kind of explanations is given.

## 2.1 Context-Based Explanations

In general, explanations in early KBS were based on canned text and rule-based explanations. Canned text may be associated with each part of the knowledge base or even each rule, explaining what the part or rule is doing. Rule-based explanations consist of information during the system's reasoning in the form of "why" a question is asked and after the problem solving by asking "how" a conclusion was reached. There are severe shortcomings with both types, cf. e.g. [5]. For canned text there is, e.g., the problem that all questions and answers must be anticipated in advance and all these answers have to be provided in the system, which is an impossible task for larger systems. Rule-based explanations are, e.g., criticised for being too extensive and too detailed. Furthermore, the rules contain often a mixture of domain knowledge and control information, which may be a problem. It is easy to generate this kind of explanations in a system, though.

Context-based explanations are a completely different way of dealing with explanations, which has impact on the whole knowledge system design. Chandrasekaran and Swartout state that "knowledge systems based on explicit representations of knowledge and methods with information about how and from what their knowledge was obtained, are the foundations for producing good explanations" [1].

Context-based explanations can be seen as one of the issues in second generation expert systems. The idea behind second generation expert systems is to represent both deep and shallow knowledge and explicitly represent the interactions between both knowledge types [6][7]. Then the knowledge system has a model of the domain context, which can be causal, functional, structural, etc. [8]. Two different approaches for the explanations can be distinguished, the first representing the knowledge used for the explanations in a more abstract way than in early systems, and the second utilising a different kind of knowledge to explain the conclusions [9]. The last approach is often called providing reconstructive explanations.

An example of the first of these types of explanation is NEOMYCIN [10], which gives an abstract representation of the knowledge that is the base for the explanations. The explanation mechanism interprets task structures, stored within a strategy system, to build the explanations. Another example is the XPLAIN [5] and the Explainable Expert System, EES, a further development of XPLAIN [11]. In these systems have Swartout *el al* tried to find a way to capture the knowledge that was used by the programmer to write the program to improve the explanations. In XPLAIN an automatic programmer creates a refinement structure, which is comprised of successive refinements of goals into prototype methods using domain models and domain principles. This structure is the base for the explanations.

Work with reconstructive explanations, the second approach, is done by Chandrasekaran and his associates. An interesting result from their work is a generic task methodology used for building knowledge systems to enhance explanations [12][13]. Wick and Thompson belong to this second approach with their implementation of a system called REX (reconstructive explainer) for generating reconstructive explanations [14]. A special explanation system in REX performs a complete reconstruction of how the expert system reasoned to reach a conclusion, with, for instance, new associations and the introduction of new objects not in the actual line of reasoning.

To generate context-based explanations more and deeper domain knowledge has to be included in the system. The explanations may therefore be richer and can show more of the system's domain knowledge than canned text and rule-based explanations. Moreover, the context-based explanations may be more flexible and easier to tailor to a particular user. Some of the advantages with such explanations are at the same time the drawbacks. Since more knowledge has to be included in the system the knowledge acquisition phase will be protracted. The required knowledge may be difficult to attain and, moreover, it may be difficult to reproduce it in the system. Furthermore, the architecture has to be quite advanced to be able to deal with this kind of explanations.

## 2.2 Classification of Knowledge

What kind of knowledge is to be displayed through the explanations? There are some suggestions concerning the knowledge that the system ought to present.

Clancey [15] characterises knowledge needed for explanations in MYCIN - which he argues is applicable to other KBS - in three categories:
(Cl I) strategy, which refers to a plan according to which goals and hypotheses are ordered in problem solving
(Cl II) structural knowledge, which consists of abstractions that are used to index the domain knowledge
(Cl III) support knowledge, justifying the causality between the problem features and the diagnosis, which may be somewhat redundant to the diagnostic associations.

Swartout [5] found, through a series of trials, that the questions a user would like to pose to a knowledge system, in this case Digitalis Advisor, were the following:
(Sw I) questions about the methods the program employed
(Sw II) justification of the program's actions
(Sw III) questions involving confusion about the meaning of terms.

Chandrasekaran, Tanner and Josephson [12] state that the explanations relevant to the problem solving are the main issue. Their categorisation of explanations is:
(Ch I) how well the data match the local goals, which describes how certain decisions are made and what piece of data is used to arrive at a specific conclusion
(Ch II) justification of knowledge, which involves justifying fragments of domain knowledge by explaining a certain part of the knowledge base, generally not based on a special case
(Ch III) explanation of control strategy, which clarifies the behaviour of the problem solver and the control strategy used in a particular situation.

There are resemblances between Clancey, Swartout, and Chandresekaran *et al* in terms of the categories of knowledge needed for explanations. These categories can be combined into four groups:

- problem solving strategy, including (Cl I), (Sw I), (Ch III)
- justification of the system's domain knowledge, including (Cl III), (Sw II), (Ch II)
- local problem solving, including (Cl II), (Ch I)
- term descriptions, including (Sw III)

These four groups will be elaborated upon in Section 3.2.

# 3 Presenting Domain Context

First the necessity of reproducing the domain context both as informal and formal knowledge is discussed. Then are the notions inferential and conceptual context described. A system, Analyse More, is used to illustrate the ideas.

## 3.1 Reproducing Informal and Formal Knowledge

To reproduce a domain context, it is insufficient to provide information about the formal knowledge, i.e., to only provide the knowledge needed for the reasoning [16]. This is in accordance with Wick and Thompson who state that generating explanations is a complex problem-solving activity that depends on both the actual line of reasoning and additional knowledge of the domain [14]. Wenger expresses the same opinion: One way to articulate superficial knowledge in a knowledge base is to augment it with information that explicitly provides the missing justifications for the knowledge [17]. Hence, the limitations of formalisation necessitate the inclusion of informal domain knowledge in the system. The informal knowledge would relate to and complement the knowledge in the formalisation and thereby extend the knowledge in the system. Let us exemplify this with domain knowledge from a real system, Analyse More.

Analyse More is an expert system that aims at supporting students in sampling and evaluating the quality of water in lakes [18]. The student should get an increased understanding of choice of method and interpretation of data. The investigations are coupled to the teaching in biology, physics, and chemistry. The Analyse More project was a part of a larger program initiated by The National Board of Education in Sweden for developing software for upper secondary schools in the environment protection field. The system was developed in co-operation with experts at the Swedish Environmental Protection Agency and teachers. Analyse More was implemented in Klöver [19], a shell for developing KBS. Klöver is implemented in Prolog.

The formal knowledge in Analyse More is represented as rules. These rules are divided into two groups, one for the chemical-physical evaluation of the lake, and one for the biological evaluation. The conclusions refer to the how nutritious the lake is and whether it is acid. The problem solving is based on these rules.

The informal knowledge within the domain refers to how to measure, e.g., the conductivity, the unit of measurement and the interval for the value. Another example is how to decide the species of a phytoplankton. This kind of knowledge is a complement to the rules since it is not part of the reasoning. But the knowledge is important for the user so he/she can perform the measurements and observations and hence is able to give correct input to the system. Informal context knowledge that is related to the formal knowledge is, e.g., a justification of the rule content and information about alternative ways to reach a conclusion. Some of this knowledge may be formalised but not all, e.g., the procedure when measuring the conductivity or observing the appearance of a phytoplankton.

The informal knowledge should of course be reproduced in its most natural form, as text, diagrams, pictures, animations, or sound etc.

Experiences from testing Analyse More showed that users, both students and teachers, were satisfied with the system's problem-solving and the conclusive results. It was different with the explanations though. These comprise both canned text and rule-based explanations [18]. Some of the informal knowledge mentioned above can be found s canned text, e.g. the method is described in text. When testing it was found that the users were satisfied with the canned text, even if they did not utilised the texts so often as we expected. But the rule-based explanations were not understandable, though special emphasis had been put on formulising the rules as a basis for these explanations when implementing the system [20]. One rule may be fairly understandable, but the problem is that a single "why" explanation can involve several tens of rules. The number of rules for a conclusion was also increased by the design of the rules. Information about the groups of rules has to be presented on a highly abstracted level, which could be combined with presentations of what the systems is doing at the moment.

## 3.2 Inferential and Conceptual Context

The proposition is to generate explanations based on inferential and conceptual context knowledge. The inferential context presents the actual problem solving and the knowledge this is based on. The conceptual context mirrors the domain knowledge in a broader perspective and shows different views of the domain.

### *3.2.1 Presenting the Inferential Context*

Experiences from Analyse More showed a need for explanations of the rules on a more abstract level together with information about the current reasoning. Let's start with the later task, which is the easiest one. The system displays, during the problem solving, what it is trying to show for the moment and the premises that has to be fulfilled. When a goal succeeds or fails this is also presented. During the reasoning the user participate by giving different kinds of input and it is easy to see how this input is utilised in the reasoning.

An abstract presentation of the formal domain knowledge is performed using informal knowledge directly related to the formal knowledge but also complementary information. This knowledge is structured as objects in a context tree. A rough distinction can be made between the objects according to their participation in different phases of the problem solving, see Figure 1. An object could be a goal object, in which case the system will try to conclude a value for the object. The user can provide values for some objects, so called ground objects. All objects between goal and ground objects are called intermediate objects. Their values can

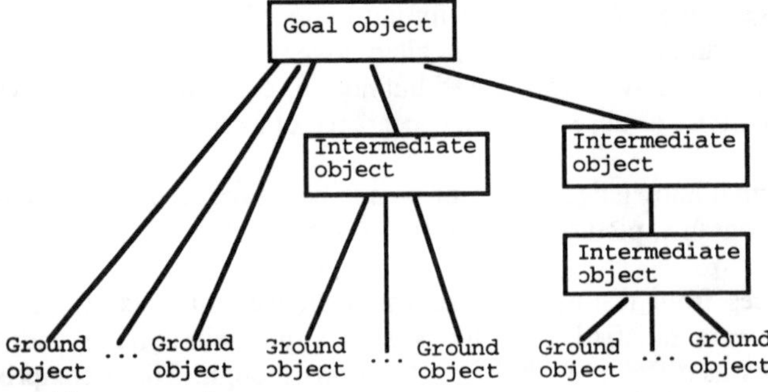


Figure 1. Different object categories.

be used in the final conclusion or in concluding values related to other intermediate objects, which will be used later on in the reasoning of goal objects.

The context tree for the chemical-physical part of Analyse More can be seen in Figure 2. The different objects in the tree have properties connected to them and these will be used for explanations. The properties are listed in Figure 3. Naturally, the properties are domain dependent but some have a more general applicability.

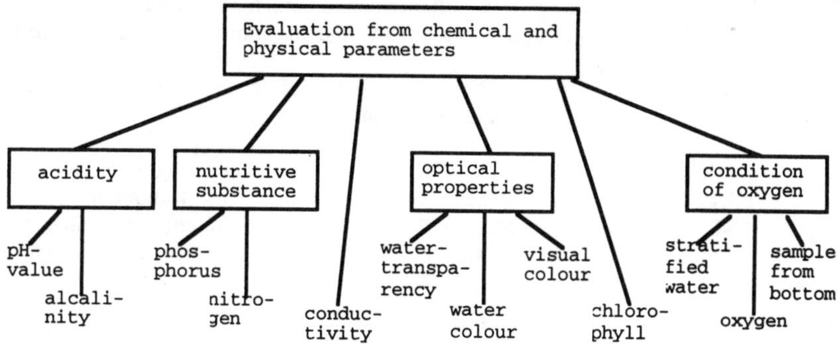


Figure 2. Objects related to the chemical-physical part in Analyse More.

When the user during the problem solving is asked for a value, e.g. for alcalinity, then he/she may ask for related information. If the object alcalinity is used in relation to several conclusions the user chooses which is currently of interest. If the answer is oligotrophic then the inferential context is presented for a branch in Figure 2. The explanation is expanded from informal knowledge about the root object '"evaluation from chemical and physical parameters: oligotrophic", the intermediate object "acidity" to the ground object "alcalinity". Only the relevant categories are used in the presentation, see Figure 4. Note that the dialogue is presented without any pretensions concerning adequate user interfaces.

| No. | Domain property | Objects |
|---|---|---|
| (1) | Justification of domain knowledge | Goal, Intermediate, Ground |
| (2) | Evaluation of conclusions or objects | Goal. Intermediate. Ground |
| (3) | Term descriptions | Goal, Intermediate, Ground |
| (4) | Totality of the objects involved when inferring a conclusion | Goal, Intermediate |
| (5) | Concordance between objects | Intermediate |
| (6) | Class of objects | Intermediate, Ground |
| (7) | General information | Goal, Intermediate, Ground |
| (8) | Order | Goal, Intermediate |
| (9) | Method for the observation or measurement of an object | Ground |
| (10) | Unit for the observation/measurement | Ground |
| (11) | Interval for the measurement | Ground |
| (12) | Observation/description of an object | Ground |

Figure 3. A categorisation of the knowledge in the context tree.

**evaluation from chemical and physical parameters: oligotrophic**
TOTALITY: Evaluating the nutriment in a lake, in this case that it is oligotrophic, comprises estimating the waters' acidity, nutritive substance, optical properties, conductivity and chorophyll.
TERM DESCRIPTIONS: A water is oligotrophic when it is poor of nutriment. Eutrophic is the opposite term to oligotrophic.
ORDER: The program will investigate the acidity first.
EVALUATION: Some tests are more important than others for a special conclusion. To conclude that the lake is oligotrophic the acidity and the nutritive substance are most influential.
GENERAL INFORMATION: In general one can say that if a lake is acid it is also oligotrophic, but an oligotrophic lake does not have to be acid.
**acidity**
TOTALITY: Alcalinity and pH-value are investigated when evaluating acidity.
EVALUATION: To conclude if the lake is acid the alcalinity is most important.
CONCORDANCE: There is a concordance between some measurements, which means that you cannot have a high value for one and a low for the other. The alcalinity and pH-value act together in such a way.
JUSTIFICATION: The buffer capacity in the surroundings is important for the acidity in the lake. This is not taken into considerations, though.
GENERAL INFORMATION: The measurements changes during the time of the year but the system does not take that into account.
**alcalinity**
CLASS OF OBJECTS: Alcalinity is the quantity hydrogen ions that is used to neutralise the bases in 1 kilo water.
JUSTIFICATION: The acidity measures how basic a liquid is.
METHOD: (*An animation of how the measurement can be performed together with a text description.*)
UNIT: Alcalinity is measured in mekv/l, which is the same as mol/l.
INTERVAL: The measurement can only be in the interval 0-4.
GENERAL INFORMATION: The Swedish Environment Protection Agency counts with margin of errors when measuring. The margin is 4% for alcalinity.

Figure 4. An explanation related to alcalinity in an oligotrophic lake.

Four groups of information that explanations ought to comprise, based on Clancey, Swartout and Chandresekarans research, were formulated in section 2.2. Let's relate our categorisation of domain knowledge in Figure 3 to the these groups.
(I) Problem solving strategy corresponds to (4), (8) and (2).
(II) Justification of the system's domain knowledge corresponds to (1), (5), (6) and (7).
(III) Local problem solving corresponds to (4), (8), (2) and (6).
(IV) Term descriptions corresponds to (3) and (7).

A discussion regarding this correspondence can be found in [20] for childhood illnesses. The categories (9)-(12), referring to the methods for measurement, the unit and the interval for measurements, and the descriptions of objects, are not incorporated in the categories (I)-(IV) above. The actual information deals with how to obtain information needed in the problem solving and supports the user in finding this data, which are important, especially since the user is an active part of the reasoning process. In contrast, the knowledge in (I)-(IV) is more directed towards explanations after the problem solving.

### 3.2.2 Presenting Conceptual Context

The conceptual context is presented through different kinds of information showing relations between objects and conclusions and conceptualisations of the domain. For instance, the relations between a measurement and a conclusion are seen in Figure 5. The user has measured the phosphorus to be 40. The other measurements are presented after importance for the current result. If the pH-value is measured to be 6.5 it does not fit in this figure and a new one is given. This looks quite different because the estimation is now that the lake is normal.

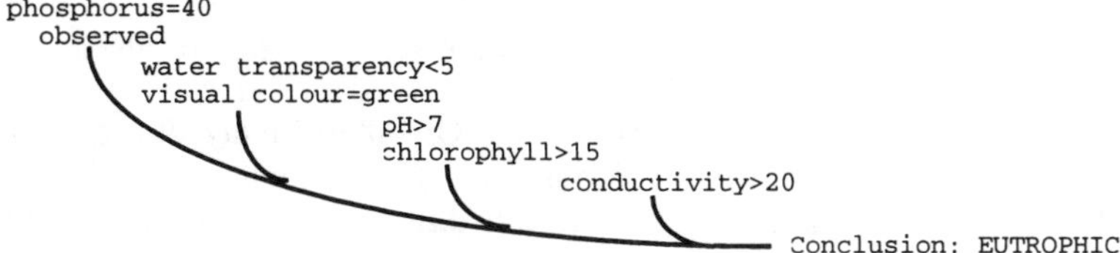


Figure 5. Relation between phosphorus and an eutrophic lake.

A simulation of the status in the lake in relation to pH-value is another example of a conceptual context. Figure 6 shows simplification of such a simulation for perches. When the pH-value gets lower the number of fishes desreases to completely vanish at 4.5. Reasons why a fish vanish may be that their food disappears, they get poisoned or they are not reproductive anymore. In Figure 7 properties for perch fishes are shown which may also be part of the conceptual context. The conceptual context is reproduced as informal knowledge in the system.

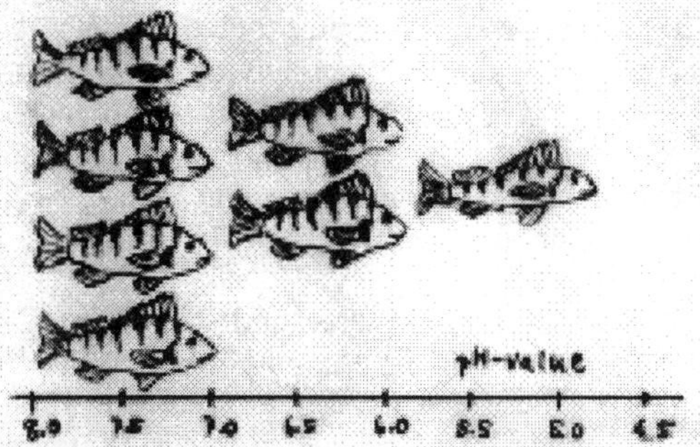


Figure 6. The relation between perches and pH-value.

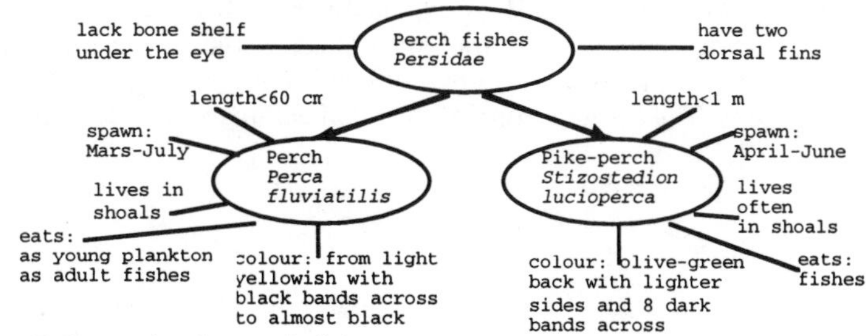


Figure 7. Properties for perch fishes.

# 4 The System Architecture

In a knowledge-based system formal knowledge is utilised in the problem solving. The meaning of the formal representation is a certain part of the informal domain knowledge. When formalising knowledge three separate and distinct "theories" are involved in the process according to Kleene [21] These theories are:

- the informal theory, IT, of which the formal system constitutes a formalisation
- the formal system or object theory, OT, and
- the metatheory, MT, in which the formal system is described and studied.

Two different perspectives can be taken in the metatheory. The metamathematical one, where the informal theory is simply disregarded and only the formal properties of the formal theory are investigated. Or, alternatively, the metatheory can examine the relation between the formal and the informal theory. Thus, the informal theory is regarded as being the intended interpretation of the incomplete formal theory. The first perspective presupposes that the informal theory is so fully understood that it can be replaced altogether by a formal theory. For KBS, this is generally not possible. The system can only have a partial axiomatisation of the formal object theory because the informal theory is only partially understood [22]. Therefore, the metatheory examines the relation between the formal and informal theory, and not only the formal theory.

The proposed system architecture is based on the three theories OT, IT and MT. Figure 8 gives an overview of the system architecture. In OT the formal knowledge is represented, e.g., as rules. IT is composed of the knowledge complementing and corresponding to OT, such as the context tree, knowledge about the statements that should be displayed during the reasoning and the conceptual context. Part of IT is also the user's contributions in the problem-solving. The user can, of course, give data but also contribute by giving a truth value to a statement, which the system has not succeeded in proving. Another alternative is that the user can decide whether a statement is equivalent to another statement, which the user can define or the system has knowledge about.

All the relations between IT and OT are administered by the metatheory. MT carries out the reasoning in the system based upon inferences in OT together with the information the user supplies. Therefore MT has the task of conducting the communication between the user and the system. This communication includes an integration of the user's contributions in IT. It also includes presentations of the system's knowledge as different kinds of explanations. Consequently, MT carries out automated reasoning about the informal knowledge stored in the system, e.g., giving the user access to relevant information and for enabling it to produce adequate presentations. The formalisation of the architecture can be found in [23].

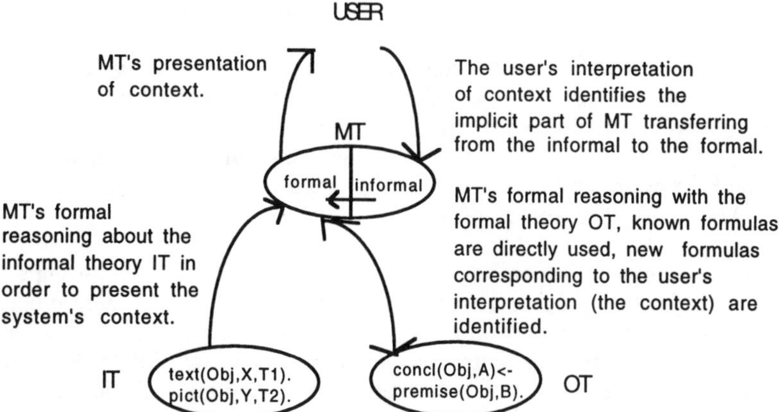


Figure 8. The semiformal metatheory and its interrelations.

The metatheory in the system has to be quite advanced, performing reasoning based on both OT and IT and integrating the user's interpretations of the informal knowledge in IT. MT represents the relations between the different kinds of knowledge. The architecture is realised in first order logic, which is capable of expressing arbitrary relations between syntactical terms. The division of the knowledge into three distinct theories gives the system a high degree of modularity. Moreover, the respective modules are expressed in their natural way, which in turn promotes clarity, making the system easy to survey. This is vital for achieving maintainability, i.e., facilitating updating and alterations to the system.

# 5 Conclusions and Further Work

This paper discusses context-based explanations. The domain context is a combination of the informal and formal knowledge in the system. Implementing context-based explanations leads to a different approach to the knowledge represented than earlier KBS and to the form in which it is represented and even how the system reasons with it. The results are that more and deeper domain knowledge is included in the system, that the explanations can be tailored to different users more easily and that they can be presented in a distinct way.

However, in contrast to Chandrasekaran and Swartout [1], the author agrees with Cawsey et al. [24] that giving explanations after the problem solving is invalid for most realistic problem situations. A well functioning system that co-operates with the user must be able to interact with the user at any time during its reasoning.

In the system architecture an informal domain theory, a formal object theory axiomatising the informal theory and a metatheory analysing the properties and interrelations between them are integrated. The grouping of objects in a context tree is used when building up the informal domain theory and the contextual knowledge coupled to each object and every property is reproduced. This architecture is to serve as a programmable schema for supporting the composition of second generation KBS.

The knowledge in the context tree satisfies the demands on explanations specified by Clancey, Swartout and Chandrasekaran and offers even more information. Objects at different levels in the context tree are connected to special domain properties. Hence, the properties can describe the context with different levels of abstraction and from different perspectives. The inferential context shows the problem solving in a top-down manner while some of the conceptual context presents it bottom-up. Problem-solving is supported by such a combination of top-down and bottom-up procedures, cf. e.g. [25].

The way of categorising the objects and then connecting the different groups with properties is a practical procedure for reproducing domain context. These properties have been used in two domains, in addition to the two domains in Analyse More. The properties are tested for diagnosing childhood illnesses [20] and in Small Business Manager [26], where the explanations regarding the cash flow behaviour in a firm were based on the categorisation.

The way to categorise knowledge coupled to a context tree has been used in two domains, where the properties were different. First the method was used for reproducing context knowledge in a matching facility [27] implemented within an EC project, easi-isae [28]. This facility is used by teachers and school leaders when searching for candidate companies for co-operation in the production of computer aided learning material and by companies trying to find teachers for the role of content provider or intellectual author in the production of such material. The method was adopted by all six of the countries co-operating within the project, but they decided the properties used locally. Secondly, the method has been used in an explorative initial study examining the requirements of specified information for different target groups, in conjunction with major accidents in the society [29]. The study shows that the types of information differ between different target groups and between accident phases. Structuring the domain context as objects in an context tree facilitated the management of the information, both the acquisition and the presentations.

To deal with the informal knowledge a number of domain properties of relevance to the tasks of diagnosis and classification are identified. It is impossible to account for all properties that might be relevant completely and the architecture should be kept open for extensions. However, a continution of the work is to analyse and identify properties for other tasks such as design and planning, etc.

As described, generating explanations during the problem solving is implemented. A task for further work is to investigate explanations afterwards, i.e. "how" explanations. Hence, the task is to investigate what kind of knowledge is suitable and how this should be presented to the user. Furthermore, tailoring the explanations to different users is an important and challenging issue.

**References**

1. Chandrasekaran B, Swartout W. Explanations in knowledge systems, the role of explicit representation of design knowledge. IEEE expert, June 1991; 47-49

2. Brézillon P, Cases E. Cooperating for assisting intelligently operators. In: Proceeding of the International Workshop on the Design of Cooperative Systems, Juan les Pins, France, 1995, pp. 370-384

3. Shadbolt N. Knowledge acquisition: breaking the bottleneck. Material from tutorial, The seventeenth annual international conference of the British Computer Society Specialist Group on Expert Systems, Cambridge, England, 1997

4. Stolze M. Task level frameworks for cooperative expert system design, AI Communications 1991; Vol.4 No. 2/3

5. Swartout WR. Explaining and justifying expert consulting programs. Proceedings of the Seventh International Joint Conference of Artificial Intelligence, Vancouver, B.C. Canada, 1981, pp. 815-823

6. Steels L. Second generation expert systems. Future Generation Computer Systems, 1985; Vol. 2, 2

7. Steels L. The deepening of expert systems. AI Communication. 1987; Vol. 1, 1

8. Steels L. Components of expertise. AI Magazine, 1990; 11(2):28-49

9. David J-M, Krivine J-P, Simmons R. Second generation expert systems: A step forward in knowledge engineering. In: David J-M, Krivine J-P, Simmons R (ed) Second generation expert systems, Springer-Verlag, 1993, pp. 3-23

10. Clancey WJ, Letsinger R. NEOMYCIN: Reconfiguring a rule-based expert system for application to teaching. Proceedings of the Seventh International Joint Conferences on Artificial Intelligence, 1981, vol. 2, pp 829-836. (Reprinted in Clancey WJ, Shortliffe EH. Readings in medical artificial intelligence, Addison-Wesley, 1984, pp. 361-381)

11. Swartout WR, Moore J. Explanations in second generation expert systems. In: David J-M, Krivine J-P, Simmons R (ed) Second generation expert systems, Springer-Verlag, 1993, pp. 543-585

12. Chandrasekaran B, Tanner MC, Josephson JR. Explanation: The role of control strategies and deep models. In: Hendler JA (ed) Expert Systems: The user interface, . Ablex Publishing Corporation, 1988, pp. 219 - 246

13. Chandrasekaran B, Johnson T. Generic tasks and task structures: History, critique and new directions. In: David J-M, Krivine J-P, Simmons R (ed) Second generation expert systems, Springer-Verlag, 1993, pp. 232-272

14. Wick RM, Thompson WB. Reconstructive expert system explanation. Artificial Intelligence 1992; 54: 33-70

15. Clancey WJ. Extensions to rules for explanation and tutoring. Artificial Intelligence 1983; 20:215-251 (Edited version in Buchanan BG, Shortliffe EH. Rule-based expert systems, Addison-Wesley, 1984, pp. 531-568)

16. Edman A, Hamfelt A. A basis for a system development methodology for user co-operative systems. In: Proceedings of the International and Interdisciplinary Conference on Modelling and Using Context, CONTEXT 97, Rio de Janeiro, Brasilia, 1997, pp. 290-302

17. Wenger E. Artificial intelligence and tutoring systems. Los Altos, CA: Morgan Kaufman, 1987

18. Edman A, Lindman Å, Sundling L. Design issues concerning explanations in an educational expert system - a case study. In: Proceedings of the Seventh PEG Conference, PEG-93, Edinburgh, Scotland, 1993, pp. 108-115

19. Edman A, Sundling L. Investeringsrådgivningssystemet Klöver (A consultative system for investments, Klöver). Computing Science Department, Uppsala University, Sweden, 1989

20. Edman A. Combining knowledge systems and hypermedia for user co-operation and learning. PhD thesis, Uppsala University, Uppsala, Sweden, 2001 http://publications.uu.se/theses/

21. Kleene SC. Introduction to meta-mathematics. Amsterdam: North-Holland, 1971

22. Hamfelt A. Metalogic representation of multilayered knowledge. PhD thesis, Uppsala University, Uppsala, Sweden, 1992

23. Edman A. & Hamfelt A. A system architecture for knowledge based hypermedia. International Journal of Human-Computer Studies, 1999; 51:1007-1036

24. Cawsey A, Galliers J, Reece S, Sparck Jones K. The role of explanations in collaborative problem solving. In: Proceedings of the ECAI-92 Workshop W15 Improving the Use of Knowledge-Based Systems with Explanations, Vienna, Austria, 1992, pp. 97-106

25. Bender-Öberg A, Edman A. Pedagogical issues for DLW - an interactive learning system. In: Proceedings of the Eighth International Prolog Education Group Conference, PEG-97, Sozopol, Bulgaria, 1997, pp. 88-96

26. Öhlmér J. Knowledge-based explanations in a decision support system. Thesis for the degree of Master Science, No. 34/98, Department of Computing Science, Uppsala University, Sweden, 1998

27. Johansson A-L. A matching facility based on a multicultural concept structure. Proceedings of the SSGRR 2000 International Conference on Advances in Infrastructure for Electronic Business, Science, and Education on the Internet, 2000 http://www.ssgrr.it/en/ssgrr2000/proceedings.htm

28. Gerret D. easi-isae Vocational training software and tool to assist intellectual authors and software developers in the production of multimedia. Project Program, Joint Call Educational Multimedia, 1997

29. Lindström, J. Målgruppsanpassad information via Internet i samband med olyckor (Specified information through the Internet in liaison with accidents). Thesis for the Degree of Master of Science Majoring in Computing Science, No. 57/99, Division of Computer and Systems Science, Department of Information Science, Uppsala University, Sweden, 1999

# Facilitating DL-based Hybrid Reasoning with Inference Fusion

Bo Hu
School of Computing, Robert Gordon University, Aberdeen, UK

Inés Arana
School of Computing, Robert Gordon University, Aberdeen, UK

Ernesto Compatangelo
Department of Computing Science, University of Aberdeen, UK

**Abstract**

We present an extension to DL-based taxonomic reasoning by means of the proposed *inference fusion*, i.e. the dynamic combination of inferences from distributed heterogeneous reasoners. Our approach integrates results from a DL-based system with results from a constraint solver under the direction of a global reasoning coordinator. *Inference fusion* is performed by (i) processing heterogeneous input knowledge, producing suitable homogeneous input knowledge for each specialised reasoner; (ii) activating each reasoner when necessary, collecting its results and passing them to the other reasoner if appropriate; (iii) combining the results of the two reasoners. We discuss the benefits of our approach and demonstrate our ideas by proposing a language ($\mathcal{DL}$(D)/S) and a reasoning system (CONCOR) which uses knowledge bases written in $\mathcal{DL}$(D)/S and supports hybrid reasoning. We illustrate our ideas with an example.

## 1 Motivation and background

Central to the *semantic web* is the development of representations which are understandable by both human beings and machines [3]. Hence, progress in the *semantic web* has boosted the research in ontological modelling and reasoning. Current approaches to ontology reasoning during the knowledge lifecycle management are based on a wide variety of structured knowledge models, each enabling different automated capabilities. Some models, such as UML [24], represent knowledge at the conceptual level. Unfortunately, most of them have an ill-defined semantics and thus do not enable any semantic deduction. Frame-based models like Protégé [23] represent knowledge at the epistemological level (i.e. they use the two generic primitives class and role). Although these models enable automated inferences such as class membership, they do not support deductions such as subsumption. Finally, models based on Description Logics (DLs) like OIL/DAML+OIL [7] broaden the spectrum of frame-based inferences with a whole set of specialised deductions based on taxonomic reasoning.

Deductive services provided by DL-based reasoners include, among others, semantic consistency check subsumption, and concept classification [6]. DL-based approaches are particularly appealing for applications such as ontology reasoning in the Semantic Web, where taxonomic reasoning has been recognised as one of the core inferences [7]. Moreover, DLs use the notions of concept (i.e. unary predicate) and role (i.e. binary relation) to model declarative knowledge in a structured way. Using different constructors defined with a uniform syntax and unambiguous semantics, complex concept definitions and axioms can be built from simple components. Therefore, DLs are particularly appealing both to represent ontological knowledge and to reason with it.

Unfortunately, the expressive power needed to model complex real-world ontologies is quite high, so that ontology reasoning was initially ruled out of the list of services to be provided by ontology management tools [9]. Nevertheless, the OIL/DAML+OIL effort has re-introduced the issue of ontology reasoning as a first-class problem, providing a solution within the framework of a DL-based, frame-centred approach [7]. However, despite its expressivity, the OIL/DAML+OIL approach does not yet provide practical support to reasoning with concrete domains or local constraints (i.e. role-value maps). This is because the knowledge model of the iFaCT DL engine [13], which provides the deductive services for the ontology inference layer, does not currently include concrete domains or role-value maps.

During the last few years, much research has been devoted to the development of more powerful reasoning systems, Although single-purposed reasoning systems have improved substantially, their homogeneous approaches are limited in two ways: (i) the expressive power of their representation is restricted in order to ensure computational tractability, completeness and decidability; (ii) the specialist nature of their reasoning means that they are only successful at carrying out particular inferential tasks. For instance, DL-based systems specialised in the construction of concept taxonomies from concept descriptions while constraint programming tools solve constraint problems. Although in the past there has been some research on the integration of hybrid homogeneous reasoning [22], little has been done on the integration of heterogeneous reasoning, e.g. the integration of DL-based and constraint-based reasoners.

Some approaches have been proposed to include *concrete domains*—and predicates on these domains—in DL-based concept definitions which are normally restricted to *abstract domains*. Despite the diversity of their representations, most of them are based on $\mathcal{ALC}$ [25] and its expressive successor $\mathcal{SHIQ}$ [15] and extend the original tableau-based algorithm [25] in different ways. It has been proved, however, that reasoning about extensions of $\mathcal{ALC}$ with concrete domains is generally intractable [19]. This problem can be mitigated only if suitable restrictions are introduced in the way of combining concept constructors [10].

Homogeneous reasoning systems (or systems with homogeneous inference algorithms) have encountered the difficulty of finding the right "trade-off" between expressiveness and computational complexity. We believe that if a knowledge model is too expressive to be analysed within the framework of DLs, then other representation and reasoning paradigms must be jointly used. Therefore, it's reasonable to consider a that a hybrid approach to heterogeneous knowledge management may provide, among other things, a wider and better support to ontology reasoning. The benefits of such an approach in the context of ontology sharing through the articulation of ontology interdependencies is highlighted in [5].

In this paper, we thus present a generic schema to extend existing DL-based systems with the ability of representing and reasoning with numeric constraints. Our idea is materialised through a hybrid modelling language $\mathcal{DL}$(D)/S, and supported by an implemented hybrid reasoning system (HRS), CONCOR.

## 2 Practical approach for hybrid reasoning

*Inference fusion* is a generic schema for dynamically integrating heterogeneous inferential engines [17]. More specifically, we focus on a particular class of *inference fusion*-based HRSs, which fuse the T-Box deductions from a DL-based taxonomic reasoning system with constraint satisfaction inferences from a constraint solver under the direction of a global reasoning coordinator.

In order to ensure the autonomy of both inferential sub-systems (hereafter, referred to as engines), there should be a reliable mechanism responsible for the communicating between them. For this purpose, we introduce the bijection, *linkage*, which is responsible for mapping the intrinsic data structures in the DL-based system to the data structures in the constraint solver and *vice versa*. *Linkages* ensure that (i) the results from one system can be fed into the other system without increasing the original computational complexity of these two systems; and (ii) no changes are required on either reasoning system, i.e. the underlying inference algorithms remain unchanged.

A Hybrid Knowledge Base (HKB), denoted as $\Pi_{\text{KB}}$, is first processed by a *parser* which fragments the descriptions and splits them into three sets, namely: (i) $\Pi_{\text{DL}}$, i.e. a set of DL-oriented statements which do not exceed the expressive power of the selected DL-based system, (ii) $\Pi_{\text{non-DL}}$, i.e. a set of non-DL statements which contains the concrete knowledge filtered out to form $\Pi_{\text{DL}}$, and (iii) $\Pi_{linkage}$, i.e. a set of *linkages* which are one-to-one relations connecting DL and non-DL statements.

As a result, instead of reasoning with constraints directly, DL-based systems provide inferential services without being aware of the existence of constraint reasoning. All the information related to concrete domains is removed from concept definitions. Thus, only the proper DL-based constructors which are admitted by the selected DL-based inferential engines are left.

The reasoning results from the non-DL system are reflected into the DL one using *linkages*. Therefore, the hybrid characteristics of our approach are evident in the "polymorphism" of *linkages* which are regarded as atomic concepts in the DL-based inferential engine while act as legal objects in the non-DL reasoning system (e.g. constrained variables in CSs).

For instance, let's assume that, in state X, all people participating in legal marriages should be at least 22 years old. In the meantime, only those who are older than 70 are counted as senior citizens. Amongst the married people, couples who have already celebrated their golden wedding anniversary should have been married for at least 50 years. The set of concepts and global constraints for this domain is as follows: Married-person who is between 22 and 100[1], Golden-couples who have been married for at least 50 years, and Senior-citizens who are between 70 and 100. Because of the difficulty of carrying out real calculations, e.g. addition of X+Y, DL-based systems may not be able to detect that a person who belongs to Golden-couple is also a Senior-citizen.

Our approach can facilitate such reasoning by splitting and redirecting knowledge to specialised reasoners. In the above example, a series of $\mathrm{AGE}_x$ will be defined as constrained variables with specified domains, e.g. 0..100. *Linkages* map a concrete variable $\mathrm{AGE}_x$ (used by the constraint solver) to an abstract atomic concept $\mathsf{Age}_x$ (referred in the DL concept definitions of Married-person, Golden-couple and Senior-citizen). Thus, the reasoning results w.r.t. $\mathrm{AGE}_x$ from the constraint solver are fed into the DL-based system. Subsequently, the subsumption relationship between Senior-citizen and Golden-couple can be detected by the DL-based (taxonomic) reasoning system.

# 3 Hybrid DL-based modelling with $\mathcal{DL}$(D)/S

In this section, the hybrid modelling language $\mathcal{DL}$(D)/S is proposed to illustrate the applicability of *inference fusion* in extending the DL-based systems. $\mathcal{DL}$(D)/S extends $\mathcal{ALC}$ with various types of concrete constraints. Note that, because of the generic characteristics of *inference fusion* and the common availability of *linkages* in DLs, the use of $\mathcal{ALC}$ is not mandatory, i.e. other DLs could have been used for our purposes.

## 3.1 Syntax and Semantics of $\mathcal{DL}$(D)/S

$\mathcal{ALC}$ concepts are built as follows. Let $\mathcal{A}$ be the set of concept names, $\mathcal{C}$ the set of arbitrary concept descriptions, $\mathcal{R}$ the set of role names and $n$ an arbitrary non-negative integer. Starting with (i) $\mathsf{A} \in \mathcal{A}$, (ii) $\mathsf{C}, \mathsf{D} \in \mathcal{C}$ and (iii) $\mathsf{R} \in \mathcal{R}$, concept terms can be defined inductively. A *concept definition* is either $\mathsf{A} \dot{\sqsubseteq} \mathsf{C}$ (partial definition) or $\mathsf{A} \doteq \mathsf{C}$ (full definition). An interpretation $\mathcal{I}$ for $\mathcal{ALC}$ is a couple ( $\Delta^{\mathcal{I}}$, $\cdot^{\mathcal{I}}$): the nonempty set $\Delta^{\mathcal{I}}$ is the domain of $\mathcal{I}$, while the $\cdot^{\mathcal{I}}$ function maps each concept to a subset of $\Delta^{\mathcal{I}}$ and each role to a subset of $\Delta^{\mathcal{I}} \times \Delta^{\mathcal{I}}$. The interpretation of $\mathcal{ALC}$ constructors is shown in Table 1. $\mathcal{ALCN}$ [15] extends $\mathcal{ALC}$ with numeric role number restrictions, i.e. $\geqslant_n \mathsf{R}$ and $\leqslant_n \mathsf{R}$.

$\mathcal{ALC}$ has been extended with the ability to describe concrete knowledge. For instance, $\mathcal{ALC}$(D) [1] extends $\mathcal{ALC}$ with constructors allowing the definition of predicates over functional roles and role chains. Sound and complete algorithms for $\mathcal{ALC}$(D) exist for A-Box reasoning provided that **D** is an *admissible* concrete domain, e.g. $\mathcal{N}$ [1]. $\mathcal{SHOQ}$(D) extends $\mathcal{ALC}$ with constructors for *concrete datatypes* used to represent numbers and strings [14]. Sound and complete algorithms exist for reasoning in $\mathcal{SHOQ}$(D) provided that suitable

[1] We assume that the life span of human being does not exceed 100 years

Table 1: Syntax and semantics of $\mathcal{ALC}$ constructors

| Constructor | Syntax | Semantics (*Interpretation*) |
|---|---|---|
| Top (Universe) | $\top$ | $\Delta^{\mathcal{I}}$ |
| Bottom (Nothing) | $\bot$ | $\emptyset$ |
| Atomic Concept | A | $A^{\mathcal{I}} \subseteq \Delta^{\mathcal{I}}$ |
| Atomic Role | R | $R^{\mathcal{I}} \subseteq \Delta^{\mathcal{I}} \times \Delta^{\mathcal{I}}$ |
| Conjunction | $C \sqcap D$ | $C^{\mathcal{I}} \cap D^{\mathcal{I}}$ |
| Disjunction | $C \sqcup D$ | $C^{\mathcal{I}} \cup D^{\mathcal{I}}$ |
| Negation | $\neg C$ | $\Delta^{\mathcal{I}} \setminus D^{\mathcal{I}}$ |
| Universal quantification | $\forall R.C$ | $\{ c \in \Delta^{\mathcal{I}} \mid \forall d \in \Delta^{\mathcal{I}} : \langle c, d \rangle \in R^{\mathcal{I}} \rightarrow d \in C^{\mathcal{I}} \}$ |
| Existential quantification | $\exists R.C$ | $\{ c \in \Delta^{\mathcal{I}} \mid \exists d \in \Delta^{\mathcal{I}} : \langle c, d \rangle \in R^{\mathcal{I}} \wedge d \in C^{\mathcal{I}} \}$ |

restrictions are introduced [1]. Meanwhile, substantial efforts have been made on the implementations, e.g. $\mathcal{ALCRP}$(D) [12] and RACER [11].

Despite the difference in expressive and deductive powers, traditional approaches which extend DLs have concentrated on enhancing the algorithm originally devised for $\mathcal{ALC}$ [25], i.e. create a tableaux containing both concept constructors and constraint predicates, during which process, the complex intervention of abstract and concrete knowledge is inevitable. Thus, adding concrete domains (e.g. numeric constraints) directly to expressive DL-based systems may result in undecidable inferential problems [19].

We introduced the hybrid modelling language $\mathcal{DL}$(D)/S (Table 2) in order to extend DLs with concrete domains while avoiding a significant increase in the computational complexity of the DL-based systems [17]. The concrete domain is formally defined as a pair $\mathcal{D} = (\Delta_{\mathcal{D}}, \Phi_{\mathcal{D}})$, where $\Delta_{\mathcal{D}}$ is a finite set of numeric and symbolic constants and $\Phi_{\mathcal{D}}$ a set of algebraic and boolean operators.

Table 2: Syntax and semantics of $\mathcal{DL}$(D)/S constructor (not in $\mathcal{ALC}$)

| Constructor | Syntax | Semantics (*Interpretation*) |
|---|---|---|
| role value constraint(D) | $\forall R_H.H$ | $\{x \in \Delta^{\mathcal{I}} \mid \forall y.\langle x, y\rangle \in R^{\mathcal{I}} \rightarrow y \in H^{\mathcal{I}}\}$ |
| role cardinality | $(rel\ v\ R)$ | $\{ c \in \Delta^{\mathcal{I}} \vert \sharp \{ d \in \Delta^{\mathcal{I}} : \langle c, d \rangle \in R^{\mathcal{I}} \}\ rel\ \lambda'(v) \}$ |
| constraint(S) | $\exists v.C[v]/\xi[v]$ | $C^{\mathcal{I}}[\lambda(v)]$ where $\xi[\lambda(v)]$ hold |

Here, $rel \in \{=\}$, H is a hybrid concept, $v$ an integer type variable and $\xi[v]$ the set of role cardinality constraints defined over $v$; $\lambda'$ an assignment mapping $v$ to a set of non-negative integers. The constraints are, therefore, specified through hybrid role successors (*hybrid concept*) H or role cardinality variables $v_1, \ldots, v_n$. The following concept contains a numeric constraint which restricts the number of airpads to be twice the number of axis:

**exists**$(\alpha, \beta)$(**and** Machine_Tool (**equal** $\alpha$ has-axis) (**equal** $\beta$ has-airpad)\
(: **with** : **begin** $\alpha = 2\beta$ : **end**))

## 3.2 Constraints in $\mathcal{DL}$(D)/S

Both global constraints over hybrid role successors and local constraints on role cardinalities are allowed in $\mathcal{DL}$(D)/S. A $\mathcal{DL}$(D)/S knowledge base ($\mathcal{DL}$(D)/S-KB) is represented as $\Omega = \mathcal{T} + \Psi$, where $\mathcal{T}$ is the set of concept definitions and multi-concept relationships (e.g. subsumption and disjointness among concepts) and $\Psi$ (short for $\Psi[\mathsf{H}_1,\ldots,\mathsf{H}_n]$) is the set of all global constraints $\psi[\mathsf{H}_1,\ldots,\mathsf{H}_n]$ defined over $\mathsf{H}_1,\ldots,\mathsf{H}_n$ or a subset of them.

Let $\lambda(\mathsf{H}^{\mathcal{I}}) \subseteq \Delta_{\mathcal{D}}$ be the assignment function which creates a concrete image (a concrete variable with associated domains) for an hybrid concept and assign a subset of $\Delta_{\mathcal{D}}$ to the concrete image, and $\lambda'(v_i) \rightarrow t_i \in \mathcal{N}$ mapping $v_i$ a non-negative integer. We have:

$$(\psi(\mathrm{H}_1,\ldots,\mathrm{H}_n))^{\mathcal{I}} \equiv \mathtt{sat}(\psi(\mathrm{H}_1,\ldots,\mathrm{H}_n)) \equiv$$
$$\bigwedge_{i=1}^{n} \forall x_i \in \lambda(\mathsf{H}_i^{\mathcal{I}}).(\exists y_1 \in \lambda(\mathsf{H}_1^{\mathcal{I}}),\ldots,\exists y_{i-1} \in \lambda(\mathsf{H}_{i-1}^{\mathcal{I}}),$$
$$\exists y_{i+1} \in \lambda(\mathsf{H}_{i+1}^{\mathcal{I}}),\ldots,\exists y_n \in \lambda(\mathsf{H}_n^{\mathcal{I}}).\psi(y_1,\ldots,y_{i-1},x_i,y_{i+1},y_n))$$

i.e. for every value of the concrete image of $\mathsf{H}_i$, there exist values in every $\mathsf{H}_j$ $(j = 1\ldots n, j \neq i)$ such that predicate $\psi$ holds. Meanwhile, the collection $\Psi[\mathrm{H}_1,\ldots,\mathrm{H}_n]$ is satisfied $\mathtt{sat}(\Psi[\mathrm{H}_1,\ldots,\mathrm{H}_n])$ *iff*

$$\mathtt{sat}(\Psi[\mathrm{H}_1,\ldots,\mathrm{H}_n]) \equiv \forall\psi \in \Psi[\mathrm{H}_1,\ldots,\mathrm{H}_n].\mathtt{sat}(\psi)$$

A $\mathcal{DL}$(D)/S-concept $\mathsf{C}/\xi$ ($\xi$ may be empty) is satisfiable w.r.t. $\xi[v_i]$ *iff* there is an assignment $\lambda'$ such that $\mathsf{C}[\lambda'(v_i)] \neq \emptyset$ and $\xi[\lambda'(v_i)]$ hold for $i = 1\ldots n$ where $\lambda'(v_i) \rightarrow t_i \in \mathcal{N}$:

$$(\exists v_i.\mathsf{C}[v_i]/\xi[v_i])^{\mathcal{I}} = \exists t_i.(\mathsf{C}^{\mathcal{I}}[t_i] \neq \emptyset \wedge \xi[t_i]) \quad (i = 1\ldots n)$$

Our hybrid concepts capture both abstract knowledge and RC constraints. However, constraints need to be "wrapped" as they cannot be directly processed by a DL-based system. Concepts containing wrapped RC constraints are said to be *normalised*.The normalisation of $\mathcal{DL}$(D)/S concepts:

**Global constraints**: (i) Generating a atomic concept for each hybrid concept H, (ii) creating a mapping between H and the corresponding constrained variable and (iii) removing all global constraints is as:

**RC-constrained concept**: (i) Replacing every sub-concept containing constraints on role cardinalities with an existential role restriction; (ii) Introducing an atomic concept for every set of constraints on role cardinalities; (iii) Removing the existential restrictions on RC variables and eliminating RC constraints by conjuncting atomic concepts at the same logical level;

**non-RC-constrained concept**: If the concept is defined with the RC constrained roles acting as the subject of numeric role cardinality restrictions, (i) creating an existential role restriction to replace every sub-concept referring to RC-constrained roles; (ii) generating a set of numeric constraints to represent the numeric role cardinality restrictions; (iii) defining an atomic concept into the HKB and conjuncting it to the original concept at the same logical level. Concepts will not be changed otherwise.

For instance, the previous Machine_Tool example is transformed into

(**and** Machine_Tool (**some** has-axis) (**some** has-airpad) C1_axis-pad)

where the RC constraint (i.e. $\alpha = 2\beta$) is replaced by C1_axis-pad introduced as an atomic concept. Meanwhile, if a concept in the same HKB is defined as

(**and** Machine_Tool (**atleast** 4 has-axis) (**atmost** 4 has-axis))

it will be normalised as:

(**and** Machine_Tool (**some** has-axis) C2_axis-pad)

where the RC constraints (e.g. $\{|\text{has-axis}| \leq 4\}$) is extracted and replaced by C2_axis-pad because that the same roles (i.e. has-axis and has-airpad) have been restricted by RC constraints in other concepts from the same HKB.

If we define that all concepts contains roles that restricted by RC constraints as RC related concept, then:

1. If two concepts C and D are RC related concepts (i.e. $\xi$ may be empty but the concept contains roles restricted by RC constraints), the subsumption relationship between $\mathcal{DL}$(D)/S concepts is defined as follows:
   - *let C' and D' be the normalised concept definitions of C and D;*
   - *let $\xi'_C$ ($\xi'_D$) be the union of original RC constraints $\xi_C$ ($\xi_D$) and those generated from the normalisation of concept C (D).*

   *Then, $D/\xi_D \sqsubseteq C/\xi_C$ if concept D' is subsumed by C', i.e. $D \sqsubseteq C$ and constraint set $\xi'_D$ entails constraint set $\xi'_C$ in model $\Sigma$, namely $\xi'_D \models_\Sigma \xi'_C$.*
2. If otherwise the normal DL-based reasoning will be carried.

The *hybrid concept* is similar to the *concrete datatype* in $\mathcal{SHOQ}$(D) [14]. However, our approach differs from the latter in three aspects. Firstly, all the concept constructors are interpreted solely in abstract domains; associations between abstract and concrete domains are realised by an assignment function through hybrid concepts. Secondly, more complex global constraints can be modelled using role value constraints. Finally, the overall inferential process is distributed across different (specialised) engines and thus the overall complexity of the reasoning task may be reduced.

# 4 Hybrid reasoning with constraints

Our *linkages* are based on two observations. Firstly, DL-based systems can specify subsumption relationships between concepts (the "told" knowledge). For instance, in the iFaCT system [13], one can specify concept A to be subsumed by concept B as (implies A B). Most other DL systems such as LOOM [20] and RACER [11] have the same functionality.

Secondly, it is possible to obtain an ordering (e.g. *quasi-ordering* [16]) with the help of constraint solvers[2]. For instance, the entailment between two set of constraints can be seen as an ordering.

## 4.1 Ordering of constraints

When domain reduction can be carried out thoroughly and the constraint system can reach a stable status, the inclusion relationships between reduced domains are passed to the DL-based system. Such approach applies to cases when (i) variable domains exist independently; (ii) their images in DL-based systems can be extracted from the rest of a KB and (iii) the extracted knowledge can be referred to as an independent object in the KB. For instance, the life-span of human beings whose domain is $0 \ldots 150$ can be isolated from others easily and defined as a atomic concept in a DL-based knowledge base.

When constrained variables appear as the role number restrictions, the domain reduction technique is not applicable. Because constraints can be considered as the set of tuples of legal values that the constrained variables can take simultaneously [26], an inclusion between different sets of tuples can actually be established and manipulated.

The relationship obtained among concrete constraints is described by a *quasi-ordering*. A formal definition on the new concept, *quasi-ordering*, is introduced as follows:

Let $\alpha$ and $\beta$ be the sets of compound labels (tuples). We say that $\alpha$ is prior to $\beta$ in a *quasi-ordering* with regard to a model $\Sigma$, if every tuple in $\beta$ also exists in $\alpha$, i.e. $\beta \models_\Sigma \alpha$. In this case, we also say that $\beta$ is tighter than $\alpha$.

Note that the ordering among constraint sets is a partial ordering as it is reflexive, transitive and anti-symmetric. In cases when such ordering are mutual, $\alpha$ and $\beta$ are equivalent.

Constraints in $\mathcal{DL}$(D)/S-KB are manipulated in two ways. Global role value constraints are removed in the sense that the same restrictions can be achieved by reducing the domains of constrained objects (i.e. maintaining a path consistency among the associated constrained domains of concrete images of the *hybrid concepts*). On the contrary, local RC constraints are enhanced by explicitly expressing the restrictions which are otherwise implicit (i.e. discover the entailments ordering and the disjointness).

## 4.2 Hybrid reasoning system, CONCOR

CONCOR is composed of four major parts: *engine interface*, *user(and KB) interface*, *internal storage* and *reasoning coordinator* which is at the heart of CONCOR. Hybrid knowledge is input into CONCOR through the *user(and KB) interface*. The *user(and KB) interface* contains a parser which checks the inputs

[2]Currently, Constraint Logic Programming (CLP) languages have been extend with the ability to tackle with different domains of computation, e.g. Boolean algebra, finite domains, *etc.* and, for part of these domains provide the decision about consistency and entailment of constraints (please refer to [18] for a detailed survey).

Figure 1: System architecture of CONCOR hybrid reasoning systems

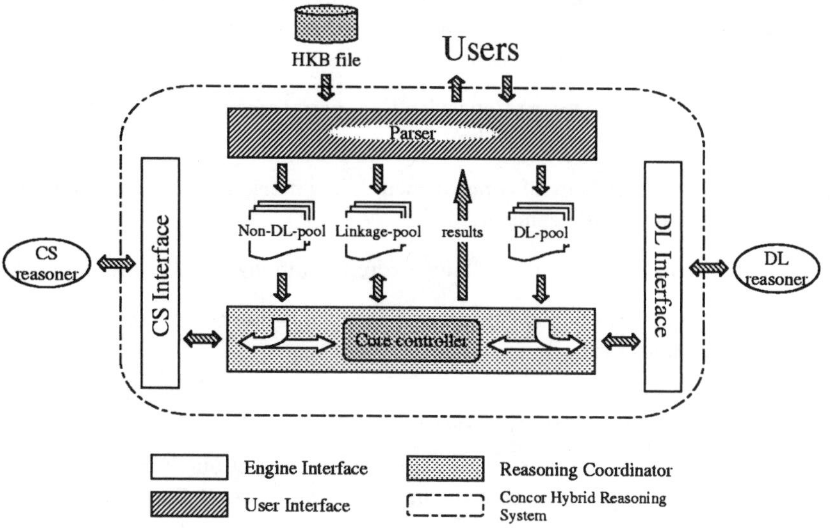

for errors such as illegal syntax and invalid constructors, i.e. those constructors that are not admitted by the selected inferential engines. Well-formed concept descriptions are normalised and translated into intermediate forms and split into non-DL, DL and *linkage* pools which are referred to as *internal storage*.

Having parsed the input HKB, the *user(and KB) interface* passes control to the *reasoning coordinator* and the latter will decide which subsequent-inferential engines (SIEs) the contents of the *internal storage* should be sent to. Communications between the *reasoning coordinator* and the SIEs are carried out through the *engine interface*. An *engine interface* associated to an engine is responsible for transferring the data and control flows to this particular engine. The *engine interface* helps to design CONCOR system in a modular manor: SIE can be replaced together with its interface, thus, theoretically the effect of exchanging SIE will not ripple off to other parts of the HRS.

The modular manor of CONCOR system is further guaranteed by introducing an intermediate language between user language and the underlying modelling languages of the selected SIEs. The intermediate language allows a standard translator to be designed for each inferential engine. It also reduces the programming tasks on any further extensions to the modelling language—only the parser residing in the User Interface need to be upgraded. Meanwhile, because the intermediate modelling language has a well-formed semantics, engine interfaces can actually be developed off-line with the help of certain tools.

CONCOR's reasoning process is as follows:

1. parse the input HKB and split it into small homogeneous parts: DL,

non-DL (global and concept-local constraints), and *linkage*;

2. check the consistency of global constraints and propagate them in order to maintain a full path-consistency by reducing the set of possible values associated with each constrained variable;

3. update DL-based descriptions with the *quasi-ordering* (domain inclusion) between constrained variables;

4. check the consistency of concept-local RC constraints w.r.t. each individual RC constrained concept;

5. obtain *quasi-ordering* (entailment ordering) among all RC constraint sets;

6. update and classify the DL-based descriptions based on the new knowledge (*quasi-ordering*).

## 4.3 Hybrid reasoning with examples

We will use a toy example to demonstrate the merits of our hybrid approach. Assume that an estate agency X maintains a database of floor plans. Each design contains certain types of constraints on the number and style of rooms. The HKB is as follows:

```
(def-primconcept 'Floorplan 'top)

(def-role 'has_room)                 (def-role 'has_bathroom)
(def-role 'has_bedroom)              (def-role 'has_internet_plug)
(def-role 'has_phone_plug)

(decl-variable 'Shape_SBaD   [square, rect, oval, rhomb, cir, tri ])
(decl-variable 'Shape_SBeD   [square, rect, oval, rhomb, cir, tri ])
(decl-variable 'Shape_SBaH   [square, rect, oval, rhomb, cir, tri ])
(decl-variable 'Shape_SBeH   [square, rect, oval, rhomb, cir, tri ])
(decl-variable 'Shape_SBaE   [square, rect, oval, rhomb, cir, tri ])
(decl-variable 'Shape_SBeE   [square, rect, oval, rhomb, cir, tri ])

(def-concept   'Ensuit_Design   '(exists (x y z)
                                   (and Floorplan
                                      (equal z has_rooms) (equal x has_bedrooms)
                                      (forall has_bedrooms Style_bed_Ensuit)
                                      (equal y has_bathrooms)
                                      (forall has_bathrooms Style_bath_Ensuit))
                                   (with :begin
                                      :body
                                         x = y,  z ≥ y + x + 1
                                      :end) ))

(def-concept   'Residence_Design   '(exists (r be ba)
                                      (and Floorplan
                                         (equal r has_rooms)
                                         (equal be has_bedrooms)
                                         (equal ba has_bathrooms)
                                      (with :begin
                                         :body
                                            r > be + ba
                                         :end) ))
```

```
(def-concept  'Hitech_Design  '(exists (x y z n1 n2)
                                  (and Floorplan
                                    (equal x has_rooms) (equal z has_phone_plug)
                                    (equal y has_internet_plug)
                                    (equal n1 has_bathrooms)
                                    (forall has_bathrooms Style_bath_Hitech)
                                    (equal n2 has_bedrooms)
                                    (forall has_bedrooms Style_bed_Hitech))
                                  (with :begin
                                    :body
                                      x > n1 + n2, y = z, y = x
                                    :end) ))
(def-concept  'Dorm_Design  '(exists (x y z)
                                (and Floorplan
                                  (equal x has_rooms) (equal y has_bedrooms)
                                  (forall has_bedrooms Style_bed_Dorm)
                                  (equal z has_bathrooms)
                                  (forall has_bathrooms Style_bath_Dorm))
                                (with :begin
                                  :body
                                    x > y + z, y = z
                                  :end) ))
(def-concept  'Modern_Design  '(exists (r pl)
                                  (and Residence_Design
                                    (equal r has_rooms) (equal pl has_phone_plug)
                                  (with :begin
                                    :body
                                      r = pl
                                    :end) ))
(def-concept  'Style_bath_Dorm    '(and room (fallin shape Shape_SBaD) ))
(def-concept  'Style_bed_Dorm     '(and room (fallin shape Shape_SBeD) ))
(def-concept  'Style_bath_Hitech  '(and room (fallin shape Shape_SBaH) ))
(def-concept  'Style_bed_Hitech   '(and room (fallin shape Shape_SBeH) ))
(def-concept  'Style_bath_Ensuit  '(and room (fallin shape Shape_SBaE) ))
(def-concept  'Style_bed_Ensuit   '(and room (fallin shape Shape_SBeE) ))
(decl-constraint  'RoomShape  :with :BEGIN
                              :BODY
                                Shape_SBaD=[square, rect, rhomb ],
                                Shape_SBeD=[square, rect, rhomb ],
                                Shape_SBaE\=[cir, oval, tri, rhomb ],
                                Shape_SBeH=[square, rect, oval ],
                                Shape_SBaE=Shape_SBeE,
                                disjoint(Shape_SBaH, Shape_SBeH)
                              :END)
```

Reasoning about the above HKB with traditional DL-based systems may be either (i) possible but at the price of computational complexity, e.g. reasoning about the individual shapes; or (ii) not feasible, e.g. the reasoning with constraints on role cardinalities.

After the hybrid reasoning, a series of nontrivial conclusions can be drawn from the above example as:

$$\text{Ensuit\_Design} \sqsubseteq \text{Dorm\_Design}$$

$$\text{Dorm\_Design} \sqsubseteq \text{Residence\_Design}$$

$$\text{Hitech\_Design} \sqsubseteq \text{Morden\_Design}$$

# 5 Conclusions and future work

We have presented a new approach which extends taxonomic (DL-based) systems by combining the results of existing non DL-based reasoning systems. This approach aims at enabling *inference fusion* by dividing an input hybrid KB into smaller components, each containing the knowledge that can be processed by a different specialised reasoning system. Results of inferences are then fused.

Benefiting from the use of independent inferential engines and the polymorphous *linkages* which are required to have consistent semantics within different systems, our approach to *inference fusion* does not depend on a specific DL-based system or constraint solver.

In order to demonstrate the feasibility and applicability of our ideas, we have presented a hybrid modelling language, $\mathcal{DL}$(D)/S which extends $\mathcal{ALC}$ and illustrated its usage in the context of *inference fusion* by means of an example.

The CONCOR architecture is proposed as the platform of carrying out *inference fusion* which has several advantages, such as system extensibility, simplicity and component isolation. Implementation of CONCOR system is completed which fuses inferences from the iFaCT DL-based system [13] and the Ecl$^i$ps$^e$ CS [4]. Small test cases have been reasoned about by CONCOR system giving promising results. Although no formal analysis of the complexity of the CONCOR system has been made, the complexity of each of its components is as follows:

- DL system: since we do not explicitly introduce any new type of reasoning or new concept constructors or operators, the complexity of the DL system remains unchanged. Meanwhile, by introducing a hybrid approach, we avoid the complex interventions between symbolic role number restrictions and other conceptual constructors by introducing the former through hybrid "wrapping" concepts. This removes one of the major sources of computational complexity [2] with regard to the extensions of DLs with concrete domains, if, again, only the DL-based inference is considered.

- Constraint reasoner: Finite Constraint Satisfaction Problems (FCSPs) are NP-complete as a general class [21]. Pragmatic results show that the performance varies from system to system. For a thorough analysis on different constraint systems, please refer to [8].

- Reasoning coordinator: on the general case, we expect its complexity to be $O(N^2)$ with regard to the number of the input constrained concepts.

A formal evaluation of CONCOR HRS and the theory of *inference fusion* using real-life examples is forthcoming.

## Acknowledgements

This work is partially supported by an Overseas Research Scholarship from the British Council and by EPSRC under the AKT IRC grant GR/N15764.

## References

[1] F. Baader and P. Hanschke. A scheme for integrating concrete domains into concept languages. In *Proc. of the 12th Intl. Joint Conf. on Artificial Intelligence (IJCAI'91)*, pages 452–457. Morgan Kaufmann, 1991.

[2] F. Baader and U. Sattler. Description Logics with Symbolic Number Restrictions. In *Proc. of the 12th European Conf. on Artificial Intelligence (ECAI'96)*, pages 283–287. John Wiley, 1996.

[3] T. Berners-Lee, J. Hendler, and O. Lassila. The Semantic Web. *Scientific American*, pages 28–37, May 2001.

[4] P. Brisset et al. *$ECL^iPS^e$ Constraint Library Manual, Rel. 5.2.* International Computers Ltd. and Imperial College London, 2001.

[5] E. Compatangelo and H. Meisel. $\mathcal{K}$–ShaRe: an architecture for sharing heterogeneous conceptualisations. In Proc. of I-KOMAT'2002-to appear.

[6] F. M. Donini et al. Reasoning in description logics. In *Foundations of Knowledge Representation*, pages 191–236. CSLI, 1996.

[7] D. Fensel, F. van Harmelen, I. Horrocks, D. McGuinness, and P. Patel-Schneider. OIL: An Ontology Infrastructure for the Semantic Web. *Intelligent Systems*, 16(2):38–45, 2001.

[8] A. Fernández and P. M. Hill. A Comparative Study of Eight Constraint Programming Languages over the Boolean and Finite Domains. *Jour. of Constraints*, 5:275–301, 2000.

[9] R. Fikes and A. Farquhar. Distributed Repositories of Highly Expressive Reusable Ontologies. *Intelligent Systems*, 14(2):73–79, 1999.

[10] V. Haarslev, C. Lutz, and R. Möller. A description logic with concrete domains and role-forming predicates. *Jour. of Logic and Computation*, 9(3):351–384, 1999.

[11] V. Haarslev and R. Möller. High Performance Reasoning with Very Large Knowledge Bases: A Practical Case Study. In *Proc. of the 17th Intl. Joint Conf. on Artificial Intelligence (IJCAI'01)*, pages 161–168, 2001.

[12] V. Haarslev, R. Möller, and A. Turhan. ABox reasoner: Progress report. In *Proc. of the Intl. Workshop on Description Logics (DL'98)*, pages 82–86, 1998.

[13] I. Horrocks. FaCT and iFaCT. In *Proc. of the Intl. Workshop on Description Logics (DL'99)*, pages 133–135, 1999.

[14] I. Horrocks and U. Sattler. Ontology Reasoning in the $\mathcal{SHOQ}$(D) Description Logic. In *Proc. of the 17th Intl. Joint Conf. on Artificial Intelligence (IJCAI'01)*, pages 199–204. Morgan Kaufmann, 2001.

[15] I. Horrocks, U. Sattler, and S. Tobies. Practical reasoning for very expressive description logics. *Logic Journal of the IGPL*, 8(3):239–263, 2000.

[16] B. Hu, E. Compatangelo, and I. Arana. A hybrid approach to extend DL-based reasoning with concrete domains. In *Proc. of the KI-2001 Workshop on Applications of Description Logics*. CEUR Proceedings, 2001.

[17] B. Hu, E. Compatangelo, and I. Arana. Coordinated reasoning with *inference fusion*. In *Proc. of the KES-2002, Sixth Intl. Conf. on Knowledge-Based Intelligent Information & Engineering Systems*. IOS Press, 2002. To appear.

[18] Joxan Jaffar and Michael J. Maher. Constraint Logic Programming: A Survey. *The Jour. of Logic Programming*, 19 & 20:503–582, 1994.

[19] C. Lutz. NExpTime-complete description logics with concrete domains. In *Proc. of the Intl. Joint Conf. on Automated Reasoning*, number 2083 in LNAI, pages 45–60. Springer-Verlag, 2001.

[20] R. MacGregor, H. Chalupsky, and E. R. Melz. *PowerLoom Manual*. ISI, University of South California, 1997.

[21] A. K. Mackworth and E. C. Freuder. The Complexity of Constraint Satisfaction Revisited. *Artificial Intelligence*, 59(1–2):57–62, 1993.

[22] B. Nebel. What is hybrid in hybrid representation and reasoning systems? In *Proc. of the 2nd Intl. Symp. on Computational Intelligence (CI'89)*, pages 217–228, 1989.

[23] N. F. Noy, R. W. Fergerson, and M. A. Musen. The knowledge model of Protégé-2000: Combining interoperability and flexibility. In *Proc. of the 12th Intl. Conf. on Knowledge Engineering and Knowledge Management (EKAW'2000)*, 2000.

[24] The Object Management Group OMG. OMG Unified Modeling Language Specification, March 2000. Available from http://www.omg.org/technology/documents/formal/uml.htm.

[25] M. Schmidt-Schauß and G. Smolka. Attributive concept descriptions with complements. *Artificial Intelligence*, 48(1):1–26, 1991.

[26] E. P. K. Tsang. *Foundations of Constraint Satisfaction*. Academic Press, 1993.

# Representing and Eliciting "If … Then Rules": An Empirical Analysis

Daniel E. O'Leary
University of Southern California
3660 Trousdale Parkway
Los Angeles, CA 90089-0441

**Abstract**

This paper investigates how knowledge representation in the elicitation process, impacts the knowledge that is solicited. In particular, this paper investigates the relationship between using different, but equivalent knowledge representations for knowledge elicitation (e.g., "If – then" and "Given"), while focusing on probability knowledge. In addition, this paper investigates other issues that can influence the knowledge elicited. Tense (present or future) of items ranked in a probability elicitation process, extent of expertise and presence of problem in a domain of their expertise, and the impact of acquiring knowledge from groups compared with individuals, also are found to impact knowledge elicited.

## 1. Introduction

The relationship between knowledge elicitation (KE) and knowledge representation (KR), used to elicit that knowledge, is fundamental to the knowledge acquisition effort (KA) necessary for intelligent systems. Typically knowledge is solicited using some knowledge representation (elicitation knowledge representation – "EKR," e.g., "if … then …" rules). In addition, that knowledge typically is represented logically in a system using some related knowledge representation (system knowledge representation – "SKR").

This paper provides an empirical analysis of relationship between using different knowledge representations that are logically equivalent, but not the same (e.g., "but" or "and"), focusing on "if … then rules," to generate probability knowledge as part of EKR. A priori, we would expect logically equivalent forms would result in the same knowledge. However, this paper does not find that conclusion. Instead, different logically equivalent representations used for knowledge elicitation can result in different orderings of probability of events. Thus, what are apparently equivalent representations ultimately can generate different knowledge.

This paper also provides an investigation as to the impact of using different tenses on knowledge elicited. Presentation of events in different tenses (e.g., present vs. future) also results in different representation of probability of events. Thus, soliciting knowledge needs to focus on the proper and consistent tense representation or probability evaluations are likely to be inconsistent.

Finally, this paper investigates the impact of using groups versus using individuals as sources for knowledge. In general, groups are better at using different, but logically equivalent representations. Fewer differences in orderings of probability knowledge are found for groups than for individuals. Thus, individuals, more than groups generate differences between logically equivalent representations.

These results are important for a number of reasons. First, the lack of conformance between logically equivalent forms means that we must be very careful when soliciting knowledge, even when using logical equivalents. Second, knowledge acquisition must be done very carefully, even down to ensuring that the appropriate tense is used, and is used on a consistent basis. Third, the results suggest that if we can solicit information from groups, we should use those opportunities, since the results are likely to be more consistent if done by a group, rather than an individual.

In order to analyze these issues, an experiment was used to ask subjects to order the likelihood of different sets of events, some with equivalent knowledge representations, in the context of three cases. In the experiment, subjects were asked to perform that analysis using either events framed in the present or future tense. In some cases, subjects were put into groups, while other subjects were not in groups, but were responsible for completing the analysis themselves.

This paper proceeds as follows. Section 2 summarizes some issues in knowledge elicitation and representation for this paper and summarizes background concepts for tense and for individual versus group knowledge elicitation. Section 3 develops the hypotheses. Section 4 discusses the empirical study. Section 5 summarizes the results. Section 6 provides a brief summary and discusses extensions.

## 2. Knowledge Elicitation, Knowledge Representation, Tense and Knowledge Sets

This section of the paper provides a brief background summary of some of the key issues discussed in this paper.

### 2.1 Relationships Between EKR and KRR

There are at least two possible relationships between knowledge represented in the elicitation process (EKR) and knowledge represented in the system (SKR). The KE effort may be done using a direct match with EKR and SKR. For example, an "if-then" rule-based system approach may be used for both EKR and SKR. If rules are needed for the knowledge representation, then, e.g., rules may be presented to the experts to ensure the proper knowledge has been elicited or rules may be used to directly gather probability information about the relationship captured in the rules.

This approach assumes that since rule knowledge is necessary for the computer program representation, the knowledge should be elicited in that form.

Alternatively, different approaches may be used for EKR and for SKR. Rules might be seen as "stiff" and difficult to explain. Further, variation is the norm in normal human communication, which is inevitably a part of knowledge elicitation. As a result, knowledge elicitation is likely to generate multiple frames in an effort to solicit knowledge. For example, the system builder may represent rule-based knowledge such as "if A then B to what likelihood" rules using a KE approach such as "given A, what is the likelihood of B," since the two are equivalent from a probability perspective. This paper finds that using an approach for EKR that is different than SKR potentially can result in lost or incorrect knowledge.

## 2.2 Scope: Knowledge Representations

Since one of the dominant forms of knowledge representation has been "if-then" rules, one of the primary concerns in this paper is with rules. In addition, since probability theory offers a normative comparison basis, the focus of this paper is on analysis of probabilistic thinking in the KE and KR processes.

Thus, this paper is specifically concerned with the impact of capturing probability information about rules using either "if-then" rule representations or an alternative approach for KE purposes. In particular, this paper analyzes the extent to which "if-then" and "given" elicit the same likelihood ordering. This paper presents empirical evidence that indicates that the probability attributed to events couched as "if-then" and "given" are not evaluated as the same. This is in contrast to probability theory, which would indicate that the conditional probabilities associated with the two sets of statements should be the same.

In addition, a closely related issue is the conjunctive construction of rules for the same comparative KE and KR. In particular, with the construction of conjunctive rules, the typical terminology employs the term "and" in order to join multiple components in a single rule. Yet EKR may make use of other terminology, such as "but" as part of the KA process. This paper presents empirical evidence that subjects do not always view those representations as having the same meaning. Event sets joined with "and" and "but" were ranked with different probability likelihoods.

As a result, these findings lead us to conclude that probability knowledge should be obtained using a set of language that matches EKR and SKR. Even logically equivalent variations in language can impact the probability attributed to event sets.

## 2.3 Tense

In addition, the placement in time of the events might also influence knowledge in the form of probability assessments. Using the future tense might translate into greater uncertainty of some events since they have not yet occurred. In addition, tense can impact the way a subject frames the problem. Language set in the past tense can suggest a specific set of events that has been experienced, thus, influencing the subject's probability judgment.

For example, one approach to gathering knowledge might focus on the future, "what is the probability that xxxx *will* win the match, given that xxxx *will* lose the first set?" Alternatively, the approach could focus on the present, "what is the probability that xxx wins the first match, given that they lose the first set?" Does soliciting knowledge in present or future tense make a difference in knowledge of probabilities? The research summarized here found that tense made a difference in probability likelihood orderings.

## 2.4 Students vs. Experts

There is a substantial literature that suggests that knowledge generated from experts is more likely to be correct than knowledge from less expert personnel, such as students, and this research does not find contrary to that (e.g., Kneale (1988) and Kelly et al. (1987)). In particular, we would expect that experts are more knowledgeable in their particular area of expertise. This paper finds that professionals make fewer errors, than students, in the analysis of problems in their domains of expertise.

### 2.5 Groups, Individuals and "Knowledge Sets"

The notion of "knowledge sets" (the terminology used here to capture the notion of a person's or group's knowledge base) argues that individuals have a knowledge base, developed from past experience, education, etc. (e.g., Simon [1981] and Lenat and Guha [1990]). That knowledge guides their solution generating processes. Subjects carry their knowledge from situation to situation. As is often argued, knowledge changes as experience and education changes. As the knowledge changes, the "knowledge set" changes.

The knowledge sets of the group and the individuals in the group are closely related. Conceivably, if one member knows something then the entire group will have access to that knowledge. The existence of an "expert" or someone knowledgeable about a particular issue allows the group to use that person's knowledge to solve the particular problem.

In general, it is assumed that the knowledge set of the group is limited, to the union of the knowledge sets of the group members. For discussion purposes, assume that the knowledge of individual i can be written as KS(i) = (k(i,1), ..., k(i,m)), where k(i,j) is some subset of knowledge, for individual i. For a group of individuals a and b, the group knowledge set would be KSg(a,b) = (k(a,1), ..., k(a,m), k(b,1), ..., k(b,m)). If the group is making judgments, then only one member may need to understand the issue in order for the group to generate a correct solution.

The notion of knowledge sets has received much application in artificial intelligence (e.g., Simon (1981) and Lenat and Guha (1990)). In addition, it is not unusual for the developers of computer systems (e.g., decision support systems and expert systems) to assume that that the use of a computer program will increase the knowledge set of the user. Effectively, those developers assume that the augmented human and computer system can function with a knowledge set limited only by the union of the two knowledge sets.

# 3. Hypotheses

This section uses the background information provided in the previous section to generate the hypothesis to be analyzed.

## 3.1 Probability Theory Hypotheses

Probability theory suggests that the intersection of two events be called "A and B," while the event A conditional on B, be called "A given B." However, there are other language representations of those sets of events. For example, in the development of expert systems, typically, the terminology "if - then" is used to capture rules. Further, in the development of decision trees, the sequential and conditional nature of the trees is typically characterized using the terminology "If A then B" (von Winterfeldt and Edwards [1986]). In addition, to represent the intersection of two events, the term "but" has been used in experiments in cognitive science (e.g., Tversky and Kahneman [1983]). Thus, if subjects follow normative theory, we would have the following null hypotheses:

Hypothesis 1: Subjects will order the probability of conditional events represented by "if-then" and "given" at the same level.

Hypothesis 2: Subjects will order the probability of the intersection of events represented by "and" and "but" at the same level.

## 3.2 Language Tense

Language tense could also impact the assessed probability relationships between sets of events. This leads to the following hypothesis, in null form.

Hypothesis 3: Subjects will order probabilities of events represented in the future tense at the same level as those in the present tense.

## 3.3 Students vs. Experts

When students are compared to professionals, in the analysis of cases in the professional's sphere of expertise, we would expect that format (e.g., "If – then" vs, "Given") would not have as much an impact for professionals. Instead, we would expect professionals to be more likely to treat logically equivalent formats as equivalent, for those problems in which they are more expert. As a result, we have the following hypothesis in null form.

Hypothesis 4: For the business cases, the professionals and students will perform at the same levels.

### 3.4 Individual vs. Groups

Since groups will have an expanded "knowledge set," we would expect groups to make fewer errors. According to the knowledge set theory, all it would take would be one person in the group to get the "right" order of events and then the group would have access to that knowledge. In null form, the hypothesis can be stated as follows:

Hypothesis 5: Groups and individuals will perform at the same level.

## 4. Experiment and Methodology

In order to test the relationship between knowledge elicited and knowledge representation, an empirical study was developed. A questionnaire, with three case studies, was designed to determine the extent to which subjects considered "if-then" the same as "given," and "and" the same as "but." In addition, the questionnaire was placed in two different formats, one future tense and the other present tense. Finally, the questionnaire was administered to students, professionals and groups of students.

### 4.1 Likelihoods

Subjects were asked to rank likelihoods of events because normative solutions existed for those likelihoods. As a result, we could assess the impact of knowledge elicitation representation and not be concerned that there existed a "better" answer than the one generated by a group of subjects or by the experimenter.

### 4.2 Subjects

Four groups of subjects were used to investigate the hypotheses. The first two groups of subjects, denoted S were students (n=52 and 50). These students were undergraduate majors in business, at a large university in the United States. Each of these subjects was given a questionnaire to complete. Each of the student subjects completed the questionnaire in a class setting.

The third group of subjects, denoted P were professional business consultants with a large professional services firm in Los Angeles, California, in the United States (n=25). It was requested that 20 to 40 consultants completed the questionnaire.

The fourth group of subjects were students, that were used to generate three person groups, that are designated as "G." These students were different than the other students (n=17, for a total of 51 students). Each set of groups received and completed a single questionnaire.

## 4.3 Questionnaire

In order to determine the probability that subjects attribute to particular representations, subjects were given a case and multiple statements about events in that case. The subjects were then asked to rank the statements, from most likely to least likely, where a 1 was attributed to the most likely. The instrument was modeled after an experiment design in Tversky and Kahneman [1983].

## 4.4 Cases

Three cases were used in the development of the questionnaire. The first case involved the analysis of a tennis scenario, as discussed above. The second and third cases were designed to have students and professionals use knowledge from their areas of expertise. One case involved a company with financial problems and the other case concerned "management control systems," a major concern of consultants. These last two cases were specific to the domain and the first one was independent of the domain of consulting expertise, to investigate whether domain expertise made a difference.

## 4.5 Event Sets

The set of events for each scenario was developed as follows. Two events A and B were each established as part of the event sets. Then other events were placed in the event set. These included (A/\B) (with both "and" and "but" used to represent the intersection), (A|B) (with both "if-then" and "given"), and other events.

As an example, in one case, "A" could be "Agassi will win the match," while "B" could be "Agassi will lose the first set." Thus, another element in the event set could be "Given that Agassi loses the first set, he will win the match."

## 4.6 Tense

In order to test the impact of tense (present or future) two separate versions of the questionnaire were developed. The two different questionnaires were each given to different groups of subjects. Subject groups saw either the present tense version or the future tense version, but not both.

## 4.7 Measurement of Outcome: Violation

The responses of the subjects were investigated to determine if the subjects treated the sets of events "If A then B" and "Given A, B," as equal, and the sets "A and B" and "A, but B" as equal. If a subject did not rank a pair equally, then that was treated as a "violation" of probability theory. This allowed us to compute "violation rates" (similar to "failure rates") associated with different cases, different tenses and with different groups of subjects. Those violation rates could then be compared to see if there were differences based on tense, level of expertise, logical representation, or individual versus group.

## 4.8 Implementation of Hypotheses

Using the information in this section, the hypotheses of section 3 were implemented as follows:

Hypothesis 1': Subjects will order the probability of conditional events represented by "if-then" and "given" correctly with no violations.

Hypothesis 2': Subjects will order the probability of the intersection of events represented by "and" and "but" correctly with no violations.

Hypothesis 3': Subjects will order probabilities of events represented in the future tense and in the present tense with the same violation percentage for each tense.

Hypothesis 4': For cases 2 and 3, the professionals and students will have the same violation percentage.

Hypothesis 5': Student groups and individuals will have the same violation percentage.

## 4.9 Statistical Evaluation of Hypotheses

For each of the hypotheses, the percentage of violations was developed for the set of pairs in the hypotheses, across subjects. For example in hypothesis 5, violation percentages were calculated for both groups and individuals for each case and for each of "If – then," and "Given." Then a test of a "difference of proportions" was used to evaluate the pairs of proportions. This test results in a "z statistic" that was used to determine statistical significance of the difference between two violation rates. In particular, the test is used to determine if for two violation rates, say $p_1$ and $p_2$, $p_1 - p_2 = 0$.

# 5. Findings

The results are summarized in tables 1 and 2.

## 5.1 "If - Then" vs. "Given" (Hypothesis 1')

Student subjects exhibited violation rates of 42% to 71%. Professional consultant subjects experienced violation rates of 36% to 64%. Although the students experienced higher violation rates, both groups exhibited substantial violations. In the case of the students and professionals for all cases and tenses, we reject the hypothesis at better than 0.001. Subjects apparently differentiate between "if-then" and "given" in their ranking of likelihoods of events.

## 5.2 "But" vs. "And" (Hypothesis 2')

Student subjects experienced violation rates of 50% to 81%. Professional consultant subjects experienced violation rates of 20% to 40%. Students had a violation rate significantly greater than the professionals. In the case of the students and professionals for all cases and tenses, we reject the hypothesis at better than 0.001 and 0.01, respectively. Subjects apparently differentiate between "but" and "and" in their likelihoods of events.

## 5.3 Impact of Tense (Hypothesis 3')

The tense, whether future or present, used to elicit knowledge can have an impact on the knowledge elicited. Tense was found to be statistically significant on the number of violation errors made by subjects in the comparison of both "if-then" and "given" and a comparison of "and" and "but."

For the case of "If-then" and "Given," the results indicate that we

- Cannot reject the hypothesis for cases 1 and 2 for both students and professionals.
- Can reject the hypothesis that tense does not make a difference for case 3 for students (at better than 0.08) and professionals (at better than 0.03).

For the case of "But" and "And," the results indicate that we

- Cannot reject the hypothesis for cases 1 and 2 for students and 1, 2 and 3 for professionals
- Can reject the hypothesis that tense does not make a difference for case 3 for students (at better than 0.001)

Tense can make a difference in the error rate of ordering likelihoods in the case of both student and professional subjects. As a result, in the knowledge elicitation process or in the knowledge represented in, e.g., rules, that the tense can have a major impact.

## 5.4 Professional Vs. Students (Hypothesis 4')

Using violation percentage as a guide, professionals outperformed students in each of cases 2 and 3, the business cases, as seen in table 1. As a result, this suggests that domain and domain understanding influences the violation percentage for ordering likelihoods of events. Seven of the eight situations were significantly different at the .07 lev l or better, with five significantly different at the .05 level or better, as seen below.

| | ("If – Then," "Given") | ("And," "But") |
|---|---|---|
| Case 2 (Future) | 0.04 | 0.03 |
| Case 3 (Future) | ---- | 0.07 |
| Case 2 (Present) | 0.03 | 0.06 |
| Case 3 (Present) | 0.05 | 0.001 |

As a result, professionals apparently differentiate themselves from the students in the quality of analysis of problems in their domain.

### 5.5 Individuals Vs. Groups (Hypothesis 5')

In all but one experimental setting it was found that student groups outperformed student individuals. In particular, the results indicate that we can reject the hypothesis of no difference at the following levels

| | ("If – Then," "Given") | ("And," "But") |
|---|---|---|
| Case 1 | 0.05 | 0.02 |
| Case 2 | 0.001 | 0.01 |
| Case 3 | ---- | 0.001 |

Groups apparently provide a strong basis for estimation of relative likelihoods.

## 6. Extensions and Summary

This section briefly discusses some extensions and provides a summary of the paper's results.

### 6.1 Extensions

The results presented here can be extended to other language issues. For example, we focused on the relationship between present and future tense for ranking probability information. The results could be extended to include a comparison that includes past tense.

In addition, the results can be extended to other sets of subjects. For example, individual data was gathered from both students and professionals. However, group data was gathered only from students. Future research could focus on professionals in groups.

Further, the results can be extended to other probability terms, such as "or." For example, studies might focus on the impact of using "either" and "or." Finally, this paper focused on probability knowledge. Future research could focus on qualitative or alternative quantitative settings.

## 6.2 Summary

Knowledge representations used in the knowledge elicitation process may differ from those ultimately used in the development of a system, or knowledge elicitation may employ multiple, but logically equivalent formats. This research indicates that if probability knowledge is solicited using multiple approaches then the two are likely to result in different probability information being solicited

The violation rates found in this research indicate that there is likely to be a difference in the probability attributed to the same set of events using different knowledge representations. Subjects attributed different likelihood rankings to "if-then," as opposed to "given." In addition, subjects also attributed different likelihood rankings to "and" and "but." As result, the probabilities elicited with rules in one format are different that the probabilities of rules elicited in another format. Further, tense was found to make a difference in the number of violations in rankings.

In addition, professionals as sources of knowledge provided fewer errors than students, in problems in their area of expertise. The fewer errors did not carry over to a general setting, the case 1, "tennis." As would be expected, domain expertise makes a difference in the domain.

Groups also make a difference in being able to provide better probability information, by not making mistakes that confuse "if ... then ... " and "given" or "but" and "and."

**References**


1. Kelly, K., Ribar, G. and Willingham, J., "Interim Report on the Development of an Expert system for the Auditors's Loan Loss Evaluation," Proceedings of the Touche Ross/University of Kansas symposium, 1987, pp. 167-188.
2. Kneale, D., "How Coopers & Lybrand Put Expertise Into Its computers," Wall Street Journal, 1988.
3. Lenat, Douglas B. and R.V. Guha, Building large knowledge-based systems: representation and inference in the Cyc project, Reading, Mass.: Addison-Wesley, [1989], c1990.
4. Simon, H., The Sciences of the Artificial, Second Edition, MIT Press, Cambridge MA, 1981.
5. Tversky, A. and Kahneman, D., "Extensional Versus Intuitive Reasoning: The Conjunction Fallacy in Probability Judgment," Psychological Review, volume 90, no. 4, October 1983, pp. 293-315.
6. von Winterfeldt, D. and Edwards, W., Decision Analysis and Behavioral Research, Cambridge University Press, 1986.

Table 1

Panel A: Comparison of "If-then" and "Given"* &

| Type | Case | Tense | N | Violation % |
|---|---|---|---|---|
| S | 1 | F | 52 | 44% |
| S | 1 | P | 50 | 42% |
| S | 2 | F | 52 | 62% |
| S | 2 | P | 50 | 68% |
| S | 3 | F | 51 | 71% |
| S | 3 | P | 49 | 57% |
| P | 1 | F | 25 | 48% |
| P | 1 | P | 25 | 60% |
| P | 2 | F | 25 | 40% |
| P | 2 | P | 25 | 44% |
| P | 3 | F | 25 | 64% |
| P | 3 | P | 25 | 36% |

Panel B: Comparison of "But" and "And"@

| Type | Case | Tense | N | Violation % |
|---|---|---|---|---|
| S | 1 | F | 52 | 56% |
| S | 1 | P | 50 | 54% |
| S | 2 | F | 52 | 56% |
| S | 2 | P | 50 | 60% |
| S | 3 | F | 52 | 50% |
| S | 3 | P | 50 | 81% |
| P | 1 | F | 25 | 36% |
| P | 1 | P | 25 | 24% |
| P | 2 | F | 25 | 32% |
| P | 2 | P | 25 | 40% |
| P | 3 | F | 25 | 32% |
| P | 3 | P | 25 | 20% |

* S stands for students, P stands for professionals, F stands for future and P stands for present.

& A violation is said to occur if statements representing (A|B) using "If-Then" and "Given" are not ranked the same.

@ A violation is said to occur if statements representing ($A \wedge B$) using "and" and "but" are not ranked equally.

Table 2

Comparison of "If-then" and "Given"* &

| Type | Case | Tense | N | Violation % |
|---|---|---|---|---|
| G | 1 | P | 17 | 18% |
| G | 2 | P | 17 | 23% |
| G | 3 | P | 17 | 47% |

Comparison of "But" and "And"@

| Type | Case | Tense | N | Violation % |
|---|---|---|---|---|
| G | 1 | P | 17 | 23% |
| G | 2 | P | 17 | 23% |
| G | 3 | P | 17 | 29% |

* G stands for groups.

& A violation is said to occur if statements representing (A|B) using "If-Then" and "Given" are not ranked the same.

@ A violation is said to occur if statements representing ($A \wedge B$) using "and" and "but" are not ranked equally.

# A Hybrid KRS to Treat Fuzzy and Taxonomic Knowledge

Rita Maria da Silva Julia
Federal University of Uberlandia, Brazil, rita@ufu.br

Fernanda Emília Muniz de Resende
Federal University of Uberlandia, Brazil, muniz@ufu.br

Antônio Eduardo Costa Pereira
Federal University of Uberlandia, Brazil, costa@ufu.br

**Abstract**

The purpose of this paper is to present a hybrid Knowledge Representation System (KRS) in which Terminological Logic (TL) and Fuzzy Logic (FL) resources are used to store and to retrieve information. Knowledge here must be related to technical subjects that deals with terms whose meanings are vague and whose definitions are dependent on taxonomic organization of other terms, such as demographic census, medical diagnosis etc. Terminological and Assertional Knowledge compose the Knowledge Base (KB). The Terminological Knowledge defines crisp and fuzzy terms by means of TL term constructors. The Assertional Knowledge describes the world by means of Predicate Calculus formulae whose variables are annotated by TL expressions. The inference engine is able to answer questions that include Natural Language (NL) fuzzy quantifiers such as *several*, *some*, *most*, *many* etc. The advantages to be gained by this hybrid approach are: the ease of expressing knowledge and of retrieving information where the definition of fuzzy terms depend on several factors (for example, the definition of the fuzzy term *tall* for human beings depends on the height, the sex and the age of individuals); the contribution of using subsumption to improve the information retrieval process in goals that are structured in terms of NL fuzzy quantifiers.

## 1 Introduction

Hybrid architectures have been largely used in KRSs. This paper proposes a hybrid KRS that combines FL and TL formalism. TLs are knowledge representation formalisms of enormous applicative interest, as they are specifically oriented to the vast class of application domains that are describable by means of taxonomic organizations of complex objects [12]. FL provides a way to deal with vagueness and make it possible to grasp vague phenomena present in NL and in the real word. The idea here is to propose a hybrid KRS that combines TL and FL formalisms to support and to improve knowledge representation and information retrieval in contexts where knowledge includes vagueness (fuzzy definitions) and taxonomic organizations of complex objects. As an example of such a context, this paper treats some statistics that are obtained in a demographic census of a population. In sections 2 and 3, a brief review of some FL and TL definitions are presented, respectively. In section 4, the KB is described. Section 5 introduces the Information Retrieval Process. Finally, conclusions are discussed in section 6.

# 2 Review of Fuzzy Logic in Natural Language

FL, based on Fuzzy Set Theory proposed by Zadeh [15], was introduced principally to provide a way to deal with vagueness and to make it possible to grasp vague phenomena present in natural language and in the real world [8]. In this way, FL is very suitable for dealing with fuzzy quantifiers like *most*, *least* and *few* [14].

Fuzzy Set is the most important concept in fuzzy logic theory. The difference between a fuzzy set and a crisp set is the boundary between the membership and the non-membership of a particular element in the set. In crisp sets this boundary is well defined and the transition from membership to non-membership is abrupt. On the other hand, for fuzzy sets, partial memberships are possible. Thus, there is a membership degree corresponding to each element of a fuzzy set.

Let $U$ be the universe of discourse. Let $x$ be a generic element of $U$. A fuzzy set $A$ in $U$ is characterized by the following membership function $\mu_A$:

$$\mu_A : U \rightarrow [0,1],$$

where $\mu_A(x)$ represents the membership degree of $x$ to $A$. In this way, $A$ is defined by [5]:

$$A = \{(x, \mu_A(x)) \mid x \in U\}.$$

Consider people and people's height. In this case, the universe $U$ is the set *People*. The property "*to be a tall person*" can be defined by the fuzzy set *TALL* which will answer the question "*what's the height degree corresponding to a person $x$?*". Considering the *tall* membership function that follows:

$$\mu_{tall}(x) = \begin{cases} 0, & \text{if height}(x) \leq 1.50\text{m}, \\ (height(x) - 1.50m)/0.30m, & \text{if } 1.50\text{m} < \text{height}(x) < 1.80\text{m}, \\ 1, & \text{if height}(x) \geq 1.80\text{m} \end{cases}$$

The membership degree of a person who is 1,60m tall to the fuzzy set *tall* is about 0.66.

## 2.1 The Semantics of Natural Language

Most formalisms and notations for writing NL grammars are similar in that they are based on the idea of phrase structure, where different phrases are combined to compose other ones more complex [11]. For example, the grammar rule

$$sentence \rightarrow noun\_phrase, verbal\_phrase$$

states that phrases of category *noun_phrase* and phrases of category *verbal_phrase* can be combined to compose a phrase of category *sentence.* Identifying phrases in this way is a good strategy since phrases are convenient handles on which semantics can be attached, what simplifies the task of associating meaning to sentences (semantical parsing). In this way, the meaning of a sentence is obtained by combining the meanings of its phrases. This paper deals with NL sentences that are quantified by fuzzy quantifiers, such as sentences

$$Q\, xs\, are\, B$$

where $Q$ is a fuzzy quantifier, like *most, many, few* etc., $x$ is a generic element of a set $U$ (universe), and $B$ is the label of a fuzzy set of $U$ describing a property of $x \in U$ (Ex: *Most people are tall*) [4, 9]. It is possible to assign a particular characteristic to the members of $U$ (as in *Most young people are tall*), in such a way as to produce sentences

$$Q\, Axs\, are\, B$$

where $A$ is a fuzzy set of $U$ describing the meaning of the assigned characteristic. [16]

*Definition 1*: The support set of a fuzzy set $B$ is defined as $\{x \in U \mid \mu_B(x) > 0\}$.

*Definition 2*: Let $B$ be a fuzzy subset of $U$. The cardinality of $B$ is defined by:

$$Card(B) = \sum_{i=1}^{n} \mu_B(x_i),\ x_i \in \text{support of } B$$

The meaning of a fuzzy set may be given by its cardinality. The meaning of a fuzzy quantifier $Q$ may be given by a function $[0,1] \rightarrow [0,1]$ whose argument $r$ is described below. For instance, the function that interprets *most* can be given by

$$Most(r) = \begin{cases} 0, & \text{if } 0 \leq r < 0.5 \\ 2r-1, & \text{if } 0.5 \leq r \leq 1 \end{cases}$$

The truth value of sentences $Q\, xs\, are\, B$ can be calculated as it follows:

$$r = \frac{Card(B)}{Card(U)} = \frac{1}{n}\sum_{i=1}^{n} \mu_B(x_i)$$

Set $Truth(Q\, xs\, are\, B) = Q(r)$

Notice that the truth value of these sentences is calculated by applying the meaning of the quantifier (function $Q$) to the ratio between the meanings of the fuzzy set $B$ and $U$ (that is, Card(B) and Card(U)). Then, calculating the truth value of these sentences corresponds to combining the meaning of its phrases. In other words, the truth values of these sentences represent their meaning.

Similarly, the truth value of $Q\,Axs\,are\,B$ could be found through the following process:

$$r = \frac{Card(B \cap A)}{Card(A)} = \frac{\sum_{i=1}^{n} min[\mu_B(x_i), \mu_A(x_i)]}{\sum_{i=1}^{n} \mu_A(x_i)}$$

Set $Truth(Q\,Axs\,are\,B) = Q(r)$

The linguistic context treated in this paper may produce more complex definition for $A$ and $B$, such as in *Most young tall individuals are thin* or *Many fat individuals are old adults.* Furthermore, in this work the information retrieval process will follow a strategy to interpret sentences quantified by NL fuzzy quantifiers that improves the one described above, whenever it is possible, by using some TL tools to simplify the interpretation of the fuzzy sets $A$ and $B$ (see section 5.4).

# 3 Terminological Logic Review

Any hybrid terminological system consists of at least two subsystems: a terminological representation system and an assertional representation system. The former subsystem represents the terminology and relationships between terms. The later is used to describe the world by means of assertions [1, 2, 7].
*Definition 3*: A *concept* may be an individual, a class of individuals, an individual property or an individual property of a class of individuals. It is usually represented by a unary predicate. *Individual Concepts* are intended to denote individuals. *Generic Concepts* denotes classes of individuals that can be classified as *Defined concepts* and *Primitive concepts.* The *Defined Concepts* are introduced by establishing all the necessary and sufficient conditions to detect whether any individual is an instance of them or not. The *Primitive Concepts* are simply terms for which no definition can be given.
*Definition 4*: *Roles* can be viewed as potential relationships between individuals of a class denoted by a concept and other individuals in the world.

# 4 The Knowledge Base (KB)

The KRS proposed is able to deal with technical knowledge that includes terms whose meanings are vague and whose definitions are dependents on taxonomic organizations of other terms. Here knowledge refers to statistics obtained in a demographic census of a population (Assertional Knowledge) and to the definition of the terminology and the relationships that were considered in the statistics (Terminological Knowledge). Initially, the Assertional Knowledge corresponds to the following set of information about each individual: *name*, *sex*, *age*, *height* and *weight.* The Terminological Knowledge establishes that these relationships (*name*, *sex*, *age*, *height* and *weight*) are primitive roles and defines concepts such as *tall*, *fat*, *child* and *adult* by means of a taxonomic organization of these primitive roles. Obviously, definitions such as *tall* and *old* can not be determinative, since both concepts are vague. That is why a hybrid formalism that combines TL and FL formalism is used to represent knowledge, since TL copes with taxonomy and FL deals with vagueness. In this way, some tools from both formalisms can be used to improve information representation and information retrieval.

## 4.1 Assertional Knowledge

Initially, the population statistics data are stored in a Database. The system retrieves the data related to each individual in the Database and stores it in the KB as formulae of Predicate Calculus whose variables are annotated by TL expressions [2, 3]. These formulae, that represent information about individuals of a population (Domain), correspond to the Assertional Knowledge.

Suppose that the Database stores the *name*, *sex*, *age*, *height* and *weight* corresponding to the individuals of a population, as shown in Table 1.

| **Name** | **Sex** | **Age** | **Height(cm)** | **Weight(kg)** |
|---|---|---|---|---|
| Mary Lawrence | Feminine | 17 | 165 | 48 |
| John Louis | Masculine | 52 | 178 | 80 |
| Annie Thomas | Feminine | 60 | 154 | 60 |
| Peter Brown | Masculine | 18 | 200 | 97 |
| Kate Stuart | Feminine | 13 | 160 | 40 |

Table 1: Individuals of a Population

The system performs a syntactical parsing of this data. In this example, where the system is applied to a population statistics subject, each formula contains just one variable that represents an individual. Consider the first individual of the Database. The parsing will produce the following formula $F_1$ to represent him:

$F_1$: individual (X/ (and (all name_is mary_lawrence) (all sex_of feminine)
(equal 17 age_of) (equal 165 height_of)
(equal 48 weigh_of)))

In $F_1$, the variable X represents the individual whose *name*, *sex*, *age*, *height* and *weight* are *mary_lawrence*, *feminine*, *17 years old*, *165 centimeters* and *48 Kg*, respectively. In this case, *name_is*, *sex_of*, *age_of*, *height_of* and *weight_of* are primitive roles, *feminine* is a primitive concept and *mary_lawrence* is an individual concept. The expression constructed by the term constructor *and* that annotates the individual variable X is a TL expression that defines the individual. The syntax and semantics of the TL expressions are described next:

#### *4.1.1 Syntax (terms constructors)*

< *fuzzy_concept* > ::= < *atom* >

| (compose_fuzzy $\mu_{fuzzy\_concept}$)
| (or_f < *fuzzy_concept* >$^+$)
| (and_f < *fuzzy_concept* >$^+$)

< *concept* > ::= < *atom* > | (*top*) | (*bottom*)
| (all < *role* > < *concept* >)
| (or < *concept* >$^+$)
| (and < *concept* >$^+$)
| (equal < *number* > < *role* >)
| (atleast < *number* > < *role* >)
| (atmost < *number* > < *role* >)
| (more_than < *number* > < *role* >)
| (less_than < *number* > < *role* >)

< *role* > ::= < *atom* >

### *4.1.2 Semantics*

Let $D$ be a non-empty set of individuals and $\varepsilon$ a function from concepts into subsets of $D$, from role into subsets of $D \times D$ and from fuzzy concepts into $D \times [0,1]$. $\varepsilon$ is an *extension function* over $D$ if and only if:

$\varepsilon$ [(compose_fuzzy $\mu_{FC}$)] $= \{(x,\mu_{FC}(x)) \mid x \in D,\ \mu_{FC}\colon D \rightarrow [0,1]\}$

$\varepsilon$ [(or_f FC1...FCn)] $= \{(x,\max(\mu_{FCn}(x)\ldots\mu_{FCn}(x)) \mid x \in D,\ \mu_{FCi}\colon D \rightarrow [0,1]\}$

$\varepsilon$ [(and_f FC1...FCn)] $= \{(x,\min(\mu_{FCn}(x)\ldots\mu_{FCn}(x)) \mid x \in D,\ \mu_{FCi}\colon D \rightarrow [0,1]\}$

$\varepsilon$ [(top)] $= D$

$\varepsilon$ [(bottom)] $= \emptyset$

$\varepsilon$ [(all R C)] $= \{x \in D \mid \forall y\ (< x, y > \in \varepsilon[\mathrm{R}] \Rightarrow y \in \varepsilon[\mathrm{C}])\}$

$\varepsilon$ [(or C1...Cn) ] $= \bigcup_{i=1\ldots n} \varepsilon$ [Ci]

$\varepsilon$ [(and C1...Cn) ] $= \bigcap_{i=1\ldots n} \varepsilon$ [Ci]

$\varepsilon$ [(equal n R)] $= \{x \in D \mid < x, y > \in \varepsilon[\mathrm{R}] \wedge y = \mathrm{n}\}$

$\varepsilon$ [(atleast n R)] $= \{x \in D \mid < x, y > \in \varepsilon[\mathrm{R}] \wedge y \geq \mathrm{n}\}$

$\varepsilon$ [(atmost n R)] $= \{x \in D \mid < x, y > \in \varepsilon[\mathrm{R}] \wedge y \leq \mathrm{n}\}$

$\varepsilon$ [(more_than n R)] $= \{x \in D \mid < x, y > \in \varepsilon[\mathrm{R}] \wedge y > \mathrm{n}\}$

$\varepsilon$ [(less_than n R)] $= \{x \in D \mid < x, y > \in \varepsilon[\mathrm{R}] \wedge y < \mathrm{n}\}$

In this way, the extension function provides the following representation for the TL complex concepts that annotate the variable X in $F_1$: *(all name_is mary_lawrence)* is represented by the set of individuals whose name is *mary_lawrence*, *(all sex_of feminine)* is represented by the set of individuals whose sex is feminine, and so on. The same semantics establishes that the TL expression that annotates X corresponds to the intersection of all these sets and it is represented by the set of individuals whose *name*, *sex*, *age*, *height* and *weight* are *mary_lawrence*, *feminin*, *17 years old*, *165 centimeters* and *48 Kg*, respectively. Therefore, this expression is represented by the first individual described in Table 1. It is interesting to notice that primitive concepts such as *feminine* and that complex concept such as *(all name_is mary_lawrence)*, *(all sex_of feminine)*, *(equal 17 age_of )*, *(equal 165 height_of)* and *(equal 48 weight_of)*, all of them represent crisp sets. In fact, either an individual belongs to one of them or not, that is, there is no uncertainty degree in establishing whether an individual belongs or not to one of these sets.

More details about syntax and semantics of TL expressions can be seen in [7, 10, 12]. Notice, however, that the semantics used in this paper is different from the one proposed in the references given. For example, there is a difference in the interpretations of concepts such as *(atleast n R)* and *(atmost n R)*. Furthermore, as in human physical characteristics context there are vague concepts, such as *child*, *adult*, *fat*, *tall* etc, here it is necessary to increase the classical TL expressions by introducing fuzzy concepts. In fact, usually it is not possible to establish, exactly, whether an individual is tall or not, for example. To deal with this kind of uncertainty, the system must count on some FL tools, such as membership degree. Following this method, here the definition of the extension function $\varepsilon$ over a Domain $D$ [12] is extended in such a way as to support the definition of fuzzy concepts. A Fuzzy concept FC can be created by the expression *(compose_fuzzy* $\mu_{FC}$*)*, whose syntax and semantics are described in sections 4.1.1 and 4.1.2. According to this semantics, a fuzzy concept FC is represented by a set of pairs $(x,\mu_{FC}(x))$, where $x$ is an individual of the Domain $D$ and $\mu_{FC}$ is a function that represents the membership degree of $x$ to the fuzzy concept FC. In this work, fuzzy concepts are represented by fuzzy sets and are used in the Terminological Knowledge context of the KB, as shown in the next section.

## 4.2 Terminological Knowledge

The concepts and the roles that characterize, respectively, the individuals of the Domain and the relationships among them are defined in the Terminological Knowledge context of the KB. In other words, the Terminological Knowledge defines crisp and fuzzy sets that represent concepts and roles. These sets are created by means of term constructors whose syntax and semantics are specified in sections 4.1.1 and 4.1.2. To create complex terms, the term constructors combine concepts and roles to produce new concepts and new roles. For example, the complex concept *(all sex_of feminine)* is constructed by combining the primitive role *sex_of* and the primitive concept *feminine*. Section 4.1 shows that a fuzzy concept FC can be created by the expression *(compose_fuzzy* $\mu_{FC}$*)*. FC is represented by a set of pairs $(x,\mu_{FC}(x))$, where $x$ is an individual of the Domain $D$ and $\mu_{FC}(x)$ is the membership degree of $x$ to the fuzzy concept FC. To create a fuzzy concept FC it is necessary to define its corresponding $\mu_{FC}$ function. This hybrid representation, including TL expressions and FL membership degree allows one to represent fuzzy concepts whose definition depends on several factors (for example, the definition of the fuzzy set *tall* (as seen below) depends on the height, the sex and the age of individuals). Notice that it corresponds to a situation more complex and more realistic than those where fuzzy concepts are defined just in terms of one crisp set (for example, the classical representation of the fuzzy set *tall* is defined just in terms of the height of the individuals (see section 2)). The definitions of the fuzzy concepts *tall*, *adult*, *old* and their corresponding $\mu$ functions are presented below:

Tall ::= (compose_fuzzy $\mu_{tall}$)

$$\mu_{tall}(x) = \begin{cases} 0, \\ \quad \text{if x} \in \varepsilon[\text{(and (all sex\_of femenine)} \\ \qquad\qquad \text{(atmost fem\_inf\_lim(age(x)) height\_of))]} \\ 1, \\ \quad \text{if x} \in \varepsilon[\text{(and (all sex\_of femenine)} \\ \qquad\qquad \text{(atleast fem\_sup\_lim(age(x)) height\_of))]} \\ \\ (height(x) - (\text{fem\_inf\_lim}(age(x)) + 1))/ \\ (\text{fem\_sup\_lim}(age(x)) - \text{fem\_inf\_lim}(age(x))), \\ \quad \text{if x} \in \varepsilon[\text{(and (all sex\_of femenine)} \\ \qquad\qquad \text{(or (atleast fem\_inf\_lim(age(x))+1 height\_of)} \\ \qquad\qquad\quad \text{(atmost fem\_sup\_lim(age(x))-1 height\_of)))]} \\ 0, \\ \quad \text{if x} \in \varepsilon[\text{(and (all sex\_of masculine)} \\ \qquad\qquad \text{(atmost masc\_inf\_lim(age(x)) height\_of))]} \\ 1, \\ \quad \text{if x} \in \varepsilon[\text{(and (all sex\_of masculine)} \\ \qquad\qquad \text{(atleast masc\_sup\_lim(age(x)) height\_of))]} \\ \\ (height(x) - (\text{masc\_inf\_lim}(age(x)) + 1))/ \\ (\text{masc\_sup\_lim}(age(x)) - \text{masc\_inf\_lim}(age(x))), \\ \quad \text{if x} \in \varepsilon[\text{(and (all sex\_of masculine)} \\ \qquad\qquad \text{(or (atleast masc\_inf\_lim(age(x))+1 height\_of)} \\ \qquad\qquad\quad \text{(atmost masc\_sup\_lim(age(x))-1 height\_of)))]} \end{cases}$$

Where:

*height* and *age* are functions $D \rightarrow$ *Integer* that take an individual as argument and that outcome, respectively, the height and the age of the individual;

*masc_inf_lim*, *fem_inf_lim*, *masc_sup_lim* and *fem_sup_lim* are functions *Integer* $\rightarrow$ *Integer* that take the age of a masculine/feminine individual as argument and that outcome, respectively, the masculine/feminine inferior height limit and the masculine/feminine superior height limit corresponding to the age of the individual (see Table 2). Notice that in the definition of the concept *tall*, the dependency on the *age*, *sex* and *height* is represented by a taxonomic organization of complex TL expressions, such as in *(and (all sex_of masculine) (atmost masc_inf_lim(age(x)) height_of))*. Further, the fuzzy characteristic of *tall* is introduced by the definition of the function $\mu_{tall}$.

| Age | Height (cm) Inferior Limit | | Height(cm) Superior Limit | |
|---|---|---|---|---|
| | Feminine | Masculine | Feminine | Masculine |
| 1 | 68 | 69 | 79 | 80 |
| ⋮ | ⋮ | ⋮ | ⋮ | ⋮ |
| 13 | 141 | 144 | 170 | 171 |
| ⋮ | ⋮ | ⋮ | ⋮ | ⋮ |
| $\geq$ 19 | 151 | 163 | 175 | 190 |

Table 2: Masculine and Feminine Height Limits - Extracted from [6]

Adult ::= (compose_fuzzy $\mu_{adult}$)

$$\mu_{adult}(x) = \begin{cases} 0, & \text{if x} \in \varepsilon[\text{(atmost 15 age\_of)}] \\ (age(x) - 15)/6, & \text{if x} \in \varepsilon[\text{(and (atleast 16 age\_of)} \\ & \qquad \text{(atmost 20 age\_of))}] \\ 1, & \text{if x} \in \varepsilon[\text{(atleast 21 age\_of)}] \end{cases}$$

Notice that the definition of the fuzzy concept *adult* depends just on the age of the individuals. This definition is obtained by means of a taxonomic organization of complex concepts such as *(atmost 15 age_of)*, *(and (atleast 16 age_of) (atmost 20 age_of))* etc.

Old ::= (compose_fuzzy $\mu_{old}$)

$$\mu_{old}(x) = \begin{cases} 0, & \text{if x} \in \varepsilon[\text{(atmost 45 age\_of)}] \\ (age(x) - 45)/15, & \text{if x} \in \varepsilon[\text{(and (atleast 46 age\_of)} \\ & \qquad \text{(atmost 59 age\_of))}] \\ 1, & \text{if x} \in \varepsilon[\text{(atleast 60 age\_of)}] \end{cases}$$

Considering the definitions given above, the semantics proposed in section 4.1.2 and the world described in table 1, the fuzzy concepts *tall*, *adult* and *old* could be represented as indicated below:

tall: $\{(mary\_lawrence, 0.54), (john\_louis, 0.52), ..., (kate\_stuart, 0.58)\}$
adult: $\{(mary\_lawrence, 0.33), (john\_louis, 1), ..., (kate\_stuart, 0)\}$
old: $\{(mary\_lawrence, 0), (john\_louis, 0.47), ..., (kate\_stuart, 0)\}$

## 4.3 Extending the KB

The information retrieval process must interpret query sentences whose composition includes NL fuzzy quantifiers and fuzzy concepts. To optimize it, the system performs an evaluation of the original KB in such a way as to calculate the membership degrees of each individual to the fuzzy concepts defined in the Terminological Knowledge. It will free the system from the burden of calculating the same membership degree each time a different goal demands it.

After calculated, the membership degrees corresponding to each individual are included in the Assertional Knowledge, such that, for example, the formula $F_1$ that represents the first individual (see section 4.1) becomes:

$F_1$: individual (X/ (and (all name_is mary_lawrence) (all sex_of feminine)
(equal 17 age_of) (equal 165 height_of)
(equal 48 weigh_of)
(equal 0 memb_degree_child)
(equal 1 memb_degree_young)
(equal 0.33 memb_degree_adult)
(equal 0 memb_degree_old)
(equal 0.54 memb_degree_tall)))

where the fuzzy concepts *child* and *young* can be defined by only changing the age intervals of *adult* definition.

# 5 Information Retrieval

The information retrieval process must interpret queries whose composition includes NL fuzzy quantifiers and NL fuzzy concepts. Such an interpretation consists of calculating the fuzzy truth value of a query. This section shows how to get advantages from the hybrid approach to retrieve information.

## 5.1 The Queries

The queries to be treated are represented by a general expression

$Q\, Axs\, are\, B$

where $A$ is a fuzzy concept that corresponds to the domain to which $Q$ will be applied to, $B$ is a NL fuzzy concept that represents a property of the elements of $A$ and $Q$ is a NL fuzzy quantifier.

Some examples of possible queries are shown below:

1. *Most children are tall.*

   $Q$: *most*; $A$: *child*; $B$: *tall.*

2. *Least fat adults are tall.*

   $Q$: *least*; $A$: fat adults (represented by the fuzzy concept *(and_F fat adult)*); $B$: *tall.*

3. *Most tall individuals are old adults.*

   $Q$: *most*; $A$: tall individuals (represented simply by the fuzzy concept *tall*); $B$: old adults (represented by the fuzzy concept *(and_F old adult)*).

## 5.2 Syntax of the Queries

A syntactical parsing translates a query $Q\,Axs\,are\,B$ into:

$$Y/Q(A,B),$$

where $Y$ is the answer variable that is annotated by the expression $Q(A,B)$.

The syntactical analysis of a query is very trivial, since the queries correspond to very simple NL sentences that can be analyzed with no difficulty by grammar rules based on phrase structure (see section 2.1).

## 5.3 Semantics of the queries

Following the same reasoning presented in section 2.1, to simplify the interpretation of a query it is convenient to model the meaning of each one of its parts (phrases). The final meaning of the query can be obtained by combining the partial meaning of its parts. The queries to be treated here are composed of the following parts (phrases):

$$Quantifier\_Domain\_Verb\_Property$$

Then, to interpret a query, the system must, first, interpret its parts. The interpretation of part $A$ (that is, the *Domain* interpretation) and the interpretation of part $B$ (that is, the *Property* interpretation) have already been presented, since $A$ and $B$ correspond to fuzzy concepts whose meanings are described in section 2.1.

The meaning of $Q$ is also given in section 2.1. Remember that $Q$ takes as argument the ratio $\frac{Card(B \cap A)}{Card(A)}$. The outcome of $Q$ is the fuzzy truth value to be retrieved as an answer to a query.

The verb *are* is used just to link $A$ and $B$. Then, its semantics is included in the interpretation of the function $Q$, which links $A$ and $B$.

As shown in section 5.1, each query is translated into an expression $Y/Q(A,B)$, where the answer variable $Y$ is annotated by the expression $Q(A,B)$, that is, by the outcome of function $Q$. This outcome corresponds to the final interpretation of the query, in other words, to the answer retrieved.

## 5.4 Retrieving Information

As introduced in section 2.1, retrieving information in this paper corresponds to calculate the truth value of queries $Q\,Axs\,are\,B$, that is:

$$Truth(Q\,Axs\,are\,B) = Q(\frac{Card(B \cap A)}{Card(A)})$$

Some examples are shown below:

1. Most_children_are_tall.

   query: $Y/Most(child, tall)$; A = child; B = tall

$$r = \frac{\sum_{i=1}^{n} min[\mu_{tall}(x_i), \mu_{child}(x_i)]}{\sum_{i=1}^{n} \mu_{child}(x_i)}$$

   Set $Truth(Most\, Axs\, are\, B) = Most(r)$

2. Least_fat adults_are_tall.

   query: $Y/Least((and\_F\; fat\, adult), tall)$; A = (and_F fat adult); B = tall

$$r = \frac{\sum_{i=1}^{n} min[\mu_{tall}(x_i), min[\mu_{fat}(x_i), \mu_{adult}(x_i)]]}{\sum_{i=1}^{n} min[\mu_{fat}(x_i), \mu_{adult}(x_i)]}$$

   Set $Truth(Least\, Axs\, are\, B) = Least(r)$, where:

$$Least(r) = \begin{cases} 1, & \text{if } 0 \leq r < 0.5 \\ 2 - 2r, & \text{if } 0.5 \leq r \leq 1 \end{cases}$$

   and the fuzzy set *fat* can be defined by considering the body mass index (BMI), that is: $BMI = weight(kg)/(height(cm)/100)^2$

The TL/FL hybrid approach proposed allows one to speed up information retrieval by extending the classical TL subsumption criteria in order to simplify the fuzzy sets *A* and *B*. This extension corresponds to include in the classical subsumption algorithm the definition of subsumption between fuzzy concepts. According to the classical definition, a crisp TL expression $E_1$ subsumes a crisp TL expression $E_2$ whenever $\varepsilon[E_2] \subseteq \varepsilon[E_1]$, where $\subseteq$ represents the inclusion symbol and $\varepsilon$ is the extension function.

In this paper this definition is extended such as to establish that a fuzzy TL expression $E_1$ subsumes a fuzzy TL expression $E_2$ whenever

$$\varepsilon[E_2] \,_F\!\subseteq \varepsilon[E_1],$$

where $_F\!\subseteq$ represents the fuzzy inclusion symbol. For example, suppose that C1 and C2 are fuzzy concepts such as shown below:

$$C1 = \{< x_i, \mu_{C1}(x_i) > | \, x_i \in U\}; \; C2 = \{< x_i, \mu_{C2}(x_i) > | \, x_i \in U\}$$

Then, C1 subsumes C2 if, $\forall x_i \in U, \mu_{C2}(x_i) \leq \mu_{C1}(x_i)$.

*Definition 5:* If a fuzzy concept C1 subsumes a fuzzy concept C2, then C2 is a simplification of the fuzzy concept (and_F C1 C2).

This definition can be used to simplify the information retrieval process, such as shown in the example that follows:

3. Most_tall individuals_are_old adults.

query: $Y/Most(tall, (and\_F\, old\, adults))$; A = tall; B = (and_F old adults)

As *adult* subsumes *old*, B can be simplified to:

B = old, and the query is simplified to: $Y/Most(tall, old)$

In this example, *definition 5* will be used to simplify the calculus of the truth value of the query. By using it, instead of being applied to the ratio expression $r_1$ below, the function *Most* will be applied to $r_2$, which corresponds to a simplification of $r_1$.

$$r_1 = \frac{\sum_{i=1}^{n} min[min[\mu_{old}(x_i), \mu_{adult}(x_i)], \mu_{tall}(x_i)]}{\sum_{i=1}^{n} \mu_{tall}(x_i)} = 0.56$$

$$r_2 = \frac{\sum_{i=1}^{n} min[\mu_{old}(x_i), \mu_{tall}(x_i)]}{\sum_{i=1}^{n} \mu_{tall}(x_i)} = 1.47/2.64 = 0.56$$

It will simplify and speed up the calculus of

$$Truth(Most\, Axs\, are\, B) = Most(r_2) = \mathit{0.12}$$

# 6 Conclusions

This paper proposes a hybrid KRS to handle technical linguistic contexts that include terms whose meanings are vague and whose definitions are obtained by taxonomic organization of other terms. To cope with these constraints, the system combines TL and FL formalisms, since TL is adequate to treat taxonomy and FL is able to deal with vagueness. This strategy corresponds to extending classical TL semantics [7, 10, 12, 13] such as to include fuzzy meanings. The strengthening of the semantics increases the expressiveness of the representation language and, consequently, increases the complexity of the algorithms as well. This trade-off between expressiveness and efficiency is a problem common to all KRS [13]. The authors believe that important advantages have been gained by this hybrid approach, that is, improvement in the expressiveness of the representation language and simplification in the information retrieval process by using subsumption criteria. A prototype of the system has been implemented. As future work, the authors intend to improve the information retrieval process by including some inference rules related to fuzzy quantifiers [5] and to analyze the computation efficiency of the system.

# References

[1] G. Bittencourt, The Integration of Terminological and Logical Knowledge Representation Languages, Elsevier Science Publishing Co., Inc., 1990.

[2] R.M. Da Silva Julia, Un Systme Hybride Pour le traitement du Langage Naturel et pour la Rcuperation de l'Information, PhD Thesis, Universit Paul Sabatier, Toulouse, France, 1995.

[3] R.M. Da Silva Julia, A.C Pereira, W.M. Arantes, A.M.S. Guillén, Improving Incremental Construction of Knowledge Bases by Using Terminological Logic Resources, IEEE'98 International Conference on SMC, San Diego, California, USA, 1998.

[4] F. Gomide and W. Pedrycz, An Introduction to Fuzzy Sets, Analysis and Design, MIT - Press, 1998.

[5] E.S. Lee, Q. Zhu, Fuzzy and Evidence Reasoning, Physica - Verlag Heidelberg, 1995.

[6] Natural Center for Health Statistics, Clinical growth charts, http://www.cdc.gov/nchs/about/major/nhanes/growthcharts/clinical_charts.htm, Revised November 21, 2000, Accessed June 6, 2002.

[7] B. Nebel, Reasoning and Revision in Hybrid Representation Systems, Published 1990 by Springer-Verlag, Berlin, Heidelberg, New York as LNAI 422, Reprinted June 1995.

[8] V. Novák, Fuzzy Set and Their Applications, Adam-Hilger, Bristol, UK, 1989.

[9] V. Novák, Fuzzy Logic: Applications to Natural Language, In: Encyclopedia of Artificial Intelligence, Second Edition, 515-521, 1992.

[10] P. F. Patel-Schneider, A hybrid, decidable, logic-based knowledge representation system, 1987.

[11] S. Russel and P. Norving, Artificial Intelligence: A Modern Approach, Prentice Hall, Inc., 1995.

[12] F. Sebastiane and U. Straccia, A Computationally Tractable Terminological Logic, 1991.

[13] M. Vilain, The Restricted Languages Architecture of a Hybrid Representation System, Proceedings IJCAI-85, Los Angeles, CA, 1985.

[14] R.R. Yager, S. Ovchinnikov, R.M. Tong, H. T. Nguyen, Fuzzy Sets and Applications: Selected Papers by L.A. Zadeh, John Wiley & Sons, 1987.

[15] L.A. Zadeh, Fuzzy Sets, Information and Control, 8, 338-353, 1965.

[16] L.A. Zadeh, A Computational Approach to Fuzzy Quantifiers in Natural Languages, Computers and Mathematics with Applications, 1983.

# SESSION 2A:

# MACHINE LEARNING 2

# SAT-Based Algorithms for Bayesian Network Inference

T. K. Satish Kumar
Gates 250, Knowledge Systems Laboratory
Stanford University, U.S.A.
tksk@ksl.stanford.edu

**Abstract**

We provide a novel method for Bayesian network inference based upon the idea of pre-compiling a given Bayesian network into a series of SAT instances. We show that this approach allows us to exploit the numerical structure of the problem domain represented by the Bayesian network and that it can be combined with the paradigm of dynamic programming to exploit both the topology and the numerical structure of the network. Because these SAT-based methods exploit both, they are assured of performing better than traditional methods that exploit only the topology of the network (sometimes referred to as "structure-based methods"). A surprising result that follows from our approach is that in domains that exhibit "high" numerical structure, we can remove the "hardness" of the Bayesian inference task into a one-time pre-compilation phase that is independent of any query, thereby achieving a fully polynomial-time randomized approximation scheme (FPRAS) for query-answering. We expect SAT-based approaches to be successful in many practical domains that exhibit good numerical structure (like the presence of monotonic/qualitative relationships between the variables of the domain).

## 1 Background and Motivation

Probabilistic reasoning is a common approach in many AI domains such as planning, diagnosis, learning etc. A Bayesian network (BN) $G$ is a graphical model for representing and reasoning with probabilistic information. It is usually a directed acyclic graph (DAG) with nodes corresponding to random variables $X = \{X_1, X_2 \ldots X_n\}$ in the system and edges corresponding to "direct" influences. Edges specify the *parent* relationships and the overall graphical structure captures the *independence* assumptions between the variables through the graph-theoretic notion of *d-separation.* Each node is associated with a domain of values that it can possibly take (we will consider only discrete and finite domains) and a conditional probability table (CPT) that indicates the probability with which it takes on a certain value given some combination of values for its parents. The set of parents of $X_i$ is denoted by $Pa(X_i)$ and we refer to $\{X\} \cup Pa(X_i)$ as the *family* of $X_i$. It is also useful to view $G$ as a "data structure" that represents the joint probability distribution of $X_1, X_2 \ldots X_n$ in a factored and compact way, exploiting the appropriate independence relationships between the variables.

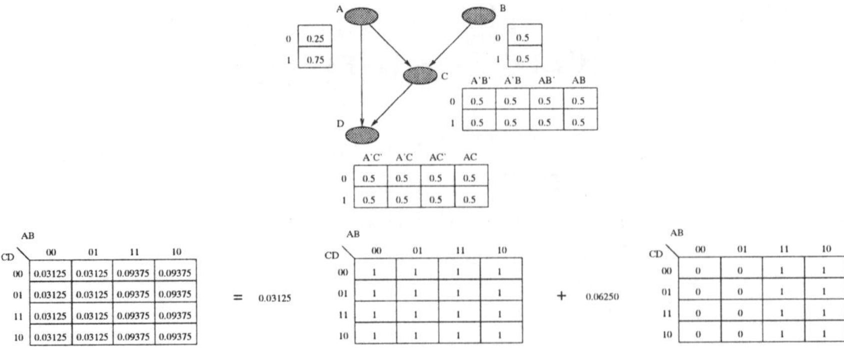


Figure 1: An example of a simple BN and a SAT representation of its joint.

Given a BN, there are many kinds of queries that we are interested in. These may include finding $P(Y = y/Z = z)$ or finding $\text{argmax}_{y \in D_Y} P(Y = y/Z = z)$. Here, $Y$ and $Z$ are subsets of $X$; and $y$ and $z$ are assignments to all the variables in $Y$ and $Z$ respectively. $D_Y$ is the just the cross product of the domains of all variables in $Y$. In this paper, we will concern ourselves only with queries of the former type—that is, to find $P(Y = y/Z = z)$. Occasionally, we will refer to $Z = z$ as the *evidence* $E$ and we will refer to queries of this type as the *BN inference problem.*

The problem of BN inference is associated with many negative results although special cases of BNs such as poly-trees have nice theoretical properties. A few of the negative results for the general case are: given a BN $G$, and an instantiation of a variable $X_i = x_{ij}$, (1) deciding whether $P(X_i = x_{ij}) > 0$ is NP-hard, (2) finding $P(X_i = x_{ij})$ is NP-hard, and (3) approximating $P(X_i = x_{ij})$ within a constant relative approximation factor $\epsilon$ is NP-hard. Despite these negative results, there are a variety of techniques that work fairly well in practice. The following methods are popular for exact inference: *clique trees and message-passing algorithms*, *cutset-conditioning*, and the use of *symbolic solutions.* The following techniques are used for approximate inference: *instantiation-based methods*, *random sampling* including *likelihood weighting* and MCMC methods like *Gibbs sampling*, *structural approximations*, and *loopy belief propagation.*

In this paper, we provide a novel method for BN inference based upon the idea of pre-compiling a given network into a series of SAT instances in disjunctive normal form (DNF). This approach is motivated by the observation of an interesting relationship between probabilities and *model counting* (the model counting problem is the problem of estimating the number of solutions to a SAT or a CSP), and the fact that there exists a fully polynomial-time randomized approximation scheme (FPRAS) for estimating the number of solutions to a SAT instance in DNF [3].

Consider the BN shown in Figure 1 that relates 4 random variables $A$, $B$, $C$ and $D$, each of which can take two values—0 or 1. The figure also shows an alternative way of representing the joint distribution of these 4 random variables—viz. $0.03125\{T\} + 0.06250\{A\}$ (see below). While the BN represents the joint exploiting the *causal* relationships and *conditional independencies* between the variables, the representation $0.03125\{T\} + 0.06250\{A\}$ exploits the *numerical structure* of the joint distribution. The numerical structure is captured by an examination of the joint and noting that it can be split up into a linear combination of Karnaugh map-like structures that represent Boolean formulas—viz. $T$ and $A$ with weights 0.03125 and 0.06250 respectively. It can be observed (proved rigorously later in the paper) that the probability of any partial assignment (say $A = 1$, $C = 0$ i.e. $AC'$) is equivalent to the same linear combination of the number of solutions to SAT instances formed by AND-ing the partial assignment with such a representation—viz. $0.03125\#(T, AC') + 0.06250\#(A, AC')$. Here, $\#(C_1, C_2 \ldots)$ refers to the number of solutions to the conjunction of the clauses $C_1, C_2 \ldots$. The intuition that we want to capture therefore is that if we can pre-compile a BN into a linear combination of SAT instances that have "neat" representations (defined formally later in the paper) and if we have an algorithm that can count the number of consistent models to a SAT in polynomial time (possibly with high precision and confidence), then we are in very good shape.

The outline of our approach is as follows. We first present an interesting relationship between probabilities and model counting. We show that the probability of a partial assignment in a BN is equal to a weighted sum of the number of solutions to a series of CSPs fixing the same partial assignment. The number of such CSPs may itself be exponential. On the face of it, this relationship does not seem very useful because not only are the number of CSPs potentially exponential, but counting the number of solutions to a CSP is $\#P$-complete. The interesting thing that we will show in the paper is that we can deal with both of these issues. First, we deal with the issue of having to consider an exponential number of CSPs by employing dynamic programming and message-passing techniques that have been used traditionally by algorithms employing clique trees for BN inference [2]. Second, we deal with the problem of counting the number of solutions to a CSP by pre-compiling it into a DNF and making use of a fully polynomial-time randomized approximation scheme (FPRAS) for counting the number of models to a SAT in DNF [3].

## 2 Probabilities and Model Counting

We show an interesting relationship between probabilities and model counting (see Figure 2). Basic definitions related to CSPs can be found in [1].

**Notation** In this section, we will use "$n$" arbitrarily and "$C$" to indicate the number of CPTs in a given BN.

**Definition** Given a set of real numbers $t_1, t_2 \ldots t_n$ a *zero-one linear combination* of $t_1, t_2 \ldots t_n$ is given by the weighted sum $x_1 t_1 + x_2 t_2 \ldots + x_n t_n$ where for all $1 \leq i \leq n$, $x_i \in \{0, 1\}$.

**Definition** A number $s$ is said to be *expressible* as a zero-one linear combi-

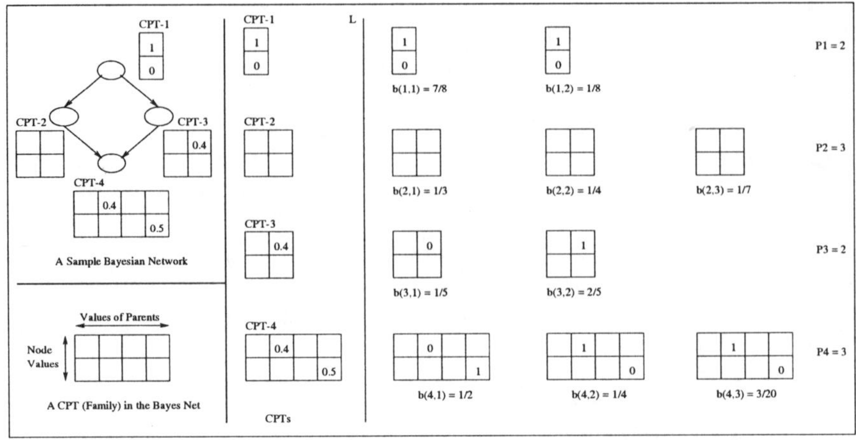


Figure 2: Shows the CPTs of a Bayes net on the left of the vertical line $L$. On the right of $L$ are the decompositions of the CPTs (for example, $0.4 = 0 \times 1/5 + 1 \times 2/5$ in CPT-3 and $0.4 = 0 \times 1/2 + 1 \times 1/4 + 1 \times 3/20$ in CPT-4). $b(i,j)$ is $b_i^j$ in text, and $Pi$ is $P_i$ in text.

nation of $t_1, t_2 \ldots t_n$ if there exist $x_i \in \{0,1\}$ for all $1 \leq i \leq n$, such that $s = x_1 t_1 + x_2 t_2 \ldots + x_n t_n$.

**Definition** A number $s$ is said to be *$\epsilon$-expressible* as a zero-one linear combination of $t_1, t_2 \ldots t_n$ if there exist $x_i \in \{0,1\}$ for all $1 \leq i \leq n$, such that $s' = x_1 t_1 + x_2 t_2 \ldots + x_n t_n$ and $|s - s'| \leq s\epsilon$.

**Definition** A *basis* $\langle b_i^1, b_i^2 \ldots b_i^{P_i} \rangle$ for $CPT_i$ is a set of positive real numbers such that all numbers in $CPT_i$ can be expressed as a zero-one-linear combination of $b_i^1, b_i^2 \ldots b_i^{P_i}$.

**Definition** An *$\epsilon$-approximate basis* $\langle b_i^1, b_i^2 \ldots b_i^{P_i} \rangle$ for $CPT_i$ is a set of positive real numbers such that all numbers in $CPT_i$ are $\epsilon$-expressible as a zero-one linear combination of $b_i^1 \ldots b_i^{P_i}$.

**Definition** Given a possible $\epsilon$-approximate basis $\langle b_i^1, b_i^2 \ldots b_i^{P_i} \rangle$ for $CPT_i$, the *$\epsilon$-$\langle b_i^1, b_i^2 \ldots b_i^{P_i} \rangle$ representation of $CPT_i$* is a table in which all the floating-point entries of $CPT_i$ are re-written as zero-one linear combinations of $b_i^1, b_i^2 \ldots b_i^{P_i}$ up to the relative approximation factor of $\epsilon$.

**Definition** The $k^{th}$ *zero-one-layer* of $CPT_i$ is a table of zeroes and ones derived from the coefficients of $b_i^k$ in the $\epsilon$-$\langle b_i^1, b_i^2 \ldots b_i^{P_i} \rangle$ representation of the corresponding numbers in $CPT_i$.

**Definition** The $k^{th}$ zero-one-layer of $CPT_i$ is defined to have *weight* $b_i^k$.

**Definition** The $k^{th}$ *CSP compilation of a CPT* is a constraint over the variables of the CPT that is derived from the $k^{th}$ zero-one-layer of the CPT such that zeroes correspond to disallowed tuples and ones correspond to allowed tuples.

**Definition** The $(k_1, k_2 \ldots k_C)$ *CSP compilation of the entire BN* is the set of constraints $S$ such that $S = \{s_i : s_i$ is the $k_i^{th}$ CSP compilation of the $i^{th}$ CPT$\}$. It is assumed that for all $1 \le i \le C$, $1 \le k_i \le P_i$.

**Definition** The *weight* of a $(k_1, k_2 \ldots k_C)$ CSP compilation of the entire network is defined to be equal to $b_1^{k_1} b_2^{k_2} \ldots b_C^{k_C}$ (assuming that for all $1 \le i \le C$, $1 \le k_i \le P_i$).

**Notation** We will use the notation $h_{ij}$ to mean the $j^{th}$ CSP compilation of the $i^{th}$ CPT. Let $A$ indicate a complete or partial assignment to the variables. If $A$ is an assignment that instantiates all the variables of $CPT_i$, then we will use the notation $h_{ij}(A)$ to indicate whether or not $A$ satisfies $h_{ij}$. If $A$ is a complete assignment for all the variables in the network, then all variables for all CPTs are instantiated and we will use the notation $CSP_{(k_1,k_2 \ldots k_C)}(A)$ to indicate whether $A$ satisfies all the constraints $h_{ik_i}$ $(1 \le i \le C, 1 \le k_i \le P_i)$. If $A$ is not a complete assignment for all the variables, then we will use the notation $\#CSP_{(k_1,k_2 \ldots k_C)}(A)$ to indicate the number of solutions to the $(k_1, k_2 \ldots k_C)$ CSP compilation of the network that share the same partial assignment as $A$.

**Theorem 1** The probability of a complete assignment $A = (X_1 = x_1, X_2 = x_2 \ldots X_n = x_n)$ is just the sum of the weights of the different CSP compilations of the BN that are satisfied by this complete assignment—i.e. $P(A) = \sum_{(k_1,k_2 \ldots k_C)} CSP_{(k_1,k_2 \ldots k_C)}(A) b_1^{k_1} b_2^{k_2} \ldots b_C^{k_C}$ (for all $1 \le i \le C, 1 \le k_i \le P_i$).

**Proof** Consider the complete assignment $A = (X_1 = x_1, X_2 = x_2 \ldots X_n = x_n)$ for all the variables. The probability of this assignment is equal to the product of the probabilities defined *locally* by each CPT. Consider $CPT_i$. Using the fact that the $t^{th}$ coefficient in the $\epsilon$-$\langle b_i^1, b_i^2 \ldots b_i^{P_i} \rangle$ representation of this local value has been written out as an allowed or disallowed tuple in the $t^{th}$ CSP compilation of that CPT, we can rewrite the local value for $A$ in $CPT_i$ as $\sum_{j=1}^{P_i} h_{ij}(A) b_i^j$. The total probability is then just the product over all local values, which is equal to $\Pi_{k=1}^{C} \sum_{j=1}^{P_k} h_{kj}(A) b_k^j$. Expanding the product, we see that it is essentially of the form $\sum_{(k_1,k_2 \ldots k_C)} b_1^{k_1} b_2^{k_2} \ldots b_C^{k_C} \{\Pi_{j=1}^{C} h_{jk_j}(A)\} = \sum_{(k_1,k_2 \ldots k_C)} CSP_{(k_1,k_2 \ldots k_C)}(A) b_1^{k_1} b_2^{k_2} \ldots b_C^{k_C}$.

**Theorem 2 (Generalized Model Counting)** The marginalized probability of a partial assignment $A$ to a set of variables $(S \subseteq X)$ is equal to the product of the weight and the number of solutions (under the same partial assignment $A$) summed over all CSP compilations of the network—i.e. $P(A) = \sum_{(k_1,k_2 \ldots k_C)} \#CSP_{(k_1,k_2 \ldots k_C)}(A) b_1^{k_1} b_2^{k_2} \ldots b_C^{k_C}$ (for all $1 \le i \le C, 1 \le k_i \le P_i$).

**Proof** From the previous theorem, we know that the probability of a complete assignment $B$ is $\sum_{(k_1,k_2 \ldots k_C)} CSP_{(k_1,k_2 \ldots k_C)}(B) b_1^{k_1} b_2^{k_2} \ldots b_C^{k_C}$ (for all $1 \le i \le C, 1 \le k_i \le P_i$). Now, the marginalized value of a partial assignment $A$ is just the sum of the probabilities of all complete assignments $B$ that agree with $A$ on the assignment to variables in $S$. That is, $P(A) = \sum_B P(B)(B(S) = A)$. Using the result of the previous theorem to expand $P(B)$, we have $P(A) = \sum_B \sum_{(k_1,k_2 \ldots k_C)} CSP_{(k_1,k_2 \ldots k_C)}(B) b_1^{k_1} b_2^{k_2} \ldots b_C^{k_C} (B(S) = A)$. Switching the two summations and noting that $\sum_B CSP_{(k_1,k_2 \ldots k_C)}(B)(B(S) = A)$ is the same as $\#CSP_{(k_1,k_2 \ldots k_C)}(A)$, we can conclude that for any partial assignment $A$, $P(A) = \sum_{(k_1,k_2 \ldots k_C)} \#CSP_{(k_1,k_2 \ldots k_C)}(A) b_1^{k_1} b_2^{k_2} \ldots b_C^{k_C}$.

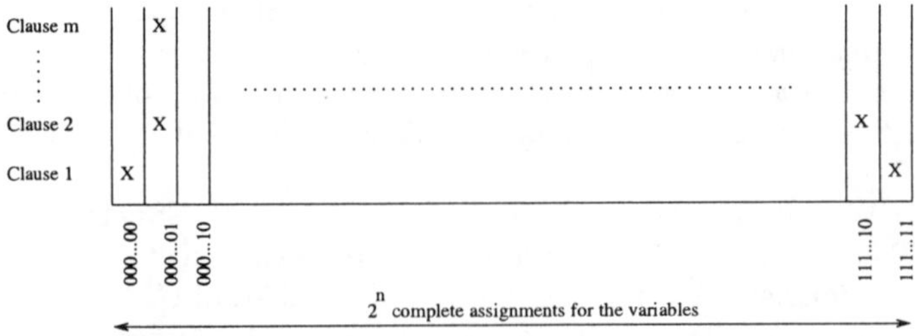


Figure 3: Illustrates the idea of *importance sampling* in the FPRAS for DNF counting.

# 3 DNF Counting

The DNF counting problem is the problem of estimating the number of solutions to a SAT in DNF (disjunctive normal form). Counting the number of solutions a SAT in DNF or CNF (conjunctive normal form) precisely, is $\#P$-complete. However, when a SAT instance is in DNF, we have a fully polynomial-time randomized approximation scheme (FPRAS) for estimating the number of solutions to it [3].

The naive way to perform sampling to estimate the number of solutions to a DNF is to choose a random assignment to all the variables as a sample; count the fraction of $N$ samples that satisfy the DNF; and scale appropriately. However, this method is not very useful because the *Estimator Theorem* for *uniform sampling* relates the number of samples $N$ with the relative approximation factor $\epsilon$ and the confidence factor $1 - \delta$ through the equation $N \geq \frac{4log_e(2/\delta)}{p\epsilon^2}$. Here $p$ is the actual fraction of satisfying assignments to the DNF and if it happens to be exponentially low, we need an exponentially large number of samples.

The idea in [3] is to leverage the extra structure present in the DNF. Let the number of variables be $n$ and let the clauses of the DNF be $C_1, C_2 \ldots C_m$. A satisfying assignment to $C_i$ is also a satisfying assignment to the whole DNF. Moreover, a satisfying assignment to a clause can be sampled *uniformly at random* by choosing an assignment of true (1) or false (0) with probability 0.5 each to all the don't-care variables in $C_i$ *independently*. Let $D_i$ be the space of satisfying assignments for clause $C_i$. Clearly, $|D_i| = 2^{\#\text{don't-care variables in } C_i}$. We want to estimate $|D|$ where $D = \cup_1^m D_i$.

Imagine a series of columns that can hold objects called *counters* (see Figure 3). Suppose that there is a column associated with each possible assignment to all the variables and suppose that for every clause, we put a counter in the column of every assignment that satisfies it. Suppose we order the clauses in some way (we can simply use the ordering in which the clauses are given to us) and throw the counters corresponding to each clause into the columns in that order. It is easy to observe that $D_i$ is the same as the set of columns in which counters corresponding to clause $C_i$ are present and $D$ is the union of all columns in which any counter is present. $|D|$ is equal to the number

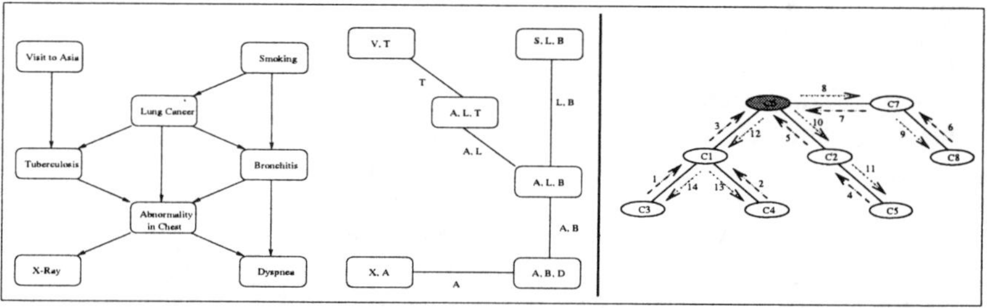


Figure 4: The left side of the figure shows an example of a BN and a clique tree over it. The right side shows an arbitrary clique with a nominated root.

of "bottom-most" counters. Estimating the number of bottom-most counters from the counters is equivalent to estimating $|D|/\sum_{i=1}^{m}|D_i|$. Since we know $\sum_{i=1}^{m}|D_i|$ precisely, we can then estimate $|D|$ as required. We have to ensure two things: (1) we can sample *uniformly at random* among all the counters, and (2) estimating $|D|/\sum_{i=1}^{m}|D_i|$ does not require an exponential number of samples. We can take care of (1) by picking a clause $C_i$ with probability proportional to $|D_i|$ and then sampling a satisfying assignment to it *uniformly at random*. We can take care of (2) by noticing that since there are no more than $m$ ($m$ is the number of clauses) counters in any column, the actual fraction of bottom-most counters $= |D|/\sum_{i=1}^{m}|D_i|$ is bounded below by $1/m$. Note that a sampled counter can be checked to see if it is a bottom-most counter in polynomial time by verifying that none of the clauses occurring before the chosen clause are satisfied by the assignment corresponding to this counter. By the *Estimator Theorem*, therefore, the number of samples required to get an $(\epsilon, \delta)$ approximation $\leq \frac{4m\,log_e(2/\delta)}{\epsilon^2}$, making the running time of the FPRAS for DNF counting polynomial in $m$, $n$, $log_e(1/\delta)$ and $1/\epsilon$.

# 4 Exploiting the Topology of the BN

We provide a brief review of the standard dynamic programming techniques used to exploit the topological structure of a BN for efficient inference. In the next section, we will show how to extend these ideas to address the issue of dealing with an exponential number of CSPs in reformulating probabilities as model counting.

Let $G$ be a BN over the variables $X = \{X_1, X_2 \ldots X_n\}$. A *cluster-tree* over $G$ is a tree each of whose nodes is associated with a cluster (a subset of $X$). Each edge is annotated with a subset of BN nodes called the *separator*. We say that a cluster tree $T$ over $G$ has *family values* if, for every $X_i$, there exists some cluster $C$ in $T$ such that $Family(X_i) \subseteq C$. We say that $T$ has the *running intersection* property if, whenever there is a variable $X_i$ such that $X_i$ is in $C$ and $X_i$ is also in $C'$, then $X_i$ is also in every cluster in the path in $T$ between $C$ and $C'$. A cluster tree that satisfies both the *family values* and the *running*

**Algorithm** Message-Passing
**Input** Clique-Tree $T$ for BN $G$
**Output** Calibration of $T$
**for** each clique $C$
  $\Pi_0(C) = 1$
**end-for**
**for** each variable $X$
  $C$ = a clique s.t. $Family(X) \subseteq C$
  $\Pi_0(C) = \Pi_0(C) \times CPT(X)$
**end-for**
Pick any clique $C_r$ as the root
*polist* = list of cliques in post order
**while** *polist* is not empty
  $C$ = next item on *polist*
  Let $C_1, C_2 \ldots C_k$ be $C$'s children
  Let $C+$ be $C$'s parent
  $\Pi(C) = \Pi_0(C) \times \times_{i=1}^{k} \mu_{C_i \to C}$
  Let $Y = C \cap C+$
  $\mu_{C \to C+} = \sum_{C \setminus Y} \Pi(C)$
**end-while**
Let *rpolist* be the reverse of *polist*
**while** *rpolist* is not empty
  Let $C$ = next item on *rpolist*
  Let $C_1, C_2 \ldots C_k$ be $C$'s children
  **for** $i = 1$ to $k$
    Let $Y = C \cap C_i$
    $\mu_{C \to C_i} = \sum_{C \setminus Y} \Pi(C)$
    $\Pi(C_i) = \Pi(C_i) \times \mu_{C \to C_i} / \mu_{C_i \to C}$
  **end-for**
**end-while**

Figure 5: Shows the working of the message-passing algorithm for clique tree calibration.

*intersection* properties is called a *clique tree* and its nodes are referred to as *cliques* (over the subset of variables in $X$ that they contain).

Before we describe how the clique tree itself is built and what parameters need to be minimized, we review how it can be used for doing Bayesian inference. Without proving the correctness of the algorithm rigorously, we provide the intuition behind how it works. The proof of its correctness can be found in [2]. Figure 4 shows an example of a BN and a clique tree over it. It also shows another (unrelated) clique tree with one of the cliques being chosen as the root. We will use this tree to illustrate the working of the message-passing algorithm provided in Figure 5.

The algorithm starts out with the goal of building a joint distribution over the variables in each clique. We refer to this as the potential $\Pi(C)$. $\Pi(C)$ is intended to resemble the true joint distribution of the variables when the algorithm terminates. The information provided in the CPTs of the BN is incorporated by assigning each CPT to some clique that contains the family of variables corresponding to that CPT. Note that because the clique tree ensures the *family values* property, we are always guaranteed of finding such a clique. After we assign CPTs to cliques, the CPTs assigned to the same clique are multiplied together.

**Definition** The multiplication ($\times$) of two distributions (potentials) $D_1$ and $D_2$ defined respectively over $\{X_{i_1}, X_{i_2} \ldots X_{i_k}\}$ and $\{X_{j_1}, X_{j_2} \ldots X_{j_h}\}$ is defined to be the distribution $D_3 = D_1 \times D_2$ over $\{X_{t_1}, X_{t_2} \ldots X_{t_r}\} = \{X_{i_1}, X_{i_2} \ldots X_{i_k}\} \cup \{X_{j_1}, X_{j_2} \ldots X_{j_h}\}$ such that $D_3(x_{t_1}, x_{t_2} \ldots x_{t_r})$ is considered as being equal to $D_1((x_{t_1}, x_{t_2} \ldots x_{t_r})|(x_{i_1}, x_{i_2} \ldots x_{i_k})) * D_2((x_{t_1}, x_{t_2} \ldots x_{t_r})|(x_{j_1}, x_{j_2} \ldots x_{j_h}))$. Here, $(x_{t_1}, x_{t_2} \ldots x_{t_r})|(x_{i_1}, x_{i_2} \ldots x_{i_k})$ indicates the projection of the first set of variables onto the second.

For the variables in any clique, there are two components that provide information about their joint distribution: (1) all the CPTs that have been assigned to that clique, and (2) any information that might come from its neighbors through the communication variables. Clearly, (1) is taken care of in the very beginning when all CPTs that have been assigned to the clique are factored in. To take care of (2), we introduce the notion of *messages*. When a clique receives a message, it multiplies it into its currently maintained potential. After all messages arrive on all incident edges for a clique and are incorporated appropriately, the correct joint is obtained. If all possible messages are sent along all edges in both directions, then the joints in each clique can be built simultaneously and consistently for each of them. Such a process is called *calibration*.

The fundamental requirement in the message-passing algorithm, however, is that the messages need to be such that a message sent from $C_i$ to $C_j$ must reflect the "cumulative information" in all of the cliques reachable from $C_j$ through $C_i$. This means, therefore, that $C_i$ must receive and incorporate messages coming from its other edges before it is ready to send a message on the edge $C_i \rightarrow C_j$. Messages are derived by marginalization over the appropriate set of variables. To be able to build the joints in all cliques consistently and simultaneously, we first notice that once we fix a root and define a tree, the leaves are in a position to send messages to their parents. This is because it is vacuously true that they have received messages on all other edges. Clearly, we can perform this bottom-up from the leaves to the root passing valid messages in one direction for each edge. Once we reach the root, it has received all messages and is in a position to send out messages in the reverse direction because its potential is now the actual joint. These messages should however be such that the message sent out on an edge does not reflect or factor in the message that was sent to the root along that edge in the opposite direction. This accounts for why we have $\Pi(C_i) = \Pi(C_i) \times \mu_{C \rightarrow C_i} / \mu_{C_i \rightarrow C}$ in Figure 5. Now it is easy to see that we can work this top-down to complete all the messages along the opposite directions of all the edges. The right side of Figure 4 shows the order in which messages are sent when $C_6$ is fixed as the root.

The running time of the above calibration algorithm is linear in the size of the tree and exponential in the size of the largest clique (see [2] for details). Constructing a clique tree that minimizes the size of the largest clique is related to the problem of finding the minimum *induced width* in the *moralized graph* of the BN and is known to be NP-hard [1]. However, certain heuristics (some based on *maximum-cardinality ordering* (*m-ordering*) [5]) work very well in practice.

Consider the goal of calibrating a given clique tree conditioned under the evidence $Z = z$. It is easy to prove that essentially the same message-passing algorithm can be applied if, at all stages, we use only those entries in the potentials that are consistent with the evidence and marginalize appropriately (see [2] for details). The complexity of this is similar to that of the original algorithm, namely, exponential in the size of the largest clique.

Given a calibrated tree $T$ (incorporating evidence $Z = z$), if we want to

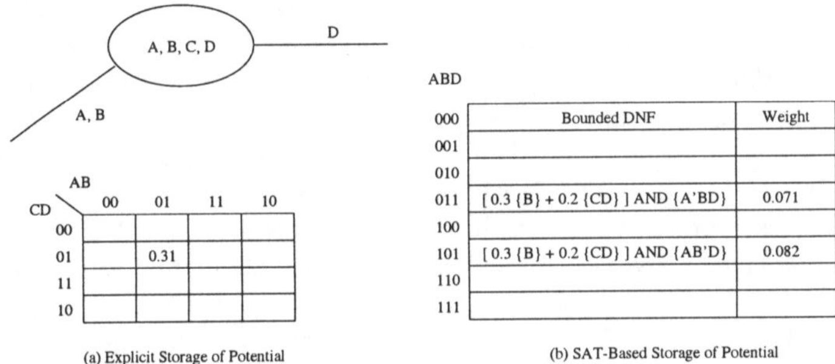


Figure 6: Compares the data structures maintained in each clique by the traditional versus the SAT-based approaches.

answer a query of the form $P(Q_i = q/Z = z)$ (for a single variable $Q_i$), it suffices to pick any clique in which $Q_i$ occurs and marginalize appropriately over the other variables. Now consider answering a query of the form $P(Q_1 = q_1, Q_2 = q_2 \ldots Q_k = q_k/Z = z)$. By Bayes' rule, we know that this is equal to $P(Q_1 = q_1, Q_2 = q_2 \ldots Q_{k-1} = q_{k-1}/Z = z, Q_k = q_k)P(Q_k = q_k/Z = z)$. Continuing this $k$ times, we notice that we can answer a query relating $k$ variables (that do not necessarily belong to a single clique) if we can answer $k$ queries on *single* variables that incorporate *varying* evidences. Since $k \leq n$, a query that relates $k$ variables can account only for a polynomial blow-up in the running time, and the dominating factor is still the size of the largest clique.

# 5 SAT-Based Message-Passing

In this section, we present methods for combining the ideas presented in previous sections. To keep the discussion simple, we will assume that all the variables can take on only two possible values—0 or 1.[1]

**Definition** A distribution (or potential) is said to have a DNF decomposition bounded by $P$ if it is possible to split it into a linear combination of Boolean formulas in DNF such that the total number of clauses is $\leq P$.

For example, the linear combination of the DNF formulas, $0.1325\{A \vee BC' \vee BD\} + 0.4\{D \vee AC'\}$ is bounded by 5. Note that in the worst case, $P$ is equal to the number of entries in the distribution. This fact is exploited in SAT-based approaches which store the initial potentials of cliques "compactly" using a DNF decomposition rather than storing them explicitly as in the previous approaches. The fundamental idea is to still make use of clique trees and message-passing, but the data structures maintained inside each clique are made more compact and efficient. We will show that this would then entail different parameters to be minimized for the clique tree that we have to work with.

[1] Clearly, this is not a serious restriction since we can use a binary encoding for larger domains.

Figure 6 compares the data structures maintained in each clique by the traditional versus the proposed SAT-based methods. Traditional approaches represent the potential of a clique by explicitly maintaining a table that is exponential in the size of the clique. In SAT-based approaches, however, we maintain a table that is exponential only in the *communication size* of that clique. The *communication* of a clique $C$ is the set of variables that $C$ shares with any of its neighbors (denoted by $C_{\odot}$) and the *communication size* is the cardinality of this set. Each entry in the table consists of two parts: (1) a *weight* field that incorporates any information that the clique may receive from its neighbors, and (2) a *DNF* field that essentially ANDs the DNF representation of the initial potential of that clique (bounded by $P$) with the particular assignment for the communicating variables corresponding to that entry (the resulting AND also has a DNF representation bounded by $P$ because the assignment forms a single clause in its DNF representation).

Suppose that all the initial potentials are such that they have DNF decompositions bounded by size $P$. Then immediately we have an algorithm that extends the message-passing algorithm and whose message-passing phase has a running time that is *polynomial* in $P$ and *exponential* not in the size of the *biggest clique* but in the size of the *biggest communication*. The truth of this claim follows from the following observation. We know that summing out variables $U \subseteq V = \{V_1, V_2 \ldots V_g\}$ in the joint over $V$ in order to obtain a marginalized joint over $V \backslash U$ is equivalent to obtaining a probability for all value assignments to variables in $V \backslash U$ and this (by the *Generalized Model Counting Theorem*) is equivalent to counting the number of models to the DNF representation of the joint by fixing different values for $V \backslash U$.

Figure 7 shows the working of message-passing algorithms that employ the SAT-based techniques for sending messages. An incoming message is incorporated by multiplying it into the currently maintained potential over the weights. An outgoing message is obtained by marginalization over the appropriate missing variables, where marginalization takes into account both the weights and the number of solutions to the DNF formulas (see Figure 7). Note that an incoming message can always be appropriately incorporated and an outgoing message can always be correctly computed because the variables over which they are defined form a subset of the variables over which the potential is maintained.

While the original message-passing algorithm incorporated evidence $Z = z$ by marginalizing only over the entries that were consistent with it, SAT-based algorithms incorporate evidence by AND-ing each DNF clause with $Z = z$. As argued earlier, such an AND-ing results in a DNF decomposition that is still bounded by $P$. Query answering over multiple variables (not necessarily belonging to the same clique) is reducible to query answering over single variables and added evidence, as explained earlier. The only difference is that for the fundamental problem of finding $P(Q_i = q)$ (for a single variable $Q_i$ belonging to clique $C$) we use $\sum_{C_{\odot}} \Pi(C_{\odot})_W \#\{\Pi(C_{\odot})_{DNF} \wedge Q_i = q\}$.

Although the message-passing phase of the SAT-based algorithm is exponential only in the size of the largest communication, the initial phase is still

**Algorithm** SAT-Based-Msg-Passing
**Input** Clique-Tree $T$ for BN $G$
**Output** Calibration of $T$
**for** each clique $C$
  $\Pi_{INIT}(C) = 1$
**end-for**
**for** each variable $X$
  $C$ = a clique s.t. $Family(X) \subseteq C$
  $\Pi_{INIT}(C) = \Pi_{INIT}(C) \times CPT(X)$
**end-for**
**for** each clique $C$
  $\Pi_0(C_\odot)_{DNF} = Decomp[\Pi_{INIT}(C)]$
  $\Pi_0(C_\odot)_W = 1$
**end-for**
Pick any clique $C_r$ as the root
*polist* = list of cliques in post order
**while** *polist* is not empty
  $C$ = next item on *polist*
  Let $C_1, C_2 \ldots C_k$ be $C$'s children
  Let $C+$ be $C$'s parent
  $\Pi(C_\odot)_W = \Pi_0(C_\odot)_W \times_{i=1}^{k} \mu_{C_i \to C}$
  Let $Y = C \cap C+$
  $\mu_{C \to C+} = \sum_{C_\odot \setminus Y} \{\Pi(C_\odot)_W \times \#\Pi(C_\odot)_{DNF}\}$
**end-while**
Let *rpolist* be the reverse of *polist*
**while** *rpolist* is not empty
  Let $C$ = next item on *rpolist*
  Let $C_1, C_2 \ldots C_k$ be $C$'s children
  **for** $i = 1$ to $k$
    Let $Y = C \cap C_i$
    $\mu_{C \to C_i} = \sum_{C_\odot \setminus Y} \{\Pi(C_\odot)_W \times \#\Pi(C_\odot)_{DNF}\}$
    $\Pi((C_i)_\odot)_W \times = \mu_{C \to C_i} / \mu_{C_i \to C}$
  **end-for**
**end-while**

Figure 7: Shows the working of the SAT-based message-passing algorithm for clique tree calibration.

exponential in the size of the largest clique (routine *Decomp* in Figure 7). The point to note however is that this is a one-time process that is independent of any query. Once we compile a BN into bounded DNF clauses for the initial potentials of all cliques, we are in a position to answer any query by a series of message-passing phases (at most $n$ phases, as explained before) over the cliques (using model counting and marginalization over a subset of the communication variables). It is this message-passing phase that is important for us at runtime and which turns out to be exponential only in the size of the largest communication for SAT-based algorithms.

Because of the above arguments, our goal is now to try and produce clique

**Algorithm** SAT-Based-Clique-Tree
**Input** BN $G$
**Output** Clique-Tree $J$ s.t.
  (1) $\Pi_{INIT}(C)$ for all $C$ has DNF representation bounded by $P$
  (2) size of max comn is minimized
$J$ = M-Ordering-Clique-Tree ($G$)
**while true**
  **if** exists edge $(C_i, C_j)$ in $J$ s.t.
    (1) $\Pi_{INIT}(C_i) \times \Pi_{INIT}(C_j)$ has DNF representation $\leq P$
    (2) $|(C_i, C_j)_\odot| < |(C_i)_\odot|, |(C_j)_\odot|$
    Merge $(C_i, C_j)$ in $J$
  **else break**
  **end-if**
**end-while**

Figure 8: An offline algorithm that tries to minimize the exponential factor (size of maximum communication) for SAT-based message-passing algorithms.

trees that minimize the size of the largest communication, keeping the DNF decompositions of the initial potentials of all the cliques still bounded by $P$. Figure 8 shows an algorithm that runs *offline* and tries to minimize the size of the largest communication while retaining the bounded DNF property. The idea is to make use of the clique tree generated using m-ordering over the moralized graph of the BN as a starting point, but collapse edges and merge cliques until we reach a point where merging them any further does not yield a benefit.[2] It is easy to note that such a merging process maintains the *family values* and *running intersection* properties required for clique trees. In domains that exhibit "high" numerical structure like the example in Figure 1, the size of the communication comes out to be 0 (the joint over all 4 variables has a neat DNF decomposition). In most practical domains, we expect that this factor will come out to be significantly lesser than the exponential factor produced by m-ordering—noting that we are always assured of doing better than this factor because we use the m-ordering as a starting point in Figure 8 to improve upon.

There are two factors that contribute to the relative approximation factor associated with SAT-based message-passing algorithms: (1) that introduced by the FPRAS algorithm for DNF counting, $\epsilon$, and (2) that associated with trying to represent the joint by a bounded DNF, $\epsilon'$. Since the SAT-based message-passing algorithm involves summations and multiplications over numbers approximated to a relative factor of $\epsilon+\epsilon'$, and since addition of $k$ numbers preserves the relative approximation factor, but multiplication compounds it by a linear factor (for small $\epsilon$ and $\epsilon'$), the compounded effect is bounded by a factor of $\epsilon + \epsilon'$ times the maximum number of multiplications any single parameter in any message undergoes. This is bounded by the number of levels in the tree that in turn is clearly bounded by the number of variables $n$, hence resulting in a total relative approximation factor of $n(\epsilon + \epsilon')$. The factor $n$ may not be very serious under the following considerations: (1) since the DNF counting algorithm is an approximation scheme, we can reduce $\epsilon$ to our choice if we correspondingly increase the running time of the algorithm (running time increases only polynomially with the factor by which we scale down $\epsilon$); (2) $\epsilon'$ is a measure of the error associated with representing the probabilities and is dependent on how "sensitive" we want our problem domain to be to exact probabilities specified in the BN.

SAT-based algorithms also provide for a framework in which we can exploit qualitative relationships between variables of a particular problem domain in the context of BN inference. By a qualitative relationship between variables $X$ and $Y$, we mean that there is some ordering on the values that $X$ can take $(x_1, x_2 \dots x_k)$ such that for any value $v$ that $Y$ can take, $P(Y = v/X = x_i)$ is monotonically increasing or monotonically decreasing with $i$. Without a rigorous discussion (due to lack of space), we claim that the idea is to consider a joint distribution on a set of variables, where subsets of them exhibit qualitative relationships. If all the numbers in the joint distribution are arranged in

[2] In most cases, even the offline decomposition of a large potential can be done simply by multiplying the decompositions of the individual potentials it incorporates and using subsequent Boolean simplification.

ascending order and discretized into intervals of appropriate resolution, we can decompose the joint into a linear combination of Karnaugh map-like structures where the weights correspond to the difference between consecutive landmarks in the discretization and the Karnaugh map structures provably exhibit "clustering" of their consistent models. Because of this clustering, it is very likely that they would have "compact" DNF decompositions.

# 6 Summary and Future Work

We presented a novel method for doing BN inference based on the idea of precompiling a BN into a representational form that allows for efficient inference, namely, a series of SAT instances in DNF. We provided techniques for exploiting both the *topology* and the *numerical structure* of the network. We showed important consequences of our approach: first, it always performs better than methods based purely on exploiting the topology of the network; second, it achieves fully polynomial-time randomized approximation schemes for domains exhibiting high numerical structure; and third, it provides a framework for exploiting qualitative relationships among variables.

Most of our future work is along two lines. On the theoretical side, we are looking into various combinatorial arguments for finding $\epsilon$-approximate bases for a given joint distribution that allow it to have a bounded DNF decomposition, including whether we can perturb it to allow for this to happen, what tradeoffs need to be made, etc. We are also interested in a more detailed study of the role of qualitative relationships. On the practical side, we are applying the theory developed in this paper to real-life scenarios requiring fast Bayesian inference algorithms like trajectory tracking, diagnosis [4], etc. We expect our approach to be successful in many real-life domains that exhibit "good" topological and numerical structure.

# References

[1] Dechter, R. *Constraint Networks.* Encyclopedia of Artificial Intelligence, second edition, Wiley and Sons, pp 276-285, 1992.

[2] Jensen, F. V. and Jensen, F. *Optimal Junction Trees.* In Proceedings of the Tenth Conference on Uncertainty in Artificial Intelligence. 1994.

[3] Karp, R., Luby, M. and Madras, N. *Monte-Carlo Approximation Algorithms for Enumeration Problems.* Journal of Algorithms 10 429-448. 1989.

[4] Kumar, T. K. S. and Dearden, R. *The Oracular Constraints Method.* Proceedings of the Fifth International Symposium on Abstraction, Reformulation and Approximation (SARA 2002).

[5] Tarjan, R. E. and Yannakakis, M. *Simple Linear Time Algorithms to Test Chordality of Graphs, Test Acyclicity of Hypergraphs, and Selectively Reduce Acyclic Hypergraphs.* SIAM Journal of Computing. 13 566-576. 1984.

# An Approach to Artificial Neural Network Training

Ireneusz Czarnowski and Piotr Jedrzejowicz
Department of Information Systems
Gdynia Maritime University
Morska 83, 81-225 Gdynia
Poland
irek, pj@wsm.gdynia.pl

Abstract

In this paper an application of a new metaheuristic called population learning algorithm (PLA) to ANN training is investigated. The paper proposes implementation of the PLA to training feed-forward artificial neural networks. The approach is validated by means of computational experiment in which PLA algorithm is used to train ANN solving a variety of benchmarking problems. Results of the experiment prove that PLA can be considered as a useful and effective tool for training ANN.

## 1. Introduction

Artificial neural networks are, nowadays, being used for solving a wide variety of real-life problems like, for example, pattern recognition, prediction, control, combinatorial optimization or classification. Main advantages of the approach include ability to tolerate imprecision and uncertainty and still achieving tractability, robustness, and low cost in practical applications. Since training a neural network for practical application is often very times consuming, an extensive research work is being carried in order to accelerate this process. Another problem with ANN training methods is danger of being caught in a local optimum. Hence, researchers look not only for algorithms that train neural networks quickly but rather for quick algorithms that are not likely, or less likely, to get trapped in a local optimum [1, 6, 14, 15].

In this paper we investigate application of the recently proposed population-based metaheurictic known as the population learning algorithm (PLA) [7]. The idea of applying population learning algorithms to train ANN has been suggested in earlier papers of the authors [2, 3, 4]. Several versions of the PLA have been designed and applied to solve variety of benchmark problems. Initial results were promising shoving good performance of the PLA as a tool for ANN training [3].

In this paper we present an extended range of the PLA implementations and validate the algorithms by means of computational experiment involving a number of well-known benchmark problems.

The paper gives details of the proposed PLA implementations and discusses the results of computational experiments carried. Conclusions include some suggestions for future research.

## 2. Population Learning Algorithm

Continuing research interest is focused on algorithms that rely on analogies to natural processes and phenomena. An important subclass of the NPB (natural processes based) class form population based methods, which also are called evolutionary algorithms.

Population based methods handle a population of individuals that evolves with the help of information exchange and self-improvement procedures. It should be noted that many different algorithms could be described within this framework. The best-known population-based algorithms are genetic algorithms, evolution strategies, evolution programming, scatter search, adaptive memory algorithms, and ant systems.

Population learning algorithms (PLA) handle population of individuals. An individual represents a coded solution of the considered problem. Initially, a massive population of individuals, known as the initial population, is generated. The number of individuals in the initial population should be sufficient to represent adequately the whole space of feasible solutions. Sufficient number of individuals relates to the need of, possibly, covering the neighbourhood of all of the local optima. Adequate representation of these neighbourhoods is related to the need of assuring that the improvement process, originated at the initial stage should be effective enough to carry at least some individuals to the highest stages of learning. The number of individuals for the particular PLA implementation is, usually, set at the fine-tuning phase.

Generating the initial population could be, simply, based on some random mechanism assuring the required representation of the whole feasible solution space. Once the initial population has been generated, individuals enter the first learning stage. It involves applying some, possibly basic and elementary, improvement schemes or conducting simple learning sessions. The improved individuals are then evaluated and better ones pass to the subsequent stage. A strategy of selecting better or more promising individuals must be defined and duly applied. At the following stages the whole cycle is repeated. Individuals are subject to improvement and learning, either individually or through information exchange, and the selected ones are again promoted to a higher stage with the remaining ones dropped-out from the process. At the final stage the remaining individuals are reviewed with a view to selecting a solution to the problem at hand.

Learning process at early stage can be run in parallel. Individuals are then grouped into classes with possibly different curricula, which are different improvement schemes. At certain level the best from all groups join together to from higher-level groups where improvement and learning process are still carried in parallel. At some stage selected individuals are brought together to complete education.

```
Begin
  Chose the number of stages M;
  For each stages i=1,...,M set the selection criterion
  SCi;
  For each stage i=1,...,M design the learning-
  improvement procedure Li;
  Generate the initial population of individuals J;
    For i=1 to M do
       For each individual in J do
         Apply the learning-improvement procedure Li;
       End for;
      Remove from J all individuals who not pass
      selection criterion SCi;
    End for
End
```

Figure 1 Structure of the PLA algorithm

At different stages of the process, different improvement schemes and learning procedures are applied. These gradually become more and more sophisticated and time consuming as there are less and less individuals to be taught.

General structure of the population-learning algorithm is shown in Figure 1.

The above pseudo-code covers simple, non-parallel version of the PLA. For the parallel PLA a scheme for grouping individuals at various stages, and the respective rules for carrying parallel computations need to be designed. Three basic PLA schemes are shown in Figure 2. Scheme a) depicts a simple, non-parallel implementation of the algorithm. Schemes b) and c) show parallel implementations. Schemes a) and b) can be used in case the improvement procedures used do not assume any information exchange between individuals or their groups. Finally, scheme c), or its variants, can be used in case some information is exchanged between individuals or groups of individuals during the learning process. Choice of the appropriate PLA scheme depends on both - computational resources available and characteristics of learning (improvement) procedures used.

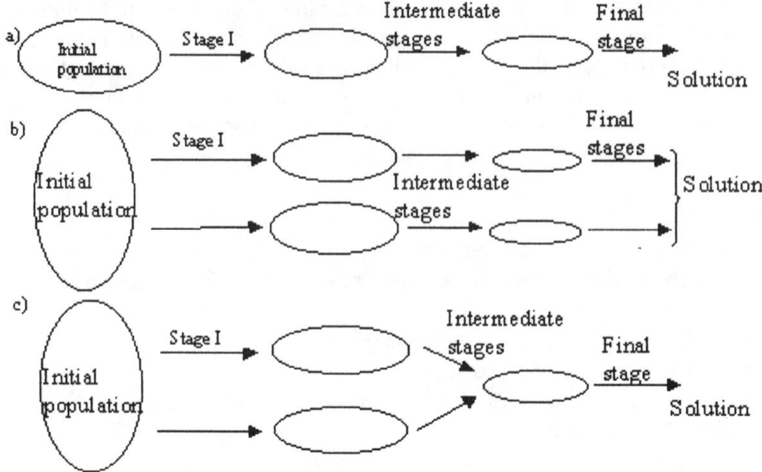


Figure 2 Three basic PLA schemes – simple (a), parallel (b), parallel with convergence (c)

# 3. PLA Implementation for ANN Training

In this paper we propose using population-learning algorithm to train artificial neural networks. Several PLA implementations are suggested. All are based on the following assumptions:

- An individual is a vector of real numbers from the predefined interval, each representing a value of weight of the respective link between neurons in the considered ANN.
- The initial population of individuals is generated randomly.
- There are five learning/improvement procedures used - standard mutation, local search, non-uniform mutation, gradient mutation and gradient adjustment.
- There is a common selection criterion for all stages. At each stage, individuals with fitness below the current average are rejected.

The suggested learning/improvement procedures are shown in the pseudo-code in Figure 3 - 7. However the procedures require some additional comments.

The first procedure – standard mutation modifies an individual by generating new values of two randomly selected elements in an individual. If the fitness function value has improved then the change is accepted.

```
Procedure L(1) { standard mutation}
Begin
  For  i=1 to J do
    For i=1 to k do {k - number of iteration}
      Select randomly two different elements x1 and
      x2 within individual i;
      Generate new random value of x1 and x2
      producing new individual;
      Calculate fitness of the new individual;
        If new fitness < old fitness then accept
        changes;
    End for
  End for
End
```

Figure 3 Pseudo-code of standard mutation

The second learning/improvement procedure exchanges values between two randomly selected elements within an individual. If the fitness function value of an individual has improved, then the change is accepted.

```
Procedure L(2) {local search}
Begin
  For i=1 to J do
    For i=1 to k do {k - number of iteration}
      Select randomly two different elements x1 and x2
      within individual i;
      Exchange values between x1 and x2 producing new
      individual;
      Calculate fitness of the new individual;
        If new fitness < old fitness then accept
        changes;
    End for
  End for
End
```

Figure 4 Pseudo-code of local search

The third learning/improvement procedure - non-uniform mutation involves modifying an individual by repeatedly adjusting value of the randomly selected element (in this case a real number) until the fitness function value has improved or until nine consecutive improvements have been attempted unsuccessfully. The value of the adjustment is calculated as:

$$\Delta(t, y) = y(1 - r^{(1-\frac{t}{T})\cdot r}),$$

where $r$ is the uniformly distributed real number from (0, 1], $T$ is equal to the length of the vector representing an individual and $t$ is a current number of adjustment.

```
Procedure L(3) {non-uniform  mutation}
Begin
  For i=1 to J do
    For t=1 to T do
      Select random point within the individual i;
      Apply non-uniform mutation;
      Calculate fitness of the new individual;
        If new fitness < old fitness then accept
        change;
    End for
  End for
End
```

Figure 5 Pseudo-code of non-uniform mutation

```
Procedure L(4) {gradient mutation}
Begin
  For i=1 to J do
    For i=1 to k do {k - number of iteration}
      Select randomly two different elements x1 and x2
      within individual i;
      Generate a random binary digit;
      Change values x1 and x2 to x1 + ξ and x2 + ξ if
      a random digit is 0 or x1 - ξ and x2 - ξ if a
      random digit is 1 producing new individual;
      Calculate fitness of the new individual;
        If new fitness < old fitness then accept
        changes;
    End for
  End for
End
```

Figure 6 Pseudo-code of gradient mutation

The fourth improvement procedure – gradient mutation changes two randomly selected elements within an individual by incrementing or decrementing their values. Direction of change (increment/decrement) is random and has identical probabilities equal to 0.5. The value of change is proportional to the gradient of an individual. If the fitness function value of an individual has improved then the change is accepted.

Number of iterations for procedures number 1,2 and 4 has to be set at the fine-tuning phase.

```
Procedure L(5) {gradient adjustment operator}
Begin
  For i=1 to J do
   α =1;
   While α > 0 do
    Apply  gradient adjustment operator;
    Calculate fitness of the new individual;
     If new fitness < old fitness then accept
     changes and break;
    α = α − 0.02 ;
   End while
  End for
End
```

Figure 7 Pseudo-code gradient adjustment operator

The fifth learning/improvement procedure adjusts the value of each element of the individual by a constant value $\Delta$ proportional to its gradient. Delta is calculated as $\Delta = \alpha \cdot \xi$, where $\alpha$ is the factor determining a size of the step in direction of $\xi$, known as a momentum. $\alpha$ has value from (0, 1]. In the proposed algorithm its value iterates starting from 1 with the step equal to 0.02. $\xi$ is a vector determining a direction of search and is equal to the gradient of an individual.

```
Seq-PLA
Begin
 Generate Initial Population;
 P = Initial population;
  For i=1 to 4 do
   Procedure L(i);
   P = Select(P);
  End for
 Procedure L(5);
 Consider best individual in P as solution;
End
```

Figure 8 Pseudo-code seq-PLA

The proposed algorithm designed to be run in a simple processor environment is shown in Figure 8.

The parallel-PLA scheme is based on the co-operation between the master worker (server) whose task is to manage computations and a number of slave workers, who act in parallel, performing computations as requested by the master. The approach allows a lot of freedom in designing population-learning process. The master worker is managing communication flow during the population learning.

It allocates computational tasks in terms of the required population size and number of iterations and also controls information exchange between slaves. The latter involves upgrading, at various learning stages, current populations maintained by all slaves with globally best individuals. Communication flow between the master and slave workers is shown in Figure 9.

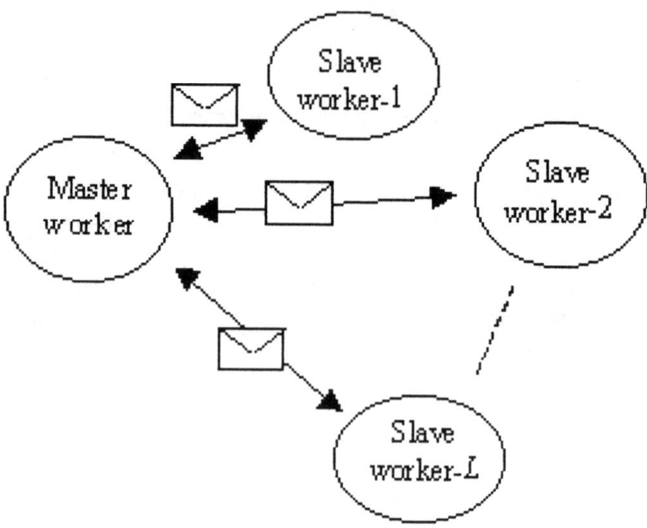


Figure 9 Communication flow between the master and slave workers

The following features characterize the proposed parallel-PLA:

- Master worker defines number of slave workers and size of the initial population for each of them.
- Each slave worker uses identical learning/improvement procedures.
- Master worker activates parallel processing.
- After completing each stage workers inform master about the best solution found so far.

- Master worker compares the received values and sends out the best solution to all the workers replacing their current worst individual.
- Master worker can stop computations if the desired quality level of the objective function has been achieved. This level is defined at the beginning of computations through setting the desired value of the mean squared error on a given set of training patterns.
- Slave workers can also stop computations if the above condition has been met.
- Computation is carried for the predefined number of stages.

A variant of the above approach, denoted parallel-PLAs, differs with respect to the strategy of using the best solution send to slaves from the master. Now the best solution is used to produce offspring by applying two types of the crossover operators - a single point crossover and a position crossover. Both are applied in turn to generate offspring from all of the current individuals for each slave.

# 4. Experiment Discussion and Results

The proposed implementations of the PLA have been used to train several neural networks applied to solving popular benchmarking classification problems - two spirals, 10-parity, Wisconsin breast cancer, Cleveland heart disease and credit approval.

ANN solving the two spirals problem has two real-valued inputs corresponding to the $x$ and $y$ coordinates of the point, and one binary target output that classifies the point as belonging to either of the two spirals coiling three times around the origin. The two spirals are constructed from 97 points given by the respective coordinates from the training set. Solving the two spirals problem appears to be a very difficult task for back-propagation networks [8, 14]. The topology of the network for this problem has been adopted from [5] where also an efficient constructive training algorithm called CASCOR was proposed. This so-called "shortcut" topology has four hidden units and 25 links with 25 weights.

In 10-parity problem ANN has to be trained to produce the Boolean "Exclusive OR" function of ten variables. A two-layer neural network with 10, 10 and 1 neurons in layers 1, 2 and 3 respectively is used.

Diagnosis of breast cancer involves classifying a tumor as either benign or malignant based on cell descriptions gathered by microscopic examination. Breast cancer databases was obtained from Dr. William H. Wolberg, University of Wisconsin Hospitals, Madison [9]. It includes 699 examples, 9 inputs and 2 outputs each. The corresponding ANN has 9, 9 and 1 neurons in layers 1, 2 and 3.

| Problem | Approach | TTV | | | 10CV | | |
|---|---|---|---|---|---|---|---|
| | | mean | max | min | mean | max | min |
| Two spirals | seq-PLA | 71.6 | 82.0 | 65.0 | 74.7 | 83.2 | 58.9 |
| Two spirals | parallel-PLA | 89.2 | 98.4 | 74.0 | 88.4 | 96.6 | 70.2 |
| Two spirals | parallel-PLAs | 91.7 | 98.0 | 80.0 | 92.0 | 98.2 | 77.0 |
| 10 parity | seq-PLA | 88.1 | 92.0 | 70.0 | 88.0 | 97.4 | 72.0 |
| 10 parity | parallel-PLA | 93.6 | 98.0 | 75.0 | 92.2 | 96.0 | 80.5 |
| Breast | seq-PLA | 95.4 | 98.5 | 78.0 | 96.4 | 98.0 | 82.2 |
| Breast | parallel-PLAs | 96.6 | 98.0 | 80.8 | 96.6 | 98.0 | 82.2 |
| Heart | seq-PLA | 81.0 | 88.0 | 62.3 | 81.3 | 89.0 | 65.0 |
| Heart | parallel-PLAs | 85.7 | 90.0 | 70.0 | 86.5 | 89.2 | 68.0 |
| Credit | seq-PLA | 82.0 | 86.4 | 63.0 | 82.6 | 87.4 | 63.0 |
| Credit | parallel-PLAs | 88.1 | 91.9 | 79.2 | 86.6 | 90.4 | 74.0 |

Table 1 Classification performance of the PLA implementations (%)

Cleveland heart disease problem involves predicting heart disease, that is deciding whether at least one of four major vessels is reduced in diameter by more than 50%. The binary decision is made based on personal data. The data set includes 303 examples with 13 inputs and 2 outputs and the corresponding ANN has 13, 13 and 1 neurons in layers 1, 2 and 3.

Credit card approval involves predicting the approval or rejection of a credit card request. The data set consists of 690 examples with 15 inputs and two outputs with a good mix of attributes. The corresponding ANN to be trained has 15, 15 and 1 neurons, respectively in layers 1, 2 and 3.

All data sets for the described problems are available at the UCI repository [10] and are often used to compare various techniques for ANN training. Data set for the 2-spirals problem is available and have been obtained from the home page http://www.cae.wisc.edu/~ece602/data/CMUbenchmark.

Computational experiment carried to evaluate the proposed PLA implementations has been based on the following quality measures:

- Correct classification ratio for the "10 cross validation" (10CV) approach.

- Correct classification ratio for the training, test and validation sets constructed using the 50%-25%-25% (TTV) principle [12].
- Mean squared error – MSE.
- Mean relative error - MRE.

| Problem | Approach | MRE | MSE | training time [min] |
|---|---|---|---|---|
| Two spirals | seq-PLA | 0.29 | 0.25 | 45.0 |
| Two spirals | parallel-PLA | 0.07 | 0.04 | 20.0 |
| Two spirals | parallel-PLAs | 0.07 | 0.04 | 18.0 |
| 10 parity | seq-PLA | 0.12 | 0.11 | 2.00 |
| 10 parity | parallel-PLA | 0.06 | 0.04 | 3.50 |
| Breast | seq-PLA | 0.02 | 0.01 | 1.50 |
| Breast | parallel-PLAs | 0.02 | 0.01 | 2.50 |
| Heart | seq-PLA | 0.21 | 0.17 | 1.50 |
| Heart | parallel-PLAs | 0.11 | 0.10 | 2.70 |
| Credit | seq-PLA | 0.20 | 0.18 | 2.50 |
| Credit | parallel-PLAs | 0.11 | 0.11 | 3.40 |

Table 2 Mean errors of the PLA implementations and the respective training times averaged over 50 runs

All artificial neural networks used in the experiment have sigmoid activation function with the sigmoid gain equal 1. Average size of the initial population in all PLA impementations has been set to 200. A maximum number of repetitions for each learning/improvement procedure has been set to 20 except for the 2-spirals problem in both - sequential and parallel versions where it has been set to 40. Each benchmarking problem has been solved 50 times and the reported values of the quality measures have been averaged over these 50 runs. All computations have been carried on the Sun Challenge R4400 and, additionally, for parallel-PLA and parallel-PLAs in PVM environment. Experiment results are shown in Table 1 and 2. In Table 3 performance of the PLA implementations is compared with some reported results from the literature.

It can be observed that PLA implementations guarantee good or even competitive level of training quality. It seems that the approach is also interesting in terms of computational time requirements. The authors have not been able to find comparable data on time performace of alternative approaches. Some conclusions can be drawn from the information on time performance of the Novel algorithm, which required 900 minutes to train ANN solving 2-spirals problem and 35 minutes to train ANN solving 10-parity problem [14].

| Problem | Approach | Literature reported accuracy | Best achieved PLA accuracy |
|---|---|---|---|
| Two spirals | Novel | 94.0 % [15] | 92.0 % |
| Two spirals | Simulated Annealing | 84.8 % [5] | 92.0 % |
| Two spirals | CASCOR | 62.0 % [15] | 92.0 % |
| Two spirals | Back Propagation | 52.0 % [15] | 92.0 % |
| Breast | Back Propagation | 96.7 % | 96.6 % |
| Breast | C 4.5 | 94.7 % | 96.6 % |
| Heart | Back Propagation | 81.3 % | 86.5 % |
| Credit | Back Propagation | 0.09 (training error) | 0.11 |

Table 3 PLA versus the reported accuracy of training algorithms. Source for the best reported: http://www.phys.uni.torun.pl/kmk/projects/datasets.html

## 5. Conclusion

Main contribution of the paper is seen as successfully applying the population based metaheuristic to training feed forward ANN. This application has resulted in proposing a new training algorithm that, in several instances, outperforms previously reported ones. It is impressively effective with respect to training ANN solving difficult 2-spirals problem as well as some other benchmarking classification problems considered difficult.

The proposed PLA seems to be a worthy and flexible training tool, which application to ANN training should be further investigated and refined. The approach seems promising in term of producing good or even excellent quality training in a reasonable time. Future research should concentrate on analysis of the PLA characteristics with a view to finding rules for effective algorithm configuration and fine-tuning, as well as on search for efficient learning/improvement procedures.

## Acknowledgements

The research has been supported by KBN, grant no. 8 T 11F020 19 2000


## References


1. Duch, W. & Korczak, J. Optimization and Global Minimization Methods Suitable for Neural Network. Neural Computing Surveys 2, 1998, http://www.icsi.berkeley.edu/~jagopta/CNS
2. Czarnowski, I., Jedrzejowicz, P., Ratajczak, E. Population Learning Algorithm - Example Implementations and Experiments. Proceedings of the Fourth Metaheuristics International Conference, Porto, 2001, 607-612
3. Czarnowski, I. & Jedrzejowicz, P. Population Learning Metaheuristic for Neural Network Training. Proceedings of the Sixth International Conference on Neural Networks and Soft Computing (ICNNSC), Zakopane, 2002
4. Czarnowski, I. & Jedrzejowicz, P. Application of the Parallel Population Learning Algorithm to Training Feed-forward ANN. Proceedings of the Euro-International Symposium on Computational Intelligence (E-ISCI), Kosice, 2002
5. Fahlman, S.E. & Lebiere, C. The Cascade-Corelation Learning Architecture. (ed.) Advances in Neural Information Processing Systems 2, Morgan Kaufmann, 1990
6. Hertz, J., Krogh, A., Palmer, R.G. Introduction to the Theory of Neural Computation. WNT, Warsaw, 1995 (in Polish)
7. Jedrzejowicz, P. Social Learning Algorithm as a Tool for Solving Some Difficult Scheduling Problems. Foundation of Computing and Decision Sciences, 1999, 24: 51-66
8. Kevin, J., Witbrock, L., Witbrock, M.J. Learning to Tell Two Spirals Adapt. Proceedings of the 1988 Connectionist Models Summer School, Morgan Kaufmann, 1998
9. Mangasarian, O.L., Wolberg, W.H. Cancer Diagnosis via Linear Programming. SIAM News, 1990, 23 (5): 1-18
10. Merz, C.J. & Murphy, M. UCI Repository of machine learning databases. [ http://www.ics.uci.edu/~mlearn/MLRepository.html ]. 'rvine, CA: University of California, Department of Information and Computer Science, 1998
11. Michalewicz, Z. Genetic Algorithms + Data Structures = Evolution Programs. Springer, Berlin, 1996

12. Prechelt, L. PROBEN 1 - A Set of Benchmark and Benchmarking Rules for Neural Network Training Algorithm. Technical Report 21/94, Fakultät für Informatik, Universität Karlsruhe, D-76128 Karlsruhe, Germany, Anonymous /pub/papers/techraports/1994/1994-21.ps.z. on ftp.ira.uka.de, 1994

13. Rutkowska, D., Pilinski, M., Rutkowski, L. Neural Networks, Genetic Algorithms and Fuzzy Logic. WN PWN, Warsaw, 1996 (in Polish)

14. Yi Shang & Wah, B.W. A Global Optimization Method for Neural Network Training. Conference of Neural Networks. IEEE Computer, 1996, 29: 45-54

15. Wah, B.W. & Minglun Qian Constrained Formulations for Neural Network Training and Their Applications to Solve the Two-Spiral Problem. Proceedings of the Fifth International Conference on Computer Science and Informatics, 2000, 1:598-601

# Genetic Algorithm Hybridized with Ruin and Recreate Procedure: Application to the Quadratic Assignment Problem

Alfonsas Misevicius

Department of Practical Informatics, Kaunas University of Technology, Studentų St. 50–416D, LT–3031 Kaunas, Lithuania
misevi@soften.ktu.lt

Abstract

Genetic algorithms (GAs) are among the widely used in various areas of computer science, including optimization problems. In this paper, we propose a genetic algorithm hybridized with so-called ruin and recreate (R&R) procedure. We have applied this new hybrid strategy to the well-known combinatorial optimization problem, the quadratic assignment problem (QAP). The results obtained from the experiments on different QAP instances show that the proposed algorithm belongs to the best heuristics for the QAP. The power of this algorithm is also demonstrated by the fact that the new best known solutions were found for several QAP instances.

## 1 Introduction

Genetic algorithms (GAs) are based on the biological process of natural selection. The original concepts of GAs were developed as far back as 1975 by Holland [1]. Many simulations have demonstrated the efficiency of GAs on different optimization problems, among them, bin-packing [2], generalized assignment problem [3], graph partitioning [4], job-shop scheduling problem [5], set covering problem [6], traveling salesman problem [7], vehicle routing [8].

The very basic definitions related to genetic algorithms and optimization problems are as follows. Let $S$ be a set of solutions of a combinatorial optimization problem with objective (fitness) function $f$: $S \rightarrow \mathrm{R}^1$. Furthermore, let $P$ be a subset of $S$. It is referred to as a population, and it is composed of individuals (solutions), $s_1$, $s_2$, ... Without loss of generality, we assume that the objective function seeks a global minimum; hence, individual $s'$ is preferred to individual $s''$ if $f(s') < f(s'')$. Genetic algorithms can then be described as follows. A fraction of $P$ is selected to be parents by use of the selection function, $\phi$: $2^S \rightarrow S \times S$. New solutions are created by combining pairs of parents; this recombination operator, $\psi$: $S \times S$, is known as a crossover. Afterward, a culling operator, $\varphi$: $2^S \rightarrow 2^S$, is applied to the previous generation and the offsprings to determine which individuals survive to form the next generation. In addition, the individuals of the population undergo a mutation, $\zeta: S \rightarrow S$, to prevent a premature loss of diversity within the population.

There exist many variants in the choice of how select, cross (recombine), mutate, and cull the individuals of the population. For example, one can maintain one large population, or several smaller, parallel sub-populations. One can choose to replace all the individuals of the current population with offsprings of every generation, or one can replace only the worst individual by the best offspring. When designing crossover, mutation procedures, many more variations and modifications are available. For the details, the reader is addressed to [9, 10 & 11].

This paper is organized as follows. In Section 2, a hybrid genetic approach is outlined. Section 3 describes the application of the proposed hybrid algorithm to the quadratic assignment problem (QAP). The results of the computational experiments on the various QAP instances are presented in Section 4. Section 5 completes the paper with concluding remarks.

## 2 Genetic Algorithm Hybridized with Ruin and Recreate Procedure

Standard genetic algorithms rely on the concept of biological evolution. State-of-the-art genetic algorithms, often referred to as hybrid genetic algorithms, are based rather on cultural – idea – evolution. While in nature genes are typically not changed during an individual's lifetime, ideas are usually modified before passing to the next generation. In contrast to classical GAs, hybrid GAs incorporate a mechanism for the improvement of the individuals at every generation. An improvement procedure is to be applied to each offspring and/or mutated individual. All the solutions of the initial population are also improved before starting the iterative process of GA. So, instead of (random) solutions, hybrid GA operates with the improved – elite – solutions. This leads to a more effective algorithm when comparing it with a pure genetic algorithm.

In principle, any local search concept based algorithm can be applied at the improvement phase of the hybrid GA. In the simplest case, a greedy (or steepest) descent (also known as "hill climbing") algorithm can be used. Yet, it is possible to apply more sophisticated algorithms, like simulated annealing or tabu search. In this paper, we propose to hybridize the genetic algorithm with a procedure that is based on so-called ruin and recreate (R&R) principle [12].

The heart of the R&R approach, which bears resemblance to a variable neighbourhood search [13], is to obtain better optimization results by a destruction (reconstruction) of an existing solution and a following rebuilding (improvement) procedure. By applying this type of treatment frequently, one seeks for high quality solutions. So, R&R can be thought of as an iterative process of reconstructions and improvements applied to solutions. The advantage of the R&R approach over the well-known random multistart method is that, instead of generating new solutions from scratch, a better idea is to reconstruct (a part of) the current solution: continuing search from this reconstructed solution may allow to escape from a local optimum and to find better solutions.

```
procedure hybrid_genetic_algorithm
  generate (or construct) initial population P
  foreach s∈P do ruin_and_recreate(s,"recreate first")
  repeat // main cycle //
    for c:=1 to C_offspr do begin // cycle of offspring generation and improvement //
      select s′,s″ ∈ P
      s‴ := crossover( s′,s″ )
      ruin_and_recreate( s‴ ,"recreate first")
      P := P ∪ { s‴ }
    end // for //
    update P
    if entropy(P)<threshold then
      foreach s∈P\{s_best} do ruin_and_recreate(s,"ruin first")
  until termination criterion is satisfied
end // hybrid_genetic_algorithm //
```

Figure 1 Template of the hybrid genetic algorithm.
Note. The function "entropy" is described in Section 3.2.5

```
procedure ruin_and_recreate(s,option)
  if option="ruin first" then s := ruin(s)
  s* := recreate(s)
  s := s*
  for q:=1 to Q_RR do begin  // cycle consisting of Q_RR iterations //
    s~ := ruin(s)            // ruin (reconstruct) the current solution (individual) //
    s* := recreate( s~ )     // try to improve the ruined solution //
    if s* is better than s then s := s*
  end // for //
end // ruin_and_recreate //
```

Figure 2 Template of the ruin and recreate procedure

One of the favourable features of the proposed hybrid strategy is that the large population of solutions is not necessary: small size of the population is compensated by high performance of the ruin and recreate procedure. Another distinguishing feature is related to the mutation. As the R&R procedure has a stochastic behaviour, there is no need in mutation operator unless the population undergoes some kind of reconstruction. It takes place when a premature convergence of the algorithm occurs. As a convergence criterion, a measure (threshold) of entropy of the population is used. The templates of both the resulting hybrid GA and the R&R procedure are presented in Figures 1, 2. More thoroughly, we discuss the components of the hybrid genetic algorithm in the next section in the context of the quadratic assignment problem.

# 3 Application to the Quadratic Assignment Problem

## 3.1 The Quadratic Assignment Problem

The quadratic assignment problem is formulated as follows. Let two matrices $\boldsymbol{A} = (a_{ij})_{n\times n}$ and $\boldsymbol{B} = (b_{kl})_{n\times n}$ and the set $\Pi$ of permutations of the integers from 1 to $n$ be given. Find a permutation $\pi = (\pi(1), \pi(2), ..., \pi(n)) \in \Pi$ that minimizes

$$z(\pi) = \sum_{i=1}^{n}\sum_{j=1}^{n} a_{ij} b_{\pi(i)\pi(j)} .$$

The context in which Koopmans and Beckmann [14] first formulated this problem was the facility location problem. In this problem, one is concerned with locating $n$ units on $n$ sites with some physical products flowing between the facilities, and with distances between the sites. The element $a_{ij}$ is the "flow" from unit $i$ to unit $j$, and the element $b_{kl}$ represents the distance between the sites $k$ and $l$. The permutation $\pi = (\pi(1), \pi(2), ..., \pi(n))$ can be interpreted as an assignment of units to sites ($\pi(i)$ denotes the site what unit $i$ is assigned to). Solving the QAP means searching for an assignment $\pi$ that minimizes the "transportation cost" $z$.

An important area of the application of the quadratic assignment problem is computer-aided design (CAD), more precisely, the placement of electronic components into locations (positions) on a board (chip) [15]. Other applications of the QAP are: campus planning [16], hospital layout [17], image processing (formation of grey densities) [18], typewriter keyboard design [19], etc. (see, for example, [20]).

It has been proved that the QAP is NP-hard [21]. Problems of size, say $n>30$, are not, to this date, practically solvable in terms of obtaining exact solutions. Therefore, heuristic approaches have to be used for solving medium- and large-scale QAPs: ant algorithms [22], simulated annealing [23], tabu search [24]. Starting from 1994, several authors applied genetic algorithms to the QAP, first of all, [25, 26, 27 & 28].

## 3.2 A Hybridized Genetic Algorithm for the Quadratic Assignment Problem

All we need to do by creating our genetic algorithm (we will call it GAHRR – Genetic Algorithm Hybridized with Ruin & Recreate procedure) is to design the genetic operators and ruin and recreate procedure as a local improvement procedure. The details of these components (in the context of the quadratic assignment problem) are described below.

### 3.2.1 Initial Population Generation

The initial population $P$ ($P \subset \Pi$) is obtained by generating random permutations that are passed through the improvement (ruin and recreate) procedure – the same one that is used at further phase, i.e. within the genetic operators. The size of the population, $PS$ ($PS=|P|$), depends on the size of problem ($n$), and is relatively small (we tried the sizes in the range $[\lfloor \sqrt{n} \rfloor, 2 \cdot \lfloor \sqrt{n} \rfloor]$).

### 3.2.2 Selection Rule

For the parents selection, we applied a rank based selection rule [28]. In this case, the position, $u$, of the parent (solution) actually selected within the sorted population is determined according to the formula $u = \lfloor v^{\rho} \rfloor$, where $v$ is a uniform real random number from the interval $[1, PS^{1/\rho}]$, where $PS$ is the population size, and $\rho$ is a real number in the interval [1, 2] referred to as a selection factor ($SF$). It is obvious that the larger the value of $SF$, the larger probability of selecting better parents.

### 3.2.3 Crossover Operator

The crossover operator produces an offspring (child) that shares some characteristics from both of his parents. The permutation structure is to be preserved. Our crossover is based on the one due to Tate and Smith [28]. Its very formal description is as follows:

$TSX(\pi_1, \pi_2)$ // Tate & Smith's crossover //
// input: $\pi_1$, $\pi_2$ – parents; output: $o$ – offspring ($\pi_1, \pi_2, o \in \Pi$) //
$\forall i \in \{1, 2, ..., n\}$:
  $o(i)$ := if(randint(1,2)=1, if($\pi_1(i)$ not assigned, $\pi_1(i)$,0), if($\pi_2(i)$ not assigned, $\pi_2(i)$,0)), once $\pi_1(i)$ (or $\pi_2(i)$) is assigned it is no longer considered in future assignments;
$\forall i \in \{1, 2, ..., n\}$:
  if $o(i) = 0$ then $o(i) := j \mid j \in \{k \mid k$ is not assigned$\}$
end // $TSX$ //

Notes. 1. The function if($x$,$y_1$,$y_2$) returns $y_1$ if $x$=TRUE, otherwise it returns $y_2$. 2. The function randint($x$,$y$) returns integer random, uniformly distributed number between $x$ and $y$.

We have slightly enhanced the TSX crossover as described below:

$OTSX(\pi_1, \pi_2)$ // optimized Tate & Smith's crossover //
// input: $\pi_1$, $\pi_2$ – parents; output: $o$ – offspring ($\pi_1, \pi_2, o \in \Pi$) //
$o := \arg\min_{i=1,...,M} z(o_i)$, where $o_i$ is returned by $i$th call of TSX crossover
end // $OTSX$ //

So, only the best child among $M$ children – elite child – is passed through the subsequent improvement procedure. The value of $M$ should not be very large ($0.1n \le M \le n$, for example, $M=0.3n$).

The number of crossovers, i.e. the offsprings created per one generation is controlled by a corresponding parameter, $C_{offspr}$. Usually, $C_{offspr}$ is between 1 and 4 when dealing with small populations.

### 3.2.4 Improvement Procedure: Ruin and Recreate Procedure

Ruin and recreate procedure contains three main components: a solution recreation procedure (local search procedure), a ruin procedure (solution mutation (or reconstruction) procedure), and a candidate acceptance criterion.

Recreation Procedure. In our algorithm, we use the tabu search methodology based algorithm as a recreation procedure, more precisely, a modified version of the robust tabu search algorithm due to Taillard [24].

Let $N$: $\Pi \rightarrow 2^{\Pi}$ be a neighbourhood function that defines for each $\pi \in \Pi$ a set $N(\pi) \subseteq \Pi$ – a set of neighbouring solutions of $\pi$. A $\lambda$-exchange neighbourhood function, $N_\lambda(\pi)$, is defined as follows $N_\lambda(\pi) = \{\pi' \mid \pi' \in \Pi, d(\pi, \pi') \leq \lambda\}$, where $d(\pi, \pi')$ is the "distance" between solutions $\pi$ and $\pi'$: $d(\pi, \pi') = \sum_{i=1}^{n} \operatorname{sgn} |\pi(i) - \pi'(i)|$. For the QAP, the commonly used case is $\lambda = 2$, i.e. the 2-exchange function $N_2$. In this case, a transformation from the current solution $\pi$ to the neighbouring one $\pi'$ can formally be defined by using a special operator – 2-way perturbation, $p_{ij}$ ($i,j = 1, 2, ..., n$): $\Pi \rightarrow \Pi$, which exchanges $i$th and $j$th elements in the current permutation. (Notation $\pi' = \pi \oplus p_{ij}$ means that $\pi'$ is obtained from $\pi$ by applying perturbation $p_{ij}$.) The framework of the local search algorithm can then be described as follows. Initialize tabu list, $\boldsymbol{T} = (t_{ij})_{n \times n}$, and start from an initial solution $\pi$. Continue the following process until a predetermined number of trials is executed: a) find a neighbour $\pi''$ of the current solution $\pi$ in such a way that $\pi'' = \arg\min_{\pi' \in N_2'(\pi)} z(\pi')$, where $N_2'(\pi) = \{\pi' \mid \pi' \in N_2(\pi), (\pi' = \pi \oplus p_{ij} \text{ and } p_{ij} \text{ is not tabu}) \text{ or } z(\pi') < z(\pi''')\}$ ($\pi'''$ is the best so far solution); b) replace the current solution $\pi$ by the neighbour $\pi''$, and use as a starting point for the next trial; c) update the tabu list $\boldsymbol{T}$. The detailed template of the tabu search based recreation procedure for the QAP is presented in Appendix A (Figure A1). Note: the parameter $\alpha$ controls how many recreation trials one has to perform.

Ruin Procedure. A ruin (or mutation) of the current solution is achieved by performing a "move" in the neighbourhood $N_\lambda$, where $\lambda > 2$. This can be modelled by generating $\mu = \lfloor(\lambda+1)/2\rfloor$ sequential elementary perturbations, like $p_{ij}$. Here, the parameter $\mu$ is referred to as a ruin rate ("strength"). We can add more robustness to the R&R procedure if we let vary the parameter $\mu$ in some interval, say $[\mu_{min}, \mu_{max}] \subseteq [2, n]$, during the execution of the algorithm. In our implementation, $\mu$ is varied sequentially within the interval $[\mu_{min}, \mu_{max}]$ starting from $\mu_{min}$: once maximum value $\mu_{max}$ has been reached (or a better locally optimum solution has been found) the value of $\mu$ is dropped to the minimum value $\mu_{min}$, and so on. The detailed template of the ruin procedure is presented in Appendix B (Figure B1).

Note that, for the convenience, the parameters $\beta_{\min}$, $\beta_{\max} \in (0,1]$ are used instead of $\mu_{\min}$, $\mu_{\max}$ respectively ($\mu_{\min} = \max(2, \lfloor\beta_{\min}\cdot n\rfloor)$, $\mu_{\max} = \max(2, \lfloor\beta_{\max}\cdot n\rfloor)$).

Candidate Acceptance Criterion. In our algorithm, we accept only the best locally optimal solution as a candidate for the ruin (mutation). The candidate solution at $q$th iteration is defined according to the following formula $\pi^{(q)} = \text{if}\left(z(\pi^{\bullet}) < z(\pi^{(q-1)}), \pi^{\bullet}, \pi^{(q-1)}\right)$, where $\pi^{(q)}$ is the candidate solution at the current iteration, $\pi^{(q-1)}$ is the solution before the last recreation execution (the best so far solution), and $\pi^{\bullet}$ is the solution after the last recreation execution.

The number of iterations, $Q_{RR}$, plays a role of the termination criterion for the R&R procedure. The number of iterations of the R&R procedure used at the initial population generation (initialization) phase is equal to $R\cdot Q_{RR}$, where $R$ ($R\geq 1$) is a factor (aspect ratio).

### *3.2.5 Updating the Population*

As a standard, updating (culling) of the population takes place each time before going to the next generation. After $k$ ($k = C_{offspr}$) offsprings have been added to the population, its members are sorted (according to the increasing values of the objective function; $k$ solutions with the greatest objective function value are then removed away from the population to keep the size of the population constant. A different kind of the update is performed when the premature convergence of the algorithm is observed. We identify the convergence by means of an entropy measure. The entropy of the population is defined in the following way [25]:

$$E = \sum_{i=1}^{n}\sum_{j=1}^{n} e_{ij} \Big/ n\log n,$$

where $e_{ij} = \begin{cases} 0, m_{ij} = 0 \\ -\frac{m_{ij}}{m}\log\frac{m_{ij}}{m}, \text{otherwise} \end{cases}$, $m$ is the size of the population, and $m_{ij}$ represents the number of times that the unit $i$ is assigned to the site $j$ in the current population.

This normalized entropy takes values between 0 and 1. So, if $E$ is close enough to zero ($E\leq 0.01$), we state that the algorithm has converged – further improvements of the individuals are unlikely. In this case, we update the population in such a way that all the individuals of the population but the best undergo a deep reconstruction (mutation). The R&R procedure with the ruin being performed at the start serves as a reconstruction procedure. In addition, the ruin rate as well as the number of iterations of R&R are slightly increased. After the reconstruction, the algorithm proceeds with the new population in an ordinary way.

The process is continued until the stopping criterion is satisfied, i.e. the algorithm has performed a total number of $N_{gen}$ generations.

# 4 Computational Experiments and Results

We have carried out a number of computational experiments in order to test the performance of the algorithm GAHRR. A wide range of the QAP instances taken from the quadratic assignment problem library QAPLIB [29] were used. The types of the QAP instances that we use are as follows:

(a) randomly generated instances (these instances are randomly generated according to a uniform distribution; in QAPLIB, they are denoted by tai20a, tai25a, tai30a, tai35a, tai40a, tai50a, tai60a, tai80a, tai100a (short notation tai∗a));

(b) real-life like instances (they are generated in such a way that the entries of the data matrices resemble a distribution from real-life problems; the instances are as follows: tai20b, tai25b, tai30b, tai35b, tai40b, tai50b, tai60b, tai80b, tai100b (tai∗b)).

For the comparison, we used the robust tabu search (RTS) algorithm due to Taillard [24], and the genetic hybrid algorithm (GHA) due to Fleurent and Ferland [25]. The first one belongs to the most powerful algorithms for the problems of type (a), whereas the second one is among the best algorithms for the problems of type (b).

As a performance measure, the average deviation from the best known solution is chosen. The average deviation, $\theta_{avg}$, is defined according to the formula $\theta_{avg} = 100(z_{avg} - z_b)/z_b$ [%], where $z_{avg}$ is the average objective function value over $W$ ($W$=1, 2, ...) restarts (i.e. single applications of the algorithm to a problem instance), and $z_b$ is the best known value (BKV) of the objective function. (BKVs are from [29].)

The values of the parameters of the algorithm GAHRR for the particular problem types are presented below:

| Problem types | Parameters | | | | | | | |
|---|---|---|---|---|---|---|---|---|
| | $PS$ | $N_{gen}$ | $C_{offspr}$ | $SF$ | $Q_{RR}$ | $R$ | $\alpha$ | $(\beta_{min}, \beta_{max})$ |
| (a) | $\lfloor\sqrt{n}\rfloor$ | 30 | 1 | 1.1 | 4 | 3 | 10 | $\begin{cases}(0.2, 0.3), n \geq 50\\(0.25, 0.35), 30 \leq n < 50\\(0.3, 0.4), n < 30\end{cases}$ |
| (b) | $2\lfloor\sqrt{n}\rfloor$ | 80 | 4 | 1.7 | 8 | 3 | 0.01 | (0.45, 0.55) |

The parameters of the algorithm GHA are similar to those of GAHRR: the population size, $PS'$ (it is equal to min(100, 2$n$)); the number of generations, $N'_{gen}$; the number of offsprings per generation, $C'_{offspr}$ ($C'_{offspr} = 2$); the selection factor, $SF'$ ($SF'$=2.0); the number of iterations of the improvement procedure, i.e. robust tabu search procedure, $Q'_{RTS}$ (it is chosen to be equal to 4$n$). The same number of iterations is both in initialization phase and in subsequent evolution phase.

The only control parameter of RTS is the number of iterations, $Q_{RTS}$. The value of $Q_{RTS}$ as well as the value of $N'_{gen}$ were chosen in such a way that all the algorithms use approximately the same computation (CPU) time. Some differences of run time are due to non-deterministic behaviour of the tabu search based recreation procedure used in GAHRR. In most cases, they are insignificant and cannot influence the results obtained.

The results of the comparison, i.e. the average deviations from BKV, as well as the approximated CPU times per restart (in seconds) are presented in Tables 1, 2. The deviations are averaged over 10 restarts. CPU times are given for the x86 Family 6 processor. The best values are printed in bold face (in addition, in parenthesis, we give the number of times that BKV is found (if $\theta_{avg}>0$)).

Table 1 Comparison of the algorithms on randomly generated instances

| Instance name | $n$ | BKV | RTS | | GHA | | GAHRR | |
|---|---|---|---|---|---|---|---|---|
| | | | $\theta_{avg}$ | $t$ | $\theta_{avg}$ | $t$ | $\theta_{avg}$ | $t$ |
| tai20a | 20 | 703482 | 0.061 (8) | 3.5 | 0.411 (2) | 3.3 | **0** | 3.2 |
| tai25a | 25 | 1167256 | 0.052 (8) | 8.3 | 0.382 (2) | 7.7 | **0** | 7.4 |
| tai30a | 30 | 1818146 | 0.044 (6) | 14.5 | 0.362 (4) | 13.4 | **0.002** (9) | 12.5 |
| tai35a | 35 | 2422002 | 0.327 (0) | 23 | 0.643 (0) | 21 | **0.163** (5) | 19 |
| tai40a | 40 | 3139370 | 0.556 (0) | 25 | 0.618 (0) | 33 | **0.451** (0) | 25 |
| tai50a | 50 | 4941410 | 0.962 (0) | 52 | 0.871 (0) | 55 | **0.668** (1) | 49 |
| tai60a | 60 | 7208572 | 1.122 (0) | 83 | 1.047 (0) | 86 | **0.910** (0) | 82 |
| tai80a | 80 | 13557864 | 0.825 (0) | 200 | 0.917 (0) | 190 | **0.739** (0) | 190 |
| tai100a | 100 | 21125314 | 0.731 (0) | 430 | 0.967 (0) | 440 | **0.629** (0) | 450 |

Table 2 Comparison of the algorithms on real-life like instances

| Instance name | $n$ | BKV | RTS | | GHA | | GAHRR | |
|---|---|---|---|---|---|---|---|---|
| | | | $\theta_{avg}$ | $t$ | $\theta_{avg}$ | $t$ | $\theta_{avg}$ | $t$ |
| tai20b | 20 | 122455319 | **0** | 3.4 | 0.045 (9) | 4.1 | **0** | 3.1 |
| tai25b | 25 | 344355646 | **0** | 5.9 | **0** | 7.8 | **0** | 5.6 |
| tai30b | 30 | 637117113 | 0.000 (8) | 10 | **0** | 13.5 | **0** | 9.7 |
| tai35b | 35 | 283315445 | **0** | 17 | 0.094 (6) | 22 | **0** | 15 |
| tai40b | 40 | 637250948 | **0** | 25 | **0** | 27 | **0** | 27 |
| tai50b | 50 | 458821517 | 0.114 (4) | 47 | 0.033 (9) | 55 | **0** | 49 |
| tai60b | 60 | 608215054 | 0.125 (2) | 81 | 0.014 (6) | 87 | **0** | 82 |
| tai80b | 80 | 818415043 | 0.394 (0) | 185 | 0.353 (2) | 190 | **0.001** (5) | 195 |
| tai100b | 100 | 1185996137 | 0.279 (0) | 390 | 0.045 (3) | 370 | **0.015** (3) | 410 |

It turns out that the efficiency of the algorithms depends on the type of the problems (instances) being solved. For the randomly generated instances (instance family tai*a), the results are not as good as for real-life like instances (instance family tai*b). Nevertheless, the results from Tables 1, 2 show promising efficiency of the proposed hybrid genetic algorithm. In most cases, the algorithm GAHRR appears to be superior to other two efficient algorithms. For a number of instances, for example, tai20a, tai25a, tai30a, tai80b, GAHRR produces much more better results than other algorithms (the record difference in results was achieved for the instance tai80b (see Table 2)).

The performance of the algorithm GAHRR can be improved either by a more accurate tuning of the control parameters (we call this direction "the parameter improvement based direction"), or modifying some components of the algorithm ("the algorithm's idea improvement based direction") (Some directions of the enhancement of the algorithm's idea are outlined in Section 5.) The results obtained by using different values of the parameters $PS$, $C_{offspr}$, $SF$ and $Q_{RR}$ are presented in Table 3. The values of the parameters are as follows:

$PS=2\cdot\lfloor\sqrt{n}\rfloor$, $C_{offspr}=\lfloor 0.25\cdot PS\rfloor$, $SF=1.7$, $Q_{RR}=\lfloor 0.1n\rfloor$ (column a);

$PS=3\cdot\lfloor\sqrt{n}\rfloor$, $C_{offspr}=\lfloor 0.25\cdot PS\rfloor$, $SF=1.7$, $Q_{RR}=\lfloor 0.1n\rfloor$ (column b);

$PS=2\cdot\lfloor\sqrt{n}\rfloor$, $C_{offspr}=\lfloor 0.5\cdot PS\rfloor$, $SF=1.7$, $Q_{RR}=\lfloor 0.1n\rfloor$ (column c);

$PS=2\cdot\lfloor\sqrt{n}\rfloor$, $C_{offspr}=\lfloor 0.25\cdot PS\rfloor$, $SF=2.0$, $Q_{RR}=\lfloor 0.1n\rfloor$ (column d);

$PS=2\cdot\lfloor\sqrt{n}\rfloor$, $C_{offspr}=\lfloor 0.25\cdot PS\rfloor$, $SF=1.7$, $Q_{RR}=\lfloor 0.15n\rfloor$ (column e).

$R$, $\alpha$, $\beta_{min}$, $\beta_{max}$ remain unchanged:

$$R=\begin{cases}2, n\le 30\\ 3, 30<n\le 80\\ 4, n=100\end{cases},\ \alpha=\begin{cases}0.1, n\le 25\\ 0.2, 25<n\le 40\\ 0.3, 40<n\le 80\\ 0.5, n=100\end{cases},\ \beta_{min}=0.45,\ \beta_{max}=0.55.$$

Table 3 Computational results of GAHRR.
Note. $t_{avg}$ denotes the average CPU time (in seconds) needed to find the best known solution under condition that all the 10 restarts of GAHRR succeeded in finding the best known solution

| **Instance name** | $t_{avg}$ | | | | |
|---|---|---|---|---|---|
| | **(a)** | **(b)** | **(c)** | **(d)** | **(e)** |
| tai20b | **0.05** | 0.06 | **0.05** | 0.06 | 0.06 |
| tai25b | 0.24 | 0.22 | **0.2** | 0.26 | 0.28 |
| tai30b | 0.6 | 0.6 | 0.55 | **0.45** | 0.65 |
| tai35b | 2.2 | 2.4 | **1.7** | 6.6 | 2.3 |
| tai40b | 1.5 | 2.0 | **1.3** | 1.4 | 1.8 |
| tai50b | 6.6 | 8.9 | **6.5** | 7.0 | 13.0 |
| tai60b | 25.0 | 21.0 | 22.0 | **20.0** | 28.0 |
| tai80b | 148.0 | 176.0 | **130.0** | 212.0 | 310.0 |
| tai100b | **690.0** | 990.0 | 800.0 | >3600 | 1800.0 |

Increasing the population size, as expected, does not improve the results, i.e. the average time needed to search for the best known solution. Also, the variation of the parameter *SF* does not influence the quality of the results considerably, except the instance tai100b. Somewhat unexpected results were obtained by modifying the number of iterations $Q_{RR}$ – as $Q_{RR}$ increases, the average search time increases as well. One of the reasons for this might be a "stagnation phenomenon" of the ruin and recreation process when the number of iterations is increased. A better idea, therefore, is to increase the number of offsprings generated per generation. This leads to very promising results as shown in Table 3 (column c). We see that, for the small and medium instances, GAHRR finds the best known solutions extremely quickly. For the large instances, however, "stagnations" can be observed. Nevertheless, GAHRR was successful in finding a number of new best solutions for the QAP instances corresponding to the elaboration of grey frames. Instances of this type are described in [18 & 30] under the name grey_$n_1$_$n_2$_$m$, where $m$ is the density of the grey ($0 \le m \le n = n_1 \cdot n_2$), and $n_1 \cdot n_2$ is the size of a frame. New solutions for the instance family grey_16_16_* are presented in Table 4.

Table 4 New best known solutions for grey density problems

| Instance name | $n$ | Previous best known value[a] | New best known value |
|---|---|---|---|
| grey_16_16_26 | 256 | 2426606 | 2426298 |
| grey_16_16_45 | 256 | 8677670 | 8674910 |
| grey_16_16_46 | 256 | 9134172 | 9129192 |
| grey_16_16_77 | 256 | 29928042 | 29895152 |
| grey_16_16_83 | 256 | 35447648 | 35444806 |
| grey_16_16_84 | 256 | 36409340 | 36397376 |
| grey_16_16_86 | 256 | 38393344 | 38376438 |
| grey_16_16_90 | 256 | 42621464 | 42608826 |

[a] comes from [30].

# 5 Concluding Remarks

The method that has been widely applied to many fields of computer science, among them optimization problems, is the genetic approach. In this paper, we introduce a new hybrid genetic strategy for a difficult optimization problem, the quadratic assignment problem.

The central idea is that the use of the genetic algorithm succeeds in search only if it disposes of an efficient and robust local search procedure. So, we propose to hybridize the genetic algorithm with a very promising procedure – the ruin and recreate procedure. The most important features of this approach are as follows:

a) a small population is enough to seek for high quality solutions, b) the standard mutation operator is substituted by the ruin and recreate procedure, c) mutations take place only if the entropy of the population approaches zero. All these features coupled with additional modifications of the genetic operators resulted in an algorithm (GAHRR) that allowed to achieve very good results with small amount of the computation time. The results from the comparison with the robust tabu search algorithm and other efficient genetic algorithm show that the new hybrid algorithm produces better results than other two algorithms, which are among the most powerful heuristics for the QAP. The outstanding performance of GAHRR is also corroborated by the fact that the new best known solutions were found for the largest available QAPs (so-called problems of grey densities).

There are several possible directions of the modification of the proposed hybrid algorithm: a) improving the performance of the existing components of the algorithm; b) trying to use two or more sub-populations (instead of the single population) and allowing some sort of migrations of the individuals between sub-populations; c) implementing other crossover operators, like a distance preserving or cycle crossover; d) introducing additional components, for example, so-called "don't look bit" mechanism.

It might also be worthy applying the genetic algorithm presented above for other combinatorial optimization problems, like the traveling salesman problem or the graph-partitioning problem.

## Acknowledgements

Author is grateful to Prof. E. Taillard for providing the code of the robust tabu search algorithm. He also would like to thank Prof. C. Fleurent for the paper that helped coding the hybrid genetic algorithm.

### References

1. Holland JH. Adaptation in natural and artificial systems, University of Michigan Press, Ann Arbor, MI, 1975
2. Falkenauer E, Delchambre A. A genetic algorithm for bin packing and line balancing. Proceedings of the IEEE international conference on robotics and automation (RA92), Nice, France, 1992
3. Chu PC, Beasley J.E. A genetic algorithm for the generalized assignment problem. Comput Oper Res 1997; 24:17–23
4. Bui TN, Moon BR. Genetic algorithm and graph partitioning. IEEE Trans Comput 1996; 45:841–855
5. Yamada T, Nakano R. A genetic algorithm applicable to large-scale job-shop problems. In: Männer R, Manderick B (eds) Parallel problem solving from nature 2, North-Holland, Amsterdam, 1992, pp 281–290
6. Beasley JE, Chu PC. A genetic algorithm for the set covering problem. Eur J Oper Res 1996; 94:392–404
7. Merz P, Freisleben B. Genetic local search for the TSP: new results. Proceedings of the 1997 IEEE international conference on evolutionary computation, 1997, pp 159–164

8. Blanton J (Jr), Wainwright RL. Multiple vehicle routing with time and capacity constraints using genetic algorithms. In: Forrest S (ed) Proceedings of 5th international conference on genetic algorithms, Morgan Kaufmann, San Mateo, CA, 1993
9. Davis L. Handbook of genetic algorithms, Van Nostrand, New York, 1991
10. Goldberg DE. Genetic algorithms in search, optimization and machine learning, Addison-Wesley, Reading, MA, 1989
11. Mühlenbein H. Genetic algorithms. In: Aarts E, Lenstra JK (eds) Local search in combinatorial optimization, Wiley, Chichester, 1997, pp 137–171
12. Schrimpf G, Schneider K, Stamm-Wilbrandt H, Dueck V. Record breaking optimization results using the ruin and recreate principle. J Comput Phys 2000; 159:139–171
13. Mladenović N, Hansen P. Variable neighbourhood search. Comput Oper Res 1997; 24:1097–1100
14. Koopmans T, Beckmann M. Assignment problems and the location of economic activities. Econometrica 1957; 25:53–76
15. Hu TC, Kuh ES (ed). VLSI circuit layout: theory and design, IEEE Press, New York, 1985
16. Dickey JW, Hopkins JW. Campus building arrangement using TOPAZ. Transp Res 1972; 6:59–68
17. Elshafei AN. Hospital layout as a quadratic assignment problem. Oper Res Q 1977; 28:167–179
18. Taillard E. Comparison of iterative searches for the quadratic assignment problem. Location Sci 1995; 3: 87–105
19. Burkard RE, Offermann J. Entwurf von schreibmaschinentastaturen mittels quadratischer zuordnungsprobleme. Z Oper Res 1977; 21:121–132
20. Burkard RE, Çela E, Pardalos PM, Pitsoulis L. The quadratic assignment problem. In: Du DZ, Pardalos PM (eds) Handbook of combinatorial optimization, Vol.3, Kluwer, 1998, pp 241–337
21. Sahni S, Gonzalez T. P-complete approximation problems. J ACM 1976; 23:555–565
22. Gambardella LM, Taillard E, Dorigo M. Ant colonies for the quadratic assignment problems. J Oper Res Soc 1999; 50:167–176
23. Bölte A, Thonemann UW. Optimizing simulated annealing schedules with genetic programming. Eur J Oper Res 1996; 92:402–416
24. Taillard E. Robust taboo search for the QAP. Parallel Comput 1991; 17:443–455
25. Fleurent C, Ferland JA. Genetic hybrids for the quadratic assignment problem. In: Pardalos PM, Wolkowicz H (eds) Quadratic assignment and related problems. DIMACS series in discrete mathematics and theoretical computer science, Vol.16, AMS, Providence, 1994, pp 173–188
26. Lim MH, Yuan Y, Omatu S. Efficient genetic algorithms using simple genes exchange local search policy for the quadratic assignment problem. Comput Optim Appl 2000; 15:249–268
27. Merz P, Freisleben B. A genetic local search approach to the quadratic assignment problem. Proceedings of the seventh international conference on genetic algorithms (ICGA'97), Morgan Kaufmann, 1997, pp 465–472
28. Tate DM, Smith AE. A genetic approach to the quadratic assignment problem. Comput Oper Res 1995; 1:73–83
29. Burkard RE, Karisch S, Rendl F. QAPLIB – a quadratic assignment problem library. J Glob Optim 1997; 10:391–403
30. Taillard E, Gambardella LM. Adaptive memories for the quadratic assignment problem. Tech. report IDSIA-87-97, Lugano, Switzerland, 1997

# Appendix A

```
function recreate(π,n,α) // recreation procedure (based on tabu search) for the QAP //
  // π – the current permutation, n – problem size, α – n-factor (α>0) //
  τ := max(1,⌊α·n⌋)            // τ – the number of iterations //
  h_min := 0.4n, h_max := 0.6n  // lower and higher tabu sizes //
  π* := π                      // π* denotes the best so far permutation //
  for i:=1 to n−1 do for j:=i+1 to n do store the objective function difference δ_ij=Δz(π,i,j)
  T:=0
  h := randint(h_min,h_max)
  i:=1, j:=1, k:=1, K:=n(n−1)/2 // K – size of the neighbourhood N_2 //
  improved := FALSE
  while (k≤τ) or improved do begin // main cycle of the recreation //
    δ_min := ∞ // δ_min – minimum difference in the objective function values //
    for l:=1 to K do begin
      i := if(j < n,i,if(i < n − 1,i + 1,1)) ,  j := if(j < n, j + 1,i + 1)
      tabu := if(t_ij≥k,TRUE,FALSE), aspired := if(z(π)+δ_ij<z(π*),TRUE,FALSE)
      if ((δ_ij< δ_min) and not tabu) or aspired then begin δ_min := δ_ij, u := i, v := j end // if //
    end // for l //
    if δ_min < ∞ then begin
      π := π ⊕ p_uv   // replace the current permutation by the new one //
      if z(π)<z(π*) then π* := π
      improved := if(δ_uv<0,TRUE,FALSE)
      for l:=1 to n−1 do for m:=l+1 to n do update the difference δ_lm
      t_uv := k+h
      if k mod 2h_max = 0 then h := randint(h_min,h_max)
    end   // if //
  end      // while //
  return π*
end // recreate //
```

Figure A1 Template of the recreation procedure for the QAP

# Appendix B

```
function ruin(π,n,μ) // ruin (mutation) procedure for the QAP //
  // π – the current permutation, n – problem size, μ – ruin rate (2≤μ≤n) //
  π* := π, new_local_optimum := FALSE
  for k:=1 to μ do begin // main cycle of the ruin procedure //
    i := randint(1,n), j := randint(1,n−1)
    if i≤j then j := j+1
    π := π ⊕ p_ij   // replace the current permutation by the new one //
    if z(π)<z(π*) then begin
      π* := π, new_local_optimum := TRUE
    end   // if //
  end      // for k //
  if new_local_optimum then π := π*
  return π
end // ruin //
```

Figure B1 Template of the ruin procedure for the QAP

# ECCLAT: a New Approach of Clusters Discovery in Categorical Data

Nicolas Durand
IP and Network Laboratory, France Telecom R&D Caen
France

Bruno Crémilleux
GREYC CNRS-UMR 6072, University of Caen
France

**Abstract**

In this paper we present a new approach for the discovery of meaningful clusters from large categorical data (which is an usual situation, e.g., web data analysis). Our method called ECCLAT (for Extraction of Clusters from Concepts LATtice) extracts a subset of concepts from the frequent closed itemsets lattice, using an evaluation measure. ECCLAT is generic because it allows to build approximate clustering and discover meaningful clusters with slight overlapping. The approach is illustrated on a classical data set and on web data analysis.

## 1 Introduction

Discovering the structure and relationships within data is an important problem in many application areas. For instance, in analyzing market basket data, it is interesting to find clusters (i.e. groups) of customers having similar characteristics (or close to each other) while customers in different groups are dissimilar, or to find groups of similar products. On the other hand, for some years, there has been a considerable interest in web data analysis in order to create new applications and services (e.g. clusters of user accesses, clustering of web sessions). In such contexts, it is important to have knowledge discovery methods on categorical data that are both relevant and efficient to tackle the enormous amount of data. In this paper, we focus on a method to discover meaningful clusters from large categorical data sets. We will see below that this approach is quite different from usual clustering techniques. In the following discussion, each data record is called an *example* (or a *transaction* in the data mining context) and is described by *attributes*.

Let us recall that the general meaning of clustering is decomposing or partitioning examples into groups so that the examples in one group are similar to each other and are as different as possible from the examples in other groups.

The conceptual classification methods [4, 9, 19] produce clusters of examples described by categorical attributes. They do not produce directly a clustering. Indeed, these methods create a hierarchy of concepts, generally represented by a lattice [11]. Every concept can be seen as a cluster with its properties (i.e. items) and examples. Even if the number of concepts is smaller than the number of all combinations of items, this number remains very high in real-world applications. We will see in Section 3 the KDD's results (the frequency [2] and the efficiency to extract condensed representations like frequent closed itemsets [3, 20, 22]). Unfortunately, the number of concepts remains high and the hierarchy can not be used nor presented to an expert. Nevertheless, in Section 3, we will show that such clusters can provide a starting point to get a clustering. Furthermore, in many practical applications like web mining, this discovery of meaningful clusters (and not necessarily a clustering) may be of great help. For instance, in a clustering of web pages, it is understandable and useful to obtain a page in two (or more) clusters in order to retrieve it from several kind of queries. In fact, it corresponds to several points of view to classify pages. These clusters can also be used to browse and follow new paths through a hyper-document [5]. The situation is analogous to the discovery of visitor profiles or pre-fetching: several distinct groups (or clusters) may have overlaps between their interests. In the medical area, such meaningful clusters can be used to search for prognostic factors [7].

In this paper, we propose an efficient method to produce a set of clusters from a large set of categorical data with a minimum overlapping ("approximate clustering") or a slight overlapping to catch all the similarities between examples. The behavior of the method is parametrized by the user. Clusters are a subset of concepts from the frequent closed itemsets lattice and are selected according to an evaluation measure.

In the next section, we present related work. In Section 3, we introduce the minimal properties required for discovering interesting clusters from large databases. We will see that the frequent closed itemsets are relevant candidates to be clustered. In Section 4, starting from the frequent closed itemsets (seen as clusters), we propose a method called ECCLAT (for Extraction of Clusters from Concepts LATtice) to select the most interesting concepts gathering similar examples. ECCLAT is able to build a set of clusters with a minimum overlapping or a slight overlapping. In the latter case, the clusters which will be used, will depend on the point of view adopted. In Section 5, we give practical uses of ECCLAT to produce clusters and clustering from categorical data and logs of a proxy server. Our conclusions are presented in Section 6.

## 2 Related Work

The clustering methods developed in the literature can be identified in three types [15]: those based on an attempt to find the optimal partition into a specified number of clusters (for instance, the standard $K$-means method), those based on a hierarchical attempt to discover cluster structure (like the centroid-based agglomerative hierarchical clustering), and those based on a probabilistic model for the underlying clusters (there is an assumed probability model for each component cluster). Some methods have been developed to handle categorical data [10, 12, 14].

Usual criterion functions yield satisfactory results for numeric attributes but are not appropriate when examples include categorical attributes. It is not easy to define distances between values of categorical attributes [6]. The most common way of adapting such measures is to count the overlap of attributes having same values in two examples [18]. This technique may fail to capture the complexity and subtlety of the problem domain. For instance, Guha et al. [12] show that large clusters can be split even though examples in the cluster are well connected. There are several commonly used similarity measures such as the Cosine and the Jaccard similarity coefficients used for document clustering. Nevertheless, these measures have drawbacks. For instance, the Jaccard coefficient fails to capture the natural clustering of not so well-separated examples described with categorical attributes [12].

Among other things, due to the development of web usage mining (e. g., to identify strong correlations among user interests by grouping their navigation paths), there is a tendency for clustering with categorical attributes and recent research in Knowledge Discovery in Databases (KDD) revisits this question. More precisely, two main families of clustering methods based on association rules exist [1]. Association rules represent something like "It is frequent that when properties $A_1$ and $A_2$ are true within an example, then property $A_3$ tends to be true. As usual in this community, we refer to an attribute-value a pair as an *item* (for instance, `country = 'England'`).

Han et al. [13] present a method of association rules hypergraph k-partitioning. It takes a set of association rules and declares the items in the rules to be vertices, and the rules themselves to be hyperedges. Since each association rule has a direction, the algorithm combines all rules with the same set of items, and uses an average of the confidence of the individual rules as the weight for a hyperedge. Clusters are then found by a hypergraph partitioning method [16]. A clustering of items is obtained, but examples are not straightforwardly ranked into clusters. Ronkainen [21] defines similarities between items in large data sets to form hierarchies of clusters of items using agglomerative techniques. This family of methods produces a clustering of items and it may not be easy to rank examples within clusters.

So, the second family of methods starts by building a partition of examples. Wang et al. [24] suggest a clustering algorithm which groups examples in order to minimize intra-cluster and inter-cluster costs. Typically, an intra-cluster cost measures differences between elements within the cluster and an inter-cluster cost indicates the duplication of items among different clusters. This strategy gives a partition of the examples, but it is not able to derive easily a characterization of each cluster.

# 3 Understanding Required Properties for Clusters

In this section, we present the minimal properties required for discovering interesting clusters and how these properties are taken into account in large databases.

### 3.1 Concepts Lattice

Let $\mathcal{D} = (\mathcal{T}, \mathcal{I}, \mathcal{R})$ be a data mining context, $\mathcal{T}$ a set of examples (i. e. transactions), $\mathcal{I}$ a set of items (denoted by capital letters), and $\mathcal{R} \subseteq \mathcal{T} \times \mathcal{I}$ is a binary relation between examples and items. In the following, we use the term of *transaction* instead of *example* because it is the most common term in KDD. Each couple $(t, i) \in \mathcal{R}$ denotes the fact that the transaction $t$ is related to the item $i$. A transactional database is a finite and non empty multi-set of transactions. Table 1 provides an example of a transactional database consisting of 8 transactions (each one identified by its Id) and 9 items denoted $A \ldots I$. This table is used as support for the examples in the rest of the paper. An itemset is a subset of $\mathcal{I}$ (note that we use a string notation for sets, e.g., $AB$ for $\{A, B\}$). A transaction $t$ supports an itemset $X$ iff $X \subseteq t$.

| Id | Items |
|---|---|
| 1 | $A$ $B$ $C$ |
| 2 | $A$ $B$ $C$ |
| 3 | $A$ $B$ $C$ |
| 4 | $D$ $E$ |
| 5 | $D$ $E$ $H$ |
| 6 | $A$ $D$ $E$ $F$ $G$ $H$ |
| 7 | $A$ $F$ $G$ $I$ |
| 8 | $H$ $I$ |

Table 1: A transactional database

Given $\mathcal{D}$, there is a unique ordered set which describes the inherent lattice structure defining natural groupings and relationships among the transactions and their items. This structure is known as a concepts lattice or Galois lattice [11][25]. Each element of the lattice is a couple $(T, I)$ composed of a set of transactions and an itemset. Each couple (named *concept* by Wille [25]) must be a complete couple with respect to $\mathcal{R}$, which means that the following two properties (noted $f$ and $g$) are satisfied. For $T \subseteq \mathcal{T}$ and $I \subseteq \mathcal{I}$, we have:

$$f(T) = \{i \in \mathcal{I} | \forall t \in T, (t, i) \in \mathcal{R}\}$$
$$g(I) = \{t \in \mathcal{T} | \forall i \in I, (t, i) \in \mathcal{R}\}$$

$f(T)$ associates with $T$, items common to all transactions $t \in T$, and $g(I)$ associates with $I$, transactions related to all items $i \in I$. In other words, $T$ is the largest set of transactions described by the items found in $I$, and symmetrically, $I$ is the largest set of items common to the transactions supporting $I$. For instance, in Table 1, the couple composed of transactions 1, 2 and 3 on one side and the items $ABC$ on the other side is a concept of the lattice whereas there is no couple composed of transactions 1, 2 (since transaction 3 shares the same items as transactions 1 and 2). The idea of maximally extending the sets is formalized by the mathematical notion of *closure* in ordered sets and the operators $h = f \circ g$ and $h' = g \circ f$ are the Galois closure operators.

The idea of maximally extending the sets is on the core to highlight meaningful clusters. Indeed, for a group of transactions, we prefer to simply produce the single itemset which is composed of the maximal number of items shared by the group. The key point is to capture the maximum amount of similarity among the data. The next section defines the notion of closed itemsets and shows that only frequent closed itemsets are relevant in the discovery of meaningful clusters.

## 3.2 Frequent Closed Itemsets

Let $X$ be an itemset. $X$ is a closed itemset iff $h(X) = X$. In other words, a closed itemset is a maximal set of items (with respect to set inclusion) shared by a set of transactions. Then, a candidate cluster is a concept of the closed itemsets lattice and is composed of an itemset $X$ and its transactions $g(X)$.

In our example (see Table 1), $ABC$ is a closed itemset because it is the maximum set of items shared by transactions containing at least $ABC$. On the contrary, $AB$ is not a closed itemset since it is not a maximal group of items common to the data: all transactions having the items $AB$ also get the item $C$. In other words, we can add item $C$ to $AB$ without decreasing its frequency.

The frequency of $X$ is $\mathcal{F}(X) = |g(X)|$ (where as usual $|\ldots|$ denotes the cardinality of a set). Note that we use here the absolute frequency (a number of examples $\leq |\mathcal{T}|$) instead of the relative frequency $|g(X)|/|\mathcal{T}|$ in $[0, 1]$. An itemset $X$ is *frequent* if its frequency is at least the frequency threshold $minfr$ fixed by the user. For the following, $X$ denotes a frequent closed itemset, and $L$ the set of the frequent closed itemsets. The frequency is fundamental to extract reliable clusters. It allows to take into account the "importance" (in term of "weight") of a candidate cluster and discard clusters which do not rely on sound relationships within data. A cluster with too few transactions would not be kept by a user. From large databases, there are efficient algorithms [3, 20, 22] to compute the frequent closed itemsets and give the associated transactions.

Let us come back to our example (Table 1). If we set *minfr* to 2, $DE$ is frequent because its frequency is 3 (transactions 4, 5 and 6 contain $DE$) and $DEF$ is not frequent (its frequency is 1 since only transaction 6 contains $DEF$). Seven frequent closed itemsets are extracted from Table 1 (Table 2 shows these frequent closed itemsets, noted FCI, with their frequencies).

These two points (the capture of the maximum amount of similarity - i.e. closed itemsets - and the notion of frequency) are the basis of the method of selection of meaningful clusters that we present below.

| FCI | Transactions | Homogeneity | Concentration | Interestingness |
|---|---|---|---|---|
| I | 7 8 | 0.333 | 0.416 | 0.375 |
| H | 5 6 8 | 0.272 | 0.344 | 0.308 |
| AFG | 6 7 | 0.6 | 0.266 | 0.433 |
| DE | 4 5 6 | 0.545 | 0.511 | 0.528 |
| ABC | 1 2 3 | 1 | 0.5 | 0.75 |
| A | 1 2 3 6 7 | 0.263 | 0.406 | 0.334 |
| DEH | 5 6 | 0.666 | 0.266 | 0.466 |

Table 2: Interestingness of frequent closed itemsets (FCI)

# 4 ECCLAT: Extraction of Clusters from Concepts LATtice

Starting from the frequent closed itemsets (seen as clusters), we propose here a method, based on the definition of a cluster evaluation measure, to select the most interesting concepts gathering similar transactions.

## 4.1 Cluster Evaluation Measure

As we have seen, a relevant cluster has to be as homogeneous as possible and should gather "enough" transactions. Translated into the usual clustering framework, it means that we have to maximize the intra-cluster similarity (which we call *homogeneity*) and minimize the inter-clusters similarity. We use a *concentration* measure to limit the overlapping of transaction's between clusters (a relevant cluster should concentrate some transactions). We will see that a slight overlapping may be understandable and useful in some applications.

Let us start by defining homogeneity and concentration. For homogeneity, we want to favor clusters having many items shared by many transactions. Homogeneity of a cluster $X$ is computed from its size, $\mathcal{F}(X)$ (i.e. its number of transactions) and a divergence measure. The *divergence* is the number of items not in $X$, for each transaction of $g(X)$.

$$homogeneity(X) = \frac{\mathcal{F}(X) \times |X|}{divergence(X) + (\mathcal{F}(X) \times |X|)}$$

where $divergence(X) = \sum_{t \in g(X)} |t - X|$.

We have $0 \leq homogeneity(X) \leq 1$. If a cluster is pure (i.e. $\forall t \in g(X)$ $f(t) = X$), its divergence is equal to 0, and its homogeneity equals 1. The more a cluster supports transactions with items not belonging to $X$, the more its homogeneity tends towards 0. Let us remark that the homogeneity of a cluster $X$ depends only on $X$ and can be computed simultaneously to $X$.

Following our previous example, Table 2 gives all frequent closed itemsets with their transactions, homogeneity and concentration measures.

We have $homogeneity(ABC) = (3 \times 3)/((0+0+0)+(3 \times 3)) = 1$: all items of each transaction supporting $ABC$ belong to $ABC$. For $DE$, $homogeneity(DE) = (3 \times 2)/((0+1+4)+(3 \times 2)) = 0.545$: transaction 5 has an item which diverges (i.e. does not belong to the closed $DE$) and four items diverge for transaction 6.

For concentration, we want to favor clusters having transactions appearing the least in the whole set of clusters. Concentration limits the overlapping of transactions between selected clusters. Concentration of a cluster $X$ is defined by taking into account the number of clusters where each transaction appears.

$$concentration(X) = \frac{1}{|g(X)|} \times \sum_{t \in g(X)} \frac{1}{\mathcal{F}'(t)}$$

where $\mathcal{F}'(t)$ is the number of clusters where $t$ occurs (i.e. absolute frequency of $t$ in $L$).

We have $0 < concentration(X) \leq 1$. If all transactions $g(X)$ occur only in $X$, then $concentration(X) = 1$. The more frequent are the transactions of $g(X)$ in the whole set of clusters, the more $concentration(X)$ tends towards 0.

In our example, we have $concentration(ABC) = 1/3 \times (1/2+1/2+1/2) = 0.5$ (each transaction supporting $ABC$ belongs to two closed frequent itemsets). For $DE$, $concentration(DE) = 1/3 \times (1/1+1/3+1/5) = 0.511$. Transaction 4 only supports the closed itemset $DE$ while transaction 5 supports three closed itemsets and transaction 6 supports five closed itemsets.

Finally, we define the *interestingness* of a cluster as the average of its homogeneity and concentration. We have $0 \leq interestingness(X) \leq 1$.

$$interestingness(X) = \frac{homogeneity(X) + concentration(X)}{2}$$

We have $interestingness(ABC) = (1+0.5)/2 = 0.75$ (the most interesting cluster in our example) and $interestingness(DE) = (0.545+0.511)/2 = 0.528$.

The idea is to select clusters with high interestingness and the next section presents an algorithm for this task.

## 4.2 Clusters Procedure: Selection Algorithm

We use the interestingness defined above to select clusters from the frequent closed itemsets lattice. An innovative feature of ECCLAT is its ability to produce a clustering with a minimum overlapping between clusters (which we call "*approximate clustering*") or a set of clusters with a slight overlapping. This functionality depends on the value of a parameter called $M$. $M$ is an integer corresponding to a number of transactions not yet classified that a new selected cluster must classify. If $minfr$ is low, all transactions appear at least in one frequent closed itemset. So with $M = 1$, we assure to classify all transactions in the selected cluster. Nevertheless, a slight overlapping between clusters may appear. $M$ should be set near 1 if we are interested in discovering meaningful clusters. The more the value of $M$ increases, the more the overlapping decreases but some transactions may not belong to any cluster. We refer to these unclustered transactions as *trash* (i.e. remaining transactions are grouped in a trash cluster). Experimental results (see Section 5) show that the choice of a value of $M$ near $minfr$ performs good results in approximate clustering.

The sketch of the algorithm is the following. First, the interestingness of each cluster of $L$ is computed ($L$ is the set of the frequent closed itemsets, see Section 3.2). The cluster having the highest interestingness is selected. Then as long as there are transactions to classify (i.e. which do not belong to any selected cluster) and clusters remain, we select the cluster having the highest interestingness and containing at least $M$ transactions not yet classified.

The results of the method are linked to the value of $M$. Let us illustrate these different behaviors with our example. Let us start with $M = 1$. The cluster which has the highest interestingness (see Table 2) is $ABC$, so it is selected. Transactions 1, 2 and 3 are classified. Then cluster $DE$ is chosen and transactions 4, 5 and 6 belong to this cluster. Transactions 7 and 8 remain. Cluster $DEH$ is skipped because neither transaction 7 nor transaction 8 supports it. Then cluster $AFG$ is selected because it classifies transaction 7. Transaction 8 is the only remaining one. Finally, cluster $I$ is selected. All transactions are classified in four clusters. We get the following overlapping: transaction 6 is both in $DE$ and $AFG$ and transaction 7 belongs to $AFG$ and $I$. Intuitively, when we observe transactions 6 and 7 (see Table 1), there is no sound reason to classify them in one cluster or the other. Note that item $A$ appears in two clusters.

With $M = 2$, we get clusters $ABC$, $DE$ and $I$. $AFG$ is not selected because it only classifies one remaining transaction. There is no overlapping and we obtain a partition. Note that here $M = minfr$.

With $M = 3$, only two clusters are selected ($ABC$ and $DE$) and a trash cluster is built with transactions 7 and 8.

From the computational point of view, it is obvious that the lower $minfr$, the more there are frequent closed itemsets and more time is required. With regard to $M$, the higher $M$, the number of constraints that needs to be checked between clusters increases and this reduces system efficiency.

# 5 Experiments

We have tested our method on the well-known data set Mushroom[1], and on proxy server logs coming from France Telecom R&D.

## 5.1 Clustering the Mushroom Data Set

The Mushroom data set includes 8124 transactions and 116 items. Each transaction has a class value (`edible` or `poisonous`). For experimentation purposes, the class is ignored, but it is used afterwards for the assessment of

[1] http://www.ics.uci.edu/~mlearn/MLRepository.html

the results. To simplify presentation of results, we use a relative value (i.e. percentage) for $minfr$ and $M$. For instance, since the total number of data is 8124, $minfr = 5\%$ means 406 transactions using an absolute frequency ($5\% = 0.05 \simeq 406/8124$).

| $minfr$ % | No. of frequent closed itemsets | No. of selected clusters | ratio % |
|---|---|---|---|
| 50 | 44 | 10 | 22.7 |
| 40 | 113 | 13 | 11.5 |
| 30 | 301 | 21 | 6.9 |
| 20 | 888 | 30 | 3.4 |
| 10 | 3581 | 61 | 1.7 |
| 5 | 9738 | 144 | 1.5 |

Table 3: Number of selected clusters according to the $minfr$ value (Mushroom, $M = 1$)

Table 3 shows the number of closed frequent itemsets and the number of selected clusters for different values of $minfr$. In order to discover all meaningful clusters, we set $M$ to 1. The number of selected clusters is much lower than the number of frequent closed itemsets. When $minfr$ decreases, we see that the number of selected clusters does not increase as much as the number of frequent closed itemsets (in other words, ratio decreases).

| M | No. of selected clusters | No. of transactions in trash | No. of common transactions (avg.) |
|---|---|---|---|
| 1 (0.01%) | 144 | 0 | 40 |
| 101 (1.25%) | 43 | 60 | 29 |
| 203 (2.5%) | 28 | 44 | 28 |
| 304 (3.74%) | 21 | 60 | 15 |
| 406 (5%) | 17 | 340 | 7 |
| 507 (6.2%) | 13 | 442 | 16 |
| 609 (7.5%) | 11 | 572 | 16 |
| 812 (10%) | 9 | 479 | 73 |

Table 4: Results of ECCLAT according to the $M$ value (Mushroom, $minfr = 5\%$)

Table 4 gives the number of selected clusters, the number of transactions in the trash cluster and the average number of common transactions between all pairs of selected clusters (i.e. overlapping) according to $M$ ($minfr = 5\%$). With $M = 1$ all transactions are classified (because $minfr$ is low enough), but some overlapping remains. One observes that with $M = 5\%$ (which is also the *minfr* value) the overlapping is minimal. Too large a value of $M$ leads to a trash cluster with many transactions and an increase of overlapping. Experimentally, $M = minfr$ is a good choice to achieve an approximate clustering.

For $minfr = 5\%$ (9738 frequent closed itemsets) and $M = minfr$, we obtain 16 clusters and a trash cluster (see Table 5)[2]. Slight overlapping involves only clusters 14 and 16.

| cluster | #poisonous | #edible |
|---|---|---|
| 1 | 0 | 432 |
| 2 | 0 | 432 |
| 3 | 0 | 432 |
| 4 | 0 | 432 |
| 5 | 648 | 0 |
| 6 | 648 | 0 |
| 7 | 432 | 0 |
| 8 | 432 | 0 |
| 9 | 432 | 0 |
| 10 | 432 | 0 |
| 11 | 0 | 768 |
| 12 | 0 | 512 |
| 13 | 352 | 96 |
| 14 | 288 | 896 |
| 15 | 0 | 416 |
| 16 | 72 | 560 |
| trash | 180 | 160 |

Table 5: An approximate clustering with ECCLAT (Mushroom, $minfr$=5%)

| cluster | #poisonous | #edible |
|---|---|---|
| 1 | 0 | 94 |
| 2 | 0 | 13 |
| 3 | 0 | 6 |
| 4 | 26 | 682 |
| 5 | 30 | 2631 |
| 6 | 37 | 121 |
| 7 | 61 | 69 |
| 8 | 287 | 0 |
| 9 | 3388 | 61 |
| 10 | 77 | 372 |
| 11 | 0 | 9 |
| 12 | 10 | 19 |
| 13 | 0 | 21 |
| 14 | 0 | 110 |

Table 6: A clustering with the method of Wang et al. (Mushroom)

It is interesting to compare these results with those provided by the method of Wang et al. [24] (see Table 6). This method produces 14 clusters which are obtained hierarchically (by splitting trash clusters) and using several *minfr* values. Results given by our approach seem more understandable: 13 clusters among 17 are pure and we did not use a hierarchical decomposition requiring several values for *minfr*. Let us recall that we used a low value for *minfr*, which is possible because ECCLAT is based on efficient algorithms for frequent closed itemsets mining with regard to the step of extraction of candidate clusters.

## 5.2 Proxy Server Logs

In this experiment, we used some proxy server logs coming from France Telecom R&D. This data contained 136 transactions and 17,270 items. Items are

[2]The fact that several clusters have the same number of transactions is an amazing coincidence.

keywords of the HTML pages browsed by 136 users of a proxy-cache, over a period of 1 month. 18,162 pages were viewed. For every page, we extracted at most 10 keywords with an extractor based on the frequency of significant words. This extractor was developed at France Telecom R&D, and used in several studies, notably the variability of the users' thematic profile [17].

| $minfr$ % | No. of frequent closed itemsets | No. of selected clusters | ratio % |
|---|---|---|---|
| 60 | 84 | 8 | 9.52 |
| 55 | 295 | 8 | 2.71 |
| 50 | 981 | 10 | 1.01 |
| 45 | 4482 | 13 | 0.29 |
| 40 | 21507 | 16 | 0.07 |
| 35 | 109237 | 25 | 0.02 |

Table 7: Number of selected clusters according to the $minfr$ value (Proxy server logs, $M = 1$)

Table 7 represents the number of selected clusters with $M = 1$. As previously, the number of selected clusters is much lower than the number of frequent closed itemsets.

| M | No. of selected clusters | No. of transactions in trash | No. of common transactions (avg.) |
|---|---|---|---|
| 1 (0.7%) | 16 | 0 | 50 |
| 3 (2.2%) | 9 | 3 | 40 |
| 7 (5.1%) | 5 | 14 | 31 |
| 10 (7.3%) | 4 | 21 | 30 |
| 13 (9.5%) | 4 | 12 | 45 |
| 27 (20%) | 3 | 14 | 28 |
| 40 (30%) | 2 | 45 | 0 |
| 54 (40%) | 2 | 45 | 0 |

Table 8: Results of ECCLAT according to the $M$ value (Proxy server logs, $minfr = 40\%$)

Table 8 gives the number of selected clusters, the number of transactions in the trash cluster and the average number of common transactions between all pairs of selected clusters according to $M$ ($minfr = 40\%$). When the value of $M$ increases, note that the number of selected clusters lowers drastically. All transactions are ranked in a cluster with $M = 1$ with an average overlapping of 50 transactions.

In this experiment, we obtain clusters of users according to their interests (consulted keywords). We think that it is useful that all users are classified in at least one cluster (which is allowed with $M = 1$) and the overlapping is suitable for some applications. For instance, a user may be included in a cluster corresponding to `fishing` and `England` and also in a cluster characterized by `bike` and `mountain`. The overlapping allows to retrieve such a user from several kind of queries (i.e. taxonomies corresponding to several points of view). Note that a "pure" clustering algorithm (i.e. producing a partition of transactions) assigns the user to a single cluster, that means a single point of view. The obtained clusters can also be used for personalization (e.g., web pages), for recommendation of web sites or documents to users, and also for the prefetching of information on a proxy-cache [8, 23] (for example, for the selected clusters, we can load in the cache documents indexed by the keywords of clusters).

## 6 Conclusion

We propose a new method (ECCLAT) to build approximate clustering and discover meaningful clusters from categorical data. Such clusters correspond to concepts selected from the frequent closed itemsets lattice. With regard to the step of extraction of candidate clusters, efficiency of algorithms for frequent closed itemsets mining allows to tackle large databases. Furthermore, we think that it is an original use of the frequent closed itemsets. Unlike existing techniques, our approach does not use a global measure of similarity between transactions but is based on an evaluation measure of a cluster. The number of clusters is not fixed beforehand.

ECCLAT is generic because it allows to build an approximate clustering where overlapping is minimized or to discover a set of clusters with a slight overlapping. We claim that in some situations, like web mining applications, a set of clusters (and not necessarily a partition) is required. For instance, overlapping is suitable to cluster pages or web page suggestion.

We have tested our method on the well-known Mushroom data set where we looked for an approximate clustering, and on web data coming from France Telecom R&D where we searched clusters of users. In all experiments, we show that the number of selected clusters is very low with respect to the number of frequent closed itemsets.

As exceptions are common in real-world data, further work will be to relax the constraint of closure to allow for some exceptions in a cluster.

## References

1. Agrawal, R. & Imielinski, T. & Swami, A. Mining Association Rules between Sets of Items in Large Database. In Proceedings of ACM SIGMOD 93, pages 207-216, ACM Press, 1993

2. Agrawal, R. & Srikant, R. Fast Algorithms for Mining Association Rules. In Proceedings of the 20th VLDB Conference, Santiago, Chile, 1994

3. Boulicaut, J.F. & Bykowski, A. Frequent Closures as a Concise Representation for Binary Data Mining. In Proceedings of the Fourth Pacific-Asia Conference on Knowledge Discovery and Data Mining, PAKDD 00, volume 1805 of LNAI, pages 62-73, Kyoto, Japan, 2000. Springer-Verlag

4. Carpineto, C. & Romano, G. Galois: An Order-Theoretic Approach to Conceptual Clustering. In Proceedings of the 10th International Conference on Machine Learning, ICML 93, pages 33-40, Amherst, USA, June 1993

5. Crémilleux, B. & Gaio, M. & Madelaine, J. & Zreik, K. Discovering Browsing Paths on the Web. In Proceedings of the 7th International Conference on Human-System Learning, pages 9-18, Paris, France, 2000. Europia

6. Das, G. & Mannila, H. Context-based Similarity Measures for Categorical Databases. In Proceedings of the Fourth European Conference on Principles and Practice of Knowledge Discovery in Databases, PKDD 00, volume 1910 of LNAI, pages 201-210, Lyon, France, 2000. Springer-Verlag

7. Durand, N. & Crémilleux, B. & Henry-Amar, M. Discovering Associations in Clinical Data: Application to Search for Prognostic Factors in Hodgkin's Disease. In Proceedings of the 8th Conference on Artificial Intelligence in Medecine in Europe, AIME 01, volume 2101 of LNAI, pages 50-54, Cascais, Portugal, July 2001. Springer-Verlag

8. Durand, N. & Lancieri, L. Study of the Regularity of the Users' Internet Accesses. In Proceedings of the 3rd International Conference on Intelligent Data Engineering and Automated Learning, IDEAL 02, volume 2412 of LNCS, pages 173-178, Manchester, UK, August 2002. Springer-Verlag

9. Fisher, D.H. Knowledge Acquisition via Incremental Conceptual Clustering. Machine Learning, 2:139-172, 1987

10. Ganti, V. & Gehrke, J. & Ramakrishnan, R. CACTUS: Clustering Categorical Data Using Summaries. In Proceedings of the 5th ACM SIGMOD International Conference on Knownledge Discovery and Data Mining, pages 73-83, New-York, August 1999

11. Godin, R. & Missaoui, R. & Alaoui, H. Incremental Concept Formation Algorithms based on Galois (concept) Lattices. Computational Intelligence, 11(2):246-267, 1995

12. Guha, S. & Rastogi, R. & Shim, K. ROCK: A Robust Clustering Algorithm for Categorical Attributes. In Proceedings of the 15th International Conference on IEEE Data Engineering, ICDE 99, pages 512-521, 1999

13. Han, E.H. & Karypis, G. & Kumar, V. & Mobasher, B. Hypergraph Based Clustering in High-Dimensional Data Sets : a Summary of Results. Bulletin of the Technical Commitee on Data Engineering, 21(1), 1998

14. Huang, Z. Extensions to the K-Means Algorithm for Clustering Large Data Sets with Categorical Values. Data Mining and Kownledge Discovery, 2(3):283-304, 1999

15. Jain, A.K. & Dubes, R.C. Algorithms for Clustering Data. Prentice Hall, Englewood Cliffs, New Jersey, 1988

16. Karypis, G. & Han, E.H.S. Concept Indexing: a Fast Dimensionality Reduction Algorithm with Applications to Document Retrieval and Categorization. Technical Report TR-00-0016, University of Minnesota, 2000

17. Legouix, S. & Foucault, J.P. & Lancieri, L. A Method for Studying the Variability of Users' Thematic Profile. In Proceedings of WebNet2000, Association for the Advancement of Computing in Education (AACE), San Antonio, 2000

18. Liu, W.Z. & White, A.P. Metrics for Nearest Neighbour Discrimination with Categorical Attributes. In Proceedings of the Seventh International Annual International Conference of the British Computer Society Specialist Group on Expert Systems (ES 97), Cambridge, UK, 1997

19. Michalski, R.S. & Stepp, R.E. Learning from Observation: Conceptual Clustering. In Michalski, R. S. & Carbonell, J. G. & Mitchell, T. M. (eds), Machine Learning, An Artificial Intelligence Approach, volume 1, pages 331-363. Morgan Kauffmann, 1983

20. Pasquier, N. & Bastide, Y. & Taouil, R. & Lakhal, L. Efficient Mining of Association Rules Using Closed Itemset Lattices. Information Systems, 24(1):25-46, Elsevier, 1999

21. Ronkainen, P. Attribute Similarity and Event Sequence Similarity in Data Mining. Technical Report C-1998-42, University of Helsinki, October 1998

22. Stumme, G. & Taouil, R. & Bastide, Y. & Pasquier, N. & Lakhal, L. Computing Iceberg Concept Lattices with TITANIC. Journal on Knowledge and Data Engineering, 2002

23. Wang, J. A Survey of Web Caching Schemes for the Internet. ACM Computer Communication Review, 29(5):36-46, October 1999

24. Wang, K. & Chu, X. & Liu, B. Clustering Transactions Using Large Items. In Proceedings of the ACM Conference on Information and Knowledge Management, CIKM 99, USA, 1999

25. Wille, R. Ordered Sets, chapter Restructuring Lattice Theory: an Approach based on Hierachies of Concepts, pages 445-470. Reidel, Dordrecht, 1982

# SESSION 2B:

# KNOWLEDGE REPRESENTATION AND REASONING 2

# Reverse Engineering Ontologies from Performance Systems

Debbie Richards
Department of Computing
Division of Information and Communication Sciences
Macquarie University
Sydney, Australia
Email: richards@ics.mq.edu.au

Abstract

Considerable effort is associated with the development, validation and integration of ontologies. This paper suggests that an alternative, or possibly complementary approach, to engineering ontologies is to retrospectively and automatically discover them from existing data and knowledge sources in the organization and then to combine them if desired. The method offered assists in the identification of similar and different terms and includes strategies for developing a shared ontology. The approach uses a data analysis technique known as formal concept analysis to generate an ontology. The approach is particularly strong when used in conjunction with a rapid and incremental knowledge acquisition and representation technique, known as ripple-down rules. However, any data that can be converted into a crosstable (a binary decision table) can also use the approach. The ontological representation is not as rich as many others but we have found it useful for uncovering higher-level concepts and structure that were not explicit in the performance data. If richer models are required our approach may provide a quick way of developing a first draft and gaining initial ontological commitment.

## 1. An Overview

The alternative technique proposed for ontological engineering in this paper begins with rapid development of a performance system using Multiple Classification Ripple Down Rules (MCRDR) [14] followed by automatic generation of an ontology in the form of an abstraction hierarchy using Formal Concept Analysis (FCA) [45, 46]. MCRDR incrementally and rapidly acquires and validates the knowledge on a case-by-case basis. Cases are used to motivate and validate the knowledge acquired. Figure 1 shows the process involved. MCRDR use cases found naturally in a domain to assist the user with classification of those cases and development of rules to cover the cases. The technique is very simple. Classification of cases and rule development are part of the same task. An expert runs an inference on a case using the current knowledge in the knowledge base (KB). If the expert agrees with the system assigned conclusion they review another case. If they disagree they assign the correct conclusion, which may involve adding that conclusion to the set of valid conclusions. Next the expert picks some features in the case, which provide a justification of the new conclusion and form the rule conditions. The rules are then automatically translated into crosstable format. FCA uses the crosstable to generate higher-level concepts by taking intersections of shared rule conditions. The concepts are ordered using subsumption (≤) to generate a complete lattice. It is also feasible to use records in a database as the basis of the crosstable. Ideally a machine learning algorithm should be used on the dataset prior to translation to a crosstable to remove irrelevant attributes. This is not necessary when rules are used as input since the relevant features have been identified by the expert during knowledge acquisition. The ontology developed is based on validated knowledge, real examples and there is strong ontological commitment between the performance and explanation system. Let us examine reverse engineering, MCRDR and FCA in more detail.

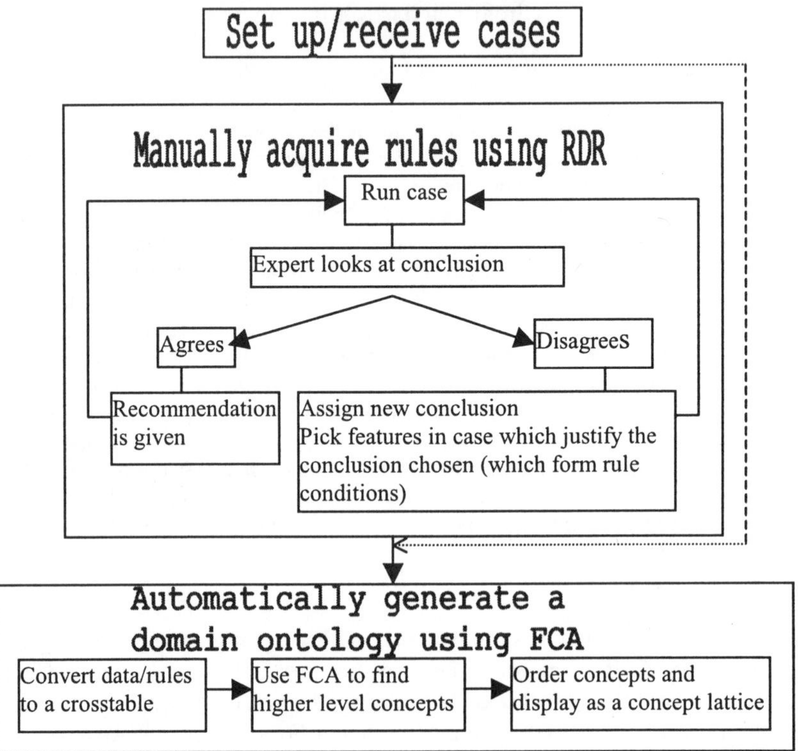


*Figure 1: A process model for reverse engineering a domain ontology. MCRDR will classify cases and identify salient features before application of FCA. Alternatively, examples/cases can be used directly as input into the final phase. As KA in MCRDR is incremental and on a case-by-case basis the process is iterative.*

## 2. Reverse Engineering an Ontology

Reverse engineering has been described as uncovering 'secrets' in the original artifact not apparent in the development of the product [26]. Unlike the majority of knowledge-based systems (KBS) approaches, the development of an MCRDR KBS does not require the user, typically the domain expert, to structure their knowledge, specify relationships between concepts or to provide abstract concepts. We can therefore view the retrospective discovery of an ontology from an MCRDR KB as reverse ontological engineering. As described above, in the MCRDR approach the domain expert enters rules in response to reviewing system recommendations for cases. The conclusion and rule conditions (features in the case) become an exception rule to the rule which gave the misclassification. To assist the user and provide online validation, cases which prompt a rule to be added are stored in association with the new rule (these are known as cornerstone cases) and shown to the user when an exception rule needs to be added. The features selected to form the exception rule must distinguish between the current case and the cornerstone case(s) for the rule which misfired. See Figure 2 for an example of a partial MCRDR KB. The expert may also stop an existing rule and add a new rule at the first level if they do not agree with the features in the parent rule. In standard rule-based systems, validation of the entire knowledge base may be needed each time one rule is added [36]. From experience with over a dozen currently deployed systems and through experimentation we have found that the time to acquire and validate a rule in an MCRDR KB is constant at approximately one rule per minute. Most of that time is taken up with deciding on the preferred wording of the conclusion. The order of cases seen will affect the compactness and time to maturity of an RDR KB but does not noticeably impact inferencing time. When FCA is applied the KB is restructured using term subsumption and the order is even less of an issue. MCRDR have found commercial success in the domains of pathology report interpretation (LabWizard [19]) and help-desk applications [15]. Knowledge bases with over 7,000 rules have been developed in less than a month. Key features of MCRDR that have assisted easy knowledge acquisition are the use of:

1. an exception structure for knowledge representation which provides local patching of the rules; and
2. the use of cases to motivate, assist and validate the acquisition of new knowledge.

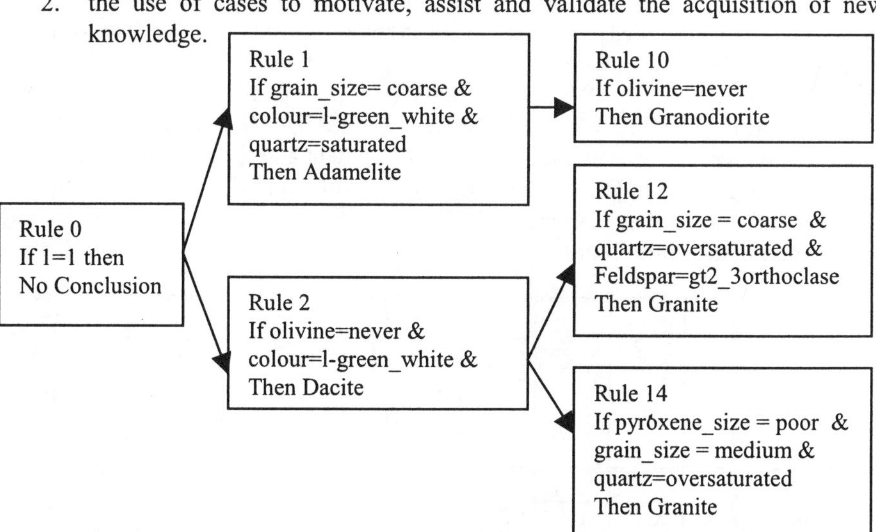


*Figure 2: A partial MCRDR for the domain of Igneous Rocks. Two levels of decision lists are shown. The children of true parents are evaluated against the case. The last true rule on each pathway is reported as the conclusion/s.*

Once we have the performance system we use FCA to uncover the structure and higher-level concepts. A concept in FCA is comprised of a set of objects and the set of attributes which are shared by those objects. In our usage of FCA we treat each rule as an object (identified by its rule number and conclusion code) and the rule conditions as the attributes [31]. In Figure 3 we have translated three of the rules in Figure 2 into a crosstable by picking up the rule conditions from all ancestors. We have selected the rules for the granite family of rocks, but we could have developed an ontology including all 6 rules in Figure 2 (or the whole KB). This representation is known as a formal context in FCA and is used to generate concepts. FCA works by finding intersections of rule conditions in different rule objects. These intersections represent higher-level concepts shared by the primitive concepts. The ability to show higher levels of abstraction than were originally specified means that the lattice does more than just restructure or re-represent the original low-level concepts. The terms, structure and coverage of the ontology will depend on the content of the rules (which are directly related to the content of the cases), or the content of the data records if mining from databases. Once the concepts have been generated they are ordered using term subsumption to produce a concept lattice. The concept lattice is visualized as a line diagram. The line diagram based on the formal context in Figure 3 is given in Figure 4. From Figure 4 we can identify what features these three types of granite share and what features distinguish them from one another. To find attributes that belong to a concept follow all ascending paths. Objects sharing an attribute are reached by descending paths. In the supremum (top concept) we can see that they share the features COLOUR is LIGHT_GREEN_WHITE and OLIVINE is NEVER. They are further distinguished from one another by other attributes. We can see that granodiorite %GR000 shares the attribute GRAIN_SIZE=COARSE with granite %GR001 but that they differ in their QUARTZ content, with granodiorite having QUARTZ=SATURATED and granite having QUARTZ=OVER-SATURATED. Granite is similar to microgranite %GR002 in the QUARTZ content but differs in GRAIN_SIZE which is MEDIUM. Granite also takes into account the FELDSPAR content and tbe rule for microgranite includes PYROXENE=POOR. The diagram raises the question of whether there a relationship between PYROXENE and FELDSPAR. If there is rules 12 and 14 may be considering the same features.

| | 1=1 | Grain-size=coarse | Colour=light_green_white | Colour=light_green_white | Quartz =saturated | Olivine= Never | Quartz =over-saturated | Feldspar= GT2-3 Orthoclase | Grain-size= medium | Pyroxene= poor |
|---|---|---|---|---|---|---|---|---|---|---|
| 10-%GR000 | X | X | X | X | X | X | | | | |
| 12-%GR001 | X | X | X | X | | X | X | X | | |
| 14-%GR002 | X | | X | X | | X | X | | X | X |

*Figure 3: A formal context for the rules 10-%GR000(Grandiorite), 12-%GR001(Granite) and 2-%GR002(Microgranite)*

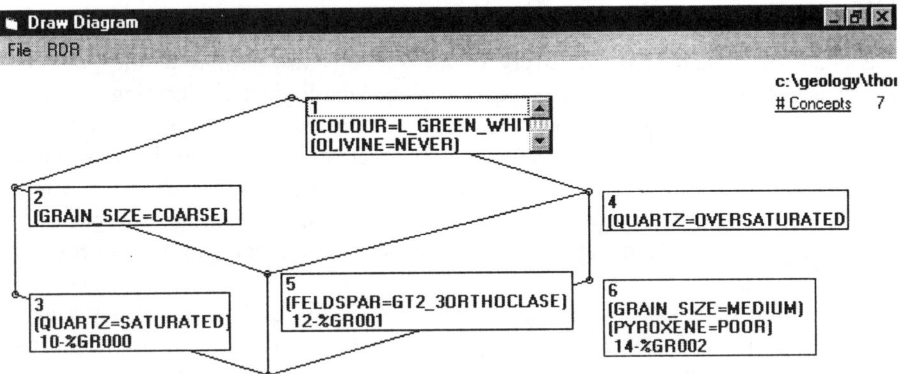


*Figure 4: The line diagram for the formal context in Figure 3 showing the relationship and structure between rules 10-%GR000(Grandiorite), 12-%GR001(Granite) and 14-%GR002(Microgranite).*

Our ability to generate a concept lattice from rules is not restricted to tasks of classification or MCRDR KBs. Most RDR have been developed for classification tasks but they have also been applied to causal modeling, configuration, design, simulation and search control problems. The same knowledge acquisition and representation technique has been applied to these problems but the inference engine has been modified in some cases, generally requiring additional cycles and sometimes input from the user for conflict resolution between alternatives. However, the generation of an ontology from the rules is the same regardless of the type of domain or task. Work has also been done which looks at the generality of using FCA for creating concept lattices from any propositional knowledge representation that can be mapped into a crosstable, known as a formal context. The line diagram shown in Figure 5 uses rules from an animal knowledge base shipped with CLIPS 5.1. The use of FCA to generate lattices from databases is well established and used in a number of large companies [43].

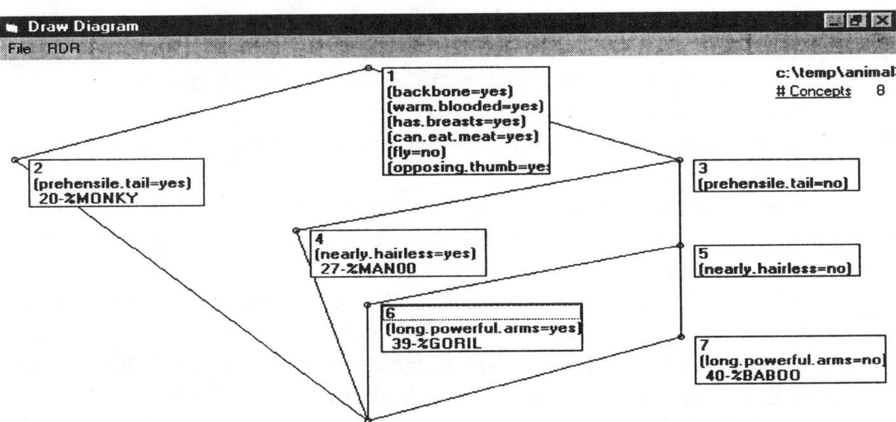


*Figure 5: Finding the animals closest to man using CLIPS 5.1 Animal KBS. From the line diagram we can see that the monkey is separated the most from man and the gorilla and baboon are the most similar.*

## 3. To Engineer or Reverse Engineer

The goals of retrospective discovery of an ontology are similar to the goals of ontological engineering and reverse engineering. Ontological engineering supports reuse and sharing of knowledge. Although we do not need the ontology for knowledge acquisition using MCRDR, we are interested in reusing the knowledge acquired for inferencing or consultation for alternative uses such as tutoring, modeling, explanation, critiquing and 'what-if' analysis. Since we go straight from data to rules without the development of an intermediate model we need to reverse engineer models.

The notion of cost-saving using reverse engineering of knowledge bases may seem absurd if we view ontologies as a solution to the problem of acquiring knowledge. Ontologies are seen as a means of obtaining a wealth of structured, and hopefully already validated, knowledge that can be used in the development of KBs. Unfortunately, many of the difficulties associated with the KA bottleneck, such as the unwillingness or the inability of experts to articulate their knowledge, difficulty in understanding and formalizing the conceptual model of another person, the lack of agreement on terms and the unreliability and variability of models, also hamper ontology acquisition. We seem to have a chicken and egg problem. To address the ontology acquisition bottleneck, there is a strong focus on the sharing and reuse of ontologies. One approach is the development of libraries of reusable ontologies containing components which could be assembled together. However, integration of ontologies is itself seen "as a challenging task" [22, p.53]. This problem occurs due to the content, partitioning and structure of concepts and the variability in the knowledge representation used. An even bigger impediment to the reusable library of ontologies approach appears to be the *interaction problem,* which contests the notion that problem solving knowledge and domain knowledge are two distinct components of a KBS. These two types of knowledge are difficult to separate since the domain knowledge needed will be strongly affected by the type of problem and the method of inference [3]. None of these approaches are an easy or complete solution to the high cost of developing ontologies. Russ et. al. [33] offer a discussion of the tradeoffs between reusability and usability of ontologies and conclude that current tools do not provide a practical solution.

Noy and Musen [23] offer two solutions to the problem of integration:

1. merging multiple ontologies into one;
2. aligning ontologies in a way that allows sharing and reuse of information between them.

The latter can be assisted by adopting specific principles for the development of a *core ontology* [41]. Like any standard gaining acceptance amongst competing alternatives is difficult.

The ability to generate a term-subsumption hierarchy using our approach could possibly be used as a framework for comparing and combining existing ontologies, or parts thereof, similar to the approach proposed by [44]. We have developed a framework based on MCRDR and FCA which allows multiple knowledge bases to be combined [30]. Describing a concept using an intensional and extensional definition assists in determining whether terms are being used in a similar way. For example, Figure 6 shows a line diagram which includes the rules for classifying the rock Diorite (coded as %DI000) from 5 different KB, identified as C1, C2, C3, C5 and L3. While we don't have space to explore all that can be learnt from this lattice, we draw attention to the different ways in which the feature grainsize is used. We can see that experts C3 and C1 consider the grainsize of Diorite to be coarse. C2 and L3 consider the grainsize to be medium. This difference in perception is made explicit in the lattice. A difference in terminology is shown in concept 6, where expert C5 considers the grainsize for Diorite to be coarsely-crystalline. This appears to match the view of experts C1 and C3. Another difference in terminology could be [Olivine=No] (concept 7 expert L3) and [Olivine=Never] (concept 8 expert C1). We reconcile similar terms by using a table for mapping synonyms, hypernyms and hyponyms. The use of mappings is a common (e.g. [9]) alternative approach to the use of core ontologies suggested above [41]. The framework we have developed includes conflict detection, negotiation and resolution strategies. We determine which resolution strategy to use based on a four-state model of comparison [34]. See [30] for details regarding the reconciliation framework.

Another feature shown in Figure 6 is the ability to provide a case in support of a rule. This is particularly useful for conflict resolution. In the KA technique offered by standard FCA (that is FCA without MCRDR) the user is asked to offer a counterexample if they do not agree with the implications derived by the system. Coming up with such examples is often difficult. As can be seen in Figure 6, the case associated with concept number 8 has been popped up. This rule states that Expert C1 believes IF [Colour=Mesocratic], [Olivine=Never], [Quartz=Possibly], [Grain_Size=Coarse] THEN the rock is Diorite (%DI000). No other experts are in complete agreement with this expert. The ability to show the case gives the experts a concrete example to consider and saves the C1 expert from having to think up, find or recall an example.

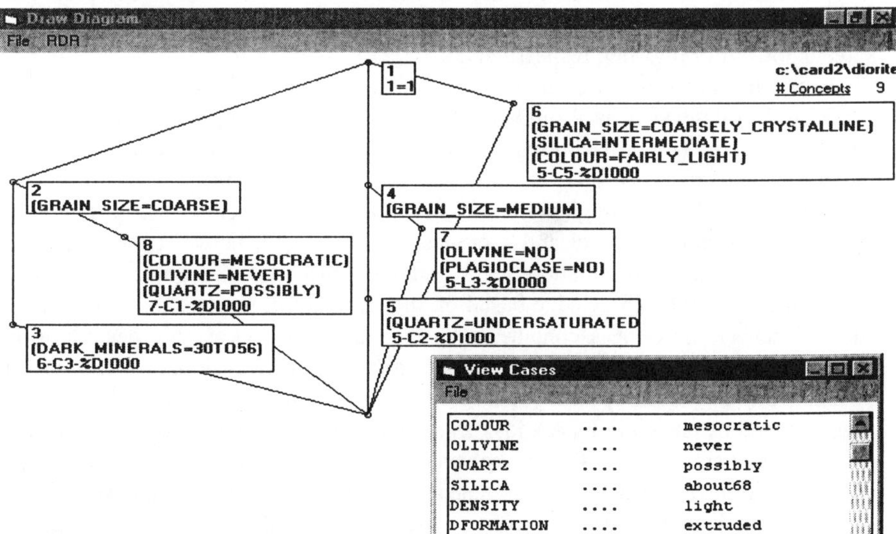


*Figure 6: A line Diagram showing how different KB can be compared and how a case can be popped up to assist in reconciliation of conflict between multiple sources of expertise.*

Apart from savings in time and effort, automatic generation of an ontology from a rule-base reduces validation overheads as there is high fidelity between the two. We avoid the interaction problem by concentrating on contextualised domain knowledge. The ontological commitment made is directly related to the cases that have been seen. Also, the rules represent performance knowledge based on the visible and everyday behaviour of the domain expert (which is: see case, assign conclusion, select features to justify conclusion) and may be executed for validation with real cases. Rather than starting with models, which by their very nature are imperfect representations, we start with real cases for acquisition and validation of the rules.

## 4. A Comparison to other Approaches

Most approaches are founded on the basic assumptions that the cost of knowledge acquisition is higher than the cost of building the ontology and that KA will more easily follow once the ontology is available. While progress is being made on a number of fronts, the MCRDR/FCA approach challenges these assumptions and allows ontology building to follow knowledge acquisition in domains where cases and a domain expert exist.

The current use of ontologies in the MCRDR/FCA approach is for the purpose of modelling domain knowledge. GenSim [16] shares this purpose however their main focus is on simulation and prediction of experimental results and GenSim is restricted to the domains of molecular biology and biochemistry. As previously mentioned, the motivation for adding FCA techniques into MCRDR was the desire to provide an environment that allowed knowledge to be reused in multiple ways for various activities and decision styles. Other similarly motivated work are Protégé [28] and the work on reusing the knowledge in MYCIN [4], however both approaches targeted a particular reuse activity such as automatic development of screens for KA or tutoring, respectively.

A key difference between the ontology developed using FCA and a semantically organised ontology such as WordNet [21] is the use of term subsumption for concept structuring. While WordNet uses a hierarchy of superclasses and subclasses this hierarchy, known as synsets, is based upon the sense or meaning of the word. However, the FCA ontologies are not simply syntactical representations. FCA is focused at the concept level and provides the connection between the names and definitions at the representation level and the objects at the object level. FCA restructures the RDR knowledge based on the terms used, not based on the order of rules. When we describe a conclusion by its rule conditions we are describing the meaning of that conclusion. Most ontologies focus on the intensional description of a concept, but the philosophically based notion of a formal concept defined by its intension and extension in FCA adds meaning and assists in comparison of concepts.

Another distinguishing feature between FCA and WordNet, or other lexically-based ontologies, is that FCA does not develop one or more hierarchies which are broken up into nouns, verbs, adjectives, etc. The type of terms which appear in a concept lattice are directly dependent on the type of terms used in the formal context. The Generalized Upper Model (GUM) [1] provides a level of abstraction which is in between lexical knowledge and conceptual knowledge. It may be that some benefit can be achieved by including a lexically-based ontology into the FCA ontology so that semantically equivalent terms can be identified and possibly automatically reconciled. Unlike GUM, which has separate hierarchies for concepts and relationships, the FCA concept lattice combines concepts and relationships into the one structure. The combination seems to be more visually comprehensible.

The use of taxonomies in the organization of ontologies is common [22]. The structure of these taxonomies varies with some approaches having one large taxonomy e.g. CYC [12], Sowa's ontology [37], GUM, GenSim, and noun sysnets in WORDNET, or a number of smaller ontologies e.g. TOVE [11]. In some sense MCRDR/FCA offers both approaches. The user may choose to develop a concept lattice of the whole KB or a collection of KBs or many smaller lattices can be generated based on restricted contexts (or rules subsets). Due to the limitations of displaying and navigating around large graphs and computational complexity issues the latter approach is recommended and we thus offer various techniques for selecting rules/conclusions to include in a formal context. The FCA concept lattice is closest to the implicit taxonomy found in PLINIUS that is structured using the subsumption relation. The PLINIUS Project [42] does not use the hierarchical-axiomatic approach used by most other projects for building ontologies. At a surface-level the construction of the PLINIUS ontology is similar to the FCA technique in that it begins with a set of atomic concepts. Elements of these sets are combined to define other concepts. PLINIUS uses rules in its construction kit for determining sub and superconcepts rather than term subsumption. PLINIUS is very domain specific and it is not known if it can be extended beyond the domain of chemistry. Although the FCA concept lattices tend to be domain specific this feature is due to the nature of the knowledge contained in the KBS. There is no particular restriction on the domain that they can describe. Two further significant differences are that the FCA concept lattice is automatically generated from the primitive concepts and is able to represent properties belonging to an object.

In addition to containing a taxonomy of concepts, most ontologies include a set of meaningful properties and categories [22]. Some ontologies will allow explicit specification of axioms. This is not possible in an MCRDR KB. The absence of axioms in MCRDR and FCA reflects the strongly held view of knowledge applying within the context of a case or example. MCRDR is able to handle knowledge which goes beyond first-order logic but this knowledge is not always clearly displayed in the concept lattice. For example a default rule will appear in the top concept in the lattice but it is not labeled or otherwise identified as a default. Similarly, context is handled in MCRDR through its exception structure and the storage of cases which prompt new knowledge to be added. As shown in Figure 6, cases associated with a particular node on the lattice may be shown and the exception structure can be found in the lattice although it may not be as obvious as in the original MCRDR format (compare Figures 2 and 4).

There are a number of ontological approaches such as [8, 40] that concurrently perform KA and develop the ontology. The Methontology [8] ontology-development process includes specification, acquisition and conceptualization of domain knowledge, integration with existing ontologies, evaluation and automatic implementation into Ontolingua. In such approaches, ontological engineering is not a prerequisite task to KA but a complementary task that can be used to assist and validate the knowledge being acquired. What makes MCRDR/FCA so unusual is that KA does not involve the specification of the user's conceptual model and the ontology is truly automatic and can only be generated after KA has occurred. Similar to the approach offered by ROCHS, mentioned below, it may be desirable to integrate the MCRDR/FCA approach with another ontological approach to improve the systematic acquisition of knowledge or to speed up the growth of the KB. However, since MCRDR is fundamentally an incremental KA technique designed to deal with cases as they occur (and since the current approach results in rapid development anyway) such changes to the approach may be counterproductive.

Ontologies are used in data mining by a number of approaches. In some approaches the output of data mining is an ontology. Omelayenko [24] has surveyed a number of approaches to learning ontologies. He divides the approaches broadly into two main categories depending on whether they involve machine-learning (ML) or manual construction. Omelayenko found, and we agree, that the combination of both techniques tended to offer the best results by combining the speed of machine learning with the accuracy of a human. Omelayanko also found that ML results in flat homogeneous structures often in propositional form. Flat structures do not support queries at multiple level. We have proposed [32] using FCA on rule bases (possibly output by other datamining techniques) to develop these multilevel rules.

Others have used ontologies to guide the discovery of multi-level rules (e.g the ParkaDB approach [39]. In ParkaDB an ontology (in the form of a concept hierarchy) together with frequency counts are used to determine which concepts should be included in a rule. The ontology provides the background knowledge to guide the discovery process. A number of similar approaches that use concept taxonomies (e.g. [35]) have also been developed but these are based on traditional relational database technology and require transformation to a generalized table as part of the preprocessing which can result in over-generalisation. DeGraaf et al. [10] use a prespecified taxonomy to suggest interesting association rules, which they define as unexpected rules that do not fit with the taxonomy. Intuitively it is appealing but the approach obviously relies on the development of a complete and valid taxonomy. ParkDB does not require such preprocessing but supports dynamical generalization of data without over generalization. Our approach is different to all of these in that we do not use a concept hierarchy to develop rules. Instead we use rules to develop a concept hierarchy which may lead to higher level rules being uncovered. Thus we avoid the substantial effort required in first developing the hierarchies and the difficult task of validating them. Given any string or substring and using set intersection, term subsumption and lectical ordering we are able to find all combinations using that string. Some concepts will include attributes and/or objects at different levels of abstraction such as the objects mammal and dog will appear in individual and shared concepts. The combination of multi-level concepts allows us to perform queries at and across multiple levels.

The connection between FCA and ontologies was first made in the work in Web Analysis and Visualisation Environment (WAVE) [17] which defines an "ontology as a specification of a concept lattice". However, our application of FCA to rules bases is novel. Other MCRDR work using conceptual hierarchies includes: Ripple-down rules Oriented Concept Hierarchy System (ROCHS) [20], Nested MCRDR (NRDR) [2] and the discovery of class relationships from MCRDR KBS [38].

## 5. Conclusion and Future Work

RDR and MCRDR have been evaluated empirically [7] and experimentally [6]. Of greater concern to the approach described in this paper is the evaluation of the role and use of ontologies as part of the MCRDR approach. Some evaluation has been done concerning the value of the concept lattice for explanation, exploring and learning about a domain [29]. Part of this evaluation involved obtaining four different MCRDR KB from the fields of pathology, agriculture, geology and chemistry. The MCRDR rules were used to develop FCA lattices. The lattices were used by a beginner (level lower than novice) to answer questions and learn about the domain. The knowledge 'learnt' after about 1 hour of generating and browsing the lattices was written down and shown to domain experts who were asked to comment on the validity and value of what had been learnt. In the first 3 domains each expert found that the understanding gained was valid for that domain. Experts from the pathology and agricultural domains were impressed by the depth of understanding which the beginner appeared to have. In the geology and pathology case studies, where the beginner and expert were able to interact, the lattices provided a valuable communication channel for discussing key ideas and modifying hypotheses. The rules in the chemistry domain tended to have single conditions which resulted in few intersections between rules and uninteresting lattices so there was very little in terms of higher level concepts, structure or relationships to learn from that knowledge source. While such an experiment is not conclusive it does indicate that the ontologies represented in the concept lattice offers knowledge at a greater depth which extends beyond offering an alternative graphical view of the rules.

The work by Predigger [25] which takes a many-valued context and derives concept graphs which show on the edges the nature of the relationships between the vertices would provide an even richer representation. Just as it is necessary in the MCRDR/FCA approach for a human to initially provide the label for any abstractions uncovered, the nature of the relationship, apart from the subsumes relation, would need to be supplied as this information is not automatically derivable from the KB. The work by Priss and Old [27] which extends FCA to Relational Concept Analysis (RCA) considers relationships other than subsumption will be investigated as a possible means of generating and displaying more kinds of relationships between concepts. As suggested in the Section 4, if the MCRDR/FCA approach were extended to allow the use of other ontologies such as WordNet it may be possible to automatically label the edges with the relationship type. Integration is not an easy task. Asking the user to supply relationship names could be more efficient and accurate. Another lesser problem is that the labeling of edges will decrease the number of concepts that can be shown before comprehensibility is lost. Increased expressibility in a representation always comes with a cost.

It would be interesting to explore the ramifications of ontologies for MCRDR from a theoretical standpoint. Sowa's ontology is philosophically motivated and seeks to address a number of theoretical issues concerning ontologies. The similarity between Sowa's fundamental principles of ontology design as distinctions, combinations, and constraints [37] is embodied in the FCA set-theoretic approach and the use of difference lists, cornerstone case lists (which identify related cases) and rules in MCRDR. A key difference between the constraints used by Sowa and those found in MCRDR KB is that in Sowa's ontology the ontology developer is responsible for identifying logical constraints. In MCRDR, the use of cases constrains what can be represented in the rules.

As mentioned before, building an ontology from an RDR KB means that we are starting with validated knowledge. Validation of each rule extends beyond the cornerstone case. Each time a case is seen it is validated against the whole KB. If any case is deemed to be incorrect based on that rule, an exception rule is added. In our commercial version of MCRDR we record how many cases have visited a rule and been accepted. Selection of which rules to include in the generation of an ontology could be made on the basis of these statistics. A rule that has been visited by many cases can be seen to be more important and more reliable than one that has rarely been exercised or that has been frequently patched.

There are many open issues in the field of ontological engineering. Until definitive answers are found, alternatives such as that offered by MCRDR/FCA deserve some consideration. The alternative offered is to rapidly acquire knowledge and use that knowledge to automatically reverse engineer an ontology.

**Acknowledgments**
RDR research is supported by Australian Research Council grants.

## References

[1] Bateman, J.A., Magnini, B. and Rinaldi, F. (1994) The Generalised Italian, German, English Upper Model. *Workshop on Comparison of Implemented Ontologies at 11th European Conf. on Artificial Intelligence (ECAI'94),* Aug.8-12, Amsterdam, The Netherlands.

[2] Beydoun, G. and Hoffmann, A. (1997) Acquisition of Search Knowledge, In Enric Plaza and Richard Benjamins (eds), *Knowledge Acquisition, Modeling and Management. 10th European Workshop, EKAW'97*, LNAI 1319, Springer-Verlag, 1-16.

[3] Bylander, T. and Chandrasekaran, B. (1988) Generic Tasks in Knowledge-Based Reasoning: The Right Level of Abstraction for Knowledge Acquisition In B.R. Gaines and J.H. Boose (eds.) *Knowledge Acquisition for KBSs*, Academic Press, London.

[4] Clancey, W.J., (1986) From GUIDON to NEOMYCIN and HERACLES in Twenty Short Lessons: ORN Final Report 1979-1985 *AI Magazine*, August 1986, 40-60.

[5] Compton, P. and Jansen, R., (1990) A Philosophical Basis for Knowledge Acquisition. *Knowledge Acquisition* 2:2

[6] Compton, P., Preston, P. and Kang, B. (1995) The Use of Simulated Experts in Evaluating Knowledge Acquisition, *Proceedings 9th Banff Knowledge Acquisition for Knowledge Based Systems Workshop* Banff. Feb 26 - March 3 1995.

[7] Edwards, G., Compton, P., Malor, R, Srinivasan, A. and Lazarus, L. (1993) PEIRS: a Pathologist Maintained Expert System for the Interpretation of Chemical Pathology Reports *Pathology* 25: 27-34.

[8] Fernandez Lopez, M., Gomez-Perez, A., Pazos Sierra, A., and Pazos Sierra, J. (1999) Building a Chemical Ontology Using Methontology and the Ontology Design Environment *IEEE Intelligent Systems* 14(1) January/February 1999.

[9] Gennari, J.H., Tu, S.W., Rothenfluh, T.E. and Musen, M.A. (1994) Mapping Domains to Methods in Support of Reuse Int. Journal of Human-Computer Studies 41:399-424.

[10] Graaf, de, J., M., Kosters, W., A. and Witteman, J., J., W. (2000) Interesting Association Rules in Multiple Taxonomies, Proc. of the 12th Belgium-Netherlands Artificial Intelligence Conf.

[11] Gruninger, M. and Fox, M.S. (1995) Methodology for the Design and Evaluation of Ontologies *Workshop on Basic Ontological Issues in Knowledge Sharing* 19-20 Aug., Montreal, Quebec.

[12] Guha, T.V., and Lenat, D.B. (1990) CYC:A Mid-Term Report *AI Magazine* 11(3):32-59.

[13] Jasper, R. and Uschold, M. (1999) A Framework for Understanding and Classifying Ontology Applications In *Proc. of the 12th Workshop on Knowledge Acquisition, Modeling and Management (KAW'99),* 16-21 October, 1999, Banff.

[14] Kang, B., Compton, P. and Preston, P (1995) Multiple Classification Ripple Down Rules: Evaluation and Possibilities *Proceedings 9th Banff Knowledge Acquisition for Knowledge Based Systems Workshop* Banff. Feb 26 - March 3 1995, Vol 1: 17.1-17.20.

[15] Kang, B., Yoshida, K, Motoda, H, and Compton, P. (1997) Help Desk with Intelligent Interface *Applied Artificial Intelligence* 11:611-631.

[16] Karp, P.D. (1993) A Qualitative Biochemistry and its Application to the Regulation of the Trytophan Operon In L. Hunter (ed.) *Artificial Intelligence and Molecular Biology* Menlo Park, AAAI Press, California: 289-325.

[17] Kent, R. E. and Neuss, C. (1995) Creating a 3D Web Analysis and Visualization Environment *Computer Networks and ISDN Systems*, 28:109-117.

[18] Kietz, J.-U., Maedche, A. and Volz, R. (2000) A Method for Semi-Automatic Ontology Acquisition from a Corporate Intranet. WS "Ontologies and Text", co-located with *EKAW'2000,* Juan-les-Pins, French Riviera, October 2-6, 2000.

[19] Lazarus, L. (2000) Clinical Decision Support Systems: Background and Role in Clinical Support, http://www.pks.com.au/CDSS_White_Paper_doc.pdf

[20] Martinez-Bejar, R., Benjamins. R., Compton,, P., Preston, P. and Martin-Rubio, F. (1998) A Formal Framework to Build Domain Knowledge Ontologies for Ripple-Down Rules-Based Systems. In Gaines, B. and Musen, M. (eds) *Eleventh Workshop on Knowledge Acquisition, Modeling and Management (KAW'98),* Banff, Alberta, Canada, 18-23 April, 1998, Vol 2:SHARE.13.

[21] Miller, G. A. (1990) WORDNET: An On-Line Lexical Database, *Int. Journal of Lexicography* 3-4:235-312.

[22] Noy, N. F. and Hafner, C. D. (1997) The State of the Art in Ontology Design: A Survey and Comparative Review *AI Magazine* Fall 1997 18(3): 53 - 74:

[23] Noy, N. F. and Musen, M. A. (1999) SMART: Automated Support for Ontology Merging and Aligning In *Proceedings of the 12th Workshop on Knowledge Acquisition, Modeling and Management (KAW'99),* 16-21 October, 1999, Banff.

[24] Omelayenko B., (2001) Learning of Ontologies for the Web: the Analysis of Existent Approaches, In: Proceedings of the International Workshop on Web Dynamics, held in conj. with the 8th Int. Conf. on Database Theory (ICDT'01), London, UK, 3 Jan. 2001.

[25] Predigger, S. (1999) The Lattice of Concept Graphs of a Relationally Scaled Context In W. Tepfenhart and W. Cyre *Proceedings fo the 7th International Conference on Conceptual Structures; Standards and Practices (ICCS-99)* Blacksburg, VA, USA, July 12-15, LNAI-1640, Springer Verlag, Berlin: 401-414.

[26] Pressman, R. (2000) 5th Edn. *Software Engineering: A Practitioner's Approach* (European Adaptation), McGraw Hill, Berkshire.

[27] Priss, U. and Old, J. (1998) Information Access through Conceptual Structures and GIS In *Information Access in the Global Information Economy Proceedings of the 61st Annual Meeting of ASIS'98* :91-99 also http://php.indiana.edu./~upriss/papers/asis98.ps

[28] Puerta, A. R, Egar, J.W., Tu, S.W. and Musen, M.A. (1992) A Multiple Method Knowledge Acquisition Shell for Automatic Generation of Knowledge Acquisition Tools *Knowledge Acquisition* 4(2).

[29] Richards, D. (1998) An Evaluation of the Formal Concept Analysis Line Diagram In Slaney, J., Antoniou. G and Maher, M.J. (eds) *Poster Proc. of 11th Australian Joint Artificial Intelligence Conf. AI'98* 13-17 July 1998, Brisbane, Australia, 121-133.

[30] Richards, D. (2000) Reconciling Conflicting Sources of Expertise: A Framework and Illustration In P. Compton, A. Hoffmann, H. Motoda and T. Yamaguchi1 (eds) *Proceedings of the 6th Pacific Knowledge Acquisition Workshop* Sydney December 11-13,2000, 275 – 296.

[31] Richards, D. and Compton, P. (1997) Uncovering the Conceptual Models in Ripple Down Rules In Dickson Lukose, Harry Delugach, Marry Keeler, Leroy Searle, and John F. Sowa, (eds) (1997), *Conceptual Structures: Fulfilling Peirce's Dream, Proceedings of the Fifth International Conference on Conceptual Structures (ICCS'97),* August 3 - 8, University of Washington, Seattle, USA, LNAI 1257, Springer Verlag, Berlin, 198-212.

[32] Richards, D. and Malik, U. Multi-Level Knowledge Discovery in Rule Bases, *Applied Artificial Intelligence*, Taylor and Francis Ltd. (accepted 2002).

[33] Russ, T., Valente, A., MacGregor, R. and Swartout, W. (1999) Practical Experiences in Trading Off Ontology Usability and Reusability In *Proceedings of the 12th Workshop on Knowledge Acquisition, Modeling and Management (KAW'99),* 16-21 Oct., 1999, Banff.

[34] Shaw, M.L.G. and Gaines, B.R., (1988) A Methodology for Recognising Consensus, Correspondence, Conflict and Contrast in a Knowledge Acquisition System in *Proceedings of the 3rd Knowledge Acquisition for Knowledge-Based Systems Workshop,* November 1988, Banff, Canada.

[35] Singh, L., Scheuermann, P. and Chen, B. (1997) Generating Association Rules from SemiStructured Documents Using an Extended Concept Hierarchy. In *Proceedings of the 6th International Conference on Information and Knowledge Management.* Las Vegas, Nevada, USA, 1997, pp. 193-200.

[36] Soloway, E, Bachant, J. and Jensen, K. (1987) Assessing the Maintainability of XCON-in-RIME: Coping with Problems of a very Large Rule Base *Proceedings of the Sixth Int. Conf. on Artificial Intelligence*, Seattle, WA: Morgan Kaufman, Vol 2:824-829.

[37] Sowa, J. F. (1995) Top-Level Ontological Categories *International Journal of Human-Computer Studies* 43(5-6): 669-685.

[38] Suryanto, H. and Compton, P. (2000) Discovery of Class Relations in Exception Structured Knowledge Bases In *Proceedings of the 8th International Conference on Conceptual Structures; Logical, Linguistic and Computational Issues (ICCS-2000)* Darmstadt, Germany, 14-18 August, Springer Verlag, Berlin.

[39] Taylor, M., Stoffel, K. and Hendler J. (1997) Ontology-based Induction of High Level Classification Rules In *SIGMOD Data Mining and Knowledge Discovery workshop proceedings*. Tuscon, Arizona, 1997.

[40] Uschold, M. and Gruninger, M. (1996) Ontologies: Principles, Methods and Applications. *Knowledge Engineering Review* 11(2):93-155.

[41] Valente, A. and Breuker, J. (1996) Towards Principled Core Ontologies In B.Gaines and M. Musen (eds.) *Proceedings of the 10th Workshop on Knowledge Acquisition, Modeling and Management (KAW'99),* Banff.

[42] Van de Vet, P. E., Speel, P. -H. and Mars, N.J. (1994) The PLINIUS Ontology of Ceramic Materials. 11th European Conf. on Artificial Intelligence (ECAI'94) *Workshop on Comparison of Implemented Ontologies*, 8-12 Aug., Amsterdam, The Netherlands.

[43] Vogt, Frank and Wille, Rudolf (1995) TOSCANA - A Graphical Tool for Analyzing and Exploring Data *Knowledge Organisation* 22(2):78-81.

[44] Weinstein, P. and Birmingham, W. P. (1999) Comparing Concepts in Differentiated Ontologies In *Proceedings of the 12th Workshop on Knowledge Acquisition, Modeling and Management (KAW'99),* 16-21 October, 1999, Banff.

[45] Wille, R. (1982) Restructuring Lattice Theory: An Approach Based on Hierarchies of Concepts In Ordered Sets (Ed. Rival) pp:445-470, Reidel, Dordrecht, Boston.

[46] Wille, R. (1992) Concept Lattices and Conceptual Knowledge Systems Computers Math. Applic. (23) 6-9: 493-515.

# Ontology, Knowledge Management, Knowledge Engineering and the ACM Classification Scheme

John Kingston
AIAI, School Of Informatics, University of Edinburgh
Edinburgh, Scotland
J.Kingston@ed.ac.uk

Abstract

The purpose of this paper is to test the theory of multiple perspectives being necessary for completeness in ontologies by applying it to the task of placing "knowledge management" and "knowledge engineering" within the ACM classification scheme. The thesis of this paper is that a multi-perspective analysis of the ACM classification scheme, along with a published extension for AI subjects, should demonstrate some of the principles on which the classification is based, and therefore help in deciding where knowledge management and knowledge engineering (and knowledge acquisition) should appear in the classification. Some implications for ontology building are discussed.

## 1 Introduction

Much work is being carried out these days on the classification of objects or concepts in a standardised manner; such a classification is often referred to as an *ontology*. Various researchers are promoting different ontologies, approaches to building ontologies, standards for ontologies, and so on. Such work is valuable and worthy of respect, but often a single ontology cannot describe an object or concept fully. It is proposed in [1] (with a case study in [2]) that representing an object or concept completely may require up to six ontologies, covering *who, what, how, where, when and why* perspectives, and furthermore that these perspectives may recur at different levels of abstraction, from an "organisational" level right down to a "system implementation" level. This is referred to as a *multi-perspective modelling* approach. The contents of the "what" perspective on knowledge are typically resources of some kind; the "how" perspective contains methods or techniques; the "who" perspective will typically contain agents; the "where" perspective will demonstrate external connections; the "when" perspective will include control and constraints; and the "why" perspective will include justifications and goals.

The purpose of this paper is to test the theory of multiple perspectives being necessary for completeness in ontologies by applying it to the task of placing "knowledge management" and "knowledge engineering" within the ACM classification scheme. This task arose from a request by the librarian of the Artificial Intelligence library at the University of Edinburgh. For several years, the AI library has been classifying its collection according to the ACM classification scheme, along with an extension to the Artificial Intelligence section of the scheme that was published in the AI magazine in 1985 [3]. However, recent interest in knowledge management from commercial and research organisations, along with a grant from EPSRC to develop a Master's Training Package in Knowledge Management and Knowledge Engineering, has led to an influx of books and other materials on these topics. There is no entry in the current ACM scheme for knowledge management, and although there is an existing category for knowledge engineering in the extended version of the scheme (as a subclass of Learning), the librarian had noticed that books on knowledge engineering were being classified in four different places, which suggests that there may be a problem with the current classification scheme.

The thesis of this paper is that a multi-perspective analysis of the ACM classification scheme and the AI extension should demonstrate some of the principles on which the classification is based, and therefore help in deciding where knowledge management and knowledge engineering should appear in the classification.

## 2 The ACM Classification Scheme and the Scientific Datalink extension

The ACM classification scheme [4] was first published in 1964, with seven top level topics. In its third revision, produced in 1998, the number of top level categories had increased to 11 (see Table 1), along with major extensions of lower level categories.[1]

| | |
|---|---|
| A | General literature |
| B | Hardware |
| C | Computer systems organisation |
| D | Software |
| E | Data |
| F | Theory of computation |
| G | Mathematics of computing |
| H | Information systems |
| I | Computing methodologies |
| J | Computer applications |
| K | Computer milieux (philosophy, legislation, administration) |

**Table 1: Top level of the 1998 ACM classification scheme**

[1] The report [4] accompanying the 1998 classification suggests that another major revision is needed, but because deletion of categories would render historical indexes inaccurate, it was decided that a major revision would be delayed; and in addition, categories that were considered redundant would be "retired" rather than being deleted from the hierarchy.

Artificial Intelligence appears in the ACM classification scheme as a subcategory of one of the newer top level categories, "Computing Methodologies", alongside "symbolic and algebraic manipulation", "computer graphics", "simulation and modelling", "document and text processing", and others. The subcategories of AI (apart from General and Miscellaneous, which appear in every list of subcategories) are Applications and Expert Systems; Automatic Programming; Deduction and Theorem Proving; Knowledge Representation Formalisms and Methods; Programming Languages and Software; Learning; Natural Language Processing; Problem Solving, Control methods and Search; Robotics; Vision and Scene Understanding; and Distributed Artificial Intelligence. Each of these has some suggested interest areas (i.e. a partial list of possible subcategories); for Applications and Expert Systems, for example, the current list of interests includes (among others) cartography, games, industrial automation, law, medicine and science, natural language interfaces, mathematical aids and prosthetics. It's immediately clear to readers familiar with the Artificial Intelligence field that, however valid this classification was when it was developed, it does not reflect the current levels of interest in the field very well: an obvious example is cartography, which is listed as a fourth level classification here, but nowadays would probably not even make it to the fifth level – it might be regarded as a subclass of "Geographical applications" which in turn would be a subclass of "Medicine and Science". Similarly, it's hard to believe that a new classification would grant "Distributed Artificial Intelligence" the same level of prominence as "Applications and Expert Systems". The original classification may have been based on what was known at the time, on the political preferences of the ACM committee[2], or on some other basis. However, this highlights the need to understand the principles on which ontological decisions are based to be noted.

In 1985, David Waltz was invited by Scientific Datalink, a division of Comtex Scientific Corporation to extend the AI classification to account for some of the subdivisions of AI, to aid Comtex in indexing the series of AI memos and reports that they had been gathering. The resulting classification, which has been published by Waltz in AI Magazine [3], retains all of the above top level categories except for "Distributed Artificial Intelligence", which is replaced by "Specialized AI Architectures". Two new categories are also added: "Cognitive Modelling and Psychological Studies of Intelligence", and "Social and Philosophical issues". The contents of most categories have been significantly expanded: continuing the earlier example, "Applications and Expert Systems" now has 19 subcategories, including the 7 proposed as "interests" by the ACM, and these 19 subcategories have up to 11 sub-sub-categories or even sub-sub-sub-categories. Space prevents the replication of the entire classification here, but four of the nineteen categories are described in detail in Table 2.

---

[2] To illustrate "political preferences", AIAI helped to carry out a project to merge four ontologies of "scientific knowledge management" (i.e. academics and their publications) prepared by different universities into one "reference ontology" [5]. When the four original ontologies were compared, it was noted that there were many similarities, but if a research group's own special interest area appeared in the ontology, it was classified at a higher level in its own ontology than in the others' ontologies.

| **I.2.1. Applications and Expert Systems** | **Subcategories** |
|---|---|
| 1.0 Cartography | |
| 1.1 Games | Chess, Checkers, Backgammon, Bidding Games, Wagering Games, War Games, Other |
| 1.2 Industrial Applications | Automatic Assembly, Parts Handling, Inspection, Welding, Planning for Production, Inventory |
| 1.3 Law | |
| 1.4 Medicine and Science | Medical Applications, Chemical Applications, Biological Applications, Geological Applications |
| 1.5 Natural Language Interfaces | |
| 1.6 Office Automation | |
| 1.7 Military Applications | Autonomous Vehicles, Integration of Information, Decisions Aids, Target Tracking, Communication |
| 1.8 Business and Financial | Tax experts, Investment, Financial Planning, Information Storage and Retrieval |
| 1.9 Natural Language Processing Applications | |
| 1.10 Mathematical Aids | |
| 1.11 Education | Tutoring systems, Intelligent Computer-aided Instruction, Aids to learning Programming, Curriculum Design |
| 1.12 Library Applications | |
| 1.13 Engineering Automation | Computer System Design, VLSI Design Aids, CAD/CAM, Programming Aids |
| 1.14 System Troubleshooting | |
| 1.15 Expert Systems | Expert System Languages and Aids for Building Expert Systems, Acquisition of Expert Knowledge, Plausible Reasoning, Representation of Expert Knowledge, Generation of Explanations, Expert Systems based on Simulation and Deep Models, User Interfaces for Expert Systems, Validation of Expert Systems |
| 1.16 Prosthetics | |
| 1.17 Aviation Applications | |
| 1.18 Applications, Other | |
| **I.2.4 Knowledge Representation** | |
| 4.0 Frames and Scripts | Defaults, Stereotypes and Prototypes, Generation of Expectations, Frame Languages, Frame-Driven Systems, Inheritance Hierarchy |
| 4.1 Predicate Logic | First Order Predicate Calculus, Skolem Functions, Second Order Logic, Modal Logics, Fuzzy Logic |
| 4.2 Relational Systems | Relational Data Bases, Associative Memory |
| 4.3 Representation Languages | |
| 4.4 Representations (Procedural and Rule-Based) | Production Rule Systems, Knowledge Bases |
| 4.5 Semantic Networks | |
| 4.6 Connectionist Systems | |
| 4.7 Multiple Agent/Actor Systems | |
| 4.8 Constraints | |

| | |
|---|---|
| 4.9 Discrimination Trees and Networks | |
| 4.10 Belief Models | |
| 4.11 Representation of the Physical World | |
| 4.12 Representation of Natural Language Semantics | |
| **I.2.6 Learning** | |
| 6.0 Analogies | Geometric Analogies, Natural Language Analogies, Structural Analogies, Functional Analogies |
| 6.1 Concept learning | Near-Miss Analysis, Version Spaces, Schema Acquisition and Generalisation, Learning of Heuristics, Credit and Blame Assignment, Conceptual Clustering |
| 6.2 Induction | Statistical Methods, Inductive Inference |
| 6.3 Knowledge Acquisition | Advice Taking and Learning by Being Told, Learning from Examples, Learning by Observation, Learning from Experience, Learning by Discovery |
| 6.4 Knowledge Engineering | Dialogues with Experts, Knowledge Base Stability, Knowledge Base Consistency |
| 6.5 Language Acquisition | Acquisition of Grammar, Learning of Concepts through Language |
| 6.6 Parameter Learning | |
| 6.7 Associative Learning | |
| 6.8 Learning of Skills | |
| 6.9 Developmental and Incremental Learning | |
| 6.10 Evolutionary Models for Learning | |
| **I.2.8 Problem Solving, Control methods and Search** | |
| 8.0 Backtracking | |
| 8.1 Dynamic Programming | |
| 8.2 Graph and Tree Search Strategies | Depth first, Breadth first, Best first, Branch & Bound, Hill Climbing, Minimax, Alpha-Beta, A*, Beam, Dependency-Directed Backtracking, Constraint Propagation, Relaxation Methods, Marker Passing, Bidirectional, Data-Driven/Top-Down |
| 8.3 Heuristic Methods | Nature of Heuristics, Heuristic Control of Search, Strategies, Default Reasoning, Closed World Heuristics, Induction and Evaluation of Heuristics, Qualitative Reasoning and Envisionment |
| 8.4 Plan Execution, Formation, Generation | Means-End Analysis, Forward Chaining, Backward Chaining, Weak methods, Generate and Test, Hierarchical Planning, Metaplanning and Multiple Goals, Plan Verification, Plan Modification |
| 8.5 Matching | |

**Table 2: Part of the Scientific Datalink AI classification scheme**

# 3 Dimensions of classification: classes, subclasses and multi-perspective modelling

The ACM classification scheme is considered to be a four-level, hierarchical taxonomy. A "taxonomy" is defined in Merriam-Webster's dictionary as "a classification, especially an orderly classification of plants and animals according to their presumed natural relationships". Taxonomies are typically used to represent one class of objects or concepts and its sub-types; that is, objects/concepts that possess all the defining features[3] of the higher level object/concept plus a couple of extra features. A 'true' taxonomy therefore includes only one relationship between objects or concepts; one object/concept is a subclass (or "a kind of") the other.[4]

However, when ontologies are built to represent the relationships between tasks, activities, philosophies, or other conceptual entities, it's often difficult to connect them all using only subclass relationships; maybe there are no obvious taxonomic groupings, or maybe there is a more obvious grouping according to function, form, role or relevance. An example of a "more obvious" grouping can be found in vegetable classification; while it might possibly be helpful to know that the Linnaean classification of (most) tomatoes places them alongside aubergines and potatoes in the Nightshade genus of the Potato family, many gardeners would probably prefer to see tomatoes classified alongside other vegetables that grow on vines, vegetables that grow in greenhouses, or even vegetables that are served in salads. An example of "no obvious groupings" can be found by looking at cars. Possible classifications include "saloon", "hatchback", "sports car", etc (based largely on form, but also on role) or "petrol engine cars", "diesel engine cars" and "alternative fuel engine cars" (based on function), but such subdivisions seem less "natural" than the higher level classes – and yet taxonomies are supposed to be based on "presumed natural relationships".

In fact, the whole issue of "natural" versus "artificial" classification has been a major subject of academic debate. A good summary is produced by Wilkins [6] who argues that "all classifications are artificial, but some have a degree of naturalness about them" and quotes R.G. Millikan who proposes that a "natural" concept can be determined by making a historical investigation of how an object and its name came about, and then determining what the name refers to today in most cases.[5] The

[3] There is much debate in psychological circles about what constitutes a "defining feature". Interested readers might look at the work of Rosch on "typicality" [7].

[4] There is also a variant of 'subclass' – 'instance-of' – that allows for individual members of classes; so an object can be an instance of a class. Strictly speaking, therefore, a taxonomy allows two types of relationship between objects and concepts.

[5] This is a highly simplified summary; there is an entire journal devoted to classification. Wilkins' complete summary quotation is: "All classifications are artificial, but some have a degree of naturalness about them. Natural classifications are the result of a refinement of the intension of terms based on a very broad and generally culture-neutral set of observations. Species names, indeed all taxa names, are terms with a proper function assigned by the history of their use, and which may change as new evidence is arrived at."

practical result of these "artificial" distinctions is that taxonomies are sometimes based on relationships other than 'subclass'. Common ones are 'part of', 'causes/produces', and 'has property'[6]. In the next section, an analysis of the ACM classification will be carried out to determine what relationships are actually used.

# 4 The ACM Classification scheme: analysis

The ACM classification covers several of the multiple perspectives. The perspectives covered include "what" is needed for a computer system (hardware and software), "how" to build a computer system (techniques), and "why" systems are built (computing milieux). The categories also cover different levels of abstraction: some categories consider the contents of the computer itself (hardware, software, computer systems organisation, data, information systems) while other categories consider the computer as a single concept in the context of applications (computing methodologies, computer applications, computing milieux). There's also a third level of detail to be found in the two theoretical categories (*Theory of Computation* and *Mathematics of Computing*) which provide the foundational techniques for computer systems organisation, data and information systems. See Table 3 for a summary.

| | **What** | **How** | **Why** | **When** | **Where** | **Who** |
|---|---|---|---|---|---|---|
| **Computer applic-ations** | Computer Applic-ations | Computing Method-ologies | Computer milieux | | | |
| **What goes inside a computer** | Hardware, Software | Computer Systems Organisation, Data, Information Systems | | | | |
| **Theoret-ical level** | | Theory of Computation, Mathematics of Computing | | | | |

**Table 3: Top level categories from the ACM scheme, classified according to multi-perspective modelling**

This organisation is broadly mirrored in the organisation of some of the second level categories in the ACM classification scheme. For example, the subclasses of *Computer Systems Organisation* are *Processor Architectures* and *Computer-Communication Networks* (two disjoint components that are necessary for a functioning hardware system, aka *Hardware* and *Software* at the top level); while *Special Purpose and Application Based Systems* and *Computer systems*

[6] Each of these relationships can be broken down into a number of distinct relationships, but this level of detail is beyond the scope of this paper. For an example, see [8] on the breakdown of 'part of'.

*implementation* look at the "what" and "how" perspectives on hardware construction "applications". There's also a subcategory for *Performance of systems*, which probably falls under the "when" perspective.

The subclasses of Information Systems, Data and Software all use a similar multi-perspective classification scheme. Not all of the second level categories and their decompositions fit neatly into this multi-perspective framework, however. The subdivisions of *Computer Applications* appear to be closer to a taxonomy, in that their second level breakdown consists of different areas of study or different disciplines which reads like a list of university faculties (*Administrative data processing, Physical sciences and engineering, Life and medical sciences, Social and behavioural sciences, Arts and Humanities).* While disciplines are not strictly speaking subclasses of "computer applications", they do (or should) form a single coherent subclass of a (hypothetical) taxonomy of knowledge.[7] The two top-level categories with a theoretical leaning also have sub-categories that reflect different areas of study in the disciplines of (applied) mathematics and (applied) logic.

A third approach is found in the *Hardware* category; its subcategories name different areas of hardware design (*Control structures, Arithmetic and logic structures, Memory structures, Input/Output and Data Communications, Register-transfer-level implementation, Logic Design* and *Integrated Circuits*), each of which includes the same small set of sub-sub-categories: *Design Styles, Design Aids*, and (until it became a separate category in the 1998 classification), *Performance and reliability*. It seems, therefore, that the Hardware category is decomposed into its second level using the 'part of' relation instead of the 'subclass' relation (i.e. each subcategory is a "part of" the hardware of a computer system rather than a subclass) while a multi-perspective approach is used at the third level, which explains the recurrence of the same subcategories at this level.

# 5 The Scientific Datalink AI extension: analysis

As with the ACM classification, each of the four categories of the Scientific Datalink AI classification (as reproduced in Table 2) can be broken down into subgroups.

- *Applications and Expert Systems* has nineteen subcategories, seven of which are drawn from the "interests" in the ACM classification scheme. Most of these are concerned with different domains in which expert systems have been applied (similar to the ACM's taxonomic breakdown of Computer Systems Applications into different disciplines), but I.2.1.15 ("Expert Systems") and I.2.1.5 ("Natural Language Interfaces") are more concerned with techniques for expert system construction, and I.2.1.14 ("System Troubleshooting") focuses on a particular task rather than on a domain. The distinction between tasks and domains, which

---

[7] If the subcategories were relabelled "Applications in <Discipline>" rather than just <Discipline>", the taxonomic connection would be much clearer.

is a key tenet of the CommonKADS methodology for knowledge engineering [9], corresponds to the distinction between "how" and "what" in multi-perspective modelling.

- Most of the subcategories of *Knowledge Representation* are concerned with different knowledge representation formalisms – the "what" of knowledge representation. Frames and Scripts, Predicate Logic, Procedural & Rule-based Representations, Semantic Networks, Constraints and Connectionist Systems all fall into this category. The odd ones out are Representation of the Physical World and Representation of Natural Language Semantics; while these have some correlation with representation formalisms (e.g. simulation models with Representation of the Physical World), these two categories are primarily concerned with knowledge representation as a task rather than a formalism -- i.e. with "how" rather than "what".
- Several subcategories of *Learning* deal with different methods of learning (by analogy; induction; associative learning), others deal with subjects to be learned (Concept learning; Language Acquisition; Learning of Skills). So here there is a multi-perspective decomposition; some subclasses represent "what" subcategories while others represent "how". And then there's Knowledge Acquisition and Knowledge Engineering. Knowledge Acquisition is apparently categorised under "learning" because its subcategories include learning from examples (i.e. induction), learning by observation, learning from experience and learning by discovery. Yet several popular knowledge acquisition techniques are not covered here at all – and while there is a category named "Acquisition of Expert Knowledge" (I.2.1.15.1) two levels down from "Applications and Expert Systems", the popular techniques are classified in various different places rather than being collected together in I.2.1.15.1. Protocol analysis, for example, is categorised under I.2.11 Cognitive Modelling and Psychological Studies of Intelligence, while the analysis of interview transcripts is most closely covered under Dialogues with Experts, which is considered to be one of only three subcategories of Knowledge Engineering. The reader is left with a strong feeling that Knowledge Acquisition and Knowledge Engineering are underspecified, incomplete, and (possibly as a result) misclassified.
- The final category considered here, *Problem Solving, Control Methods and Search* seems to be something of a catch-all category for methods of controlling inference in AI programs. It has six subcategories, two of which are (unsurprisingly) *Heuristic Methods* and *Graph and Tree Search Strategies.* It also has categories for *Backtracking, Dynamic Programming, and Matching*, which are concerned with the implementation of rule-based systems, and finally a category for *Plan Execution, Formation and Generation.* Control knowledge is slightly difficult to categorise within a multi-perspective framework. In theory, it should be "meta-how" knowledge (i.e. knowledge about the process of controlling processes); in practice, it often includes information about the ordering or processes and the timing of key inputs and outputs to a process, and thus consists of "when" knowledge. This is particularly true of knowledge about planning.

To summarise: Scientific Datalink's AI extension to the ACM classification seems to stick with a formula where formalisms/resources ("what" knowledge) are mixed with methods/techniques ("how" knowledge) to generate subcategories. A taxonomic breakdown is also used (for Applications).

# 6 Correct classification of Knowledge Management, Knowledge Engineering and Knowledge Acquisition

Having carried out this detailed analysis, it is time to use the principles identified to meet the original goal of this paper: to determine where Knowledge Management and Knowledge Engineering should be classified. Knowledge Acquisition will be considered too.

## 6.1 Correct classification of Knowledge Engineering

Knowledge Engineering has been variously classified as "the design and development of knowledge based systems"; "application of logic and ontology to the task of building computable models of some domain for some purpose"; "[the study of] the development of information systems in which knowledge and reasoning play pivotal roles"; and "[a] scientific methodology to analyze and engineer knowledge". Using the classifications identified earlier, it's clear that knowledge engineering is primarily application-focused (as opposed to concerned with the internal function of knowledge based systems or theoretical principles of knowledge); and that it focuses on the task of system development (i.e., "how" knowledge). From this analysis, the following classifications of *Knowledge Engineering* are possible:

- Knowledge Engineering could be a subclass of *I.2.1 Applications and Expert Systems*. Unfortunately, *Applications and Expert Systems* uses a largely taxonomic breakdown; but there are two subcategories of *Applications and Expert Systems* that are concerned with techniques for expert system construction. These do not fit well with in the taxonomic breakdown of I.2.1, but would be appropriate siblings for Knowledge Engineering.
- Knowledge Engineering could sit alongside Software Engineering as a subcategory of *D. Software* in the ACM classification. The primary objections to this are the "political" ones – there's much more interest and activity in Software Engineering than in Knowledge Engineering, which makes it difficult to place them at the same level.
- Knowledge Engineering could be a subcategory of *D.2 Software Engineering*. This is probably the most "principled" place to put it, since knowledge engineering is indeed a subcategory of software engineering – it is software engineering for a specialised type of software system. However, this conflicts with the current basis of decomposition of Software Engineering, which is by subtasks rather than a "taxonomy" of types of software.

- Knowledge Engineering could appear alongside *Representation of the Physical World* and *Representation of Natural Language Semantics* as a "how" category under *I.2.4 Knowledge Representation* in the AI extension. The difficulty with this is that the focus of Knowledge Representation is very much on the internals of a knowledge based system, whereas the focus of Knowledge Engineering is on applications, so there is a clash in levels of abstraction.
- Finally, Knowledge Engineering could be left in its current location as a subcategory of *I.2.6 Learning*. This is probably the worst option of all, since knowledge engineering techniques (with accompanying knowledge models) are only appropriate for software that *doesn't* rely on learning as its primary input method, since it's hard to analyse knowledge that has not yet been learned.

In summary, there is no ideal location for Knowledge Engineering in the ACM or Scientific Datalink hierarchies. Since a proposal is needed, a "tie-breaker" can be found in the current subcategory *I.2.1.15 Expert Systems* of *I.2.1.Applications and Expert Systems*. This subcategory actually has a number of knowledge engineering subtasks as its subcategories already. For the sake of backward compatibility, therefore, I.2.1.15 should be left in its current position in the hierarchy, but be renamed to "Expert Systems and Knowledge Engineering".

## 6.2 Correct classification of Knowledge Acquisition

Once the classification of Knowledge Engineering has been decided, the correct classification of Knowledge Acquisition is fairly easy to determine, for Knowledge Acquisition is a subtask of Knowledge Engineering. Indeed, there is already a category I.2.15.1 named "Acquisition of Expert Knowledge". The only difficulty lies in determining where to classify those topics that are currently subclasses of *I.2.6.3 Learning: Knowledge Acquisition*. Since the Learning section needs to revised anyway to take account of (a) the removal of Knowledge Engineering and (b) the presence of Induction but the absence of two related technologies, Case Based Reasoning and Neural Networks[8], it is proposed that the subcategories of I.2.6.3 are either transferred to other categories under Learning (for example, *I.2.6.3.1, Learning from Examples*, would be appropriate for this) or moved to *I.2.1.15.1, Acquisition of Expert Knowledge.*

## 6.3 Correct Classification of Knowledge Management

Deciding where to classify knowledge management is difficult because there is considerable disagreement about the best approach to knowledge management. A good working definition of knowledge management would be "the deliberate design of artifacts with the intent to improve the use of knowledge within an organisation",

---

[8] There are existing Scientific Datalink categories for Connectionist systems under Knowledge Representation, and Connectionist Architectures under *I.2.12 Specialised AI Architectures*, but there is no explicit category for "how" to build neural networks. There is so much work on neural networks these days that it probably deserves its own separate category.

but a range of artifacts have been suggested, from knowledge based systems (thus considering knowledge management as an early stage in knowledge engineering) through to communication forums (considering knowledge management as a process of community interaction in which knowledge-based technology has no part to play). A good survey is given by Binney [10] in which he identifies a "KM spectrum" where knowledge management activities are classified according to their overall goal. Applications that embed knowledge in organisational transactions lie at the "technology-focused" end of the spectrum whereas applications that support innovation and creation of new knowledge lie at the "community-focused" end of the spectrum. Between these two extremes can be found "analytical KM" (the use of knowledge to interpret vast amounts of material); "asset management" KM; "process-based" KM (the codification and improvement of organisational processes); and "developmental" KM (increasing the competencies or capabilities of an organisation's knowledge workers).

KM is therefore generally application-focused; it can be focused on "what", "how", "who" or even "why" depending on the KM approach that is taken; and Binney's decomposition of KM is focused on "how" a particular goal should be achieved. From this analysis, options for classification of Knowledge Management would be:

- As a subclass of *I.2.1.15 Applications and Expert Systems*, alongside Knowledge Engineering;
- As a subclass of *I.2.4 Knowledge Representation*; however, the arguments against this are the same ones that applied to Knowledge Engineering;
- As a subclass of *I.2.13 Social and Philosophical Issues [in Artificial Intelligence]*. This, however, is more of a theoretical perspective while Knowledge Management is more focused on applications;
- As a subclass of *H.4 Information Systems* in the ACM classification scheme. This removes the commitment that a KM system must be knowledge-based in some fashion, and thus encompasses more of the various KM approaches than would otherwise be the case, but it's debatable whether or not Knowledge Management should appear at the same level as Database Management – for despite the similarity in terminology, these are really quite different tasks;
- As a subclass of *H.4.1 Office Automation* underneath *H.4 Information Systems*. H.4.1 already contains a category for Workflow management, which is a key enabling technology for process-based KM, and a category for Groupware;
- As a subclass of *H.4.2 Types of Systems* underneath *H.4 Information Systems*. This category currently includes "Decision support systems (e.g. MIS)" and "Logistics", both of which are reasonably application-focused and also focus on "how" tasks are done.

It seems that there are advantages in taking "Knowledge Management" outside the Artificial Intelligence classification and using the Information Systems classification instead, since some knowledge management approaches are based on software that is not knowledge based. The final recommendation is that Knowledge Management should be a subclass of *H.4.2 Types of [Information] Systems*, since it fits better alongside other types of systems (decision support systems and logistics) than alongside its own enabling technologies (workflow systems and groupware). A new category is therefore proposed, to be labelled *H.4.2.3 Knowledge Management.*

# 7 Discussion

It has been shown that the ACM classification, and Scientific Datalink's extension, are based on two or three different structuring principles: sometimes taxonomic, sometimes based on "what" knowledge, (which implies that the subcategory is something that is used for, or produced by the top level category; it is a resource in the most general sense of the word), and sometimes based on "how" knowledge – i.e. techniques for, or methods to achieve the top level category. In addition, the Hardware category has a 'part of' decomposition, and some political considerations come into play as well.

What does this tell us about the ACM classification, about multi-perspective modelling, and about ontologies in general? It tells us that if an ontology tries to use "natural" categories, then it will almost certainly be developed using multiple perspectives; so the original thesis of this paper, that multiple ontologies from different perspectives are needed for completeness, is borne out. However, the "what" and "how" perspectives are much more common than the "who", "when", "where" and "why", so it seems that while six ontologies from different perspectives may be necessary, two – with appropriate attention to whether the ontology is focused on theoretical principles, system internals, or applications -- will often be sufficient.

It also tells us that "political" considerations – the level of interest in a subject – have considerable weight when determining the level of various categories in the ontology. The underlying message of this is that there is no canonical way of determining when a set of subcategories is complete – or at least, no way that is sufficiently widely accepted to override political concerns. Some guidance on category completeness may be available from other research; to give an example, "System Troubleshooting" has been identified as the only subcategory of *I.2.1.15 Applications and Expert Systems* that represents an application-focused task. However, a set of "knowledge based tasks" has been proposed by the CommonKADS methodology [11], and one of them (diagnosis) can be instantiated to "troubleshooting". This implies that all the other knowledge based tasks should be eligible, or even expected to make an appearance in I.2.1.15; examples might be "artifact design", "system monitoring", and "selection/ assessment". But this set of tasks is not theoretically proven to be complete; in fact, the original author of this set of tasks has since revised his opinions and proposed that the tasks above are actually composed from a smaller set of five or six "primitive" tasks [12]. So while published sets of categories such as this can be pragmatically useful to ontology developers, they rarely actually solve the problem of canonically determining all possible members of a category.

The ACM classification scheme itself, along with its AI extension, is detailed, widely accepted, and reasonably principled, and so should continue to be used. Some revisions are needed, though (especially under I.2.6 Learning in the AI extension), and it is worth questioning why *Hardware* uses a different decomposition principle from the rest of the scheme: is this an artifact of political lobbying, or is there a "natural" principle here that could be extended to other areas of the classification?

Finally, the new classifications proposed by this paper have classified Knowledge Engineering and Knowledge Management very differently. This raises the issue of the purpose of a classification: should it be carried out according to ontological principles for robustness, or should it be organised to place relevant subjects close to others, to facilitate serendipitous browsing? The case of knowledge management is a difficult one because there are different opinions about it – some books on knowledge management will draw heavily on techniques from knowledge engineering and will serve as useful precursors to knowledge engineering projects, while other books will have little or no relevance to knowledge engineering. An intriguing alternative to the ontological approach would be to use learning techniques to create an entirely new classification scheme based on cluster analysis (using references, keywords, or other criteria); an examination of this approach is suggested for future research.

## References

1. Kingston J.K.C., *Multi-Perspective Modelling: A Framework for Re-usable Knowledge.* Forthcoming.
2. Kingston J.K.C. and Macintosh A.L., Knowledge Management through Multi-Perspective Modelling: Representing and Distributing Organizational Memory. Proceedings of ES '99, Cambridge, 1999.
3. Waltz D.L., Scientific Datalink's Artificial Intelligence Classification Scheme. The AI Magazine, Spring 1985, pp.58-63.
4. N. Coulter et al, Report of the CCS Update Committee. http://www.acm.org/class/1998/ccsup.pdf, 1998.
5. Kingston J.K.C., Developing a Reference Ontology for Scientific Knowledge Management. Proceedings of AAAI-02 Workshop on Ontologies and the Semantic Web, AAAI-02, Edmonton, Canada, 29 July 2002.
6. Wilkins J., Natural and Artificial Classification, http://www.users.bigpond.com/thewilkins/papers/artifnat.html, 1997.
7. Rosch E., Natural categories. Cognitive Psychology 4: 328 – 350, 1973.
8. Artale A., Franconi E., Guarino N. & Pazzi, L. Part-Whole Relations in Object-Centered Systems: an Overview. Data and Knowledge Engineering, 20(3): 347-383. 1996.
9. Schreiber A.Th., Akkermans J.M. et al, Engineering and Managing Knowledge: The CommonKADS Methodology. University of Amsterdam, Amsterdam, 1998.
10. Binney D.,The knowledge management spectrum – understanding the KM landscape. Journal of Knowledge Management, 2001, 5(1):33-42.
11. Breuker, J.A., Model Driven Knowledge Acquisition. ESPRIT project 1098 KADS, Deliverable, A1, 1987.
12. Breuker J.A., Problems in Indexing Problem-Solving Methods, Proceedings of the Workshop on Problem Solving Methods, IJCAI-97, Nagoya, Japan, August 1997.

# How Habermas' Action Types Can Influence KBS Design

Gareth Owen Jones and Andrew Basden
Information Systems Institute, University of Salford,
Salford, M5 4WT, U.K.
G.O.Jones@salford.ac.uk, A.Basden@salford.ac.uk

Abstract

Knowledge based systems (KBS) encapsulate human expertise in such as way that the user not only obtains expert advice but can explore the knowledge underlying it. This has allowed KBSs a variety of possible roles beyond the traditional consultancy role - such as checklist, communication, training and knowledge refinement. Each role demands different features of the KBS. So knowing in what roles a KBS may assist its users can help the designers focus on those features that are most important and avoid wasting effort on other features. These roles can be understood by means of Habermas' Theory of Communicative Action. This paper discusses how consideration of Habermas' action types might influence the design of knowledge based systems.

Keywords: KBS roles, KBS design, usability features, explanation, Habermas Theory of Communicative Action.

## 1 Introduction

"The technology forms only one part of the system - the people and procedures are just as important" [1] is a lesson learned in many KBS projects over the past 20 years. Because of this, the design of knowledge based systems (KBS) often includes not only a high quality knowledge base but also usability features such as hypertext linkages to related information [2], trapping of input errors [3], identification of inconsistencies [4], context-specific explanation [3], the ability to ask "What if?" and "Why?" [5], ability to override the KBS's reasoning [6], sensitivity curves to highlight critical dimensions [2], and many more. Such features are often seen as 'frills' when compared with theoretically more interesting issues such as knowledge acquisition techniques and knowledge representation formalisms, but they often make the difference between a usable and unusable KBS. This paper suggests that usability features can be theoretically interesting if we view them from the standpoint of philosophy.

KBS designers must decide which features to include and exclude, what types of explanation facilities are needed, how accurate and complete the knowledge base (KB) must be, and so on, but the theoretical basis for such decisions has not been widely discussed. Lack of theoretical basis can lead to uncertainty and wasted or misdirected effort during the development process (for example, when effort is devoted to acquiring full, accurate knowledge when it is not required). Sometimes the KBS must be substantially redesigned after it is in use because its features cannot support the roles in which it is actually used. It would be useful if there were some way of predicting which features might be useful, what types of explanation facility are likely to be needed, and the desired levels of knowledge accuracy and completeness in the light of intended or potential use of the KBS. The theory proposed in this paper opens up a principled approach to doing just this.

## 1.1 Roles, Benefits and Features

What features will be useful in a KBS are often determined by the roles the KBS will play and the benefits the users might expect from it [7]. If we see KBSs as artefacts that human beings use to facilitate their activity, then what is important is not the technological basis of the KBS, but the benefits it provides via its features and characteristics in the working situation.

The benefits to be expected are closely connected with the roles the KBS plays in its relation to its user. Basden [7] gave an early list of such roles he had found to be important in practical applications, with corresponding benefits. The list has stood the test of time and, though updated a decade later [8], was little changed:

> **Consultancy role**: By making inferences from questions put to the user, the KBS provides advice and expert guidance to the user; the benefit is that the expertise available to the user is enhanced. For example, the ELSIE KBS [6] was designed to assist quantity surveyors when setting budgets for office buildings - but was used in other roles too.
>
> **Checklist role**: By posing relevant questions to the user the KBS helps the user ensure they do not overlook important issues. The main function of KBS inference is to carefully select the questions. The results of inference are less important, leading to comments like "But its only a glorified checklist" - hence the name of the role. It was found that ELSIE was used in this role because the surveyors were legally liable for their services to clients.
>
> **Training role**: The KBS takes the user through expert scenarios by means of questions and results and, in doing so, imparts training.
>
> **Communication role**: By means of questions, results and explanations, the KBS conveys knowledge to its user(s), resulting in a form of communication. The communication can be from the KBS creator to the users, or between two users. KBS used thus have two benefits over written or visual media such as video: they can communicate the sophisticated structure of interconnected concepts, and can let the user see how that knowledge can be 'activated' in their own specific situations. A KBS that provided an arbitration service [9] can be seen as fulfilling this role.
>
> **Knowledge refinement role**: The KBS stimulates the user to reflect on, and question, their own knowledge of the domain so that their knowledge

is refined. It was found that ELSIE was used to stimulate clients to question their requirements.

**Knowledge collection role**: As a by-product of the activities of any of the above, the KBS can collect information about the users' situations, which provides the host organization with high quality knowledge.

**Monitoring role**: The KBS repeatedly seeks information about a continuously varying situation (e.g. process plant or the stock market) and highlights any unusual phenomena so users can take action.

**Programmed system role**: The KBS is designed to run automatically, often without a human user, and thus KBS technology is used largely as a programming language, the benefit over conventional languages being its ability to handle declarative knowledge and uncertainty.

**Demonstration vehicle**: The KBS is used to demonstrate possible use or benefits of KBS technology in any of the above roles.

For each role, different features of the KBS become important. For example a KBS designed for a consultancy role must possess full and accurate knowledge, while one designed for a communication or knowledge refinement role requires powerful explanation and what-if facilities instead, but does not always require accurate knowledge. Therefore, if it is known in which roles a KBS will be used, it is often possible to identify the features that should be designed into the KBS and the characteristics of its KB.

Many KBSs are used in several roles. Though designed for one role, it is often found they become used in unanticipated ways because of the flexibility in their design. For example, the ELSIE system was designed for the consultancy role but proved particularly useful in the checklist and even the knowledge refinement roles [10].

## 1.2 The Need for Theoretical Justification

The list of roles above emerged from practice but it has never been theoretically justified nor grounded in theory. So it is not clear how the roles relate to each other nor even whether the list above is complete. Nor is it clear why certain features are required for each role. It would benefit the development process and facilitate discussion between developers and users concerning the design of the KBS if theory were available about what roles there are, what features are required for each role, and what shape those features should take.

To understand such roles requires treating KBS as a social, not technical, science. While agent architectures, such as Bratman's BDI [11], might provide theory for designing agents that stand in place of human beings, they are of little help when designing a KBS to aid human tasks, especially those of an ill-structured sort; the 'beliefs', 'desires' and 'intentions' of which Bratman speaks are those represented in the technical agent while those of the human user are often not representable within the machine. However, a body of research has developed which has underscored the social nature of knowledge and the social elements of power, subjective meaning, human interests and consensus and conflict in information system design (ISD) [12]. Such a contribution has been seminal, and from this research useful development methods have emerged (multi-view, ANT, ETHICS and Critical Systems to name but a few). Central to many of these is the philosophy of Jürgen Habermas.

This paper examines the possibility that Habermas' Theory of Communicative Action could provide such a theoretical underpinning, and that the detailed picture of each action type provided by Habermas and others can identify which features it would be useful to include in a KBS when it is to fulfil each role.

# 2 Habermas' Theory of Communicative Action

Habermas' philosophical approach is to explain the world as a whole with principles to be discovered in reason. His social theory is centred on communication and seeks to clarify the conditions, means, contents, constraints and objectives of all socially organised human behaviour [13]. Indeed, [14] proposes that Habermas' action types exhaust all social action. If this is so, Habermas' action types cover all possible roles in which a KBS might be used by people and should provide the theoretical underpinning we seek to clarify and scope the roles of KBS.

## 2.1 Habermas' Typology of Communicative Action Types

All action types have a success aspect, which is defined as the appearance in the world of a desired state [13:285]. Habermas' use of the concept 'action' is very broad, incorporating any form of symbolic expression (verbal behaviour and text) and interlinked behaviour sequences such as occur in markets, courts or warfare [14]. Habermas' first key distinction is between purposive-rational action, when an actor seeks to achieve success in an objectified world, and cultural action, when actors seek understanding as a means to success. These two classes of action are further broken down as follows:

Purposive-rational Action (oriented to direct success):
- IA: Instrumental Action
- SA: Strategic Action
- DmA: Dramaturgical Action

Cultural Action (oriented to understanding):
- NRA: Normatively Regulated Action
- CA: Communicative Action
- DvA: Discursive Action

### *2.1.1 Instrumental Action (IA)*

Habermas defines IA as "actors... seek[ing] to reach their goals in an effective and most efficient fashion [by] employing predictions drawn from physical and behavioural models" [13:127-128]. These models are constructed by objectifying the 'world' [15] where everything, including human beings, is regarded as a more-or-less controllable object [14]. Success is thus dependant upon valid empirical knowledge and appropriate technical tools and theoretical models.

### *2.1.2 Strategic Action (SA)*

The difference between IA and SA is that success in strategic action is dependent on other actors, each of which is oriented to his own success and behaves co-operatively only to the degree that this fits his egocentric calculus of utility [13:87-88]. These acting subjects achieve their ends by following decision rules [16]. Though recognised as full human beings, the other actors are treated as 'opponents' to control for one's own purposes - as in game theory. These actions can be either open (war) or covert (indoctrination) and a prerequisite for success is that the actors have an accurate set of facts and a correct picture of the relevant relationships.

### *2.1.3 Dramaturgical Action (DmA)*

Goffman [17] first used the term, dramaturgical, in his work, 'The Presentation of Self in Everyday Life' and it is used by Habermas to describe the way an actor wishes to express himself to an audience when putting himself on 'stage'. Habermas distinguishes between a subject capable of free-will expression and an observable object with such properties as extension, weight and colour, to demonstrate the dramaturgical action of human actors [13:91]. Encounter and performance are key concepts in which participants form a visible public for each other and perform for one another, hence, attributes of style, aesthetic expression and formal qualities play an important role [13:90,92]. Dramaturgical action can be of a strategic nature, where stylistic features are employed to project a certain impression to an audience treated as opponents rather than as a public [13:90,93].

### *2.1.4 Normatively Regulated Action (NRA)*

NRA starts the action types that are cultural. It includes the social world and the social group to which an actor belongs as a role- playing subject [13:85]. NRA is so termed because the social group establishes norms to define a common predictable social world in which actors may orientate [13:88] and success is defined by these 'constraints' [14]. Members of any group can expect other actors to behave in accordance with and with reference to these norms [13:89], a simple example of which is drivers conforming to the highway-code [14].

### *2.1.5 Communicative Action (CA)*

"Communicative action focuses on [reaching] a common agreement and understanding of social norms, meaning and values, and on maintaining social relationships" (Habermas, quoted in [14]). The central concept in CA is interpretation: negotiations between people that allow them to achieve a consensus understanding. Habermas draws particular attention to validity claims, which are directed toward the truth of facts, the rightness of norms and the sincerity of the actor [18] and in such action the actor is confronted with a system of worlds: the objective world assumed in teleological action and the inter-subjective social world assumed in normatively regulated action [14].

*2.1.6 Discursive action (DvA)*

Discursive action is an expression of the 'concept of communicative rationality' and the 'central experience of the unconstrained, unifying, consensus bringing force of argumentative speech' [13:10]. (Strictly speaking, Habermas saw DvA as a level within CA, but many treat it as a distinct form of action, and we do so here.) It is in discursive action that validity claims are challenged, enabling consensus about the situation at hand. In DvA it is the speaker rather than the content of discourse that is challenged, and the 'force of the better argument' determines which claims are upheld via 'inter-subjective conviction' [13:36]. 'Ideal discourse' requires conditions free of threats in which all participants are able to question validity claims and all listen to reason [19:151].

## 2.2 Worlds

To Habermas, the various types of action involve three 'worlds', objective, subjective and social. These worlds are what we can or do talk about, have explicit concepts for or are aware of. All action types involve the objective world of facts, DmA, CA, DvA involve the subjective world of feelings and NRA, CA, DvA involve the social world of right and wrong.

But Habermas posits a fourth 'world', the lifeworld, which the action types do not involve but rather are carried out within, as their linguistic and cultural framework. The lifeworld comprises the "reservoir of taken-for-granteds, of unshaken convictions that participants ... draw upon in ... processes of interpretation" [20:124-127]. The 'taken-for-granteds' involve shared tacit agreements or disagreements, either about technical matters, or, in NRA, CA and DvA, about inter-subjective social world of values, norms, feelings and quality of life.

Thus, to engage in each type of action we employ knowledge of the worlds that the action type involves, we do so within the framework of the lifeworld. When we use a KBS to aid a particular type of action, knowledge from the relevant worlds is encapsulated in the KB, and the lifeworld forms the environment within which the KBS and its users operate.

# 3 Applying Habermas' Action Types to KBS Design

In this section, in the light of the previous sentence, we attempt to apply Habermas' thinking to the process of KBS design. We find that the design of the KBS is strongly influenced by the action type that the KBS is intended to serve, by Habermas' worlds and by the lifeworld of the user. Typically, KBS have been designed to give advice to aid purposive-rational types of action, but it is often found that the use to which they are actually put is more in line with the cultural action types. In real life use, a KBS might aid the user in a number of ways, so the implications the intended purpose has for its design should not be too rigidly applied.

We consider a number of factors in this light. First, we consider the correspondence between KBS roles and Habermas' action types. A discussion of different types of world leads into considering how content and style of knowledge and the degrees of accuracy and completeness needed in the KB can vary with action type. In its turn, this can influence the knowledge acquisition process. Then features of the KBS that the user experiences during a session are discussed, together with what types of explanation are needed for each action type. Note that the more usual technical discussions about whether the KBS should operate by a goal or data directed inference process, what knowledge representation languages should be employed, etc. are not discussed because they are little affected by the action type of the user. Table 1 summarizes the whole discussion.

## 3.1 Roles of KBS

We can see a correspondence between Habermas' action types and Basden's [7] roles of KBS.

- ♦ In a consultancy role, the results and explanations a KBS gives are designed to increase the user's success in whatever task they are undertaking. This is directly equivalent to IA.
- ♦ In a checklist role, the KBS ensures that its users do not overlook important issues. In most cases such issues are related to norms of the situation, so we can see that a checklist role KBS assists NRA.
- ♦ As might be expected, the communication role corresponds almost exactly with Habermas' CA. In this role, several users gain a shared understanding when they use the KBS together, discussing each question as it arises. By making clear the interrelationships in the domain of knowledge and 'activating' the knowledge in the KBS to show how it works in specific situations of interest, such a KBS can clarify areas of misunderstanding, including contextual misunderstandings, and can stimulate consensus.
- ♦ In a training role, the KBS is used to impart knowledge, either by means of explanation or by giving the user practice with simulated situations. This can be seen as assisting CA in which the participants are the designer and the user of the KBS, but it might also be seen as a type of SA since in training we are trying to achieve success in changing human beings.
- ♦ In a knowledge refinement role, the questions, results, etc. of the KBS stimulate users to question their beliefs and assumptions. This corresponds quite closely with DvA. One of the authors was involved with such a KBS

in the early 1980's, used by managers of business sectors in a company to reflect on the various aspects of the quality of their sector. Holding overview knowledge about these aspects of business, the KBS would pose probing questions, then ask the user to express their beliefs and explore reasons for them. This system was so highly valued that it was made company secret and never reported in the literature. The knowledge refinement role, however, is not always social; in one example [21], a corrosion expert took responsibility for constructing the KBS and, in the process, discovered gaps in his knowledge. He then undertook laboratory experiments to obtain the knowledge to fill these gaps. Correspondence between the knowledge refinement role and DvA is not total.

♦ The knowledge-collection role is less easy to align with Habermas' action types. But in some cases the purpose of collecting information is to allow the host organization to exert power over, or adapt to, the users, so in such cases, the KBS serves SA.

♦ In the monitoring or programmed system roles a KBS would seem to serve IA, but in a more restricted way than in the consultancy role.

♦ In a demonstration role, the KBS is used by the user to present something of their purpose or person, and thus we can see a similarity with DmA (dramaturgical action). What is demonstrated is usually one of the other roles, so how DmA affects the design of a KBS will depend not so much on DmA itself but on which other roles are being demonstrated. This echoes Lyytinen's [14] view that dramaturgical action (DmA) is of marginal interest to information systems design. However, the user interface assumes greater importance because of the audience.

Thus we can see that many of the important roles in which KBS can usefully correspond with Habermas' action types. Though not total, the correspondence is sufficient to propose that we can replace most of the roles with action types and benefit from the exposition that Habermas made thereof.

Sometimes a KBS can be used to support several types of action. The budget module of the ELSIE KBS [6] is an interesting case. Initially designed for a consultancy role, it was also used in the checklist and knowledge refinement roles. That is, it was used to assist IA, NRA and DvA or at least CA. Its ability to support these three types of action arose from the features designed into it, such as what-if, overriding and various types of explanation, which happened to support these other types of action, as we discuss below. Its knowledge contained not only physical, spatial and numeric calculations about office buildings, but also human preferences about such things as quality of finishes.

## 3.2 KBS Knowledge Types

The type of knowledge that is sought during elicitation for encapsulation in the KB is determined by the type of world that the users' actions involve. For IA the knowledge is of the objective world, of the pre-human aspects (mathematical, physical, biological), and may often be represented in logic. SA includes objectified knowledge about human action and response, which is often treated probabilistically (e.g. probability that share prices will rise) because human action is difficult to predict. For DmA the KB must also include knowledge from the subjective world, which often means asking users to express such things as preferences or feelings on a sliding scale, and finding suitable algorithms to take these into account.

For NRA, the KB should encapsulate knowledge about relevant norms and issues from the social world, with appropriate ways of representing compliance with norms. It is important to ensure that all relevant aspects of the situation in which the KBS is to be used are included, and the Multi-Aspectual Knowledge Elicitation (MAKE) method [22] was designed to achieve this.

For CA and DvA, knowledge from all three worlds is needed. In particular, the KB must contain significant amounts of knowledge on how to encourage effective communication (CA) or stimulate self-reflection in the user (DvA). It is tempting to assume such knowledge is simple enough to represent procedurally (e.g. present result then ask user's opinion) but it is often much more complex. In ELSIE [6], for example, 50% of the code was for enabling exploration, what-iffing and overriding and presenting explanations. Recognising this, and planning for it, can improve efficiency during development.

## 3.3 Completeness and Accuracy of Knowledge

The size and difficulty of the knowledge acquisition process depends not only on how complex and voluminous the domain knowledge is, but also on how complete and accurate a knowledge base need be. For some action types it is not always necessary to achieve full completeness or accuracy.

Completeness and accuracy are difficult concepts and always relative to the purpose of KBS. 'Complete' means that all areas or major topics that experts in the domain would deem it is necessary to cover have been represented in the KB, while 'incomplete' means that some might be missing. 'Accuracy' is related to how much we can trust the KBS to not mislead its users in any of the areas or topics in the domain. In particular, omitting contextual knowledge can make the KBS 'brittle' in use, suddenly letting the user down without warning [24].

In IA and SA, where there is direct action in an objectified world oriented to success, accuracy needs to be as high as the available knowledge permits. Accuracy may be less important for NRA, but completeness is paramount. With CA, both completeness and accuracy of domain knowledge that is represented in the KB are less important; what is important is to represent the users' and designer's own interpretations as completely and accurately as possible within the social context of use. This is often achieved via the explanation facilities rather than the inferences made in the KB (the main purpose of which are to disclose the interpretations). DvA is similar to CA but completeness and accuracy are mildly important because users are loath to question their assumptions unless they trust the knowledge framework in the KB.

## 3.4 Knowledge Acquisition Strategy

The boundary between world and lifeworld is not always clear and the KB will usually include some knowledge from the latter as well as the former. Difficulty in knowledge acquisition is partly due to the 'taken-for-granted' nature of the lifeworld, but this can be reduced by a knowledge acquisition strategy that recognises that knowledge can exist in different forms [23,24]:

> **E, Experience**, is heuristic knowledge that individuals actually use in their everyday situations. It is efficient in use because it has assumed a form that is specific to the individual, their usual ways of working and the contexts they ordinarily meet.
>
> **U, Understanding**, is knowledge that is generally (agreed to be) true by the community of experts across a range of contexts, and its inclusion tends to make a KB more robust - but it is not always available.
>
> **CPS, Context-Dependent Problem-Solving**, is knowledge of the context, the strategy adopted for the action being carried out, and characteristics of the individual that holds it.

Approximately, U corresponds to Habermas' worlds and CPS to lifeworld. E (heuristics) is a fusion of U with CPS, in which the latter takes the form of tacit assumptions. A KB can contain all three forms of knowledge, but each has a different impact on the quality of the KBS, as discussed in [8,24]. Inclusion of U makes the KBS robust across many contexts and users and provides higher quality explanations, and the inclusion of CPS in explicit form makes it easier to adapt to specific contexts. The inclusion of E can be problematic, leading to brittleness and poor quality explanations, but it is often E that is obtained during knowledge acquisition. However techniques are available for converting E into explicitly separate U and CPS [e.g. 8].

The importance of each depends on the type of action the KBS is designed to support. For IA and SA, all three (U, E, CPS) may be explicitly represented in the KB, but for SA the CPS can be more difficult to define, leading to a greater dependence on E and thus to a higher risk of 'brittleness'. For NRA, the knowledge must often be valid across many contexts, so U is particularly important. For CA and DvA, CPS is often important because of the need to make cultural meanings or other assumptions explicit during the operation of the KBS, but there must always be a core of U to facilitate shared understanding or useful reflection.

In some DvA KBSs, a core KB is built using the above methods but the users add knowledge to it or modify it each time the KBS is used. Allowing users to modify the KB can lead to inconsistencies with knowledge in the KB of which the users are unaware. The first knowledge that users will bring into the KB will be their E, their immediate perceptions and beliefs, and as such it will be subjective and context dependent. It may be that these problems can be reduced by guiding the users to separate out U from CPS.

## 3.5 Session Structure

The session structure refers to what the user experiences during the process of interacting with the KBS. The basic structure is a sequence of questions, results, and explanations of each at various points.

In a KBS that supports IA, this basic session structure may suffice, but for all other types it is useful to augment it with other features. In SA, where fallible inferences are made about human beings, it is often useful to include a facility by which the user can override the inferences made by the KBS. In ELSIE, for example, inferred quality factors, building sizes, costs of various elements of the building could all be overridden. For NRA, facilities that enable the user to evaluate their situation according to the norms, or vice versa, can be useful - visual indications such as bar charts and traffic lights can be very useful.

For CA, the users' understanding may be enhanced by two types of facility that open up, respectively, the structure and behaviour of the knowledge. Understanding of structure of the knowledge can be achieved by facilities for semantic exploration, such as graphical rendering of the inference net or the step-by-step exploration offered by the Istar Knowledge Server [25]. Understanding of behaviour of the knowledge, especially around critical values, can be expedited by sensitivity analyses [2] and 'what-if' facilities [5].

DvA is supported by facilities not normally found in a KBS. While the emphasis in KBS designed for most action types is to help the user to believe the knowledge conveyed by the KBS, the emphasis in DvA is on encouraging the user to disbelieve. The user is invited to question both the knowledge in the KBS and their own knowledge. In the company-secret KBS mentioned above, the session was split into several parts, each concerned with an aspect of business. Each part was composed of a few questions, a request for the user to declare their own beliefs, a declaration of the KBS' belief, an invitation to explore areas of disagreement, an invitation to alter previously given answers and, crucially, an invitation to select either their own beliefs or those of the KBS.

## 3.6 Explanation Type

The explanation facility seeks to communicate the meaning of the knowledge handled by users and KBS during the session. For purposive-rational actions this need only explain what the questions or result texts mean. But to assist cultural action, oriented towards understanding, the explanation facilities should also disclose the rationality and normativity of the domain. To aid NRA, the explanation focuses on the normative element of the knowledge (in ELSIE this included necessary building elements such as roof, walls, foundations, and various regulations), especially of why norms are, or are not, relevant, and on what would happen if the norms were transgressed (which could involve 'what-if' facilities). CA and DvA are aided by facilities that disclose the semantic structure of the knowledge and allow cultural meanings to be investigated. For DvA explanation is also needed of departures from expectations and why arguments are valid or invalid. 'Why not' facilities are useful.

The KBS users' lifeworld is a set of 'taken-for-granteds', so the use of the KBS could be jeopardised if users make assumptions that are incompatible with those made by the designers of the KBS or with each other. The style of explanation (and indeed of all the questions and results) must therefore be tailored to the type of lifeworld the users will operate within. Unfortunately, Habermas gives little guidance on the inner structure of the lifeworld, but we can note that, for IA and SA, it contains largely technical matters, while, for NRA, CA and DvA, it includes values, norms, feelings and the like and so explanation facilities for it must be more sophisticated.

# 4 Conclusion

The KBS community has seldom employed philosophical theory to underpin the notion of KBS as an element in a human social context, and consequent developmental implications. Applying the principles of Habermas' Theory of Communicative Action has been a useful exercise because it presupposes that the KBS is a social tool. We have seen how this apparently abstract philosophical notion can provide very concrete guidance to KBS designers about which features should or should not be included. These are summarised in Table 1. In conclusion, a number of points might be noted.

One is that most of the effects are visible at the knowledge level rather than at the symbol level [26], because Habermas' action types and their corresponding worlds speak of human purpose rather than symbol manipulations or structures. At the knowledge level we have been able to distinguish different roles the KBS might fulfil and benefits that users receive therefrom and have discussed different types of knowledge, different requirements for accuracy and completeness of the KB, different forms of knowledge and their corresponding knowledge acquisition strategies. We have discussed the shape of the user's interaction with the KBS during the session, and how different types and styles of explanation can support the various action types.

We have not found it necessary to discuss issues that have traditionally exercised debates in the KBS community, such as knowledge representation languages and ontology structures, data- versus goal-directed reasoning, graph search, or the validity of various types of inexact reasoning. These are largely symbol level issues. It is, of course, necessary to attend to these during implementation of the KBS (for example, 'what if' and 'why not' facilities involve graph search), but since they are not visible at the knowledge level, they are not much affected by the Habermasian action types.

In these discussions we have drawn mainly on experience in real-life use of KBS to find examples of facilities that have already been implemented in KBSs. But it may be that reflection upon Habermasian action types might suggest new types of facility hitherto not currently seen in KBS.

Though Habermas' theory is not without its problems (we have encountered some above, and deeper problems are discussed in [27,28]), it has nevertheless proved most useful in this study in providing a reference point from which to explore the nature, purpose and desired features of KBSs. It can challenge the knowledge engineer to develop methodology of a more social and participative nature, where understanding and context are made explicit and open to amendment and validation.

## Acknowledgements

This research is partly supported by the UK EPSRC via the C-SanD project: Creating, Sustaining and Disseminating Knowledge for Sustainable Construction (GR /r20564 GR/r21332 GR/r20274). The project includes staff from Loughborough University , LSE and University of Salford . Further details available at www.c-sand.org.uk.

## References

1. Brown P. Barclaycard Fraudwatch - a KBS for detecting credit card fraud. In: Land L (ed) Knowledge Based Systems Usage. McGraw Hill, 1995, pp 147-56.
2. Devlukia J, McMahon C, Williams JS. Rover Group: a knowledge-based approach for fatigue analysis of automotive parts. In: Land L (ed) Knowledge Based Systems Usage. McGraw Hill, 1995, pp.125-46.
3. Green K. British Telecom SPOP expert system application. In: Land L (ed) Knowledge Based Systems Usage. McGraw Hill, 1995, pp.157-63.
4. Baker DM. AEA Environment and Energy: CRISIS - an expert assistant in criticality accident dosimetry In: Land L (ed) Knowledge Based Systems Usage. McGraw Hill, 1995, pp.79-89.
5. Muggeridge L. Institute of Chartered Accountants of Scotland: Assessing professional expertise using expert systems. In: Land L (ed) Knowledge Based Systems Usage. McGraw Hill, 1995, pp.173-81.
6. Brandon P, Basden A, Hamilton I, Stockley J. Expert Systems: The Strategic Planning of Construction Projects. The RICS/Alvey Research, Quantity Surveyors Division of The Royal Institution of Chartered Surveyors in collaboration with The University of Salford, 1988.
7. Basden A. On the application of expert systems. International Journal of Man-Machine Studies, 1983, 19:461-477.
8. Basden A, Watson ID, Brandon PS. Client Centred: An Approach to Developing Knowledge Based Systems. Council for the Central Laboratory of the Research Councils, U.K, 1995.
9. Cheng P. British Sugar: Expert decision support system in production monitoring. In: Land L (ed) Knowledge Based Systems Usage. McGraw Hill, 1995, pp.193-203.
10. Castell AC, Basden A, Erdos G, Barrows P, Brandon PS. Knowledge Based

Systems in Use: A Case Study. In: Proc. Expert Systems 92 (Applications Stream). British Computer Society Specialist Group for knowledge based systems, 1992.

11. Bratman MF, Israel DJ, Pollack ME. Plans and resource bounded practical reasoning. Computational Intelligence, 1988, 4:349-55.

12. Hirschheim R, Klein HK, Newman M. Information Systems Development as Social Action: Theoretical Perspective and Practice. Omega, 1991, 19(6):587-608.

13. Habermas J. The Theory of Communicative Action, Volume 1: Reason and rationalisation in society. Thomas McCarthy (tr). Polity Press in association with Blackwell Publishers Ltd, Oxford, 1984.

14. Lyytinen K. Information Systems Development as Social Action: Framework and Critical Implications. Jyvaskylan Yliopisto, Jyvaskyla, 1986.

15. Ngwenyama KO, Lee AS. Communication Richness in Electronic Mail: Critical Social Theory and the Contextuality of Meaning. MIS Quarterly, 1997, 21(2):145-167.

16. Lyytinen K, Klein HK. The Critical Theory of Jurgen Habermas as a Basis for a Theory of Information Systems. In: Mumford E (ed), Research Methods in Information Systems. Elsevier, B.V. (North-Holland), 1985, Chapter 12.

17. Goffman E. The Presentation of Self in Everyday Life. Anchor Books, New York, 1959.

18. Kunneman H. The Truth Funnel: A Communicative Theory Perspective on Science and Society. Meppel, The Netherlands: Boom (in Dutch), (1986).

19. Habermas J. The Theory of Communicative Action, Band 1. Suhrkamp Verlag, Frankfurt am Main, Germany (in German), 1985.

20. Habermas J. The Theory of Communicative Action, Volume II: Lifeworld and System: A Critique of Functionalist Reason. Beacon Press, Boston, 1987.

21. Hines JG, Basden A. Experience with the use of computers to handle corrosion knowledge. British Corrosion Journal, 1986, 21(3):151-156.

22. Winfield MJ. Multi-Aspectual Knowledge Elicitation. PhD Thesis, University of Salford, Salford, U.K., 2000.

23. Ngwenyama OK, Klein HK. An exploration of expertise of knowledge workers: towards a definition of the universe of discourse for knowledge acquisition. Information Systems Journal, 1994, 4:129-140.

24. Attarwala FT, Basden A. A methodology for constructing Expert Systems. R&D Management, 1985, 15(2):141-149.

25. Basden A. Some technical and non-technical issues in implementing a knowledge server. Software - Practice and Experience, 2000, 30:1127-1164.

26. Newell A. The Knowledge Level. Artificial Intelligence, 1982, 18:87-127.

27. Wilson FA. The truth is out there: the search for emancipatory principles in information systems design. Information Technology and People, 1997, 10(3):187-204.

28. Jones GO, Basden A. How Habermas' Action Types can influence KBS design and use. European Confenence on I.T. Evaluation, ECITE, Paris, July 2002.

| Social Action Type | Instrumental | Strategic | Dramaturgical | Normatively Regulated | Communicative | Discursive |
|---|---|---|---|---|---|---|
| **Roles of KBS** | Consultancy | Training, Collection | Demonstration | Checklist | Communication | Knowledge refinement |
| **Knowledge Types** | Objective | Objectified | Obj. + Subjective | Obj.+Social: multi-aspectual norms | Obj. + Social + Subjective | Obj. + Social + Subjective |
| **Important forms of knowledge** | U, CPS, E | U (if available), CPS, E | Depends on what is being demo'd | U of multiple aspects | CPS with U | U with CPS, modified by user |
| **KB Accuracy** | Important | Important | Depends | Less important | Unimportant. KB must well reflect human interpretation | Mildly important. As CA. |
| **KB completeness** | Important | Important | Depends | Paramount | Less important | Mildly important |
| **Session Structure** | Qns, results, explanations | Qns, override, results, explanations | User interface is important | Qns, results, explanations, assessment against norms | Qns, results, explanations, semantic explor'n sensitivity anal. | As CA, plus comparison of user's view with that of KBS |
| **Types of Explanation** | Inference structure and meaning of terms | Inference structure and meaning of terms | Depends; UI is important | Why norms are relevant | Semantic structure, cultural meanings | As CA, plus argumentation, departure from expectations |

Table 1. How Habermasian Action Types can influence KBS design

# Business Service Components: a Knowledge Based Approach

Stefania Bandini, Sara Manzoni and Paolo Mereghetti
Dipartimento di Informatica, Sistemistica e Comunicazione
Università degli Studi di Milano – Bicocca
Via Bicocca degli Arcimboldi 8
20126 – Milano, Italy
{bandini,manzoni,paolo.mereghetti}@disco.unimib.it

**Abstract**

The work described in this paper deals with the definition of an empirical model to classify components, and the development of a knowledge–based system to capture and organize the knowledge of the experts, as well as, technical documentation associated with components. The objective is to provide developers with a comprehensive tool that addresses the problem of managing (i.e. selecting, configuring, integrating and deploying) COTS components to deliver tailored software systems. The goal of the system is to support the decision process of business managers, software consultants and architects in the definition and design of services for a variety of specific application domains, mainly in the area of Electronic Business. The system should also support the engineers in the specification of software architectures that realize those services.

## 1 Introduction

Software development process defines which activities are important and in which order they have to be carried on in order to manufacture, deploy and maintain software systems. In the last decade the world of software development has rapidly evolved. In particular, the diffusion of computer networks, such as the Internet, has changed the perspective to view the development processes. Moreover, Internet–oriented information systems have been evolving into complex service platforms responding to increasing needs for business service support. Such software systems are perceived as collections of interacting components, instead of as single, often huge, bundles. Component–based reference frameworks have been developed to support the creation of complex business services by assembling a collection of independently developed macro–components within a multi–tier middleware infrastructure.

In this scenario, developers aim to increase the quality of the systems and reduce the development costs through the adoption of the so called commercial off–the–shelf components (COTS). According to [7], the term COTS means a software product, supplied by a vendor, that has specific functionality as part of a system, a piece of pre–built software that is integrated into the system and must be delivered with it to provide operational functionality or to sustain maintenance efforts.

For the purposes of this paper, we focus on the development of business component systems, which can be defined as a set of cooperating business components assembled to deliver a solution to a business problem [7]. In turn, a business component is a component, typically a COTS component, which implements a single autonomous business concept.

Building software systems out of components has changed the development process. In the simplest form, three activities have to adressed: COTS identification in the requirement analysis phase, COTS selection in the design phase, and COTS integration and testing to deliver the complete system [5, 6]. Even if this is a simplification of a real development process, it is adequate to the purposes of this paper. This assumption has been confirmed in other works [7]. The reader may refer to [3] for a detailed discussion on development processes and to [5] for component–based development processes. *Component identification* is associated with requirement analysis phase. The activity consists of the definition of the functionalities that will be part of the final system, along with the interaction among such functionalities. This is a high–level process in which software engineers concentrate on the business logic. At the same time, the gross system architecture is defined by the identification of relationships between business components. The next phase deals with *component selection* and it is associated with the design process. The activity consists of the definition of the actual system architecture, which means that the gross architecture and the business functionalities undergo a consistency verification to identify missing functionalities. Then, candidate business components are identified and a preliminary compatibility check is carried on. The third phase consists in the integration of candidate COTS components (*integration phase*) and in the development of new software. The development of new software addresses two needs: the development of adapters to integrate COTS components, and the implementation of missing functionalities. Integration requires a in–depth understanding of the environment surrounding each business component, that is, communication protocols and the services it relies on. There are two possibilities, with a number of intermediate situations in between. On one hand, there are components that are already compatible since they rely on the same infrastructure and use the same communication paradigms. On the other hand, there are components that rely on different infrastructures and adopt different communication paradigms. In the latter case, integration implies a possibly huge effort in designing and implementing adapters to achieve the desired integration.

The issue of defining a right process to include components is affected by a number of issues related to the status of component technologies. In fact, there is lack of standard definitions that establish rules to develop, configure, integrate and deploy components. Currently, there are proposals for standards (Enterprise Java Beans, CORBA component model, Microsoft DCOM/.NET) that are not yet mature and, most important, are not completely accepted by the Information Technology community [9]. Therefore, software developers have to deal with a plethora of pseudo–standards, and proprietary solutions. Despite this lack of conceptual and formal models and methodologies, the development of business service platforms drastically changed the technology solution scenario. For instance, e–business technology provides a key competitive advantage for many companies, responding to hard operational requirements (robustness, scalability, etc.).

Therefore, component–based development is already perceived as a viable way to deliver quality software reducing the overall costs. Moreover, component–based solutions are required by Internet–based business service software that requires inter–operability among independent actors to deliver e–business applications. For example, an e–commerce application may require the presence of a merchandize supplier, a financial intermediary, and a delivery organization. Each of these actors usually provide services through applications that need to be integrated to deliver the e–commerce system.

The design and development of business services define a new and dynamic software architecture domain that requires novel solutions to cope with the rapid growth of technology–based business models and new kinds of domain–specific applications. The knowledge about these solutions is owned by professional practitioners with different skills and different roles in a development team. The knowledge ranges from strategic to engineering and it supports different concerns. For example, the expert knowledge is used to address marketing strategy design activities, to define the set of services offered to users, to address project planning, to select a suitable technology to cope with development constraints. Business managers, software architects and engineers are the main experts involved in problem solving activity and, in many cases, their empirical knowledge supports all the process: rapid development, configuration, customization and deployment.

To carry on the activities identified so far, a huge amount of detailed and precise information is needed. Unfortunately, documentation of software products is hard to produce and maintain due to continuous changes in the environments and in the functionalities. Moreover, available documentation is written is natural languages, hence with a number of unavoidable ambiguities that introduce uncertainty to identify and qualify the provided functionalities. This is a well–known problem that has not a solution yet: formal and semi–formal languages (e.g., UML [1]) support the description of the component syntax, but no effective counterpart exists for semantic description.

Over these common problems about documentation, the lack of models and standards to describe, design and compose software components introduce a considerable overhead. The reality is that formal and precise description of components is not usually available. According to [6], the only way to cope with the missing and incomplete information problem is to grasp the desired knowledge from human experts that can supply additional information derived by practices and experience.

The work described in this paper deals with the definition of an empirical model to classify components, and the development of a knowledge–based system to capture and organize the knowledge of the experts, as well as, technical documentation associated with components. The knowledge–based approach to support software development process has already been investigated and validated [8]. This paper focuses on components providing business services and its objective is to provide developers with a comprehensive tool that addresses the problem of managing (i.e. selecting, configuring, integrating and deploying) COTS components to deliver tailored software systems. The goal of the system is to support the decision making process of business managers, software consultants and architects in the definition and design of services for a variety of specific application domains, mainly in the area of Electronic Business. The system should also support the engineers in the specification of software architectures that realize those services.

# 2 The component model

For the purposes of this paper, an effective component model needs to capture those features that are useful to address system development issues identified in the previous section.

The proposed component model refers to the following component definition [5]:

1. A component is a self–contained software construct that has a defined use, has a run–time interface, can be autonomously deployed and is built with foreknowledge of a specific component socket;

2. A component socket is software that provides a well–defined and well–known interface to supporting infrastructure into which the component will fit;

3. A component is built for composition and collaboration with other components.

From this component model, two different types of components have been derived: *Business Components* (BC), that maps to definition 1, and *Middleware Service Components* (MSC), that maps to definition 2. Relationship between components has been defined according to definition 3.

## 2.1 Business Components and Middleware Service Components

A business component is the implementation of a business concept, that is a specific *functionality*. For example, a credit–card system component implements the business logic that deals with the process of payment by credit card. The semantics of a business component are defined by the functionality it provides. It has been assumed that functionalities are associated with BCs by definition. This assumption has been introduced to overcome the lack of practical and precise means to describe functionalities in detail, and to adopt criteria that are common practice: components implement well–known functionalities

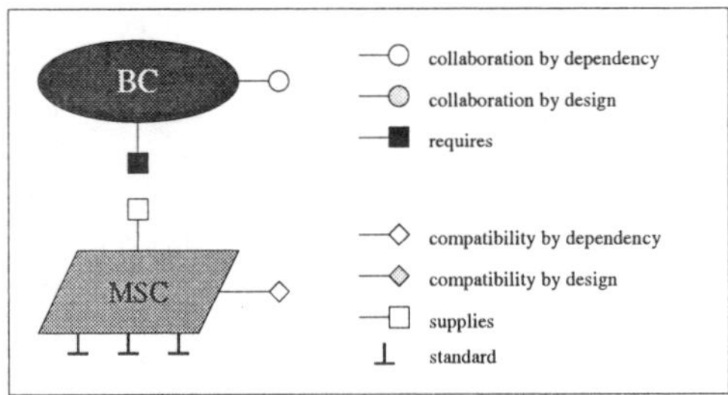


Figure 1: Relationships defined on BCs and MSCs

(i.e., concepts), and experts use that knowledge to assembly software systems. Functionalities associated with BCs rely on services that are supplied by MSC components. In other words, MSCs define the environment for business components, and therefore support BC inter–operation. An Enterprise Java Bean (EJB) container is an example of MSC that defines the services an EJB component can access and, in particular, how it communicates with other EJB components.

As shown in Figure 1 two sets of relationships have been defined to deal with Business Components and Middleware Service Components, respectively.

Business components support three kinds of relationships. *Collaboration by dependency* and *collaboration by design* that is defined between BCs only; and *requires* relation that involves MSCs. Collaboration by dependency refers to a well–known relation between two different BCs, that is, it states that a component requires another component to provide its functionality. For example if in the configuration task, there is a BC that supplies the billing functionality, it has been assumed that also a BC that supplies the tax handler functionality must be included since the two functionalities are logically correlated. Collaboration by design means that a communication between two BCs is defined by the designer. For example, the designer can state that a BC that supplies the catalog manager functionality needs one that supplies inventory management functionality to address the specific requirements of a system. The *requires* relation encapsulates the need of a BC for services. Such services are supplied by one or more MSCs, hence the requires relation cannot be applied between two BCs.

Similarly to the collaboration relation that holds for BCs, the *compatibility* relation has been introduced for MSCs. The compatibility relation can be classified in compatibility *by dependency* and *by design*. Compatibility by dependency means that a well–known compatibility relation is defined between two MSCs. For example, it is well–known by domain experts that the Tomcat web server and the JBoss EJB container can be used together to develop web–based applications. The compatibility by design relations are deduced by configuration requirements, as shown in section 3.2.2. In the work described in this paper, compatibilities by design have been derived by experience in de-

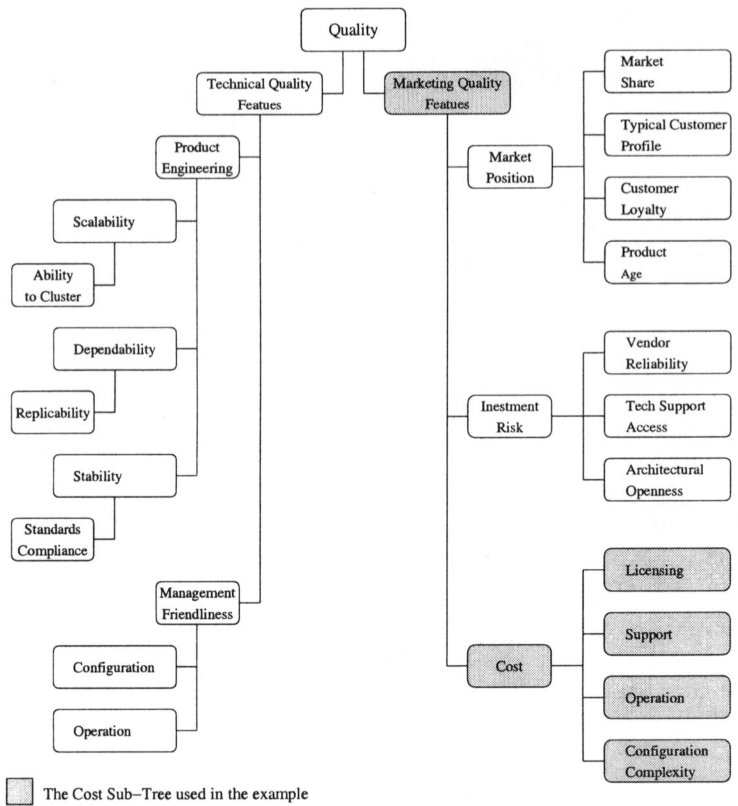


Figure 2: Quality Features Tree

signing architectures for e–commerce systems. The *supplies* relation represents the different services supplied by the MSCs and can be viewed as the logical counterpart of the BCs requires relation. In addition a MSC can *comply* to standards. Standards deal with communication protocols to define data exchange and interaction protocols between components. Examples of standards are CORBA, XML, HTTP, SSL and TCP/IP protocol.

COTS software products described according to the proposed component model set up the Component Repository (Comp–Rep), a database of components that, following the terminology adopted for component–based architectures, realize a set of services by providing an implementation for them.

## 2.2 Quality value component description

BCs and MSCs are also described by a set of quality features that are organized into a tree–structured hierarchy. Each product in the Comp–Rep has an associated Quality Tree, whose values are populated by an expert that is responsible for it. Each node $n$ represents a quality feature and has a value $q(n)$ associated with it. For simplicity, in this discussion it has been assumed $q(n) \in \{1,\ldots,10\}$ (or other small range of ordered values) for each $n$. Also, it has been assumed that the ordering is consistent across each $n$: a higher value for a feature always denotes "better" performance for that feature. We further assume that $q(n)$ is defined for each $n$ in the tree. In 3.2.1 it will be shown how to specify a set of quality values in the Comp–Rep queries, in order to select only the items that exhibit those desired quality values.

In the quality tree, different branches represent different quality features, while each level in the hierarchy corresponds to a specific level of granularity for a particular quality feature. Thus, children of a particular feature node refine the quality metrics for that feature. The rationale behind this structure is to let Comp–Rep users select products whose description is stored in the Comp–Rep based on only a fragment of the quality features, as needed. This fragment can be either vertical (a detailed characterization of a specific feature), or horizontal (a high–level characterization of multiple features), or a combination of both.

Figure 2 shows the quality tree that has been adopted in the development of supporting tool described in section 3. The tree–structure is based on the separation between *Marketing Quality Features* and *Technical Quality Features*. Each branch can be extended arbitrarily to include and refine quality values. For example, the marketing quality features have been refined adding three categories: *market position*, *investment risk* and *cost*. Cost category has been further specified in *licensing*, *support*, *operation* (e.g. dedicated staff, etc.) and *configuration*. Through further refinements, users can achieve a fine grain specification to meet their needs.

# 3 The supporting tool

This section describes the knowledge–based system that has been developed to support the decision making process of business managers, software consultants and architects in the definition and design of e–business services. Two types of knowledge are implemented into the supporting tool. The first one concerns the implementation of the component model above described, while the second one encapsulates the knowledge that experts use for component selection and integration tasks. After an overview of the tool architecture (section 3.1), a description of the logical steps the tool must go through will be given in section 3.2.

## 3.1 The tool software architecture

Due to the need to access the tool using a web browser, its implementation has been based on the EJB (Enterprise Java Bean) technology. Figure 3 shows the schema of the tool architecture.

The *Tool Configurator Bean* is a façade and it is used to wrap the user requests and handle them by calling the *Tool Configurator Context*. The Tool

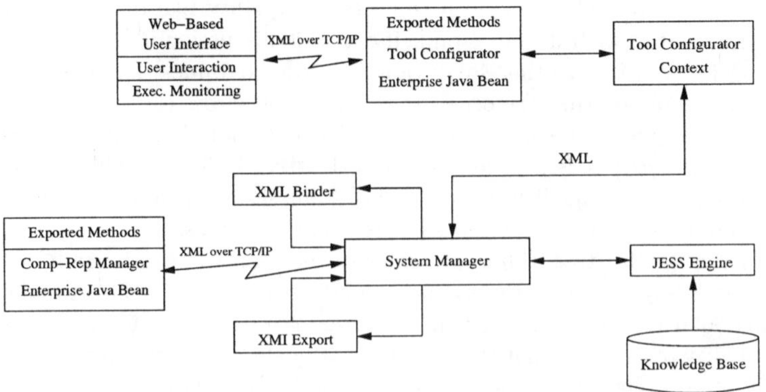


Figure 3: The tool architecture

Configurator Context is in charge of handling the *state–sensitive* user input. It mantains an internal state that is used to syncronyze tool questions with user answers on the web front-end. The *System Manager* is the module that coordinates the use of the different modules in order to complete the configuration task. Since all the information exchanged between the System Manager, the user interface (through the Tool Configuration Context) and the *Comp–Rep Manager* are represented according to the XML standard, a *XML Binder* has been included to transform the XML content in Java objects that can be used during the configuration process. The System Manager is also in charge of managing the *Knowledge Base* module. The Knowledge Base module is composed by two different parts; the knowledge base and the expert system shell (JESS the Java Expert System Shell [2]) that manages the knowledge base. Also the Comp–Rep Manager is EJB based and it is completely indipendent. Both the requests to the Comp–Rep Manager and the results are expressed in XML. The output representation can be either in XML or XMI (XML Metadata Interchange). In the latter case the *XMI Exporter* module is used to transform the Java objects in the corresponding XMI representation.

## 3.2 The knowledge–based module

The tool input can be a set of BCs, a set of functionalities or a mix of both. Also the collaboration by design relations are part of the tool input. If the input includes functionalities, the tool uses the criteria described in 3.2.1 to identify and select a suitable BC that implements each given functionality.

The knowledge about compatibilities by dependency associated with components is used by the tool to complete the input adding components and needed relations. For example if the input contains a BC that implements the billing functionality and a BC that implements the tax handler functionality is not present, the tool includes that component and applies a collaboration by dependency relation between the two BCs. So if the billing functionality is present and the tax management functionality is not, the tool adds this functionality in the configuration proposal. As it will be better described in session 3.2.2, the tool is based on the *generate and test* approach, that is, after the input completion and the component selection phases, the tool generates an hypothesis of solution and then tests if it is a suitable one.

### *3.2.1 Component selection*

Comp–Rep users may select products based on their quality features, using a sort of "query–by–example" mechanism that reflects quality requirements for a given class of products. A query is a tree template that is isomorphic to the features tree defined above. A node $n$ in the query tree ($Q$) either contains a pair $(e(n),\mu(n))$, or its value is undefined. The expression $e(n)$ is either a constant value $e(n) = c$ in the same range as the corresponding quality feature in the quality tree, or it is a constraint of the form "$e(n)\ rel(e(n))\ val(e(n))$". $val(e(n))$ is the value that must be satisfied by the value $e(n)$ according to the relational operator $rel(e(n))$. The supported relational operators include $<$, $\leq$, $>$, and $\geq$. The number $\mu(n)$ is a weight and represents the relevance of the query node, relative to all other expression nodes in the query tree.

Nodes of tree $Q$ with an associated value expression form the set $def(Q)$. Nodes in $def(Q)$ for which $rel(e(n))$ is defined form the set $rel(Q) \in def(Q)$. Finally, nodes whose value is undefined are simply not considered by the query evaluation algorithm.

The goal of the query is to fetch a predefined (maximum) number of trees that satisfy the relational constraints or that satisfy a relaxed version of the constraints. This is achieved by fetching a limited-size answer set and then ranking it. Component ranking relies upon three functions computed for each tree in the answer set: its distance from the query tree, a quality indicator, and a constraint violation index. Specific ranking criteria can be defined using these three functions, as exemplified below.

**Distance:** given a product tree ($P$) and a query tree ($Q$), we apply the usual definition of distance to each pair of corresponding nodes:

$$\delta(P,Q) = \left[ \sum_{n \in def(Q)} \mu(n) \cdot \Big[q(n) - val(e(n))\Big]^2 \right]^{\frac{1}{2}}$$

**Quality Indicator:** this indicator provides an estimate of the global quality of a product tree compared to the query tree. The larger this number, the better the quality. It is defined as follows:

$$\alpha(P,Q) = \sum_{n \in def(Q)} \mu(n) \cdot \Big|q(n) - val(e(n))\Big| \cdot \Big[q(n) - val(e(n))\Big]^2$$

**Constraint Violations Indicator:** this function counts the number of constraint violations, it is defined as follows:

$$\beta(P,Q) = \sum_{n \in rel(Q)} f(q(n), e(n))$$

where $p(q(n), e(n)) = \big(q(n) rel(e(n)) val(e(n))\big)$ is a predicate, and

$$f(q(n), e(n)) = \begin{cases} 0 & \text{if } p(q(n), e(n)) \text{ is true,} \\ 1 & \text{if } p(q(n), e(n)) \text{ is false} \end{cases}$$

Given these three functions, several ranking criteria can be defined. For example the ranking algorithm can first look for small distances with no constraint violations, then for increasing large distances, and finally relaxes the constraints. An alternate ranking may instead proceed by increasing the distance (starting from zero), picking smallest distance first within a given radius, then relaxing the constraints within the radius, then increasing the radius, and so on.

The Comp–Rep is populated by experts that can enter quality values at any level of the quality tree depending on the available information. For example, an expert that is very confident about the cost structure of a product may enter the corresponding information at the leaf level (licensing, support cost, etc.) for the cost sub–tree (see Figure 2). At the same time, he may omit all the value assignments below, say, the "investment risk" feature.

Since it has been assumed earlier that each tree node must have a value, and experts are allowed to enter partial quality information, a mechanism for assigning the missing values, both upwards and downwards, has been defined. Users may associate quality requirements with their queries into the Comp–Rep, by specifying a quality query tree that is isomorphic to that of the quality tree. In practice, the user will likely use a "wizard–like" interactive interface to input her quality requirements. Users are presented with simple, high level questions in order to assess their propensity to risk, their technology and software budget and their expected levels of connections (customer targets). The tool then constructs the tree template that represents the query, and submits it to the module responsible for the product selection.

#### *3.2.2 Compatibility issues*

The generate phase starts with the identification of all the MSCs that supply at least one of the services required by the BCs. It might be the case that none of the MSCs that are available to the tool provides a required service [12, 13]. To handle this situation, the concept of *ghost–MSC* has been introduced. Such ghost components are included to complete the system architecture. The tool will advise designers of the characteristics that the ghost–MSC must have in order to satisfy the configuration requirements. Then the user is in charge of either implementing such service or supplying new components.

A configuration proposal is composed by the set of BCs (with the collaboration and requires relationships), the set of MSCs that satisfies the services required by the BCs and the set of compatibility by design relationships. The tool deduces the compatibility by design relations between the MSCs using the information on the relations between BCs (see below for a detailed description).

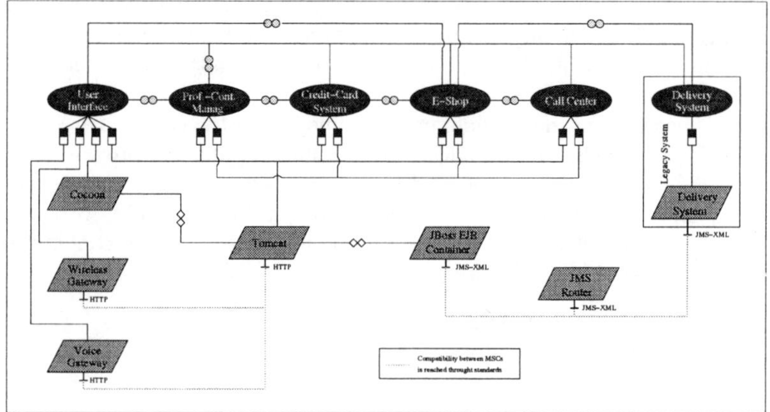


Figure 4: An example of the tool output

The aim of the test phase is to validate the configuration proposal and eventually to modify it in order to propose a suitable system architecture. If the configuration proposal contains only one MSC, the test phase is trivial and it is a suitable system architecture because the MSC is able to supply all the services required.

In the case that the configuration proposal contains two or more MSCs, the set of MSCs with the compatibility relationships are tested. The configuration output is an architecture proposal as shown in Figure 4. The output is a set of BCs and MSCs completed with all the collaboration, compatibility, require and supply relations.

Both the generate phase and the test phase follow a knowledge–base approach. Since only empirical and informal knowledge is used by the experts in their decision making process, this approach seems to be the most appropriate (other examples of this approach for the configuration problem can be found in [10] and [11]). After a knowledge–acquisition campaign conducted with a team of business managers, software consultants and architects, the acquired empirical knowledge was represented in a *rule–based* form and integrated into the tool. The knowledge–acquisition campaign was conducted following a well known methodology for the design and development of knowledge based systems [4].

The knowledge–base of the tool is partitioned into two distinct sets of rules, performing respectively the generate and test phases. The rules of the first set, are responsible for generating the compatibility by design relationships among MSCs that belong to the configuration proposal. The second one tests every compatibility by design relations and, if necessary, adapts the configuration proposal adding needed components. In order to explain how the tool performs the compatibility issue, in the following some examples of rules of both sets will be shown. For instance, referring to the code listed below, if a collaboration relationship by dependency or by design exists (line 4 "collaboration_compatibility" rule in the example) between two BCs (?bc_1 and ?bc_2 in lines 2 and 3), compatibility by design relations between the MSCs that supply services to the BCs are applied (lines 10 and 11). This rule is applied only if the solution is not present in the configuration (line 8) and the two BCs are distinct (line 7). If two MSCs (?msc_x and ?msc_y in lines 14 and 15) provide services to the same BC (condition expressed in line 16), a compatibility by design relation is applied between them ("single_bc_compatibility" rule). Also in this case the rule is applied only if the solution is not present in the configuration (line 18) and the MSCs are distinct (line 17).

```
1    (defrule collaboration_compatibility
2      (BComponent (name ?bc_1))
3      (BComponent (name ?bc_2)
4         (collaborations ?bc_1 ?bc_2)
5      (solution ?msc_x ?bc_1)
6      (solution ?msc_y ?bc_2)
7      (neq ?msc_x ?msc_y)
8        (not(pair (MSC1 ?msc_y) (MSC2 ?msc_x)))
9      =>
10     (definstance pair (new Pair ?msc_x
11       ?msc_y)))
12
13   (defrule single_bc_compatibility
14     (solution ?msc_x ?bc_1)
15     (solution ?msc_y ?bc_2)
16       (intersection$ ?bc_1 ?bc_2)
17     (neq ?msc_x ?msc_y)
18       (not(pair (MSC1 ?msc_y) (MSC2 ?msc_x)))
19     =>
20     (definstance pair (new Pair ?msc_x
21 ?msc_y)))
```

A pair of MSCs between which a compatibility by design has been applied is considered compatible if a compatibility by dependency between them is present in the Comp–Rep (Figure 5a). Another way is to find in the Comp–Rep a third component (called from now on *MSC Adapter*) that has a compatibility by dependency relationship with them (Figure 5b). The difference between Figure 5b and 5f is that the compatibility between the second MSC and the MSC Adapter is obtained using the standards that both comply with. In Figure 5c it is shown that it is possible to make compatible two MSCs using two MSC Adapters. In this case the type of the relationships between the four components are compatibility by dependency. The case shown in Figure 5d is very similar to that shown in 5c, the only difference is that the compatibility between the two MSC Adapters is reached using standards. Figure 5e shows that two MSCs can be compatible if there are some standards supported by them.

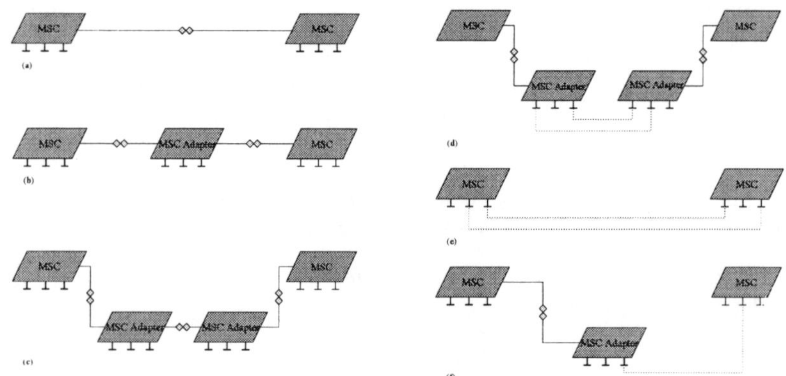


Figure 5: Some examples of possible configurations that satisfy the compatibility relationship between MSCs

# 4 Conclusions and future work

The paper has presented a knowledge–based tool developed in order to support business managers, software architects and engineers in the design process of COTS–based system solutions. The tool has been designed and developed according to expert knowledge and experience. The knowledge–base of the tool implements a model for software component configuration based on component classification in Business Components (BC – components providing business services) and Middleware Service Components (components providing services to BCs), on relations among both types of components, and on configuration knowledge derived from expert experience.

The developed tool has been preliminary tested and validated by a team of domain experts on case studies. The team of experts that tested the tool has reported its great usefulness in their everyday activity (rapid development, configuration, customization and deployment of software systems). The work presented in this paper is the intermediate result of an ongoing project regarding knowledge–based approach to configuration problem. Future activities that regard this project will deal with the refinement of component selection criteria and a further investigation of the role that standards play in the automated component integration.

# References

[1] Booch G., Rumbaugh J. and Jacobson I., *The Unified Modelling Language - User Guide*, Addison Wesley, 1999, ISBN 0201571684.

[2] Friedman-Hill E., *JESS, the Rule Engine for the Java Platform*, http://herzberg.ca.sandia.gov/jess/

[3] Garg P. K. and Jazayeri M., editors, *Process-Centered Software Engineering Environments* IEEE Computer Society Press, 1995, ISBN 0-8186-7103-3

[4] Guida G., Tasso C., *Design and Development of Knowledge–Based Systems* John Wiley & Sons, Chichester, 1994, ISBN 0-471-92808-9

[5] Herzum P., and Sims O., *Business Component Factory*, OMG Press, Wiley, 2000.

[6] Morisio M., Seaman C., Parra A., Basili V., Condon S., Kraft S., *Investigating and Improving a COTS-Based Software Development Process*, Proceedings of the 22nd International Conference on Software Engineering (ICSE 2000), Limerick, Ireland, June 2000.

[7] Morisio M., Seaman C., Basili V., Parra A., Kraft S., Condon S., *COTS–Based Software Development: Processes and Open Issues*, Journal of Systems and Software, December 2001.

[8] Seacord R., Mundie D., Boonsiri S., *K-BACEE: Knowledge-Based Automated Component Ensemble Evaluation* published in proceedings of the 2001 Workshop on Component-Based Software Engineering, Warsaw, Poland, September 4-6, 2001, IEEE Computer Society.

[9] Szyperski C., *Component Software: Beyond Object-Oriented Programming*, Addison Wesley Longman, 1998, ISBN 0201178885.

[10] Soininen T., *An Approach to Knowledge Representation and Reasoning for Product Configuration Task*, Acta Polytechnica Scandinavica, Mathematics and Computing Series (No. 111), Espoo 2000, ISBN 9516665608.

[11] Soininen T., Niemela I., Tiihonen J., Sulonen R., *Representing Configuration Knowledge With Weight Constraint Rules*, Answer Set Programming: Towards Efficient and Scalable Knowledge Representation and Reasoning, AAAI Spring 2001 Symposium, Stanford.

[12] Yakimovich D., Travassos G., Basili V., *A Classification of Software Components Incompatibilities for COTS Integration*, Software Engineering Laboratory Workshop, NASA/Goddard Space Flight Center, Greenbelt, Maryland, December 1999.

[13] Yakimovich D., Bieman J., Basili V., *Software Architecture Classification for Estimating the Cost of COTS Integration*, Proceedings of the 21st International Conference on Software Engineering (ICSE) 1999, Los Angeles, California, pp. 296-302, June 15-21, 1999.

# SESSION 3A:

# KNOWLEDGE ACQUISITION

# Capturing Consensus Knowledge from Multiple Experts

Faezeh Afshar, John Yearwood and Andrew Stranieri
School of Information Technology and Mathematical Science
University of Ballarat, Victoria, Australia
f.afshar@ballarat.edu.au

Abstract

The acquisition of knowledge from multiple experts for the development of intelligent decision support systems is difficult in that divergent opinions are often held so strongly that consensus cannot be reached. Yet, disagreement is a common feature in fields such as law, science and engineering. A model for eliciting common ground amongst experts without the involvement of extensive knowledge engineer resources is presented. The model, called Consult, enables experts to elicit a set of arguments that are plausible for an issue. The process involves three steps. A knowledge engineer initially elicits a set of arguments consistent with the generic actual argument model (GAAM) from one expert. A process based on the Delphi method is then used to anonymously elicit suggested modifications from other experts. The Borda Count voting system is used in the third phase to elect modifications preferred by experts. In this way, Consult semi-automates knowledge acquisition by capturing a consensus view from multiple experts.

## 1. Introduction

The knowledge acquisition bottleneck identified by Buchanan et al [1] almost two decades ago still remains a hurdle to the development of intelligent decision support systems. This problem typically arises from difficulties an expert experiences in articulating personal knowledge, which is often tacit or quite intricate. The problem is magnified when expertise from more than one expert is sought.

The use of multiple opinions not only helps to reveal different analyses of a given problem, but also can eventually strengthen expert consensus. Together, individual views provide a broader view and description of the problem. According to Clemen and Winkler [2], Linstone and Turoff [3], most experts know how to solve problems, but each of the individual experts may not be able to explicitly specify the overall framework of analysis. Therefore, it is assumed that when experts' opinions are pulled together, collectively, as a group they offer sufficient knowledge for building a knowledge base. Furthermore, by considering the acquired knowledge of other experts new pieces of knowledge are triggered that otherwise may not be captured.

Often, within scientific, engineering, legal and many other fields, there is not complete agreement among experts. Gaines and Shaw [4] noted that domain experts disagree with other experts in the domain and even overtime with themselves. LeClair [5] indicates that there are times when domain experts present conflicting solutions to the same problem. In addition, agreement and disagreement about domain knowledge is dynamic in nature and evolves and changes over time.

The search for ontologies that is currently the subject of substantial research aims to alleviate the knowledge acquisition bottleneck where multiple experts are involved because each expert can express personal knowledge within a standard framework. However, the underlying ontological and terminological assumptions used in ontology are often not adequately expressed or sufficiently agreed upon between experts [6].

Richards [7]] proposes that an approach that aims to explicitly capture and reconcile different and conflicting viewpoints is required. The clear demarcation between concepts and beliefs that experts share from those they do not share can facilitate the process of knowledge articulation and lead to the identification of consensus.

The problem of reconciling multiple points of view has been studied for some time. The knowledge acquisition framework advanced some time ago by Gaines and Shaw [4] provides limited assistance in dealing with inconsistencies. Trice [8] debugs two knowledge bases in order to achieve consensus. However, this relies on the unlikely assumption that the terminology and the assumptions underlying the two knowledge bases are identical.

Richards [7] captures knowledge from each expert in separate knowledge bases using the Ripple-Down rules approach advocated by Compton et al [9]. A process resolving Ripple-Down rule conflict involves face-to-face meetings. Face to face meetings are time consuming and, being non-anonymous, are complicated by emotional and power based issues. An early knowledge acquisition method advanced by Boose [10] based on the repertory grid test focuses on using knowledge from multiple sources but offers only little guidance for reaching consensus and does not fully consider the resolution of inconsistencies.

The problem of representing multiple perspectives has been peripheral to study of group decision support systems (GDSS). One stream of research in GDSS, exemplified by Shaw [11] is based on the sociology of group interactions and aims to discover the cognitive or psychological processes of individuals involved in group interactions. The other is based on the development of technology to support collecting, managing, presenting and coordinating information that might be useful in decision situations [12]. Neither approach places emphasis on the representation of different perspectives and strategies for the facilitation of their reconciliation. More recently, argumentation models have been applied to this problem.

Stranieri *et al* [13]] distinguish argumentation research into those approaches that model and support the process of engaging in a dispute dialectically from those that use argumentation to structure or organise knowledge. For example, the Zeno program [14], assists experts in the dialectical process of discussion and debating using argument concepts. The use of argumentation and the underlying non-monotonic logic based engine identifies inconsistencies for experts to resolve without guiding the resolution process in any way.

Yearwood and Stranieri [15] describe a non-dialectical argumentation approach that aims to apply argumentation concepts to structure knowledge in a domain. Their Generic/Actual Argument Model (GAAM) based on a variation of the Toulmin layout of arguments [16]. This model has been applied to represent knowledge in family law [17], Copyright regulation [18] and refugee law [15]. In all of those studies generic arguments were elicited manually from experts.

Consult (CONsensus views and a Shared Understanding of the Leading Tree) is a multi expert KA model which aims to semi-automate the KA process by capturing a consensus view based on a shared understanding of multiple domain experts. This model adopts some of the advantages of the group communication method of Delphi [3].

The Consult system described in this paper is based on the GAAM, although future research is aimed at illustrating that the Consult method can be applied with knowledge represented in other ways. Two features of the GAAM model that make it particularly suitable for representing multiple perspectives are:

- There are two levels of argument within the model; generic arguments and actual arguments. Generic arguments capture arguments at a sufficient level of generality for all experts agree. Generic arguments are similar to an ontology but are more domain specific. Actual arguments represent personal instantiations of generic arguments that represents user's beliefs. Section 2 of this paper describes the GAAM .
- The layout of claims and premises is kept entirely separate from inference mechanisms applied to premises to infer claims. In this way, multiple users can agree on a layout of claims, called a generic argument tree in the GAAM model without committing to a single inference procedure. Two users may apply different inference procedures on the same premises to infer different claims thereby disagreeing on the value inferred while agreeing on the layout of claim and premises.

In this paper a four-step process for the elicitation of generic arguments in a domain from multiple experts is advanced:

1. With a single expert, draft a generic argument tree that will be used as a starting point by the multiple experts.
2. Each expert, independently and anonymously suggests the addition of new nodes to the tree and advances their reasons for the relevance of the desired additions.
3. Each expert, suggests changes to the tree and advances their reasons for the desired change. This is a variant of the Delphi technique described by Linstone and Turoff, [3] and used successfully in software engineering.
4. All experts vote on the suggested changes so that a clear choice is made. The voting method is the Borda preferendum described by Saari [19].

Steps three is repeated until no more changes are suggested. The outcome of step four is said to represent knowledge at a sufficiently, general level for consensus. The generic tree ultimately elicited represents an understanding of the domain that all experts share.

The Consult method has been implemented as an extension of the Argument Developer program which implements the GAAM described by Yearwood and Stranieri [20]. Used with the GAAM, Consult enables a group of experts to identify the layout of claims that they all agree on. Users of the system ultimately developed, will no doubt instantiate the arguments in different ways for a diversity of views.

The GAAM model is described in the next section of this paper. Following that each step of the Consult process is described with an example.

## 2. Phase One. Eliciting Initial Generic Arguments

The first phase of the Consult process involves the generation of an initial set of generic arguments. This phase involves one expert in Consultation with the knowledge engineer. A generic argument is a structure that is sufficiently general so as to capture the variety of perspectives displayed by users of the knowledge base. Figure 1 represents a generic argument in refugee law. A generic argument has the following components:

- A claim variable and appropriate values that represent the arguments assertions. For example, the Figure 1 argument claim is that an applicant for refugee status is 'very likely', or 'likely', or 'possibly', or is 'unlikely' to have a well founded fear of persecution. When a generic argument is instantiated to construct an actual argument, for example by a refugee applicant then one of these values is selected (presumably the 'very likely' value). Experts in refugee law in our trials agree that these four values are appropriate.
- One or more data variables and values. *Real chance of persecution* and *prospects for relocation* to another part of the applicant's home country are data items, or premises that are used to infer *well founded fear.*
- Each data variable is relevant for a reason. This is often a statute in generic arguments in law.
- One or more inference mechanisms are specified in the generic argument that can be invoked to infer a claim value from data item values. An inference mechanism may be a rule, procedure, or, in the case of 'myHuman' an unspecified discretion a decision maker has.
- Reasons for the appropriateness of inference procedures
- Any number of context variables and values setting the context in which the generic argument applies

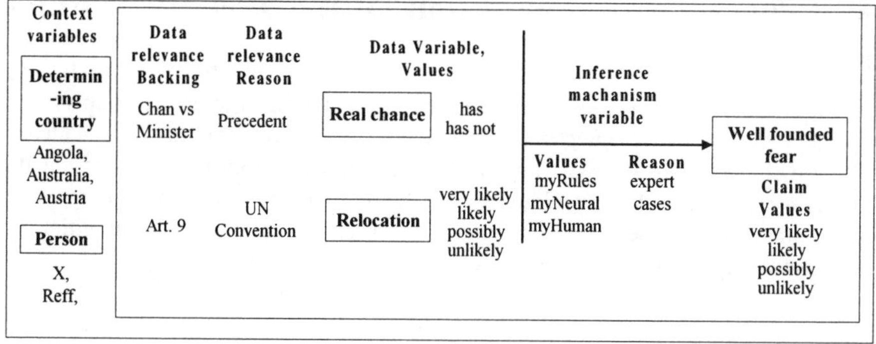


**Figure 1. The GAAM's Argumentation template**

Each data item in a generic argument can be the claim of another argument. Generic arguments are thereby linked together to form a tree of arguments. Figure 2 illustrates part of the generic argument tree relating to refugee status as it appears in Consult. Only the claim and data items appear in the tree. The user performs a mouse click to display the entire generic argument associated with any claim.

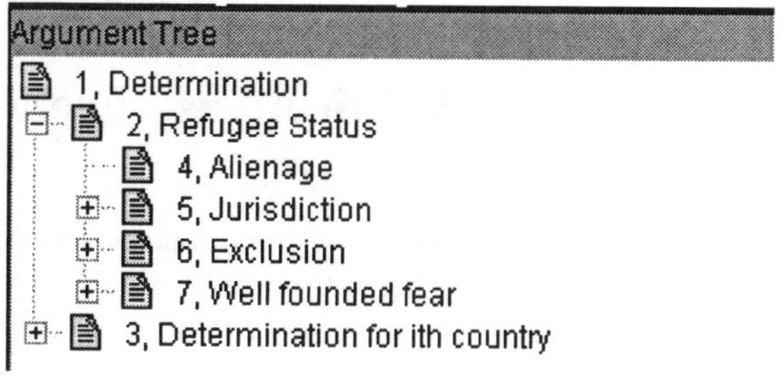


**Figure 2. Part of the refugee law generic tree in Consult**

The tree illustrated in Figure 2 was elicited with experts from the Refugee Review Tribunal of Australia by the authors operating as knowledge engineers. In the next phase, this initial tree is made available to multiple experts for suggestions. This phase is currently being performed so results to date are illustrative only and are described in the next section.

# 3. Phase Two. Completion Of the Tree By Multiple Experts

In this phase, using the GAAM knowledge representation structure, the experts add any node that is not presented in the tree in any form; a node should not be added in the tree if there already exist any node that could be modified to represent the expert's perspective. This would eliminate the redundancy of the data and the need for summarization. The outcome of this phase as shown in Figure 3 is an initial KB to be modified by all participated experts.

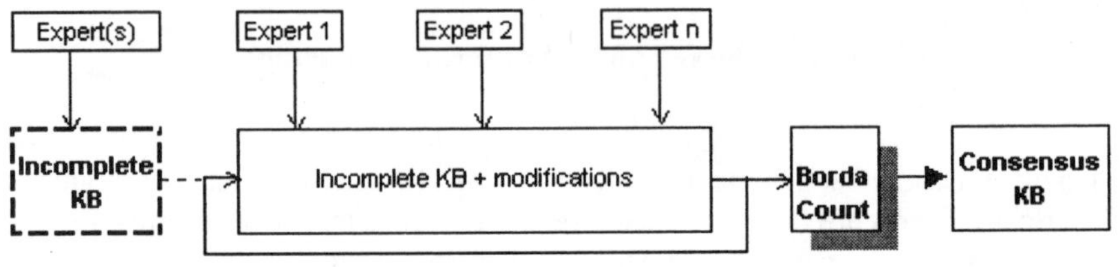


**Figure 3. The construction of initial KB by incremental knowledge acquisition of domain experts**

# 4. Phase Three. Modifications From Multiple Experts

Figure 4 illustrates the process of eliciting suggested modifications. The initial tree elicited from Phase 2 is first made available to one expert. The initial tree and the first expert's suggestions for modification including reasons are then made available to the second expert. When all experts have had an opportunity to make a contribution Phase 4 is invoked and all suggestions are voted on.

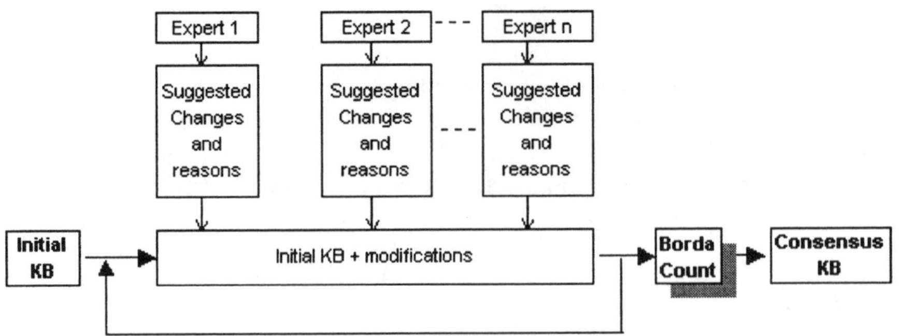


**Figure 4. The experts' changes and reasoning to KB to achieve consensus view**

Consult allows the collaboration of experts in dynamically contributing their knowledge to the system and to modify and evolve the system, as shown in Figure 5. In this approach experts are all the creators of the resulting decision support system, so feel a sense of ownership. Unlike most other groupware the goal of our approach is not only to provide a means of communication between multiple experts to express their ideas and conflicting views but also to facilitate the generation of new concepts and the refinement of those already presented.

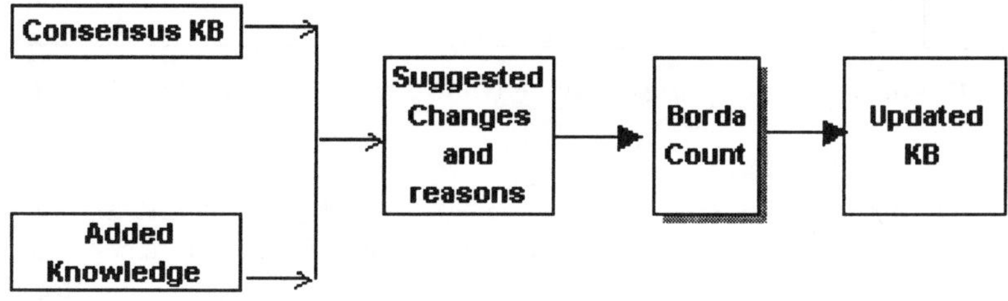


**Figure 5. The process of updating the KB**

Each expert in Phase 3 is permitted to make the following types of suggestions:

- Remove, modify or add claim, data or context variables
- Remove, modify or add variables values
- Remove, modify or add reasons for relevance of data items
- Remove, modify or add acceptable inference mechanisms
- Remove, modify oı add reasons for inference mechanisms

Figure 2 illustrates that the relevant data items in the generic argument that has *refugee status* as its claim are; *alienage*, *jurisdiction*, *exclusion* and *well founded fear*. The *refugee status* claim refers to whether or not the applicant ought to be considered a refugee or not. A data item in this argument is the *well founded fear* claim illustrated in Figure 1. Another relevant data item refers to *jurisdiction* and represents the claim that the Tribunal clearly has, or does not have jurisdiction to assess the case. For example, if the applicant has not lodged an application within specified time limits, the Tribunal no longer has jurisdiction to make a ruling on refugee status according to relevant statutes. The root of the tree is the *determination* claim. In most cases, the determination is simply the refugee status result. However, there are some cases where the assessment of refugee status may be positive yet the final determination is not.

Table 1 illustrates suggestions that experts have made in a sample trial of the Consult system.

| Node No : 5 | Parent No : 2 |
|---|---|
| **Suggestion** | *Move to Parent Node 1* |
| **Supporting reason 1** | Jurisdiction does not impact on refugee status decision |
| **Supporting reason 2** | The jurisdiction issue is a separate decision from the refugee status decision |
| **Supporting reason 3** | Jurisdiction impacts on the ultimate determination but has nothing to do with refugee status |
| **Contrary reason 1** | The Tribunal considers jurisdiction issues together with refugee status issues |

**Table 1. Reasons for and against moving Node 5 from Parent 2 to Parent 1**

The Consult approach allows each expert to work asynchronously and independently of the others avoiding the numerous issues of face-to-face communication. In face-to-face communications individual experts sometimes submit themselves to biase. Follow the leader tendencies can diminish individual creativity and minority views may not be heard adequately. In Consult there is no need to bring experts together. This allows knowledge elicitation by a geographically dispersed panel of experts, and anonymity permitted by Consult diminishes problems with group interaction identified by Stasser [21] and others [22] [23] [24] [25].

This phase of the Consult process is similar to the Delphi technique described by Linstone and Turoff [3]. The Delphi Method is a structured process for gathering information from multiple experts. In its standard form, a questionnaire is distributed to each expert and responses are anonymously collated by the Delphi moderator. Responses form the basis of a subsequent questionnaire. This process is repeated until a stopping criteria is met. Since its inception, the Delphi Method has been used in a wide range of fields such as forecasting, software engineering and management.

Consult has much in common with the Delphi process but its goal is different. The objective of Consult is to construct a well defined structure, the generic argument tree. Furthermore, all suggestions are advanced by participating experts themselves. Whereas in Delphi the initial questionnaire and all the subsequent changes to it are done by intervention of the moderator. Consensus in the Consult approach, is the result of experts reflections on the reasoning others have advanced for modifications and not the result of statistical findings perceived by a Delphi moderator.

## 5. Phase Four. Voting

The achievement of consensus on a generic argument tree between multiple experts is a central objective of the Consult model. Experts in any field have a unique mental model for understanding and interpreting domain knowledge. This interpretation and understanding evolves with experience. According to Gordon and Morrow [26], mental models are built by experiencing significant aspects of our physical and social world. Therefore each individual interprets the world and creates their mental models differently.

A voting process is used to reach the goal of capturing the consensus on the generic arguments. The Borda Count (BC) is adopted for the voting process in Consult. The Borda Count is a decision-making methodology that is not majoritarian. The voters rank each suggestion with a limited number of points. Points for each option are then summed and the winning suggestion scores more points than others. Saari, [19] claims that the Borda Count appears to be a unique method in representing the true wish of voters as long as voters express their preferences honestly and do not attempt to manipulate the result. There is little risk of this occurring in the context of a knowledge engineering exercise so it is well suited to the task of identifying a consensus view amongst experts.

Figure 6 illustrates the screen from Consult that relates the result of a Borda Count on votes for each reason associated with the suggestion to move Node 5 to parent 1. The move was carried with a Borda Count result of 80%. This is reported as carried with 80% consensus.

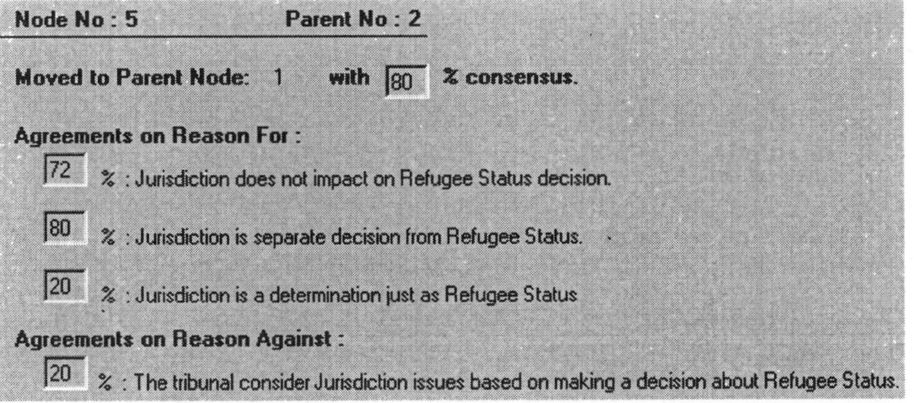


**Figure 6. The result of the Borda Count for the suggestion to move node 5 to parent 1**

# 6. Conclusion

Consult provides a means for capturing the opinions of multiple experts that involves the resources of a knowledge engineer only marginally more than if a single expert was involved. The approach initially involves a knowledge engineer in consultation with a single expert to elicit a representation of knowledge to be used as starting point for multiple expert acquisitions. In the current work knowledge is gathered in the form of generic arguments consistent with the generic actual argument model advanced by Yearwood and Stranieri [15]. However, future applications of the Consult method are planned that involve other knowledge formalisms in order to identify the extent to which the approach is appropriate for other formalisms.

Once an initial set of generic arguments is elicited from a single expert, others are invited to make suggestions. Suggestions are invited from experts anonymously, avoiding well documented pitfalls of face-to-face meetings in a process that is similar to the Delphi method. However, whereas the Delphi method requires a moderator to collate results for subsequent iterations, in Consult, experts themselves are invited to reflect upon the views of others. This encourages deliberation prior to an election on each suggestion. The election occurs as the third phase of the Consult process and is performed using the Borda Count method. This is a preferential voting system known to produce fair results as long as voters are honest.

The Consult process is currently being trailed with a group of experts in refugee law. Soon, another trial will commence to elicit opinions regarding a politically sensitive issue related to Australian aborigines in order to determine the extent to which the Consult method can be applied more generally than a knowledge acquisition device for multiple experts towards a model of deliberative democracy.

## References

1. Buchanan B, Barstow D, Bechtal R, et al. Constructing an expert system. In: Hays-Roth F, Waterman D, Lenat D (eds) Building Expert systems. Addison-Wesley, MA, 1983
2. Clemen RT, Winkler RL. Limits in the precision and value of information from dependent sources. Operations Research 1985; 33: 427-442
3. Linstone HA, Turoff M. The Delphi Method, Techniques and Applications. Addison-Wesley Publication Company, London, Amsterdam, Don Mills, Ontario, Sydney, Tokyo, 1975
4. Gains BR, Shaw ML. Comparing the Conceptual Systems of Experts. The 11th International Joint Conference on Artificial Intelligence 1989; 633-638
5. LeClair SR. A Multi expert Knowledge System Architecture for Manufacturing Decision Analysis. Ph.D. Dissertation, Arizona State University, Tempe, Arizona, 1985
6. Skuce D. Conventions for Reaching Agreement on Shared ontologies. In: Gaines B, Musen M (eds) Proc. 9th BANFF Knowledge Acquisition for Knowledge-Based Systems Workshop. SRDG Publications, Banff, Alberta, Canada, 1995, pp. 3-19
7. Richards D. Negotiating a Shared Conceptual Model using Groupware. In: Proceedings of the 11th Australasian Conference on Information Systems, 6-8 December. Brisbane, Australia, 2000
8. Trice A, Davis R. Consensus knowledge acquisition information technologies group, Working Paper. MIT School of Management, 1989
9. Compton P, Edwards G, Srinivasan A, et al. Ripple-down-rules: Turning Knowledge Acquisition into Knowledge Maintenance. Artificial Intelligence in Medicine 1992; 47-59

10. Boose J. Expertise Transfer for Expert Systems Design. Elsevier, Amsterdam, 1986
11. Shaw ME. Group Dynamics: The Psychology of Small Group Behavior. third ed. McGraw Hill, New York, 1981
12. Vogel D, Nunamaker J. Group Decision Support System Impact: Multi methodological Exploration. In: Galegher J, Kraut R, Egido C (eds) Proceedings of Conference on Technology and Cooperative Work (Tucson, Arizona, February 25-28). National Science Foundation, Bell Communications, University of Arizona, Tucson, 1988
13. Stranieri A, Zeleznikow J, Yearwood J. Argumentation structures that integrate dialectical and non-dialectical reasoning. To appear in Knowledge Engineering Review 2002;
14. Gordon TF, Karacapilidis N. The Zeno argumentation framework. In: Proceedings of the Sixth International Conference on AI and Law. ACM Press. New York City, NY, USA, 1997
15. Yearwood J, Stranieri A. The integration of retrieval, reasoning and drafting for refugee law: a third generation legal knowledge based system. In: Seventh International Conference on Artificial Intelligence and Law, ICAIL. ACM Press. 1999
16. Toulmin SE. The uses of argument, . Cambridge University Press, Cambridge, England, 1958
17. Stranieri A, Zeleznikow J, Gawler M, et al. A Hybrid rule- neural approach for the automation of legal reasoning in the discretionary domain of family law in Australia. Artificial Intelligence and Law 1999; 153-183
18. Stranieri A, Zeleznikow J. Copyright regulation with argumentation agents. Information and Communication Law 2000.; 10: 123-137
19. Saari DG. Basic geometry of voting. Springer, Berlin, New York, 1995
20. Yearwood J, Stranieri A. An argumentation shell for knowledge based systems. In: Proceedings of IASTED International conference on Law and Technology. 2000
21. Stasser G. Information Salience and the discovery of hidden profiles by decision making groups: a "thought experiment." Organisational Behaviour and Human Decision Processes 1992; 156-181
22. Turoff M, Hiltz SR. Computer Based Delphi Processes. Cited at:http://eies.nJit.edu/~turoff/Papers/delphi3.html, 2002
23. Scheibe M, Skusch M, Schofer J. Experiments in Delphi Methodology, supported by the Urban Systems Engineering Center, Northwestern University. In: Linstone HA, Turoff M (eds) The Delphi Method, Techniques and Applications. Addison-Wesley Publication Company, London, Amsterdam, DonMills, Ontario, Sydney, Tokyo, 1975, pp. 262-288
24. Damian D, Eberlein A, Shaw M, et al. Studies in Distributed Software Requirements Engineering. In: Proceedings of the 12th Workshop on Knowledge Acquisition, Modelling and management, KAW. Banff, 1999
25. Diehl M, Stroebe W. Productivity loss in brainstorming groups: toward the solution of a riddle. Journal of personality and social psychology 1987; 497-509
26. Gordon HB, Morrow DG. Mental models in narrative comprehension. Science 1990; 44-48

# Improving Collaborative Personalized TV Services *
## A Study of Implicit and Explicit User Profiling

David Wilson, Barry Smyth, and Derry O' Sullivan

Smart Media Institute
University College Dublin
{david.wilson,barry.smyth,dermot.osullivan}@ucd.ie

**Abstract.** As part of an ongoing research programme in personalized TV services, we have been developing a range of personalization and recommendation techniques that are well suited to the TV domain. In this paper we describe recent work on the application of data mining methods as a means of extracting programme similarity knowledge from shallow user profiles in order to address the sparsity problem normally associated with collaborative-filtering techniques. In particular, we compare the use of implicit behavioural profile data from Físchlár—a deployed online personal video recorder system—with the use of explicit user-rating profile data from PTVplus—a deployed online personal electronic programme guide—as employed in our earlier work. We evaluate the approach to show that it benefits from superior personalization accuracy across a range of experimental conditions, and that the benefits extend to implicit as well as explicit user profiling.

## 1 Introduction

Recent years have seen dramatic changes in the TV sector on a number of fronts. The advent of Digital TV services has offered consumers a greater range of channels and programming content in addition to a host of interactive services. In parallel, new breeds of TV-based consumer devices have emerged, such as personal video recorder (PVR) technologies (e.g., TiVo, WinTV). With the availability of this unprecedented array of video and TV content consumers are faced with a new challenge of how to search and browse for relevant content in an intuitive and efficient way. The personal electronic programme guide (pEPG) is one answer to this challenge that provides users with an interface to programming content that is personalized to their needs. Such systems employ user profiling and information filtering techniques to learn about the viewing preferences of individual users in order to pro-actively promote programmes that are relevant to an individual user.

As part of our ongoing research programme into personalized TV services we have been developing a range of personalization and recommendation techniques that are well suited to the TV domain. In this paper we describe recent work on the application of data mining methods to extract programme similarity knowledge from shallow

* The support of the Informatics Research Initiative of Enterprise Ireland is gratefully acknowledged.

item-rank profiles in order to address the sparsity problem normally associated with collaborative filtering (CF) techniques. We evaluate our approach to show that it benefits from superior personalization accuracy across a range of experimental conditions. Our earlier work in this area employed only explicit ratings-based user profiles as the central source of preference information. In this paper we focus on new results from the collection of implicit behavioural profile data by monitoring the use of an online server-based PVR system called Físchlár (www.fischlar.dcu.ie) [1] .

## 2 Digital TV Services Background

As a background for the current work we focus on two important technologies: a personalized TV listings service called PTVplus (www.ptvplus.com) [3] ; and Físchlár, an online video recording, playback and browsing service. PTVplus is a Web-based personalized TV listings service that automatically learns about the viewing preferences of individual users by monitoring their online behaviour and how they rate specific programmes. PTVplus uses a combination of content-based and collaborative filtering techniques to pro-actively compile TV guides that are personalized for the preferences of an individual user. PTVplus is an ideal example of a pEPG.

Físchlár is a separate online system that focuses on the recording, playback and browsing of video content. It is a server-based system that allows Web-users to interactively schedule TV programmes for recording so that they may be archived and played back at a later date. Físchlár also incorporates sophisticated video analysis and browsing capabilities to allow users to efficiently browse through recorded content by recognising and extracting key frames within video content to serve as a programme summary. Both PTVplus and Físchlár have been deployed and currently attract thousands of users on a regular basis. Recently there has been an opportunity to couple both systems, which solves a number of critical problems that both experienced on their own. For example, users of the Físchlár system were hampered by a rudimentary static electronic programme guide as the primary recording and playback interface. The result was the need to browse through many pages of listings content in order to locate a programme to record. By integrating PTVplus' personalized TV listings service it is now possible to offer users a far more effective personalized EPG interface.

Moreover, one of the key problems with the PTVplus system has been the fact that it has always been disconnected from the TV domain; in the sense that users could not access the PTVplus listings through their TV set and so the tasks of locating programming content and viewing programming content were separated. One implication of this is that user preferences could only be gathered by asking users to provide explicit preferences information, either in the form of programme lists or programme ratings. By integrating PTVplus and Físchlár technologies users can now access TV listings and view programming content from a single location and interface. Furthermore, by monitoring the behaviour of a Físchlár user, by analysing the recording, playback and browsing behaviour, it should be possible to infer their programme preferences directly, without the need for explicit preference information. In the remainder of this paper we describe our recommendation technique and focus experiments on the issue of explicit versus implicit profiling in the context of programme recommendation within the Físchlár-PTVplus system.

## 3 Improving TV Programme Recommendation

Modern recommender systems typically employ collaborative, content-based filtering techniques, or some combination thereof [5–7, 4, 8–10]. PTVplus, for example, employs a combination of case-based reasoning and collaborative filtering. In this research, we are interested in improving the collaborative recommendation component employed by PTVplus and the Físchlár-PTVplus combination.

Collaborative techniques incur a cost in gathering enough profile information to make accurate user similarity measurements. This *sparsity problem* tells us that, on average, two users are unlikely to have rated many of the same items and so there will be little direct overlap between their profiles. This is problematic when it comes to retrieval, because it means that there may be no direct way to measure the similarity between two profiles unless we have access to additional knowledge that allows us to compare non-identical profile items. Our approach applies automatic data mining techniques to extend the similarity relationships between programme items.

Previous work has demonstrated the validity of using data mining techniques with CF and CBR for recommendation and its effect in combating the sparsity problem [11]. Data mining techniques have been used in other recommendation research [12]; our approach differs with respect to use of the knowledge generated. We use association rules to augment standard collaborative filtering algorithms rather than using these rules directly to provide recommendations.

## 4 Mining Programme Similarity Knowledge

There are many automated techniques that could be used to derive programme item similarity knowledge. The approach we have chosen is to apply data mining techniques (see [13] for an overview), in particular the *Apriori* algorithm [14], to extract association rules between programmes in user-profile cases. By discovering hidden relationships between TV programmes, we may be able to cover more potential profile matches and, at the same time, make more informed recommendations [11]. For example, under conventional collaborative filtering techniques, a person that likes *X-Files* and *Frasier* would not normally be comparable to a person that likes *Friends* and *ER*, but discovering a relationship between *Frasier* and *Friends* would provide a basis for profile comparison.

### 4.1 Item Similarities

By treating user profiles as transactions and the rated programmes therein as itemsets, the Apriori algorithm can be used directly to derive a set of programme-programme association rules and confidence levels. We have limited this phase of the work to rules with single-programme antecedents and consequents. Confidence values are taken as probabilities and used to fill in a programme-programme similarity matrix, which provides the additional similarity knowledge necessary to compare non-identical profile items [11].

Since the matter of additional similarity coverage rests in populating the similarity matrix as densely as possible, a natural extension suggests itself. The rules can be chained together ($A \Rightarrow B$ and $B \Rightarrow C$ imply $A \Rightarrow C$) to provide indirect programme relationships. A choice then has to be made as to how the indirect rule confidence will be calculated (e.g., minimum, maximum, or some combination of the confidences in the potential paths); our experiments present results from a number of different models. Rule similarity knowledge that is generated by Apriori, we refer to as *direct*, and additional derived knowledge as *indirect*.

Building such item-item similarity knowledge to address the sparsity problem is similar in spirit to item-based collaborative techniques [15]. The item-based collaborative approach uses rating overlaps to build item-item similarities, and suggested items are then retrieved in direct comparison to the elements that comprise a user profile. The direct nature of such item retrieval, however, recalls direct content-based item recommendation, as well as the potential cost in terms of diversity.

## 5 Recommendation Strategy

The availability of item similarity knowledge facilitates a new type of similarity-based recommendation strategy that combines elements from case-based and collaborative recommendation techniques [11]. It facilitates the use of more sophisticated CBR-like similarity metrics on ratings-based profile data, which in turn make it possible to leverage indirect similarities between profile cases, and so generate improved recommendation lists. This new recommendation strategy consists of two basic steps:

1. The target profile, $t$ is compared to each profile case, $c \in C$, to select the $k$ most similar cases.
2. The items contained within these selected cases (but absent in the target profile) are ranked according to the relevance to the target, and the $r$ most relevant items are returned as recommendations.

### 5.1 Profile Matching

The profile similarity metric is presented in Equation 1 as the weighted-sum of the similarities between the items in the target and source profile cases. In the situation where there is a direct correspondence between an item in the source, $c_i$, and the target, $t_j$, then maximal similarity is assumed (Equation 2). However, the nature of ratings-based profile cases is such that these direct correspondences are rare and in such situations the similarity value of the source profile item is computed as the mean similarity between this item and the $n$ most similar items in the target profile case $(t_1, ..., t_n)$ (Equation 3).

$$PSim(t, c, n) = \sum_{c_i \in c} w_i \cdot ISim(t, c_i, n) \tag{1}$$

$$ISim(t, c_i, n) = 1 \;\; if \; \exists \, t_j \, \epsilon \, t : \; t_j = c_i \quad (2)$$

$$= \frac{\sum_{j=1..n} sim(t_j, c_i)}{n} \quad (3)$$

Notice, that if $n = 1$ and there is a perfect one-to-one correspondence between the target and source profile cases, then this profile similarity metric is equivalent to the traditional weighted-sum similarity metric used in CBR. Figure 1 demonstrates how these equations work on example profiles using rules and their associated confidences.

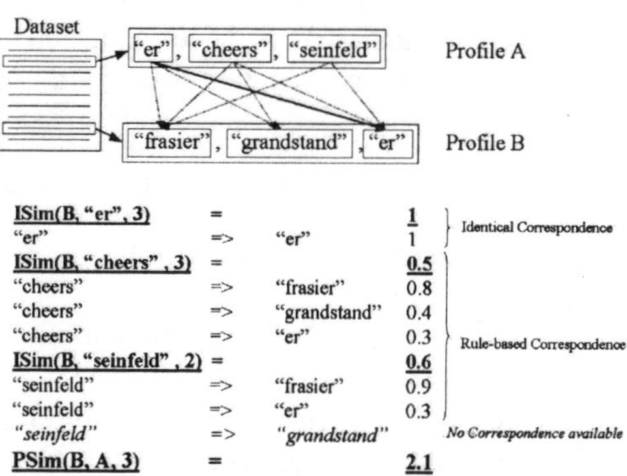


| | | | | |
|---|---|---|---|---|
| **ISim(B, "er", 3)** | = | | **1** | Identical Correspondence |
| "er" | => | "er" | 1 | |
| **ISim(B, "cheers", 3)** | = | | **0.5** | Rule-based Correspondence |
| "cheers" | => | "frasier" | 0.8 | |
| "cheers" | => | "grandstand" | 0.4 | |
| "cheers" | => | "er" | 0.3 | |
| **ISim(B, "seinfeld", 2)** | = | | **0.6** | |
| "seinfeld" | => | "frasier" | 0.9 | |
| "seinfeld" | => | "er" | 0.3 | |
| *"seinfeld"* | => | *"grandstand"* | | *No Correspondence available* |
| **PSim(B, A, 3)** | = | | **2.1** | |

**Fig. 1.** Profile/Item Matching Example.

## 5.2 Recommendation Ranking

Once the $k$ most similar profile cases ($\hat{C}$) to the target have been identified a set of ranked item recommendations can be produced. There are three factors to consider when ranking these recommendations. First, we want to give priority to those items that have a high similarity to the target profile case. Second, items that occur in many of the retrieved profile cases should be preferred to those that occur in few profile cases. Finally, items that are recommended by profiles that are similar to the target should be preferred to items that are recommended by less similar profiles. Accordingly we use each of these factors as multiplicands to compute the *relevance* of an item, $c_i$, from a retrieved profile case, $c$, with respect to the target profile, $t$, as shown in Equation 4; where $C' \subseteq \hat{C}$ is the set of retrieved profile cases that contain $c_i$.

$$Rel(c_i, t, \hat{C}) = ISim(c_i, t, k) \cdot \frac{|C'|}{|\hat{C}|} \cdot \sum_{c \epsilon C'} PSim(c, t, k) \quad (4)$$

# 6 Experimental Evaluation

## 6.1 Setup

In order to evaluate our approach to mining and applying similarity knowledge, we conducted an initial series of experiments using data from 622 PTVplus user profiles [11]. The first set of experiments were designed to investigate the performance characteristics of our chosen data mining algorithm within the PTVplus domain. The second set of experiments tested the potential for mining additional similarity knowledge using the chaining paradigm (see Section 4.1), in terms of relationships between programme items. The third set of experiments tested the potential of the approach for improving actual recommendation quality. In this work, we have conducted the experimental series using both explicit user-rating profiles and implicit behavioural profiles from Físchlár.

**Datasets** - We conducted our experiments using 5 further datasets:

1. Físchlár dataset consisting of 650 explicit user profiles of similar form to those in the PTVplus dataset.
2. Físchlár behavioural datasets each consisting of 650 implicit ratings profiles made by the video library system:
   (a) Record - Profiles created using requests received for programme recordings;
   (b) Browse - Profiles created using requests received to browse programmes;
   (c) Play - Profiles created using requests received to view programmes;
   (d) Combined - A combination of the above behaviours;

**Algorithms** - The following recommender models are used in the experiments:

1. Collaborative Filtering Model - These algorithms provide full functionality of existing CF systems. Due to required comparative analysis, we also implement an extended version of CF which also ranks items deemed relevant to the user (see Section 6.5).
2. Direct Model - Here, we simply take the rules generated by the Apriori algorithm for use in our recommender system.
3. Indirect Models -This model provides an extension to the direct model by combining confidences in rule paths to chain rules; currently we simply combine these probabilities using addition, average, maximum, minimum and multiplication.

For experimental runs, we examined only positively rated items, leaving negative ratings for future work.

## 6.2 Tuning Data Mining

Previous experiments demonstrate how we tune the Apriori algorithm to provide optimal results for use in our recommendation techniques. It was found that the number of rules generated (and rule accuracy) is more dependent on confidence than on support [11]. A similar pattern emerged in results from our other datasets; we therefore chose representative support levels (PTVplus and Físchlár: 5%, Record, Play, Browse and Combined: 10%) for the remainder of the experiments. These support values were chosen as they allowed optimal rule generation within a range of confidence values. Having different representative support values highlights an important difference between dataset density; the PTVplus dataset was sparser than both the implicit and explicit Físchlár datasets. To corroborate this fact, we use a density metric (Equation 5) adapted from [15]:

$$Density(Dataset) = \frac{Number\ of\ nonzero\ entries}{Number\ of\ total\ entries} \quad (5)$$

where the number of total entries is calculated by multiplying the number of users by the number of items that have been rated at least once; the number of nonzero entries is the total number of ratings overall in the dataset. Table 1 shows the results of this metric on the 6 datasets (using Físchlár explicit profiles as the baseline):

| Dataset | Density | Percentage Increase |
|---|---|---|
| Físchlár | 0.00358 | - |
| PTVplus | 0.00575 | 60% |
| Record | 0.00809 | 126% |
| Play | 0.00843 | 135% |
| Combined | 0.01182 | 230% |
| Browse | 0.01191 | 233% |

**Table 1.** Dataset Density

As dataset coverage governs rule harvesting, sparsity causes lower rule generation at high support values, which necessitates dropping to low support values to find more rules with higher confidences.

### 6.3 Increasing Similarity Coverage

In the next set of experiments, we were interested in evaluating the degree to which similarity coverage could be improved by the generated rule sets. For the first experiment, the density of the generated item-item similarity matrix was taken as our measure of similarity coverage. We varied Apriori confidence levels from 40% to 5% at 5% intervals. On each run we generated the Apriori direct rule set, as well as a maximal indirect rule set by chaining direct rules and filled in the item similarity matrix, taking the matrix density relative to the items that participated in the rule set. Results for PTVplus showed direct item similarities provide an average of 10% coverage, but there is a marked increase for the indirect similarity rules (65% coverage in the best case).

Of course, the Apriori method does not generate association rules for every profile programme, and in fact Apriori ignores a great many programmes because their frequency fails the Apriori threshold tests. Nevertheless when we add these newly generated rules to the full item-item matrix, we found an increase in density from 0.6% to

2.6%. Again, a similar pattern was found in the Físchlár (.17% to .65%) dataset [11] as well as Combined (.04% to .26%), Browse (.044% to .29%), Record (.05% to .14%) and Play (.06% to .17%).

### 6.4 Recommendation Quality : Accuracy

With encouraging results for increasing the similarity coverage, we designed experiments to test the effect of this new similarity knowledge on recommendation quality. Based on our earlier experiments, we chose representative confidence levels of 10% for the PTV, Físchlár, Play and Record datasets and 30% on Browse and Combined datasets. Using these specified levels, we have shown an item-item matrix coverage increase when moving from CF to both direct and indirect rule approaches.

The final experiment tested the accuracy of recommendation on both datasets. After generating direct and indirect similarity rules, a profile case is selected from the case-base. A parameterized percentage of the items in the selected case are removed from consideration. The remainder of the profile case is then used as the basis for retrieval, using our similarity metric and recommendation ranking. Accuracy was calculated using three metrics:

**Metric 1:** Percentage of removed items that were recommended in each case.
**Metric 2:** Percentage of profiles in which at least one removed item was recommended.
**Metric 3:** A combination of the above: percentage of removed items that were recommended, given a recommendation could be made.

Metrics 1 and 2 give us an overall sense of each model's performance whereas metric 3 provides a more localised account of how well each model functions. Hence we are more concerned about the performance of the first 2 metrics in these experiments as they give us a better sense of model accuracy. In the following experiments we use indirect models (Add, Av, Max, Min and Mult (see Section 6) as well as direct (DR), CF (Collaborative Filtering) and CFRR (Collaborative Filtering with Recommendation Ranking (see Section 6.5)) models when testing.

We were most interested in looking for uplift in recommendation quality when comparing our CBR technique (using direct and indirect similarity rules) to a pure collaborative filtering technique. We tested the effect of our recommendation ranking function by correlating rank score/numerical rank and item success.

On the PTVplus dataset, results of the first metric showed that using direct rules (20%) outperformed indirect rules (18%), which in turn outperformed pure CF (8%). A similar pattern was seen in the other metrics except for metric 3 which showed pure CF having a higher accuracy (30%) than either CBR method (Direct: 24%, Indirect: 30%) (Figure 2). Físchlár data provided similar evidence to PTV; metric 1 showed rule techniques outperforming their collaborative counterparts (CF: 4%, Direct: 15%, Indirect: 12%). Metrics 2 and 3 confirmed these findings; however metric 3 showed CF (34%) outperforming both CBR methods (Direct: 21%, Indirect: 18%) (Figure 3).

Behavioural datasets (Figures 4, 5, 6, 7) demonstrated a similar trend; increases for direct over indirect rules range from 9% to 16% on metric 1, 10% to 18% on metric 2 and 2% to 16% on metric 3. Increases for direct rules over collaborative filtering

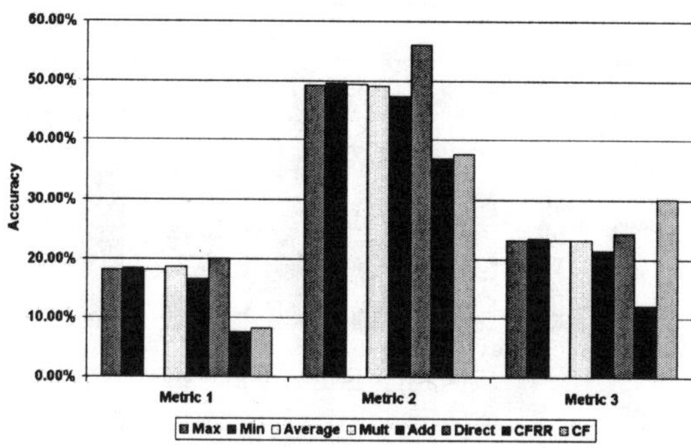


**Fig. 2.** PTVplus recommendation accuracy.

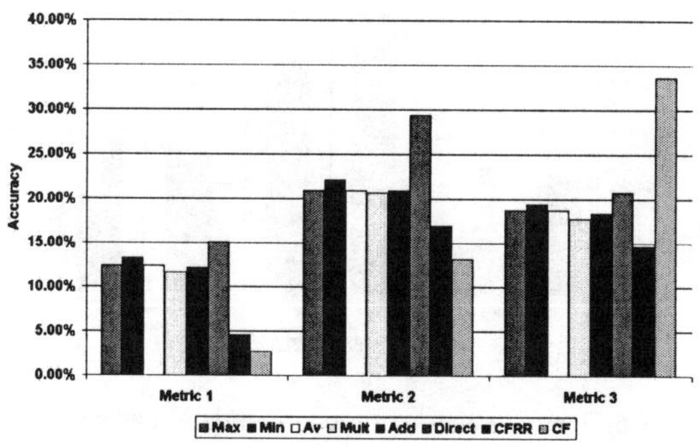


**Fig. 3.** Físchlár recommendation accuracy.

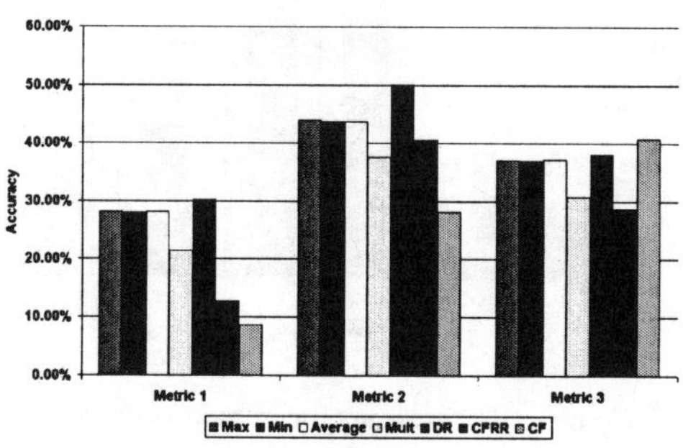


**Fig. 4.** Play behaviour recommendation accuracy.

vary from 110% to 200% on metric 1, 25% to 50% on metric 2 and 4% to 12% on metric 3. These results again demonstrate the positive effect of our technique to enhance recommendation accuracy.

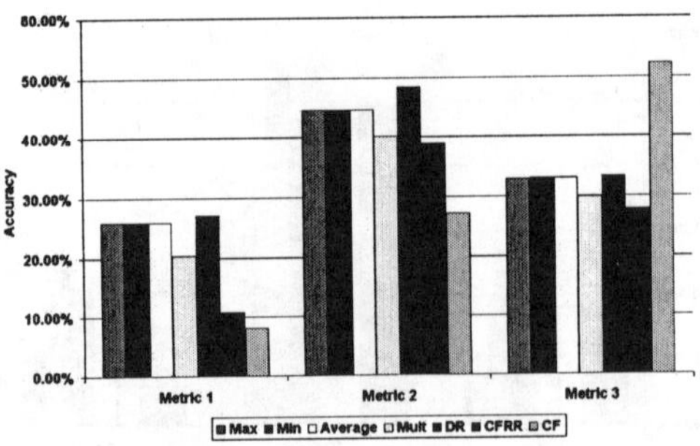


**Fig. 5.** Record behaviour recommendation accuracy.

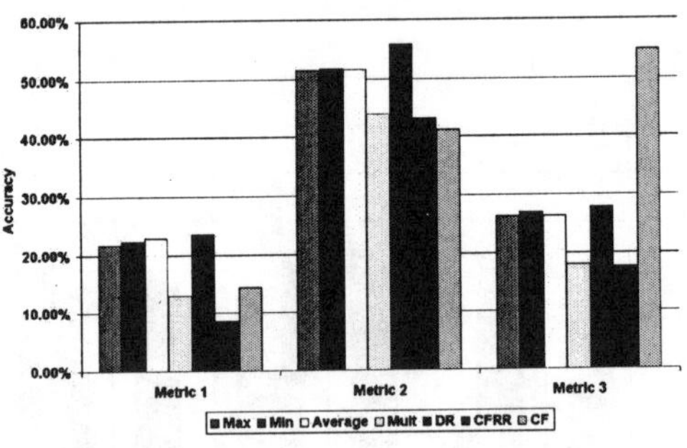


**Fig. 6.** Browse behaviour recommendation accuracy.

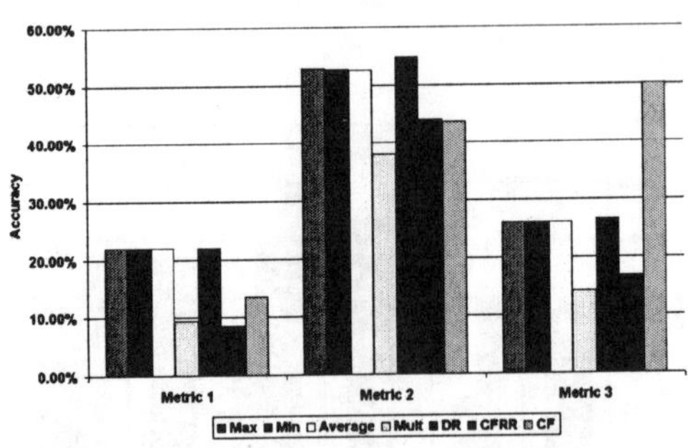


**Fig. 7.** Combined behaviours recommendation accuracy.

These results may indicate that more densely populated profile case-bases favour CF techniques, an issue that bears further study for possible multi-strategy approaches. They also suggest that indirect rules may not be as useful as their direct counterparts; another possibility is that these rules are generating high quality recommendations which are not present in our profile cases.

### 6.5 Recommendation Quality : Ranking Correlation

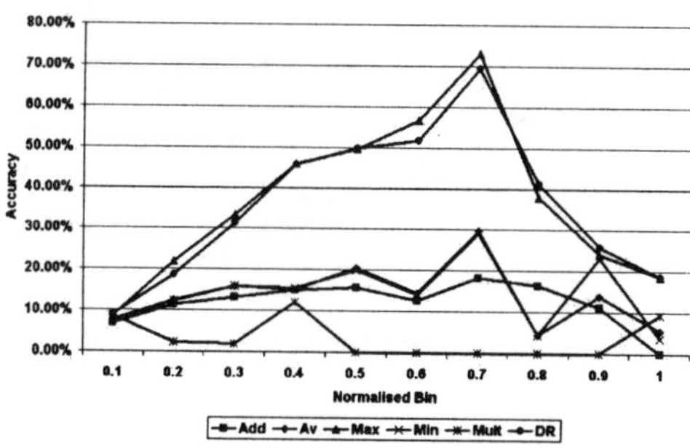


**Fig. 8.** PTVplus recommendation rank score accuracy.

In order to test our recommendation ranking function against pure CF methods, we used a tailored version of our recommendation ranking method. For each unique item in our list of recommended profiles $c_i$, where $C' \subseteq C$ is the set of retrieved profiles that contain $c_i$, and a target $t$:

$$Rel(c_i, t) = \frac{|C'|}{|C|} \cdot \sum_{c \epsilon C'} CFSim(c, t) \qquad (6)$$

where $CFSim(c, t)$ is the standard collaborative filtering similarity found by calculating the percentage of overlapping programmes between profiles $c$ and $t$. We then test our ranking functions by finding correlations between the score/rank of an item and its success over all profiles. For recommendation score, we normalize the score and then find the number of successes in each bin (0 - 1.0 in 0.1 increments); for rank, our bins contain all the successes at each rank position over all profiles. PTVplus results show that certain models provide uplift from direct to indirect rules (8% increase rank, 4% increase score) (Figure 8) and CF techniques (52% rank). Percentage increases are calculated by averaging the correlations over all bins for each model and using this to compute the increase between the models required. We found that score binning proved extremely inaccurate under CF with little or no correlation to be found.

With the Físchlár dataset, however, the minimal chaining model gave highest accuracy. Direct rules outperform indirect (14% rank, 24% score) and CF (56% rank) techniques (Figure 9). Behavioural datasets generally indicate direct rules having best ranking correlation followed by indirect rules with collaborative filtering using recommendation ranking performing lowest. The performance of different mathematical models under indirect rules varies greatly; future work aims to discover how these chaining models affect certain datasets into giving contrasting results.

Our final graphs discuss the use of implicit and explicit datasets, both for recommendation and testing. In this experiment, we performed tests using both behavioural and

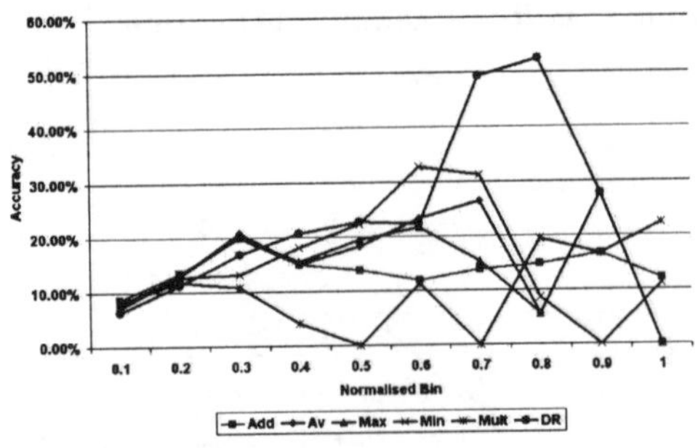


**Fig. 9.** Físchlár recommendation rank score accuracy.

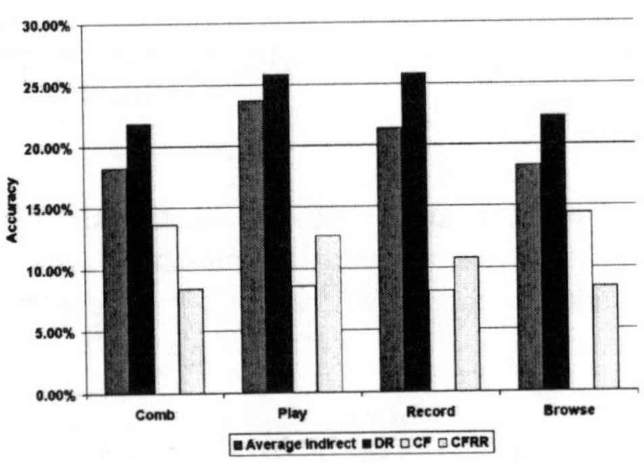


**Fig. 10.** Comparison of Accuracy on user rules and behavioural datasets.

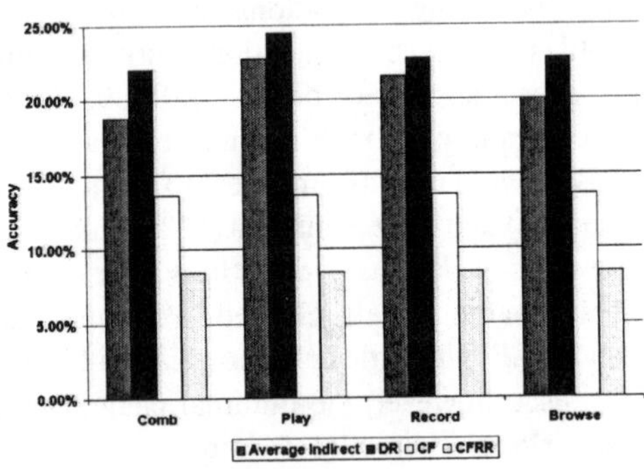


**Fig. 11.** Comparison of Accuracy on behavioural rules and combined dataset.

user-rated datasets, varying which dataset we used in rule generation/recommendation testing. This allows us to see both the effect and usefulness of implicit ratings in rec-

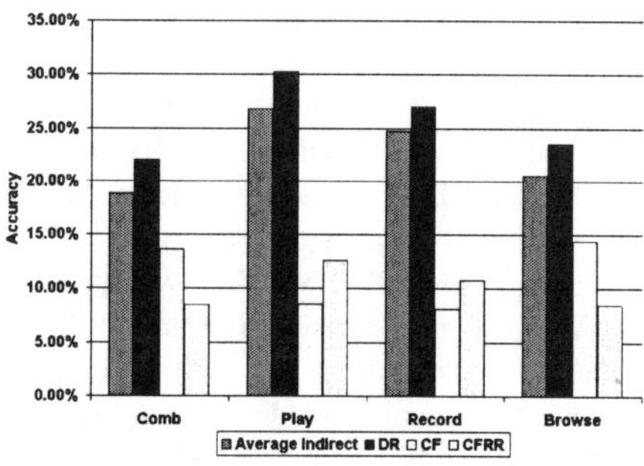


**Fig. 12.** Comparison of Accuracy on behavioural rules and datasets.

ommendations. Each of these comparison graphs (Figures 10, 11, 12) display results of the first accuracy metric discussed earlier (see Section 6.4). Using rules generated from explicit profiles, higher accuracy is seen when testing on implicit (Fig. 3) rather than explicit (Fig. 10) profiles. We also see from the comparison graphs that the play dataset outperforms all other behaviours; as this includes the combined behaviours, we may only presume that one or both of the remaining behaviours is introducing noise into the system. This theory is confirmed in Figures 11 and 12; using individual behavioural datasets in testing provides higher accuracy then using combined datasets. Future work will further investigate the use of implicit profiles in recommender systems, both as an aid to, and comparative method of, our recommender technique.

## 7 Conclusion and Future Work

We have described a data mining approach to ameliorating the problem of sparse similarity knowledge in profile-based recommendation systems, and we have demonstrated that it provides superior personalization accuracy. Moreover, we have shown that our technique works well with implicit behavioural profiles as well as explicit user-rating profiles. This grounds the usefulness of our approach in real user action. It also demonstrates the close relation of implicit and explicit approaches to personalization, which will have an impact on the direction of personalization development in the combined Físchlár-PTVplus system. Overall, the results provide good evidence in support of the view that learning similarity knowledge through profile mining makes it possible to improve overall recommendation quality.

Our future work will investigate the effects of these algorithms on further data sets using multiple antecedents and consequents in data mining, inclusion of negative ratings, investigation of multi-strategy (CF and rule-based) approaches and analysis of alternatives to rule chaining for extending item-item matrix coverage. We would also like to compare data mining to item-based collaborative metrics [15], both in measures such as Mean Absolute Error, as well as in terms of recommendation diversity.

## References


1. Smeaton, A.F., Murphy, N., O'Connor, N.E., Marlow, S., Lee, H., McDonald, K., Browne, P., Ye, J.: The Físchlár Digital Video System: A Digital Library Of Broadcast TV Programmes. In: Proceedings of the first ACM/IEEE-CS joint conference on Digital Libraries, ACM Press (2001) 312–313
2. Lee, H., Smeaton, A., O'Toole, C., Murphy, N., Marlow, S., O'Connor, N.: The Fischlar Digital Video Recording, Analysis and Browsing System. In: Proceedings of RIAO'2000: Content-Based Multimedia Information Access, pp. 1390-1399, 2000. (2000)
3. Smyth, B., Cotter, P.: Surfing the digital wave: Generating personalised TV listings using collaborative, case-based recommendation. (In: Proceedings of the 3rd International Conference on Case-based Reasoning. Munich, Germany.)
4. Smyth, B., Cotter, P.: Personalized electronic programme guides. Artificial Intelligence Magazine **21** (2001)
5. Herlocker, J., Konstan, J., Borchers, A., Riedl, J.: An algorithmic framework for performing collaborative filtering. In: Proceedings of the 1999 Conference on Research and Development in Information Retrieval: SIGIR-99. (1999)
6. Konstan, J., Miller, B., Maltz, D., Herlocker, J., Gordon, L., Riedl, J.: Grouplens: Applying collaborative filtering to usenet news. Communications of the ACM **40** (1997) 77–87
7. Shardanand, U., Maes, P.: Social information filtering: Algorithms for automating "word of mouth". In: Proceedings of ACM CHI'95 Conference on Human Factors in Computing Systems. (1995) 210–217
8. Good, N., Schafer, J.B., Konstan, J.A., Borchers, A., Sarwar, B.M., Herlocker, J.L., Riedl, J.: Combining collaborative filtering with personal agents for better recommendations. In: Proceedings of the 1999 Conference of the American Association of Artifical Intelligence (AAAI-99). (1999) 439–446
9. Soboroff, I., Nicholas, C.: Combining content and collaboration in text filtering. In: Proceedings of the IJCAI-99 Workshop on Machine Learning for Information Filtering. (1999)
10. Balabanović, M., Shoham, Y.: Fab: Content-based, collaborative recommendation. Communications of the ACM **40** (1997) 66–72
11. O'Sullivan, D., Wilson, D., Smyth, B.: Using collaborative filtering data in case-based recommendation. In: Proceedings of the 15th International FLAIRS Conference (FLAIRS 2002), AAAI Press (2002) 121–125
12. Lin, C., Alvarez, S., Ruiz, C.: Collaborative recommendation via adaptive association rule mining. In: Proceedings of the Web Mining for E-Commerce Workshop (WebKDD'2000). (2000)
13. Hipp, J., Nakhaeizadeh, U.G.: Mining association rules: Deriving a superior algorithm by analyzing today's approaches. In: Proceedings of the 4th European Symposium on Principles of Data Mining and Knowledge Discovery. (2000)
14. Agrawal, R., Mannila, H., Srikant, R., Toivonen, H., Verkamo, A.I.: Fast discovery of association rules. In Fayyad, U.M., Piatetsky-Shapiro, G., Smyth, P., Uthurusamy, R., eds.: Advances in Knowledge Discovery and Data Mining. AAAI Press (1996) 307–328
15. Sarwar, B.M., Karypis, G., Konstan, J.A., Riedl, J.: Item-based collaborative filtering recommender algorithms. In: Proceedings of the Tenth International World Wide Web Conference. (2001)

# Personalized Information Ordering: A Case Study in Online Recruitment*

Keith Bradley[1], Barry Smyth[1, 2]
[1]Smart Media Institute, Department of Computer Science,
University College Dublin, Dublin 4, Ireland
Keith.Bradley@ucd.ie

[2]Changing Worlds Ltd.,
South County Business Park, Leopardstown, Dublin 18, Ireland
Barry.Smyth@changingworlds.com

Abstract

Traditional search engine techniques are inadequate when it comes to helping the average user locate relevant information online. The key problem is their inability to recognize and respond to the implicit preferences of a user that are typically unstated in a search query. In this paper we describe CASPER, an online recruitment search engine, which attempts to address this issue by extending traditional search techniques with a personalization technique that is capable of taking account of user preferences as a means of classifying retrieved results as relevant or irrelevant. We evaluate a number of different classification strategies with respect to their accuracy and noise tolerance. Furthermore we argue that because CASPER transfers its personalization process to the client-side it offers significant efficiency and privacy advantages over more traditional server-side approaches.

## 1 Introduction

Online recruitment services are among the most popular applications on the Internet. However their usability is compromised by the information overload problem, as users must frequently search through hundreds or thousands of job adverts for a given query. The CASPER project [1-5] seeks to enhance such services by incorporating user profiling and similarity-based reasoning techniques to provide users with more personalized information retrieval [3, 6] using JobFinder, an Irish recruitment site, as an application test-bed.

The following scenario typifies the problems facing online recruitment applications that rely on traditional information retrieval techniques. A user

* The support of the Informatics Research Initiative of Enterprise Ireland is gratefully acknowledged.

specifies a query for a software development job with a salary of £25k. However, they are actually looking for a permanent C++ job, with a salary in excess of £25k in Dublin. In other words the query is incomplete and this will ultimately limit the accuracy of the search results. Moreover, two users with the same query will receive the same results even though they may have different implicit preferences – a second user with the same incomplete query but looking for a LISP job in Cork, will not want to see information on Dublin or C++ jobs. This scenario is not unusual in the context of Web search in general. Many Web users are not information retrieval experts and tend to construct poor search queries that are generally broad and incomplete. For example, most Web search queries contain only 2 or 3 search terms.

CASPER's solution is a two-stage search engine that selects job cases not just according to their similarity to the target query, but also according to their relevance to the specific user in question, based on that user's interaction history [2, 3, 5]. During stage one, job cases are ranked according to their similarity to the query by using a standard similarity metric, which calculates a similarity score between query features and corresponding job case features; each case is made up of a fixed set of features such as *job type*, *location*, *salary*, etc (see also [7]). This server-side stage produces a ranked list of job cases according to their similarity to the target query (see also [8]).

The second stage, a client-side process, emphasizes personalized *information ordering*. It reorders the results according to their relevance to the user by comparing each result to the user's learned search profile. Each profile specifies the job cases that the user has previously liked or disliked based on past feedback. Each stage-one result is associated with a *relevance score* by comparing it to the $k$ most similar user profile cases. For instance if the result is similar to many positive profile cases it gets a high relevance score, while if it is similar to negative cases it gets a low score.

Thus, priority is given to jobs that are *similar* to the target query and *relevant* to the user. If a user has previously liked jobs in the Dublin area, then the second retrieval stage will prioritize job cases from these locations in the future, even if the user does not specify a location constraint in a query.

In this paper we build on earlier work by proposing and evaluating a variety of different classification techniques as the basis for CASPER's personalized information ordering technique.

## 2 System Architecture

The outline system architecture for CASPER is presented in Figure 1. CASPER is a client-server system with search functionality shared between the server and client-side components. The server-side component is equivalent to a traditional search-engine in the sense that it takes a user's query and compares it to job cases in the job case-base to identify the best matches. However, unlike a traditional search engine, this process is based on a similarity-based retrieval technique rather than on an exact-match technique. This means that relevant jobs can be identified even though they share no features with the original user query.

Each job case is made up of a fixed set of features such as job type, salary, key skills, minimum experience etc. An example of a typical job case is visible in Figure 1. During retrieval the user's search query or *target query* is compared on a feature-by-feature basis to each of the job cases. A standard weighted-sum similarity metric is used to compute the similarity between each job case and the target query, based on the similarity of corresponding features.

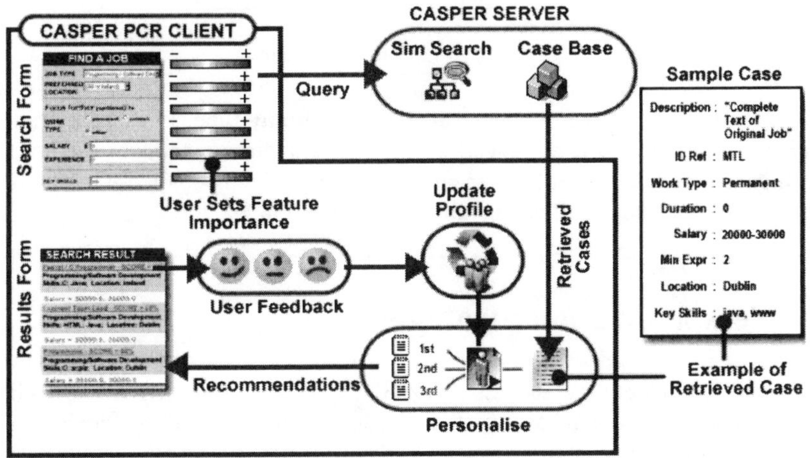


**Fig 1.** CASPER System Architecture.

As it stands this retrieval approach is still ignorant of the implicit needs of individual users, and therefore the retrieval results are not personalized. This motivates the need for the second stage of retrieval, which is capable of personalizing the retrieval results on the client-side. The client-side personalization technique views the personalization task as a classification problem. In other words, personalizing the server-side retrieval results amounts to classifying each suggested job candidate as either relevant or irrelevant for a given user. To do this we use a nearest-neighbor type classification approach that uses graded job cases in a target user's profile as a basis for classification.

User profiles are composed of a series of shortened job descriptions and the users' rating for each job. Part of a user profile is shown below in Figure 2. Only job features that actively contribute to job similarity are retained for the profile. Features such as location, salary, required experience, contract type and required skills are retained in the job case base, while all other elements such as contact details are discarded. This reduces the amount of space required to store the profile on the client side. The users rating of each profile element is also included and reflects how much they liked or disliked a given job. These ratings are expressed in a scale ranging from 0 (meaning strongly disliked) to (1 meaning strongly liked). A user profile is then made up of a series of these profile elements, and is only restricted in size by the amount of space available on the client-side to store the profile.

| Feature | Value |
|---|---|
| Type | Permanent |
| Location | Dublin |
| Salary | €25000-€30000 |
| Experience | 2 |
| Skills | Java, C |
| Rating | 0.7 |

**Fig. 2.** A user profile element.

Users are free to view and update their profile at any time. Profile generation is currently driven by user selection of relevant items, though methods for intelligently selecting profile elements are currently being studied. One particular method of automated profile generation is discussed in Section 4.

# 3 Personalization Strategies

Of course, ultimately the success of CASPER depends critically on its ability to reorder search results in a way that accurately reflects the preferences of an individual user. This in turn, relies on the way that CASPER classifies search results as either relevant or irrelevant on the client-side. In this paper we are interested in evaluating a range of different classification strategies that may be used for the purpose of personalization. These strategies, which are described in the following sections, differ in the way that they evaluate the relevance of a candidate job in the context of its nearest-neighbour jobs stored in the user's client-side profile. In each case, the strategy in question returns a classification score in the range of 0 to 1, where 1 corresponds to maximal relevance.

## 3.1 Uniform Similarity (US)

The first strategy (Equation 1) compares a candidate case *cc* to the user's profile *P* and classifies it depending on its mean similarity to the *k* nearest elements of the users profile without taking the user's interest rating for a profile element into account.

$$Classify\,(cc,P,k) = \frac{\left(\sum_{i=1}^{k} Sim(cc,p_i)\right)}{k}, \qquad (1)$$

*where* $p_i$ *is the ith closest profile element to cc*

## 3.2 Weighted Similarity (WS)

This strategy shown in Equation 2 below classifies a candidate *cc* by its mean similarity to the *k* nearest profile elements weighted by the graded interest score originally given to those profile elements by the user. In this way candidate jobs that are similar to profile jobs liked by the user in the past receive more emphasis and contrarily candidates similar to profile jobs disliked by the user receive less emphasis.

$$Classify\ (cc, P, k) = \frac{\left(\sum_{i=1}^{k} Sim(cc, p^{w}{}_{i}).w_i\right)}{k}, \tag{2}$$

$$where\ p^{w}{}_{i}\ is\ the\ ith\ closest\ weighted\ profile\ element\ to\ cc$$

## 3.3 Uniform Voting (UV)

This strategy (Equation 3) classifies a candidate *cc* as either interesting *1* or uninteresting *0* based on a comparison between its mean similarity to the *k* nearest positive profile elements $p^{+} \varepsilon P$, and its mean similarity to the *k* nearest negative profile elements $p^{-} \varepsilon P$. A profile element is said to be positive or relevant to a user if the interest score given to it by a user exceeds a threshold of 0.7, otherwise it is taken to be a negative or irrelevant element. If the mean similarity of *cc* to the nearest positive elements exceeds its mean similarity to the nearest negative elements then it is classed as relevant and vice versa.

$$Classify\ (cc, P, k) = \begin{cases} 1 & if \quad \dfrac{\left(\sum_{i=1}^{k} Sim(cc, p^{+}{}_{i})\right)}{k} > \dfrac{\left(\sum_{i=1}^{k} Sim(cc, p^{-}{}_{i})\right)}{k} \\ 0 & otherwise \end{cases} \tag{3}$$

$$where\ p^{+}{}_{i}\ is\ the\ ith\ closest\ positive\ profile\ element\ to\ cc\ and$$
$$p^{-}{}_{i}\ is\ the\ ith\ closest\ negitive\ profile\ element\ to\ cc$$

## 3.4 Weighted Voting (WV)

The final strategy (Equation 4) again takes the user's original graded classification of a profile element into account. It classifies a candidate *cc* based on a comparison between its mean similarity to the nearest positive profile elements weighted by user score $p^{w+} \varepsilon P$, and its mean similarity to the nearest negative profile elements weighted by user score $p^{w-} \varepsilon P$. If the mean similarity of *cc* to the positive elements exceeds its mean similarity to the negative elements then it is classed as interesting and vice versa.

$$Classify\ (cc,P,k)=\begin{cases}1 & if\ \dfrac{\left(\sum\limits_{i=1}^{k} Sim(cc,p^{w+}{}_i).w_i\right)}{k} > \dfrac{\left(\sum\limits_{i=1}^{k} Sim(cc,p^{w-}{}_i).w_i\right)}{k} \\ 0 & otherwise\end{cases} \quad \textbf{(4)}$$

*where* $p^{w+}{}_i$ *is the ith closest weighted positive profile element to cc and* $p^{w-}{}_i$ *is the ith closest weighted negitive profile element to cc*

## 3.5 Example Retrieval Session

A typical retrieval session begins when a user submits a query. The user describes their ideal job in terms of its features. For the purpose of this example we will assume only three features are of interest namely location, salary and skills.

Consider two job hunters, A and B, who submit an identical query to the job retrieval system. Their ideal job shown in Figure 3 is located in Dublin, has a salary of €25000 and requires a knowledge of Java.

| Feature | Value |
|---|---|
| Skills | Java |
| Location | Dublin |
| Salary | €25000 |

**Fig. 3.** The ideal job desired by both users.

These queries are sent to the first stage of the Casper system which performs a similarity-based retrieval for each query. Since both queries are identical the results returned are also identical. In this case no jobs that perfectly match the target description can be found. However the similarity search did retrieve jobs with similar skills in the closest possible location to the target as shown in Figure 4.

| Result 1 | Feature | Value |
|---|---|---|
| | Skills | Java, C++ |
| | Location | Dublin |
| | Salary | €25000 |
| | Score | 0.8 |

| Result 2 | Feature | Value |
|---|---|---|
| | Skills | Java |
| | Location | Cork |
| | Salary | €25000 |
| | Score | 0.8 |

**Fig. 4.** Search results returned by the first stage.

At this stage of the retrieval the results seem equally relevant to both job hunters. Both results are rated as 80% similar to the target despite the fact that these people probably have different tastes and expectations.

The second stage of the process takes place on the client-side and personalizes these results with respect to the individual's profile. The user profile is made up of descriptions of jobs previously examined and rated by the job seeker. In the case of A we see that their profile, shown in Figure 5, contains two jobs and indicates a strong dislike for C++ (shown by their rating profile element 1 with 0.4). Otherwise this element is a perfect match for our ideal job. By contrast A seems much more willing to accept a change in location as shown by their rating of the second profile element with 0.8

| (1) | Feature | Value |
|---|---|---|
| | Skills | C++ |
| | Location | Dublin |
| | Salary | €25000 |
| | Score | 0.4 |

| (2) | Feature | Value |
|---|---|---|
| | Skills | Java |
| | Location | Tralee |
| | Salary | €25000 |
| | Score | 0.8 |

**Fig 5:** The user profile of A.

The results are personalized by comparing them in turn to each profile element. Each of the personalization strategies discussed previously use different methods to calculate a personalized score. For example the Weighted Similarity method would give Result 1 a relevance score equal to the mean product of its similarity to each profile element times the users score for that element (Equation 2). If the similarity of Result 1 to profile element 1 is 0.8 and it's similarity to profile element 2 is 0.6 then the relevance of Result 1 to the profile is ((0.8*0.4)+(0.7*0.6))/2 = 0.37. The final personalized score for Result 1 is then the product of this relevance score and its original similarity to the target query (0.37*0.8) = 0.3.

If the similarity of Result 2 to profile element 1 is 0.5 and its similarity to profile element 2 is 0.8 then its personalized score would be the product of its relevance to the profile ((0.5*0.4)+(0.8*0.8))/2 = 0.44 and its original similarity to the target (0.44*0.8) = 0.35. In this way we see that this person will probably be more interested in Result 2.

Conversely if our second job seeker, B, has the opposite taste to A (i.e. B finds location more important than skills) then B would probably be more interested in Result 1 than Result 2. This allows us to order the list of results for each user so that jobs they are more likely to be interested in appear higher in the list. In practice the personalisation calculation is more complex than described as more features are involved, and only the most similar elements of a users profile are used to classify the results obtained from stage one.

# 4 Experimental Evaluation

Ideally we would like to evaluate our personalization strategies using real users over an extended period of time. However such studies are generally very difficult and expensive to perform due to the cost of locating interested users. Nevertheless we are currently engaged in a real user study as part of the CASPER project.

In the meantime we have chosen to evaluate CASPER's techniques by using artificial users that can be readily generated and tested across a wide variety of experimental conditions. In this section we describe these artificial user trials focusing on the accuracy of our 4 different personalization strategies and their sensitivity to noise in the user profiles.

## 4.1 Setup

The following evaluation uses a case-base of job cases from the JobFinder system. In total there are over 900 cases describing a range of IT jobs in Ireland. Each job case is made up of a fixed set of features such as *job type*, *location*, *salary*, etc.

In order to generate each artificial user we chose an ideal job or seed job to represent the general preferences of an individual user and then select relevant and irrelevant jobs from the case-base to serve as profile elements, using the similarity between the seed and a case as a measure of user interest. During this process we eliminate seeds that are outliers; that is, we ignore seed cases that do not have a good range of relevant and irrelevant cases. In total 100 seed cases are selected to correspond to 100 artificial job seekers. Positive and negative profile elements are then chosen from this ranked list, while the remaining jobs serve as retrieval candidates for the personalization client. In this way it is possible to generate user profiles with arbitrarily many positive (relevant) and negative (irrelevant) cases. For the purpose of these experiments we chose a fixed profile size of 20 elements, 10 cases that are similar to the seed and therefore relevant to the artificial user, and 10 cases that are dissimilar and therefore irrelevant to the user.

## 4.2 Personalization Accuracy

Personalization accuracy is a key success criterion for any personalization algorithm. Ultimately a user will only value CASPER's recommendations as long as those returned are relevant to the user's query and preferences. In this experiment we evaluate the accuracy of the 4 personalization strategies by averaging their personalization accuracy over the 100 artificial users. For each user and strategy combination, we predict the relevancy score for each of the remaining cases in the job case-base (that is, those cases not present in the user's profile) and compare the classification score (that is, the predicted relevancy score for that user) to the user's "true" relevancy score; remember that this "true" relevancy score is the similarity between a case and the user's seed case. In these experiments we assume that relevancy score of 0.7 or greater indicates relevancy.

Figure 6 presents the accuracy results for each of the 4 personalization strategies for k (the number of profile cases that are used in the classification process) equal to 3. Each graph is a bar chart with each bar representing the accuracy of one personalization strategy. Each bar is divided into the following 4 sections (starting from the base) to measure the different components of personalization accuracy:

1. The number of relevant cases correctly classified as relevant.
2. The number of irrelevant cases correctly classified as irrelevant.
3. The number of relevant cases incorrectly classified as irrelevant.
4. The number of irrelevant cases incorrectly classified as relevant.

For example, the first bar in Figure 6 represents the results for the uniform similarity (US) strategy for *k=3*. It indicates that the total personalization accuracy (the percentage of cases, both relevant and irrelevant, that were correctly classified) is approximately 68%, with approximately 15% coming from relevant cases being correctly classified and the remainder coming from irrelevant cases being correctly classified. We also see that the 32% incorrect classifications are a result of irrelevant cases being incorrectly classified, with hardly any relevant cases classified incorrectly. It is worth noting at this point that the majority of cases in a given trial are, as is to be expected, irrelevant to the average user.

In general, the similarity strategies (US and WS) perform better than the voting strategies (UV and WV) with overall accuracies of 68% (US) and 95% (WS) compared to 53% (UV) and 16% (WV). All of the 4 strategies appear equally able to correctly classify relevant cases but the voting strategies fail badly when it comes to correctly classifying irrelevant cases. We also see that the increased performance of the WS strategy compared to US is based on its ability to reduce the number of irrelevant cases that were incorrectly classified by US. However, the WS strategy's extra accuracy over US does come at the expense of some relevant cases being incorrectly classified as irrelevant.

As alternative accuracy metrics we can evaluate the precision and recall characteristics of the different personalization strategies. Precision is the percentage of items retrieved that are relevant and in the context of the current work this is the percentage of cases that are classified as relevant that are actually relevant; that is, the number of correctly classified relevant cases divided by the number of correctly classified relevant cases plus the number of incorrectly classified irrelevant cases. Recall is the percentage of relevant items that are retrieved and in the context of the current work this is the percentage of relevant cases that are correctly classified. The precision and recall results for each strategy are shown in Figure 7. Noteworthy is the high precision of the WS strategy compared to the others, but its relatively poor recall characteristics. In other words, using the WS strategy, a higher portion of cases presented to the user will be relevant, but some relevant cases may be missed. In contrast the other strategies are better are identifying all of the relevant cases that exist but they will tend to also recommend many irrelevant cases to the user. In terms of CASPER and many similar recommendation systems, precision is generally assumed to be more critical than recall as a general rule since otherwise users will become frustrated by irrelevant retrieval results.

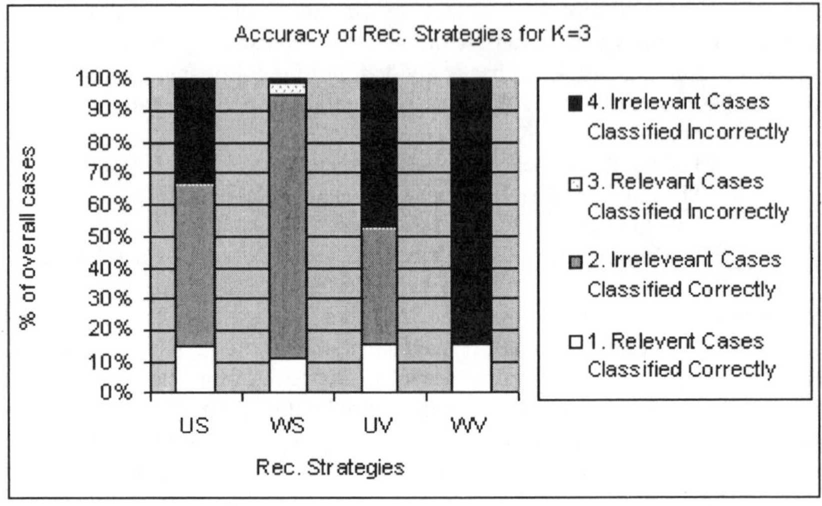


**Fig. 6.** The accuracy of each personalization strategy.

| Strategy | Precision | Recall |
|---|---|---|
| US | 32% | 98% |
| WS | 92% | 73% |
| UV | 92% | 99% |
| WV | 16% | 100% |

**Fig. 7.** Precision and recall results.

## 4.3 Noise Sensitivity

One of the shortcomings of our particular use of artificial users and the above experimental set-up has to do with the way in which we determine the likes and dislikes of an artificial user, specifically the assumed direct correlation between the similarity of a case and the user's seed and the user's "true" relevancy score for that case. In real life things are never so neat and in general we can expect user relevancy ratings to contain a level of inaccuracy or noise. This is because often people can be expected to display a degree of inconsistency in their opinions on a certain topic, especially when these opinions are rendered over a period of time. There could be many reasons for this behaviour including a persons' mood, alertness, and expertise in a given field of inquiry. A person may not be aware that Java is a similar language to C++, for example. In order to try and model this in our evaluation we introduce noise in to the user ratings varying the user's relevancy score at random within a given range. For example a user's "true" relevancy score of 0.7 might be varied randomly between 0.6 and 0.8 (0.7 +/- 10% of the maximal relevance) by introducing a noise threshold of 10%. In this way we can evaluate the impact of noise on personalization accuracy by introducing different levels of noise in to the user profiles.

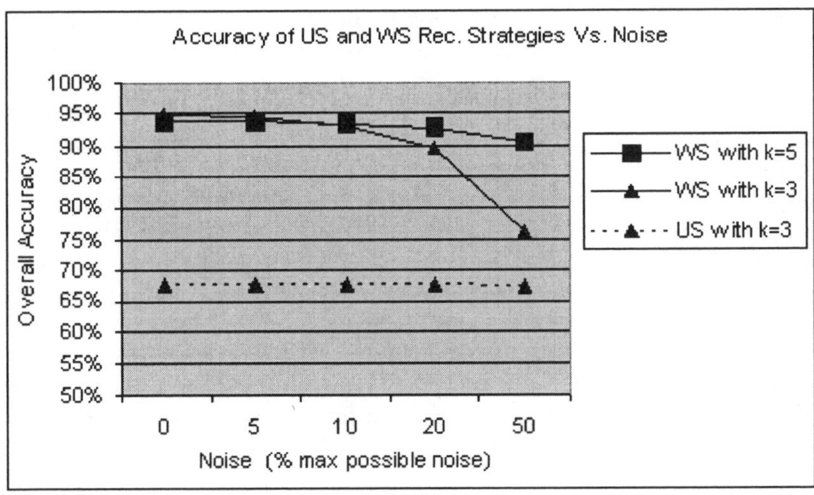


**Fig. 8** The overall accuracy of the uniform similarity (US) and weighted similarity (WS) techniques for different levels of noise.

Figure 8 shows the impact of noise on the uniform and weighted similarity metrics for noise levels from 0% up to 50%. These techniques are chosen because they significantly outperformed the uniform and weighted voting methods. Of course the US technique is essentially unaffected by noise since the user scores, which are perturbed by our noise model, do not play a role in the classification process. Hence, US accuracy is approximately 67% for all levels of noise. In contrast, noise has a significant impact on the accuracy characteristics of the WS method. As the level of noise increases, WS accuracy falls consistently from 94% at 0% noise down to 77% at 50% noise. One way to combat noise is to increase $k$ in the classification process. Very briefly, in Figure 8 we also show the accuracy characteristics for WS at $k=5$. It should be clear that at this value of $k$ the WS methods is less affected by noise with accuracy falling from approximately 93% at 0% noise to only 91% at 50% noise. Indeed, WS at $k=5$ is capable of producing similar accuracy levels with noise at 50% as WS with noise at only 20%.

Clearly, from these results we see that the WS strategy has impressive noise tolerance characteristics. It out-performs the US method at all levels of noise and has the potential to cope with extreme noise levels with a suitably chosen *k*.

# 5 Discussion

In recent years the idea of providing users with a personalized online experience has become less of a "nice to have" and more of a "must have" especially as users find it increasing difficult to cope with traditional information retrieval technologies in the face of a burgeoning World-Wide Web. Many researchers have developed a range of techniques that are capable of learning about and responding to important user preferences.

Personal Web Watcher (PWW) [9] and Letizia [10] are examples of content-based systems that recommend Web-page hyperlinks by comparing them with a history of previous pages visited by the user. Letizia uses the unused time when the user is actually reading a web page to search the adjoining hyperlinks. The user's profile is composed of keywords extracted from the various pages visited. PWW uses an offline period to generate a bag of words style profile for each of the pages visited during the previous browsing session. Hyperlinks on new pages can then be compared to this profile and graded accordingly.

GroupLens [11] is a recommendation system for Usenet news. A user's profile is created by recording the user's explicit ratings of various articles. Automatic collaborative filtering is then used to statistically compare one user's likes and dislikes with another user and to recommend articles from other similar user profiles.

PTV is a personalized TV listings service, providing users with personalized TV guides based on their learned viewing preferences [12, 13]. It employs a hybrid recommendation strategy using both content-based and collaborative methods. Its server uses explicit user gradings on various programmes, channels, and viewing times to build a profile.

CASPER's personalization technique shares many similarities with the above systems. Like PWW and Letizia it primarily uses a content-based technique, comparing the details of candidate jobs to the details of those jobs the user has previously liked and disliked. Moreover, like PTV it also relies on user ratings as part of its personalization strategy.

One significant difference between CASPER and many other personalization approaches is that CASPER employs a client-side personalization technique where user profiles are stored on the user's client and not available to any central profile repository on the server-side. This is in contrast to PTV and GroupLens, for example, which both utilise a central profile database stored on the server-side. The significance of this is twofold. First of all, it means that it is possible to share the computational load needed for personalization since the personalization process in CASPER is the responsibility of an individual user's client and this can significantly reduce the computational load on the CASPER server.

Secondly, CASPER's client-side personalization has potential privacy and security advantages over server-side methods. By storing profiles on the client-side and not releasing them to the server a user can feel more confident that they are in control of the personal profile data. This is especially important in any applications that may involve the collection of sensitive personal data, for example, medical or financial data. This advantage is not available with server-side applications.

# 6 Conclusions

This paper described recent work on the CASPER system, a Web-based, personalized online recruitment service that is capable of learning about a user's job finding preferences in order to recommend jobs to that user that not only match their explicit query but that also match their learned preferences. We have focused on CAPSER's two-stage retrieval and personalization strategy and evaluated a number of different personalization techniques. In particular we have shown the potential benefits of a weighted-similarity based classification technique for personalization. This technique has an overall classification accuracy in excess of 90% when tested on real-world job cases and artificial users, and impressive precision and recall characteristics.

**References**


1. Smyth, B., Bradley, K. and Rafter, R. "Personalization Techniques for Online Recruitment Services", Communications of the ACM 2002, 45(5): 39-40.
2. Bradley, K., Rafter, R. & Smyth B. Case-Based User Profiling for Content Personalisation. In Proceedings of the International Conference on Adaptive Hypermedia and Adaptive Web-based Systems, (AH2000), Trento, Italy, 2000
3. Bradley, K., Rafter, R., and Smyth, B.: Personalised Case Retrieval. In: Proceedings of the 10th Irish Conference on Artificial Intelligence and Cognitive Science, Cork, Ireland, 1999
4. Bradley K., Smyth B. Improving recommendation diversity, Proceedings of the Twelfth Irish Conference on Artificial Intelligence and Cognitive Science, Maynooth, Ireland, 2001
5. Rafter R., Bradley K., Smyth B.: Personalised Retrieval For Online Recruitment Services. In: Proceedings of the 22nd Annual Colloquium on IR Research, Cambridge, UK, 2000
6. Budzik, J., Hammond, K. J., Marlow, C., and Scheinkman, A: Anticipating Information Needs: Everyday Applications as Interfaces to Internet Information Sources. In Proceedings of the 1998 World Conference on the WWW, Internet, and Intranet. AACE Press, 1998
7. Balabanovic M, Shoham Y.: FAB: Content-Based Collaborative Recommender. Communications of the ACM 1997; 40(3):66-72.

8. Billsus D & Pazzani M.: Learning Collaborative Information Filters. In: Proceedings of the International Conference on Machine Learning. Morgan Kaufmann, Madison, Wisc., 1998
9. Mladenic, D.: Personal WebWatcher: Implementation and Design. Technical Report IJS-DP-7472, Department of Intelligent Systems, J. Stefan Institute, Slovenia, 1996
10. Liebermann, H.: Letizia: An agent that assists web browsing. In: Proceedings 14th International Joint Conference on Artificial Intelligence (IJCAI), 1995
11. Konstan J.A, Miller B.N., Maltz D, Herlocker J.L., Gordon L.R., Riedl J: Group Lens: Applying Collaborative Filtering to Usenet News. Communications of the ACM 1997, 40(3):77-87
12. Smyth B & Cotter P.: Surfing the Digital Wave: Generating Personalised Television Guides using Collaborative, Case-based Recommendation. In: Proceedings of the 3rd International Conference on Case-based Reasoning, Munich, Germany, 1999
13. Smyth B & Cotter P.: Sky's the Limit: A Personalised TV Listings Service for the Digital Age. In: Proceedings of the 19th SGES International Conference on Knowledge-Based and Applied Artificial Intelligence (ES99). Cambridge, UK, 1999

# KA-Tool and domain construction for AI planning applications

Ruth Aylett (r.s.aylett@salford.ac.uk) Christophe Doniat (doniat@wanadoo.fr)
Centre for Virtual Environments
University of Salford, M5 4WT Salford, UK

Abstract

KA-Tool embodies work aimed at allowing domain experts to generate a domain model for an AI planning system, carried out as part of a larger project to build an integrated set of tools for supporting AI planning. The paper outlines the overall methodology and describes how KA Tool supports it. A Domain model is generated in which can be represented by cluster of constraints shaping an Ontology of each studied case. Progress has been made towards automatic conversion into the modelling language OCL and integration with the OCL tool GIPO. We illustrate the methodology by applying it in two examples of planning.

## 1. Introduction and motivation

The effort required to construct a domain model for an AI planning system has long been recognised as a major barrier to the take-up of this technology outside the AI planning community [1]. Researchers at the Universities of Huddersfield, Salford and Durham [18] have been tackling this problem in the EPSRC-funded project PLANFORM. Its aim is to research, develop and evaluate a method and supporting high level research platform for the systematic construction of planner domain models and abstract specifications of planning algorithms, and their automated synthesis into sound, efficient programs that generate and execute plans. FIGURE 1 shows the high-level architecture of the PLANFORM system. Within this project, the domain model is represented in the object-oriented sorted first-order logic language OCL [16,19] which supports validation and checking tools as well as translation to other formalisms such as PDDL [20], the standard domain representation language used in the international Planning Competition. The toolset GIPO [26] is used to support the iterative construction and validation of an OCL model: however this still requires too much specialist knowledge of OCL and AI planning to be a suitable interface for a domain expert – one who understands the domain in which planning is to take place but lacks any specific expertise in AI planning. The KA-Tool discussed here is aimed at such domain experts. The problem of supporting knowledge acquisition directly from the domain expert, without the intervention of a knowledge engineer, has been discussed in the field of Knowledge-Based Systems (KBS) for many years [23,28]. A consensus has been reached that this may be feasible where a skeletal domain model can be provided to guide the knowledge acquisition process and both the skeleton model and the process itself can be defined through a methodology embodied in the knowledge acquisition tool [23]. The key components of the skeleton model are seen as domain ontologies combined with domain-independent problem-solving methods which have often been thought of as *generic tasks*. The

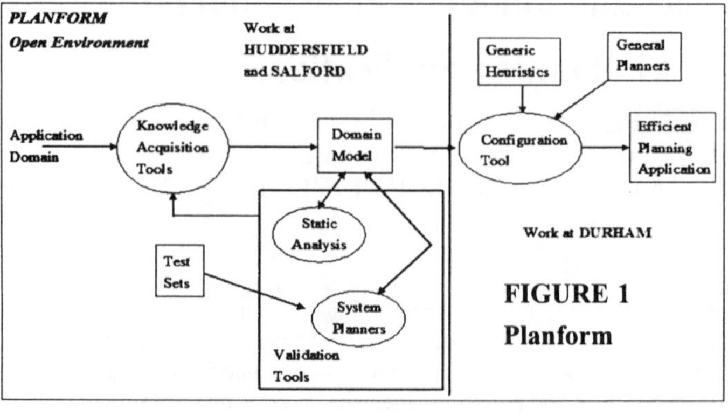


FIGURE 1
Planform

best-known – but far from only – example of such a methodology is Common KADS [25], offering libraries of configurable problem-solving components together with stereotypical configurations which can be thought of as corresponding to types of abstract problem-solving tasks such as *diagnosis by heuristic classification* or *interpretation*. It is noticeable that AI Planning has rarely been considered as part of this research (see Valente [28] for a rare exception). While in theory planning could be considered as one or more generic tasks, in practice the Knowledge Engineering community has concentrated on other generic tasks – diagnosis in particular – while AI Planning researchers have hardly been involved at all, tending to concentrate on the development of planning algorithms. The approach discussed here draws on this work in the KBS community, seeing the combination of ontologies, logics and generic problem-solving methods as a way of addressing knowledge acquisition for planning [23]. It supports the capture [2,3,27] and structuring of relevant knowledge about a domain and its intelligent behaviours [2] because they play an important role in the choice of an appropriate problem-solving method, possibly configured from complex components held in a library [28].

## 1.1 Knowledge acquisition process

The knowledge acquisition (KA) process embodied in the KA-Tool can be seen in FIGURE 2. A *question-driven process* works on protocols and on a skeleton theory derived from an ontologies library. By protocol we mean raw domain knowledge - transcripts, documents, interviews,

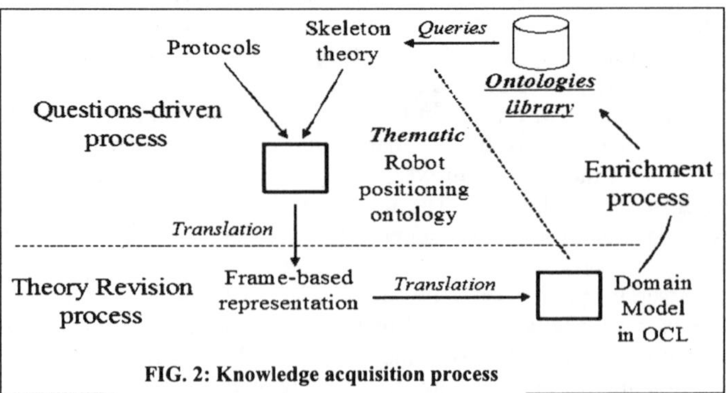


FIG. 2: Knowledge acquisition process

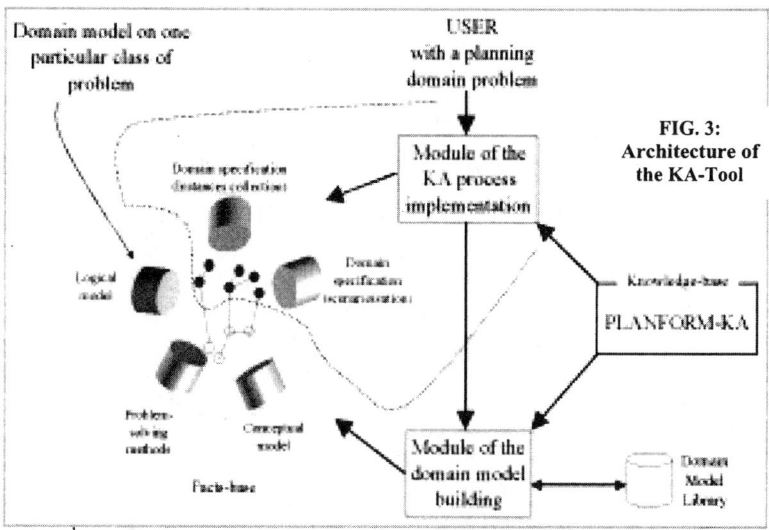


**FIG. 3: Architecture of the KA-Tool**

observations[1], created by a problem-solving episode in which experts are provided with a real-AI Planning problem, of the kind that they normally deal with, and are asked to solve it. As they do so, they are required to describe each step, and their reasons for doing what they do. The transcript of their verbal and/or text account is, in this case, called a protocol.

By problem specification we mean a definition or description of an application domain represented as a set of choices at a particular level of abstraction in an ontological hierarchy. Thus 'Entertaining a foreign visitor' and 'Drumstore', the domains used for the experiments reported later, are problem specifications. The second stage in the KA process incorporates a *theory revision process* which produces a conceptual model using a hierarchical frame system which allows easy representation of inheritance between *frames* (the relationship *kind-of*) and/or aggregation between *frames* (the relationship *part-of*) for instance. Translation into a sorted first-order logic such as that used by OCL is straightforward. Frames have an advantage over a first-order logic in that both structure and behaviour can be embodied in one generic entity. An Ontology is defined [14] as a rigorous specification of a set of specialised vocabulary terms sufficient to describe and reason about the range of situations of interest in a particular domain - a conceptual representation of the domain entities, events, and relationships. Two primary relationships of interest are abstraction (kind-of) and composition (part-of). Thus an Ontology provides a grounding of the key concepts within a domain. In principle we need both an Ontology of planning problem domains and of planning software to carry out knowledge acquisition since the premise is that the conceptual framework of the problem domain is not the same as that of the planning software – otherwise there would be little problem for the domain expert. The *question-driven process* is also used to construct a domain dictionary, in effect a partial Ontology - using the experimental approach, it is hard to make an exhaustive analysis of all domain objects. Nevertheless, the problem specification can be used

---

[1] We will used the term 'transcript' hereafter to mean a combination of transcripts, documents, interviews, observations as a whole.

to define relevant objects and relationships, using macroscopic properties that support appropriate choices. The domain dictionary is associated with (i) a particular domain, (ii) specification of a problem or problems that we want to solve, (iii) the reasoning that belongs to the studied domain and allows the specified problem to be solved. The final stage is the *enrichment process*, which adds the new partial Ontology into the existing ontologies library.

### 1.2 Overview of PLANFORM KA-Tool architecture

FIGURE 3 shows the main architecture of the PLANFORM KA-Tool – an intelligent system that contains the KA process. The user applies the *module of domain model building* to a particular problem specification. The building of a new conceptual model might be carried out with or without an existing problem specification from the *Domain model library* (Ontology). The result is recorded in this library. On the right-hand side, the overall knowledge base consists of the conceptual model of the knowledge acquisition process itself, called PLANFORM KA and the *KA-Expertise* belonging to the particular conceptual model being constructed.

## 2. Case studies and methodology

In this section, we present two case studies using our methodology, based on the problem specifications: (i) 'EVentus: Entertaining a foreign visitor to your lab at the weekend' and (ii) 'Drumstore: a logistics problem in a nuclear waste factory with eight identical robots loading and unloading drums of nuclear waste materials'. In fact, this domain was the generalization of an 'exchange an object between two robots' activity already studied by the team. We conducted these experiments, respectively with eight people and five people who verbalised their knowledge about how they would solve this problem during interviews. We chose *EVentus* because it was a planning problem drawing on general rather than specialised knowledge that was not difficult to collect. *Drumstore* was chosen because it had already been implemented as an AI planning domain within the group. The interviews contained the unstructured knowledge (discourse) and sometimes some notes such as graphics, plans and other material describing knowledge and activity (explicitly/implicitly) both about the case studies and the KA process itself. It is important to understand the level of abstraction at which such a sample problem must work. The PLANFORM toolkit as a whole will be used to create a domain model within which a number of specific tasks can be planned. Thus the experiment does not start with a specific task, but with the generic problem specification. Subjects were asked to explore the generic domain model that would be needed to plan within the domain of the problem specification and to support the solving of a number of specific tasks. Note that a more abstract version of this problem would be to replace 'your lab' with 'a lab' where this might be anywhere in the world potentially. An instance of a specific task would be something like 'Professor Stein from DFKI Germany is to be entertained on Saturday May 9th'.

### 2.1 Building a domain dictionary

The first phase gives us domain dictionaries (TABLE 1) that puts together a set of terms according to the problem specification. Next, we built a set of scenarios with the shared knowledge of these domain experts to find out how each expert defines

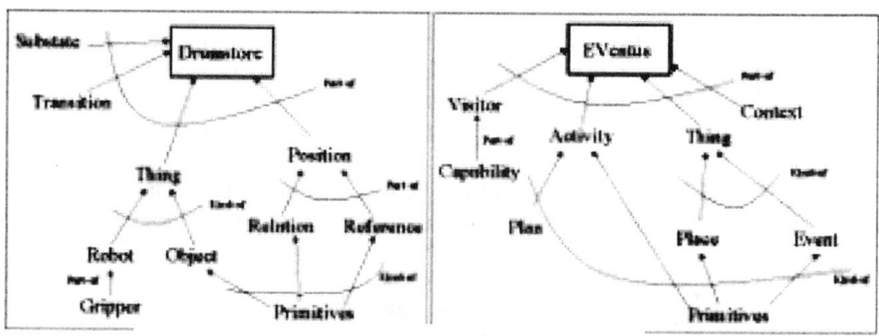


**FIG 4: Frame systems of Drumstore and EVentus.**

reasoning strategies to solve the problem specification. In KOD [29], the building and generalization of taxonomy (one of its paradigms) from examples and scenarios has been deemed useful for this KA process (See SECTION 2.2). TABLES 2 and 3 show the number of instances of each term in each scenario. We will call these outcomes *instance coverage*. This shows that knowledge about this particular specification varies between domain experts giving different number of examples of each term. This coverage gives us an idea of the experts' practice so as to build the interface of the future intelligent system.

TABLE 1

| Drumstore | EVentus |
|---|---|
| Robot | Thing |
| Thing | Activity |
| Gripper | Context |
| Object | Visitor |
| Relation | Capability |
| Reference | |

TABLE 2

| Drumstore | Terms | | | | | |
|---|---|---|---|---|---|---|
| | R | T | G | O | REL | REF |
| 1 | 5 | 1 | 3 | 7 | 2 | 3 |
| 2 | 10 | 2 | 2 | 5 | 2 | 3 |
| 3 | 20 | 5 | 5 | 12 | 1 | 3 |
| 4 | 10 | 3 | 3 | 5 | 1 | 3 |
| 5 | 5 | 1 | 4 | 7 | 2 | 2 |
| 6 | 6 | 1 | 3 | 13 | 2 | 2 |
| 7 | 8 | 1 | 5 | 7 | 2 | 3 |
| 8 | 7 | 1 | 4 | 11 | 2 | 2 |

TABLE 3

| EVentus | Terms | | | | |
|---|---|---|---|---|---|
| | T | A | C | V | Ca |
| 1 | 9 | 4 | 1 | 1 | 3 |
| 2 | 5 | 6 | 1 | 1. | 2 |
| 3 | 8 | 7 | 2 | 2 | 2 |
| 4 | 5 | 5 | 3 | 1 | 4 |
| 5 | 13 | 7 | 1 | 2 | 6 |

**TABLE 1: Domain dictionaries**
**TABLES 2 & 3: Instance coverage of Drumstore[2] and EVentus[3].**

## 2.2 Building of conceptual/epistemological model

The second extraction gives us first a conceptual model containing semantic relationships, objects and actions. We then add an epistemological model – the definition of concepts, hierarchy and structuring relationships (behaviours). A domain model is thus defined by these representations in our methodology by using a frame system as in FIGURE 4. `Drumstore` relies on the nine following generic concepts: `Thing` is a root of the domain model and describes two mobile things: `Robot` and `Object`. `Robot` depicts a real robot, which can navigate and has equipment – `Gripper` – to bring and carry some `Object` according to a `Relation/Reference` address pair (e.g. `(Object,at,beacon1)`). `Primitives` depict a set of generic concepts like `Drum (Object)`, `At`, `Near (Relation)` and

---

[2] Each Drumstore scenario is designed through the six terms as follows: Robot (R), Thing (T), Gripper (G), Object (O), Relation (Rel) and Reference (Ref).
[3] Each EVentus scenario is designed through the four terms as follows: Thing (T), Activities (A), Context (C), Visitor (V) and Capability (Ca).

Beacon (Reference). Substate and Transition depict respectively the conditions in which Robot does some tasks and the state of each task when it has taken place. EVentus contains the nine following generic concepts: Visitor is a locus of the domain model and describes a real visitor according to her/his real capacities, which are depicted by Capacity. Activity and Context describe behaviours of a visitor; Plan describes a set of alternative plans used by a visitor. Thing describes Places and Events used during the activity. Finally, Primitives depicts a set of generic concepts like a restaurant, a town (place) or an exhibition (event). One main distinction exists between these Ontologies. They include different interactions between the agent (e.g. Robot, Visitor) and its environment (e.g. thing, relation) because while the Drumstore task is state-based, the EVentus task is action-based. Additional details about the Substate, Transition and Primitives concepts are available in [16].

## 2.3 Summary

A KA process has been carried out to capture knowledge and build two domain models for particular problem specifications through two case studies: Drumstore and EVentus. The generic concept Thing is defined in both domain models with different semantics. In Drumstore, this concept represents an abstraction of *mobiles* but in EVentus, it represents an abstraction of *locations*. TABLE 4 shows the similarity between Drumstore and EVentus concepts using three main categories: Agent, Object and Task as a skeleton ontology for planning domains [29]. Note that the Task category is divided into two semantic subcategories: (i) the Drumstore task is state-based and (ii) the EVentus task is action-based. This represents a first step towards an epistemological model.

| Categories | Drumstore | EVentus |
|---|---|---|
| Agent | Thing | Visitor |
| Object | Position | Thing |
| Task | Substate | Context |
| | Transition | Activity |
| | | Plan |

**TABLE 4: Abstraction similarity between Drumstore and EVentus**

# 3. An Intelligent System: PLANFORM KA

In this section we discuss the PLANFORM KA-Tool in more detail – see FIGURE 5 for its conceptual model. As outlined above, the process component of the tool can be decomposed into a set of refinement processes – called phases – carried out by the domain expert according to an expertise. We are studying[4] a specialised version of Upper Cyc Ontology [7] (though in this work we have constructed a small ontology ourselves as representative of the AI Planning field) to start instance collection. This Ontology provides a sufficient common grounding for applications. Some concepts such as Actor or Plan are supplied in it as generic definitions, which should help the domain expert. It also includes definitions of Object and Agent categories (as in SECTION 2.3) and a

[4] Note: there is no well-founded AI Planning Ontology which can completely support the domain expert in this KA process. However, three generic concepts are: Agent, Object and Task.

fragmentary definition of the Task category. That is the case for Drumstore for instance where there are State and Transition generic concepts as parts of OCL.

## 3.1 Conceptual model of PLANFORM-KA

The conceptual model of PLANFORM-KA (FIGURE 5) relies on several interrelated generic concepts. The Domain expert generic concept depicts the subject acquiring the knowledge model, the KA-expertise generic concept features the knowledge required to build the knowledge, and the KA-Process generic concept describes the behaviour carried out by the domain expert with the tool. The KOD method (i.e. taxonomy formation paradigm) was again used to elaborate a frame system to be implemented inside the KA Tool.

## 3.2 Frame representations

For reasons of space we discuss only a subset of the frame representations for these concepts – those for Domain expert, *KA-Expertise* and *KA-Process*.

### 3.2.1 Domain expert

We consider the domain expert (DE) as the cognitive agent [15] carrying out the process of knowledge acquisition. DE has a mental model of the real world expressed in concepts. The domain expert generic concept represents the properties of this agent in relation to the carrying out of the KA-Process and is central to the overall conceptual model since there are composition relationships with concepts *KA-Process* and *KA-Expertise.*

### 3.2.2 KA-Expertise

The KA-Expertise generic concept represents the memory of our domain expert. This holds three knowledge categories: transcripts from a case study, and the related domain dictionary and domain model. The Transcript generic concept represents the properties of documents such as free-text or graphics collected in a case study. The Domain dictionary generic concept represents the properties of a domain specification expressed as a set of choices – terms – themselves organised into a set of scenarios (FIGURE 5). The Domain model generic concept represents the properties of a conceptualisation as a set of conceptual/epistemological and logical representations.

### 3.2.3 KA-Process

The KA-Process generic concept represents the process which drives knowledge acquisition and its refinement phases. The KA process starts with an instance collection phase (see FIGURE 3), i.e. the explaining of each term by providing examples of it. For example, Robot, a term of the terms in Drumstore, contains the following instances:

```
Robot R3 navigates from location S3 towards beacon B14
Robot R3 docks at beacon B14
Robot R2 grabs from beacon B15 drum D12
```

| Epistemological level | | Logical level |
|---|---|---|
| ROBOT Frame and its slots | Arity | OCL |
| Kind-of value THING = {r1,r2,r3,r4} | (1) | sorts(thing,[robot]) |
| | (1,1) | sorts(primitive_sorts,[robot]) |
| if-add <GRIPPER, create-instance(),($equiqment)> | (1) | objects(robot,[r1,r2,r3,r4]) |
| | (1,1) | |
| Sense-on domain Boolean = {true, false} | (1) | sense_on(robot) |
| | (1,1) | |
| Can_sense domain tuple (ROBOT,OBJECT,REL,REF) | (3) | can_sense(robot,object,rel,ref) |
| | (1,1) | belongs_to(gripper,robot) |
| Equipment domain GRIPPER | (1) | belongs_to(g1,r1) |
| | (1,1) | belongs_to(g2,r2) |
| | | belongs_to(g3,r3) |
| | | . . . . . . . .. |

**TABLE 5: Translation from epistemological level to logical level.**

This phase continues until the expert has provided instances for each newly defined term. The process continues with a <u>scenario creation</u> phase: the description of several scenarios – particular problems to be solved – within the scope of the given global goal (e.g. entertaining a foreign visitor; a logistics problem in a nuclear waste factory) using the previously defined instances. Finally, a scenario can be seen as a set of facts (predicates), which will be used to define some properties, constraints, plan, and goal states samples at the conceptual level. The outcome is a terminology, i.e. a set of terms and a set of scenarios. The built-in ontology is used to prompt the expert during this phase.

This bottom-up approach has also been supplemented by a top-down approach in which the ontological categories `agent`, `object` and `action`, are used to drive a question cycle in which new terms are extracted from the expert. Questions move between the categories, so that if the expert provides an `agent` term (e.g. `Robot`),

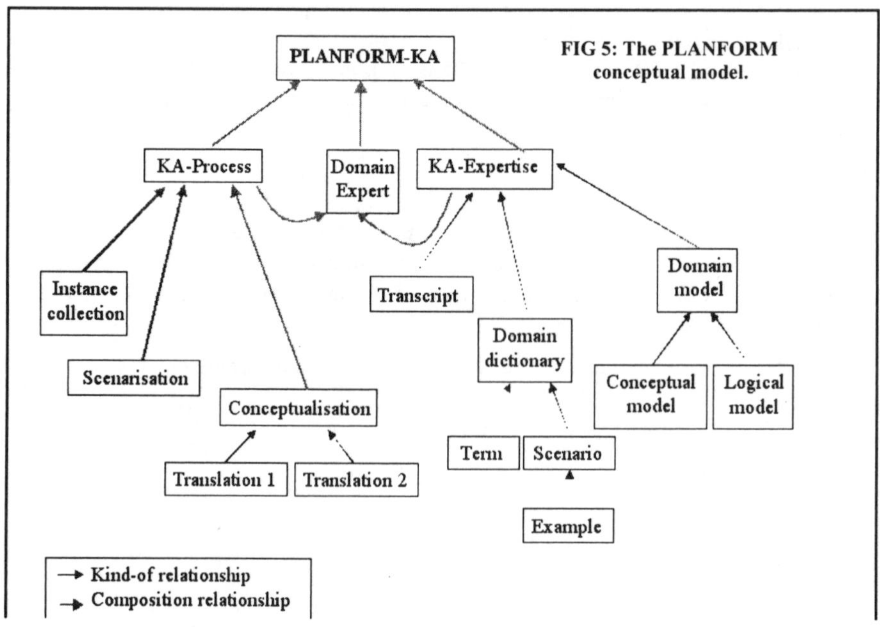

**FIG 5: The PLANFORM conceptual model.**

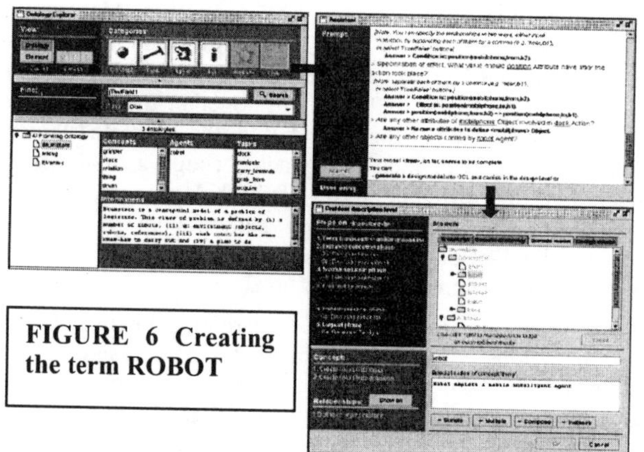

FIGURE 6 Creating the term ROBOT

they are then prompted for actions carried out by that agent and objects involved in the action. At the conceptual/epistemological level, first of all, the process automatically carries out a translation phase into the frame-based representation, so that each defined term becomes a frame. Next, the domain expert defines by hand, or through the agent-object-action question cycle, the properties of each frame. Thus, the term `Robot` becomes the `Robot` frame and belongs to the `Concept`[5] `superframe`. In the same way, a `Visitor` frame – from `EVentus` – can be defined, though space does not permit us to show it. This references a `Capability` frame holding the properties of natural abilities and skills that make the visitor able to do some activities.

A visitor could have either at least seven {Status, gender, age, budget, type, quality, nationality} or several further capabilities such as {like to try new things, accompanying other people, swim, has a budget, other}. The conceptualisation finishes with a second translation phase from the frame-based representation into sorted first-order logic, using the language OCL. In OCL, `Substate` and `Transition-substate` concepts describe respectively, the conditions before the transformation of each task and the transition when an object changes from one substate to another substate. This translation is automatic: each frame ‡[6] sort, each instance of frame ‡ object, each attribute ‡ predicate and each *part-of* relationship with its related arity ‡ a defined predicate called `belongs_to`. For example, TABLE 5 shows the `Robot` frame and its translation into OCL where gripper – equipment – of the robot. The arity of this slot (column Arity, bottom) is defined by `(1)`, i.e. this slot takes one frame gripper in the relationship at the same time and `(1,1)`, i.e. this slot allows the obligatory instantiating of one gripper's instance. As a result, the relationship and its arity of this slot translate into invariant predicates (bottom) the constraint that one robot has to have one gripper only.

## 3.3 Evaluation and results

A first demonstrator has been implemented to validate the approach of PLANFORM KA. FIGURE 6 shows the main GUI during the creation of the `Robot` generic concept in the `Drumstore` domain model. The core of the GUI is the *Assistant Prompt* (top, right hand side of FIGURE 6), which is the

---

[5] `Concept` superFrame is the generic frame, which is the root/father of all frames in the frame system.

[6] ‡ means *is translated into the type of...*

questioning system based around the `Agent-Object-Task` concepts. Meanwhile, the *Ontology Explorer* (top, left hand side of FIGURE 6) gives a view of the existing library so that it supports the Domain expert. After a typical session, the *Problem Specification Level* (bottom of FIGURE 6) puts together the specialized knowledge representations as models. One of these models is the generated logical model seen in Appendix 1 with OCL semantics and syntax through a first version of a translator: Generalising over the different phases of the KA process, we have formulated the notion of `Constraint`. Thus the `Term` generic concept – in the instance collection phase – is a kind of constraint which allows the domain expert to make a set of choices to justify the domain specification.

Next, the `Scenario` generic concept is also a kind of constraint, allowing choices in the design of task representations. Thus the task could be state-based, action-based and so forth. In the same way, the `Relationship` generic concept – in the conceptualisation phase – is a kind of constraint (FIGURE 7- top), which structures each concept. In addition, the `Arity` and `Daemon` generic concepts – from the epistemological phase – are also kinds of constraints (FIGURE 7 - bottom) on the problem-solving methods (PSM) and heuristics. Finally the `Proposition` generic concept – from the logical phase – is also a kind of constraint, representing the chosen logical language. The `Constraint` is then described as something that must be `true`. Thus in the KA process we define a cluster of constraints (FIGURE 3 – Left hand) across the several representation levels.

## 3.4 Capturing actions

The creation of a strong methodological framework for the PLANFORM KA-Tool was seen as a priority, and this has been accomplished. What is required now is to incorporate the planning-specific conceptual framework of agent, object and task in a more direct fashion. Work has begun on the generation planning operators and translation into OCL, through the question-driven agent-action-object dialogue. Given that PLANFORM KA sits within the overall PLANFORM architecture, even the generation of skeletal operators would allow use of GIPO's refinement mechanisms to fill them out into a complete form. This would require an AI planning expert to supplement the role of the domain expert but would at least automate the basic knowledge acquisition process from the expert.

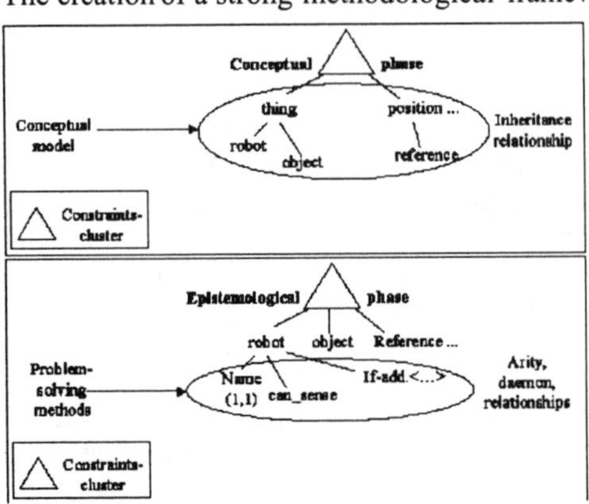


**FIG 7: Constraints-cluster on conceptual model.**

# 4. Related work

Many alternative approaches propose a set of solutions for the acquisition, the representation and the sharing/reusing of knowledge using libraries and/or strategies, since this topic has been studied extensively in the KBS community since the 1980s. Some of them are more specialised in the first extraction of knowledge proposing a generic surrogate to capture knowledge. We noticed also that most of these approaches adopt one or several implicit revision processes. We propose the KA-Tool approach – as a part of PLANFORM project – to take account of the underlying revision aspect through several stages of refinements.

Protégé [11] includes a suite of tools for editing ontologies, which can automatically generate customised editors that are accessible to domain experts. The Protégé library includes the problem-solving strategies (diagnosis) and also methods ontologies that describe the kinds of domain-independent knowledge used in strategies. Recently, researchers have investigated this topic through theory revision [13]. As Poole mentioned in [24] belief states of robots are uncertain when it adopts conditional plans. Clack [5] presents the Generic Types formulated by Fox and Long, which propose the categorisation of domains into domain classes (e.g. transportation domain) is a kind of ontology (i.e. a complex sort) deduced during the planning process to generate Generic Types. McCluskey [17] suggests in adddition an inductive process with OpMaker. The Protégé planning system is supported by a tool that captures new ontologies, and offers a library of problem-solving methods. EXPECT [9,23] used explicit representations of problem-solving strategies (propose-and-revise strategy for the configuration design task, for example) to support flexible approaches to knowledge acquisition. Blythe [4] uses expectation theory (task, critique) to capture data, object classes and preferences. Williams [30] proposes an intelligent system called SATEN to deal with theory extraction and revision from inconsistent ranking. KRAKEN is a toolset [8], which addresses several problems from domain experts who are non-logicians. PLANET [12] is an ontology for the representation of plans in the AI Planning field, which focuses on a similar approach with respect to reuse of ontology as in the more extended framework discussed here. In other approaches, the answer for a given problem is built through a combined set of different techniques (AI methodologies, for example KOD, KADS [25]) according to some generic task (diagnosis for example [21][22] or requirements engineering [6] for instance).

# 5. Conclusion and further work

Surprisingly, given the amount of work in the KBS community in general, knowledge acquisition has not been widely studied in AI planning. Yet applying planning systems to real-world problems requires a systematic approach to knowledge acquisition and a methodology supporting reuse rather than ad-hoc adaptations of specific planning systems by particular individuals whose expertise remains private and invisible. The work discussed here represents some steps in this direction.

## 5.1 Conclusion

Our work consisted in demonstrating the value of the methodology called PLANFORM KA in supporting a knowledge acquisition process. First of all, we have presented the basic steps of a methodology to build a representation of AI Planning case studies according to a given problem specifications. We have described how a cluster of constraints could help domain experts during the knowledge acquisition process and how the configuration of a cluster at any representation level can formalise the knowledge of a domain expert. Second, we have validated our KA process through the building of the case studies such as `Drumstore` and `EVentus` and shown some results as follows:

• *Instance coverage.* This allows us to study the interaction with the domain expert,

• *Two frame systems.* These introduce different abstraction levels of knowledge.

• *Three AI Planning categories*: `Agent`, which is a mobile thing like `Robot` or `Visitor`, `Object`, for example location (`Position`, `Place`, `Event`) and `Task`, which is specialised into action-based and state based representations.

• *The* `Constraint` *generic concept.* It features an abstraction of several constraints defined at different representation levels.

Finally, we are building on the question-driven interface and expect soon to generate at least outline planning operators. Putting this in the context of the overall PLANFORM project, different processes from GIPO/Opmaker, STAN/TIM and KA-Tool offer a multistrategy toolset meant to deal with the acquisition challenge, with theory revision as a backbone making it possible to build a neat underlying logical model.

## 5.2 Further work

So far, we have built a framework for an intelligent system to solve a set of issues concerning the knowledge acquisition in AI Planning. We will make a systematic survey – at the epistemological level – of other approaches like PROTÉGÉ, EXPECT or PLANET, for instance, which focus on a similar approach with respect to reuse of ontology. A particular direction is to explore the use of *Generic types*, [10] formulated by PLANFORM co-researchers Fox and Long, within the question-driven acquisition module. Currently, *Generic types* are extracted from PDDL domain models, but the FSM definitions used for this might be moved towards the domain expert through incorporation into PLANFORM KA. Thus once an expert identifies a `mobile` agent for example, the system could actively prompt for the possibility of route-following. Further case-study examples will be explored in order to assess the coverage PLANFORM KA is able to provide for domains where a domain model has already been created by hand. Finally, supporting the expert with a much larger ontology – possibly a specialised version of the CYC Upper ontology – will also be explored. This would then enable much more widespread trials of the system.

## References


1. Aylett, R.S. & Jones, S. Planner and Domain: Domain Configuration for a Task Planner. *International Journal of Expert Systems*, **9**(2), pp. 279-318. 1996.
2. Benjamins, V.R. Problem Solving Methods for Diagnosis. *PhD thesis*, University of Amsterdam, Amsterdam, The Netherlands. 1993.
3. Breuker, J. & Wielinga, B. Models of Expertise. *Knowledge Acquisition*. Guida, G. & Tasso, C. (Eds). Topics in Expert Systems Design: methodologies and tools. North Holland Publishing Company. 1989.
4. Blythe, J. Integrating expectations for different sources to help end users acquire procedural knowledge. *Proceeding of the Seventeenth International Joint Conference on Artificial Intelligence, IJCAI 2001. Vol. II – Knowledge Acquisition*, pp. 943-952. Bernhard Nebel (Ed.). Morgan Kaufmann Publishers. 2001.
5. Clark, M. Construction domains: a generic type solved. *PLANSIG'01. Workshop of UK Planning and Scheduling*. Edinburgh. 2001.
6. Cybulski, J.L. Application of Software Reuse Methods to Requirements Elicitation from Informal Requirements Texts. http://www.dis.unimelb.edu.au/staff/jacob/. 2001.

7. CycCorp. The Upper Cyc Ontology. *Available at* http://www.cyc.com/cyc-2-1/cover.html. 2002.
8. CycCorp. KRAKEN project. *Available at* http://reliant.teknowledge.com/RKF/proposals/Cycorp.html. 1999.
9. Fridman-Noy, N. & *al*. The knowledge model of Protégé-2000: combining interoperability and flexibility. *2th Int. Conf. on Knowledge Engineering and Knowledge Management (EKAW)*. Juan-les-Pins (Fce). 2000.
10. Fox, M. & Long, D. Automatic Synthesis and use of Generic Types in Planning. *AIPS'00 - Workshop on Analysis and Exploiting Domain Knowledge for Efficient Planning*. 2000.
11. Gil, Y. & Blythe, J. How Can a Structured Representation of Capabilities Help in Planning? *Proceedings of the AAAI – Workshop on Representational Issues for Realworld Planning Systems*. 2000.
12. Gil, Y. & Blythe, J. PLANET: A Shareable and Reusable Ontology for Representing Plan. *Proceedings of the AAAI – Workshop on Representational Issues for Real-world Planning Systems*. 2000.
13. Grenier, R. The complexity of theory revision. *Available at* http://www.cs.ualberta.ca/~grenier. 1998.
14. Gruber T.R. A Translation Approach to Portable Ontology Specifications. *Knowledge Acquisition*, **5**(2). pp. 199-220. 1993.
15. Hayes-Roth, B. & Hayes-Roth, F. A Cognitive Model of Planning. Representation and Reasoning. *Readings in Planning*. Morgan Kaufman Publishers. 1990.
16. Liu, D. & McCluskey, T. L. The Object Centred Language Manual - OCLh – Version 1.2. *Technical report*. School of Computing and Mathematics, University of Huddersfield. *Available at* http://helios.hud.ac.uk/planform. 1999.
17. McCluskey L. & Richardson B. The Induction Operator Descriptions from Examples and Structural Domain Knowledge. *PLANSIG'01. Workshop of UK Planning and Scheduling*. Edinburgh. 2001.
18. McCluskey T.L. & *al*. Planform. An Open environment for building planners. *Available at* http://helios.hud.ac.uk/planform. 1999.
19. McCluskey T.L. & Porteous J.M. Engineering and compiling planning domain models to promote validity and efficiency. *Artificial Intelligence*, pp. 1-65. 1997.
20. McDermott, D. & *al*. PDDL --- The Planning Domain Definition Language. *Machine Intelligence 4*. D. Michie (ed.), Ellis Horwood, Chichester (UK). 1998.
21. Mercantini, J.M., Doniat, C. & *al*. Safety Previsional Analysis Method of an Urban Industrial Site. *Scientific Journal of the Finnish Institute of Occupational Health. Serie: People and Work, safety in modern society*, pp. 105-109, 33. 2000.
22. Mercantini, J.M., Doniat, C. & *al*. Etude d'un système d'aide au diagnostic des accidents de la sécurité routière. *Information & Connaissances'99*. Palaiseau (Fce). 1999.
23. Musen, M. Modern Architectures for Intelligent Systems : Reusable Ontologies and Problem-Solving Methods. *AMIA Annual Symposium*. Chute (Eds), pp. 46-52. 1998.
24. Poole, D. Decision theory, the situation calculus and conditional plans. *Electronic articles in Computer and Information Science*. **3**(8). 1998.
25. Schreiber, G., Wielinga, B., de Hoog, R., Akkermans, H. and Van de Velde, W. CommonKADS: A Comprehensive Methodology for KBS Development. *IEEE Expert*, **9**(6), pp. 28-37. 1994.
26. Simpson, R.M., McCluskey, T. L., Zhao, W., Aylett, R. S. & Doniat, C. An Integrated Graphical Tool to support knowledge Engineering in AI Planning. *Proceedings of European Conference on Planning (ECP'01)*, Toledo, Spain. 2001.
27. Sowa, J.F. Knowledge representation: logical, philosophical and computational foundations. Brooks/Cole (Eds). 2000.
28. Valente, A. Planning models for the CommonKADS library. ESPRIT Project KADS-II. *Available at* http://www.swi.psy.uva.nl/usr/andre/publications.html. 1993.
29. Vogel, C. Le génie cognitif. Editor & Publisher: Masson (Fce). 1988.

30. Williams, M.A. Implementing Belief Revision. *Non-monotonic reasoning*. G. Antoniou (ed.). MIT Press. 1997.

## Appendix 1 – OCL model

```
domain_name(drumstore).
% Sorts
sorts(non_primitive_sorts,[thing,position]).
sorts(primitive_sorts,[robot,gripper,object,relation,reference]).
Sorts(thing,[robot,object]).
% Objects
objects(robot,[r1,r2,r3,r4]).
objects(gripper,[g1,g2,g3,g4]).
objects(object,[d1,d2,d3,d4,d5,d6,d7,d8,d9,d10,d11,d12]).
objects(relation,[near,at]).
objects(reference,[s1,s2,s3,s4,b1,b2,b3,b4,b5,b6,b7,b8,b9,b10,b11,b
1
2,b13,b14,b15,b16]).
% Predicates
predicates([
can_sense(robot,object,relation,reference),
sense_on(robot),
position(thing,relation,reference),
full(gripper),
empty(gripper),
belongs_to(robot,gripper),
in(object,gripper),
released(object),
in_range(reference,reference)]).
% Atomic Invariants
atomic_invariants([
position(r1,at,d12),position(d9,at,d4),position(r2,near,s2),
belongs_to(r1,g1),belongs_to(r2,g2),belongs_to(r3,g3),belongs_to(r4
, g4),
in_range(s1,b12),in_range(b12,s1),
in_range(s2,b15),in_range(b15,s2),
in_range(s3,b14),in_range(b14,s3),
in_range(s4,b13),in_range(b13,s4),
in_range(b13,b1),in_range(b1,b13),
in_range(b15,b13),in_range(b13,b15),
in_range(b12,b14),in_range(b14,b12),
in_range(b14,b16),in_range(b16,b14)])
```

# SESSION 3B:

# KNOWLEDGE REPRESENTATION AND REASONING 3

# Holons and Agents. Do they differ?

Adriana Giret, Vicente Botti
Departamento de Sistemas Informáticos y Computación,
Universidad Politécnica de Valencia
Valencia, Spain
{agiret, vbotti}@dsic.upv.es

**Abstract**

The future of the Manufacturing sector in the world will be determined by how it meets the challenges of the 21st century. Two paradigms promise to meet these challenges, multiagent systems and holonic systems. Currently, there is some misunderstanding about the relationships between these two approaches. The aim of this work is to make a study of all the characteristics of the holonic and the multiagent systems approach, in order to illustrate an exhaustive comparison of holons and agents.

## 1 Introduction

The future of the manufacturing sector in the world will be determined by how it meets the challenges of "new manufacturing". Such manufacturing systems will need to satisfy the following fundamental requirements [1], [2]:

- *Enterprise Integration*: In order to support global competitiveness and rapid market responsiveness.
- *Distributed Organization*: For effective enterprise integration across distributed organizations.
- *Heterogeneous Environments*: Such manufacturing systems will need to accommodate heterogeneous software and hardware in both the manufacturing and information environment.
- *Interoperability*: A heterogeneous information environment may use different programming languages, represent data with different representation languages and models, and operate on different computing platforms.
- *Open and Dynamic Structure*: It must be possible to rapidly integrate new subsystems into or remove existing subsystems from the system without stopping or reinitializing the working environment.
- *Cooperation*: Manufacturing enterprises will have to fully cooperate with their suppliers, partners, and customers for materials, supplies, parts fabrication, final product commercialization, and so on.

- *Integration of humans with software and hardware*: People and computers need to be integrated to work collectively at various stages of the product development and even the whole product life cycle.
- *Agility*: Agile manufacturing is the ability to adapt quickly in a manufacturing environment of continuous and unanticipated changes and thus is a key component in manufacturing strategies for global competition.
- *Scalability*: Expansion of resources should be possible without the disruption of previously established organizational links.
- *Fault Tolerant*: The system should be fault tolerant both at the system level and at the subsystem level so as to detect and recover from system failures at any level and minimize their impacts on the working environment.

Many manufacturing paradigms promise to meet these challenges. Two of these paradigms, distributed intelligent manufacturing systems (or agent based manufacturing systems), and holonic manufacturing systems have lately received a lot of attention in academia and industry. Currently, there is some misunderstanding about the relationship between these two approaches. Some researchers, like Bussmann [3], Brennan and Norrie [4], have clarified the basic philosophical differences among agents and holons. Nevertheless, a comprehensive comparison of all the properties of both paradigms has not yet been made. The aim of this work is to make a study of all the characteristics of holonic and multiagent approach. To this end, in the first section, we will give an overview of concepts of holonic and multiagent systems. Following, we will made a comparison of both paradigms. Finally, we will present some conclusions.

# 2 Agents and Holons

The purpose of this section is not to make an exhaustive analysis of both paradigms, but rather a brief review of the holonic and the multiagent approaches. A comprehensive study of each paradigm can be found in the specialized literature.

## 2.1 Holons

The holonic concept was developed by the philosopher Arthur Koestler [5] in order to explain the evolution of biological and social systems. On the one hand, these systems develop stable intermediate forms during evolution that are self-reliant. On the other hand, in living and organizational systems it is difficult to distinguish between 'wholes' and 'parts': almost everything at the same time is a part and a whole. These observations led Koestler to propose the word "*holon*" which is a combination of the Greek word 'holos' meaning whole and the Greek suffix 'on' meaning particle or part as in proton or neutron. The strength of holonic organization, or *holarchy*, is that it enables the construction of very complex systems that are nonetheless efficient in the use of resources, highly resilient to disturbance (both internal and external), and adaptable to changes in the environment in which they exist. Within a holarchy, holons may dynamically create and change hierarchies. Moreover, holons may participate in multiple hierarchies at the same time. Holarchies are recursive in the sense that a holon may itself be an entire holarchy that acts as an autonomous and cooperative unit in the first holarchy.

Holonic Manufacturing was first proposed as a new manufacturing paradigm in the beginning of the 1990s and has since then received a lot of attention in academic and industrial research. The application of holonic concepts to manufacturing was initially motivated by the inability of existing manufacturing systems (i) to deal with the evolution of products within an existing production facility and (ii) to maintain a satisfactory performance outside normal operating conditions [1].

Holonic Manufacturing Systems (HMS) was one of the six test cases of the Intelligent Manufacturing Systems (IMS). The task of the HMS consortium is to translate the concepts that Koestler developed for social organizations and living organisms into a set of appropriate concepts for manufacturing industries. The goal of this work is to attain in manufacturing the benefits that holonic organization provides to living organisms and societies.

The basic holonic attributes are [1]:

- **autonomy**: Each holon must be able to create, control and monitor the execution of its own plans and/or strategies, and to take suitable corrective actions against its own malfunctions.

- **cooperation**: Holons must be able to negotiate and execute mutually acceptable plans and take mutual actions against malfunctions. [6],[7].

- **openness**: The system must be able to accommodate the incorporation of new holons, the removal of existing holons, or modification of the functional capabilities of existing holons, with minimal human intervention, where holons or their functions may be supplied by a variety of diverse sources.

A holonic manufacturing system consists of autonomous, self-reliant manufacturing units called holons. A manufacturing holon is an autonomous and cooperative building block of a manufacturing system for transforming, transporting, storing and/or validating information, and/or physical objects [8]. Therefore, a manufacturing holon always contains an information processing part and, optionally, a physical processing part [6]. The general holon architecture of Christensen [6] can be seen in Figure 1.

As Figure 1 shows, the Inter-Holon Interface and the Human Interface are responsible for communication with the outer world. The Physical Processing represents the execution of manufacturing operations, such as milling or assembly. This layer is controlled by the Physical Control module. The Decision

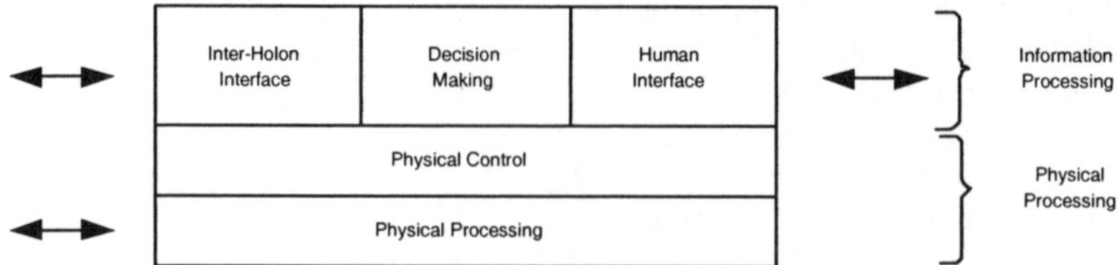


Figure 1: Holon General Architecture

Making module is the kernel of a holon that consists of other different units such as the knowledge and the actual status of a holon which are necessary for making decisions. Moreover, the Decision Making unit has control over all interfaces; and at the same time the interfaces supply the Decision Making unit with environmental information.

The multiagent's basic concepts are presented in the following subsection.

## 2.2 Agents

A Multiagent System (MAS) is made up of two or more related agents. An agent is an autonomous and flexible computational system, which is able to act in an environment [9]. Flexible means, that the agent is:

- *Reactive*, it reacts to its environment.
- *Pro-active*, it is able to try to fulfill it's own plan or goals.
- *Social*, it is able to communicate with other agents by means of some language.

Some properties which are usually attributed to agents to a greater or lesser degree for solving particular problems are [10, 11]: autonomy, social ability, rationality, reactivity, pro-activity, adaptability, mobility, veracity, benevolence.

The study of MAS began about 20 years ago, within the field of Distributed Artificial Intelligence (DAI). DAI studies group intelligent behaviours that follow from the cooperation of entities called *agents*. It studies how a group of modules cooperates to divide and share the problem knowledge and how the solution is developed.

MAS studies the coordination of intelligent behaviour among a group of (possibly preexisting) autonomous intelligent agents. It is focused on the individual behaviour from which the system behaviour follows. Today MAS is a very active area of research and is beginning to see commercial and industrial applications. MAS is centered in the social behaviour of intelligent entities and focuses mainly on investigating behaviour models, cooperation and coordination strategies, intelligent brokerage, task performance optimization, learning from own experiences, coalition formation, etc.

# 3 Comparative Study

In this section, we make a comparison between holons and agents. In a first case, following the generalized trend in the field of intelligent manufacturing systems, we indicate the motivation of both approaches; then we identify those properties that are contrasted in order to make an analysis of each one. The main goal of this section is to find out whether holons and agents are different or not, or if one is a sub-case of the other.

As pointed out by Bussmann [3], Brennan and Norrie [4] among others, both approaches differ mainly in motivation. The HS research is motivated by flexible manufacturing tasks. Therefore, it is oriented towards low-level, communication standards and low-level behaviour. On the other hand, the MAS research is motivated by programming of distributed systems. It is aimed at the social behaviour of intelligent entities and is mainly involved in the investigation of behavioural models, cooperation and coordination strategies, intelligent brokerage, performance optimization tasks, learning from own experiences, coalition creation, etc. In summary, unlike MAS, which is a broad software approach that can also be used for distributed intelligent control, HS is, by definition, a manufacturing-specific approach for distributed intelligent control.

As we have mentioned in previous sections, agents are [9]: autonomous, social, reactive, pro-active, rational, mobile, they may learn, etc. Holons, as a paradigm, have the following basic characteristics: autonomy, cooperation and reorganization (openness). In addition to these, which could be called "behavioural properties", holons have "structural properties". One of them is "recursiveness", which allows holons to be made internally of self-similar entities (holons), which again can be made of holons, and so on (until we reach an atomic level in which a new subdivision is impossible or useless for the domain application). Holons may be composed of holons which 1) may themselves be holarchies, 2) may participate in many holarchies simultaneously, and 3) may come, go, and change - that is, holons which yield dynamic holarchies. Another important structural property, as was defined by the HMS consortium [1], is that holons usually comprise an information processing part with an optional physical processing part. In the following sub-sections we are going to analyze and compare each property separately.

## 3.1 Autonomy

Autonomous entities' behaviour can be based on both their own experiences and the built-in knowledge used in constructing the entities for the particular environment in which they operate. Agents have been successfully used in domains where the degree of uncertainty and unpredictability requires processing units which are capable of autonomous action, without the direct intervention of humans or others.

Manufacturing control systems are large and complex systems which are designed to carry out a clearly defined task. However, in a manufacturing system, rarely do things go as expected. The system may be asked to do additional tasks that were not anticipated and is sometimes allowed to omit certain tasks. The resources available to perform tasks can become unavailable, and additional resources introduced. The beginning time and processing time of a task are also subject to variation. A task can take more time than anticipated or less time than anticipated, and tasks can arrive early or late. These are some of the reasons why holons are by definition autonomous entities which must be able to create, control and monitor the execution of their own plans and/or strategies, and to take suitable corrective actions against their own malfunctions [1]. In this sense, we can say that agents and holons share this property.

## 3.2 Reactivity

An agent is responsive to events that occur in its environment, where these events affect either the agent's goals or the assumptions which underpin the procedures that the agent is executing in order to achieve its goals. So, the effects of environment stimulis may be changes in the agent's goals or assumptions, or the agent's actions effecting changes in the environment. In the same way, holons need to react to changes in their environment. Such changes may affect their initial goals or may prevent the execution of the current or future planned tasks.

Let's suppose a simplified manufacturing system (see the gray area in the manufacturing processing section in Figure 2). There are three types of holons: (*i*) order holons which represent tasks in the manufacturing system; (*ii*) resource holons which are production resources in the manufacturing system, and; (*iii*) product holons, the products themselves. There is OH1 (order holon 1) processing a task to produce PH1 (product holon 1). The production process is carried out in processing steps assigned to resource holons RH1, RH2 and RH3, such that RH1 is the first processing step, RH2 is the second and RH3 the third. For some reason, RH1 takes more time for processing than the initial estimated time. RH2 and RH3 have to realize this situation which prevents the execution of their current plans. They must react in some way, for example, search for other order holons to take advantage of their production power, or stop until RH1 finishes its processing (obviously, the second alternative is less productive for the overall system performance, but it is a reactive action, too). Despite the fact that this example is a simplified and reduced one, it reflects the reactive property of holons.

There are some problems associated with holons which are composed of holons. One of these problems is: Who actually acts and/or perceives in a holarchy?. One approach is for every holarchy to have a head that is responsible for the outside interaction (interactions at its level). For inside interaction, a holon is allowed to interact with any other holons of its holarchy. This approach has been adopted, among others, by [12], [13] and [14].

A second approach is to allow to every holon of a holarchy to interact with every other holon, no matter whether the other holons are from the same

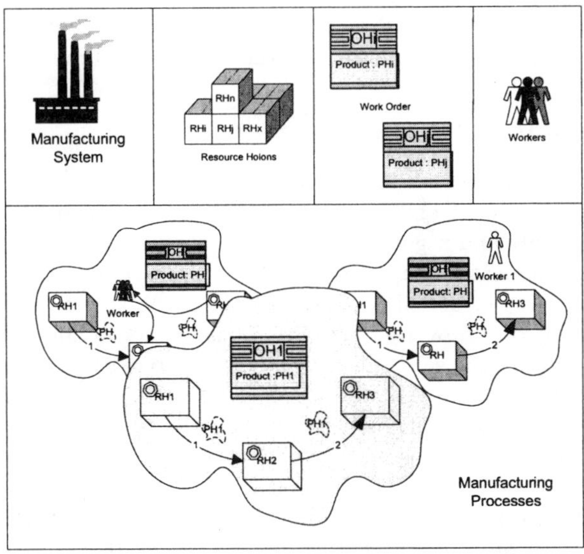


Figure 2: Example of a Manufacturing System

holarchy or from other holarchies. There is no unique outside interface, every holon of a holarchy is an interface. The holarchy behaviour will emerge as the composition of the behaviour of its constituent holons. In spite of this being the way in which biological systems are organized, it is a very complicated and hard approach to implement. Some questions associated with this approach arise: what are the effective boundaries of a holarchy/holon?, what is the identity of a holarchy/holon?, etc.

## 3.3 Pro-activity

Agents do not simply act in response to their environment, they are able to exhibit goal-directed behaviour by *tacking the initiative* [9].

As we pointed out in previews sections the domain application area of agents and holons changes constantly, preventing them from blindly executing a procedure without regard to whether the assumptions underpinning the procedure are valid. This implies that agents and holons need a balance between goal-directed (pro-active) and reactive behaviour. They will attempt to achieve their goal systematically, but they will also be able to react to new situation in time for the reaction to be of some use. Let's suppose that in the previous example, that RH1, RH2 and RH3 have as goal: "to maximize their utilization". Before RH1 begins to slow down its processing, RH2 and RH3 have a certain slot time assigned to PH1, so they look for other products to get a greater utilization of their time and processing power, i.e. to achieve their goal. When RH2 and RH3 realize that RH1 is taking more time than was expected, RH2 and RH3 must re-schedule the slot time assigned to PH1 as well as the slots time and the processing power for the new products found in their attempt to achieve their goal. This simple example reflects the pro-active property of holons.

## 3.4 Social ability

As agents usually do not act in isolation but in the presence of other agents or humans, they need social ability and interactive behaviour to communicate, co-operate, coordinate and negotiate with them. They are enabled to interact and especially communicate with other agents by agent communication languages (ACL). The variety of domains where agents can be active requires agents to have access and control over an extensive vocabulary. In addition, interacting agents need to have the same understanding of a particular vocabulary. This problem is solved by ontologies that cover every domain where agents operate.

A holon's social ability is included in its capacity for cooperation (see the next subsection), since holons need a means of communication with other holons to be able to cooperate. In the above example, the tree types of holons need social abilities to exchange information about the manufacturing process, to enable the execution of tasks. For example, OH1 needs resources to produce PH1, so OH1 interacts with resource holons RH1, RH2 and RH3 to obtain processing functionalities and specific properties of the operation, such as high quality or high throughput. On the other hand, RH1, RH2 and RH3 try to maximize their utilization, whereas PH1 at any time focuses on the next operations in order to get processed by RH1, RH2 and RH3. As can be deduced from this simple example, holons need to interact with each other, therefore, as agents, they need social ability with all its associated problems.

In manufacturing systems, people and computers need to be integrated, with access to required knowledge and information, in order to work collectively at various stages of the product development [1]. This requirement led Christensen to propose an integrated Human Interface block (see Figure 1) on his holon general architecture [6]. Each holon must always be able to cooperate with humans, whereas in MAS, human interface is implemented by one or several specialized agents who provide communication services as a whole. Nevertheless, nothing in the agent definition, prevents having agents with an integrated human interface block.

## 3.5 Cooperation

Cooperation is a means of social ability. Manufacturing enterprises have to fully cooperate with their suppliers and customers for material supply, parts fabrication, final product commercialization, and so on. Such cooperation should be in an efficient and quick-response manner. Cooperation is an imperative requirement for any complete functional model for advanced manufacturing systems [1]. Moreover, all manufacturing units cooperate in order to achieve the overall manufacturing goals. With respect to these goals, a holon never deliberately rejects the cooperation with another holon. Only when the requested actions are impossible or strongly disadvantageous to the manufacturing process, does it refuse their execution [3]. Coordination, negotiation, bargaining, and other cooperation techniques allow holons to flexibly interact with other holons in an abstract form. For cooperation, there exists a great number of specific approaches in MAS, see [15] and [16] for an overview. A sample cooperation scenario was presented in the social ability subsection.

## 3.6 Openness

Koestler [5], defines a holarachy as a hierarchy of holons which function (a) as autonomous wholes in supraordination to their parts, (b) as dependent parts in sub-ordination to controls on higher levels, (c) in coordination with their local environment. This definition leads to a heterarchy of holons which is a mixture of hierarchy and horizontal organization. As indicated by Brennan and Norrie [4], the holarchy notion can be implemented using several MAS architecture approaches for federations such as facilitators, brokers, or mediators.

Holons are able to act within multiple organizations (holarchies), which are created and changed dynamically. Real world manufacturing environments are highly dynamic because of diverse, frequently changing situations: bank rates change overnight, materials do not arrive on time, power supplies breakdown, production facilities fail, workers are absent, new orders arrive and existing orders are changed or canceled, etc [1]. Such changes lead to deviations from existing plans and schedules. It is, therefore, necessary for the working system to adapt to such a changing environment. That is why holarchies must be open organizations, which must be able to accommodate the incorporation of new holons, the removal of existing holons, the re-organization of the work load, etc. The implications of the agreed reorganization are distributed to the other holons' components. In MAS, while there are many works regarding cooperation, there is little work on reorganization [3].

## 3.7 Rationality

A rational agent is one that does the right thing, i.e. an action which causes the agent to be the most successful [17]. The actions an agent performs can be understood as goals. Galliers proposes, in [18], a definition of rationality: *...(crudely) the assumption that an agent will act in order to achieve its goals and will not act in such a way as to prevent its goals being achieved - at least insofar as its beliefs permit.* A rational agent acts according to: the percept sequence, what the agent knows about its environment, and the actions that the agent can perform. These three things will determine the success of the agent.

Although this property does not explicitly appear in the holon definition, it can be derived from a stronger definition of autonomy: *a system is autonomous to the extent that its behaviour is determined by its own experiences* [17]. And the general assumption is that a holon always attempts to obtain the best overall system performance.

### 3.8 Mental Attitudes

In recent years, a number of approaches have been proposed in DAI to specify rational agents in terms of mental attitudes such as knowledge, beliefs, wants, goals, commitment, and intention.

As was pointed out in previews sections, although manufacturing processes experience several changes and disturbances, the degree of uncertainty and unpredictability is not comparable to that of other domain applications of agents. As a consequence, manufacturing applications require less mental and social deliberation than typical applications of multiagent systems [3]. Manufacturing control units (holons) must reason about the behaviour of manufacturing system, but not about their own mental attitudes or that of other control units (holons).

### 3.9 Learning

When designing multiagent systems, it is often infeasible to foresee all the potential situations an agent may encounter and specify an agent behaviour optimally in advance. In order to overcome these design problems, agents have to learn from and adapt to their environment.

Manufacturing control units (holons) must be able to adapt changing environments and handle emergent contexts. Holarchies may be reorganized to cope with unforeseen situations. This capability can be improved with learning. For example, as pointed out by [19], some learning targets are: combinations of manufacturing resources for specific tasks, manufacturing system behaviour, support in favor of or against a decision, preconditions and postconditions for actions and tasks, types of conflicts, heuristics to solve conflicts and to negotiate, etc.

### 3.10 Benevolence

The property of benevolence is that property by which agents cooperate with other agents whenever and wherever possible. Blind benevolence has no place in modelling autonomous agents for whom cooperation will occur only when it is considered advantageous in terms of motivation to do so. The agent cannot spend all its time in new cooperations with other agents, without taking into account its current commitments and motivations. We can say that holons are benevolent entities, because when they discover a possible cooperation scenario they will cooperate.

### 3.11 Mobility

Mobile agents extend the capabilities of distributed systems by code mobility. Mobile agents are programs that can wander through a computer network and can contact other agents and agent places to perform their task.

Manufacturing control units are dedicated to continuos control of physical manufacturing components. The relationship <*controller*, *controlled unit*> is assigned beforehand and fixed throughout the manufacturing process. Moreover, all the necessary control information is in the controlled unit. Therefore, holons rarely need mobility for the execution of their tasks [3].

### 3.12 Recursiveness

Holonic Systems' basic condition is that a holon is simultaneously a whole and a part of some whole/part [1]. This means that holons can contain other inferior levels of holons, that can also be contained in another superior level of holons, being in a recursive architecture.

In the multiagent specialized literature, we have not found references about recursive agent architectures. Nevertheless, in the agent definition, nothing prevents having agents whose internal structure is composed of self-similar entities.

### 3.13 Physical and Information Processing Part

In 1994 Christensen proposed a holon general architecture [6] (Figure 1). Almost everyone in HS adopts this general architecture. An explicit separation between information processing and physical processing can be seen in this general architecture. In the MAS field, there is no such explicit separation, since an agent in its internal structure has software components that can do any kind of processing. Bussmann [3] proposes the use of multiagent systems as the allowing technology for the information processing in HS. For the physical processing part, Fletcher and Deen [20] propose functional blocks to manage real-time control for low-level process/machine interaction.

Table 1 summarizes the comparison made in previous subsections.

## 4 Conclusions

In the first section, we have presented the basic concepts of holonic systems (HS) and multiagent systems (MAS). In the third section, we have made an extensive discussion on the similarities and differences between HS and MAS. In this discussion, we have indicated that in spite of having arisen in different ways, the holonic paradigm and the agent paradigm share similar concepts. In summary, (see Table 1) we can say that a holon is a special case of an agent. There are no conventional methods for developing holonic systems. Conceptually, a holon is a special type of agent, and the technology which is used by most people who are dedicated to HS research is the multiagent system. Because of its multiple characteristics, an agent seems suitable for implementing holons. As has been proposed by many researchers, such as [4] and [3] among others, central information processing and communication with other holons and humans, and, optionally, physical control should be adopted by agents.

Table 1: Holons Vs. Agents

| **Property** | **Holon** | **Agent** |
|---|---|---|
| *Autonomy* | Yes. | Yes. |
| *Reactivity* | Yes. | Yes. |
| *Pro-activity* | Yes. | Yes. |
| *Social Ability* | Yes. Human Interface is specific of each holon. | Yes. Human Interface is generally implemented by one or several specialized agents. |
| *Cooperation* | Yes. Holons never deliberately reject cooperation with another holon. | Yes. It may compete and cooperate. |
| *Organization, Openness.* | Yes. Holarchies. | Yes. Hierarchies, horizontal organizations, heterarchies, ect. Holarchies can be implemented using several MAS architecture approaches for federations such as facilitators, brokers, or mediators |
| *Rationality* | Yes. | Yes. |
| *Learning* | Yes. | Yes. |
| *Benevolence* | Yes. | Yes. |
| *Mobility* | Holons rarely will need mobility for the execution of their tasks. | Yes. |
| *Recursiveness* | Yes. | There is no recursive agent architecture as such, but some techniques could be used to define federations that could simulate different recursive levels. |
| *Information Processing and Physical Processing* | Yes. The separation is explicit, although the Physical Processing part is optional | There is no explicit separation. |
| *Mental Attitudes* | Yes. They do not need to reason on its own mental attitudes or those of other control units. | Yes. |

Brennan and Norrie [4] say that, if the real-time requirements are important, the functional block model is the most appropriate choice; whereas, if the problem is classified as soft-real time or not-real time, agent's conventional technology may be used. We believe, based in the previous analysis, that MAS technology can be appropriate for all cases, since currently there are also real-time agent architectures available. An example is ARTIS [21], which has proven to be effective in solving hard-real time problems.

The analysis made in this work have shown that holons and agents share many properties. Among all the analyzed characteristics, recursiveness is the only one which is not present as such in the agent technology, but, in the agent specialized literature, there are some techniques that could be used to simulate it. However, we are convinced that several difficult challenges for automated systems may be tackled by giving full meaning to the agent concept: adopting a recursive definition of agents and allowing the dynamic creation of agents (organization of agents) by agents themselves. One of the most difficult challenges for automated systems is scalability and adaptation. The strength of holonic organization, or holarchy, is that it enables the construction of very complex systems from more simple self similar entities. To this end we are now working on a recursive agent definition and a formalization of the behaviour of a MAS in terms of the behaviour of its constituent agents. Our current work is addressed by the concepts developed by Koestler about recursiveness in holonic organizations and by the broadly well-known agent definitions which can be found in the specialized agent literature.

# References


[1] HMS, P.R.: HMS Requirements. HMS Server, http://hms.ifw.uni-hannover.de/ (1994)

[2] Shen, W., Norrie, D.: Agent-based systems for intelligent manufacturing: A state-of-the-art survey. Knowledge and Information Systems, an Internatinal Journal **1** (1999) 129–156

[3] Bussmann, S.: An agent-oriented architecture for holonic manufacturing control. Proc. of 1st Int. Workshop on Intelligent Manufacturing Systems, EPFL (1998) 1–12

[4] Brennan, R.W., Norrie, D.H.: Agents, holons and functions blocks: Distributed intelligent control in manufacturing. Journal of Applied Systems Studies Special Issue on Industrial Applications of Multi-Agent and Holonic Systems **2** (2001) 1–19

[5] Koestler, A.: The Ghost in the Machine. Arkana Books (1971)

[6] Christensen, J.: Holonic manufacturing systems: Initial architecture and standards directions. in First European Conference on Holonic Manufacturing Systems, European HMS Consortium, Hanover, Germany (1994)

[7] Deen, S.: A cooperation framework for holonic interactions in manufacturing. In Proceedings of the Second International Working Conference on Cooperating Knowledge Based Systems (CKBS'94 (1994)

[8] Van Leeuwen, E., Norrie, D.: Intelligent manufacturing: holons and holarchies. Manufacturing Engineer **2** (1997) 86–88

[9] Wooldridge, M., Jennings, N.R.: Intelligent agents - theories, architectures, and languages. Lecture Notes in Artificia Intelligence, Springer-Verlag. ISBN 3-540-58855-8 **890** (1995)

[10] Nwana, H.S.: Software agents: An overview. Intelligent Systems Research. AA&T, BT Laboratories (1996)

[11] Franklin, S., Graesser, A.: It is an agent, or just a program?: A taxonomy for autonomous agents. Proceedings of the Third International Workshop on Agent Theories, Architectures, and Languages. Springer-Verlag (1996)

[12] Maturana, F., Norrie, D.: Distributed decision-making using the contract net within a mediator architecture. Decision Support Systems 20 (1997) 53–64

[13] Fletcher, M., Garcia-Herreros, E., Chritensen, J., Deen, S., Mittmann, R.: An open architecture for holonic cooperation and autonomy. Proceeding of HoloMAS'2000 (2000)

[14] Brussel, V., Wyns, J., Valckenaers, P., Bongaerts, L., Peeters, P.: Reference architecture for holonic manufacturing systems: Prosa. Computers In Industry **37** (1998) 255–274

[15] O'Hare, G., Jennings, N.: Foundation of distributed artificial intelligence. John Wiley & Sons (1996)

[16] Huhns, M., Singh, M.: Readings in agents. Morgan Kaufman Publ. (1998)

[17] Russell, S., Norvig, P.: Artificial Intelligence: A Modern Approach. Prentice Hall, Englewood Cliffs, New Jersey (1995)

[18] Galliers, J.R.: A Theoretical Framework for Computer Models of Cooperative Dialogue, Acknowledging Multi-Agent Conflict. PhD thesis, Open University, UK (1988)

[19] Shen, W., Maturana, F., Norrie, D.: Learning in agent-based manufacturing systems. In Proceedings of AI & Manufacturing Research Planning Workshop (1998)

[20] Fletcher, M., Deen, M.S.: Fault-tolerant holonic manufacturing systems. Concurrency and Computation: Practice and Experience **13** (2001) 43–70

[21] García Fornes, A., Terrasa, A., Botti, V.: Engineering a tool for building hard predictable real-time artificial intelligent systems. In Proceedings of the 21th IFAC/IFIP Workshop on Real-Time Programming (1996) 177–183

# Logic Programming Agents Playing Games

Marina De Vos
Department of Computer Science, University of Bath
Bath, UK

Dirk Vermeir
Department of Computer Science, Vrije Universiteit Brussel (VUB)
Brussels, Belgium

**Abstract**

We present systems of logic programming agents (LPAS) to model the interactions between decision-makers while evolving to a conclusion. Such a system consists of a number of agents connected by means of unidirectional communication channels. Agents communicate with each other by passing answer sets obtained by updating the information received from connected agents with their own private information. As an application, we show how extensive games with perfect information can be conveniently represented as logic programming agent systems, where each agent embodies the reasoning of a game player, such that the equilibria of the game correspond with the semantics agreed upon by the agents in the LPAS.

## 1 Introduction

In this paper we present a formalism for systems of logic programming agents. Such systems are useful for modeling decision-problems, not just the solutions of the problem at hand but also the evolution of the beliefs of and the interactions between the agents.

A system of logic programming agents consists of a set of agents connected by means of unidirectional communication channels. Each agent contains an ordered choice logic program [3] representing her personal information and reasoning skills. Agents use information received from their incoming channels as input for their reasoning, where received information may be overridden by other concerns represented in their program. The resulting model is communicated to the agents listening on the outgoing channels. The semantics of the whole system corresponds to a stable situation where no agent needs to change its output.

To model a single agent's reasoning, we use ordered choice logic programs[3], an extension of logic programming which provides facilities for the direct representation of preference between rules and dynamic choice between alternatives.

Game theory [5] makes contributions to many different fields. In particular, there is a natural connection with multi-agent systems. In this paper we illustrate the use of logic programming agent systems as convenient executable representations of games, where each player corresponds with exactly one agent. We concentrate on so-called extensive games with perfect information: a sequential communication structure of players taking decisions, based on full knowledge of the past. We demonstrate that such games have a constructive and intuitive translation to logic programming agent systems where the agents/players are connected in a cyclic communication structure. The game's equilibria (Nash or subgame perfect, depending on the transformation used to construct the corresponding system) can then be retrieved as the system's answer set semantics. Moreover, the fixpoint computation of the answer sets closely mirrors the actual reasoning of the players in reaching a conclusion corresponding to an equilibrium.

## 2 Choice Logic Programming

Choice logic programs [1] represent decisions by interpreting the head of a rule as an exclusive choice between alternatives.

Formally, a *Choice Logic Program* [1], CLP for short, is a finite set of rules of the form $A \leftarrow B$ where $A$ and $B$ are finite sets of ground atoms. Intuitively, atoms in $A$ are assumed to be xor'ed together while $B$ is read as a conjunction (note that $A$ may be empty, i.e. constraints are allowed). The set $A$ is called the head of the rule $r$, denoted $H_r$, while $B$ is its body, denoted $B_r$. In examples, we often use "$\oplus$" to denote exclusive or, while "," is used to denote conjunction.

The *Herbrand base* of a CLP $P$, denoted $\mathcal{B}_P$, is the set of all atoms that appear $P$. An *interpretation* is a consistent[1] subset of $\mathcal{B}_P \cup \neg\mathcal{B}_P$. For an interpretation $I$, we use $I^+$ to denote its positive part, i.e. $I^+ = I \cap \mathcal{B}_P$. Similarly, we use $I^-$ to denote the negative part of $I$, i.e. $I^- = \neg(I \cap \neg\mathcal{B}_P)$. An atom $a$ is *true* (resp. *false*) w.r.t. to an interpretation $I$ for a CLP $P$ if $a \in I^+$ (resp. $a \in I^-$). An interpretation is *total* iff $I^+ \cup I^- = \mathcal{B}_P$. The positive complement of an interpretation $I$, denoted $\overline{I}$, equals $\mathcal{B}_P \setminus I^+$.

A rule $r$ in a CLP is said to be *applicable* w.r.t. an interpretation $I$ if $B_r \subseteq I$. Since we are modeling choice, we have that $r$ is *applied* when $r$ is applicable and $|H_r \cap I| = 1$[2]. A rule is *satisfied* if it is applied or not applicable. A *model* is defined in the usual way as a total interpretation that satisfies every rule. A model $M$ is said to be *minimal* if there does not exist a model $N$ such that $N^+ \subset M^+$.

The *Gelfond-Lifschitz transformation* for a CLP $P$ w.r.t. an interpretation $I$ is the positive logic program $P^I$ obtained from $P$ by first removing all false atoms from the head of each choice rule (e.g. a rule with more than one head atom). Afterwards, all remaining choice rules $r$ are replaced with the constraints $\leftarrow H_r, B_r$. These constraints force $P^I$ to reject interpretations that contain two true atoms that are both in the head of an applicable choice rule. A total interpretation $M$ is a *stable model* for $P$ iff $M$ is a minimal model for $P^M$. For choice logic programs the stable model and the minimal model semantics coincide[1].

The following example is a variation on the well-known prisoner's dilemma [5].

**Example 1 (Eternal Enemies)** *One day two eternal enemies, the lions and the hyaena's, meet on the African plains. Today's cause of argument is a juicy piece of meat. Both the lions and the hyaena's are keen on devouring it. To obtain their share there are two*

[1] For a set of literals $X$, we use $\neg X$ to denote $\{\neg a \mid a \in X\}$, where $\neg\neg a = a$ for any atom $a$. $X$ is consistent iff $X \cap \neg X = \emptyset$.

[2] For a a set $X$, we use $|X|$ do denote its cardinality.

*possibilities: they can either divide the piece among the members of both groups or they can fight for it with the risk of getting injured. Knowing the other group's temper it is always best to attack: either both parties are willing to fight or the peace-loving group will be chased away. However, both parties know that they get the most meat without any risk if they are both willing to share. Despite this, no pride is willing to take the risk of losing out on this free lunch. The following simple choice logic program models this eternal feud.*

$$\begin{array}{lllll} share_{lions} & \oplus & fight_{lions} & \leftarrow & \\ share_{hyaenas} & \oplus & fight_{hyaenas} & \leftarrow & \\ & & fight_{lions} & \leftarrow & share_{hyaenas} \\ & & fight_{lions} & \leftarrow & fight_{hyaenas} \\ & & fight_{hyaenas} & \leftarrow & share_{lions} \\ & & fight_{hyaenas} & \leftarrow & fight_{lions} \end{array}$$

*The program from Example 1 has one stable model* $\{fight_{lions}, fight_{hyaenas}\}$, *which explains why the two species remain enemies: neither wants to give sharing a try as they fear that the other will take advantage by attacking.*

# 3 Ordered Choice Logic Programming

An ordered choice logic program (OCLP) [2] is a collection of choice logic programs, called components, each representing a portion of information. The relevance or preciseness of each component with respect to the other components is expressed by a strict pointed partial order[3].

**Definition 1** *An* ***Ordered Choice Logic Program****, or OCLP, is a pair* $P = \langle \mathcal{C}, \prec \rangle$ *where* $\mathcal{C}$ *is a finite set of finite choice logic programs[4], called* ***components****, and "*$\prec$*" is a strict pointed partial order on* $\mathcal{C}$. *We use* $P^{\cup}$ *to denote the CLP obtained from* $P$ *by joining all components, i.e.* $P^{\cup} = \cup_{c \in \mathcal{C}} c$. *For a rule* $r \in P^{\cup}$, $c(r)$ *denotes the component from which the rule was taken (i.e. we assume that rules are labeled by the component)[5]. The Herbrand base of an OCLP* $P$ *is defined by* $\mathcal{B}_P = \mathcal{B}_{P^{\cup}}$. *An* ***interpretation*** *of* $P$ *is an interpretation of* $P^{\cup}$. *A rule* $r$ *in an OCLP* $P$ *is applicable, resp. applied, w.r.t. an interpretation* $I$, *if it is applicable, resp. applied in* $P^{\cup}$, *w.r.t.* $I$.

For two components $C_1, C_2 \in \mathcal{C}$, $C_1 \prec C_2$ implies that $C_2$ contains more general, or less preferred, information than $C_1$. Throughout the examples, we will often represent an OCLP $P$ by means of a directed acyclic graph in which the nodes represent the components and the arcs the $\prec$-relation.

[3] A relation $<$ on a set $A$ is a strict partial order iff $<$ is anti-reflexive, anti-symmetric and transitive. $<$ is pointed if there is an element $a \in A$ such that $a < b$ for all $b \in A \setminus \{a\}$.

[4] We assume that all rules are grounded; i.e. any rule containing variables has been replaced with all its ground instances.

[5] In fact, the same rule could appear in two components and thus $P^{\cup}$ should be a set of labeled rules. We prefer to work with the present simpler notation and note that all results remain valid in the general case.

**Example 2** *This year, the choice for the holidays has been reduced to a city trip to London or a fortnight stay in either Spain or Mexico. A city trip to London is rather short and Mexico is expensive. With a larger budget however, we could have both a holiday in Mexico and a trip to London. Given these considerations, there are two possible outcomes:*

- *we have a small budget and we should opt for Spain, or*
- *with a larger budget, we can combine Mexico and London.*

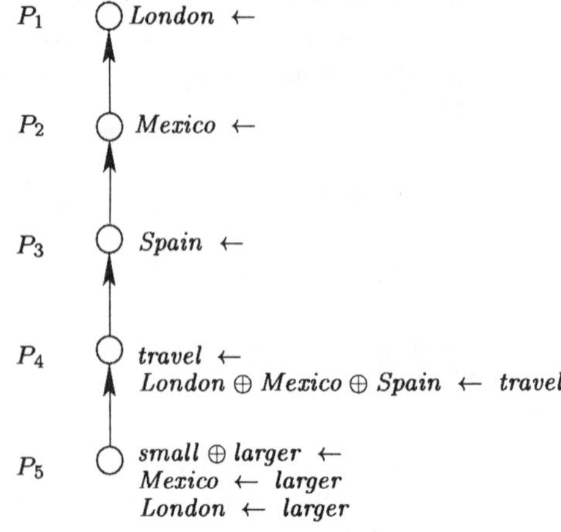


***Figure 1*** *The travel OCLP of Example 2*

*This decision problem can be conveniently represented as an OCLP, as displayed by Figure 1. The rules in the components $P_1 \ldots P_3$, express the preferences in case of a small budget. The rules in $P_4$ explain that we want to travel and, because of this, we need to make a decision concerning our destination. In component $P_5$, the first rule states that there is also the possibility of a larger budget. In this case, the two other rules in this component tell us that we can have both London and Mexico.*

*The sets: $I = \{Mexico, small, \neg Spain\}$, $J = \{travel, Mexico, small, \neg London, \neg Spain, \neg larger\}$, $K = \{travel, Spain, small, \neg larger, \neg London, \neg Mexico\}$, and $L = \{travel, London, Spain, Mexico, larger, \neg small\}$ are all interpretations for this OCLP. The interpretation $I$ makes the rule $small \oplus larger \leftarrow$ applied while the rule $London \leftarrow$ is applicable but not applied. While $J$, $K$ and $L$ are total, $I$ is not.*

When it is clear from the context that only total interpretations are considered, we will omit the negative part. If necessary it can be retrieved by means of the positive complement.

A decision involves a choice between several alternatives. In a CLP, decisions are generated by so-called *choice rules*, i.e. rules with multiple head atoms. Thus, for an interpretation $I$ of a CLP, $a$ and $b$ are alternatives if they appear together in the head of an applicable rule. For an ordered program, we will use a similar notion which takes the preference order into account. Intuitively, for a component $C$, $a$ and $b$ are alternatives w.r.t. an interpretation $I$ if there is an applicable choice rule containing $a$ and $b$ in the head, in a component that is at least as preferred as $C$.

**Definition 2** *Let $P = \langle \mathcal{C}, \prec \rangle$ be an OCLP, let $I$ be an interpretation and let $C \in \mathcal{C}$. The set of* ***alternatives*** *in $C$ for an atom $a \in \mathcal{B}_P$ w.r.t. $I$, denoted $\Omega^I_C(a)$, is defined as*[6]*: $\Omega^I_C(a) = \{b \mid \exists r \in P^{\cup} \cdot c(r) \preccurlyeq C \ \wedge\ B_r \subseteq I \ \wedge\ a, b \in H_r \text{ with } a \neq b\}$ .*

[6] $\preccurlyeq$ is the reflexive closure of $\prec$.

**Example 3** *Reconsider the interpretations I and J from Example 2. The alternatives for Mexico in $P_2$ w.r.t. J are $\Omega^J_{P_2}(Mexico) = \{Spain, London\}$. With respect to I we obtain $\Omega^I_{P_2}(Mexico) = \emptyset$, since the choice rule in $P_3$ is not applicable. When we take $P_5$ instead of $P_2$, we obtain w.r.t. J: $\Omega^J_{P_5}(Mexico) = \emptyset$.*

Atoms that are each others' alternative w.r.t. a certain interpretation $I$ will continue to be so in any extension $J \supseteq I$. In this sense, $\Omega_P$ is a monotonic operator.

Although rules do not contain negations, they can still conflict. E.g. one rule could force a choice between $a$ and $b$ while other rules could force $a$ and $b$ separately. More generally, a conflict exists for a rule $r$, which is applicable w.r.t. an interpretation $I$, if for all $a \in H_r$, there exists another rule $r_a$ such that $H_{r_a} \subseteq \Omega^I_{c(r)}(a)$.

As in [4], we use the preference relation among the components to ignore rules that are *defeated* by more preferred rules forcing different alternatives.

**Definition 3** *Let I be an interpretation for an OCLP P. A rule $r \in P^{\cup}$ is* ***defeated*** *w.r.t. I iff*

$$\forall a \in H_r \cdot \exists r' \in P^{\cup} \cdot c(r) \not\prec c(r') \wedge r' \text{ is applied w.r.t. } I \wedge H_{r'} \subseteq \Omega^I_{c(r)}(a) \ .$$

*The rule $r'$ is called a* ***defeater*** *w.r.t. I. I is a* ***model*** *of P iff every rule in $P^{\cup}$ is either not applicable, applied or defeated w.r.t. I. A model M is* ***minimal*** *iff its positive part is minimal according to set inclusion, i.e. no model N of P exists such that $N^+ \subset M^+$.*

The above definition defines a approach where a rule can be defeated by applied rules that are not less preferred as the rule at hand. This approach can be seen as credulous, as a random choice is made between two equally or unrelated alternatives. A more skeptical approach would demand that the rules are related and the defeater(s) is (are) strictly more preferred.

**Example 4** *Reconsider the interpretations J and L defined in Example 2. The rule $London \leftarrow$ is defeated w.r.t. J by the rule $Mexico \leftarrow$. The combination of the rules $Mexico \leftarrow larger$ and $London \leftarrow larger$ defeats the rule $London \oplus Mexico \oplus Spain \leftarrow$ is w.r.t. L. Only K and L are models. Model L is not minimal due to the smaller model $Z = \{travel, larger, Mexico, London, travel, \neg Spain, \neg small\}$. The minimal models K and Z correspond to the intuitive outcomes of the problem.*

For ordered programs, the minimal semantics sometimes yields unintuitive results, as demonstrated in the following example.

**Example 5** *Consider the program $P = \langle\{c_1, c_2, c_3\}, \prec\rangle$ where $c_1 = \{a \leftarrow\}$, $c_2 = \{b \leftarrow\}$, $c_3 = \{a \oplus b \leftarrow c\}$ and $c_3 \prec c_2 \prec c_1$. The minimal models are {a,b}, where no choice between a and b is forced, and {c,b}. The latter is not intuitive due to the gratuitous assumption of c.*

Unwarranted assumptions as in Example 5 can be avoided by adopting an answer set semantics, where we use a variant of the Gelfond-Lifschitz transformation to map an OCLP to an unordered CLP.

**Definition 4** *Let $M$ be a total interpretation for an OCLP $P$. The* **reduct** *for $P$ w.r.t. $M$, denoted $P^M$, is the choice logic program obtained from $P^{\cup}$ by removing all defeated rules. $M$ is called an* **answer set** *for $P$ iff $M$ is a stable model for $P^M$.*

**Example 6** *The program $P$ from Example 5 does not admit $N = \{a, b\}$ as an answer set, since $P^N = \{b \leftarrow, \ a \oplus b \leftarrow c\}$ which has only $\{b\} \neq N$ as a stable model. The minimal models $K$ and $Z$ of Example 4 are both answer sets.*

# 4 Logic Programming Agents

In this section we consider systems of communicating agents where each agent is represented by an OCLP that contains its knowledge about itself and other agents.

Agents communicate via unidirectional communication channels through which the conclusions derived by the agent at the source of the channel are passed on to the agents at the other end.

**Definition 5** *A* ***logic programming agent system****, or LPAS, is a pair $F = \langle \mathbf{A}, \mathbf{C} \rangle$ where $\mathbf{A}$ is a set of agents $a$ and $C \subset \mathbf{A} \times \mathbf{A}$ is an anti-reflexive relation representing the communication channels between agents. Moreover, each agent $a \in \mathbf{A}$ is associated with an ordered choice logic program $F_a = \langle C_a, \prec_a \rangle$.*

We will use a more convenient graph-like notation in our examples.

**Example 7** *Two witnesses discover a body lying in the park. The first witness tells the local police that she saw hair near the victim and that she did not see any blood. The second witness testifies that she saw blood and that the victim had strange bite marks. The sheriff states that this situation is a clear case of murder and passes it to the FBI. Because of the strange appearance of bite-marks and hair, the FBI passes the case to the special X-cell. In addition, the FBI states that, if the X-cell reports that a werewolf is involved, the case should be classified. Given the evidence, the X-file team has no choice but to decide that the killing was indeed done by a werewolf. This situation is represented by the LPAS depicted in Figure 2.*

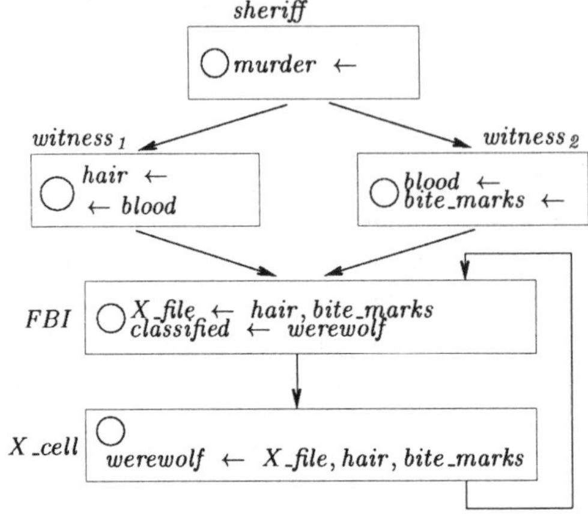


***Figure 2*** *The werewolf-killing of Example 7*

The Herbrand base of a LPAS is the union of all the Herbrand bases of the ordered choice logic programs used by the agents. An interpretation assigns a set of literals to each agent in the system. These literals may be concluded by the agent itself, based on input received through an input channel, or they may simply be accepted from other agents via an input channel.

**Definition 6** *Let $F = \langle \mathbf{A}, \mathbf{C} \rangle$ be an LPAS. The* ***Herbrand base*** *of $F$, denoted $\mathcal{B}_F$, equals $\mathcal{B}_F = \bigcup_{A \in \mathbf{A}} \mathcal{B}_A$. An* ***interpretation*** *of $F$ is a function $I : \mathbf{A} \rightarrow \mathbf{2}^{(\mathcal{B}_\mathbf{F} \cup \neg \mathcal{B}_\mathbf{F})}$ that associates a consistent set of literals (beliefs) to each agent.*
*Given an interpretation $I$, the* ***inputs*** *and* ***outputs*** *of each agent are defined by $In_I(a) = cons(\bigcup_{(b,a) \in C} I(b))$ and $Out_I(a) = I(a)$, respectively, where $cons(X) = X^+ \setminus (X^+ \cap X^-)$, i.e. the maximal positive consistent part of $X$.*

Thus, an agent sends its full set of beliefs over all outgoing communication channels. On the other hand, an agent receives as input, the beliefs of all agents connected to its incoming channels. If two agents send conflicting information to a receiving agent, the conflicts are removed.

**Example 8** *Consider the Werewolf LPAS F of Example 7. We define the interpertation I of F as:*

$$
\begin{array}{lcl}
I(sheriff) & = & \{murder\} \\
I(witness_1) & = & \{murder, hair, \neg blood\} \\
I(witness_2) & = & \{murder, blood, bite\_marks\} \\
I(FBI) & = & \{murder, hair, bite\_marks, werewolf.X\_file, classified\} \\
I(X\_cell) & = & \{murder, hair, bite\_marks, werewolf, X\_file, classified\}
\end{array}
$$

*The input of agent FBI w.r.t. I equals $In_I(FBI) = \{murder, hair, bite\_marks\}$ . The output produced by the $X\_cell$-agent w.r.t. $I_2$ is $Out_I(X\_cell) = \{murder, hair, bite\_marks, werewolf.X\_file, classified\}$ .*

An agent reasons on the basis of positive information that is received from other agents (its input) and its own program that may be used to draw further conclusions, possibly overriding incoming information. Hence, agents attach a higher preference to their own rules rather than to suggestions coming from outside.

This can be conveniently modeled by extending an agent's ordered program with an extra "top" component containing the information gathered from its colleagues. This way, the OCLP semantics will automatically allow for defeat of incoming information that does not fit an agent's own program.

**Definition 7** *Let $F = \langle \mathbf{A}, \mathbf{C} \rangle$ be a LPAS. The* ***updated version*** *of an agent $a \in \mathbf{A}$, with program $F_a = \langle \mathcal{C}_a, \prec_a \rangle$, w.r.t. a set of atoms $U \subseteq \mathcal{B}_F$, denoted $a^U$, is defined by $a^U = \langle \mathcal{C}_a \cup \{c_U\}, \prec_a \cup \{c < c_U \mid c \in \mathcal{C}_a\} \rangle$ with $c_U = \{l \leftarrow \mid l \in U\}$.*

For an interpretation to be a model, it suffices that each agent produces a local model (output) that is consistent with its input.

**Definition 8** *Let $F = \langle \mathbf{A}, \mathbf{C} \rangle$ be a LPAS. An interpretation $I$ of $F$ is a* ***model*** *iff $\forall a \in \mathbf{A} \cdot Out_I(a)$ is an answer set of $a^{In_I(a)}$.*

**Example 9** *Reconsider the Werewolf LPAS of Example 7 and its interpretation I from Example 8. It is easy to see that I is a model. Even more, it is the only model.*

For systems without cycles the above model semantics will generate rational solutions for the represented decision-problems. The next example demonstrates that systems that do have cycles may have models that contain too much information, because assumptions made by one agent may become justified by another agent.

**Example 10** *Two children have been listening to a scary story about vampires and zombies. Suddenly, they think something moved in the room and they start fantasizing about the story they just heard. The first child says that, in order to have a real zombie or vampire, the creature should be dead and be walking around. The second child agrees that vampires and zombies are both dead but still able to walk around.*

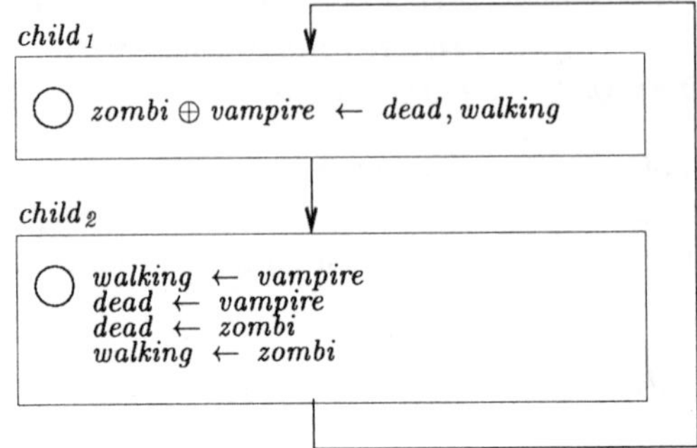


***Figure 3*** *The imagination LPAS of Example 10*

*The situation is represented by the LPAS in Figure 3. This system has three models with* $M_1(child_1) = M_1(child_2) = \{\neg vampire, \neg zombi, \neg walking, \neg dead\}$, *and* $M_2(child_1) = M_2(child_2) = \{zombi, walking, dead, \neg vampire\}$ ; *and* $M_3(child_1) = M_3(child_2) = \{vampire, walking, dead, \neg zombi\}$ . *The last two models are not realistic, since the children are just giving a description.*

To avoid such self-sustaining propagation of assumptions, we will demand that a model be the result of a fixpoint procedure which mimics the evolution of the belief set of the agents over time.

**Definition 9** *Let* $F = \langle \mathbf{A}, \mathbf{C} \rangle$ *be a LPAS. A sequence of interpretations* $I_0 \ldots I_n$ *is an* ***evolution*** *of* $F$ *iff for any* $i \geq 0$, $a \in \mathbf{A}$, $I_{i+1}(a)$ *is a model of* $a^{In_{I_i}(a)}$. *An* ***evolutionary fixpoint*** *of an interpretation* $I_0$ *is any interpretation* $I$ *that can be repeated forever in an evolution* $I_0 \ldots I_n = I$, $I_{n+1} = I$. *An* ***answer set*** *of* $F$ *is any c-evolutionary fixpoint of* $I_\emptyset$.

Thus, in an evolution, the agents evolve as more information becomes available: at each phase of the evolution, an agent updates her program to reflect input from the last phase and computes a new set of beliefs. An evolution thus corresponds to the way decision-makers try to get a feeling about the other participants. The process of reaching a fixpoint boils down to trying to get an answer to the question "if I do this, how would the other agents react", while trying to establish a stable compromise. Note that the notion of evolution is nondeterministic since an agent may have several local models. For a fixpoint, it suffices that each agent can maintain the same set of beliefs as in the previous stage.

**Example 11** *Consider the Werewolf LPAS of Example 7. The interpretation $I$ described in Example 8 is an answer set of the LPAS. The vampire-zombie LPAS of Example 10 has one answer set $I$, where*

$$I(child_1) = I(child_2) = \{\neg zombie, \neg vampire, \neg walking, \neg dead\} \ .$$

**Theorem 1** *Let $F = \langle \mathbf{A}, \mathbf{C} \rangle$ be a LPAS. An interpretation $I$ is a model for $F$ iff it is an evolutionary fixpoint of $F$.*

**Corollary 1** *Let $F = \langle \mathbf{A}, \mathbf{C} \rangle$ be a LPAS. Every answer set of $F$ is a (model of $F$.*

The reverse of the above corollary does not hold in general. A counter example is given in Example 10. However, for acyclic LPAS a one-to-one mapping does exist.

**Theorem 2** *Let $F = \langle \mathbf{A}, \mathbf{C} \rangle$ be a LPAS without cycles. An interpretation $M$ is a stable model (resp. answer set) iff $I$ is a model (resp. c-model) of $F$.*

# 5 LPAS and Game Theory

In this section we demonstrate that extensive games with perfect information have a natural formalization as logic programming agent systems. The equilibria of such games can be obtained as the answers sets of the system, where each agent represents a player, and the evolution mimics the mechanism players can use in order to come to a decision.

## 5.1 Extensive Games with Perfect Information

An extensive game is a detailed description of a sequential structure representing the decision problems encountered by agents (called *players*) in strategic decision making (agents are capable to reason about their actions in a rational manner). The agents in the game are perfectly informed of all events that previously occurred. Thus, they can decide upon their action(s) using information about the actions which have already taken place. This is done by means of passing *histories* of previous actions to the deciding agents. *Terminal histories* are obtained when all the agents/players have made their decision(s). Players have a preference for certain outcomes over others. Often, preferences are indirectly modeled using the concept of *payoff* where players are assumed to prefer outcomes where they receive a higher payoff.
Summarizing, an extensive game with perfect information, [5]), is 4-tuple, denoted $\langle N, H, P, (\succcurlyeq_i)_{i \in N} \rangle$, containing the players $N$ of the game, the histories $H$, a player function $P$ telling who's turn it is after a certain history and a preference relation $\preceq_i$ for each player $i$ over the set of terminal histories.
For examples, we use a more convenient representation: a tree. The small circle at the top represents the initial history. Each path starting at the top represents a history. The terminal histories are the paths ending in the leafs. The numbers next to nodes represent the players while the labels of the arcs represent an action. The numbers below the terminal histories are payoffs representing the players' preferences (The first number is the payoff of the first player, the second number is the payoff of the second player, ...).

**Example 12** *The game depicted in Figure 4 models an individuals' predicament in the following situation: two ladies have decided that they want fruit cake for dessert. There are two possibilities: they either bake a cake or they buy one. At the bakery shop one can choose between strawberry and cherry cake. For strawberry cake there is the possibility to have whipped cream on top. They agree that the first lady will decide on how to get the cake and, if necessary, whether a topping is wanted or not. The second lady will be picking the type of fruit cake.*

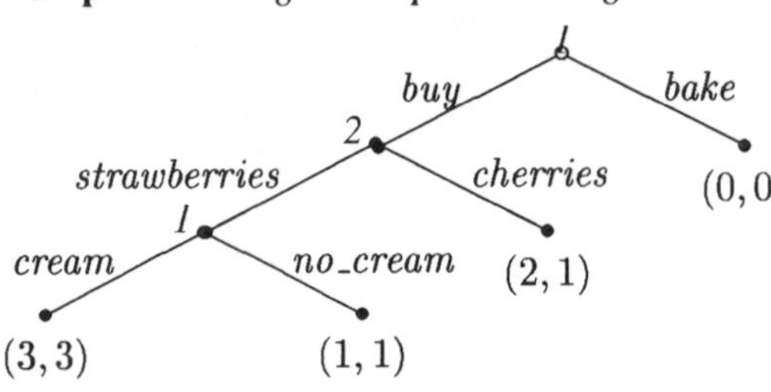


***Figure 4*** *The Cake-game of Example 12*

A *strategy* of a player in an extensive game is a plan that specifies the actions chosen by the player for every history after which it is her turn to move. A *strategy profile* contains a strategy for each player.
The first solution concept for an extensive game with perfect information ignores the sequential structure of the game; it treats the strategies as choices that are made once and for all before the actual game starts. A strategy profile is a *Nash equilibrium* if no player can unilaterally improve upon his choice. Put in another way, given the other players' strategies, the strategy stated for the player is the best this player can do[7].

**Example 13** *The game of Example 12 has two Nash equilibria:*

$$\{\{buy, cream\}, \{strawberries\}\} \textit{ and } \{\{buy, no\_cream\}, \{cherries\}\} \ .$$

Although the Nash equilibria for an extensive game with perfect information are intuitive, they have, in some situations, undesirable properties due to not exploiting the sequential structure of the game. These undesirable properties are illustrated by the next example.

**Example 14** *Being a parent can sometime be hard. Especially when your child asks for a pet. His two favorite animals are cats and spiders and you really hate spiders. However, your son prefers the cat since it is more affectionate. The game corresponding to this situation is depicted in Figure 5. This game has three Nash equilibria* $\{\{no\_pet\}, \{cat\}\}$, $\{\{no\_pet\}, \{spider\}\}$ *and* $\{\{pet\}, \{cat\}\}$.
*The strategy profile* $\{\{no\_pet, spider\}\}$ *is an unintuitive Nash equilibrium since it is sustained by the threat that the child would opt for the spider when a pet was allowed. However, the child would never go for a spider (payoff 1) since a cat is more playful (payoff 2).*

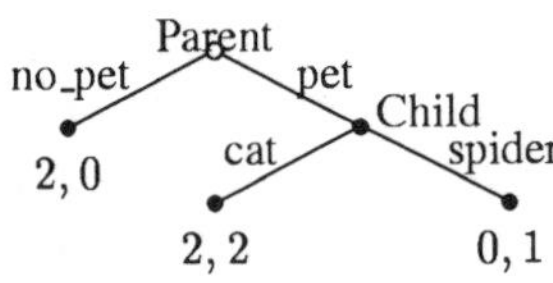


***Figure 5*** *The Spider Threat of Example 14*

[7] Note that the strategies of the other players are not actually known to $i$, as the choice of strategy has been made before the play starts. As stated before, no advantage is drawn from the sequential structure.

Because players are informed about the previous actions they only need to reason about actions taken in the future. This philosophy is represented by subgames. A *subgame* is created by pruning the tree in the upwards direction. So, intuitively, a subgame represent a stage in the decision making process where irrelevant and already known information is removed. Instead of just demanding that the strategy profile is optimal at the beginning of the game, we require that for a *subgame perfect equilibrium* the strategy is optimal after every history. In other words, for every subgame, the strategy profile, restricted to this subgame, needs to be a Nash equilibrium. This can be interpreted as if the players revise their strategy after every choice made by them or another player. Therefor, subgame perfect equilibria eliminate Nash equilibria in which the players' threats are not credible.

**Example 15** *Reconsider the game of Example 14:* $\{\{pet\},\{cat\}$ *and* $\{\{no\_pet\},\{cat\}$ *are the only subgame perfect equilibria. The unintuitive Nash equilibrium* $\{\{no\_pet\},$ $\{spider\}$ *is no longer accepted. The Cake-game of Example 12 admits only one subgame perfect equilibrium:* $\{\{buy, cream\},\{strawberries\}\}$.

## 5.2 Playing Games

We demonstrate that extensive games with perfect information have a natural formulation as multi-agent systems with a particularly simple information-flow structure between the agents. For our mapping, we assume that an action can only appear once[8]. This is not really a restriction, since one can simply use different names for these actions since they are not related. This will just have an effect on the syntax of the game and not on its semantics.

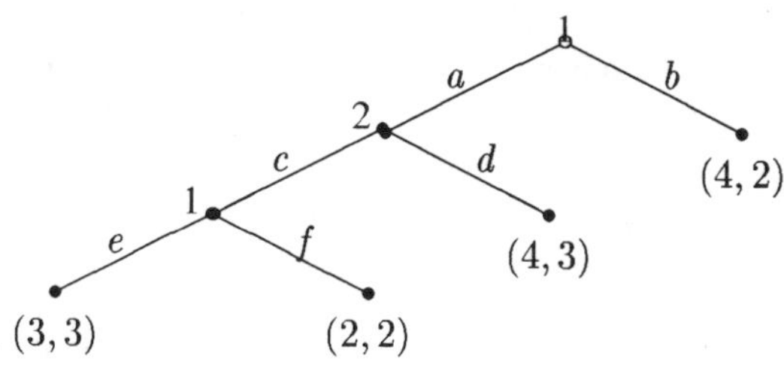


**Figure 6** *The game of Example 16*

**Example 16** *Consider the extensive game depicted in Figure 6. This game has six Nash equilibria:* $\{\{b,e\},\{c\}\}$, $\{\{b,f\},\{c\}\}$, $\{\{b,e\},\{d\}\}$, $\{\{b,f\},\{d\}\}$, $\{\{a,e\},\{d\}\}$, $\{\{a,f\},\{d\}\}$. *Three of these Nash equilibria are also subgame perfect equilibria:* $\{\{b,e\},\{c\}\}$, $\{\{b,e\},\{d\}\}$, $\{\{a,e\},\{d\}\}$.

The following transformations will be used to retrieve the Nash equilibria and subgame perfect equilibria from the game as the answer sets of the corresponding OCLP.

**Definition 10** *Let* $\langle N, H, P, (\succcurlyeq_i)_{i \in N}\rangle$ *be a finite extensive game with perfect information. The corresponding Nash LPAS* $S^n = \langle\{A^i \mid i \in N\}, C\rangle$ *with* $S^n_{A^i} = \langle\{C_{A^i}\}, \prec_i\rangle$ *constructed as follows:*

*1.* $C_{A^i} = \{C^i_u \mid \exists h \in Z \cdot u = U_i(h)\}$ ;

2. $\forall C^i_u, C^i_w \in \mathcal{C}_{A^i} \cdot C^i_u \prec_i C^i_w$ *iff* $u > w$ ;

3. $\forall h \in (H \setminus Z), P(h) = i \cdot (A(h) \leftarrow) \in C^i_w, \forall C^i_n, n \neq w \cdot C^i_w \prec_i C^i_n$ ;

4. $\forall h = h_1 a h_2 \in Z, P(h_1) = i \cdot a \leftarrow B \in C^i_u$ *with* $B = \{b \in [h]^9 \mid h = h_3 b h_4, P(h_3) \neq i\}$ *and* $u = U_{P(h_1)}(h)$ ,

5. $C(A^i) = \{A^{i+1}\}$ *for* $i \in N, i < \max N$ ,

6. $C(A^{\max N}) = \{A^1\}$ .

*The corresponding subgame LPAS* $S^s = \langle\{A^i \mid i \in N\}, C\rangle$ *where* $S^s_{A^i} = \langle\{\mathcal{C}_{A^i}\}, \prec_i\rangle$ *is defined in the same way as the Nash variant apart from step 4 which becomes:*

4'. $\forall h = h_1 a h_2 \in Z, P(h_1) = 1 \cdot (a \leftarrow B) \in C^i_u$ *with* $B = \{b \in [h2] \mid h = h_3 b h_4, P(h_3) \neq i\}$ *and* $u = U_{P(h_1)}(h)$ .

Intuitively an agents is created for each player in the game. The OCLP of such an agents contains as many component as the represented player has payoffs (step 1.). The order among the components follows the expected payoff, higher payoffs correspond to more specific components (step 2). The various actions a player can choose from a certain stage of the game are turned into a choice rule which is placed in the most specific component of the agent modelling the player making the decision (step 3). Since Nash equilibria do not take into account the sequential structure of the game, players have to decide upon their strategy before starting the game, leaving them, for each decision, to reason about both past and future. This is reflected in the rules (step 4): each non-choice rule is made out of a terminal history (path from top to bottom in the tree) where the head represents the action taken by the player/agent, when considering the past and future created by the other players according to this history. The component of the rule corresponds to the payoff the deciding player would receive in case the history was actually followed. When considering subgame perfect equilibria, we know that they do take previous actions into account, making unnecessary to reason about the past. This is reflected in step 4'. Steps 5 and 6 establish the communication between the agents in the system.

**Example 17** *For the game of Example 16, the corresponding LPAS's* $S^n$ *and* $S^s$ *are displayed in Figure 7.*

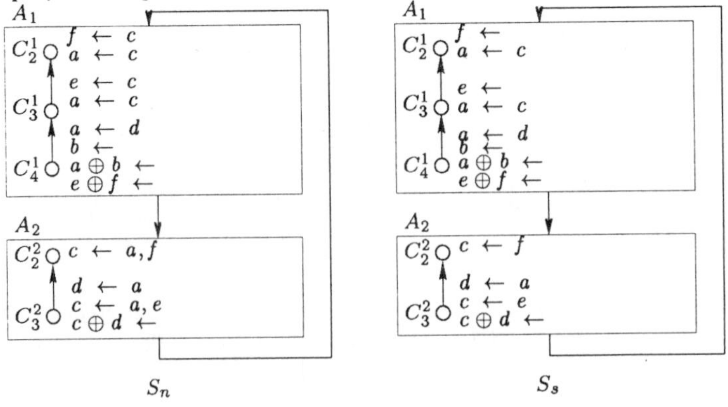


9 We use $[h]$ to denote the set of actions appearing in a sequence $h$.

***Figure 7*** *The LPAS's of Example 17*

*Notice that the answer sets for $S^n$ match exactly the Nash equilibria of the game, while the subgame perfect equilibria can be retrieved using the answer sets of $S^s$.*

**Theorem 3** *Let $\langle N, H, P, (\succcurlyeq_i)_{i \in N}\rangle$ be a finite extensive game with perfect information and let $S^n$ and $S^s$ be the corresponding LPAS's, according to Definition 10. Then, $s^*$ is a Nash equilibrium (resp. subgame perfect equilibrium) for $\langle N, H, P, (\succcurlyeq_i)_{i \in N}\rangle$ iff the interpretation $I$ with $I(a) = s^*$ for every $a \in \mathbf{A}$ is an answer set for $S^n$ (resp. $S^s$).*

For the proof of the above theorem, we demonstrate that every c-evolutionary fixpoint of $I_\emptyset$ can be constructed in $n$ iterations, with $n$ the number of players in the game. Of course, this only happens when players or agents know which actions will lead to an equilibrium state. In practice, it might take more iterations in order to find a fixpoint. Such a fixpoint computation can easily be seen as the players trying to obtain actions belonging to an equilibrium state. At first, she picks an action and sees how the other players respond to this. With this information she can update her actions. This process is carried on until a equilibrium is reached.

# 6 Relationship to Other Approaches

In this section we investigate the relationship of our approach with other formalisms. We restrict to the relationship with Game Theory, logic and agents. For a comparison with other preference based systems we refer to [2].

In the previous section we have demonstrated that OCLPs and multi-agent systems based on OCLPs provide a way to represent extensive games with perfect information in such a way that, depending on the transformation, either the Nash or subgame perfect equilibria can be retrieved as the stable models of the system. With the algorithm for the stable model computation of an OCLP, we immediately have an implementation for the equilibria of the game that the OCLP is representing. At the end of the previous section we already mentioned certain extensions to our proposed formalism in order to investigate other topics relevant to game theory, like for example information hiding and cheating. Probably the most important benefit for using logic programming for such research is its immediate return in the form of algorithms which allow for an efficient monitoring tool for the effects of the changes made.
Another aspect of logic programming that we already mentioned in the introduction, is its capability to represent more complex games. Take the Travel OCLP (Example 2) for example. If we just consider the first three components ($P_1$, $P_2$ and $P_3$), we see the representation of a very simple strategic or extensive game with a single player (the person who wants to travel). In this case the equilibrium would be $\{Spain\}$ which corresponds to the situation in which there are few dealers. From the moment that the dealers outnumber the officers two alternatives instead of just one are needed, which is impossible in game theory.

There are two main ways of relating logic and games: logic games and game logics. The former uses the games for the purpose of logic, while the latter uses logic for the purpose of game theory. Detailed information about their history can be found in [8]. Our research belongs the category of game logic and, as far as we know, we are the only ones that look at game theory in the context of logic programming. The only exception might be [6], but he simply puts game theoretic features on top of his language. We, on the other hand, do not go outside the realm of logic programming to retrieve equilibria.

Some research has already been done in the area of agents and games, although with different viewpoints. For example, [7] investigates methods to prevent agents exploiting game theoretic properties of negotiations. [6] incorporates the players of the game directly into its logic programming formalism for strategic games in order to obtain mixed strategy Nash equilibria. We, on the other hand, are interested in multi-agent systems that are able to represent, in an intuitive way, games such that agents correspond with players and models with the equilibria.

# References

[1] Marina De Vos and Dirk Vermeir. On the Role of Negation in Choice Logic Programs. In Michael Gelfond, Nicola Leone, and Gerald Pfeifer, editors, *Logic Programming and Non-Monotonic Reasoning Conference (LPNMR'99), Lecture Notes in Artificial Intelligence*, pages 236–246, Springer Verslag, 1999.

[2] Marina De Vos and Dirk Vermeir. A Logic for Modelling Decision Making with Dynamic Preferences. In *Proceedings of the Logic in Artificial Intelligence (Jelia2000) workshop*, Lecture Notes in Artificial Intelligence, pages 391–406, Malaga, Spain, 2000. Springer Verslag, 2000.

[3] Marina De Vos and Dirk Vermeir. Logic Programming Agents and Game Theory. In *Answer Set Programming: Towards Efficient and Scalable Knowledge Representation and Reasoning*, pages 27–33, American Association for Artificial Intelligence Pres, 2001.

[4] D. Gabbay, E. Laenens, and D. Vermeir. Credulous vs. Sceptical Semantics for Ordered Logic Programs. In J. Allen, R. Fikes, and E. Sandewall, editors, *Proceedings of the 2nd International Conference on Principles of Knowledge Representation and Reasoning*, pages 208–217, Morgan Kaufmann, 1991.

[5] Martin J. Osborne and Ariel Rubinstein. *A Course in Game Theory*. The MIT Press, third edition, 1996.

[6] David Poole. The independent choice logic for modelling multiple agents under uncertainty. *Artificial Intelligence*, 94(1–2):7–56, 1997.

[7] Jeffrey S. Rosenschein and Gilad Zlotkin. *Rules of Encounter. Designing Conventions for Automated Negotiation among Computers*. The MIT Press, 1994.

[8] Johan van Benthem. Logic and games. Online course notes of 1999, Stanford University.

# A Constraint Functional Logic Language for Solving Combinatorial Problems

Antonio J. Fernández*
Lenguajes y Ciencias de la Computación, Universidad de Málaga
Málaga, Spain

Teresa Hortalá-González† Fernando Sáenz-Pérez†
Sistemas Informáticos y Programación, Universidad Complutense de Madrid,
Madrid, Spain

**Abstract**

We present CFLP(FD), a constraint functional logic programming approach over finite domains (FD) for solving typical combinatorial problems. Our approach adds to former approaches as Constraint Logic Programming (CLP), and Functional Logic Programming (FLP) both expressiveness and further efficiency by combining combinatorial search with propagation. We integrate FD constraints into the functional logic language TOY. CFLP(FD) programs consist of TOY rules with FD constraints declared as functions. CFLP(FD) seamlessly combines the power of CLP over FD with the higher order characteristics of FLP.

## 1 Introduction

Declarative programming (DP) is intended to separate the problem formulation from the procedure to solve the problem itself. Well-known DP instances are logic programming (LP) on which the problem can be expressed in first-order predicate calculus and functional programming (FP) that allows to express problems in terms of higher order functions. Recently, constraint logic programming (CLP) emerged to increase both the expressiveness and efficiency of LP programs [9]. The basic idea in CLP consists of replacing the classical LP unification by constraint solving on a given computation domain. Then, different instances of the computation domain generate different CLP instances that are used in the solving of problems of distinct nature.

Among the domains for CLP, the Finite Domain (FD) [6] is one of the most and best studied since it is a suitable framework for solving discrete constraint satisfaction problems. The importance of the CLP languages based on FD is in their impact in the industry since a lot of problems in the real life involve variables ranging on discrete domains. Unfortunately, literature lacks proposals

*E-mail: afdez@lcc.uma.es. The work of this author was partially supported by the project TIC2001-2705-C03-02 funded by the Spanish Ministry of Science and Technology.

†E-mails: {teresa,fernan}@sip.ucm.es. The work of these authors has been supported by the Spanish project PR 48/01-9901 funded by UCM.

to integrate FD constraints in the functional setting. This seems to be caused by the relational nature of the FD constraints that do not fit well in FP.

Another instance of DP is functional logic programming (FLP) that emerges with the aim to integrate the declarative techniques used in both FP and LP and that gives rise to new features not existing in FP or LP [5]. This paper describes our work of integrating FD constraints as functions in the FLP language TOY [10, 11], which includes pure LP and lazy FP programs as particular cases. Our work is a contribution for further augmenting the expressive power of FLP by adding the possibility of solving FD constraint problems in the functional logic setting. As far as we know, there is no concrete realization of a pure F(L)P language embodying FD constraints. In this paper, we show the integration of FD constraints into a FLP language.

The structure of the paper is as follows: Section 2 shows our implementation of CFLP(FD). Section 3 highlights some advantages obtained from integrating constraints into a functional logic language. Section 4 introduces some program examples which show how to benefit from the integration of FLP and FD. Finally, section 5 summarizes some conclusions and points out future work.

## 2 TOY(FD) : a CFLP(FD) Implementation

This section describes part of TOY(FD), that is, our CFLP(FD) implementation that extends the TOY system to deal with FD constraints and that also shows how to increase the FLP paradigm by integrating FD constraints as functions. This implementation uses the efficient SICStus Prolog FD library [2]. (For a more detailed description of TOY and TOY(FD) see [10] and [4].)

### 2.1 Constraints as Functions

TOY(FD) provides support for six different categories of FD constraints: (1) relational constraints, (2) arithmetic constraints, (3) combinatorial constraints, (4) membership constraints, (5) enumeration constraints, and (6) statistics constraints. For reasons of space, we only briefly describe part of these categories.

Assume $L, L_1, L_2$ are lists (vectors) of integers and/or FD variables with length $n$; $X, Y, N$ are either FD variables or integer values; $V, V_1, V_2$ are integers and ***RelOp*** is a value that represents a relational operator. Suppose also that ***equiv***(***RelOp***) is a function that returns the classical arithmetic operator equivalent to the value ***RelOp*** (i.e., ***equiv***(*lt*) is '#<', ***equiv***(*eq*) is '#=', ***equiv***(*le*) is '#<=', ***equiv***(*ge*) is '#>=', ***equiv***(*gt*) is '#>' and ***equiv***(*neq*) is '#\=').

**Relational Constraints** include equality and disequality constraints in the form $e \diamond e'$ where $\diamond \in \{\#<, \#=, \#<=, \#>=, \#>, \#\backslash =\}$ and $e$ and $e'$ are either integers, or FD variables or functional expressions.

**Arithmetic Constraints** include all the classical arithmetic operators as well as the dedicated constraints 'sum/3' and 'scalar_products/4' where

- '*sum L RelOp V*' is true if $(\sum_{\mathbf{e} \in \mathbf{L}} \mathbf{e})$ ***equiv***(***RelOp***) $\mathbf{V}$ holds.

- '*scalar_products* $L_1$ $L_2$ *RelOp* $V$' is true if the scalar product of $L_1$ and $L_2$ is related with the value $V$ by the operator *RelOp*, i.e., if

$$L_1 \; *_s \; L_2 \; equiv(RelOp) \; V$$

  is satisfied with $*_s$ defined as the usual scalar product of integer vectors.

As expected, the expressions constructed from both the arithmetic and relational constraints may be non-linear.

**Combinatorial Constraints** include well-known global constraints that are useful to solve problems defined on discrete domains. For example,

- '*assignment*/2' is applied over two lists of domain variables with length $n$ where each variable takes a value in $\{1, \dots, n\}$ which is unique for that list. Then, '*assignment* $L_1$ $L_2$' is true if for all $i, j \in \{1, \dots, n\}$, and $X_i \in L_1$, $Y_j \in L_2$, then $X_i = j$ if and only if $Y_j = i$.

- '*all_different* $L$' and '*all_distinct* $L$' are true if each variable in $L$ is constrained to have a value that is unique in the list $L$ and there are no duplicate integers in the list $L$, i.e., this is equivalent to say that for all $X, Y \in L$, $X \neq Y$. The difference between both constraints is that *all_different*/1 uses a complete algorithm that maintains the domain consistency whereas *all_distinct*/1 uses an incomplete one. There are extended versions that allow one more argument which is a list of options, where each option may have one of the following values

  1. 'on value', 'on domains' or 'on range' to specify that the constraint has to be woken up, respectively, when a variable becomes ground, when the domain associated to a variable changes, or when a bound of the domain (in interval form) associated to a variable changes.
  2. 'complete true' or 'complete false' to specify if the propagation algorithm to apply is complete or incomplete.

- '*circuit* $L_1$' and '*circuit'* $L_1$ $L_2$' are true if the values in $L_1$ form a Hamiltonian circuit. This constraint can be thought of as constraining $n$ nodes in a graph to form a Hamiltonian circuit where the nodes are numbered from 1 to $n$ and the circuit starts in node 1, visits each node and returns to the origin. Also the $i$-th element of $L_1$ (resp. $L_2$) is the successor (resp. predecessor) of $i$ in the graph.

- '*element* $X$ $L$ $Y$' is true if the $X$-th element in the list $L$ is $Y$.

- '*count* $V$ $L$ *RelOp* $Y$' is true if the number of elements of $L$ that are equal to $V$ is $N$ and also $N$ *equiv*(*RelOp*) $Y$ (in the sense of FD).

**Membership Constraints** restrict variables to have values in a set of integers (i.e., an interval). The expression '*domain* $L$ $V_1$ $V_2$' is true if each element in the list $L$ belongs to the interval $[V_1, V_2]$.

**Enumeration Constraints** reactivate the search process when no more constraint propagation is possible. TOY(FD) provides the following constraints:

1. '*indomain X*' that assigns a value, from the minimum to the maximum in its domain, to $X$.

2. '*labeling Options L*' that is true if an assignment of the variables in $L$ can be found such that all of the constraints are satisfied. *Options* is a list of four elements that allow to specify the nature of the search.

# 3 Advantages of the Integration

## 3.1 Semantic Advantages

FLP languages express problems as higher order functions with logic variables, which allows one-way expression reduction. Also, in functional languages, relations cannot be expressed. However, constraint programming languages allow to express relations with a pure declarative reading (so that multi-way uses of the variables in the relation can be applied, i.e., different modes for the variables: input or output). The integration therefore allows expressing relations involving logic variables combined with functional applications.

## 3.2 Operational Advantages

Solving in logic programming languages (including functional logic) is based on different techniques including SLD resolution (logic programming), narrowing, and residuation (functional logic programming). These languages feature the concept of logic variable. A logic variable is assigned only once to at most a unique value during the search for a solution (a computation branch). Due to their nondeterminism, several solutions may exist (and, therefore, several computation branches). The multiset of solutions is characterized by all the sets of possible assignments for each variable in the goal during the computation[1]. The search space is the union of all the computation branches. Nondeterminism provides the way to formulate combinatorial problems since alternatives for rules (in FLP) or clauses (in LP) may provide different assignments to the same variable. Combinatorial problems can therefore be expressed with such languages, but an exhaustive enumerative procedure is implicitly used for the search of solutions.

Also, solving in constraint systems is based on constraint propagation and labeling. The first prunes the search space by reducing domains, and the second finds solutions by assigning values to variables.

A constraint system starts solving by propagating the effects of the constraints over the domains of variables. This means that, in general, propagation implies that each current domain will decrease its cardinality (pruning). There are several propagation algorithms in the literature which behave differently and may reach different fixed points. The fixed point is reached whenever there is no further domain reduction. These algorithms implement an iterative procedure which looks for a stable situation (fixed point), or a failure (a domain

[1] Several computation branches may lead to the same solution due to redundant alternatives.

becomes empty, i.e., there is no possibility of finding an assignment for the related variable such that all the constraints are satisfied). Finding a fixed point with non-singleton domains does not mean that there are definitely multiple solutions to the problem, and it does not even ensure that at least one solution exists. Propagation is not complete in the sense of ensuring the existence of solutions. Instead, it is used to find out what assignments definitely do not lead to a solution. The premise in this approach is to identify in advance, as soon as possible, what partial solution (where not all domains are singletons) is not a solution before trying to assign all the variables. Note that this follows a different approach than those from the enumeration techniques, which try to find solutions by simultaneously assigning values to all the variables, so that one knows that a solution is found when all variables have been assigned.

Once propagation procedure reaches a fixed point and at least one domain is not a singleton, labeling can be initiated in order to find feasible assignments. Indeed, the search for solutions could be seen at this point from an enumeration point of view. However, each time a variable is assigned to a value, propagation can be started until a fixed point had been reached. Next, a new assignment can be made, a new propagation cycle started, and so on, until a solution is computed or not found. The latter means that backtracking must be started in order to find another possible assignment. Each time a variable is labeled (assigned to a value among the possible values in its domain), a choice point must be annotated in order to try different assignments through backtracking.

Solving in a (constraint logic) system embodying logic variables, an enumerative search procedure (as those for LP and FLP), and a constraint solving procedure (propagation and labeling), allows to constrain variable domains during the enumerative search, therefore hopefully identifying a failure in advance (before the assignment of the variable). This improves efficiency since computation branches are pruned in advance with the information given by the constraints. In addition, lazy narrowing may avoid computations which are not demanded, therefore saving computation time.

Moreover, CFLPFD constraints are declared as functions so that a wrong use can be straightforwardly detected in the typical type checking process (in FLP) a priori, before execution. Therefore, this saves time in both correcting and debugging programs.

# 4 Programming in TOY(FD)

Any CLP(FD)-program can be straightforwardly translated into a CFLP(FD)-program so that CLP(FD) may be considered an instance of CFLP(FD) what determines a wide range of applications for our language. We will not insist here on this matter, but prefer to concentrate on the extra capabilities of the language. We illustrate here different features of CFLP(FD) by means of examples. We would like to emphasize that all the pieces of code are executable in TOY(FD) and the answers for example goals correspond to actual execution of the program.

## 4.1 A Scheduling Problem

Here, we consider the problem of scheduling tasks that require resources to complete, and have to fulfill precedence constraints. Figure 1 shows a precedence graph for six tasks which are labeled as $tX^{Y}_{mZ}$, where $X$ stands for the identifier of a task $t$, $Y$ for its time to complete (duration), and $Z$ for the identifier of a machine $m$ (a resource needed for performing task $tX$).

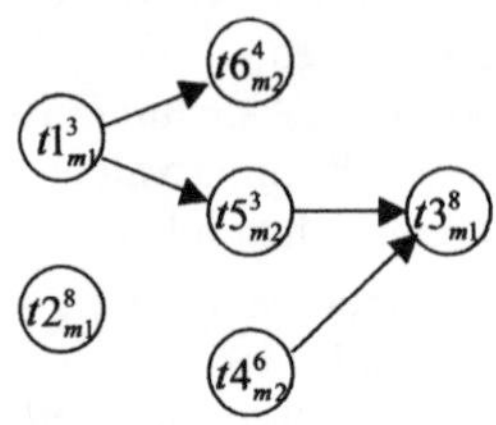

Figure 1: Precedence Graph.

The following program models the posed scheduling problem. Observe in the syntax that function arguments are not enclosed in parentheses to allow higher order applications. Also, syntactic sugar is provided for expressing Boolean functions à la Prolog. The rules that define a function follow its type declaration. The type declaration consists of the types for each argument and for the result separated by `->`. Lists adhere to the syntax as Prolog lists and **int** is a predefined type for the integers. Note also functional applications in arguments, such as `(End-D)` in the 2nd rule defining `horizon`. (Logic) Variables start with uppercase, whereas the remaining symbols start with lowercase.

```
data taskName = t1 | t2 | t3 | t4 | t5 | t6
data resourceName = m1 | m2
type durationType = int
type startType = int
type precedencesType = [taskName]
type resourcesType = [resourceName]
type task=(taskName,durationType,precedencesType,resourcesType,startType)

start :: task -> int
start (Name, Duration, Precedences, Resources, Start) = Start

duration :: task -> int
duration (Name, Duration, Precedences, Resources, Start) = Duration

schedule :: [task] -> int -> int -> bool
schedule TL Start End :- horizon TL Start End, scheduleTasks TL TL

horizon :: [task] -> int -> int -> bool
horizon [] S E = true
horizon [(N, D, P, R, S)|Ts] Start End :-
    domain [S] Start (End-D), horizon Ts Start End
```

```
scheduleTasks :: [task] -> [task] -> bool
scheduleTasks [] TL = true
scheduleTasks [(N, D, P, R, S)|Ts] TL :-
    precedeList (N, D, P, R, S) P TL,
    requireList (N, D, P, R, S) R TL,
    scheduleTasks Ts TL

precedeList :: task -> [taskName] -> [task] -> bool
precedeList T [] TL = true
precedeList T1 [TN|TNs] TL :-
    belongs (TN, D, P, R, S) TL, precedes (TN, D, P, R, S) T1,
    precedeList T1 TNs TL

precedes :: task -> task -> bool
precedes T1 T2 = (start T1) #+ (duration T1) #<= (start T2)

requireList :: task -> [resourceName] -> [task] -> bool
requireList T [] TL = true
requireList T [R|Rs] TL :- requires T R TL, requireList T Rs TL

requires :: task -> resourceName -> [task] -> bool
requires T R [] = true
requires (N1, D1, P1, R1, S1) R [(N2, D2, P2, R2, S2)|Ts] :-
    N1 /= N2, belongs R R2,
    noOverlaps (N1, D1, P1, R1, S1) (N2, D2, P2, R2, S2),
    requires (N1, D1, P1, R1, S1) R Ts
requires T1 R [T2|Ts] :- requires T1 R Ts

belongs :: A -> [A] -> bool
belongs R [] = false
belongs R [R|Rs] = true
belongs R [R1|Rs] = belongs R Rs

noOverlaps :: task -> task -> bool
noOverlaps T1 T2 :- precedes T1 T2
noOverlaps T1 T2 :- precedes T2 T1
```

A task is modeled (via the type `task`) as a 5-tuple which holds its name, duration, list of precedence tasks, list of required resources, and the start time. Two functions for accessing the start time and duration of a task are provided (`start` and `duration`, respectively) that are used by the function `precedes`. This last function imposes the precedence constraint between two tasks. The function `requireList` imposes the constraints for tasks requiring resources, i.e., if two different tasks require the same resource, they cannot overlap. The function `noOverlaps` states that for two non overlapping tasks $t1$ and $t2$, either $t1$ precedes $t2$ or vice versa. The main function is `schedule`, which takes three arguments: a list of tasks to be scheduled, the scheduling start time, and the maximum scheduling final time. These last two arguments represent the time window that has to fit the scheduling. The time window is imposed via domain pruning for each task's start time (a task cannot start at a time so that its duration makes its end time greater than the end time of the window; this is imposed with the function `horizon`). The function `scheduleTasks` imposes the precedence and requirement constraints for all of the tasks in the scheduling. Precedence constraints and requirement constraints are imposed by the functions `precedeList` and `requireList`, respectively.

With this model, we can submit the following goal, which defines the set of tasks, and asks for a possible scheduling in the time window (1,20):

```
Tasks == [(t1,3,[],[m1],S1), (t2,8,[],[m1],S2),   (t3,8,[t4,t5],[m1],S3),
          (t4,6,[],[m2],S4), (t5,3,[t1],[m2],S5), (t6,4,[t1],[m2],S6)],
schedule Tasks 1 20, labeling [] [S1,S2,S3,S4,S5,S6]
```

## 4.2 A More Involved Example

A more interesting example comes from the hardware arena. In this setting, many constrained optimization problems arise in the design of both sequential and combinational circuits as well as the interconnection routing between components. Constraint programming has been shown to effectively attack these problems. In particular, the interconnection routing problem (one of the major tasks in the physical design of very large scale integration - VLSI - circuits) have been solved with constraint logic programming [12].

For the sake of conciseness and clarity, we focus on a constraint combinational hardware problem at the logical level but adding constraints about the physical factors the circuit has to meet. This problem shows some nice features of TOY for specifying issues such as behavior, topology and physical factors.

Our problem can be stated as follows. Given a set of gates and modules, a switching function, and the problem parameters maximum circuit area, power dissipation, cost, and delay (dynamic behavior), the problem consists of finding possible topologies based on the given gates and modules so that it meets the switching function and it commits to the constraint physical factors.

In order to have a manageable example, we restrict ourselves to the logical gates NOT, AND, and OR. We also consider circuits with three inputs and one output, and the physical factors aforementioned.

In the sequel we will introduce the problem by first considering the features TOY offers for specifying logical circuits, what are its weaknesses, and how they can effectively be solved with the integration of constraints in TOY(FD).

*Example 1. FLP Simple Circuits.* Here we show the FLP approach that can be followed for specifying the problem stated above. We use patterns to provide *intensional* representation of functions. The alias `behavior` is used for representing the type `bool` → `bool` → `bool` → `bool`. Functions of this type are intended to represent simple circuits which receive three Boolean inputs and return a Boolean output. Given the Boolean functions `not`, `and`, and `or` defined elsewhere, we specify three-input, one-output simple circuits as follows.

```
i0, i1, i2 :: behavior              notGate :: behavior -> behavior
i0 I2 I1 I0 = I0                    notGate B I2 I1 I0 = not (B I2 I1 I0)
```

```
i1 I2 I1 I0 = I1
i2 I2 I1 I0 = I2

andGate, orGate :: behavior -> behavior -> behavior
andGate B1 B2 I2 I1 I0 = and (B1 I2 I1 I0) (B2 I2 I1 I0)
orGate B1 B2 I2 I1 I0 = or (B1 I2 I1 I0) (B2 I2 I1 I0)
```

Functions `i0`, `i1`, and `i2` represent inputs to the circuits, that is, the minimal circuit which just copies one of the inputs to the output (in fact, this can be thought as a fixed multiplexer - selector). They are combinatorial modules as depicted in Figure 2. The function `notGate` outputs a Boolean value which is the result of applying the NOT gate to the output of a circuit of three inputs. In turn, functions `andGate` and `orGate` output a Boolean value which is the result of applying the AND and OR gates, respectively, to the outputs of three inputs-circuits (see Figure 2).

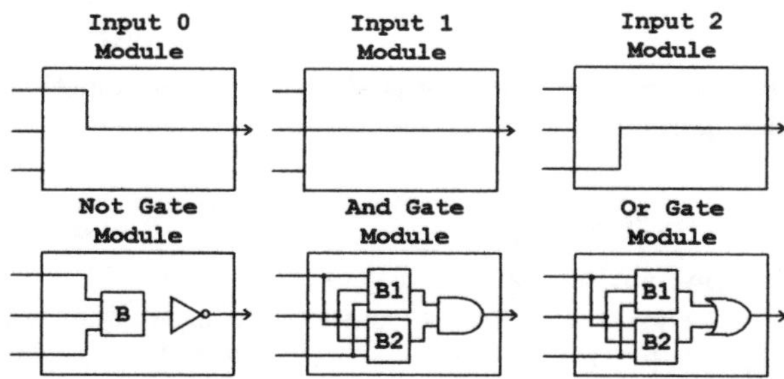


Figure 2: Basic Modules.

These functions can be used in a higher order fashion just to generate or match topologies. In particular, the higher order functions `notGate`, `andGate` and `orGate` take behaviors as parameters and build new behaviors, corresponding to the logical gates NOT, AND and OR. For instance, the multiplexer depicted in Figure 3 can be represented by the following pattern:

```
orGate (andGate i0 (notGate i2)) (andGate i1 i2)
```

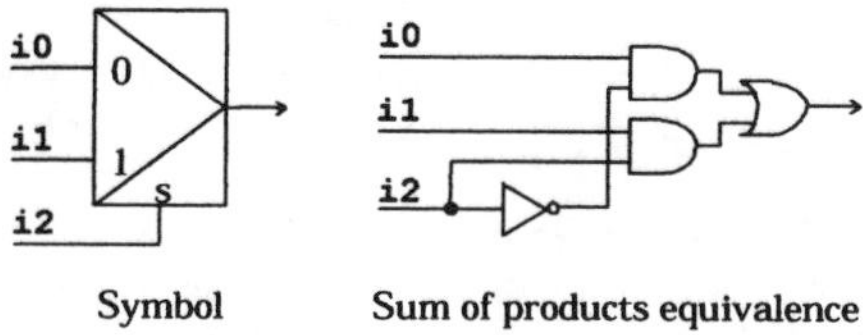


Figure 3: Two-Input Multiplexer Circuit.

This first-class citizen higher order pattern can be used for many purposes. For instance, it can be compared to another pattern or it can be applied to actual values for its inputs in order to compute the circuit output. So, with the previous pattern, the conjunctive goal:

```
P == orGate (andGate i0 (notGate i2)) (andGate i1 i2),
O == P true false true
```

is evaluated to `true` and produces the substitution `O == false`. The rules that define the behavior can be used to generate circuits, which can be restricted to satisfy some conditions. If we use the standard arithmetics, we could define the following set of rules for computing or limiting the power dissipation.

```
power :: behavior -> int
power i0 = 0
power i1 = 0
power i2 = 0
power (notGate C) = notGatePower + (power C)
power (andGate C1 C2) = andGatePower + (power C1) + (power C2)
power (orGate C1 C2) = orGatePower + (power C1) + (power C2)
```

Then, we can submit the following goal (provided the function `maxPower` acts as a problem parameter that returns just the maximum power allowed for the circuit)

```
power B == P, P < maxPower.
```

in which the function `power` is used as a behavior generator[2]:

As outcome, we get the following solutions (computed answers): {⟨`i0`, {`P==0`}, {}, {}⟩, ⟨`i1`, {`P==0`}, {}, {}⟩, ⟨`i2`, {`P==0`}, {}, {}⟩, ⟨`not i0`, {`P==1`}, {}, {}⟩, ..., ⟨`not (not i0)`, {`P==2`}, {}, {}⟩, ... }, where each solution is denoted by a set of 4-tuples $\langle E, \sigma, C, \delta \rangle$, where $E$ is a TOY expression, $\sigma$ is the set of variable substitutions, $C$ is a set of disequality constraints, and $\delta$ is the set of pruned domains. Declaratively, it is fine; but our operational semantics requires a head normal form for the application of the arithmetic operand `+`. This implies we reach no more solutions beyond ⟨ `not ( ... (not i0) ... )`, `maxPower`, {}, {}⟩ because the application of the fourth rule of `power` yields to an infinite computation. This is solved by recurring to successor arithmetics where `notGatePower`, `andGatePower` and `orGatePower` are of type `nat`, i.e.:

```
data nat = z | s nat

plus :: nat -> nat -> nat
plus z Y = Y
plus (s X) Y = s (plus X Y)

power' :: behavior -> nat
power' i0 = z
power' i1 = z
power' i2 = z
power' (notGate C) = plus notGatePower (power' C)
power' (andGate C1 C2) =plus andGatePower (plus (power' C1) (power' C2))
power' (orGate C1 C2) = plus orGatePower (plus (power' C1) (power' C2))

less :: nat -> nat -> bool
less z (s X) = true
less (s X) (s Y) = less X Y
```

[2]Equivalently and more concisely, `power B < maxPower` could be submitted, but doing so we make the power unobservable.

So, we can submit the goal `less (power' P) (s (s (s z)))`, where we have written down explicitly the maximum power (3 power units).

With the second approach we get a more awkward representation due to the use of successor arithmetics. The first approach to express this problem is indeed more declarative than the second one, but we get no termination. FD constraints can be profitably applied to the representation of this problem as we show in the next example.

*Example 2. CFLP(FD) Simple Circuits.* As for any constraint problem, modelling can be started by identifying the FD constraint variables. Recalling the problem specification, circuit limitations refer to area, power dissipation, cost, and delay. Provided we can choose finite units to represent these factors, we choose them as problem variables. A circuit can therefore be represented by the 4-tuple state ⟨area, power, cost, delay⟩. The problem formulation consists of attaching this state to an ongoing circuit so that state variables reflect the current state of the circuit *during* its generation. By contrast with the first example, we do not "generate" and then "test", but we "test" when "generating", so that we can find failure in advance. A domain variable has a domain attached indicating the set of possible assignments to the variable. This domain can be reduced during the computation. Since domain variables are constrained by limiting factors, during the generation of the circuit a domain may become empty. This event prunes the search space avoiding to explore a branch which is known to yield no solution. Let's firstly focus on the area factor. The following function generates a circuit characterized by its state variables.

```
type area, power, cost, delay = int
type state = (area, power, cost, delay)
type circuit = (behavior, state)

genCir :: state -> circuit
genCir (A, P, C, D) = (i0, (A, P, C, D))
genCir (A, P, C, D) = (i1, (A, P, C, D))
genCir (A, P, C, D) = (i2, (A, P, C, D))
genCir (A, P, C, D) = (notGate B, (A, P, C, D)) <==
      domain [A] ((fd_min A) + notGateArea)  (fd_max A),
      genCir (A, P, C, D) == (B, (A, P, C, D))
genCir (A, P, C, D) = (andGate B1 B2, (A, P, C, D)) <==
      domain [A] ((fd_min A) + andGateArea)  (fd_max A),
      genCir (A, P, C, D) == (B1, (A, P, C, D)),
      genCir (A, P, C, D) == (B2, (A, P, C, D))
genCir (A, P, C, D) = (orGate B1 B2, (A, P, C, D)) <==
      domain [A] ((fd_min A) + orGateArea)  (fd_max A),
      genCir (A, P, C, D) == (B1, (A, P, C, D)),
      genCir (A, P, C, D) == (B2, (A, P, C, D))
```

The function `genCir` has an argument to hold the circuit state and returns a circuit characterized by a behavior and a state. (Please note that we can avoid the use of the state tuple as a parameter, since it is included in the result.) The template of this function is like the previous example. The difference lies in that we perform domain pruning during circuit generation with the membership constraint `domain`, so that each time a rule is selected, the domain variable representing area is reduced by the size of the gate selected by the operational mechanism. For instance, the circuit area domain is reduced by a number of `notGateArea` when the rule for `notGate` has been selected. For domain reduction we use the reflection functions `fd_min` and `fd_max`, which respectively return the minimum and maximum values of a variable.

This approach allows us to submit the following goal:

```
domain [A] 0 maxArea, genCir (Area, Power, Cost, Delay) == Circuit
```

which initially sets the possible range of area between 0 and the problem parameter area expressed by the function `maxArea`, and then generates a `Circuit`. Recall that testing is performed during search space exploration, so that termination is ensured because the add operation is monotonic. The mechanism which allows this "test" when "generating" is the set of propagators, which are concurrent processes that are triggered whenever a domain variable is changed (pruned). The state variable delay is more involved since one cannot simply add the delay of each function at each generation step. The delay of a circuit is related to the maximum number of levels an input signal has to traverse until it reaches the output. This is to say that we cannot use a single domain variable for describing the delay. Therefore, considering a module with several inputs, we must compute the delay at its output by computing the maximum delays from its inputs and adding the module delay. So, we use new fresh variables for the inputs of a module being generated and assign the maximum delay to the output delay. This solution is depicted in the following function:

```
genCirDelay :: state -> delay -> circuit
genCirDelay (A, P, C, D) Dout = (i0, (A, P, C, D))
genCirDelay (A, P, C, D) Dout = (i1, (A, P, C, D))
genCirDelay (A, P, C, D) Dout = (i2, (A, P, C, D))
genCirDelay (A, P, C, D) Dout = (notGate B, (A, P, C, D)) <==
  domain [Dout] ((fd_min Dout) + notGateDelay) (fd_max Dout),
  genCirDelay (A, P, C, D) Dout == (B, (A, P, C, D))
genCirDelay (A, P, C, D) Dout = (andGate B1 B2, (A, P, C, D)) <==
  domain [Din1, Din2] ((fd_min Dout) + andGateDelay)(fd_max Dout),
  genCirDelay (A, P, C, D) Din1 == (B1, (A, P, C, D)),
  genCirDelay (A, P, C, D) Din2 == (B2, (A, P, C, D)),
  domain [Dout] (maximum (fd_min Din1) (fd_min Din2)) (fd_max Dout)
genCirDelay (A, P, C, D) Dout = (orGate B1 B2, (A, P, C, D)) <==
  domain [Din1, Din2] ((fd_min Dout) + orGateDelay) (fd_max Dout),
  genCirDelay (A, P, C, D) Din1 == (B1, (A, P, C, D)),
  genCirDelay (A, P, C, D) Din2 == (B2, (A, P, C, D)),
  domain [Dout] (maximum (fd_min Din1) (fd_min Din2)) (fd_max Dout)
```

Observing the rules for the AND and OR gates, we can see two new fresh domain variables for representing the delay in their inputs. These new variables are constrained to have the domain of the delay in the output but pruned with the delay of the corresponding gate. After the circuits connected to the inputs had been generated, the domain of the output delay is pruned with the maximum of the input module delays. Please note that although the maximum is computed *after* the input modules had been generated, the information in the given output delay has been propagated to the input delay domains so that whenever an input delay domain becomes empty, the search branch is no longer searched and another alternative is tried. Putting together the constraints about area, power dissipation, cost, and delay is straightforward, since they are orthogonal factors that can be handled in the same way. In addition to the constraints shown, we can further constrain the circuit generation with other factors such as fan-in, fan-out, and switching function enforcement, to name a few. Then, we could submit the following goal:

```
domain [A] 0 maxArea, domain [P] 0 maxPower, domain [C] 0 maxCost,
domain [D] 0 maxDelay, genCir (A,P,C,D) == (B, S),
switchingFunction B == sw
```

where `switchingFunction` could be defined as the function that returns the result of a behavior `B` for all its input combinations, and `sw` is the function that returns the intended result (`sw` is referred as a problem parameter, as well as `maxArea`, `maxPower`, `maxCost`, and `maxDelay`).

# 5 Conclusions and further work

We have presented CFLP(FD), a functional logic programming approach to FD constraint solving, which we think may be profitably applied to solve typical problems in the artificial intelligence area. We have shown how FD constraints can be defined as functions and therefore integrated naturally on FLP languages. Due to its functional component, CFLP(FD) provides better tools, when compared to CLP(FD), for a productive declarative programming. Due to the use of constraints, the expressivity and capabilities of our approach are clearly superior to both those of the functional and purely constraint programming approaches.

We have also presented the language TOY(FD) for CFLP(FD). Our proposal can be applied to a wide range of problems which include all CLP(FD) applications and typical uses of functional programming for combinatorial problems.

Moreover, we have shown by example the benefits of integrating FLP and FD. In particular, we have formulated a CFLP(FD) solution for a hardware design problem to show how to apply FD constraints to a functional logic language, which benefits from both worlds, i.e., taking functions, higher order patterns, partial applications, non-determinism, logical variables, and types from FLP and domain variables, constraints, and propagators from the FD constraint programming. This leads to a more declarative way of expressing problems which cannot be reached from each counterpart alone. Note also that our approach is far more declarative than other constraint programming systems as algebraic constraint programming languages (OPL [7], AMPL [3]), mainly since they do not benefit neither from complex terms and patterns nor from non-determinism.

Due to space limitations, we have not presented formally the CFLP(FD) framework in this paper and this is the subject of a further paper (in preparation). For the interested reader we briefly say that for the execution mechanism of the language we have seamlessly integrated constraint solving into a sophisticated, state-of-the-art execution mechanism for lazy narrowing.

Our implementation translates CFLP(FD)-programs into Prolog-programs in a system equipped with an efficient constraint solver [8].

In addition, we claim that our approach can be extended to other kind of interesting constraint systems, such as non-linear real constraints, constraints over sets, or Boolean constraints, to name a few. For this reason, we plan to generalize the CFLP(FD) setting to a generic constraint domain $X$ as done in the CLP setting [9].

# References

[1] N. Beldiceanu. *Global Constraints as Graph Properties on a Structured Network of Elementary Constraints of the Same Type.* 6th International Conference on Principles and Practice of Constraint Programming, Springer LNCS 1894, pp:52–66, Singapore, 2000.

[2] M. Carlsson, G. Ottosson and B. Carlson. *An Open-Ended Finite Domain Constraint Solver.* 9th International Symposium on Programming Languages: Implementations, Logics and Programs, Springer LNCS 1292, pp:191–206, Southampton, 1997.

[3] R. Fourer, D. M. Gay and B. W. Kernighan. *AMPL: A Modeling Language for Mathematical Programming.* Scientific Press, 1993.

[4] A. J. Fernández, T. Hortalá-González and F. Sáenz-Pérez. *TOY(FD): User Manual, latest version,* July, 2002. Available at `http://www.lcc.uma.es/~afdez/cflpfd/`.

[5] M. Hanus. *The Integration of Functions into Logic Programming: A Survey.* The Journal of Logic Programming (Special issue "*Ten Years of Logic Programming*"), 19-20:583–628, 1994.

[6] P. Van Hentenryck. *Constraint Satisfaction in Logic Programming.* The MIT Press, 1989.

[7] P. Van Hentenryck. *The OPL Optimization Programming Language.* The MIT Press. 1999.

[8] T. Hortalá-González and F. Sáenz-Pérez. *Interfacing a Functional Logic Language with a Finite Domain Solver.* 11th International Workshop on Functional and (Constraint) Logic Programming, Grado, Italy, 2002.

[9] J. Jaffar and M. J. Maher. *Constraint Logic Programming: A Survey.* The Journal of Logic Programming, 19/20:503–582, 1994.

[10] F. J. López-Fraguas and J. Sánchez-Hernández. *TOY: A Multiparadigm Declarative System.* 10th International Conference on Rewriting Techniques and Applications, Springer LNCS 1631, pp. 244–247, Trento, 1999. The system and further documentation including programming examples is available at `http://babel.dacya.ucm.es/toy` and `http://titan.sip.ucm.es/toy`.

[11] M. Rodríguez-Artalejo. *Functional and Constraint Logic Programming.* Constraints in Computational Logics, Springer LNCS 2002, pp. 202–270, 2001.

[12] N. F. Zhou, *Channel Routing with Constraint Logic Programming and Delay.* 9th International Conference on Industrial Applications of Artificial Intelligence, pp. 217-231, Gordon and Breach Science Publishers, 1996.

# OO Analysis Patterns as UML Metalevel Collaborations

Angeles Manjarrés
Dpto. Int. Artif., UNED, Senda del Rey s/n, 28040 Madrid, Spain
amanja@dia.uned.es

Simon Pickin, Gerson Sunyé, Damien Pollet, Jean Marc Jézéquel
IRISA-INRIA, Campus de Beaulieu, 35042 Rennes, France
{gsunye, dpollet, spickin, jezequel}@irisa.fr

Abstract.

A criticism that could be made of the most commonly-used AI development methodologies, in particular that based on the widely-known KADS-CommonKADS expertise model, is the unsuitability of the available techniques for specifying and reusing knowledge-model patterns. In this article, we investigate the alternative of formulating knowledge model patterns as OO analysis patterns. We seek to take advantage of research on design pattern specification, aimed at modelling patterns by means of structural and behavioural "meta-level" constraints. We illustrate our argument with the formulation of an OO "assessment pattern".

## 1. Introduction

With the increase in complexity of software, knowledge engineering methods have begun to show their value in areas outside that of traditional Knowledge-Based System (KBS) development, as stated in [1]. As the frontiers separating knowledge engineering from the rest of software engineering become steadily more diffuse, it would seem to be an appropriate time to seek a rapprochement from which both sides could derive significant benefit. On the software engineering side, OO techniques and in particular Object-oriented Analysis and Design (OAD) plays an increasingly pivotal role. While recognising the contribution that AI techniques can make in OO development methodologies, in this article we deal with the contribution that OO techniques can make in AI development methodologies.

The most common AI methodological perspective on software development is that of the widely-used KADS and CommonKADS expertise model [1], this also being the basis of many other methodologies. Several objections could be made to the conventional expertise model approach, in which the analysis phase is centered: informality, with some exceptions (e.g. (ML)2, see [2]), of the most widely-used notations (the case of the CML [3], lack of support for the development process, lack of autonomy of analysis with respect to later stages of the development cycle due to the adoption of a functional perspective and, finally, unsuitability of the notations for expressing the essence of knowledge-model patterns. In the last few years a more formal approach to both specification and reuse as well as development environments incorporating verification and validation [4][5][6][7][8] have been proposed. However, it is not clear how the methods and tools which these efforts have lead to could be adapted to achieve widespread acceptance outside of a research environment; model reuse based on a task/ method/ domain trichotomy is inevitably complex.

Reuse has always been a prime objective of the OO approach and the current advances in component-based software are taking place largely in the OO domain. In the last decade, reuse considerations have also lead to the development of the pattern concept and the compilation of pattern libraries at the design, implementation and analysis levels. The latest version of CommonKADS [1] recognises the widespread acceptance of OO techniques and languages and the interest of recent work on patterns. Accordingly, it attempts a kind of symbiosis of the earlier versions of the methodology with OAD ideas, by proposing the use of notations of the UML [9], the standard OAD specification language, and even proposing a OO design-level reference architecture for "knowledge-intensive systems" and recommending its implementation with OO languages. However, CommonKADS continues to defend a functional analysis perspective whose essential purpose is to maintain the clear decoupling between categories of knowledge (tasks, methods and domains, principally) which supposedly makes separate reuse possible.

In [10] and [11] we asserted that OO analysis techniques constitute a valid, and on occasions more appropriate, approach than the usual AI analysis perspectives. It is therefore of interest to integrate OO techniques in AI methodologies not only in the design phases but also in analysis, including high-level analysis, e.g. using UML. In this article, we investigate the possibility of describing AI knowledge model patterns (i.e. recurrent abstract knowledge models; "task templates" in CommonKADS terminology) as OO analysis patterns by applying results obtained in the patterns field reported in [12][13], concerning modelling patterns as UML meta-level collaborations. In Section 2 we present the description frameworks for recurrent abstractions in both AI methodologies and OO methodologies. We illustrate our approach by presenting, in Section 3, a sketch of the well-known assessment task template and then, in Section 4, a corresponding UML description of the assessment pattern. In Section 5 we point out some limitations of the expertise model perspective and highlight the interest of describing AI knowledge model patterns as OO analysis patterns via the UML metamodel. Finally, in Section 6, we draw conclusions from our modelling experience.

# 2. Recurrent Abstractions in AI and OO

## 2.1 Knowledge Model Patterns in AI

The analysis phase of most AI development methodologies is centred around a CommonKADS-style expertise model, which is based on the separation of knowledge into three categories:

1. the *inference knowledge*, described as the functional specification of the basic information-processing units (*inferences*) used, their input and output being specified abstractly as *domain roles*,
2. the *domain knowledge*, containing the *domain schemas* (characterizing the entities that are to play the *domain roles*) and *rule types*, as well as the *knowledge bases* (including the corresponding instances).
3. the *task knowledge*, consisting of the *task goal*, described as an input-output pair, and the *Problem Solving Method (PSM)*, which solves the task in the sense of decomposing it into subtasks -until the level of inferences is obtained -, plus the control flow in which the subtasks are to be embedded.

In such a framework, there are held to be three types of separately reusable model entities: tasks, PSMs and ontologies. Dependencies between entities are treated in the so-called assumptions [8]; the way in which assumptions are dealt with in order to effect the reuse has more recently been encapsulated in the notion of adapters [5]. Component libraries have been compiled dealing with different levels of the development process and exhibiting differing degrees of abstraction and formality.

As stated in the introduction, the analysis notations most widely used in the context of AI methodologies have been rather informal. In addition they are not well-suited to capturing the essence of the very "recurrent patterns" which the highly abstract analysis libraries are supposed to compile, resulting in over-restriction. In practice, this difficulty is avoided by a loose conception of reuse, in which uncontrolled modifications of the pattern are allowed. Such practises make a systematic approach to re-use difficult.

Attention has turned to making the analysis libraries more manageable and formalising the process of reusing the different components (see [14][5][6][7]). Formal languages introduced in the last few years ([4]) are more well suited for describing knowledge model patterns. Specific formal notations for assumptions have also been proposed. Assumptions are considered essential for characterizing the precise competence of PSMs. In [8] the development of a KBS is viewed as a process of introducing and refining assumptions. Formalisation enables automatic support for the specialisation of generic models in which their constraints (expressed by assumptions) are respected, as well as allowing assumption verification & validation.

In spite of the interest of the results obtained, it is not clear how these methods and tools could achieve widespread acceptance outside of a research environment. An approach using different types of supposedly separately-reusable components, whose interdependencies have to be addressed by introducing complex entities such as adapters into the architecture, could be criticised for being cumbersome and overly complex.

## 2.2 OO Patterns

The notion of "software pattern", one of the main advances in OO design in the 1990s, derives from the ideas of Alexander concerning design in the fields of architecture and urban development [15]. Following Alexander, a pattern is "a recurring solution to a common problem in a given context and system of forces", and a pattern language is defined to be "a collection of patterns together with a set of rules or guidelines for combining them in order to solve larger problems". Since our interest is in techniques for specifying AI knowledge models, we focus on the so-called "analysis" or "conceptual patterns", commonly understood as high-level abstractions occurring across a range of domains [16].

While work on analysis patterns is relatively scarce, in the design pattern field solutions have been proposed to many of the problems which arise in specifying them precisely. We believe that the results obtained are readily translatable to other kinds of patterns. Among the approaches, we are particularly interested in those based on the UML. We mentioned above that notations for the expertise model representation are not well-suited to representing knowledge-model patterns. Similar problems have been identified when trying to represent design patterns in UML. Thus, the choice of using OMT structure diagrams in [17] led to several interpretation errors. Indeed, this type of diagram can only represent models in terms of classes, associations or methods. It is not adapted to capturing the essence of a pattern, which is more properly expressed in terms of "roles" that are played by classes, attributes, associations or methods. The use of parameterized collaborations in UML, with the notions of Classifier Role and Association Role, is a promising approach which, however, still suffers from several deficiencies (see [13]). In brief, the role concept is limited to classes and associations, and the representation of pattern-specific constraints is deficient.

We have adopted the approach presented in [12][13], which also uses collaborations to represent patterns, but at the meta-model level. Meta-level collaboration diagrams and a meta-level profile are defined to facilitate modelling patterns and representing their occurrences. This proposal gives the UML enough reflexive capacity to model design patterns as structural and behavioural "meta-level" constraints. The role of these constraints in specifying patterns in OO methodologies is similar to that of the assumptions in specifying knowledge model patterns in AI methodologies.

# 3. Assessment Pattern: Expertise Model

To facilitate reuse at a high-level of abstraction, reusable combinations of the basic components of an expertise model commonly occurring across a large range of domains have been identified and specified as the so called "task templates"[1]. They consist, firstly, of a task knowledge model and an inference knowledge model and, secondly, of a specification of a typical domain schema that would be required for the application of the corresponding method. We will illustrate how the different types of knowledge are described by briefly presenting the assessment task template, as formulated in [1]. The task definition, the inference diagram of a common method and its control execution specification are shown in Figures 1, 2 and 3, respectively.

```
TASK assessment;
  ROLES: INPUT: case-description:"The case to be assessed";
         OUTPUT: decision:"the result of assessing the case";
END TASK assessment;
```

Figure 1 Assessment task definition, in CML [1].

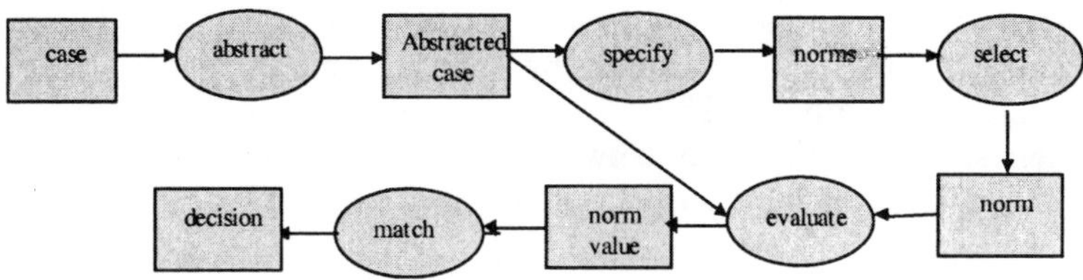


Figure 2 Inference diagram of an assessment-with-abstraction method [1] .

```
WHILE
  HAS-SOLUTION abstract(case-description->abstracted-case)
            DO case-description := abstracted-case ;
END WHILE
specify(abstracted-case-> norms) ;
REPEAT      select(norms-> norm) ;
            evaluate(abstracted-case + norm->norm-value) ;
            eval-results:=norm-value ADD eval-results ;
     UNTIL HAS-SOLUTION match(evaluation-results->decision) ;
END REPEATED
```

Figure 3 Execution control definition, in CML. [11]

The goal of the assessment task is to characterize a case in terms of a decision class on the basis of a set of domain-specific norms or criteria. According to the method, first, some of the case data must be abstracted, the abstractions required being those that present the data in the form used in the norms. The abstract inference is repeated until no more abstractions can be made, and the abstracted features are added to the case. After abstraction, those norms which are applicable to this case are selected and evaluated with respect to the case data, producing a set of truth values. Finally, it is checked whether the results of the evaluation leads to a decision.

```
INFERENCE abstract;
       ROLES: INPUT:case-description;
              OUTPUT:abstracted-case;
              STATIC:abstraction-knowledge;
SPECIFICATION:  "Input is a set of case data, output is the same set
of data extended with an abstracted feature that can be derived from
the data using the corpus of abstraction knowledge";
END INFERENCE abstract;
```

Figure 4 *abstract* inference [1]

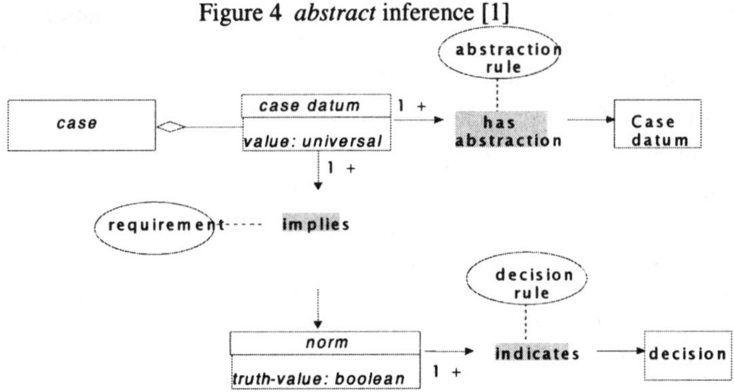


Figure 5. Method-specific ontology [1].

The inference knowledge is illustrated in Figure 4. Finally, in Figure 5 the method-specific ontology is illustrated by showing entities that are to play the domain roles, and rule-types. Thus, a *case* is specified as a composition of *case datum*. Abstraction dependencies between *case data* are represented by the *has abstraction* relation, which has an associated *abstraction* rule-type.

# 4. Assessement Pattern: UML Representation

As already stated, we have applied the pattern-representation approach proposed in [12][13], based on modelling collaborations in the UML metamodel.

The collaborations described in the UML standard belong to the base modelling level (i.e. the software modelling level), termed the M1 level. In an application of an M1-level collaboration, each of the roles described is played by one or several entities from the modelling level below, the M0 level, thus by run-time entities. M1-level collaborations can be represented by diagrams of two types: "object-level" and "specification-level" (S-diagrams). The entities shown in a UML S-diagram are roles. Such a diagram can be used to specify a parameterized collaboration containing roles with no identified class. A use of such a collaboration is a mapping from these roles to concrete classes, in accordance with the specified multiplicity. The UML standard provides a notation for the use of a parameterized collaboration. It then recommends modelling a pattern structure and its occurrence using a parameterized collaboration defined via an S-diagram and this collaboration-use notation respectively.

In [12] it is proposed instead to model pattern structures using collaborations which belong to the meta-modelling level, termed the M2 level. For this, S-diagrams are transported to the M2-level and are used in conjunction with several M2-level stereotypes1, part of a profile for pattern description. Analogously to the M1-level case, in an application of an M2-level collaboration, each role is played by one or several entities from the modelling level below, the M1 level, thus by a software model entity. Such an application can thus be viewed as an assignment of one or several M1 entities (class, attribute, operation, etc. of the model), in accordance with the specified multiplicity, to each participant of the collaboration. It can therefore be identified with an occurrence of the described pattern. The UML notation for pattern occurrence can be carried over to this new approach since the notation for M1-level collaboration use extends in a natural way to M2-level collaboration application. Note that it is a true extension since, as we have seen, the roles in an M2-level collaboration can be played by M1 entities other than classes. Further advantages of this approach are discussed in [13].

We now show how the Assessment pattern can be specified using this approach. We stress that, in contrast to the task/method/domain trichotomy of the expertise models, an OO pattern is characterised by a perspective unifying data and functionality. Thus, in the following description we distinguish only between structural and dynamic aspects of the Assessment pattern.

---

1 Strictly speaking, such diagrams should be defined using the MOF (level M3).

## 4.1 Structural Aspects

The structural aspects of an OO analysis pattern concern both domain knowledge and task & inference knowledge. The structural representation of the assessment pattern (Figure 6) describes the constraints that should be respected by the elements of a class diagram which participate in a pattern occurrence in order to accomplish the roles.

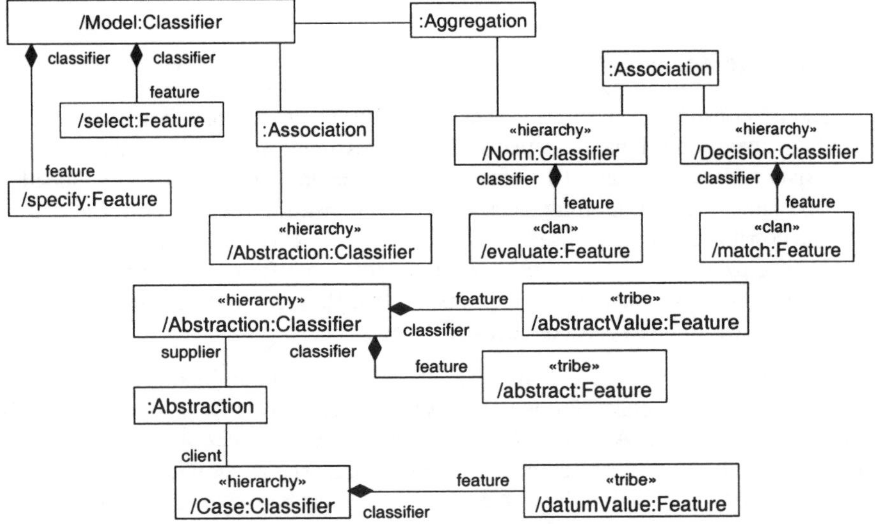


Figure 6. Meta-level Collaboration of the assessment pattern.

The main participant class is represented by the Model classifier role, which owns two role features, select and specify. Meta-level properties of an "assessment method schema" are described without unnecessarily constraining its structure. Thus, what is called a feature in the UML metamodel, can be an operation, an attribute or a method.

Certain meta-characteristics of the domain concepts that will assume the specified roles can be additionally expressed using stereotypes. A «hierarchy» is a set of classes, sharing a common super class. The concepts of clan and tribe were defined by Eden [18]. A «clan» is a set of behavioural features that share the same signature and are defined by different classes of the same hierarchy. Finally, a «tribe» is set of behavioural features, where each feature is a clan. The role Model has two relationships, with two different classifier roles, Abstraction and Norm, both stereotyped «hierarchy», which means that these roles can be played by a hierarchy of classes. Since the evaluate() method can be overloaded, it is stereotyped «clan». Analogously, the role Case represents a hierarchy of classes that implements the role datumValue. This role is stereotyped «tribe», meaning that it can be played by different features (or clans of features), having different signatures.

A less abstract pattern could be specified by assigning the meta-class operation (a subclass of the meta-class feature) to the roles corresponding to the inferences identified in the assessment task template (select, specify, etc). The declarative specification of the operations and their signatures are also seen as structural aspects of OO models and could then be included in the structural representation of the pattern making use of the parameter meta-class. The declarative specifications could be either included in the attribute specification of the meta-class, expressed in any declarative language (since this attribute is of type string) or specified by means of preconditions, invariants and postconditions attached to the operation as constraint meta-classes.

## 4.2 Dynamic Aspects

The "static" constraints previously specified have to be completed with temporal constraints specifying dynamic aspects of the assessment method (for instance, that there exists a precise order to the features to be called, that is, abstract, specify, select and match). It is important to note that this constraints cannot be expressed in OCL, the constraint language used in conjunction with UML [19]. We are currently investigating possible solutions such as the use of some form of temporal logic or the adaptation of UML sequence diagrams, so that they could describe behavioural constraints at the required level of abstraction.

With respect to the rule-type CommonKADS construct, in our perspective it can be seen as a type of meta-constraint which plays an essential role in an analysis pattern commonly occurring in AI tasks. The very abstract representation of this pattern, that we will call the Rule inference mechanism pattern, is shown in Figure 7. It exhibits associations (playing the role rule_dependency) bound to certain constraints (rules), meaning that the satisfaction of these associations is conditioned by a specific kind of rule verification. The functionality of the operation (an inference) is to obtain the instances connected via these associations by evaluating the corresponding constraints. The evaluation method operates on the constraints as a rule_inference_mechanism.

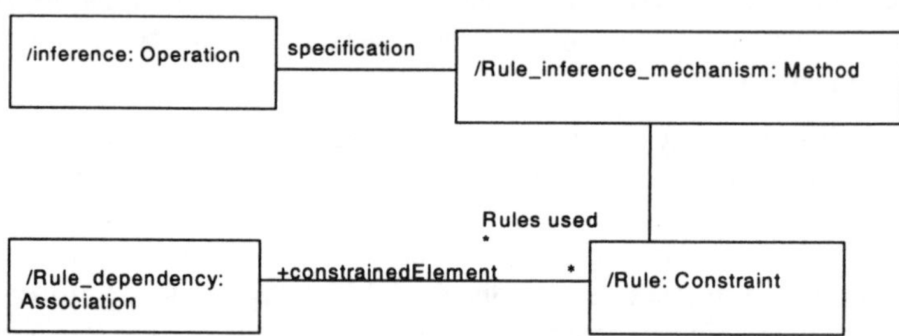


Figure 7 The *Rule inference mechanism pattern*

The rule type Abstraction of the assessment pattern is thus represented by using a combination of stereotypes (specific to an AI analysis pattern profile), as illustrated in Figure 8.

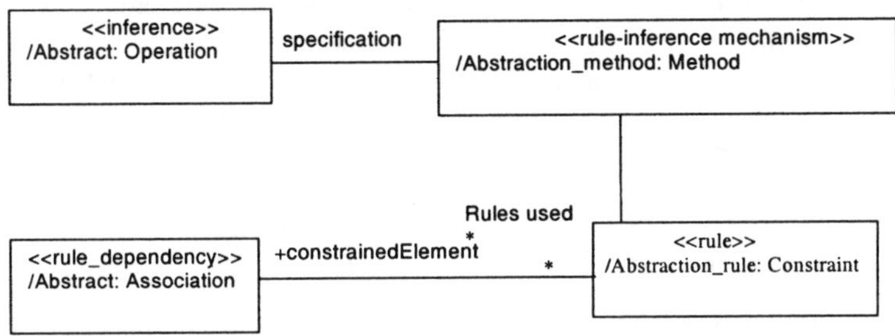


Figure 8 The *Abstract* rule-type

## 4.3 A Pattern Ocurrence Example

Figure 9 introduces a simple UML diagram, representing an application example of the assessment pattern. The chosen example, "the housing application", has been specified in [1] as an instantiation of the assessment task template. The collaboration usage is symbolized by an ellipse and represents an occurrence of the assessment pattern. The links between the collaboration usage and the classes represent the roles played by each class. The constraints specified for the assessment pattern have to be respected by its occurrences. Thus, the class Residence Assessment must implement at least two methods (corresponding to the roles select and specify of the pattern). As for the role datumValue, stereotyped «tribe», it is played by several attributes, e.g. name, address, city, etc.. Finally, since the classifier role Norm is stereotyped as a «hierarchy», several clauses can be used to determine if a residence can be allocated to an applicant; these classes then overload the evaluate() method.

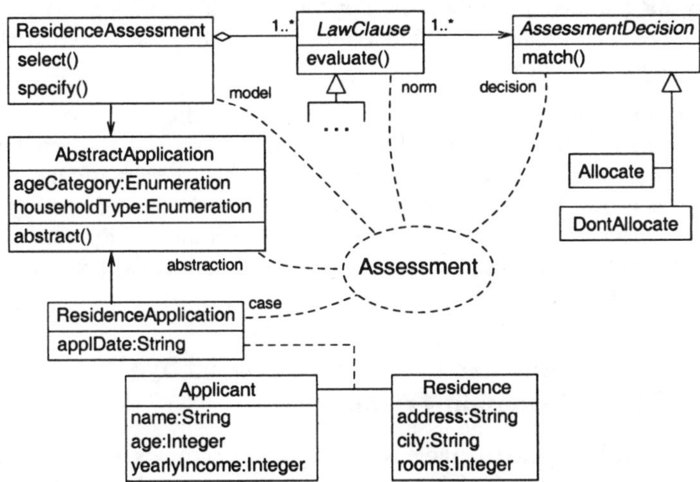


Figure 9. Class model in "the housing application", illustrating the occurrence of the assessment pattern.

As for the rule types, the role played by the association relating the classifier roles Model and Abstraction is here assumed by the relation which links

AbstractApplication and ResidenceApplication. By way of example we show the OCL corresponding to the associated constraint (content of the attribute bodyExpression in the meta-model) in the ResidenceApplication context:

```
self.applicant.age<35implies
self.AbstractApplication.agecategory=young
```

# 5. Discusion

In this section we confront the two approaches previously illustrated. Note that, though some of the limitations indicated in this section are specific to the CommonKADS task template approach to knowledge-model pattern definition, viz, overspecification and informality, other shortcomings are shared by other approaches based on the expertise model, since they mainly concern the functional approach and the expediency of the task/method/domain trichotomy.

## 5.1 Avoiding Over-Specification by a Meta-Level Description

The specification of the assessment task template is informal and, at the same time, overspecified. The use of an imperative pseudo-code almost inevitably leads to overspecification of the method. Given that the specialisation of PSMs is conceived as a strict hierarchical refinement process model reuse possibilities are limited. For example, the decision to use loops, rather than recursion, unnecessarily proscribes correct alternative solutions (see Figure 3). The inferences could also be said to be overspecified. Thus, the constraints on the output of the abstract inference (see Figure 4) concerns the structuring of the domain in the design phase. Finally, domain schemas (see Figure 5) make explicit a domain structure which is not mandatory for the method application, nor for the task resolution. Thus, case-data would be more appropriately modelled as attributes of the class case (but "tribes" of attributes cannot be modeled).

The semi-formal notations used for task template specifications, being essentially the same as the textual and graphical notations used to specify concrete knowledge models, are not suitable for expressing the high level of genericity and abstraction required. This is also the reason for the lack of characterization of rule-types, which are actually "meta-rules". In the OO pattern, both structural and dynamic meta-level properties of an "assessment method schema" are described without unnecessarily constraining its structure.

## 5.2 Simplifying the Reuse Complexity Caused by the Task/Method/Domain Trichotomy

Reuse in an expertise model framework involves a complex process of selection and adaptation of elements which are claimed to be separately reusable but whose coupling is subject to strong restrictions. Whilst the introduction of adapters to formalise the process of selecting and adapting the different components may be a positive step in this context, it does little to reduce the complexity of reuse.

For the case of CommonKADS the situation is worse since, in task templates, assumptions linking different model components are not really treated. Template descriptions do not explicitly specify the binding between the roles appearing in the inference structure and the concepts provided in the domain schema, nor the constraints about such a binding, which should exhibit a meta-level character. Inferences are in fact meta-inferences about which certain meta-properties are to be expressed: in any given application, a family of inferences with families of associated roles (norm & norm-value) must be associated to the evaluate inference.

In addition, independent reuse of tasks, methods and domains leads to the development of applications which do not preserve the principles of data encapsulation. In the OO assessment pattern, features are already encapsulated in the entitites which are to play the different roles, so that designs preserving data encapsulation principles are promoted. Due to the OO unified perspective, assumptions of the method about the domain are captured in the pattern structure itself, as well as in the stereotypes and constraints.

With respect to the emphasis on the method specification in knowledge engineering, it should be emphasized that OO pattern specifications are also intended to capture dynamic aspects, although at a high abstraction level. Though these aspects are not yet well studied, in Section 4 we pointed to possible solutions which we are currently investigating.

## 5.3 Beyond the Functional Perspective

As an example, we have chosen the assessment task for its simplicity and because it is well-known. For this task, the functional perspective cannot be said to be inadequate. This would not be the case, however, for systems with significant dynamic behaviour, particularly both those containing a strongly interactive component (e.g. decision-support systems and intelligent-tutoring systems) and those strongly reactive (e.g. robots). In both these cases, patterns of dynamic behaviour could not be adequately represented in the expertise model framework.

In our opinion (shared by [4]), in spite of the developments reported on in [1] current expertise-model approaches are still oriented towards centralised, monolithic reasoning and it may prove difficult to adapt them to the parallel and distributed context. The OO approach has, on the other hand, already made great progress in this direction.

Finally, the constrained view of methods is partly imposed by an essentially functional perspective which is recognised to be geared towards the procedural programming paradigm. The specifications derived from these knowledge patterns will, in our view, not be abstract enough to belong to the Newell knowledge level.

## 5.4 Modelling the Idiosyncracies of Knowledge-Intensive Systems

Rule-types are assumed to play an important role in the reasoning processes. However, in task template specifications they are not bound in any way to the inferences in which they take part. Additionally, introducing a rule-type construction in the domain knowledge model can be called into question. In a rule based system paradigm, rules are indeed considered as static knowledge, data on which a generic inference engine operates. However, in a functional paradigm, the type of knowledge specified in a rule-type belongs to the inference level, inferences often being the result of causal reasoning over a list of chained rules. Classifying such rules as static domain knowledge, can then be rather confusing since in a functional paradigm functions and data are supposed to be clearly distinguished. Expressing rule-types as meta-level constraints binding domain and inference concepts (as in the OO assessment pattern) would be more appropriate.

Finally, although the scope of recent knowledge engineering is not restricted to traditional KBSs, we should not lose sight of the fact that AI is still the main field of application. Thus, modelling of tasks characteristic of AI systems such as learning tasks should not be neglected. Recent OO developments in the areas of reflection and metaprogramming provide a promising basis for the modelling of these tasks.

## 5.5 Preserving Structure

The preservation of the conceptual structure of the domain in the application, from analysis to synthesis, is a desirable characteristic that has received a good deal of attention from AI methodologists, e.g. [20]. In [1] a "structure preserving" reference architecture for translating an expertise analysis model into an OO design is proposed by representating the expertise meta-model as abstract classes at the OO base-level. This rather contrived mapping between models, close to perverting the OO language constructs, is not what is commonly understood as "structure preserving" and is unlikely to lead to efficient and easily-maintainable implementations. As previously stated, a functional analysis is not easily refined to a programming paradigm other than the procedural one.

OO analysis patterns are reusable in distinct implementation paradigms, promoting well-structured modular designs. Structure preservation is particularly well supported by the OO paradigm and it can be expected that well-known OO design patterns should be discernable from OO analysis patterns.

## 5.6 Reaching a Suitable Compromise Formality-Informality

The lack of formality of the task template reuse approach contrast swith the effort of recent years in formalising the reuse process. However, while recognising the important contribution that formal methods can make, it should be recognised that they often fall down on ergonomical rather than technical reasons. OAD languages are viewed by many as a suitable compromise between formality and flexibility. The UML metamodel defines a relatively formal abstract syntax underlying the different graphical views. A valuable line of current research seeks to embed formal models behind UML's user-friendly graphical syntax.

## 5.7 Closing the Software-Knowledge Engineering Gap

A large and growing part of software development is currently conceived from an OO perspective. The use of patterns is being integrated into OO development.

Modelling patterns at the UML meta-level opens the way for automatic processing of pattern applications in CASE tools such as [21] – e.g. providing automatic support for the specialisation of generic models ensuring that their constraints are respected, recognizing generic model occurrences within source code (reverse engineering), etc. – and the use in such tools of pattern libraries. Though this ongoing work is mainly concerned with design patterns, much of it also applies to analysis patterns and is of undoubted interest for AI development support based on analysis patterns.

# 6. Conclusions and Future Work

In this article we have proposed the formulation of AI knowledge model patterns as OO analysis patterns. In particular, we have taken advantage of valuable research work done on design pattern specification concerning modelling patterns using structural and behavioural "meta-level" constraints. A library of these OO patterns (a "pattern language") could then constitute the counterpart of the widespread AI analysis libraries. We have experimented with the definition of an "assessment pattern" in analogy to the well known "assessment task template" as a meta-level collaboration. The pertinence of using meta-level modelling constructs such as «tribe» or «rule», when defining knowledge model patterns has been illustrated.

We are currently investigating the following two aspects of AI analysis pattern modelling in the OO paradigm: the question of specifying PSMs at an adequate level of abstraction and the successive specialisation of patterns, and the criteria for defining stereotypes in the context of UML profiles for AI pattern description.

Other promising research directions continuing this work include: AI design patterns and their relation with the analysis patterns; identifying suitable design patterns occurring in common AI patterns (such as a *rule inference mechanism design pattern* as well as a structural-reflective and a behavioural-reflective design patterns for learning analysis patterns); the specification of design patterns for different types of learning and the support of the development of AI systems based on OO patterns using OO CASE tools, such as those reported on in [21].

## References

1. Schreiber G, Akkermans H, Anjewierden A et al.. Knowledge Engineering and Management. The CommonKADS Methodology. MIT Press, 2000.
2. Van Harmelen F, Balder J. (ML)2: A Formal Language for KADS Models of Expertise. Knowledge Acquisition 1992; 4: 127-161.
3. Schreiber G, Wielinga B, Akkermans J, Van de Velde W, Anjewierden A. CML: The CommonKADS conceptual modelling language. In: Steels L, Schreiber A TH, Van de Velde W (eds.), proceedings of European Knowledge Acquisition Workshop'94. Springer-Verlag, 1994 pp 1-25 (Lecture Notes in Artificial Intelligence no. 236).
4. Van Eck P, Engelfriet J, Fensel D, Van Harmelen F, Venema Y, Willems, M. A Survey of Languages for Specifying Dynamics: a Knowledge Engineering Perspective. IEEE Transactions on Knowledge and Data Engineering, 2001.

5. Fensel D, Benjamins R. Key Issues for Automated Problem-Solving Methods Reuse. In H. Prade (ed.), proceedings of 13th European Conference on Artificial Intelligence (ECAI-98). John Wiley and Sons, 1998, pp 63-67.
6. Fensel D, Benjamins R, Motta E, Wielinga R. UPML: A framework for knowledge system reuse. In: Proceedings of International Joint Conference in Artificial Intelligence. Estocolm, Swden, 1999.
7. Fensel D, Motta E. Structured Development of Problem Solving Methods. IEEE Transactions on Knowledge & Data Engineering 2001; 13,(6): 913-932
8. Fensel D, Straatman R. The essence of problem solving methods: Making assumptions for efficiency reasons. In Shadbolt N, O'Hara K, Schreiber G (eds.) Advances in Knowledge Acquisition. Springer-Verlag, 1996, pp 17-32 (Lecture Notes in Artificial Intelligence no 1076)
9. OMG UML Specification. Object Management Group (OMG), Framingham, Massachusetts, USA. Version 1.4, September 2001.
10. Manjarrés A, Pickin S. Describing Generic Expertise Models as O.O. Analysis Patterns: the Heuristic Multi-Attribute Decision Pattern. Expert Systems, 2002; 19, no. 3 (28): 142-169.
11. Manjarrés A., Pickin S. Describing AI Analysis Patterns with UML. In: Evans A, Kent S, Selic B (eds) proceedings of UML 2000, UML 2000 - The Unified Modeling Language. Advancing the Standard. Springer-Verlag, 2000. (Lecture Notes in Computer Science no. 1939).
12. Le Guennec A, Sunyé G, Jézéquel JM. Precise Modeling of Design Patterns. In: Evans A, Kent S, Selic B (eds), proceedings of UML 2000, UML 2000 - The Unified Modeling Language. Advancing the Standard. Springer Verlag, 2000. (Lecture Notes in Computer Science no. 1939).
13. Sunyé G, Le Guennec A, Jézéquel JM. Design Pattern Application in UML. In: Bertino E (ed) proceedings of ECOOP'2000. Springer Verlag, 2000. (Lecture Notes in Computer Science no. 1850).
14. Benjamins VR, Plaza E, Motta E et al.. An Intelligent Brokering Service for Knowldege Component reuse on the WWW. In: proceedings of 11th Workshop on Knowledge Adquisition, Modeling and Managment '98. Banff, Canadá, 1999.
15. Alexander C, Ishikawa S, Silverstein M. A Pattern Language. Oxford Univ. Press, 1977.
16. Fowler M. Analysis Patterns: Reusable Object Models Addison-Wesley, 1997
17. Gamma E, Helm R, Johnson R, Vlissides J. Design Patterns: Elements of Reusable Object-Oriented Software. Addison-Wesley, 1995.
18. Eden AH. Precise Specification of Design Patterns and Tool Support in Their Application. Ph.D. thesis, University of Tel Aviv, 1999.
19. Warmer JB, Kleppe A. The object constraint language: precise modeling with UML. In Booch G, Jacobson I, Rumbaugh J. Eds. Addison-Wesley, 1999.
20. Van Harmelen F, Aben M. Structure-preserving Specification Languages for Knowledge-Based Systems, International Journal of Human-Computer Studies 1996, 44.
21. Ho WM, Pennaneac'h F, Plouzeau N. Umlaut: A framework for weaving UML-based aspect-oriented designs. In: proceedings of Technology of object-oriented languages and systems (TOOLS Europe). IEEE Computer Society, 2000, pp 324-334 (volume 33).

# SESSION 4:

# CONSTRAINT SATISFACTION AND SCHEDULING

# A Hybrid AI Approach to Staff Scheduling

Graham Winstanley
School of Computing & Mathematical Sciences
University of Brighton
g.winstanley@bton.ac.uk

Abstract

Assigning staff to specific duties according to their contract, qualifications, skills, etc. within a working environment characterised by multi-disciplinarity and statutory regulations is problematic. This paper discusses an approach to nurse rostering, using a strategy of distributing the computational effort required in the scheduling process. The technique involves a hybrid approach that devolves responsibility for different aspects of the problem. In the pre-processing stage, the staff to be rostered are treated as semi-autonomous agents, each equipped with heuristics to guide their initial assignment. Compilation of individual rosters is followed by a scheduling phase in which a constraint solving agent applies constraint logic programming (CLP) techniques in the generation of 'acceptable' rosters.

## 1. Introduction

The generation of work allocation schedules can generally be summarised as the assignment of staff to particular time slots in order to satisfy given criteria. Time slots may be specified shifts, or they could be temporal intervals with dynamic start and end times. The criteria can be simple or complex, sometimes involving legal, corporate and safety issues in addition to heuristics that govern individuals and ever-changing institutional policies. The rostering of nurses is widely accepted as an important and challenging intellectual problem that belongs to the class NP-complete. Many studies have been undertaken in the area, using techniques such as mathematical programming [1] heuristic methods [2] and constraint satisfaction techniques [3], [4], [5], [6]. There are even commercially available systems, whose authors claim that their products are capable of wide application [7]. In all these cases, the authors are in agreement that the combinatorial search problem is the most difficult to solve. Heuristic methods such as that proposed in [2] attempt to circumvent the search problem by identifying specific rules that could be applied to progressively fill in a roster. However, although such methods are efficient in initial search space pruning, i.e. pre-processing, they are generally not complete.

Mathematical programming continues to be used for this class of problem and does provide completeness, but with the always-present overhead of an enormous search space. Constraint logic programming (CLP) has been widely used in recent times, but almost always within a hybrid architecture that commonly includes a high degree of user interaction and heuristic pre-processing [3]. CLP offers what appears to be an ideal vehicle for the solution of scheduling problems such as nurse rostering. The high-level nature of logic programming is augmented by the seamless integration of one or more constraint solvers, thus allowing the programmer the comfort of modelling the problem and its constraints declaratively. With this approach, the programming steps are, in outline: model the problem, declare the constraints, and apply a specific search algorithm to find a satisfactory or optimised solution. Modelling includes the definition of variables, data and data structures, domains of variables, etc. Declaring constraints on the problem variables is catered for by the syntax rules of the constraint solver and can be unary, binary or n-ary. Search is the final step and is always necessary with problems of realistic scale. It proceeds by systematically instantiating variables from their domains and testing all constraints on that variable and any variable related to it (via constraints) [8], [9].

Unfortunately, CLP, or in fact any of the above-mentioned techniques alone, is not capable of solving the nurse scheduling problem, even when esoteric methods such as double-modelling are employed [4]. In our study there were a total of 18 nurses and 11 possible working shifts. For a one month scheduling period this amounts to a search space of $11^{(18*28)}$, however this is reduced slightly by reducing the domain size. Most successful systems appear to be based on the application of several methods of representation and reasoning, and this is the approach adopted in our work. Another unfortunate fact is that no two nurse rostering situations appear to be identical. This means that one solution, based commonly on the identification of symmetries and applicable heuristics becomes so specific to that particular situation, that its generality is lost. Commercial systems allow the user to predefine the 'business rules' in a kind of 'system tuning' process, but this places the emphasis very much on the knowledge and skill of the person(s) assigned to optimise the system for each application. Our approach has been to partition the problem into its identifiable components and perform a solution in a number of phases, including heuristic methods and CLP.

Results from the use of the system on a hospital medical ward within the UK NHS have been successful. Additionally, the application of the Staff Work Allocation Tool (SWAT) on the ward has proved to be an invaluable vehicle for gaining a better understanding of the interplay of constraints at various levels, i.e. from individual to institutional, and national levels.

## 2. Distributing the problem

Initial research into the process of rostering identified the naturally distributed nature of the problem. In many ways it resembled industrial domains characterised by team working, and particularly interdisciplinary collaboration. Complexity in such domains has been shown to be solvable using a multi-agent approach in which individuals are represented by semi-autonomous software agents that are able to solve problems local to themselves, but also to co-operate together to achieve predefined global goal(s) [10]. In producing a nurse roster, one person is usually given the (unenviable) task of allocating staff to shifts, i.e. time slots, for each day in a scheduling window of commonly one month. In doing that job, he/ she must be aware of the skill and/ or qualification profile of the staff, and be fully cognisant of all requirements and constraints which control how the finished roster should look. In some large hospitals, such rosters may be produced centrally, but experiences have shown that most commonly the task is performed by a staff member on the ward that is being rostered, and in our case that process was characterised by a great deal of local negotiation. Each staff member knew their qualifications and nursing grade. Each one had some preference for working patterns and each individual had the opportunity to request certain shifts on certain days or weeks. Over a period of several months, patterns seemed to evolve that serve to make the scheduler's job (apparently) easy. However, in many cases, partly due to requests that 'upset' the preset patterns, annual leave, sickness, etc., the task becomes very difficult indeed.

The agent-based metaphor adopted in our work assumes the following: Each staff member could be given a copy of the blank ward roster. Individual rosters could then be produced, based on peoples' knowledge of their own situation as it relates to the roster. Relationships may exist between individuals that result in constraints between them, but essentially negotiation would be assumed to have taken place before individual schedules are produced, i.e. the definition of preferred patterns of work would be accomplished prior to scheduling. The staff member assigned to the task of ward scheduling would then collate individual schedules into a ward roster. Given the unlikely situation that no deviations from the agreed preferred shift patterns had taken place, through requests say, the resulting ward roster should be, by definition, satisfactory without further effort. In the far more usual case, the roster production task would involve minor 'shuffles' of shifts. An optimal solution to this would be to minimise such perturbations, and an approach to dealing with this method of final ward rostering is discussed later in this paper.

The problem has the following characteristics:

1. Staffing comprises 'trained' staff and 'untrained' staff. Trained staff are professionally qualified and registered. Untrained staff are commonly referred to as auxiliary, or nurse assistants. To cater for the inevitable over-constrained case, the hospital has the benefit of a 'nursing bank.'

2. Requests are generally honoured. The Ward Manager is responsible for approval, but once this has been given, requests are treated as hard constraints.

3. On each and every day, there should be a predefined staff establishment and shifts are standardised as: Early full, Late full, Late half and Long day

4. There should be no 3 consecutive long days. If a staff member has worked two long days already, the next shift must be a day off.

5. In our approach, days off are used generically for any day not spent on the ward, i.e. including annual leave, sickness, study leave, etc. in order to reduce the number of shifts and therefore the search space [11].

6. Bank staff should be employed only when necessary. In practice, established staff members are commonly asked to work extra shifts. This poses some interesting problems in automating the process, but our solution has focused on the incorporation of bank shifts to address the over-constrained case.

Agents are defined in our system for each member of nursing staff, with a common architecture. Information pertinent to each agent is stored, and specific pre-processing is carried out at the individual agent level before the roster management phase.

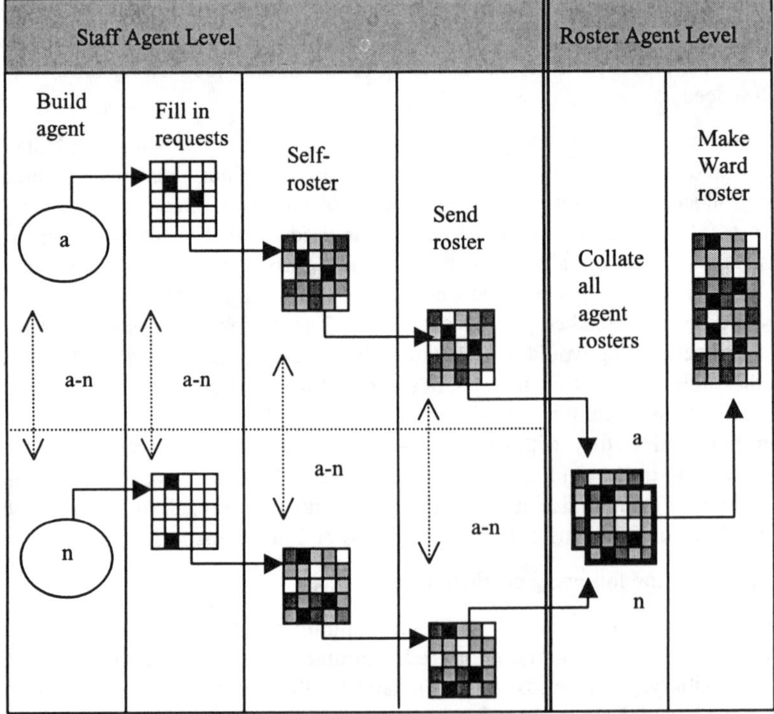


Figure 1. Sequential phases involved in producing a ward staff roster

The various phases involved in the process are shown diagrammatically in Figure 1. With reference to this figure, our solution to the rostering problem involves a number of phases, based on the following assumptions:

- Each agent should be capable of 'filling in' their own part of a ward schedule and taking part in a collective and possibly negotiated agreement.

- Preferred working patterns represent a 'starting point' for scheduling. In an ideal situation, these shift patterns, when collated together, would provide a working solution for the ward establishment for the day/ week / month. In practice, changes would almost always be required.
- Requests for specific duties, leave, etc. are evaluated at the local, i.e. individual agent, level. Once these requests are accepted, they must be honoured.
- Production of the final ward roster is the responsibility of the Roster Manager Agent. This agent is controlled by a number of higher-level constraints pertinent to the ward, the institution and beyond.

# 3. Architectural issues

The architecture of the SWAT System is based on the object-oriented knowledge system Kappa-PC , loosely coupled with the ECL$^i$PS$^e$ Constraint Logic Programming System. Each staff member is represented as an agent with the following components:

- A 'core' profile component. This component holds data on staff name, grade, qualifications, contracted hours of work, status and preferred working shift patterns.
- A request component that doubles up to contain the initial individual schedule. This component holds data on any requests that have been processed and agreed by the Request Manager Agent.
- A personal constraint component that holds specific types of constraint, e.g. 'X must work with Y.' The data in this component is accessed when defining new preferred work patterns and when processing requests.
- A communications component which currently relays object messages. There is no specific agent communication language or protocol at work.

An object called 'Nurse' is defined, with subclasses 'Trained', 'Untrained' and 'Bank', and three methods: 'BuildAgent', 'RemoveSelf' and 'SelfSchedule.' BuildAgent takes data obtained from the user interface and creates and appropriately names the above agent components. Figure 2 shows the agent architecture as an object hierarchy for 2 nurses in each of the 3 categories. In this figure, solid lines signify class/ subclass relationships, and dotted lines signify instance relationships.

In addition to the nurse agents, there are also three manager agents defined: 'RequestManager', 'RotaManager' and 'InterfaceManager', which are equipped with methods to deal with individual requests for days off, shifts, etc., invoking the initial scheduling system and controlling the interface to the user and the Roster Manager Agent, which exists and operates outside the object-oriented environment described in this section.

Figure 3 shows the main interface to the system. Using this interface, it is possible to view, add, delete and modify staff details, view requests and initial rosters for each staff member. It has facilities to view, add, delete or modify requests, and it is from here that initial and final ward scheduling is invoked.

With reference to Figure 3, and Figure 1, in the process of producing individual rotas for each agent, the following stages have taken place:

1. Requests are made for days selected from the (main) month displayed on the interface. Rules exist to validate requests and ensure that, once accepted, they persist through subsequent reasoning phases.

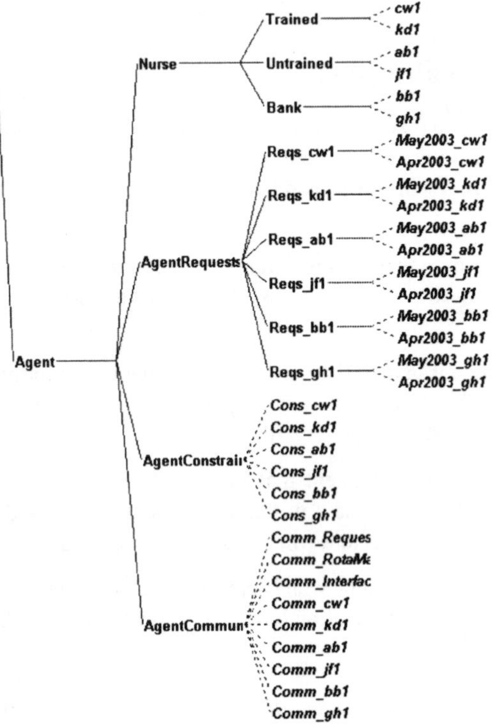


Figure 2. The object hierarchy for the nurse agent

2. A forward-chaining inference process invokes 'self-scheduling.' For each agent defined within the system and labelled as 'active', the process involves four phases:

   Phase 1: Scans the month on a day-to-day basis and assigns requests with a numerical value to signify a hard constraint. Requests are processed first and are always honoured after being accepted by the backward-chaining inference process.

Phase 2: Scans the month on a day-to-day basis and checks for requests being in conflict with preferred assignments. If such conflicts are detected, this phase records the details.

Phase 3: This phase takes the data recorded in Phase 2 and re-allocates shifts that were preferred, but have now changed due to requests. Modifications to the shift pattern for the week in question are minimised.

Phase 4: This is only active when preferred shifts are de-selected. This phase involves a large and complex rule set that effectively labels each day with a shift according to predefined soft constraints.

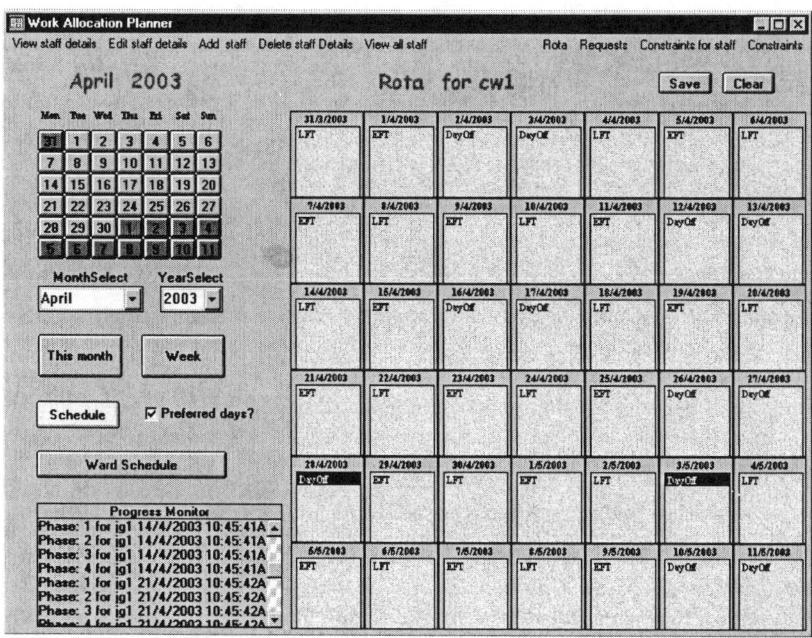


Figure 3. The system's main interface

Figure 3 shows that the staff member 'cw1' had requested the day off on Monday 28 April and Saturday 3 May, and that the 'normal' preferred shifts for that week had been slightly modified. Agent schedules are stored as ASCII files, and the Roster Manager Agent is subsequently invoked on that data. The first file contains data on the (short) names for each agent, their contracted time and their possible shifts

The second data file holds the actual initial schedules in the Prolog-style format shown below:

```
data([(1 ,apr ,2003 ,eft ,6 ,cwl),
(2 ,apr ,2003 ,dof ,6 ,cwl),
:
:
(28 ,apr ,2003 ,dof ,9 ,cwl) ]).
```

This indicates that the staff member 'cwl' has an early full trained shift on 1 April, 2003, and it comes about as a preferred shift. This agent has requested a day off on 28 April.

# 4. The Roster Manager Agent

Corporate constraints are crucial in any ward roster. They govern the number of staff at various levels, they dictate the patterns of work, and they control staff working hours. Every hospital ward has a staff establishment, i.e. the number and spread of personnel for each day in order to comply with legal standards and the guidelines developed and agreed at the corporate level. In the SWAT System, these constraints are modelled and applied at the ward level, compiling individual agents' rosters and applying its constraints to each day and to all staff. These constraints include:

1. Number of trained and untrained staff per day. The constraints have a lower and upper limit.
2. Staff should not be scheduled for a work pattern that leads to their contracted hours of work being exceeded. This is quite a powerful constraint since the hours of work 'value' can be manipulated to cater for overtime in a controlled way. It is also possible to facilitate the inclusion of bank staff during the many occasions when a roster is simply impossible with the available staff (holidays, sickness, etc.).
3. Certain staff working patterns are 'preferred.'

The roster manager is responsible for collating individual rosters for one month, and applying specific constraints. Its task is to create viable rosters according to constraints propagated from the individual agent phase, and to corporate constraints at the ward level. However, minimal changes should be made to the initial roster because this represents the 'ideal' situation according to the wishes and preferences of individual staff. In other words, repairs should be made only when necessary, and those repairs should cause minimal disruption to the initial roster.

The ECL$^{i}$PS$^{e}$ Constraint Logic Programming platform [12] was used in the production of the final roster subsequent to the agent self-scheduling and roster compilation phases. This platform facilitates the conceptual modelling of the nurse rostering problem in Prolog style, and readily provides a mapping between that model and the program required to solve the problem, i.e. the design model. It has the great advantage of being a constraint solver at a high level, closely integrated with the Prolog programming language, and it is equipped with a number of constraint solving methods within its libraries. The facility to define a high-level specification of the problem at the conceptual level and to similarly define constraints at the design level, leads to the ability to rapidly produce such models and to experiment with them. In combinatorial problem domains, this method of design-by-experimentation is tractable.

Modelling in ECL$^i$PS$^e$ follows closely the principles adopted in the agent-based component of the SWAT System. Each agent produces and communicates a matrix of shifts, with data filled in for each day of a one-month staffing period. This data is in the form of a list with the following structure:

{day, month, year, shift_type, constraint_hardness, staff}

Other data is communicated, such as the range of possible shifts for each agent, i.e. the domain for each agent. Status information is also available, such as trained or untrained.

This is incorporated into the system as a number of supporting structures, and two key arrays are defined:

1. A two-dimensional array with axes for days (1-28) and staff (1-18). Each cell of this array is constrained to be instantiated by values from the domain of values for the relevant agent. The cells are then filled in from data provided by the agent-based component of the SWAT System, and become 'tentative values' for later constraint solving.
2. An identical array, but this time having only (initially) uninstantiated variables. This array provides the structure for the variables and the constraint solving process. As constraint-solving proceeds, values are chosen and evaluated according to the constraints on them and between other values.

In this structure, there are i staff and j days. Each cell of the array is a variable Vi,j that must be instantiated to a shift type, including non-shifts, i.e. days off, n total staff and t total days to schedule.

The first, and most important constraint at the ward level relates to the staff establishment on the ward for each day. This constraint, in ECL$^i$PS$^e$ syntax is defined as:

```
shift_occurrences(et,Day_list,N1), N1#>=2, N1#<=3      % et=early trained
shift_occurrences(eut,Day_list,N2), N2#>=2, N1#<=3     % eut=early untrained
shift_occurrences(lt,Day_list,N3), N3#>=2, N1#<=3      % lt=late trained
shift_occurrences(lut,Day_list,N4), N4#>=2, N1#<=3     % lut=late untrained
```

Where the 'shift_occurrences' constraint is based on the built-in ECL$^i$PS$^e$ 'occurrences' constraint. The 'et' argument signifies early trained, etc., Day_list is a list of variables made available for each day, i.e. {Vi,j} for $n \geq i \geq 1$ and for j = the day in question. The SWAT System loops through all $t \geq j \geq 1$, applying these constraints, which generally say that "for each day, there should be at least 2 trained on an early and late shift, but at most 3, and there should be at least 2 untrained on an early and late shift, but at most 3." The specific shift types that correspond to these abstract shift types are defined within the shift_occurrences constraint itself. These constraints are also equipped with annotation that controls propagation and specifies the ECL$^i$PS$^e$ repair library, but this has been ommitted for reasons of clarity.

It is important to constrain the system to give staff only those combinations of shift types that sum to their contracted hours. This constraint is quite easy to model in ECL$^i$PS$^e$, as shown below:

```
add_them(Z31,Z32,Z33,Z34,Z35,Z36,Z37,Z22):-
        (Z31 + Z32 + Z33 + Z34 + Z35 + Z36 + Z37) #=Z22.
```

where Z31 to Z37 are variables that hold the time value for each shift assigned, and Z22 is the contracted hours value for the staff in question. It declares that the summation of assigned shifts is constrained to be equal to the contracted work time. The system loops through $n \geq i \geq 1$ and for each week within the one-month period.

The assignment of shifts according to constraints on their patterns is catered for in the system as below. For each staff i, and for $t \geq j \geq 1$, R=the hardness value of Vi,j. A value of 9 signifies that the shift should be assigned exactly as it appears in the equivalent cell in the tentative value array (Init_shift_array). A value of 6 means that the value can be changed, so long as the new value $\in$ {domain of i}. P is Vi,j and P2 is the tentative value of Vi,j.

```
(R == 9) -> (P = P2)   % if a hard constraint, then impose the tentative value
```

The constraint 'no more than two consecutive long days' is defined as:

```
Q is Shift_array[I,J-1],                        % Q is yesterday's shift
Q2 is Shift_array[I,J-2],                       % Q2 is the day before's
  ((Q#=ldt) #/\ (Q2#=ldt)) #=> (P#=dof)         % #/\ is the 'and' constraint
  ((Q#=lda) #/\ (Q2#=lda)) #=> (P#=dof)         % #=> is the 'then' constraint
```

which says that 'if the last two days were long days, for trained and untrained, then the next day must be a day off. Other constraints have been experimented with to cater for informal patterns, such as early shifts before days off and late shifts after days off. However, in practice these were seen to frequently over-constrain the problem and are commonly violated in practice. These constraints have a similar structure to the one shown above and remain in the system as optional features.

The strategy described below is designed to reduce the search complexity by addressing the problem in four one-week chunks. Complexity and tractability issues are also important in the algorithm chosen for search itself. To deal with the common problem of no roster being possible with staff numbers available, the algorithm first tries for a solution with all available staff. If no roster is possible, a bank shift is added and search begins again. This continues until all possible bank hours have been utilised, and if no roster can be found under these circumstances, the system terminates, reporting a failure.

The algorithm controlling the Roster Manager is, in outline:

*Read in data for each agent into a number of non-logical variable structures*
*Create arrays for initial shift values, status, staff domains, staff work hours*
*Apply domains to initial and final shift arrays*
*Until a consistent set of value assignments has emerge, i.e. one that satisfies all constraints*
*For each week in the one-month scheduling period*
    *Set the initial shift array to its tentative values (from the previous phase)*
    *Apply constraints: staff numbers and patterns, hours worked*
    *Search: The systematic search for values consistent with the applied constraints*
  *If no set of value assignments can be made then*
    *If there are bank staff hours left then*
      *Increase bank staff hours by one shift*
      *Restart search*
    *Else*
      *Terminate with failure*
  *Else*
    *Terminate with a satisfactory roster*

# 5. The Roster Manager search strategy

The strategy that underpins the SWAT System assumes an initial tentative assignment of all staff to shifts according to their preferences and personal constraints. Therefore, a constructive labelling approach that iteratively searches for values would be unnecessarily complex. Our methodology involves the 'repair' of tentative values in an effort to satisfy the constraints defined at the roster manager level. At one extreme, the tentative values satisfy all constraints, and are accepted as given. At the other extreme, all tentative values may have to be changed and search complexity is at its theoretical maximum for the nature and scale of the problem at hand. In the case of manual nurse rostering, this repair strategy is common, and in practice has never been seen to reach the worst case. Various move-based strategies have been proposed to deal with this type of problem, notably [13], [14]. We have chosen to use the iterative improvement/ backtracking hybrid algorithm [14], which has been termed 'weak-commitment search.' In weak-commitment search, constraints are defined on variables and the tentative values of variables. In the case of constraint violations occurring, search for variable assignments is guided by a heuristic that chooses to instantiate a variable with a value from its domain that minimises constraint violations with the tentative values of unlabelled variables. This heuristic is due to [13] and is called 'min-conflict.' When a situation arises where no value can be found that satisfies all of these constraints, this combination of assignments is remembered as a 'no-good' constraint and the combination will not be tried again. Search is then restarted with the current value assignments as the new tentative values. This approach to search has important implications for automation of the current nurse rostering problem. It assumes (requires) a tentative solution, which is tested against all constraints. In the case of a failure at this stage, a value is chosen from the domain of a variable that causes the minimum conflict with the tentative values of the as yet unlabelled variables. A partial solution is therefore built in a sensible way by 'repairing' only those tentative assignments that are seen to be problematic. If no consistent value assignment can be made for any variable, then instead of backtracking to the last variable assignment, weak-commitment search abandons the whole path, recognising and storing the fact that this was a 'no-good' assignment set, and therefore should not be tried again. It is this weak commitment to the current branch in the search space that gives the algorithm its name. Once a dead end has been reached, the algorithm stores the bad assignment set as a no-good constraint, and starts the whole process again from scratch. However, the current value assignment set becomes the new set of tentative values. The assumption here is that this represents a 'better' solution than the previous one and does not throw away the manipulative work of the previous stage of the search.

# 6. Experiences with the system

The SWAT System has been tested on a hospital medical ward as detailed in this paper and has performed at least as well as manual scheduling according to reports from those responsible for rostering on that ward. Experience indicates that there are many aspects to the production of a workable roster that includes: the ability to negotiate 'on the fly' with staff immediately before roster publication, and commonly afterwards. Although the removal of this kind of 'bartering' is generally considered a good thing by those involved in the rostering process, the automated schedules were regularly criticised for being too rigid. However, this appears to have cultural roots, since once the system had produced a sequence of such rosters, criticisms became less frequent. The fact that the final rosters reflected the initially chosen preferred shifts allowed the Ward Manager to refine these patterns over time in such a way that harsh changes were mostly minimised.

Evaluation of the system occurred in two ways. The first measure of success involved user satisfaction, from the point of view of the scheduler and of the staff being rostered. The second involved the time taken to produce a roster. On average, using preferred shifts, the initial heuristic phase was completed in approximately 3 minutes. The final rosters were created as a secondary phase in a similar time. Using weak-commitment search, the number of restarts (equivalent to backtracks in backtracking search) was commonly one or two, but never more than 5. The ward currently uses a paper diary to record requests, and this became the primary source of data entry for phase one. However, considerable simplification and standardisation of requests and request types were required. Future versions will constrain requests to specific types. Initial individual rosters are accessed in the Phase 1 system, and the final ward roster is output as an ASCII file for publication in a spreadsheet format. At present there is no feedback from Phase 2 to Phase 1 other than the ability to manually criticise the two roster types and make changes to preferred shift patterns. This mixed initiative approach has many advantages, none the least in staff appreciation, but there is obvious scope for automation and adaptation.

# 7. Conclusions

The system has been in use for several months and has been successful in producing timely and accurate ward staff rosters. The hybrid approach taken in the development of the SWAT System, along with its agent-based architecture, has proven to be natural and intuitive for this class of problem. Devolving initial scheduling to software agents representing individual staff was a core development decision and has proved to be an effective solution to the problem. Agents can be dynamically created, activated, modified in and deleted from the system, and each one reasons locally, but provides sufficient information to the roster manager agent to facilitate the creation of ward rosters based on CLP techniques. The ECL$^{i}$PS$^{e}$ system allowed us to model the problem and facilitate the dynamic nature of information passed from Phase 1. Constraints were relatively easy to define and test in this system, and the search strategy used resulted in a reduced search space. It should be noted that combinatorial space and time complexity remains and can cause severe problems in the worst case, but experience has indicated that this is unlikely, especially with the incorporation of 'bank staff' to cater for the over constrained situations.

There remains much research to undertake. Our heuristic Phase 1 could easily be replaced by a distributed CLP system, but at the moment some degree of flexibility would be lost at the pre-processing stage where information can be acquired, stored, manipulated and generally reasoned with quite efficiently at the heuristic level. A partial constraint satisfaction solution, in which a range of 'soft constraints could be defined and allowed to be violated in a controlled way in the quest for a 'good' solution would also be useful. However, our experiences and experiments with such approaches has led us to believe that, in the case of nurse rostering, these extra overheads have a marginal effect on the final product.

# 8. References

1 Miller, H.E., Pierskalla, W.P., Rath G.J. Nurse scheduling using matematical programming, In Operations Research, Vol. 24, No.8, pp857-870, 1976.

2 Isken, M.W., Hancock W.M. A heuristic approach to nurse scheduling in hospital units with non-stationary, urgent demand and a fixed staff size, Journal of the Society for Health Systems, Vol.2, No.2, 1991.

3 Abdennadher, S., Schlenker, H. INTERDIP – An Interactive Constraint Based Nurse Scheduler, Proceedings of the 1st Int. Conf. on The Practical Application of Constraint Technologies and Logic Programming, PACLP99, London, 1999.

4 Cheng, B.M.W., Lee, J.H.M., Wu J.C.K. A Nurse Rostering System Using Constraint Programming and Redundant Modelling, IEEE Transactions on Information Technology in Medicine, Vol.1, pp44-54, 1997.

5 Weigel, R., Faltings, V.B., Choueiry B.Y. Context in Discrete Constraint Satisfaction Problems, 12th European Conference on AI (ECAI96), pp205-209, Budapest, Hungary, 1996.

6 Scott, S., Simpson, R. Case Bases Incorporating Scheduling Constraint Dimensions: Experiences in Nurse Scheduling, In Advances in Case-Based Reasoning (EWCBR98), Springer Verlag Lecture Notes in AI, 1998.

7 Shibutzit. www.shibutzit.com Accessed April 2002

8 Kumar, V. Algorithms for Constraint Satisfaction Problems: A Survey, AI Magazine Vol.13, No.1, pp32-44, 1992.

9 Jaffar, J., maher M. Constraint Logic Programming: A Survey, Journal of Logic Programming, Vol.19, No.20, pp503-582, 1994.

10 Nunez, J., Winstanley, G., Griffiths R. N. A Reluctance-Based Cost Distribution Strategy for Multi-Agent Planning, The International Journal of Applied Intelligence, Special Issue on *Intelligent Adaptive Agents*, Vol.9 pp39-55. Kluwer Academic Publishers, The Netherlands, 1998.

11 Freuder, E.C. Eliminating interchangeable values in constraint satisfaction problems, Proceedings of the 9th National Cnference on Artificial Intelligence (AAAI-91), pp227-233, 1991.

12 Wallace, M., Novello, S., Schimpf, J. ECLiPSe : A Platform for Constraint Logic Programming, IC-Parc, 1997. http://www.icparc.ic.ac.uk/eclipse/reports/eclipse/eclipse.html, Accessed July 2001.

13 Minton, S., Johnston, M. D., Philips A. B., Laird P. Minimizing conflicts: a heuristic repair method for constraint satisfaction and scheduling problems, Artificial Intelligence, Vol. 58., pp 161-205, 1992.

14 Yokoo, M. Weak-commitment Search for Solving Constraint Satisfaction Problems, Proceedings of 12th Nat. Conf. On Artificial Intelligence, WA, USA, pp 313-318, 1994.

# A Contention-Oriented Timeslot Selection Heuristic for School Timetabling

Alvin C. M. KWAN
CITE, The University of Hong Kong
Pokfulam Road
Hong Kong SAR, China
alvin@cite.hku.hk

Ken C. K. CHUNG
A.K. Technology Co.
Flat C, 6/F, Block 5, Site 9
Whampoa Garden, Hunghom
Hong Kong SAR, China
kenchung@geocities.com

Abstract

Direct heuristic is widely used in scheduling applications, e.g., timeslot selection in school timetabling. Timeslot selection concerns which timeslot, among a number of applicable timeslots, be chosen for a yet-to-assign lesson. In this paper, we propose a timeslot selection heuristic based on the notion of timeslot contention among lessons. Due to the generality of the heuristic, it can be applied to other problem domains that involve disequality constraints such as examination timetabling problem. The new heuristic has been studied both analytically and empirically. Experimental results drawn from a set of real timetabling problem instances have shown that the new heuristic outperformed a variant of small-domain-first heuristic in terms of the timetable completion rate despite the similarity in both heuristics' computational load.

## 1 Introduction

Direct heuristic has been employed in scheduling research, in particular, school timetabling, for decades [13, 5]. An area that direct heuristic has been applied in school timetabling is for lesson and timeslot selection. Lesson selection is concerned with which lesson (or lecture) to choose for scheduling next. Timeslot selection concerns to which timeslot that a selected lesson should be scheduled.

In recent years, there is a growing interest in formulating the timetabling problem as a constraint satisfaction or constrained optimization problem [15, 12]. A straightforward formulation for the *school timetabling problem* (STP) that fits the constraint model [14] is to treat lessons (and the relevant resources required such as teachers, teaching venues and classes of students) as variables, the feasible timeslots during which the lessons (and its relevant resources) can be held as the variables' domains, and the corresponding timetabling requirements as constraints. With such a formulation, one may see that lesson and timeslot selection in school timetabling correspond to variable and value selection in constraint satisfaction. In this paper, we adopt such a problem formulation and focus our discussion on a timeslot selection heuristic based on the notion of timeslot contention.

In line with the work of Haralick and Elliott [4], the usual timeslot selection philosophy is to assign a selected lesson to a timeslot that imposes least restriction to the yet-to-assign lessons. The question is how the degree of restriction be measured. In this research, such a degree of restriction is measured according to how intensive those yet-to-assign lessons contend for a timeslot. Based on this notion, we propose a contention-oriented timeslot selection heuristic called *COTS*.

In the next section, a scenario to illustrate the working mechanism of COTS is given. The working mechanism of COTS, detailed with an illustrative example, is given in Section 3. Empirical results of COTS on a set of real STPs are presented in Section 4. The relationship between COTS and some relevant research is discussed in Section 5. Conclusion is given in the last section.

# 2 The Scenario

Suppose all but the following four lessons of a STP (shown in Table 1), which adopts a 3-day timetable, with four periods organized in two 2-period blocks each day, have been successively scheduled onto a master timetable.

**Table 1**. Lessons yet to be scheduled.

| *Lesson ID* | *Class ID* | *Teacher* | *Room* | *Subject* | *Duration (in periods)* |
|---|---|---|---|---|---|
| L1 | 1A | Andrew | 101 | Math | 1 |
| L2 | 1A | Bill | Playground | Phy. Ed. | 1 |
| L3 | 1B | Andrew | Playground | Phy. Ed. | 2 |
| L4 | 1C | Cary | 102 | Math | 1 |

Without loss of generality, we further assume that for each of the above lessons, there exist some infeasible timeslot(s) for the concerned lesson because either at least one of its required resources at those timeslots is taken up by some already scheduled lesson, or the placement of the lesson to those timeslots will cause some constraint violation (e.g., teacher's daily load limit requirement). Feasible timeslots of lessons for L1, L2, L3 and L4 are labeled by their names in Figure 1. The ampersand '&' stands for a conjunction whereas the vertical bar '|' stands for an exclusive or. For instance, both L1 and L4 can be scheduled at Period 2, Day 1 since they contend for no common resources. Either L1 or L2, but not both, can be scheduled at Period 4, Day 2 as they both need Class 1A. Despite the first periods of Days 2 and 3 are free, lesson L3 cannot be scheduled there because the second periods for the days are infeasible for the double-period lesson.

| | Day 1 | Day 2 | Day 3 |
|---|---|---|---|
| Period 1 | L2 | L3 | L3 |
| Period 2 | L1 & L4 | (L1 \| L2) & L4 | L2 & L4 |
| Recess | | | |
| Period 3 | L1 & L4 | - | (L1 \| L2 \| L3) & L4 |
| Period 4 | - | L1 \| L2 | L1 \| L3 |

**Figure 1**. Feasible timeslots for lessons L1, L2, L3 and L4.

# 3 How COTS works

The design of COTS is based on the observation that constrained events need to contend to use a shared pool of feasible resources. Despite a similar idea has been exploited in scheduling research for more than a decade [10], the authors are unaware of any application of the idea in the design of timeslot selection strategy. In the context of school timetabling, COTS estimates the degree of contention of each timeslot (i.e., resource) with respect to the selected lesson (i.e., constrained event). If the selected lesson is an element of a set of concurrent lessons, other elements of the relevant concurrent lesson set are also treated as parts of the selected lesson. The timeslot with the lowest degree of contention should be assigned to the selected lesson.

## 3.1 The Procedure

COTS starts to work after a constrained event is selected to be scheduled next. The COTS procedure, accompanied by an illustrative example based on the STP scenario given in Section 2, is given below.

1. Identify the set of yet-to-assign events that need to use at least one resource required by the selected event, e.g., class of students, rooms or teachers for a STP. For ease of reference, we call such a set of events, which includes the selected event, the relevant event set. (In our STP example, assuming that L1 is chosen to be labeled next, L1, L2 and L3 will be added to the relevant event set because L2 requires Class 1A and L3 requires Andrew as L1 does. L4 is not selected as it shares no common resources with L1.)

2. For each event in the relevant event set, compute the probability that each of its feasible values may be used. A feasible value is a value assignment such that all the resources needed by the constrained event are available. Unless there is some prior knowledge on value preferences, it is assumed that each feasible value has an equal chance of being selected. (In our STP example, the chance that each of the feasible timeslots is selected for Lessons L1, L2 and L3 is described in Figures 2, 3 and 4 respectively.)

| | Day 1 | Day 2 | Day 3 |
|---|---|---|---|
| Period 1 | | | |
| Period 2 | 0.167 (1/6) | 0.167 (1/6) | |
| Recess | | | |
| Period 3 | 0.167 (1/6) | | 0.167 (1/6) |
| Period 4 | | 0.167 (1/6) | 0.167 (1/6) |

**Figure 2.** Chance of each of the six feasible timeslots being selected for the single-period lesson L1.

| | Day 1 | Day 2 | Day 3 |
|---|---|---|---|
| Period 1 | 0.2 (1/5) | | |
| Period 2 | | 0.2 (1/5) | 0.2 (1/5) |
| Recess | | | |
| Period 3 | | | 0.2 (1/5) |
| Period 4 | | 0.2 (1/5) | |

**Figure 3.** Chance of each of the five feasible timeslots being selected for the single-period lesson L2.

| | Day 1 | Day 2 | Day 3 |
|---|---|---|---|
| Period 1 | | 0 | 0 |
| Period 2 | | | |
| Recess | | | |
| Period 3 | | | 1 |
| Period 4 | | | 1 |

**Figure 4.** Chance of the only feasible timeslot being selected for the double-period lesson L3.

3. For each feasible value of the selected event, add up the probability of that value being used by the relevant event set. Note that the resultant value reflects a degree of contention and must not be interpreted as a probability. COTS will assign the feasible value with the smallest resultant value, i.e., the least contended value, to the selected event. (In our example, the degrees of contention for timeslots of L1 are given in Figure 5. Since both Periods 2 and 3 in Day 1 are least contended, one of them is arbitrarily chosen to be assigned to L1. It is important to note that neither of the choices will reduce the numbers of feasible timeslots for L2 and L3. The number of feasible timeslots for L4 will not be affected too as L1 and L4 do not contend for any common resource.)

| | Day 1 | Day 2 | Day 3 |
|---|---|---|---|
| Period 1 | | | |
| Period 2 | 0.167 | 0.367 | |
| Recess | | | |
| Period 3 | 0.167 | | 1.367 |
| Period 4 | | 0.367 | 1.167 |

**Figure 5**. Degree of contention of each feasible timeslot for the single-period lesson L1.

To define the degree of contention more formally, we need to use some notational symbols as presented in Table 2.

**Table 2.** Notational symbols.

| *Symbol* | *Description* |
|---|---|
| $N$ | The number of constrained events (or variables) |
| $M$ | The number of possible resources (or values) for the constrained events (or variables) |
| $E_i$ | A constrained event (or a variable) |
| $E_{ij}$ | A resource (or value) $j$ is assigned to a constrained event (or a variable) $E_i$ |
| $A_{ij}$ | Feasibility of resource (or value) $j$ for $E_i$. $A_{ij}$ = 0 if resource (or value) $j$ is infeasible for $E_i$, otherwise $A_{ij} = 1$. |
| $S_i$ | The set of all feasible resources (or values) for $E_i$ |
| $\|S_i\|$ | The number of feasible resources (or values) for $E_i$ |
| $ES_i$ | The relevant event set with respect to $E_i$ |
| $\|ES_i\|$ | Size of the relevant event set with respect to $E_i$ |
| $C_{ij}$ | Degree of contention of resource $i$ for $E_i$ |

The probability that a resource $j$ is assigned to a constrained event $E_i$ is defined by the following function:

$$\begin{aligned} &Prob(E_{ij}) = 1/|S_i| \quad \text{if } A_{ij} > 0\text{; and} \\ &Prob(E_{ij}) = 0 \quad \text{otherwise.} \end{aligned} \tag{1}$$

The degree of contention for the $j$-th timeslot of the constrained event $E_i$ is

$$C_{ij} = \sum_{i=1}^{|ES_i|} Prob(E_{ij}) \tag{2}$$

In the timetabling example given earlier, $i$ and $j$ correspond to the lesson index and the timeslot index respectively.

## 3.2 Dealing with Multi-period Lessons

So far, the concerned lesson is of one-period long. For a multi-period lesson, the degree of contention for the concerned timeslots is defined to be the product of the lesson length (in periods) and the maximum degree of contention for the concerned timeslots. Suppose L3 is selected to be scheduled next, the degree of contention for its only successive timeslot will be *max*(1.367, 1.167) x 2 = 2.734 where *max* selects the maximum value from its input parameters (see Figure 6). More formally, the degree of contention for an $n$-period lesson starting at the $k$-th timeslot is defined by

$$n \times \max_{j=k}^{k+n-1} C_{ij} \tag{3}$$

| | Day 1 | Day 2 | Day 3 |
|---|---|---|---|
| Period 1 | | 0 | 0 |
| Period 2 | | | |
| Recess | | | |
| Period 3 | | | 1.367 |
| | | | 1.167 |

*Multiply the lesson length to the maximum degree of contention for the concerned timeslots*

**Figure 6**. Degree of contention of each feasible timeslots for the double-period lesson L3.

## 3.3 Dealing with Concurrent Lessons

So far, all concerned lessons are simple. How does COTS work if concurrent lessons (probably due to class splitting) are involved? A beauty of COTS is that concurrent lessons can be dealt with in a similar way as simple lessons except that the selected lesson is now a set of concurrent lessons instead.

Assuming that L1 and L4 are split-and-combined mathematics class for students from 1A and 1C and to be scheduled next, the relevant event set is L1-4 and the set of feasible timeslots for the concurrent lesson is depicted in Figure 7.

| | Day 1 | Day 2 | Day 3 |
|---|---|---|---|
| Period 1 | | | |
| Period 2 | 0.25 (1/4) | 0.25 (1/4) | |
| Recess | | | |
| Period 3 | 0.25 (1/4) | | 0.25 (1/4) |
| Period 4 | | | |

**Figure 7**. Chance of each of the four feasible timeslots being selected for the concurrent lessons L1 and L4.

Since L2 and L3 are elements of the relevant event set (of the concurrent lesson), the degree of contention of each of their feasible timeslots has to be taken into consideration (as indicated in Step 3 of COTS procedure) in the construction of the degree of contention for each feasible timeslot of the concurrent lesson (which is shown in Figure 8).

| | Day 1 | Day 2 | Day 3 |
|---|---|---|---|
| Period 1 | | | |
| Period 2 | 0.25 | 0.45 | |
| Recess | | | |
| Period 3 | 0.25 | | 1.45 |
| Period 4 | | | |

**Figure 8**. Degree of contention of each feasible timeslot for concurrent lessons L1 and L2.

As both Periods 2 and 3 in Day 1 are least contended, either of them can be assigned to the concurrent lessons L1 and L4. Once again, these choices do not induce any removal of feasible timeslots from L2 or L3 in the relevant event set.

## 3.4 A Desirable Property

If an event requires one resource from a resource pool for its scheduling, it is preferable to allot a resource to that event such that the resource is not usable for other events. By doing so, the sizes of the resource pools of other events will not be reduced as a result of the event scheduling. COTS ensures such a desirable property be enforced in its execution.

*Theorem*

For a constraint satisfaction problem (CSP) that involves disequality constraints only, if there exist values in a variable domain such that those values do not appear in the domain of any constraining variable, COTS will always select one of those values when the variable is chosen for labeling.

*Proof*

Suppose there are $n$ values in the effective domain of the variable, the chance that any of the values be selected is $1/n$ according to Step 2 of the COTS procedure. For those values that appear in the domain of any constraining variable, a positive value will be added to $1/n$ as shown in Step 3 of the COTS procedure. Since COTS always picks a value associated with the smallest $C_{ij}$, those values that are not constrained by other variables will have a smaller $C_{ij}$ than the others, and will thus get selected.

*Q.E.D.*

In fact, the previous timetabling example does demonstrate the mentioned property of COTS. Suppose L1 is to be scheduled next. As illustrated in Figure 1, it is obvious that the choice should be either Periods 2 or 3 of Day 1 because both choices will not reduce the number of usable timeslots for other yet-to-assign lessons. In fact, COTS does make the right selection as shown in Figure 5.

## 3.5 Complexity Analysis

First of all, a list is created for the relevant event set of each constraint event and this can be achieved in $O(MN)$ time. By caching those relevant event sets at the beginning, Step 1 of the COT procedure can be completed in constant time. Since the maximum size for each relevant event size is no more than $N$ and the number of resources is $M$, Step 2 can be performed in $O(MN)$ time. As to Step 3, the maximum number of addition operation to be done on each resource is equal to the size of the relevant event set, which is bound by $N$. As there are at most $M$ resources, the time to complete Step 3 is again bound by $O(MN)$. Thus the worst-case complexity of the COTS procedure is $O(MN) + O(1) + O(MN) + O(MN)$, which is equal to $O(MN)$.

# 4 Experiments

## 4.1 Experimental Design

We have implemented COTS and the COTS-based variable ordering strategy in a simple non-backtracking timetabling algorithm that leaves any unscheduled lessons at the end of its execution (see Figure 9), which in fact is part of the initialization procedure of a school timetabling system that we are developing for the Hong Kong Education Department.[1] The algorithm uses no other heuristics or meta-heuristics and this allows us to study the newly proposed heuristic without the need of worrying too much on the potential complication due to interactions between different heuristics.

```
procedure Timetabling()
  // Initialization
  L ← {L1,L2,…,Ln}; // n = no. of lessons
  LS ← ∅;   // LS = set of scheduled lessons
  LU ← ∅;   // LU = set of unscheduled lessons
  // Ti = timetable of lesson Li
  T ← {T1,T2,…,Tn};
  for each Ti ∈ T
    // Ti = set of m feasible timeslots for Li
    Ti ← {TS1,TS2,…,TSm};
  end-for
  // Scheduling process
  while L ≠ ∅
    select Li from L according to some
       lesson selection strategy;
    L ← L - {Li};
    if Ti ≠ ∅
      select TSi ∈ Ti according to some
        timeslot selection strategy;
      Li ← TSi; // assign lesson to timeslot
      LS ← LS + {Li}; // record scheduled lesson
    else
      LU ← LU + {Li}; // record unscheduled lesson
    endif
  end-while
end-procedure
```

**Figure 9.** A simple non-backtracking timetabling algorithm that leaves any unscheduled lessons at the end of its execution

[1] In addition to constraint propagation, the school timetabling system makes use of other techniques including local search and constraint relaxation. Details are omitted here due to space limitation.

We applied the timetabling algorithm, with various lesson and timeslot selection heuristic combinations, to tackle three real school timetabling problem instances. Those test instances were obtained from one grammar primary school, one grammar secondary school and one former pre-vocational secondary school and they are the main school types in Hong Kong. A brief description of those problems is given in Section 4.2.

Two performance indicators, namely the timetable completion rate and the time required, were adopted to evaluate the effectiveness of COTS. The timetabling algorithm is implemented in Java 2 and all experiments were run on a 700MHz Pentium III® processor with 128 megabytes of memory. Four variants of the timetabling algorithm, which differ in the choice of the lesson and timeslot selection heuristics, were implemented and they are shown in Table 3.

**Table 3**. Lesson and timeslot heuristics selected for testing the effectiveness of COTS.

| *Algorithm variant* | *Lesson selection heuristic* | *Timeslot selection heuristic* |
|---|---|---|
| A1 | Random | Best-fit |
| A2 | Random | COTS |
| A3 | K-value | Best-fit |
| A4 | K-value | COTS |

In order to establish a fairer environment for results comparison and analysis, both algorithm variants A1 and A2 selected lessons for timetabling in exactly the same order. Note that K-value heuristic is a variant of small-domain-first heuristic derived for school timetabling. As to the best-fit timeslot selection heuristic, it places a selected lesson to some period block such that the degree of fragmentation in the resultant class timetable is minimized. These two heuristics have been reported to be effective in school timetabling [7]. Note that each of the algorithm variants mentioned in Table 3 was run on each of the three problem instances 10 times and the results (including the time spent and the timetable completion rate) were collected for analysis.

## 4.2 The Problem Instances

Three real school timetabling problem instances were picked to test the proposed heuristics. Those problem instances involve a rather structured timetable in the sense that students are assigned to different classes such that students of the same class are required to take lessons together most of the time. Occasionally, a class may be split into groups to attend different subject lessons.[2] A more complicated situation arises when groups from different classes are asked to attend a subject lesson together whereas other groups from the same classes are asked to attend some other subject lessons at the same time.

[2] A class may also be split into groups to attend concurrent lessons of the same subject in order to improve the teacher-to-student ratio.

The instances involve a number of complicated timetabling requirements such as lessons of some subjects must not be held in the same day for a class and parallel teaching on one (or more subjects) for one (or more classes). A description of the most important 25 timetabling requirements for those schools can be found in [6]. Table 4 gives some basic data reflecting the problem structures and sizes. For ease of reference, the instances are named CHC2, PLK and EDPS respectively. Note that CHC2 and PLK were obtained from two high schools whereas EDPS was obtained from a junior school.

**Table 4.** Structures and sizes of the tested timetabling problem instances

| | *CHC2* | *PLK* | *EDPS* |
|---|---|---|---|
| Timetable structure | 6 days, 8 periods | 5 days, 9 periods | 5 days, 9 periods |
| Period block Pattern | 3-period block – Recess – 2-period block – Lunch – 3-period block | 3-period block – Recess – 3-period block – Lunch – 3-period block | 3-period block – Recess – 2-period block – Recess – 2-period block – Lunch – 2-period block |
| No. of classes | 13 | 15 | 30 |
| No. of teachers | 25 | 34 | 43 |
| No. of rooms | 18 | 29 | 36 |
| No. of lessons | 549 | 594 | 908 |
| No. of multi-period lessons | 151 | 199 | 436 |
| No. of special lessons | 111 | 212 | 93 |

Most of the data shown in Table 4 are self-explanatory. The only remark to make is about special lessons. A special lesson is a lesson that has to be scheduled with at least one other lesson simultaneously. Examples of special lesson are lessons that involve co-teaching by multiple teachers (at the same venue) and lessons (of the same or different subjects) that involve teaching by multiple teachers at different venues. In general, STPs of junior schools like EDPS tend to have less special lessons when compared to STPs of high schools. The existence of special lessons tends to make its corresponding STP more difficult to solve. Thus PLK is expected to be harder to solve than the other two problems, which can be reflected by leaving a larger percentage of lessons remaining unscheduled at the end of the timetabling process. Also note that due to a comparatively large problem size, EDPS is expected to take more time to solve than the other two problems.

Readers are also reminded that the timetabling tasks are hard to accomplish due to the existence of a large number of multi-period lessons in the test instances. Scheduling of multi-period lessons is in general more difficult than that of single-period lessons because multi-period lessons are typically not allowed to be scheduled across a recess or lunch break. When examining the test instances, we found that multi-period lessons occupy more than half of their available timeslots.

Table 5 gives the medium, mean and maximum utilization rates of classes, teachers and rooms for each problem. Note that the utilization rate of a resource is defined as the number of required timeslots divided by the number of available timeslots for that resource. As we understand, those utilization rates given in Table 5 are comparatively higher than the corresponding utilization rates in most other countries.

**Table 5**. Resource utilization of the tested timetabling problem instances

| *Utilization* | *CHC2 (high school)* | *PLK (high school)* | *EDPS (junior school)* |
|---|---|---|---|
| Class (medium) | 100% | 100% | 100% |
| Teacher (medium) | 76% | 78% | 83% |
| Room (medium) | 85% | 67% | 82% |
| Class (mean) | 100% | 100% | 100% |
| Teacher (mean) | 70% | 76% | 81% |
| Room (mean) | 82% | 64% | 79% |
| Class (max.) | 100% | 100% | 100% |
| Teacher (max.) | 79% | 100% | 92% |
| Room (max.) | 94% | 89% | 89% |

Table 5 reflects some typical features of the STPs in Hong Kong schools.

- Class utilization rates are typically 100%, i.e., classes have no free period.
- Both teacher and room utilization rates in junior schools are high and this makes timetabling difficult.
- Teacher utilization rate in junior schools is typically higher than that in secondary schools.
- Room utilization in high schools appears to be lower than that of junior schools. Note that such an observation can be deceiving because high schools tend to have more special classrooms such as laboratories which are not suitable for general teaching. Thus, the room utilization in schools that include a substantial number of technical subjects (like PLK) in their curriculum may appear to be low, but effectively as high as other schools.

Readers are reminded that the effective room utilization rates should be higher than the given figures because of teaching venues like playground cannot be used for general teaching. Furthermore, school timetabling requirements may further reduce the number of feasible timeslots for a teaching venue. For example, in CHC2, no physical education lessons can be held on playground when a music lesson is held in the hall, which is next to the playground. In fact, when those factors are considered, the mean room utilization of CHC2 is around 93%.

## 4.3 Results Analysis

The averaged timetable completion rate and run time (over the ten runs) for executing the algorithm variants given in Table 3 on each problem instance are shown in Table 6.[3] Note that the performance variation of all tested heuristic combinations in individual runs is small.

**Table 6**. Averaged performance of different heuristic combinations on the tested problem instances

| *Heuristic combination* | | | *Averaged timetable completion* | | | *Averaged run time (in seconds)* | | |
|---|---|---|---|---|---|---|---|---|
| *Code* | *Lesson* | *Timeslot* | *CHC2* | *PLK* | *EDPS* | *CHC2* | *PLK* | *EDPS* |
| A1 | Random | Best-fit | 88.59% | 81.75% | 81.92% | 27 | 24 | 33 |
| A2 | Random | COTS | 93.43% | 89.33% | 91.24% | 29 | 24 | 31 |
| A3 | K-value | Best-fit | 96.23% | 93.83% | 96.61% | 27 | 27 | 32 |
| A4 | K-value | COTS | 96.97% | 95.12% | 97.8% | 27 | 24 | 31 |

By comparing the performance of heuristic combinations A1 and A2, it is clear that without the aid of any lesson selection heuristic, COTS outperforms the best-fit timeslot selection heuristic significantly (5-10% improvement in timetable completion dependent on the problem instance selected) without increasing the computational effort. In practical timetabling, lesson selection heuristics are always used. Thus we applied the K-value heuristic, a variant of small-domain-first heuristic, as the lesson selection heuristic and reran the experiments using the best-fit (i.e., heuristic combination A3) and COT (i.e., heuristic combination A4) for timeslot selection again. The edge of COTS over the best-fit heuristic is still clear, with an improvement of 0.7% to 1.3% for the tested problems. Although the figures appear to be small, it is very significant from the timetabling viewpoint because it is well known that placing lessons onto a nearly full timetable is hard.

# 5 Discussion

A value selection strategy based on the notion of least-restrictive-first is used to tackle an instance of examination timetabling problem in [3]. Unfortunately, the strategy is rather problem specific and cannot be extended to other examination timetabling problems, not to say other timetabling problems. Although COTS was originally derived for school timetabling problem, the heuristic is rather generic and can be applied to any CSP that involves disequality constraints.

In [8], a random timeslot selection approach is adopted. A benefit of this approach is that instances of a subject lesson tend to be distributed across a class timetable more evenly. A rule-based timeslot selection mechanism that aims at reducing class timetable timeslot fragmentation is proposed in [7]. Their mechanism also adopts a random factor to cope with the spreading constraint. Unlike the aforesaid research, COTS does not address the issue of spreading in its design. We purposely leave that out in COTS design because we believe that the

[3] Readers are reminded that the algorithm is only part of the initialization procedure of a sophisticated school timetabling system, which does tackle all test instances successfully.

spreading requirement should be modeled as an explicit constraint rather than an implicit requirement in the design of a timeslot selection strategy. Furthermore, this allows COTS to be used for solving CSPs with no spreading requirement.

A contention-oriented heuristic worth mentioning is the ORR heuristic, which is designed for constraint-directed job-shop scheduling [10]. In fact, the underlying ideas of COTS and ORR are similar. They are devised based on the observation that some variables related by a disequality compete to be assigned to the same value. Both heuristics estimate the degree of contention for a value by finding a probabilistic estimate of each variable's individual demand for the value. Having said that, COTS is devised for value ordering whereas ORR is made for variable ordering. Furthermore, ORR considers a single resource for scheduling an activity of a job whereas COTS concerns multiple resources (e.g., class, teacher and room) in its operation.

An interesting property of COTS is that in variable labeling, if applicable, it always selects a value that is unusable for any constraining variable. Alternative ways to achieve a similar effect is to delay the labeling of such a kind of under-constrained variables [16, 17].

Another widely adopted value selection heuristic is the min-conflict heuristic [9]. An example use of the heuristic in course timetabling is described in [12].[4] The essence of the min-conflict heuristic is to choose a value for a variable such that the number of violated constraints for that variable assignment is minimized. Min-conflict is typically used with a complete but inconsistent solution whereas COTS is employed with a partial but consistent solution. While min-conflict minimizes the number of constraint violations, COTS minimizes the degree of contention for values among unlabelled variables. Apparently, the sort of contention reasoning adopted by min-conflict appears to perform at a coarser level than that of COTS.

# 6 Conclusion

The benefit of adopting sophisticated heuristics in constraint directed scheduling is demonstrated in [10, 2, 1]. We have demonstrated with cogent evidence that the same notion is applicable in school timetabling too.

Since the working of COTS relies on a reasonable estimation of the number of remaining feasible timeslot(s) for the yet-to-assign lessons, we conjecture that a search method that imposes a higher degree of local consistency would facilitate the working of COTS better. Further experiments are needed to verify this conjecture. However, care must be exercised in the experimental design in order to distinguish the potential performance gain due to the higher consistency algorithm from the gain due to the better performance of COTS.

In this research, we only exploit the notion of contention in timeslot selection in school timetabling. However, the same notion should also be applicable in

---

[4] Unlike many other research, Scharef applies min-conflict heuristic in a local search on a partial solution instead of all variables when a deadend is met.

value ordering that involves variables related by a disequality competing to be assigned to the same value, e.g., other types of timetabling problem and variants of graph coloring problem. We believe that COTS may be useful in the design of variable ordering strategies and a related study is undergoing. Another interesting area that worth investigating is whether COTS can enhance local search that generates complete but inconsistent solution in its course of problem solving.

# References

[1] Beck, J.C. Heuristics for scheduling with inventory. *Scheduling*, 5:43-69, 2002.

[2] Beck, J.C., Davenport, A.J., Sitarski, E.M. & Fox, M.S. Texture-based heuristics for scheduling revisited. In: *Proceedings of the National Conference on Artificial Intelligence (AAAI)*, 241-248, 1997.

[3] David, P. A constraint-based approach for examination timetabling using local repair techniques. In: Burke, E., Ross, P. (Eds.), *Practice and Theory of Automated Timetabling II*, Lecture Notes in Computer Science, vol. 1408. Springer, 169-186, 1997.

[4] Haralick, R.M. & Elliott, G.L. Increasing tree search efficiency for constraint satisfaction problems. *Artificial Intelligence*, 14: 263-313, 1980.

[5] Junginger, W. Timetabling in Germany – a survey. *Interfaces*, 16: 66-74, 1986.

[6] Kwan, A.C.M., Chung, K.C.K. & Yip, K.K.K. Data Modeling for School Timetabling - A Case Study. In: *Proceedings of the 5th IASTED International Conference on Computers and Advanced Technology in Education*, 211-215, 2002.

[7] Kwan, A.C.M. & Lam, H.L. Efficient heuristics for high school timetabling in Hong Kong. In: *Proceedings of the ICSA 8th International Conference on Intelligent Systems*, 155-160, June 1999.

[8] Lajos, G. Complete university modular timetabling using constraint logic programming. In: Burke, E., Ross, P. (Eds.), *Practice and Theory of Automated Timetabling*, Lecture Notes in Computer Science, vol. 1153. Springer, 146-161, 1995.

[9] Minton, S., Johnston, M.D., Philips, A.B. & Laird, P. (1992) Minimizing conflicts: a heuristic repair method for constraint satisfaction and scheduling problems. *Artificial Intelligence,* 58: 161-205.

[10] Sadeh, N. *Lookahead techniques for micro-opportunistic job-shop scheduling*. PhD thesis, Carnegie-Mellon University. CMU-CS-91-102, 1991.

[11] Schaerf, A. A survey of automated timetabling. *Artificial Intelligence Review*, 13 (2): 87-127, 1999.

[12] Schaerf, A. Combining local search and look-ahead for scheduling and constraint satisfaction problems. In: *Proceedings of the International Joint Conference on Artificial Intelligence*, 1254-1259, 1997.

[13] Schmidt, G. & Strohlein, T. Timetabling construction – an annotated bibliography. *The Computer Journal*, 23(4): 307-316, 1979.

[14] Tsang, E. *Foundations of constraint satisfaction.* Academic Press, 1993.

[15] Yoshikawa, M., Kaneko, K., Nomura, Y. & Watanabe, M. A constraint-based approach to high-school timetabling problems: a case study. In: *Proceedings of the 12th National Conference on Artificial Intelligence (AAAI-94)*, 1111-1116, 1994.

[16] Choueiry, B.Y. & Faltings, B. A decomposition heuristic for resource allocation. In: *Proceedings of the 11th European Conference on Artificial Intelligence*, 585-589, 1994.

[17] Meisels, A. & Ovadia, E. Assigning resources to constrained activities. In: Burke, E., Erben, W. (Eds.), *Practice and Theory of Automated Timetabling III*, Lecture Notes in Computer Science, vol. 2079. Springer, 213-223, 2001.

# CSP - There is more than one way to model it

Gerrit Renker, Hatem Ahriz and Ines Arana

School of Computing, The Robert Gordon University
Aberdeen, Scotland, UK.

**Abstract**

In this paper, we present an approach for conceptual modelling of constraint satisfaction problems (CSP). The main objective is to achieve a similarly high degree of modelling support for constraint problems as it is already available in other disciplines. The approach uses diagrams as operational basis for the development of CSP models. To facilitate a broader scope, the use of available mainstream modelling languages is adapted. In particular, the structural aspects of the problem are visually expressed in UML, complemented by a textual representation of relations and constraints in OCL. A case study illustrates the expositions and deployment of the approach.

## 1 Introduction

Conceptual models are widely used for problem analysis, abstracting complicated and unwieldly reality into compact and tangible form. The strength of visual models in particular lies in the ability to represent the structure of complex data in a terse and condensed fashion [12]. Conceptual models allow the analysing expert to gain a better understanding of the problem requirements. Visual models are a useful tool to discuss and structure concepts among several developers and to communicate this knowledge to even non-domain experts in an understandable form.

Constraint-based reasoning has successfully been used to solve problems throughout a wide diversity of domains and industrial applications [15]. As a result of more than 30 years of research, this discipline is well defined and understood, and a variety of efficient solving methods does exist. Although constraint problems can already be expressed in a variety of (dedicated) programming languages, coding normally requires specialized expert knowledge. Other computing disciplines like database or software design have been benefiting from conceptual modelling in the form of analysis and design methodologies with a wide range of (visual) tool support for a long while. For applications of constraints however, we do not find the same degree of support for modelling and design in terms of tools, notations and methodologies.

We have been comparing modelling constructs in semantic data modelling, knowledge engineering and formal software specification. Analyzing the commonalities of these approaches with respect to their usefulness for constraint problems has enabled us to formulate a minimal set of requirements for constraint modelling. This has resulted in the modelling approach taken in the RECOP (*REpresenting COnstraint Problems*) project. The main objective of this approach is to achieve a comparable degree of modelling support for the (re-) formulation of CSPs, as it is already available for the analysis and design of databases and general software. As a secondary goal, we aim at a suitable re-use of broadly and publicly available modelling standards, to facilitate a broader scope of applicability.

The outline of the paper is as follows. Section 2 presents the results of our analysis to isolate useful constructs for constraint modelling. In section 3, we present our integrated modelling approach and give reasons for the underlying design decisions. The use of the approach illustrated by a case study in section 4. We relate to existing work in section 5 and conclude in section 6.

# 2 Requirements of Constraint Modelling

In this section, we analyze the common tasks in setting up a constraint problem and point out the constructs which have shown to be useful for modelling. A discussion of existing modelling approaches for constraints follows in section 5.

## 2.1 Constraint acquisition

Initially, a problem description may often be ambiguous and appear informally in natural language. Eventually, a machine-interpretable implementation has to be unambiguous and solve precisely what has been stated as initial problem. The modelling process can thus be viewed as working on a concept at various levels of abstraction and detail. The conceptual model helps to record knowledge gained during the analysis. Following this reasoning, the precise extent and definition of *constraints* appearing in a problem may initially be unclear to a developer who solves a CSP, or develops an application with constraint-based reasoning. Constraints have to be identified and defined during the design. This cognitive process is understood as *constraint acquisition* and forms a branch of current constraint research [24].

## 2.2 Dynamic versus static CSPs

CSPs can be distinguished according to the degree of dynamic change involved. Purely static CSPs remain unchanged over the lifetime, and so are associated models. The other extreme are purely dynamic CSPs, in which all involved constraints are potentially subject to change. Here, a model can at best be used to reflect the changes. All other cases involve at least a core set of static constraints for which a model can be built. Depending on the individual case, work can be done either with the core model, or the model can be updated whenever changes (e.g. constraint addition) become apparent.

## 2.3 Common modelling tasks

The process of formulating a CSP so that the search space is minimized and possible symmetries are broken is similar in concept to the design of a relational database, in which the objective is to minimize the amount of unnecessary links and redundant information stored in tables. In relational database design, this is typically achieved via normalisation [19]. Similar, but less standardised, guidelines for the design of CSPs can be found throughout the literature, e.g. in [20]. This section covers only a selection of the better known modelling techniques. Not specific to the modelling of CSPs is the often used approach of dividing large, complex problems into easier solvable subproblems. More important is the problem of selecting the right representation (model) [32, 20, 16, 22], as using the right model can significantly reduce search effort. By detecting and purposefully breaking *symmetries* in a model, further solver effort can be spared. In some situations it may even pay to choose an alternative model of the problem, which exhibits more symmetry that can be broken. Clusters of individual constraints can in many cases be replaced by global constraints such as `alldifferent()`, `atmost()` and the like [20]. Adding *redundant constraints* (which are entailed by the CSP) to the model can further improve solution convergence. A study in [31] has shown that adding entailed constraints can make a problem path consistent prior to solver execution. Finally, a clever exploitation of inheritance (where available) can group sets of behaviourally equivalent constraints into a much reduced number of *class constraints* [25].

## 2.4 Relational basis of a CSP

A constraint is a relation that must hold for one or more variables. It can be expressed in *extensional* form by explicitly stating the (non-) valid tuples, or it can be represented in *intensional* form using a formula. A CSP is commonly defined as follows.

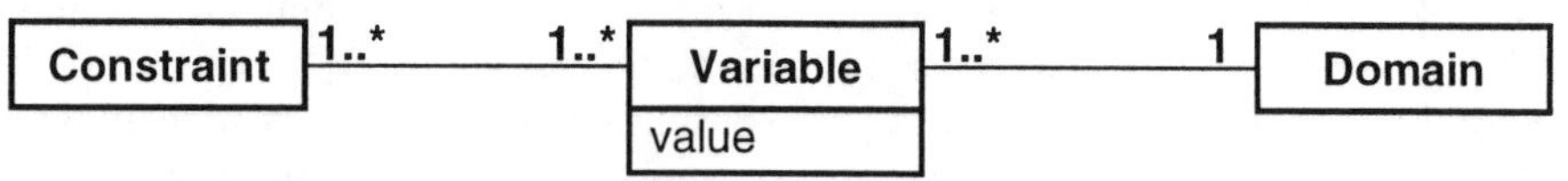


Figure 1: Constraint Satisfaction Problem (CSP)

**Definition 1.** *A constraint satisfaction problem (CSP) is a 3-tuple* $\langle V, D, C\rangle$, *in which* $V = \{x_1, .., x_n\}$ *represents the set of variables* $x_i$ *of the CSP.* $D = \{d_1, .., d_n\}$ *represents the set of all domains in the problem; a bijection from* $D$ *to* $V$ *associates one domain* $d_i$ *with each variable* $x_i$. *The set* $C$ *contains all the constraints* $c_i$ *of the problem, such that* $c_i$ *yields* `true` *if constraint* $c_i$ *is satisfied. A solution* $D_{Sol}$ *to the CSP is a subset of the Cartesian product* $D_{Cart} = d_1\ x\ ..\ x\ d_n$ *such that* $\forall\, c_i \in C:\ c_i = true$.

Figure 1 illustrates this definition in UML [18]; a variable has exactly one domain, but may be associated with multiple constraints.

The procedure that computes the solution(s) to a CSP can in turn be expressed in terms of a relation, as it assigns the subset $D_{Sol} \subseteq D_{Cart}$ to the elements in $V$. If the constraints in $C$ are too restrictive, the problem is over-constrained and $D_{Sol} = \{\}$. Solving a CSP can be expressed in relational algebra [19] in terms of applying the *selection operator* $\sigma$ on $D_{Cart}$, $D_{Sol} = \sigma_F(D_{Cart})$. The logical formula $F$ of the selection operator $\sigma$ comprises the conjunction of all constraints $c_i \in C$. This connection of constraint problems and relational algebra has been pointed out in form of discussing the analogies between solving CSPs and relational databases throughout the literature [8, 34, 28].

We therefore argue that it does make sense to base a modelling paradigm for CSPs on a (visual) expression of relations. Semantic data models, for example, offer a rich variety of notations for categorically different forms of relations [29].

## 2.5 Structural abstraction

The traditional CSP representation (figure 1) is restricted in expressivity and offers limited abstraction capabilities. Considering that a domain is a special form of a unary constraint, the representation in figure 1 can be further reduced. As a result, it leaves this form of CSP representation to comprise only entities with just a single attribute (the variables) and allowing only one type of relationship between the entities (the constraints).

Many real-life problems exhibit a fair degree of texture [30], hence an adequate expression of structure and aggregation is required [25]. Further, entities can have more than a single attribute and relationships (constraints) can be complex and involve several levels of abstraction [7]. Organizing the inherently flat structure of CSPs (fig. 1) into a hierarchy of subtypes and supertypes (ISA hierarchy, [19]) has several advantages. First, it allows a drastic gain in abstraction. Paltrinieri for example uses such a hierarchy for constraint solving and is able to completely express the semantics of 168 constraints of a bridge building CSP by just 7 class constraints [25]. Second, domains with a high inherent degree of structure, such as configuration problems [30, 5], can adequately be modeled. Last, an important benefit of abstraction via ISA-hierarchies lies in the improved facilities for constraint visualisation and debugging. CSPs can conventionally be visualized by constraint graphs, in which variables appear as vertices and constraints as (hyper-) edges. This form of representation does not allow structural abstraction and it does not scale well for problems of a larger size. Current visualisation methods like Goualard's S-boxes [13] are therefore based on a hierarchical restructuring of given source code, effectively arranging the program constraints into an inclusion hierarchy, which is conceptually close to an ISA hierarchy. Rather than re-introducing structure for debugging purposes into a finished program, we argue that it makes more sense to use structure as an integral part of the design process.

# 3 Modelling approach for constraint problems

This section presents the constructs we have found most useful for modelling CSPs. The basis of the approach (which relates to OO analysis) is subsequently introduced and our methodology is presented. This is illustrated by the case study in section 4.

## 3.1 Choosing the constructs

Following the reasoning in section 2.4, we have decided to center modelling around the expression of relations between entities. Experiences in semantic data modelling [29] have shown that using a single type construct of relationships leads to semantic overloading, i.e. several categorically different kinds of relationships have to be represented by the same construct. We have therefore chosen to use several different relationship constructs that were successfully used for modelling in knowledge engineering [6], object-oriented analysis [14, 27, 17] and semantic data models [19, 29]. These are attribute access, association, aggregation and ISA[1] relationships. Attribute relations allow to conceptually build complex entities (types) from simple (atomic) ones. Deployment of attribute and ISA relationships allows to achieve the structural abstraction discussed in section 2.5. As a result of employing these constructs, the developer can work with the model at various levels of detail (cf. section 2.1), information about a given type can be isolated from that about its attributes and subtypes. Aggregation allows a similar abstraction, from the constituent parts to a whole. These basic relationship types correspond to an analytical decomposition of the real world; the colour 'attributed' to a car is conceptually different from its 'associated' driver. Traditionally, research into object-oriented analysis has been enthusiastic in that virtually everything could potentially be modelled using objects (or frames, [6]). Quoting [17, p. 235]: *"An OO way of thinking can be used to develop* any *kind of system – whether or not the system is implemented using OO technology"*.

A central guideline of the RECOP project has been that simple things should be simple to express, whereas complex things should not be prohibited. We have thus rooted our modelling approach on OO concepts, while giving the developer enough freedom to integrate his own systematics. Modelling is a human activity, and there may be as many different approaches (or even methodologies) as there are different kinds of developers. This is confirmed by the sheer multitude of different modelling approaches in database modelling [19], OO analysis [27, 17] and software modelling [14]. The use of the above relationship types represents the intersection of modelling in disparate disciplines and should be applicable to a range of different methodologies. For the graphical notation, we have further chosen to use UML [18], since it has refined modelling notions of the past decade, captures all the above types and permits even further nuances. For instance, associations can be expressed in five ways; association class, binary, $n$-ary, qualified and derived association. In addition to this, UML is widely

[1] in this text, we use ISA and specialization/generalization relationship interchangeably.

available. Many developers are already familiar with UML, and CASE tools exist on virtually every platform. We have also looked at the Alloy modelling language [9], but abandoned the idea, as Alloy does not support attribute relationships and there is currently no support for basic types like integers, real numbers or strings. Also, it is less widely supported as UML.

Regarding the graphic notation, the number of visually expressible relations is naturally limited, as research into new diagrammatic notations has shown [11]. Thus, an accompanying textual notation for logical formulae (as proposed in [25]) is a good complement to the diagrams, whose strength is the terse expression of problem structure. Out of these considerations, we have further found it useful to adopt the Object Constraint Language (OCL) [33] of the UML for our purposes. OCL was initially intended as textual addendum to UML, to describe object behaviour at runtime. We are using and extending OCL for the declarative specification of constraints. The fact that it combines a form of first-order predicate logic with a rich variety of additional expressions has made it interesting to test whether the language is sufficiently expressive for constraint problems. We have achieved very promising results in our case studies and include an example problem for evaluation in section 4.

## 3.2 Constraint Representation

In analogy to the usual definition of a CSP (sec. 2.4), we now define the object-oriented representation that we use in the RECOP project.

**Definition 2.** *An object - oriented CSP (OOCSP) is a CSP in which the variables in $V$ are represented either as classes or as attributes of classes, the constraints $C$ as associations between the elements of $V$ and the domains in $D$ are represented as unary constraints over the elements of $V$. A solution to an OOCSP can be represented as a fully instantiated object graph in which the assignments to the elements in $V$ satisfy both the constraints in $D$ and $C$.*

It is important to point out that the OOCSP representation is primarily used for modelling purposes. It is not imperative to actually implement each entity as an object.

## 3.3 General methodology

Figure 2 illustrates the different modelling stages. Reading from left to right, the aim is to increase the degree of precision, up to the implementation level. Starting with the problem specification, a *conceptual model* is developed, clarifying the requirements of the problem. The definition of entities in OOCSP representation provides the building blocks for the *structural model*, visualized in UML. Graphical notation is well suited to represent the structural aspects, but less effective for precisely documenting the details of a system specification. To this avail, the *algebraic model* is build from the structural one, using a textual OCL representation to resolve ambiguities of the graphical model and

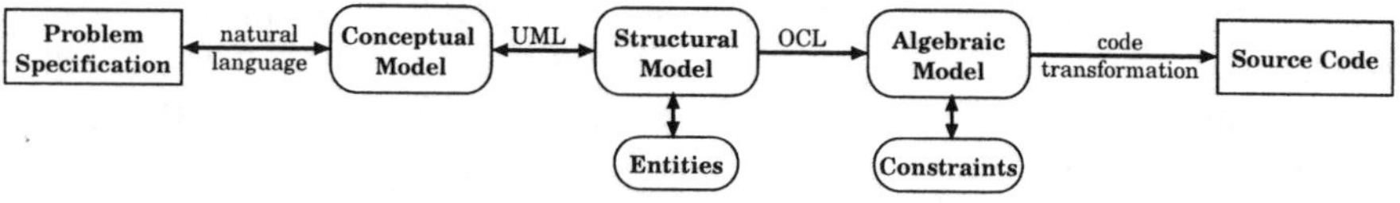


Figure 2: Design Process

to define the constraints. The algebraic model marks the end of the modelling process, having achieved a concise and unambiguous model, whose specification is precise enough to support the implementation.

Summarizing, the general modelling process involves three steps:

1. identification of the main entities in the problem
2. definition of the structural model, visualized in UML
3. definition of the algebraic model, using textual OCL representation

# 4 Case Study

We now illustrate the use of the approach on a particular CSP, the steel mill slab design problem [2, 3]. This problem belongs to a class of difficult problems, in which the structure of the problem is not fully known at the begin of the solving process. The problem is comparable to the popular warehouse location problem [26, 16]. A brief outline of OCL is provided to clarify the expositions.

## 4.1 A Sketch of OCL

The Object Constraint Language (OCL) [33] is fully integrated into the UML standard and is used to define the well-formedness of the UML meta-model as well as for other meta-models within the OMG [23]. The description of the various OCL concepts and their use fills an entire book [33]. Thus, we can only introduce the most prominent concepts here.

OCL allows to further specify associations, in annotated form directly in the diagram or via a separate text file. A separate OCL expression always begins with the class context it refers to. From this context, expressions and navigations throughout the entire diagram are possible, using the role names at association ends or class names with lower case first letter. Apart from the built-in types such as `Integer`, `Real`, `Boolean` and `String`, a rich notation for collection types is provided in OCL by the `Sequence`, `Bag` and `Set` types. Expressions on collection types always relate to the (navigation) context they are stated in, so that the notation remains unambiguous. Among a variety of set-theoretic operations, universal (`forAll`) and existential (`exists`) quantification are supported. To distinguish operations on collections from those on objects, the arrow symbol (`->`) is used in place of the usual dot. All navigations, classes and attributes of the UML model are accessible in OCL, thus allowing to post constraints on any element of the diagram. The built-in types allow modelling in both finite and continuous domains. Additionally, if non-standard domains are required, the type extension mechanism of UML can be used [18, p. 484]. The special `OCLType` class permits access to the meta-level of the model, which allows further modifications and provides room for extensions. The fact that OCL is a typed modelling language greatly simplifies the verification of models.

## 4.2 Problem specification

The problem involves coordinating steel orders with a given system of steel production. A mill produces steel in units of slabs, which are classified by their weight dimension. Only a finite number of weight classes can be produced. Input orders are characterized by the weight of the requested steel and a required route through the steel mill, indicated by a colour name.

<table>
<tr><td>Order</td><td>1</td><td>2</td><td>3</td><td>4</td><td>5</td><td>6</td><td>7</td><td>8</td><td>9</td></tr>
<tr><td>Weight</td><td>2</td><td>3</td><td>1</td><td>1</td><td>1</td><td>1</td><td>1</td><td>2</td><td>1</td></tr>
<tr><td>Colour</td><td>Red</td><td colspan="2">Green</td><td>Blue</td><td colspan="3">Orange</td><td colspan="2">Brown</td></tr>
</table>

Table 1: Instance data for input orders (taken from [2])

The design problem comprises determining number and dimension of steel slabs such that all orders are fulfilled and the total slab capacity is minimised. The task is thus an optimisation problem with an a priori unknown structure of slabs, having as cost function the sum of the allocated slab weights. The following constraints apply:

**C1** orders can not be split between slabs.

**C2** the total weight of orders assigned to a slab must not exceed its capacity.

**C3** the number of different colours per slab is restricted to `maxColours`.

The problem is introduced in [2]. Three slab sizes *(1,3 and 4)* and five colours *(Red, Green, Blue, Orange and Brown)* are available. Table 1 shows the problem instance data for the input orders.

## 4.3 Structural model

The structural model is presented in figure 3. The problem centers around the relation between the sets of orders and slabs, this is reflected in by the two classes `Order` and `Slab`. The third class, `SDP`, is mainly a utility class to contain data relevant to problem instances. Informally, the diagram reads as '*the steel mill slab design problem (SDP) is composed of orders and associated steel slabs*'. The constraint C1 is already encoded as multiplicity constraint: each instance of `Order` is associated with exactly one `Slab` instance.[2]

[2] it can redundantly be expressed using `context Order inv: slab->size() = 1`

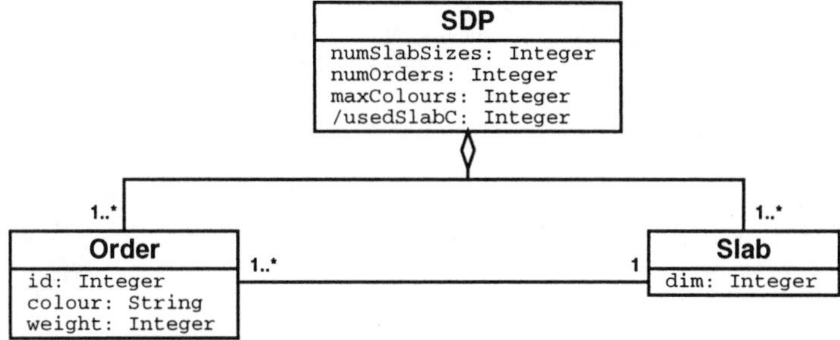


Figure 3: Structural model of the steel mill slab design problem

## 4.4 Constraints

### *4.4.1 Multiplicity Constraints*

The problem instance data affects the multiplicities of several entities, as follows.

```
context SDP inv:
    numOrders = order->size() and
    numSlabSizes = slab.dim->asSet()->size()
```

Note the stacked operation on `Slab`. Since multiple occurrences of slab sizes can be expected, the navigation to `Slab` forms a bag, whose duplicates are eliminated by the `asSet()` conversion [23, p. 6-43]. The `size()` operator is then applied to the resulting set, yielding the number of different slab sizes in the problem.

### *4.4.2 Domain constraints*

Domains are represented as unary constraints. First, the instantiation value for `maxColours` and the domain for the slab (weight) dimension are stated.

```
context SDP inv:
    maxColours = 2

context Slab inv:
    Set{1,3,4}->includes(dim)
context Order inv:
    Set{'Red', 'Green', 'Blue', 'Orange', 'Brown'}->includes(colour)
```

The first expression limits the number of different colours per slab to two. The last two expressions state that the value of the respective attribute is contained in the specified set, which is converse to the mathematical notation (value $\epsilon$ domain). Next are the instantiation values for the `Order` class, effectively translating table 1 into OCL:

```
context Order inv:
    id = 1 implies (weight = 2 and colour = 'Red') and
    id = 2 implies (weight = 3 and colour = 'Green') and
    id = 3 implies (weight = 1 and colour = 'Green') and
    id = 4 implies (weight = 1 and colour = 'Blue') and
    id = 5 implies (weight = 1 and colour = 'Orange') and
    id = 6 implies (weight = 1 and colour = 'Orange') and
```

```
id = 7 implies (weight = 1 and colour = 'Orange') and
id = 8 implies (weight = 2 and colour = 'Brown') and
id = 9 implies (weight = 1 and colour = 'Brown')
```

#### *4.4.3 Main constraints*

As C1 is already encoded as multiplicity constraint in the diagram (figure 3), the capacity (C2) and colour (C3) constraints remain and are encoded as follows.

```
context Slab inv:
    dim >= order.weight->sum()
    and
    order.colour->asSet()->size() <= sDP.maxColours
```

The first expression represents the weight constraint C2 and asserts that the value for `dim` of every `Slab` instance is never below the sum of all associated order weights. The second expression represents C3 and also uses the conversion into a set before counting the number of distinct colours, which is then related to the constant `maxColours` via the navigation to `SDP`.

#### *4.4.4 Additional and implied constraints*

After formulating the essential problem constraints, further constraints can be added to prohibit using flawed problem instance data. As an example, we add the constraint that the constant `maxColours` must not exceed the number of colours available in the problem instance.

```
context SDP inv:
    maxColour <= order.colour->asSet()->size()
```

The main objective behind adding implied constraints is improving solution convergence by adding redundant information (cf. section 2.3). As an example, it can be concluded from C1 that the number of slabs will not exceed the number of orders, which is coded as follows.

```
context SDP inv:
    slab->size() <= numOrders
```

For an in-depth treatment of breaking symmetries and using implied constraints in the steel mill slab design problem, see [2] and in particular [3].

#### *4.4.5 Cost function*

The objective function in this optimisation problem is the consumed total slab capacity, which is stated as derived value `usedSlabC` in figure 3.

```
context SDP inv: -- how to calculate the derived value usedSlabC
    usedSlabC = slab.dim->sum()
```

#### *4.4.6 Solution*

Figure 4 shows a solution, which was derived in [3]. For perspicuity, the instance of SDP and the otherwise resulting 13 aggregation links are left out in the object diagram. The total cost evaluates to `usedSlabC = 13`, which is optimal in that the total weight of the slabs equals the total weight of the orders (cf. table 1).

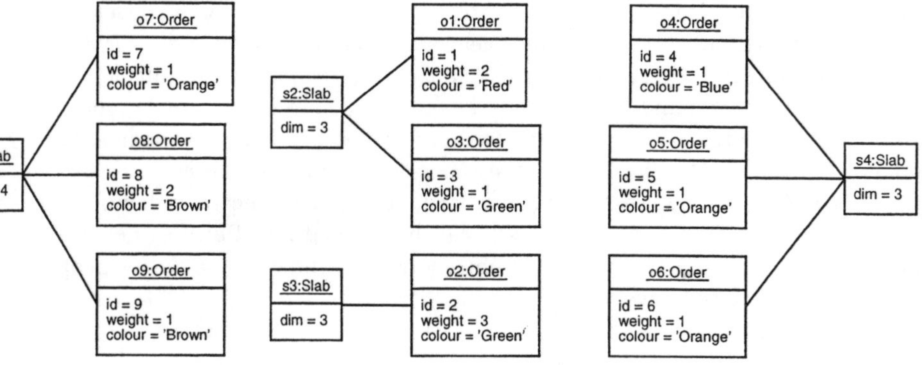


Figure 4: A solution to the example problem (values taken from [3])

# 5 Related Work

A survey on industrial applications of constraints in [15] points out a need for a modelling paradigm in constraint programming and notes that mastering current constraint techniques involves a non-trivial learning period. The evaluation of a questionnaire poll in [1] regarding the needs of constraint programmers shows "*a strong demand for graphical tools*". The recent introduction of the constraint modelling languages EaCL [21] and OPL [26] (with extensions in [10, 28]) have presented a simplified and possibly more user-friendly way of formulating constraint problems. Both are however textual constraint programming languages. Felfernig [5, 4] uses UML diagrams for the construction of configuration knowledge bases. Configuration problems often have highly structured domains and employ (in comparison to CSPs in general) relatively simple constraints. The results in [4] displayed a successful solution for knowledge acquisition and automated generation of the configuration knowledge bases. The principle of the approach lies in the use of a UML extension mechanism, which allows to encode domain-specific knowledge as special instances of UML constructs. These results are very encouraging to continue our work.

To the best of our knowledge, we are currently not aware of any other approach or case studies that adapt available modelling standards like UML and OCL to support work on conceptual modelling in the set-up of general constraint problems.

# 6 Conclusion

In this paper we have presented our UML-based modelling approach for the conception of problems that use constraint-based reasoning. We presented an example problem to study and evaluate its use. We see the main benefits of our approach in the introduction of a more user-friendly paradigm for constraint problems with visual support. It further simplifies the incorporation of constraints into mainstream software engineering, since many developers are already familiar with UML approaches. It can help to exploit constraint-based reasoning in non-AI applications and to avoid the paradigm shift between traditional programming languages and special-purpose constraint languages. Non-constraint programmers can use the models independently of the host language. Models can be shared between CASE tools and over the network using the (XML Metadata Interchange) standard. Last, the concept is helpful for knowledge reuse, as (i) recurring tasks can be banned into libraries or design patterns [14] and (ii) the format of the models is understandable by people other than the initial developer.

# References

[1] A. Aggoun, F. Bueno, M. Carro, and et al. CP Debugging Needs and Tools. In Mariam Kamkar, editor, *Proceedings of AADEBUG '97*. Linköping University Electronic Press, 1997.

[2] Alan M. Frisch, Ian Miguel, and Toby Walsh. Modelling a Steel Mill Slab Design Problem. In Christian Bessiere, editor, *Proceedings of the IJCAI-01 Workshop on Modelling and Solving Problems with Constraints*, pages 39–45, 2001.

[3] Alan M. Frisch, Ian Miguel, and Toby Walsh. Symmetry and Implied Constraints in the Steel Mill Slab Design Problem. In *Proceedings of the CP'01 Workshop on Modelling and Problem Formulation*, pages 8–15, 2001.

[4] Alexander Felfernig, Gerhard Friedrich, and Dietmar Jannach. Generating Product Configuration Knowledge Bases from Precise Domain Extended UML Models. In *Proceedings of the 12th International Conference on Software Engineering and Knowledge Engineering (SEKE'2000), Chicago, Illinois, USA*, pages 284–293, 2000.

[5] Alexander Felfernig, Gerhard Friedrich, and Dietmar Jannach. Conceptual modeling for configuration of mass-customizable products. *Artificial Intelligence in Engineering*, 15(2):165–176, April 2001.

[6] Avelino J. Gonzalez and Douglas D. Dankel. *Engineering of Knowledge-Based Systems*. Prentice-Hall, 1993.

[7] Pierre Berlandier. The Use and Interpretation of Meta Level Constraints. In Miguel Filgueiras and Luis Damas, editors, *Proceedings of the 6th Portuguese Conference on Artificial Intelligence (EPIA '93)*, volume 727 of *Lecture Notes in Computer Science*, pages 271–280. Springer, 1993.

[8] Frans Coenen, Barry Eaglestone, and Mick Ridley. Verification, Validation and Integrity Issues in Expert and Database Systems: Two Perspectives. *Expert Update*, 3(3):26–42, 2000.

[9] Daniel Jackson. Alloy: A Lightweight Object Modelling Notation. Technical report, MIT Laboratory for Computer Science, 2001.

[10] Pierre Flener and Brahim Hnich. The Syntax and Semantics of ESRA. Technical report, Department of Information Science, Uppsala University, Sweden, March 2001.

[11] J. Gil, J. Howse, and S. Kent. Constraint Diagrams: A Step Beyond UML. In *Proceedings of TOOLS USA '99.* IEEE Computer Society Press, 1999.

[12] J. Gil, J. Howse, and S. Kent. Formalizing Spider Diagrams. In *Proceedings of IEEE Symposium on Visual Languages (VL-99)*, pages 130–137. IEEE Computer Society Press, 1999.

[13] Frédéric Goualard and Frédéric Benhamou. A Visualization Tool for Constraint Program Debugging. In *Proceedings of The 14th IEEE International Conference on Automated Software Engineering (ASE-99)*, pages 110–118. IEEE Computer Society, 1999.

[14] Hans van Vliet. *Software Engineering: Principles and Practice.* John Wiley and Sons, 2nd edition, 30 August 2000.

[15] Helmut Simonis. Building Industrial Applications with Constraint Programming. In H. Comon, C. Marché, and R. Treinen, editors, *Constraints in Computational Logics: Theory and Applications*, volume 2002 of *LNCS*, chapter 6, pages 271–309. Springer-Verlag, 2001.

[16] ILOG, France. *Ilog solver 4.4, User's Manual*, 1999.

[17] James J. Odell. *Advanced Object-Oriented Analysis and Design Using UML.* Cambridge University Press, sigs reference library edition, 1998.

[18] James Rumbaugh, Ivar Jacobson, and Grady Booch. *The Unified Modeling Language Reference Manual.* Object Technology Series. Addison-Wesley, 1999.

[19] Jeffrey D. Ullman. *Principles of Database and Knowledge-Base Systems Vol. 1.* Computer Science Press, 1988.

[20] Kim Marriott and Peter J. Stuckey. *Programming with Constraints: An Introduction.* The MIT Press, 1998.

[21] P. Mills, E. Tsang, R. Williams, J. Ford, and J. Borrett. EaCL 1.5: An Easy abstract Constraint optimisation Programming Language. Technical Report CSM-324, University of Essex, 1999.

[22] B. A. Nadel. Representation selection for constraint satisfaction: A case study using n-queens. *IEEE Expert*, 5(3):16–23, June 1990.

[23] OMG. Object Constraint Language Specification. In *OMG Unified Modeling Language Specification, Version 1.4, September 2001*, chapter 6. Object Management Group, Inc., Needham, MA, Internet: http://www.omg.org, 2001.

[24] Barry O'Sullivan, Eugene C. Freuder, and Sarah O'Connell. Interactive Constraint Acquisition. In *Working Notes of the First International Workshop on User-Interaction in Constraint Satisfaction at CP-01*, 2001.

[25] Massimo Paltrinieri. Some Remarks on the Design of Constraint Satisfaction Problems. In Alan Borning, editor, *Second International Workshop on Principles and Practice of Constraint Programming (PPCP-94)*, volume 874 of *LNCS*, pages 299–311. Springer, 1994.

[26] Pascal Van Hentenryck. *The OPL Optimization Programming Language.* The MIT Press, January 1999.

[27] Peter Coad and Edward Yourdon. *Object Oriented Analysis.* Prentice-Hall, 2nd edition, 1991.

[28] Pierre Flener. Towards Relational Modelling of Combinatorial Optimisation Problems. In Christian Bessière, editor, *Proceedings of the IJCAI'01 Workshop on Modelling and Solving Problems with Constraints*, 2001.

[29] Richard Hull and Roger King. Semantic Database Modeling: Survey, Applications, and Research Issues. *ACM Computing Surveys (CSUR)*, 19(3):201 – 260, September 1987.

[30] Daniel Sabin and Eugene C. Freuder. Configuration as Composite Constraint Satisfaction. In George F. Luger, editor, *Proceedings of the (1st) Artificial Intelligence and Manufacturing Research Planning Workshop*, pages 153–161. AAAI Press, 1996.

[31] Barbara M. Smith. How to Solve the Zebra Problem, or Path Consistency the Easy Way. In Bernd Neumann, editor, *Proceedings of the 10th European Conference on Artificial Intelligence (ECAI 92)*, pages 36–37. John Wiley and Sons, Ltd, 1992.

[32] Edward Tsang. *Foundations of Constraint Satisfaction.* Academic Press, 1993.

[33] Jos B. Warmer and Anneke G. Kleppe. *The Object Constraint Language: Precise Modeling with UML.* Addison Wesley, 1999.

[34] Kit ying Hui and Peter M. D. Gray. Developing Finite Domain Constraints - A Data Model Approach. In John W. Lloyd and et al., editors, *Proceedings of the First International Conference on Computational Logic (CL-00)*, volume 1861 of *LNAI*, pages 448–462. Springer, 2000.

# A Polynomial Algorithm for Continuous Non-binary Disjunctive CSPs

Miguel A. Salido, Federico Barber
Departamento de Sistemas Informáticos y Computación,
Universidad Politécnica de Valencia,
46020 Valencia, Spain
{msalido, fbarber}@dsic.upv.es

**Abstract**
Nowadays, many real problems can be modelled as Constraint Satisfaction Problems (CSPs). Some CSPs are considered non-binary disjunctive CSPs. Many researchers study the problems of deciding consistency for *Disjunctive Linear Relations (DLRs)*. In this paper, we propose a new class of constraints called *Extended DLRs* consisting of disjunctions of linear inequalities, linear disequations and non-linear disequations. This new class of constraints extends the class of DLRs. We propose a heuristic algorithm called DPOLYSA that solves Extended DLRs, as a non-binary disjunctive CSP solver. This proposal works on a polyhedron whose vertices are also polyhedra that represent the non-disjunctive problems. We also present a statistical preprocessing step which translates the disjunctive problem into a non-disjunctive and ordered one in each step.

## 1 Introduction

Nowadays, many researchers have studied linear constraints in operational Research (OR), constraint logic programming (CLP) and constraint databases (CBD). Subclasses of linear constraints over the reals have also been studied in temporal reasoning, [2, 7], where the main objectives are to study the consistency of a set of binary temporal constraints, to perform value elimination and to compute the minimal constraints between each pair of variables.

Many real problems can be represented as disjunctive linear relations (DLRs) over the reals [2, 7]. The problem of deciding consistency for an arbitrary set of DLRs is NP-complete [12]. It is very interesting to discover classes of DLRs for which consistency can be decided in PTIME [7].

In [8], Lassez and McAloon studied the class of *generalized linear constraints*, this includes linear inequalities (e.g., $x_1+2x_3-x_4 \leq 4$) and disjunctions of linear disequations (e.g., $3x_1 - 4x_2 - 2x_3 \neq 4 \vee x_1 + 3x_2 - x_4 \neq 6$). They proved that the problem consistency for this class can be solved in polynomial time.

Koubarakis in [7] extends the class of *generalizad linear constraints* to include disjunctions with an unlimited number of disequations and *at most one* inequality per disjunction. (e.g., $3x_1 - 4x_2 - 2x_3 \leq 4 \vee x_1 + 3x_2 - x_4 \neq 6 \vee x_1 + x_3 + x_4 \neq 9$). This class is called *Horn constraints*. He proved that deciding consistency for this class can be done in polynomial time.

In [4], Jonsson and Bäckströn present a new formalism called *Horn Disjunctive Linear Relations (Horn DLRs)* that extends the class of Horn constraints since instead of managing only one inequality per disjunction, Horn DLRs can manage one linear relation of the form $\alpha r \beta$ where $\alpha, \beta$ are linear polynomials and $r \in \{<, \leq, =, \geq, >\}$ per disjunction (e.g., $3x_1 - 2x_3 = 4 \vee x_1 + x_2 - 2x_4 \neq 6 \vee 2x_1 - x_2 + x_3 \neq 5$).

In this paper, we extend DLRs to include disjunctions with an arbitrary number of linear inequalities, linear disequations and non-linear disequations. For example:

$$2x_1 + 3x_2 - x_3 \leq 6 \ \vee \ x_1 + 5x_4 \leq 9 \ \vee \ 2x_1 - x_3 + x_5 \neq 3 \ \vee \ x_2^3 - \sqrt[3]{x_3} \neq 2$$

The resulting class will be called the class of *Extended DLRs*. Moreover, our objective is not only to decide consistency, but also to obtain one or several solutions and to obtain the minimal domain of the variables.

It is well known that these objectives only can be achieved in exponential time. In an attempt to achieve these objectives in polynomial time, we propose an incomplete algorithm called "Disjunctive Polyhedron Search Algorithm" (DPOLYSA) that manages Extended DLRs as a disjunctive non-binary CSP solver. DPOLYSA is a polynomial heuristic algorithm that solves Extended DLRs in most of the times. This algorithm runs a preprocessing step in which the algorithm translates the disjunctive problem into a set of non-disjunctive ones generated by means of a technique based on sampling from finite populations. The set of constraints of each non-disjunctive problem is ordered in ascending order with respect to the number of vertices satisfied in a hypothetical polyhedron. Furthermore, when the problem is reduced to a non-disjunctive one, DPOLYSA applies a non-disjunctive CSP solver called POLYSA [11]. POLYSA manages the non-disjunctive CSP creating a polyhedron by means of the Cartesian Product of some variable domain bounds. This Cartesian Product generates a polyhedron with $n^2$ random vertices in each polyhedron face. Therefore, the computational complexity is $O(n^3)$. DPOLYSA efficiently manages non-binary CSPs with many variables, many disjunctive constraints and very large domains. This proposal overcomes some of the weaknesses of other typical techniques, like *Disjunctive Forward-Checking* and *Disjunctive Real Full Look-ahead*, since its complexity does not change when the domain size and the number of atomic constraints increase.

# 2 Preliminaries

Briefly, a disjunctive constraint satisfaction problem (DCSP) that DPOLYSA manages consists of:

- A set of variables $X = \{x_1, ..., x_n\}$.
- A continuous domain of values $D_i$ for each variable $x_i \in X$.
- A set of disjunctive constraints $C = \{c_1, ..., c_p\}$ restricting the values that the variables can simultaneously take.

A solution to a DCSP is an assignment of a value from its domain to every variable, so that at least one constraint per disjunction is satisfied. The objective in a DCSP may be: to determine whether a solution exists; to find one solution, many or all solutions; to find the minimal variable domains; to find an optimal, or a good solution by means of an objective or multi-objective function defined in terms of certain variables.

## 2.1 Notation and definitions

We will summarize the notation that is used in this paper.

*Generic*: The number of variables in a CSP will be denoted by $n$. The domain of the variable $x_i$ is denoted by $D_i$. The disjunctive constraints are denoted by $c$ with an index, for example, $c_1, c_i, c_k$, and the atomic constraints from a disjunctive constraint $c_i$ are denoted by $c_{ip} : p \in \{1..t\}$. The *arity* of a constraint is the number of variables that the constraint involves, so that a non-binary constraint involves any number of variables. When referring to a non-binary CSP, we mean a CSP where some or all of the constraints have an arity of more than 2. Also, all disjunctive constraints have $t$ atomic constraints and all atomic constraints have the maximum arity $n$.

*Variables*: To represent variables we use $x$ with an index, for example, $x_1, x_i, x_n$.

*Domains*: The continuous domain of the variable $x_i$ is denoted by $D_i = [l_i, u_i]$, so that the domain length of the variable $x_i$ is $d_i = u_i - l_i$.

*Constraints*: Traditionally, constraints are considered *additive*, that is, the order of imposition of constraints does not matter. All that matters is that the conjunction of constraints be satisfied [1]. Our framework internally manages the constraints in an appropriate order with the objective of reducing the temporal and spatial complexity.

Let $X = x_1, ..., x_n$ be a set of real-valued variables. Let $\alpha, \beta$ be linear polynomials (i.e. polynomials of degree one) over $X$. A *linear relation* over $X$ is an expression of the form $\alpha r \beta$ where $r \in \{<, \leq, =, \neq, \geq, >\}$. Particularly, a *linear disequation* over $X$ is an expression of the form $\alpha \neq \beta$ and a *linear equality* over $X$ is an expression of the form $\alpha = \beta$. In accordance with previous definitions, the constraints that we are going to manage are linear relations of the form:

$$Inequalities : \sum_{i=1}^{n} p_i x_i \leq b \tag{1}$$

$$Disequations : \sum_{i=1}^{n} p_i x_i \neq b \tag{2}$$

$$Non-linear\ \ Disequations : F(x) \neq b \tag{3}$$

where $x_i$ are variables ranging over continuous intervals and $F(x)$ is a non-linear function. Equalities can be written as conjunctions of two inequalities, using the above constraints. Similarly, strict inequalities can be written as the conjunction of an inequality and a disequation. Thus, we can manage all possible relations in $\{<, \leq, =, \neq, \geq, >\}$.

These expressions are examples that DPOLYSA can manage:

$(2x_1 - 3x_2 - 5x_3 + x_4 \leq 4)$, $(4x_2^4 + 2x_3 - 2x_5^3 \neq 4)$, $(x_1 + 4x_2 + 5x_3 + 4x_4 < 4)$, $((2x_1 - 3x_2 \leq 4) \vee (x_3 + x_4 \leq 5) \vee (3\sqrt[3]{x_1} + 2x_2^3 - x_4 \neq 5))$

The first and second constraints are managed directly by DPOLYSA, the third constraint is transformed into two constraints:

$(x_1 + 4x_2 + 5x_3 + 4x_4 \leq 4) \wedge (x_1 + 4x_2 + 5x_3 + 4x_4 \neq 4)$

The last constraint is a disjunctive constraint with 3 atomic constraints. Thus, the solution must satisfy one of them.

The following tractable formalisms can be trivially expressed in order to be managed by our proposal DPOLYSA.

**Definition 1** *A Horn constraint [7] is a disjunction $c_i = c_{i_1} \vee c_{i_2} \vee, ..., \vee c_{i_t}$ where each $c_{i_k}, k = 1, ..., t$ is a weak linear inequality or a linear disequation, and the number of inequalities among $c_{i_1}, ..., c_{i_n}$ does not exceed one. If there are no inequalities, then a Horn constraint is called negative. Otherwise it is called positive. Horn constraints of the form $c_{i_1} \vee \cdots \vee c_{i_t}$ with $t \geq 2$ are called disjunctive.*

**Example.** The following are examples of Horn constraints:

$$x_1 + x_2 - 2x_3 \leq 6, x_1 - 3x_3 + x_4 \neq 3,$$
$$2x_1 - x_3 - x_4 \leq 3 \vee 2x_1 - x_2 + x_4 \neq 4 \vee x_3 - 2x_5 + x_6 \neq 8,$$
$$x_1 - x_2 - x_3 \neq 3 \vee -x_1 - 2x_3 - 4x_4 \neq 8,$$

The first and the third constraints are positive, while the second and the fourth are negative. The third and fourth constraints are disjunctive.

**Definition 2** *Let $r \in \{\leq, \geq, \neq\}$. A Koubarakis formula [6] is a formula of either of the two forms: (1) $(x - y)rc$ or (2) $xrc$.*

**Definition 3** *A simple temporal constraint [2] is a formula of the form: $c \leq (x - y) \leq d$.*

**Definition 4** *A simple metric constraint [5] is a formula of the form: $-cr_1(x - y)r_2d$, where $r_1, r_2 \in \{<, \leq\}$.*

**Definition 5** *A CPA/single interval formula [9] is a formula of one of the following two forms: (1) $cr_1(x - y)r_2d$ ; or (2) $xry$, where $r \in \{<, \leq, =, \neq, \geq, >\}$ and $r_1, r_2 \in \{<, \leq\}$.*

**Definition 6** *A TG-II formula [3] is a formula of one of the following forms: (1) $c \leq x \leq d$, (2) $c \leq x - y \leq d$ or (3) $xry$, where $r \in \{<, \leq, =, \neq, \geq, >\}$.*

Following, we present some definitions that are applied in the paper.

**Definition 7** *Given two points $x, y \in R$, a convex combination of $x$ and $y$ is any point of the form $z = \lambda x + (1-\lambda)y$, where $0 \leq \lambda \leq 1$. A set $S \in R$ is convex if and only if it contains all convex combinations of all pairs of points $x, y \in S$.*

**Definition 8** *An Extended DLR is a disjunction $c_i = c_{i_1} \vee c_{i_2} \vee, ..., \vee c_{i_t}$ where each $c_{i_k}, k = 1, ..., t$ is a linear inequality, a linear disequation or a non-linear disequation. A negative Extended DLR is an Extended DLR without inequalities. Otherwise it is called positive. Extended DLRs of the form $c_{i_1} \vee \cdots \vee c_{i_t}$ with $t \geq 2$ are called disjunctive. Each $c_{i_k}$ is called atomic constraint.*

**Example.** The following are examples of Extended DLRs:

$$x_1 + x_2 - 2x_3 \leq 6, x_1 - 3x_3 + x_4 \neq 3,$$
$$2x_1 - x_3 - x_4 \leq 3 \vee 2x_1 - x_2 + x_4 \leq 4 \vee x_3^2 + x_5 + \sqrt[3]{x_6} \neq 12,$$
$$x_1^4 - x_2 - x_3^2 \neq 3 \vee -x_1 - 2x_3^5 - 4x_4 \neq 8,$$

The first and the third constraints are positive while the second and the fourth are negative. The third and four constraints are disjunctive.

**Definition 9** *A continuous CSP whose variables are ranged in non unitary domains, that is, each domain $D_i = [l_i, u_i] : l_i < u_i$, then the CSP is called non-single CSP.*

**Theorem 1** *A non-single CSP with a finite set of negative Extended DLRs is consistent.*

**Proof:**(Proof by Contradiction.) Suppose the CSP is not consistent, that is, there is no point inside the polyhedron generated by the cartesian product of the variable domain bounds:

1.- This polyhedron is a hyperplane $S \subseteq R^{n-1}$ of the entire space $R^n$ and a disequation deletes this hyperplane. However this contradicts the fact that CSP is non-single.

2.- Every point inside the polyhedron is deleted by one or more hyperplanes. These hyperplanes represent the negative disequations. However, there exists an infinite number of points, so an infinite number of disequations is necessary to cover all points $p \subset S$. Again this contradicts the fact that there exists a finite number of disequations.

**corollary** A *non-single CSP* with disjunctive constraints with at least one disequation per disjunction is consistent.

**Proof:** Without loss of generality, we can select a disequation for each disjunctive constraint. The resultant set of constraints is a set of negative constraints. By Theorem 1, this set of constraints is consistent, so the entire problem is consistent.

# 3 Specification of DPOLYSA

DPOLYSA is considered to be a CSP solver that manages Extended DLRs. A general scheme of DPOLYSA is presented in Figure 1. Initially, DPOLYSA runs a preprocessing step in which two algorithms are carried out: the *Constraint Selection Algorithm (CSA)* that selects the non-disjunctive problem that is more likely to be consistent and later the *Constraint Ordering Algorithm (COA)* that classifies the resultant constraints in order to study the more restrictive constraints in first place. Then, using the resultant ordered and non-disjunctive problem, POLYSA [11] carries out the consistency study as a classic CSP solver.

## 3.1 Preprocessing Step

Solving disjunctive constraint problems requires considering an exponential number of non-disjunctive problems. For example, if the problem has disjunctive constraints composed by two atomic constraints, the number of non-disjunctive problems is $2^k$, where $k$ is the number of disjunctive constraints.

Here, we propose CSA that obtains the non-disjunctive problem that is more likely to satisfy the problem. This algorithm can be compared with the sampling from a finite population in which there is a population, and a sample is chosen to represent this population. In this context, the population is the convex hull of all solutions generated by means of the Cartesian Product of variable domain bounds. This convex hull may be represented by a polyhedron with $n$ dimensions and $2^n$ vertices. However, the sample that the heuristic technique chooses is composed by $n^2$ items (vertices of the complete polyhedron)[1]. These items are well distributed in order to represent the entire population.

With the selected sample of items ($n^2$), CSA studies how many items $v_{ij}$ : $v_{ij} \leq n^2$ satisfy each atomic constraint $c_{ij}$ . Thus, each atomic constraint is labelled $c_{ij}(p_{ij})$, where $p_{ij} = v_{ij}/n^2$ represents the probability that $c_{ij}$ satisfies the entire problem. Thus, CSA classifies the atomic constraints in decreasing order and selects the atomic constraint with the highest $p_{ij}$ for each disjunctive constraint.

As we remarked in the preliminaries, constraints are considered *additive*, that is, the order in which the constraints are studied does not make any difference [1]. However, the constraint ordering algorithm (COA) carries out an internal ordering of the constraints. If some constraints are more restricted than others, these constraints are studied first in order to reduce the resultant problem. Thus, the remaining constraints are more likely to be redundant. However, if the remaining ones are not redundant, they generate less new vertices, so the temporal complexity is significantly reduced.

COA classifies the atomic constraints in ascending order with respect the labels $p_{ij}$. Therefore, the preprocessing step has translated the disjunctive non-binary CSP into a non-disjunctive and ordered CSP in order to be studied by the CSP solver.

**Example:** Let's take a problem with three variables ($n = 3$), three disjunctive constraints ($k = 3$) with two atomic constraints per disjunction ($t = 2$):

$$c_1 : c_{11} \vee c_{12}$$

[1] The heuristic selects $n^2$ items if $n > 3$, and $2^n$ items, otherwise

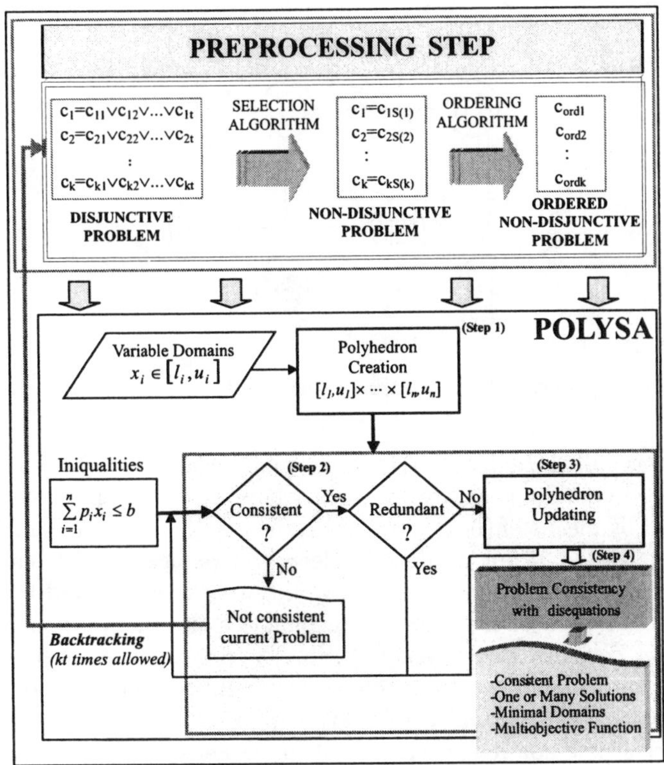


Figure 1: General Scheme of the Disjunctive Polyhedron Search Algorithm

$$c_2 : c_{21} \vee c_{22}$$
$$c_3 : c_{31} \vee c_{32}$$

The algorithm checks how many items (from a given sample: 8 items) satisfy each atomic non-binary constraint and orders them afterwards. Let's assume the following results:

$$v_{11} = 2,\ v_{12} = 6;\ \ v_{21} = 7,\ v_{22} = 4;\ \ v_{31} = 0,\ v_{32} = 7$$

$$p_{11} = 2/8 = 0.25, p_{12} = 0.75, p_{21} = 0.87,\ p_{22} = 0.5, p_{31} = 0, p_{32} = 7/8 = 0.87$$

$$\begin{array}{lcl} c_1 : c_{11}(0.25) \vee c_{12}(0.75) & & c_1 : c_{12}(0.75) \vee c_{11}(0.25) \\ c_2 : c_{21}(0.87) \vee c_{22}(0.50) & \overrightarrow{ordering} & c_2 : c_{21}(0.87) \vee c_{22}(0.50) \\ c_3 : c_{31}(0.00) \vee c_{32}(0.87) & & c_3 : c_{32}(0.87) \vee c_{31}(0.00) \end{array}$$

The selected constraints are: $(c_{12}, c_{21}, c_{32})$, so DPOLYSA will run the corresponding non-disjunctive problem. (See Figure 2)

## 3.2 DPOLYSA: CSP solver

When the preprocessing step has been carried out, DPOLYSA runs the CSP solver that studies the resulting non-disjunctive and ordered problem. This

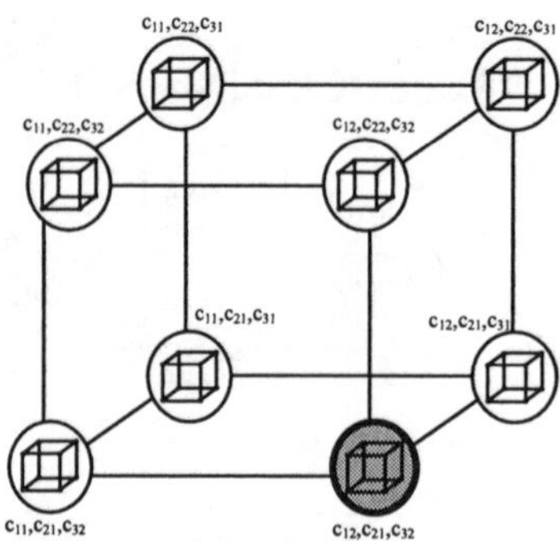


Figure 2: The process of translation process into non-disjunctive problems

CSP solver is called *POLYSA* [11]. The main steps of POLYSA are shown in Figure 1. POLYSA generates an initial polyhedron (step 1) with $2n^3$ vertices created by means of the Cartesian Product of the variable domain bounds ($D_1 \times D_2 \times ... \times D_n$), but randomly selects the vertices so that each polyhedron face maintains $n^2$ vertices that have not ever been selected by any other adjacent face. POLYSA manages the inequalities and disequations in two different steps. For each inequality, POLYSA carries out the consistency check (step 2). If the inequality is non consistent, POLYSA returns 'not consistent current problem' and DPOLYSA backtracks to the preprocessing step in order to select a new non-disjunctive problem. Otherwise, POLYSA determines whether the inequality is not redundant, and updates the polyhedron (step 3), (i.e.) DPOLYSA eliminates the not consistent vertices and creates the new ones. Finally, when all inequalities have been studied, DPOLYSA studies the consistency with the disequations (step 4). Therefore, the solutions to CSP are the all vertices, as well as all the convex combinations between any two vertices that satisfy all disequations.

It must be taken into account that when the current non-disjunctive problem is not consistent, POLYSA finishes its execution and DPOLYSA backtracks to the preprocessing step in order to select the following best set of non-disjunctive constraints. In the worst case, DPOLYSA backtracks $kt$ times, if the problem is not consistent (where $k$ is the number of disjunctive constraints and $t$ is the number of atomic constraints per disjunction). If DPOLYSA did not run a preprocessing step, then it would be necessary to check $t^k$ non-disjunctive problems in order to study all possibilities. However, experimental result show us that $kt$ backtracking steps was enough for us to study correctly 95% of the problems.

Finally, DPOLYSA can obtain some important results such as:

- The problem consistency: if the polyhedron is not empty.
- One or many problem solutions: solutions to CSP are all vertices and all convex combinations between any two vertices satisfying all disequations.

- The minimal variable domains: these domains are updated (reduced) when each inequality is studied.
- The vertex of the polyhedron that minimizes or maximizes some objective or multi-objective function: the objective function solution is an extreme point of the resultant polyhedron.

It must be taken into account that the DPOLYSA might fail due to the fact that the polyhedron generated by the heuristic does not maintain all the vertices of the complete polyhedron.

**Theorem 2** *POLYSA is correct* $\forall n \in N$

**Proof:** POLYSA is correct $\forall n \in N$ because the resulting polyhedron is convex and is a subset of the resulting convex polyhedron obtained by the complete algorithm HSA [10]. So, we can conclude that POLYSA is correct $\forall n \in N$.

**Proposition 3** *For* $n < 12$, *POLYSA is complete*

**Proof:** POLYSA generates $2n^3$ vertices; when $n < 12$, this number is greater than $2^n$. Hence the algorithm is complete since all vertices are covered.

# 4 Analysis of DPOLYSA

DPOLYSA spatial cost is determined by the number of vertices generated. Initially, in the preprocessing step, DPOLYSA studies the consistency of the $n^2$ items with the atomic constraints, where $n$ is the number of variables, so the spatial cost is $O(n^2)$. Then, DPOLYSA generates $2n^3$ vertices. For each inequality (step 2), DPOLYSA might generate $n$ new vertices and eliminate only one. Thus, the number of polyhedron vertices is $2n^3 + k(n-1)$ where $k$ is the number of disjunctive constraints. Therefore, the spatial cost is $O(n^3)$.

The temporal cost can be divided into five steps: Preprocessing step, initialization, consistency check with inequalities, updating and consistency check with disequations. In the preprocessing step, CSA checks the consistency of the sample with each atomic constraint, so the temporal cost is $O(ktn^2)$. The atomic constraint ordering in the disjunctive constraints is carried out in $O(ktlog(t))$. COA only classifies the selected set of $k$ atomic constraints in decreasing order. Thus, the temporal cost of the preprocessing step is $O(ktn^2)$, where $t$ is the maximum number of atomic constraints in a disjunctive constraint. The initialization cost (step 1) is $O(n^3)$ because the algorithm only generates $2n^3$ vertices. For each inequality (step 2), the consistency check cost depends linearly on the number of polyhedron vertices, but not on the variable domains. Thus, the temporal cost is $O(n^3)$. Finally, at the worst case the cost of updating (step 3) and the consistency check with disequations depends, on the number of vertices, that is $O(n^3)$. Thus, the temporal cost is: $O(ktn^2) + O(n^3) + kkt \cdot (O(n^3) + O(n^3)) + O(n^3) \Longrightarrow O(k^2tn^3)$. Note that, in practice, this complexity is smaller because the heuristic technique statistically obtains the most appropriate non-disjunctive problem at the preprocessing step, so it is not necessary to try the $n$ allowed possibilities.

# 5 Evaluation of DPOLYSA

In this section, we compare the performance of DPOLYSA with some of the CSP solvers. We have selected Forward-checking (FC) and Real Full Look-ahead (RFLA)[2] because they are the most appropriate techniques that can manage this CSP typology . We have used a PIII-800 with 256 Mb. of memory and Windows NT operating system.

The random generated problems depended on five parameters $< n, c_{\leq}, c_{\neq}, d, t >$, where $n$ was the number of variables, $c_{\leq}$ the number of disjunctive inequalities, $c_{\neq}$ the number of disequations, $d$ the length of variable domains and '$t$' the number of atomic inequalities per disjunction. To evaluate the behavior of the algorithms with the selected domains, we fixed the domain length to their maximum values in Figures 4, 6 and 7. In Figures 3 and 5, we fixed the maximum bounds of the variable domains. These random domains could be lower. The problems were randomly generated by modifying these parameters. We considered all constraints with non-null coefficients, that is $p_i \neq 0 \; \forall i = 1...n$. Thus, each of the graphs shown sets four of the parameters and varies the other one in order to evaluate the algorithm performance when this parameter increases. We tested 100 test cases for each type of problem and each value of the variable parameter, and we present the mean CPU time for each of the techniques. Five graphs are shown below. (Figures 3, 4, 5, 6, 7) which correspond to the five significant parameters. Each graph summarizes the Mean CPU time for each technique. Here, for unsolved problems in 200 seconds, we assigned a 200-second run-time. Therefore, this graph contains a horizontal asymptote in $time = 200$.

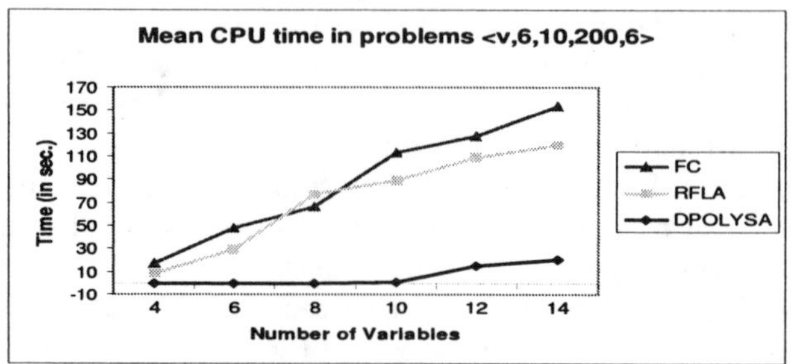


Figure 3: Mean CPU Time when the number of variables increases

In Figure 3, the number of disjunctive inequalities, the number of disequations, the maximum bounds of the variable domains and the number of atomic inequalities were set $< n, 6, 20, 200, 6 >$, and the number of variables was increased from 4 to 14. The variable domains were randomly chosen between

[2]Forward-checking and Real Full Look-ahead were obtained from CON'FLEX, which is a C++ solver that can handle constraint problems with continuous variables and disjunctive constraints. It can be found in: http://www-bia.inra.fr/T/conflex/Logiciels/adressesConflex.html.

$[-200, 200]$, so the variables took different domains: $[l, u] \subseteq [-200, 200]$. The graph shows a global view of the behavior of the algorithms. The mean CPU time in FC and RFLA increased faster than DPOLYSA, which only increased its temporal complexity polynomially. When the unsolved problems were set to time=200, and the others maintained their real time cost, we observed that FC was worse than RFLA. However, DPOLYSA always had a better behavior and was able to solve all problems satisfactorily.

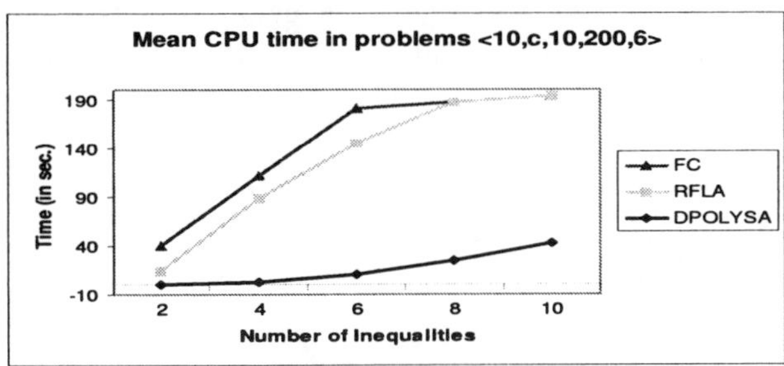


Figure 4: Mean CPU Time when the number of disjunctive inequalities increases

In Figure 4, the number of variables, the number of disequations, the domain length and the number of atomic inequalities were set $< 10, c, 40, 200, 6 >$, and the number of random disjunctive inequalities ranged from 2 to 10. In this case, the domain length was fixed, so that all variable domains were $[-200, 200]$.

The graph shows that the mean CPU times in FC and RFLA increased exponentially and were near the horizontal asymptote for problems with 10 disjunctive inequalities. However, DPOLYSA only increased its temporal complexity polynomially. The number of unsolved problems increased in FC and RFLA much more than in DPOLYSA. Also, the behavior of FC and RFLA was worse in fixed domains than in random domains. This can be seen in Figure 3 when $v = 10$ and Figure 4 when $c = 6$. In both cases the problem is $< 10, 6, 40, 200, 6 >$ and the mean CPU time is different in both graphs.

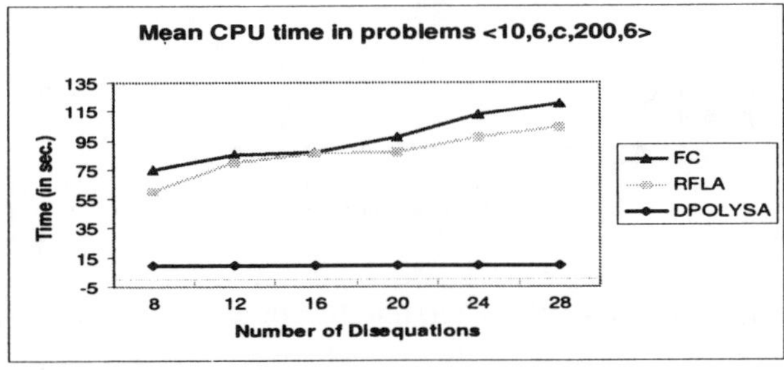


Figure 5: Mean CPU Time when the number of disequations increases

In Figure 5, the number of variables, the number of disjunctive inequalities, the domain length and the number of atomic inequalities were set $< 10, 6, c, 200, 6 >$, and the number of random disequations ranged from 6 to 26. The variable domains were randomly chosen between $[-200, 200]$. The graph shows that the behavior of FC and RFLA got worse when the number of disequations increased. DPOLYSA did not increase its temporal complexity due to the fact that it carried out the consistency check of the disequations in low complexity. The number of unsolved problems was very high for both FC and RFLA, while DPOLYSA had a good behavior. Note that DPOLYSA was proved with an amount of $10^5$ disequations and it solved them only in a few seconds ($< 3$ sc.)

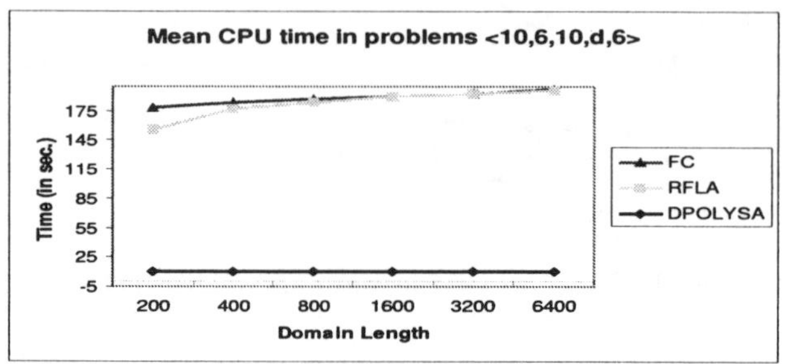


Figure 6: Mean CPU Time when the number of domain length increases

In Figure 6, the number of variables, disjunctive inequalities, disequations and atomic inequalities were set $< 10, 6, 10, d, 6 >$, and the domain length was increased from $[-200, 200]$ to $[-6400, 6400]$.

The graph shows that the behavior of FC and RFLA got worse in all domain length. DPOLYSA had a constant temporal complexity because this complexity is independent from the domain length. The number of unsolved problems was very high for both FC and RFLA, while DPOLYSA had a good behavior.

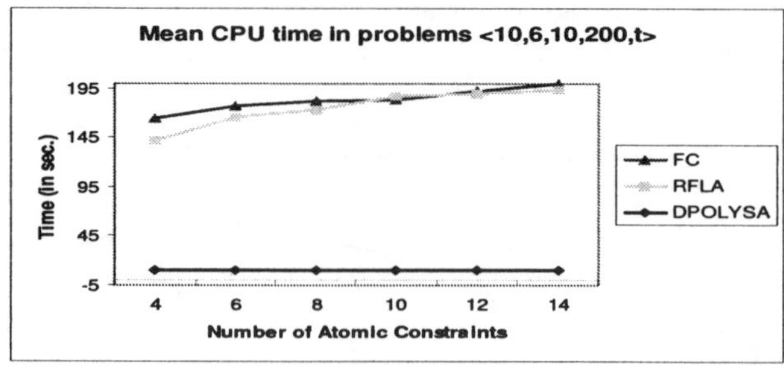


Figure 7: Mean CPU Time when the number of atomic constraints increases

In Figure 7, the number of variables, disjunctive inequalities, disequations, and the domain length were set $< 10, 6, 10, 200, t >$, and the atomic inequalities were increased from 4 to 14. In this case, the domain length was fixed to $[-200, 200]$. To study the behavior of the algorithms when the number of atomic inequalities increased, we chose $t-1$ non-consistent atomic inequalities and only one inequality atomic constraint. That is, if the number of atomic inequalities was 8, the random constraint generator generated 7 non-consistent atomic inequalities and 1 consistent constraint. Thus, we could observe the behavior of the algorithm when the number of atomic inequalities increased. FC and RFLA had worse behavior than DPOLYSA. DPOLYSA makes a preprocessing step in which it selects the most appropriate non-disjunctive problem. Also, this preprocessing step is made in polynomial time, so the temporal cost is very low.

**Remark 1** . *These tests were stopped at 200 seconds because it is the limit in which RFLA and FC had solved most of the problems. Between 200 and 1000 seconds, less than 3% of problems were solved by FC and RFLA.*

We present a comparison between RFLA and FC using the proposed preprocessing step (RFLA with preprocessing and FC with preprocessing) and not using it (RFLA without Preprocessing and FC without Preprocessing) in Table 1. The random generated problems had the following properties: the number of variables, the number of disequations, the variable domain length and the number of atomic inequalities were set $< 5, c, 5, 10, 2 >$ and the number of disjunctive inequalities were increased from 5 to 25. It can be observed that the preprocessing step reduced the number of constraint tests in both algorithms. The difference between FC without preprocessing and FC with preprocessing would increase if the number of atomic constraints were higher than 2.

| | **Number of disjunctive constraints** | | | | |
|---|---|---|---|---|---|
| **Algorithm** | 5 | 10 | 15 | 20 | 25 |
| FC without Preprocessing | 24 | 44 | 64 | 84 | 104 |
| FC with Preprocessing | 14 | 24 | 34 | 44 | 54 |
| RFLA without Preprocessing | 18.2 | 56.1 | 77.8 | 162.6 | 504.1 |
| RFLA with Preprocessing | 10.6 | 38.8 | 41.3 | 85.1 | 262.2 |

Table 1: Average number of constraint tests in problems $< 5, c, 2, 10, 2 >$.

# 6 Conclusions

In this paper, we have extended the class of DLRs to include disjunctions with an arbitrary number of linear inequalities, linear disequations and non-linear disequations. This new class of constraints called *Extended DLRs* subsumes several other classes of constraints. Moreover, our objective is not only to decide consistency, but also to obtain one or several solutions and to obtain the minimal domain of the variables. To achieve this objective, we have proposed an algorithm called DPOLYSA that solves the class of Extended DLRs as a non-binary disjunctive CSP solver. This proposal carries out two preprocessing algorithms. CSA translates the disjunctive problem into a non-disjunctive one and COA classifies the atomic constraints in an appropriate order. Then, POLYSA runs the resulting non-disjunctive problem.

# References


[1] R. Bartk, 'Constraint programming: In pursuit of the holy grail', *in Proceedings of WDS99 (invited lecture), Prague, June*, (1999).

[2] R. Dechter, I. Meiri, and J. Pearl, 'Temporal constraint network', *Artificial Intelligence*, **49**, 61–95, (1991).

[3] A. Gerevini, L. Schubert, and S. Schaeffer, 'Temporal reasoning in time graph i-ii', *SIGART Bull 4*, **3**, 21–25, (1993).

[4] P. Jonsson and Backstrom C., 'A linear programming approach to temporal reasoning', *In Proceedings of AAAI-96*, 1235–241, (1996).

[5] H. Kautz and P. Ladkin, 'Integrating metric and temporal qualitative temporal reasoning', *In Proc. 9th National Conference Artificial Intelligence (AAAI-91)*, 241–246, (1991).

[6] M. Koubarakis, 'Dense time and temporal constraints with ¡¿', *In Proc. 3rd International Conference on Principles of Knowledge Representation and Reasoning (KR-92)*, 24–35, (1992).

[7] M. Koubarakis, 'Tractable disjunction of linear constraints', *In Proc. 2nd International Conference on Principles and Practice of Constraint Programming (CP-96)*, 297–307, (1999).

[8] J.L. Lassez and K. McAloon, 'A canonical form for generalizad linear constraints', *In Advanced Seminar on Foundations of Innovative Software Development*, 19–27, (1989).

[9] I. Meiri, 'Combining qualitative and quantitative constraints in temporal reasoning', *Artificial Intelligence*, **87**, 343–385, (1996).

[10] M.A. Salido and F. Barber, 'An incremental and non-binary CSP solver: The Hyperpolyhedron Search Algorithm', *In Proceedings of Constraint Programming (CP-2001), LNCS 2239*, 799–780, (2001).

[11] M.A. Salido and F. Barber, 'POLYSA: A polinomial algorithm for non-binary constraint satisfaction problems with <= and <>', *In Proceeding of EPIA-2001 Worshop on Constraint Satisfaction and Operation Research (CSOR01)*, 99–113, (2001).

[12] E. Sontag, 'Real addition and the polynomial time hierarchy', *Information Processing Letter*, **20**, 115–120, (1985).

# SESSION 5:

# NATURAL LANGUAGE PROCESSING

# Representing Requirements in Natural Language as Concept Lattices

Debbie Richards and Kathrin Boettger
Department of Computing,
Division of Information and Communication Sciences,
Macquarie University, Sydney, Australia
{richards@ics.mq.edu.au}

**Abstract**

We have developed a *viewpoint development* approach to identify and reconcile differences between stakeholder requirements. The initial phase in our approach seeks to provide a formal solution to the problem of converting requirements descriptions in natural language into a computer processable representation. After the group brainstorms the functional requirements in the form of *use cases*, natural language descriptions are entered by individual stakeholders for each alternative viewpoint. LinkGrammar is used by ExtrAns to translate the use case sentences into flat logical forms (FLFs). FLFs are used to create crosstables. Formal Concept Analysis uses the crosstables to develop a graphical representation of the viewpoints and to assist comparison of terms and concepts. We call our approach RECOCASE as we offer a CASE (computer aided software engineering) tool to assist with viewpoint RECOnciliation. This paper focuses on the translation of natural language into crosstables to allow the generation of *concept lattices* and subsequent comparison of viewpoints.

## 1 Overview

Many software projects do not go as expected [2, 13]. One critical part of the software development process is the definition of requirements. *Requirements definition* aims to establish a shared understanding of all stakeholder requirements. *Viewpoint development* has been proposed (e.g. [3, 4, 9]) as one possibilty to gain a more representative, complete and consistent shared understanding. To capture viewpoints we capture use cases in natural language as this approach is becoming well accepted for requirements specification and humans find specification of requirements in natural language more natural and manageable than in a formal representation. However we want to do some reasoning and rerepresentation of the requirements using a computer to allow identification and reconciliation of differences between viewpoints.

We start with brainstorming the main chunks of functionality from the user's point of view in the form of *use cases* [6]. Next, viewpoints of functional requirements are captured from individual stakeholders as they enter natural language descriptions of their requirements for each *use case* and/or *scenario*. LinkGrammar is used by ExtrAns to translate natural language sentences into flat logical forms (FLFs). FLFs are used to create *crosstables.* Formal Concept Analysis (*FCA*) [14, 15] is used to develop a graphical representation of the viewpoints. Apart from the potential benefits of a visual representation and its popularity for modelling object-oriented systems, we were attracted to *FCA* for this task as we wanted to allow users to enter requirements in their own words and then perform comparison of terms and concepts. We then apply the various resolution strategies and operators that are part of our framework to develop a shared conceptual model of the requirements.

We call our approach RECOCASE as we offer a CASE (computer aided software engineering) tool to assist with viewpoint RECOnciliation. Our framework is not discussed in this paper as it was introduced in [10, 11]. This paper focuses on the translation of natural language into crosstables to allow generation of *concept lattices* using *FCA*.

# 2 Introducing the Process and the Foundational Concepts

To translate use cases in natural language into concept lattices we use the following process.

1. Each viewpoint agent enters their use case description into the RECOCASE-tool
2. The sentences are passed to ExtrAns, converted into FLFs and returned
3. The FLFs are processed using RECOCASE-logic to form verb and noun phrases
4. The sentences and phrases become the objects and attributes of a formal concept and represented as a crosstable
5. The crosstable is used by FCA to generate a concept lattice

An introduction to the basic concepts and theories used in this process are given next. Use cases and scenarios are introduced in section 2.1. LinkGrammar and ExtrAns are described in sections 2.2 and 2.3 respectively. *FCA* is described in section 2.4.

## 2.1 The Use Case Concept and the Scenario Concept

Ivar Jacobson was the first who applied the concept of *use cases* to software development as part of his object-oriented software engineering (OOSE) method. Following [6], a *use case* represents a complete course of events in a system from the user's perspective and describes the interaction between the system and an *actor*. An *actor* is a role played in relation to the system and can include an individual, groups, another system or hardware device. Using the terminology of object-oriented software development *scenarios* are instances of *use cases*.

A *scenario* is a concrete, focused and informal description of one possible behaviour of the system interacting with an *actor*. *Scenarios* are formalized into *use cases*.

*Use case* and *scenario* descriptions provide a textual description of such things as *use case* name, *actors*, preconditions, postconditions, trigger, main flow and alternative flows. Our work is primarily concerned with the main flow which is the step-by-step sequence of actions from trigger to achievement of postconditions. The textual description of the main flow is translated into FLFs using Link Grammar and ExtrAns.

## 2.2 LinkGrammar

LinkGrammar is a parser of English based on the link grammar theory. It returns all alternative syntactic dependencies between the words of a sentence. The syntactic structure consists of a set of labeled links connecting pairs of words. To find a syntactic structure LinkGrammar uses a dictionary which contains linking requirements of words. The words of a syntactic structure are connected in such a way, that the links satisfy the linking requirements for each word of the sentence (satisfaction), that the links do not cross (planarity) and that all words form a connected graph (connectivity) [12]. For example LinkGrammar provides the following syntactic structure for the sentence 'The ATM customer inserts the ATM card into the card reader.'

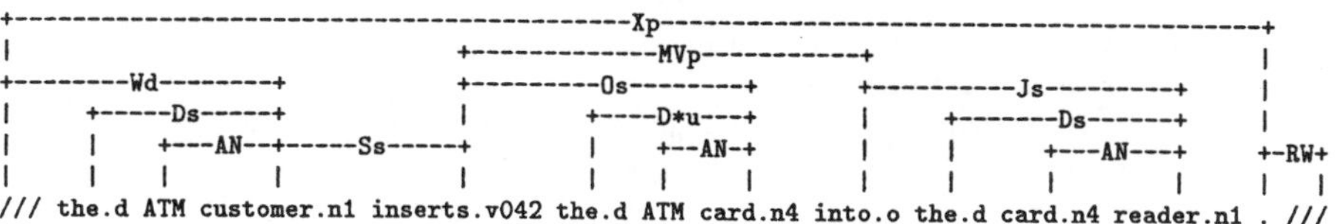

```
+----------------------------------------Xp-----------------------------------------+
|                                    +-------------MVp-----------+                     |
+---------Wd--------+                +---------Os--------+       +----------Js---------+  |
|        +-----Ds-----+              |          +----D*u---+     |      +-------Ds------+  |
|        |       +---AN--+-----Ss-----+          |     +--AN-+    |      |       +---AN---+  +-RW+
|        |       |      |            |          |     |     |    |      |       |        |  |   |
/// the.d ATM customer.n1 inserts.v042 the.d ATM card.n4 into.o the.d card.n4 reader.n1 . ///
```

'S' connects the noun 'customer' to the finite verb 'insert', which is a transitive verb and again connected through 'O' with its object 'card'. 'AN' connects the noun-modifier 'ATM' with the noun 'customer'. The object 'card' is connected also through 'AN' with the noun modifier 'ATM'. 'D' connects determiners to nouns. 'customer', 'card' and 'reader' are in this way conntected with the determiner 'the'. 'MV' connects verbs and adjectives to modifying phrases which follow the verb like adverbs, preprositional phrases and subordinating conjunctions. In this example the verb 'insert' is connected through 'MV' with the preposition 'into', which introduces a prepositional phrase. To the right the preposition 'into' is connected to its object 'reader' through 'J'.

## 2.3 ExtrAns

ExtrAns is an answer extraction system, extracting answers from a collection of technical documents. The documents are first preprocessed by a tokeniser to separate the sentences. In a second step ExtrAns uses LinkGrammar to get the syntactic structures of the document sentences. Then a pruner filters obviously wrong structures using a set of rules for the application words and domains. Since LinkGrammar does not carry out any morphological analysis a lemmatiser generates the lemmas of the inflected word forms. A disambiguator which is trained with data of the application domain is then used to resolve ambiguities. This disambiguator uses statistical knowledge in contrast to syntactic information which are used to resolve pronominal anaphors in a following step. These partially disambiguated dependency structures are used by ExtrAns to create FLFs as semantic representation for the core meaning of each sentence. For processing reasons these FLFs are translated into Prolog facts. The query is also translated into its logical form and converted into a Prolog query which is run against the facts of the sentence of the technical documents to retrieve the answer [8].

FLFs consist of a conjunction of predicates where all variables are existentially closed. consist of a conjunction of predicates. To make this logical form expressive enough, the logical form generator of ExtrAns uses the abstract concepts *object*, *event*, and *property*.

| | |
|---|---|
| object | The predicate 'object(customer,o1,[x1])' is introduced by the noun 'customer' with the meaning that 'o1 is the concept that the object x1 is customer'. The concept 'o1' can then be used in construction with adjectives or in expressions of identity. |
| event | The predicate 'evt(insert,e1,[x1,x2])' is introduced by the verb 'insert' and means that 'e1 is the concept that x1 inserts x2'. The concept 'e1' can then be used to express modification by adverbs, prepositional phrases, etc. |
| property | The predicate 'prop(into,(p1,[e1,x1])' is introduced by the preposition 'into' to describe the concept 'p1' which means 'p1 is the concept that the event e1 is connected with x1 by into'. Properties can also be introduced by adjectives and adverbs. |

These abstract concepts are used in other predicates of the FLFs.

| | |
|---|---|
| compound noun | The predicate 'compound_noun(x1,x2)' connects 'x1' and 'x2' as compound nouns. |
| genitive | The predicate 'genitive(x1,x2)' stands for 'x1's x2'. |
| holds | The predicate 'holds(e1)' means that the event 'e1' actually exists. No information is given in those cases where ExtrAns has not enough information to assume the existence. 'holds' can also be connected with the concepts 'property' and 'object'. |
| if | The predicate 'if(op1,x1,x2)' describes the concept 'op1' as 'x2 if x1'. |
| and | The predicate 'and(op2,[x1,x2])' represents the logical operator 'and' and defines the concept 'op2' as 'x1 and x2'. |
| or | The predicate 'or(op3,[x1,x2])' represents the logical operator 'or' and defines the concept 'op2' as 'x1 or x2'. |
| not | The predicate 'not(op4,x1)' represents the logical operator 'not' and describes the concept 'op4' by 'not x1'. |

### 2.4 Formal Concept Analysis

*Formal Concept Analysis* was founded by Rudolf Wille in 1980 at the TH Darmstadt, Germany. *FCA* is a mathematical approach to data analysis based on the based on the lattice theory of Birkoff [1]. *FCA* is usually used for data analysis tasks to find, structure and display relationships between concepts, which consist of attributes and objects. Thus this method assists development of domain models.

A *formal context* is a triple (G, M, I). G is a set of objects, M a set of attributes and I a binary relation $I \subseteq G \times M$ between objects and attributes. If $m \epsilon M$ is an attribute of $g \epsilon G$ then $(g, m) \epsilon I$ is valid. A *crosstable* is a typical representation of a *formal context* in tabular form. The rows represent the objects and the columns represent the attributes. A cell is marked if the particular object has the corresponding attribute.

A *formal concept* (A,B) of the *formal context* (G, M, I) is defined as a pair of objects $A \subseteq G$ and attributes $B \subseteq M$ with $B := \{m \epsilon M | \forall g \epsilon A : (g, m) \epsilon I\}$ and $A := \{g \epsilon G | \forall m \epsilon B : (g, m) \epsilon I\}$. A natural *subconcept / superconcept* relationship $\leq$ of *formal concepts* can be defined as $(A_1, B_1) \leq (A_2, B_2) \Leftrightarrow A_1 \subseteq A_2$ or, equivalently $(A_1, B_1) \leq (A_2, B_2) \Leftrightarrow B_2 \subseteq B_1$. Thus a *formal concept* $C_1 = (A_1, B_1)$ is a *subconcept* of the *formal concept* $C_2 = (A_2, B_2)$ if $A_1$ is a subset of $A_2$ or $B_1$ is a superset of $B_2$. $C_2$ is called *superconcept* of *formal concept* $C_1$.

A *concept lattice* is an algebraic structure with certain infimum and supremum operations. The set of concepts and their relations can be visualised as a line diagram. It allows the investigation and interpretation of relationships between *concepts*, objects and attributes. The nodes of the graph represent the *concepts*. Two *concepts* $C_1$ and $C_2$ are connected if $C_1 \leq C_2$ and if there is no *concept* $C_3$ with $C_1 \leq C_3 \leq C_2$. Although it is a directed acyclic graph the edges are not provided with arrowheads. Instead the convention holds that the *superconcept* always appears above its *subconcepts*. The top element of the graph is the *concept* $(G, G')$ and the bottom element the *concept* $(M', M)$. To find all attributes belonging to an object, one starts with the node which represents the object, and follows all paths to the top element. In this way one also finds all *superconcepts* of a *concept*. To find all *subconcepts* of a *concept* one follows all paths to the bottom element. Our application of *FCA* to natural language and use cases is novel. In order to apply *FCA* we need to determine the objects and attributes of the *crosstable*. We consider this next.

# 3 FLF Translation into Crosstables

Words and morphemes are the smallest meaningful units in language, but for the most part, humans communicate in phrases and sentences with each other [5]. Therefore this approach considers each sentence as an object. The question is now, what are the attributes of a sentence ?

If RECOCASE creates one attribute for each predicate representing a word of the sentence then the *concept lattice* would not be readable in most cases. As an example the *concept lattice* of the three sentences:
1. 'The customer inserts the card in the ATM.'
2. 'The ATM checks if the card is valid.'
3. 'The ATM gives a prompt for the code to the customer.'
where an attribute is created for each predicate of the FLFs, is given in figure 1.

To make the lattice more readable and assist reconstruction of the sentence we want to group words into phrases. To achieve this we transpose the FLFs into word phrases using what we call RECOCASE-logic. For example the algorithm used to

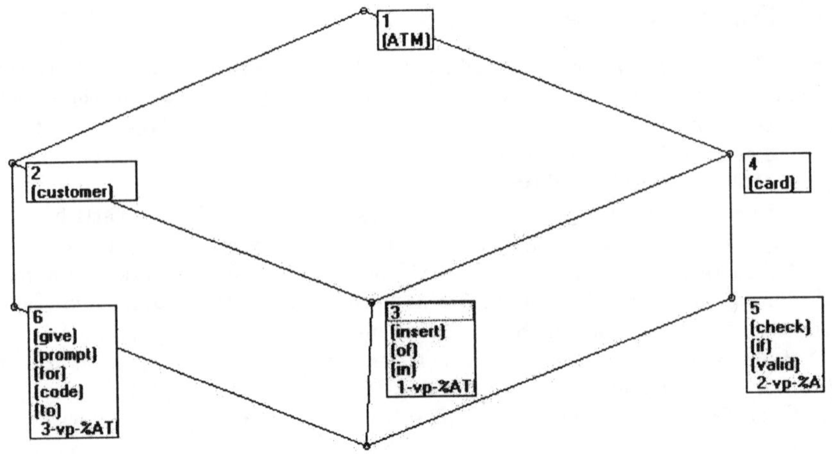


Figure 1: Detailed Representation of Three Simple Natural Language Sentences

Table 1: Crosstable for sentences 1-3

| | 1 | 2 | 3 | 4 | 5 | 6 | 7 | 8 | 9 | 10 |
|---|---|---|---|---|---|---|---|---|---|---|
| s1 | x | x | x | x | | | | | | |
| s2 | | | | | x | x | x | | | |
| s3 | | | | | x | | | x | x | x |

Table 2: Columns for crosstable in Table 1

| | | |
|---|---|---|
| **1** customer | **5** ATM | **9** prompt for code |
| **2** insert | **6** check | **10** to customer |
| **3** card of customer | **7** if valid card | |
| **4** in ATM | **8** give | |

create these word phrases and described in the following part of this section transposes the FLFs of the sentence 'The customer inserts the card in the ATM.' into the phrases 'customer', 'insert', 'card of customer' and 'in ATM'. Thus the sentences/steps of the use case description are the objects and the phrases are the attributes. Table 1 shows the crosstable for sentences 1-3 produced using RECOCASE-logic. Figure 2 shows the *line diagram* based on the crosstable in Table 1. We can see a much clearer structure in figure 2 than we could see for the same sentences in figure 1 which simply took each word individually.

The translation of FLFs into crosstable attributes follows an algorithm which uses graph theory. The algorithm contains two main parts. The first part includes building a graph representing the FLFs of a sentence. The nodes of the graph represent the words of the FLF predicates and the edges represent the relations between them. The relation between words of the predicates is derived from the FLFs. At a coarse level the algorithm, called RECOCASE-logic, is looking for the main event, object or

Table 3: Relations between Words or Word Phrases of the Predicates

| # | nodes | relation between nodes | relation derived from | nodes combined to |
|---|---|---|---|---|
| 1 | A, B | compound_noun(A,B) | compound_noun(A,B) | $A $B |
| 2 | A, B | genitive(A,B) | genitive(A,B) | $A's $B |
| 3 | A, C | prop (A, ...,[C]) | prop (A,B,[C]) | $C $A |
| 4 | A, C | prop (A, ...,[C,...]) | prop (A,B,[C,D]) | $C $A ... |
| 5 | A, D | prop (A,...,[...,D]) | prop (A,B,[C,D]) | $C ... $A |
| 6 | A, C | evt(A,...,[C]) | evt(A,B,[C]) | $C $A |
| 7 | A, C | evt(A,...,[C,...]) | evt(A,B,[C,D]) | $C $A ... |
| 8 | A, D | evt(A,...,[...,D]) | evt(A,B,[C,D]) | ... $A $D |
| 9 | if, A | if(...,B) | if(A,B) | if $B ... |
| 10 | if, B | if(A, ...) | if(A,B) | if ... $A |
| 11 | while, B | while(..., B) | while(A,B) | while $B ... |
| 12 | while, A | while(A, ...) | while(A,B) | while ... $B |
| 13 | until, B | until(..., B) | until(A,B) | until $B |
| 14 | until, A | until(A, ...) | until(A,B) | $A until |
| 15 | A, B | and(A,B) | and(A,B) | $A and $B |
| 16 | A, B | or(A,B) | or(A,B) | $A or $B |
| 17 | not, A | not(A) | not(A) | not $A |

property which is defined by the predicate 'holds'. If the FLF of a sentence does not contain the predicate 'holds', the root 'A' is defined through 'if(A,B)', 'while(A,B)' or 'not(A)' in this sequence. For the main event, object or property a node is created as root. RECOCASE-logic is looking for predicates of the FLF which are connected with the main event, object or property and creates nodes representing the words of the predicates. Table 3 lists possible relations and the predicates which they are derived from. If all predicates, which are connected with the main event, object or property, are investigated each node of the graph is considered in the same way. By this RECOCASE-logic extends the graph until all nodes are considered. The second part includes the reduction of the graph to nodes representing the crosstable attributes. In a certain sequence all edges are considered and if possible the nodes which are connected by these edges combined. Thus RECOCASE-logic reduces the graph. The final nodes represent the crosstable attributes.

The algorithm uses the fact that the FLFs can be converted into a graph where all nodes are connected. This is based on Melcuk's [7] proof of the fact that all words for sentences of most natural languages form a connected graph, which is used by LinkGrammar to find the syntactic structure of a sentence.

In the following section the algorithm is described in pseudocode. A, B, C and D are variables which stand for the words of the FLF predicates or for the created phrases as a result of the reduction of the graph, respectively. $A stands for the content of the variable A. A := $B means that the content of variable B is assigned to the variable A.

The translation from FLF into crosstable representation involves the following steps:

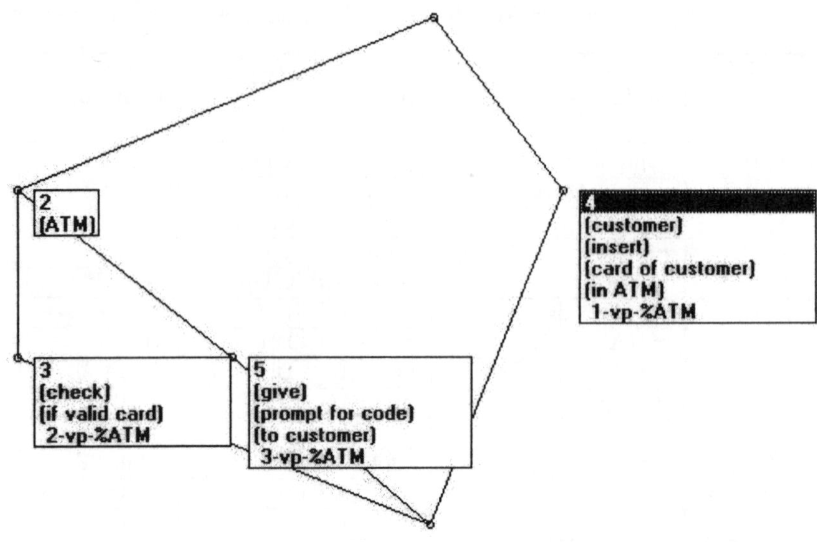


Figure 2: Representation of sentences in RECOCASE

```
for each sentence
  % === build graph

    define empty graph G

    % look for root
    if ('holds(A)' exists in FLF)
      root := $A
    else if ('if(A,B)' exists in FLF)
      root := $A
    else if ('while(A,B)' exists in FLF)
      root := $A
    else if ('not(A)' exists in FLF)
      root := $A

    add root to G
    while (not (all knots of graph G are considered))
      K =  knot of G, which is not considered yet
      while (component C exists, which is connected with K in FLF)
        add C as knot to G
        connect C with K
        mark kind of relation at edge
            % kind of relations: if, while, not, property (prop),
```

```
      %                         object (object),
      %                         event (event), compound noun, genitiv
    mark C as considered

% === create attributes for crosstable

  for all edges
    connect knots of edge in the following way
      % this means to reduce the graph
      for all edges which are of type compound_noun(A,B)
        B := $A + $B

      for all edges which are of type genitive(A,B)
        A := $B $A

      for all edges which are of type not(A)
        A := 'not' + $A

      for all edges which are of type prop (A,B,[C])
        if (not (A is the root and A is an event))
          A := $A + $C
      for all edges which are of type prop (A,B,[C,D]) connecting A and D
        D := $A + $D
      for all edges which are of type prop (A,B,[C,D]) connecting A and C
        if (not (C is the root and C is an event))
          C := $C + $A

      for all edges which are of type evt(A,B,[C])
        if (A is not the root)
          A := $C + $A
      for all edges which are of type evt(A,B,[C,D]) connecting A and D
        if (A is not the root)
          A := $A + $D
      for all edges which are of type evt(A,B,[C,D]) connecting A and C
        if (A is not the root)
          C := $C + $A

      for all edges which are of type if(A,B) connecting if and B
        if := 'if' + $B
      for all edges which are of type if(A,B) connecting A and if
        if (not (A is the root))
          A := $A + 'if'

      for all edges which are of type while(A,B) connecting while and B
        while := 'while' + $B
      for all edges which are of type while(A,B) connecting A and while
        if (not (A is the root))
          A := $A + 'while'

      for all edges which are of type until(A,B) connecting until and B
```

```
    until := 'until' + $B
  for all edges which are of type until(A,B) connecting A and until
    if (not (A is the root))
      A := $A + 'until'

  for all edges which are of type and(A,[B1,B2,...,Bn])
    if (not (A is the root))
      A := $B1 + 'and'
       ...
      A := $Bn
  for all edges which are of type or(A,[B1,B2,...,Bn])
    if (not (A is the root))
      A := $B1 + 'or'
       ...
      A := $Bn

for all knots of G
  create attribute
```

ExtrAns provides the following FLF for the sample sentence 'The ATM customer inserts the ATM card into the card reader.' :

```
holds(e4),
object(customer,o1,[x3])
compound_noun(x2,x3)
object(ATM,o2,[x2])
evt(insert,e4,[x3,x7])
object(card,o3,[x7])
compound_noun(x6,x7)
object(ATM,o2,[x6])
prop(into,(p8,[e4,x11])
object(reader,o5,[x11])
compound_noun(x10,x11)
object(card,o6,[x10])
```

Figure 3 shows the steps involved in creation of the graph for this sample sentence.

Ia) RECOCASE-logic finds 'insert' as main event through the predicates 'holds(e4)' and 'evt(insert,e4,[x3,x7])' and creates the first node e4:'insert', called root or main node of the graph, which is the starting point for all further activities.

Ib) RECOCASE-logic looks for nodes which are directly connected with the root. The predicates 'evt(insert,e4,[**x3**,x7])' and 'object(customer,o1,[**x3**])' give the information that e4:'insert' has to be connected to x3:'customer' by 'evt(e4,...,[x3,...]'. A node x7:'card' has to be connected to the root because of the predicates 'evt(insert,e4, [x3,**x7**])' and 'object(card,o3,[**x7**])' which refers to the relation 'evt(e4,...,[...,x7])'. The predicate 'prop(into,(p8,[e4,x11])' connects a node into:'into' with e4:'insert'. The relation between them is marked as 'prop (into, ...,[e4,...])'.

Ic) RECOCASE-logic considers the node x3:'customer', which has to be connected with a node x2:'ATM' because of 'object(customer,o1,[**x3**])', 'compound_noun(**x2**,**x3**)' and 'object(ATM,o2,[**x2**])'. The relation to the node x3:'customer' is marked as 'compound_noun(x2,x3)'.

Id) RECOCASE-logic considers the node x7:'card', which has to be connected with a node x6:'ATM' because of the predicates 'object(card,o3,[**x7**])', 'compound_noun (**x6**,**x7**)' and 'object(ATM,o2,[**x6**])'. The relation to the node x7:'card' is marked as 'compound_noun(x6,x7)'.

Ie) RECOCASE-logic considers the node into:'into' which has to be connected to a node x11:'reader' because of the predicates 'prop(into,(p8,[e4,**x11**])' and 'object(reader,o5,[**x11**])'. The relation is marked as 'prop (into,...,[...,x11])'.

If) RECOCASE-logic considers the node x11:'reader'. It has to be connected with a node x10:'card' because of the predicates 'object(reader,o5,[**x11**])', 'compound_noun(**x10**,**x11**)' and 'object(card,o6,[**x10**])'. The relation is marked as 'compound_noun(x10,x11)'.

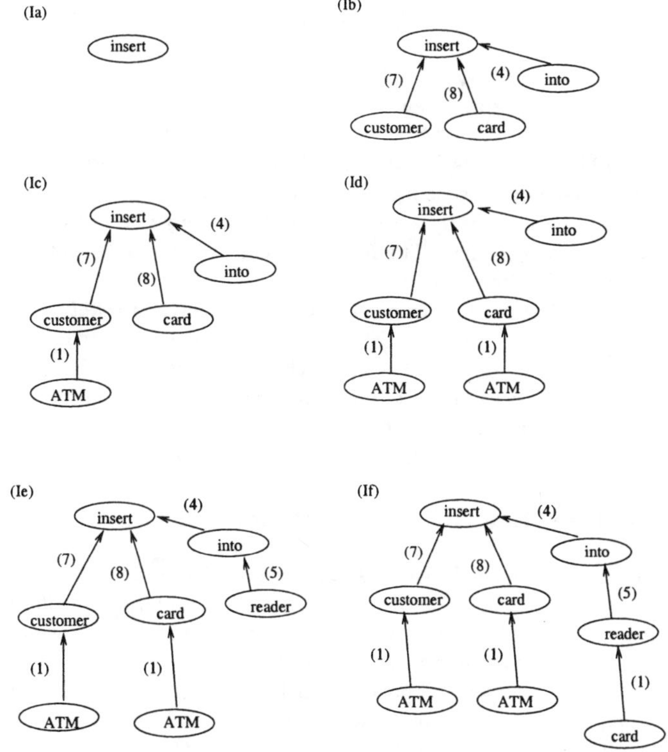


Figure 3: Step of Creation the Graph of the Sentence 'The ATM customer inserts the ATM card into the card reader.'

In a second step RECOCASE-logic reduces the graph to the crosstable attributes. Figure 4 shows the steps involved in the reduction of the graph to crosstable attributes for the sample sentence.

IIa) RECOCASE-logic considers all edges which are of type 'compound_noun(A,B)' and combines the nodes which are connected through these edges to the node B:'A

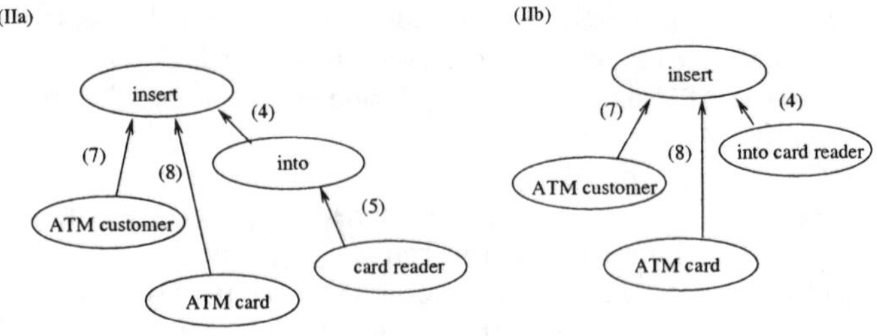


Figure 4: Step of Reducing the Graph of the Sentence 'The ATM customer inserts the ATM card into the card reader.'

B'. Thus the nodes x3:'customer' and x2:'ATM' get combined to x3:'ATM customer', the nodes x7:'card' and x6:'ATM' to x7:'ATM card' and the nodes x10:'card' and x11:'reader' to x11:'card reader'. Since x2:'ATM', x7:'ATM' and x11:'card' are not connected with other nodes these nodes are deleted.

IIb) Following the algorithm the nodes into:'into' and x11:'card reader' get connected to into:'into card reader'. The node x11:'card reader' get deleted because this node is not connected to other nodes.

If all sentences are translated using RECOCASE-logic a *crosstable* can be created. The words or word phrases form the set of attributes where no word or phrase should exist twice. All translated sentences form the set of objects. Viewpoints can be compared by taking the set of objects for each use case description for each viewpoint and generating a combined crosstable and *concept lattice.*

# 4 Conclusion and Future Work

Many approaches to the formalisation of requirements begin with the assumption that requirements already exist in computer processable format such as a tabular or logical representation. We see this assumption as a major impediment to formal approaches becoming accessible to most organisations. While we offer our own viewpoints based approach, we believe the work reported which transforms natural language into a crosstable is beneficial for many other formal requirements engineering techniques.

Only a small amount of the work conducted in the RECOCASE project has been presented in this paper. Other parts of the project include:

- the RECOCASE process model
- the RECOCASE group decision support system approach
- development of the RECOCASE-tool to capture, edit and compare viewpoints
- the development of guidelines for specifying use case descriptions
- the specification of a controlled language to improve translation into FLFs and implementation of verification rules to assist the user in keepng to the controlled language

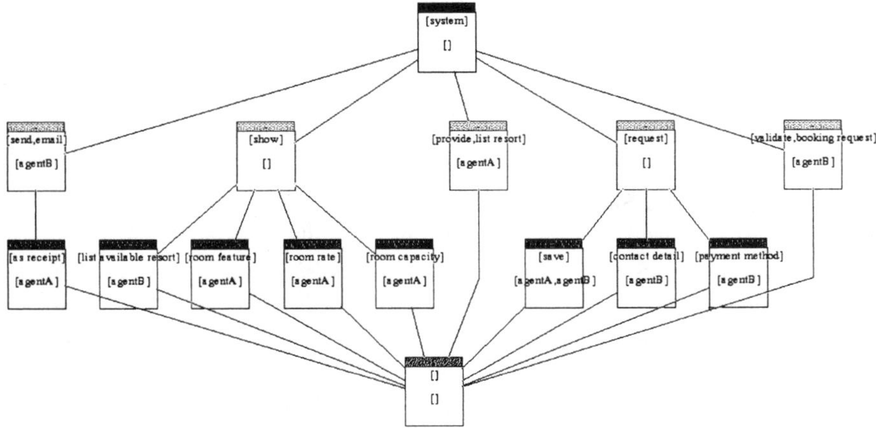


Figure 5: *Concept Lattice* for the Booking Room Use Case based on the sentences using the word 'system' from Agent A and Agent B viewpoints
*To read the diagram start at a bottom node containing the owner of the sentence (agent A and/or agent B). Follow ALL ascending paths to pick up the phrases in the sentence. Nodes with more than one owner represent shared sentences. Nodes which share superconcepts (higher nodes) show shared phrases and may indicate partially shared sentences. A higher node with an owner shown in the node (see far left) shows a sentence subsumed by another sentence, in this case a sentence in another viewpoint.*

We have conducted initial evaluations on the comprehensibility of the line diagram as a way of analysing and comparing use case descriptions. Our study involved 201 second year analysis and design students who answered questions using line diagrams OR the original textual descriptions. Five different line diagrams were considered, four of which included multiple viewpoints in the one diagram. One is shown in Figure 5. Our findings show that the line diagram could be understood accurately by 58% of our subjects after a 5 minute introduction, questions were up to 80% more likely to be correct when using the line diagram as opposed to textual sentences and that 61% of students preferred using the line diagram over sentences to answer the questions. Answering the questions using the diagrams was up to 9.9 times faster than using sentences. We are about to conduct evaluations of the group process. In particular we want to see how quickly a group facilitator can be trained to select features of interest to explore in the diagrams and to lead a project team in application of our resolution strategies. With the results of these evaluations we will revise each aspect of our project. Our ultimate goal is to offer an approach and a tool that provides a rigorous way of capturing a more complete and representative set of user requirements.

# References


[1] Birkhoff, G., (1967)*Lattice Theory*, American Mathematical Society, Providence, Rhode Island

[2] Constantine, L. L. and Lockwood, L. A. D., (1999) *Software for Use : A Practical Guide to the Models and Methods of Usage-Centered Design*, ACM Press

[3] Darke, P. and Shanks, G., (1997) *Managing User Viewpoints in Requirements Definition*, 8th Australasien Conference on Information Systems

[4] Easterbrook, S. and Nuseibeh, B. (1996) *Using Viewpoints for Inconsistency Management* BCSEEE Software Engineering Journal January 1996, 31-43

[5] Fromkin, V., Rodman, R., Collins, P. and Blair, D., (1996) *An introduction to language*, 3th edition, Harcourt Brace & Company, Australia

[6] Jacobson, I., (1992) *Object-Oriented Software Engineering*, Addison-Wesley

[7] Melcuk, I., (1988)*Dependency Syntax: Theory and Practice*, State University of NY Press

[8] Molla, D., Schwitter, R., Hess, M. and Fournier, R., (2000) *Extrans, an answer extraction system* T.A.L special issue on Information Retrieval oriented Natural Language Processing

[9] Mullery, G. P. (1979) *CORE - a method for controlled requirements expression* In Proceedings of the 4th International Conference on Software Engineering (ICSE-4), IEEE Computer Society Press, 126-135.

[10] Richards, D. and Menzies, T., (1998)*Extending the SISYPHUS III Experiment from a Knowledge Engineering to a Requirement Engineering Task*, 11th Workshop on Knowledge Acquisition, Modeling and Management (KAW'98), Banff, Canada, SRDG Pub.,Dept. of Comp. Sci., Uni. of Calgary, Calgary, Canada, Vol 1:SIS-6.

[11] Richards, D. and Zowghi, D., (1999) *Maintaining and Comparing Requirements*, Proc. of the Fourth Australian Conference on Requirement Engineering ACRE'99, Macquarie University, Sydney, 29-30 September,

[12] Sleator, D. D. and Temperley, D., (1991) *Parsing English with a Link Grammar*, Technical Report CMU-CS-91-196, Carnegie Mellon University, School of Computer Science, Pittsburgh, PA

[13] van Vliet, H., (2000)*Software Engineering, Principles and Practice*, John Wiley & Sons Ltd, England,

[14] Wille, R., (1982) *Restructing Lattice Theory: An Approach Based on Hierarchies of Concepts*, Ordered Sets, D. Reichel, Dordrecht, pp. 445-470

[15] Wille, R., (1992)*Concept Lattices and Conceptual Knowledge*, Computers and Mathematics with Applications, 23, pp. 493-522

# Natural Language Understanding Using Generative Dependency Grammar

Stefan Diaconescu
SOFTWIN, Technical Director,
Str. Fabrica de Glucoza Nr. 5, Sect.2, 72246 Bucharest, Romania

Abstract

This document presents a new kind of grammars: the Generative Dependency Grammar (GDG) and GDG with Feature Structure (FS) represented as Attribute Value Tree (AVT). This type of grammars is based on dependency trees (DT) and a generative process. GDG will eliminate some issues of Dependency Grammars DG (for example the missing of phrasal categories) and Generative Grammars GG (the problem of discontinuous structures) and will merge the advantages of the two types of grammar (GG - the representation of phrasal categories; GDG - the handling of discontinuous structures as gaps and non projective constructions). We present the generation process and the unification in GDG. Some properties of AVT and a logical representation of AVT are presented too. GDG is useful in grammar representations for natural language understanding, machine translation and data retrieval.

## 1 Introduction

If we will make a series of approximations that we will consider as satisfying for natural language understanding, we can start in language phenomenon analysis from the following considerations:

*Level 0 of analysis*: We will consider the reality as being partitioned in a discrete set of entities and relations between these entities.

*Level 1 of analysis*: We will consider that the humans build about the reality a vision that consist of entities representations and relations representations. This vision is generally not unique for all the humans. We will name this level the internal level of representation.

*Level 2 of analysis (or linguistic level):* We will consider that the linguistic expression of the representation of the entities and of the relations between the entities is made using entities names (words) and syntactic structures that merge these names in statements (about representations and therefore indirectly about reality). The entities names and the syntactic structures are specific to each natural language.

Let us take an example. We suppose that the "cats eat mice". This is the level 0 that is formed from three entities (the cats, the mice and the fact to eat) and two relations (between the cats and the fact to eat and between the fact to eat and the mice). A representation about these three entities and two relations is formed in the mind of an observer. This is the level 1 of analysis. Finally, the observer can build the statement "Cats eat mice". This is the level 2 of analysis. In this statement we find the three entities and two relations. The syntax served to build the statement as a sequence of words. The relations and the entities founded in the level 1 of analysis served to chose the appropriate words for the level 2. We will try to find a representation for the level 1 and a method to obtain the level 1 from the level 2. The level 1 of analysis can be considered the semantic level. The relation between the level 1 and the level 0 is not a semantic problem but a *truth problem* (is there a level 0 corresponding to level 1?). The level one of analysis has as best representation the Generative Dependency Grammar (GDG). GDG is a sort of combination between Dependency Grammar (DG) and Generative Grammar (GG).

DG (Tesnière [17], Gaifman [5], Mel'cuk [10] [11], Hellwig [6], Hudson [7], McCord [8], Starosta [15], Milward [12]) tries to represent entities (as words) and relations between entities (words). They use dependency trees (DT) that contains usually words as nodes and relations (oriented links between words). We will take from DG the idea of the "relation" that we consider that express somehow the semantics.

GG (Chomsky [4]) try to express a process to obtain phrases starting from a root symbol and using some generative rules. We will take from GG the idea of the "sequence" of words that we consider that express somehow the syntax.

In this paper we will present the background elements of GDG.

## 2 The Generative Dependency Grammar Definition

Definition: A generative dependency grammar GDG is an 8-tupple $GDG = \{N, T, P, A, SR, CR, t_0, R\}$ where:

- $N$ is the set of non-terminals $n$ i.e. the set of the syntactic categories that can be described having a name and a structure. A non-terminal can be decomposed in others elements from $N, T, P, A, SR, CR$. The name of a non-terminal will be written between <...>.

- $T$ is the set of the terminals $t$ i.e. the set of the words that can be found in the lexicon or can be obtained by applying some flexional rules on words from the lexicon. The terminal will be written between "...".

- $P$ is the set of pseudo-terminals $p$ i.e. the set of the non-terminals that contain only terminals. When we will describe a dependency tree or a grammar we will not cover all the words from the lexicon because in this case the number of rules from the grammar can be too big. So we can say that some non-terminals that we name pseudo-terminals (for example some nouns or some verbs) will never be described in the grammar. The name of a pseudo-terminal will be written between %...%.

- $A$ is the set of the procedural actions $a$ i.e. the set of the routines that can be used to represent a certain portion of the text that we analyze. For example a number represented like a sequence of digits or a mathematical formula or even an image with a certain significance that appear in a text can be "replaced" in grammars or dependency trees by a certain procedural action. The name of a procedural action will be written between #...#.

- $SR$ is the set of the subordinate relations $sr$ i.e. the set of the relations between $N$, $T$, $P$, $A$, $CR$, respecting some rules. The links that enter in an $sr$ come from one element that is considered to be subordinated to the elements that receive links that comes from this $sr$. The name of an $sr$ will be written between @...@.

- $CR$ is the set of the coordinate relations $cr$ i.e. the set of the relations between $N$, $T$, $P$, $A$, $SR$, respecting some rules. The links that enter in a $cr$ come from some elements that are considered to be coordinated each other but also from some other elements. The links that come from the coordinated elements (usually 2) are named fixed entries. The other entries are named supplementary entries. The name of a $cr$ will be also written between @...@.

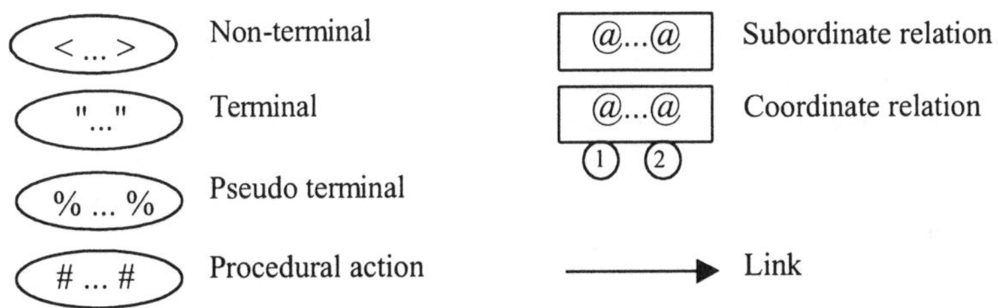


Figure - 1. Graphical symbols

- $t_0$ belongs to N and is named root symbol.

- $R$ is a set of numbered rules of the form $(i)\ n_i$->$(s_i, q_i)$ where; $n_i$ belongs to $N$; $s_i$ is a sequence of elements from $N \bigcup T \bigcup P \bigcup A$ (we will note also *ntpa* such an element), $q_i$ is a dependency tree having nodes from $s_i$ and oriented labels from $SR \bigcup CR$ and $i = 1, 2, 3, \ldots$

The next conditions must be respected:

- All non-terminals from $s_i$ must be found one time and only one in $q_i$. Terminals, pseudo-terminals and direct actions from $s_i$ can be found at most one time in $q_i$.

- All terminals, pseudo-terminals and direct actions from $q_i$ must be found one time and only one in $s_i$.

- Eventually, $q_i$ can be empty. If $s_i$, and/or $q_i$ contain the same non-terminal, terminal, pseudo-terminal, direct action, subordinate relation or coordinate relation many times, then the apparition of the same element will be differently labeled in order to distinguish them.

- An *ntpa* can have zero or one output (i.e. a link oriented from the *ntpa* to other element) that goes to an *sr* or to a *cr* on fixed entries and zero, one or many inputs (i.e. links from other elements that are oriented to the *ntpa*) that come from an *sr*. It will be noted by *ntpa*($i_1$, $i_2$, ...) or by *ntpa()* if no entry is available.

- An *sr* has always an output that goes to an *ntpa* or to a *cr* on a supplementary entry and one input that comes from an *ntpa* or from a *cr*. It will be noted by *sr*($i_1$).

- A *cr* can have zero or one output that goes to an *sr* or to a *cr* on fixed entry and can have m>=2 fixed inputs that come from *ntpa* or from *cr* and zero, one or many supplementary inputs that come from *sr*. It will be noted by *cr*($f_1$, $f_2$,... / $s_1$, $s_2$, ..) if it has supplementary inputs (where $f_1$, $f_2$, ... are fixed entries and $s_1$, $s_2$, ... are supplementary inputs) or by *cr*($f_1$, $f_2$,...) if it has not supplementary inputs. We will consider $m = 2$ because this is used about correlative constructions that have two members.

The *ntpa*-s and the links between them will constitute a dependency tree DT. The graphic notations to represent DT are showed in the figure 1.

We can summarize the types of links as follows:

1. ntpa output -> sr input
2. ntpa output -> fixed cr input
3. sr output -> ntpa input
4. cr output -> sr input
5. cr output -> fixed cr input
6. sr output -> supplementary cr input

An important feature of the DT is the head. A head in a DT is a node that has only inputs and has no output. An *ntpa* node can be head; it has inputs of type 3 (i.e. from *sr* relation). A *cr* node can be head; its fixed inputs are of type: 2 (from *ntpa*) and 5 (from other *cr*) and its supplementary inputs are of type 6 (from *sr*). An *sr* relation cannot be head. A dependency tree has one and only one head.

A DT can be described using a BNF notation as follows:

<dependency tree>::= <ntpa sequence>|<cr sequence>
<ntpa sequence> ::= ntpa(<ntpa entries>)|ntpa()
<ntpa entries> ::= <sr sequence>,<ntpa entries>|<sr sequence>
<sr sequence> ::= sr(<sr entries>)
<sr entries> ::= <dependency tree>,<sr entries>|<dependency tree>
<cr sequence> ::= cr(<fixed groups>/<supp. entries>)|cr(<fixed groups>)
<fixed groups> ::= <fixed group>;<fixed groups>|<fixed group>
<fixed group> ::= <dependency tree>,<fixed group>|<dependency tree>

A dependency tree that do not contains non-terminals will be named final tree.

_Example:_ Let's take an example that contains a gap: "*I gave a book to the boy and a doll to the girl*". A grammar that can generate such a phrase is:

(1) <phrase> -> ( <nominal group> <verbal group>, <nominal group>( @$r_1$@( <verbal group>())))
(2) <nominal group> -> ( "I", "I"())
(3) <verbal group> -> ( <verb> <direct-indirect gap coordination>, <verb>( <direct-indirect gap coordination>()))
(4) <verb> -> ( "gave", "gave"())
(5) <direct-indirect gap coordination> -> ( <direct-indirect gap coordination member> "and" <direct-indirect gap coordination member'>, @$r_2$@( <direct-indirect gap coordination member>(), <direct-indirect gap coordination member'>() / @$r_3$@( "and"())))

(6) <direct-indirect gap coordination member> -> ( <direct> <indirect>, @$r_4$@( <direct>(), <indirect>()))
(7) <direct> -> ( <indefinite article noun>, <indefinite article noun>())
(8) <indefinite article noun> -> ( “a” <noun>, <noun>( @$r_5$@( “a”())))
(9) <indirect> ->( “to” <definite article noun>, “to”( @$r_6$@(<definite article noun>())))
(10) <definite article noun> -> ( “the” <noun>, <noun>( @$r_7$@( “the”())))
(11) <noun> -> ( “book”, “book”())
(12) <noun> -> ( “boy”, “boy”())
(13) <noun> -> ( “doll”, “doll”())
(14) <noun> -> ( “girl”, “girl”())

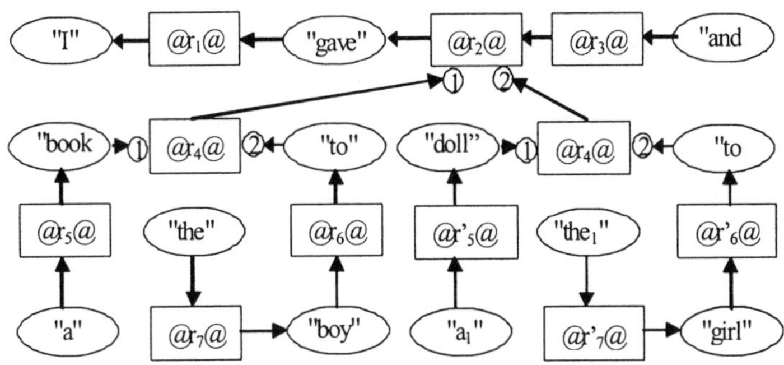


Figure 2 – An example of DT

We noted by *@$r_1$@, @$r_2$@, ...* the relations. In a good description of a grammar these relations can have more appropriate names like: relation between subject and predicate, relation between article and noun, etc. For a certain natural language the number of the types of these relations cannot be too big.

The relation *@$r_4$@* will be a special kind of relation (of the type *cr* – coordinate relation) that links together the two parts (direct part and indirect part) of this gap. We can name this relation a direct-indirect gap relation. Of course, other kinds of gap relations can be defined.

The final DT for the phrase will be:

“I”( @$r_1$@( “gave”( @$r_2$@( @$r_4$@( “book”( @$r_5$@( “a”)), “to”( @$r_6$@(“boy”( @$r_7$@( “the”()))))), @r’$_4$@( “doll”( @r’$_5$@( “a’”())), “to”( @r’$_6$@( “girl”( @r’$_7$@( “the$_1$”())))) / @$r_3$@( “and”())))))

We will explain in the next sections how this final DT can be generated from the grammar. In the figure 2 we represented this final DT.

# 3 Non-Terminal Dependency Tree Substitution

We will name non-terminal dependency tree a DT that has a non-terminal as head. We will name coordinate DT a DT that has a coordinate dependency as head. Let us take a non-terminal DT *w* that contains a non-terminal DT $n = n'(u_1, u_2, ...)$

where $n'$ is a non-terminal and $u_1$, $u_2$, ... are DTs that act as entries in the non-terminal $n'$. It is possible that $n'$ has no entries at all. It is possible too, that $n'$ have zero outputs (if it is a head of $w$) or one output that go somewhere in the tree $w$. To *substitute* $n$ from $w$ by a DT $q$ means to obtain a new tree $r$ that will replace $n$ in $w$. If $q = q'()$ is a DT without entries, then $r = q'()$. If $q = q'(v_1, v_2, ...)$ is a non-terminal DT where $q'$ is a non-terminal and $v_1$, $v_2$, ... are dependency trees that act as entries in the non-terminal $q'$, then $r = q'(u_1, u_2, ..., v_1, v_2, ...)$. If $q = q'(v_1, v_2 / t_1, t_2, ...)$ is a coordinate relation DT where $q'$ is a coordinate relation, $v_1$, $v_2, ...$ are DTs that act as entries in the fixed entries of the coordinate relation $q'$ and $t_1$, $t_2, ...$ are DTs that act as entries in the supplementary entries of the coordinate relation $q'$ (it is possible that $q'$ has no supplementary inputs at all.), then $r = q'(v_1, v_2 / t_1, t_2, ..., u_1, u_2, ...)$.

# 4 Generation in a Generative Dependency Grammar

We consider 2 rules *(i)* $n_i$->$(s_i, q_i)$ and *(j)* $n_j$->$(s_j, q_j)$ of a GDG. We consider also that $s_i$ and $q_i$ contains $p_j$. We will obtain a new rule *(k)* $n_k$->$(s_k, q_k)$ as follows:
- $s_j$ will replace $n_j$ from $s_i$ obtaining $s_k$;
- $q_j$ will *substitute* $n_j$ from $q_i$ obtaining $q_k$;
- $n_k = n_j$.

We will say that the rule *(k)* is immediately generated from the rule *(j)* using the rule *(i)*. Let us suppose that we have a phrase $s_n$ that contains only terminals. Let us suppose that, by applying a sequence of generations (starting with a rule that has a root symbol in the left side), we will obtain finally a rule *(h)* $n_h$->$(s_h, q_h)$ where $s_h$ is a phrase. We will consider too that in $n_h$ there are not non-terminals, pseudo-terminals was replaced by matching terminals taken from the lexicon and direct actions was replaced by what results from their execution. The execution of a direct action has as result a terminal or a sequence of terminals that are considered as a single terminal. We will say that $s_h$ is completely generated by the grammar GDG (or that $s_h$ is accepted by the grammar GDG). In this case, $q_h$ will be the final dependency tree of the phrase $s_h$.

Remark: When a grammar rule is applied many times, all the elements of the rule are differently labeled for each application.

Example: Using the grammar from the *Example 1* (section 2) we can generate the DT as follows:

(15)(1, 2) <phrase> -> ( “I” <verbal group>, “I”( @r1@( <verbal group>())))
(16)(15, 3) <phrase> -> ( “I” <verb> <direct-indirect gap coordination>, “I”( @r1@( <verb>( <direct-indirect gap coordination>()))))
(17)(16, 4) <phrase> -> ( “I” “gave” <direct-indirect gap coordination>, “I”( @r1@( “gave”( <direct-indirect gap coordination>()))))
(18)(17, 5) <phrase> -> ( “I” “gave” <direct-indirect gap coordination member> “and”<direct-indirect gap coordination member’>, “I”( @$r_1$@( “gave”( @$r_2$@( <direct-indirect gap coordination member>(), <direct-indirect gap coordination member’>() / @$r_3$@( “and”())))))))

We can continue the generation process and we will obtain finally:

(31)(30, 14) <phrase> -> ( "I" "gave" "a" "book" "to" "the" "boy" "and" "$a_1$" "doll""$to_1$" "$the_1$" "girl", "I"( @$r_1$@( "gave"( @$r_2$@( @$r_4$@( "book"( @$r_5$@( "a"())), "to"( @$r_6$@("boy" ( @$r_7$@( "the"()))))), @$r'_4$@( "doll"( @$r_5$@( "$a_1$"())), "$to_1$"( @$r'_6$@("girl" ( @$r'_7$@( "$the_1$"())))) / @$r_3$@( and"()))))))

In the right side of the rule we obtained the surface text "I" "gave" "a" "book" "to" "the" "boy" "and" "$a_1$" "doll" "$to_1$" "$the_1$" "girl" and the DT (see the figure 2):

"I"( @$r_1$@( "gave"( @$r_2$@( @$r_4$@( "book"( @$r_5$@( "a"())), "to"( @$r_6$@("boy" ( @$r_7$@( "the"()))))), @$r'_4$@( "doll"( @$r_5$@( "$a_1$"())), "$to_1$"( @$r'_6$@("girl" ( @$r'_7$@( "$the_1$"())))) / @$r_3$@( and"())))))

# 5 GDG with Feature Structure

One of the problem that arise when a GG is used is the great number of rules. This number can be controlled if we use a low number of metalinguistic symbols that can express a high number of linguistic situations. We will present such a formalism that is of type FS (feature structures). FS types are used for example in the PATR grammars (Shieber [14]) or in HPSG (Pollard [13]). In fact PATR or HPSG use AVM – Attribute Value Matrix. Instead of AVM we will define an AVT – Attribute Value Tree. We will consider also that the attribute are indexed or not indexed. If an attribute is indexed than in a certain context (for example in a grammar description rule) this attribute must take the same value for each *ntpa* that has associated the attribute. If an attribute is not indexed then in the same context this attribute can take any value from his value set.

An AVT can be described syntactically as follows:

1. <AVT> -> {<label>:<not labeled AVT>}|{<label>}|<not labeled AVT>
2. <not labeled AVT> -> < indexed AVT >|< non indexed AVT >
3. <indexed AVT> -> [<AVT content>]
4. <non indexed AVT> -> (<AVT content>)
5. <AVT content> -> <label>:<feature content>|<feature content>|<label>
6. <feature content> -> <attribute> = <attribute value list>
7. <attribute value list> -> <attribute value element>, <attribute value list>| <attribute value element>
8. <attribute value element> -> <attribute value><AVT>|<attribute value>

The rule 1 express the fact that an AVT can have a label – the AVT label definition. The AVT label can be used later alone in the same context and this mean that the label must be substituted with its definition. The rule 5 express the fact that an attribute with his list of values can have a label – the attribute list label definition. This label can be used later alone in the same context and this mean that the label must be substituted with its definition. In this case the label is also a marker for the attribute so two attributes with different labels (markers) must be considered as different attributes. Usually a context is formed by the left hand of a rule and one alternant from the right hand of the rule in a GG. The labels defined here are a sort of generalization of reentrancy from HPSG.

*Definition:* A GDG with feature structure is a GDG where each *ntpa* can have associated an AVT. The AVT associated with the non-terminal from the left side of the rules have always only indexed attributes.

Example: Let us have the next statement in Romanian language: "*Apele* (the waters) *linistite* (still) *sunt* (are) *adânci* (deep)" that means "The still waters are deep".

We will not use all the grammatical categories implied in the analysis of this statement but only few as an illustration. We will consider that the lexical class (verb, adjective, noun, ...) will be represented also like an attribute "class" that will have these values.

Usually, the statement to be analyzed is first of all annotated i.e. each word will have attached his lemma and a particular AVT (that have only one value for each attribute. Each word can have many interpretations. For example "sunt" can represent the third person plural (are) or the first person singular (am). Though, for the sake of simplicity, we will consider only one interpretation for each word.

The annotated statement will be:

"Apele" *apa*[class = noun] [gender = feminine] [number = plural] "linistite" *linistit* [class = adjective] [gender = feminine] [number = plural] "sunt" *fi* [class = verb] [person: III] [number = plural] [mode = indicative] [voice = active] [time = present] "adânci" *adânc* [class = adjective] [gender = feminine] [number = plural]

We noted in italics the lemmas.

A GDG with features that can generate this statement can be as follows:

(1) <phrase> -> ( <nominal group> [gender = masculine, feminine, neuter] [number = singular, plural] [person = I, II, III] <compound nominal predicate> [gender = masculine, feminine, neuter] [number = singular, plural] [person = I, II, III], <nominal group>( @$r_1$@( <compound nominal predicate> ())))

(2) <nominal group> [gender = masculine, feminine, neuter] [number = singular, plural] [person = I, II, III] -> (%noun% [class = noun] [gender = masculine, feminine, neuter] [number = singular, plural] %adjective% [class = adjective] [gender = masculine, feminine, neuter] [number = singular, plural], %noun%(@$r_2$@(%adjective% ())))

(3) <compound nominal predicate>[gender = masculine, feminine, neuter] [number = singular, plural] [person = I, II, III] -> (%verb% [class = verb] [gender = masculine, feminine, neuter] [number = singular, plural] [mode = indicative] [voice = active] [time = present, future, imperfect past] %adjective% [class = adjective] [gender = masculine, feminine, neuter] [number = singular, plural], %verb%(@$r_3$@(%adjective% ())))

As we can see we used pseudo terminals for nouns, verbs, adjectives, so this grammar can generate a set of statements.

# 6 AVT Properties

The labels are used in AVT only in order to reduce the length of the description. Before any AVT operation the labels must be substituted with their definition. During this substitution the eventually reccursivity must be identified. The reccursivity are not accepted.

AVT themselves are used also in order to represent more compactly a greater number of *ntpa-s*. How many such *ntpa-s* represent an AVT? The AVT associated with such an *ntpa* will be named EC (exclusive combination). An EC will have for each attribute only one value. We can compute how many paths are in an AVT, how these paths can be enumerated, how many EC-s are in an AVT and others proprieties. We explain here only how we can enumerate the EC-s in an AVT.

In order to enumerate (generate) all the EC-s in an AVT we will use the notations $\prod$ (and "*") that will mean "string concatenation" and $\sum$ (and "+") that will mean "string alternatives". With these notations, the enumeration of the EC-s will be made with the next recursive formulas:

- *LES(T)* = $\prod_k AES(A_k)$ is the set of EC (LES = List Exclusive Set) in an AVT T that has on the first level an attribute list $A_k$.

- *AES(A)* = $\sum_i VES(A/a_i)$ is the set of EC-s that pass through the attribute A (AES = Attribute Exclusive Set) that has a list of values $a_i$.

- *VES(A/a)* = $\prod_j A/a * AES(A_j)$ is the set of EC-s that contain the attribute value a of the attribute A (VES = Value Exclusive Set) if *a* has associated an attribute list. If *a* has not associated an attribute list then *VES(A/a)=A/a*.

# 7 Logical Interpretation of an AVT

We will give a logical interpretation of an AVT, i.e. a logical expression that correspond to an AVT. Using such an expression we can make in a more simple way some operations with AVT-s. In the enumeration of the EC-s we will consider that the sign "*" will represent the logical operation "*and*" and the sign "+" will represent the logical operation "*or*". In this case LES(T) of an AVT T can be "read" as a logical expression. As in any ordinary logical expression we will have:

$a/a_l * a/a_l = a/a_l$
$a/a_l + a/a_l = a/a_l$

and we will have all the others proprieties of the logical operators.

Because $(a/a_i)$ and $[a/a_i]$ represent the indexing type, we will introduce also the next conventions:

$(a/a_i) * (a/a_i) = (a/a_i)$
$(a/a_i) + [a/a_i] = [a/a_i]$
$[a/a_i] * (a/a_i) = [a/a_i]$
$[a/a_i] + [a/a_i] = [a/a_i]$

This means that the indexing has a priority against non indexing.

Because an attribute can not have in the same time two different value we will consider:

$(a/a_i) * [a/a_j] = \text{false}$
$(a/a_i) * (a/a_j) = \text{false}$
$[a/a_i] * (a/a_j) = \text{false}$

[a/$a_i$] * [a/$a_j$] = false
where i #j and "false" as "true" have all the proprieties from logical expressions.

The next rule must always be respected by a logical expression in order to be an AVT transformation:

Each term of a disjunction must contain at least one factor that has the same attribute name.

So, in each disjunction we must have something of the form:

A/$x_1$...+ A/$x_2$...+ A/$x_3$... + A/$x_4$ ...

We can use the logical representation of an AVT to make some operations and optimizations.

*Example*

S = [a = a1[b = b1, b2][c = c1, c2], a2(b = b1, b2)][e = e1, e2]
LES(S) = [a/a1] * [b/b1] * [c/c1] * [e/e1] + [a/a1] * [b/b1] * [c/c2] * [e/e1] +
[a/a1] * [b/b2] * [c/c1] * [e/e1] + [a/a1] * [b/b2] * [c/c2] * [e/e1] +
[a/a2] * (b/b1) * [e/e1] + [a/a2] * (b/b2) * [e/e1] +
[a/a1] * [b/b1] * [c/c1] * [e/e2] + [a/a1] * [b/b1] * [c/c2] * [e/e2] +
[a/a1] * [b/b2] * [c/c1] * [e/e2] + [a/a1] * [b/b2] * [c/c2] * [e/e2] +
[a/a2] * (b/b1) * [e/e2] + [a/a2] * (b/b2) * [e/e2]

By applying different logical transformations we will obtain:

LES(S) = ([a/a1] * ([c/c1] + [c/c2]) + [a/a2]) * ([b/b1] + [b/b2]) * ([e/e1] + [e/e2])

# 8 The Transformation of a Logical Expression into an AVT

In the above section we explained how to obtain a logical expression representing an AVT. On this logical expression, some logical transformation can be executed. Finally, the logical expression can be transformed again in an AVT. We will show the method using the example from the section 7. We will consider as starting form that do not contains parenthesis and all the transformations described in 7 was applied.

LES(S) = [a/a1] * [b/b1] * [c/c1] * [e/e1] + [a/a1] * [b/b1] * [c/c2] * [e/e1] +
[a/a1] * [b/b2] * [c/c1] * [e/e1] + [a/a1] * [b/b2] * [c/c2] * [e/e1] +
[a/a2] * [b/b1] * [e/e1] + [a/a2] * [b/b2] * [e/e1] +
[a/a1] * [b/b1] * [c/c1] * [e/e2] + [a/a1] * [b/b1] * [c/c2] * [e/e2] +
[a/a1] * [b/b2] * [c/c1] * [e/e2] + [a/a1] * [b/b2] * [c/c2] * [e/e2] +
[a/a2] * [b/b1] * [e/e2] + [a/a2] * [b/b2] * [e/e2]

a) We count the apparitions of each attribute in EC-s (an attribute can appear only one time in a EC because we considered the expression already simplified). In our case we will obtain:

a: 12, b: 12, c: 8, e: 12

b) We count how many EC-s there are. Here we obtain 12. The attributes that appears in all the EC-s will be the attributes that will appear on the first level of the tree. In our case we will have something of the form:

[a = ...]
[b = ...]

[e = ...]

We create a number of EC groups equal with the number of the EC-s that have the maximum number of apparitions. Each group contains all the EC-s from the expression. We consider that each group is associated with an attribute from those EC-s that had the apparition number equal with the number of EC-s from the current sub expression.

LES(S) = ([a/a1] * [b/b1] * [c/c1] * [e/e1] + [a/a1] * [b/b1] * [c/c2] * [e/e1] +
[a/a1] * [b/b2] * [c/c1] * [e/e1] + [a/a1] * [b/b2] * [c/c2] * [e/e1] +
[a/a2] * [b/b1] * [e/e1] + [a/a2] * [b/b2] * [e/e1] +
[a/a1] * [b/b1] * [c/c1] * [e/e2] + [a/a1] * [b/b1] * [c/c2] * [e/e2] +
[a/a1] * [b/b2] * [c/c1] * [e/e2] + [a/a1] * [b/b2] * [c/c2] * [e/e2] +
[a/a2] * [b/b1] * [e/e2] + [a/a2] * [b/b2] * [e/e2]) *
([a/a1] * [b/b1] * [c/c1] * [e/e1] + [a/a1] * [b/b1] * [c/c2] * [e/e1] +
[a/a1] * [b/b2] * [c/c1] * [e/e1] + [a/a1] * [b/b2] * [c/c2] * [e/e1] +
[a/a2] * [b/b1] * [e/e1] + [a/a2] * [b/b2] * [e/e1] +
[a/a1] * [b/b1] * [c/c1] * [e/e2] + [a/a1] * [b/b1] * [c/c2] * [e/e2] +
[a/a1] * [b/b2] * [c/c1] * [e/e2] + [a/a1] * [b/b2] * [c/c2] * [e/e2] +
[a/a2] * [b/b1] * [e/e2] + [a/a2] * [b/b2] * [e/e2]) *
([a/a1] * [b/b1] * [c/c1] * [e/e1] + [a/a1] * [b/b1] * [c/c2] * [e/e1] +
[a/a1] * [b/b2] * [c/c1] * [e/e1] + [a/a1] * [b/b2] * [c/c2] * [e/e1] +
[a/a2] * [b/b1] * [e/e1] + [a/a2] * [b/b2] * [e/e1] +
[a/a1] * [b/b1] * [c/c1] * [e/e2] + [a/a1] * [b/b1] * [c/c2] * [e/e2] +
[a/a1] * [b/b2] * [c/c1] * [e/e2] + [a/a1] * [b/b2] * [c/c2] * [e/e2] +
[a/a2] * [b/b1] * [e/e2] + [a/a2] * [b/b2] * [e/e2])

We can see that if we will develop this expression and we make some simplifications we will obtain the initial expression.

c) From each EC of a group we will eliminate the attributes that are associated with others groups.

LES(S) = ([a/a1] * [c/c1] + [a/a1] * [c/c2] + [a/a1] * [c/c1] + [a/a1] * [c/c2] + [a/a2] +[a/a2] + [a/a1] * [c/c1] + [a/a1] * [c/c2] + [a/a1] * [c/c1] + [a/a1] * [c/c2] + [a/a2] + [a/a2]) * ([b/b1] * [c/c1] + [b/b1] * [c/c2] + [b/b2] * [c/c1] + [b/b2] * [c/c2] + [b/b1] + [b/b2] + [b/b1] * [c/c1] + [b/b1] * [c/c2] + [b/b2] * [c/c1] + [b/b2] * [c/c2] + [b/b1] + [b/b2]) * ([e/e1] + [e/e1] + [e/e1] + [e/e1] + [e/e1] + [e/e1] + [e/e2] + [e/e2] + [e/e2] + [e/e2] + [e/e2] + [e/e2])

d) We will simplify the expressions from the parenthesis by keeping one sample from each combination and by applying transformations of the type x * y + x = x.

LES(S) = ([a/a1] * [c/c1] + [a/a1] * [c/c2] + [a/a2]) * ([b/b1] + [b/b2]) * ([e/e1] + [e/e2])

e) In each group we take as common factor the attribute (and value) of the attribute associated with this group:

LES(S) = ([a/a1] * ([c/c1] + [c/c2]) + [a/a2]) * ([b/b1] + [b/b2]) * ([e/e1] + [e/e2])

We will apply the steps (a) – (e) for each most inside parenthesis (for each attribute value). We continue this process until all the most inside parenthesis will contain only one attribute. In our case we already obtained the most inside parenthesis with only one attribute.

f) We can transform now the expression in an AVT using the next procedure:

f1) For each sequence of the type *([x/x1] + [x/x2] + [x/x3] + ...)* or *((x/x1) + (x/x2) + (x/x3) + ...)* we apply the transformation *[x = x1, x2, x3, ...]* respectively *(x = x1, x2, x3, ....)*. (Normally we can not have this kind of sequences with different index types, but anyway the index has a priority against not index). In our case we will have:

S = ([a/a1] * [c = c1, c2] + [a/a2]) * [b = b1, b2] * [e = e1, e2]

f2) For all the sequences of the type *[x/x1] * (sequence)* or *(x/x1) * (sequence)* we apply the transformation into *[x/x1(sequence)]* respectively *(x/x1(sequence))*. In our case we have:

S = ([a/a1[c = c1, c2]] + [a/a2]) * [b = b1, b2] * [e = e1, e2]

f3) For all the sequences of the type ([x/sequence$_1$] + [x/sequence$_2$] + [x/sequence$_3$] + ...) or ((x/sequence$_1$) + (x/sequence$_2$) + (x/sequence$_3$) + ...) we apply the transformation into [x = sequence$_1$, sequence$_2$, sequence$_3$, ...] respectively (x = sequence$_1$, sequence$_2$, sequence$_3$ ). In our case we have:

S = [a = a1[c = c1, c2]], a2] * [b = b1, b2] * [e = e1, e2]

f4) For all the sequences of the type *[sequence$_1$] * [sequence$_2$] * [sequence$_3$] ...* we apply the transformation into *[sequence$_1$] [sequence$_2$] [sequence$_3$] ...* . In our case we have:

S= [a = a1[c = c1, c2]], a2] [b = b1, b2] [e = e1, e2]

We obtained a well formed AVT.

# 9 The Unification

We can define different operations/notions on the AVT: intersection (the common part of two AVT-s), difference (what it is in the first AVT and is not in the second AVT), sorted AVT (using total order relation on names of attributes and attribute values), AVT normalization (the "less deep" form of an AVT), etc. The most important operation is the unification that will make possible the substitution of a non-terminal from right side of a rule with a the rule that have in the left side the appropriate non-terminal. The substitution process is more complicated and we have not the space to fully explain it here. We will give only the definition of the unification.

*Definition*: Two *ntpa*-s having associated AVT-s are unifiable if they have the same name and the unifier of the two AVT-s exists (i.e. it is not empty). (If the two *ntpa*-s have not associated AVT-s then they are unifiable only if they have the same name.)

*Definition*: A unifier of two AVT-s is an AVT corresponding to an a expression obtained making a logical "*and*" between the logical forms of the two AVT-s.

<u>*Example*</u>: Let us have two *ntpa*-s with the same name and with two AVT-s associated, S an T:

S = [a = a1, a2, a3, a4] [b = b1, b2, b3] [c = c1, c2[f = f1][g = g1, g2]]
[d = d1, d2[f = f2, f3][g = g1, g3, g4]]

T = [c = c1[h = h1], c2, c3] [d = d1, d2[g = g3, g4, g5]] [e = e1, e2, e3, e4]

The unifier R of S and T is R = S * T. We transform S and T in their logical form. We execute all the needed operations on the expression R * T. Finally, using the method described in section 8 we obtain:

R = [a = a1, a2, a3, a4] [b = b1, b2, b3] [c = c1] [h = h1]
[d = d1[g = g3, g4], d2[f = f2, f3][g = g3, g4]] [e = e1, e2, e3, e4]

The calculus can be complicated but it is not a problem to implement it in a computer program.

# 10 Conclusions

We think that the GDG with feature structure have the power to represent the linguistic information and they do not imply an excessively difficulty to be used (tough it is not a trivial task to make a good description of a grammar). Using a GDG we can parse texts and obtain dependency trees associated to a source text.

There are many directions in which GDG can be (and was) extended. For example we can define GDG with many DT-s in the right side of the rules. This will facilitate the description of the recursive rules. The GDG we defined uses a kind of relations that can be named *direct relations* because they link directly *ntpa*-s that are found in the current rule. We can define a more complicated sort of relations: *indirect relations* that link external *ntpa* to the current rule. These relations will facilitate too the writing of the grammar rules, especially for long distance relation between phrase parts, without the necessity to have all these parts in the same rule.

There are at least few domains where these GDG can be used: the machine translation, the data retrieval, the language understanding. In the machine translation, these DT can describe relatively easily complex linguistic structures equivalences. In the data retrieval, on these DT can be formulated logical clauses that gather all the information from the source text. The number of the types of relations between the terminals and direct actions that we find in final dependency tree is not too big so a set of supplementary logical clauses can complete the grammar description. Using the clauses obtained from the final dependency trees and these supplementary clauses, complex inferences can be made on the dependency trees. We consider that the DT built by an analysis using GDG capture the "meaning" of the texts so it can serve to natural language understanding.

Based on GDG formalism presented here we realized a specialized language GRAALAN (GRAmmar Abstract LANguage) that has a set of other features also. The logical and linguistic background of this language was defined and we presented in this paper only some elements of this background. Using GRAALAN we started to build a GDG with feature structure of the Romanian language. The Romanian language has a very difficult grammar with quite free word order. For example, only to express the accord between a multiple regent and a subordinate (in gender, number, animation, order) there are about 1350 situations that must be observed. We realized so far the description of the general rules for regent – subordinate relation (nominal – attributes, verbs – adjuncts, subjects - predicates) and we partially realized the description of nominal – attributes relation.

## References

1. Covington, Michael A. *A Dependency Parser for Variable-Word-Order Languages*, Research Report AI-1990-01, The University of Georgia, Athens, Georgia, 1990

2. Covington, Michael A. 1994 *Discontinuous Dependency Parsing of Free and Fixed Word Order*, Research Report AI-1992-02, The University of Georgia, Athens, Georgia, 1994
3. Bröker, Norbert *How to define a context free backbone for DGs: Implementing a DG in the LFG formalism*, Papers of the Workshop on the Processing of Dependency-based Grammars (COLING-ACL'98), 1998, pp.29-38
4. Chomsky, Noam *Generative Grammar: Its Basis, Development and Prospects.* Studies in English Linguistics and Literature, Special Issue, Kyoto University of Foreign Studies, 1988
5. Gaifman, H. *Dependency Systems and phrase structure systems*, Information and Control, 1965, pp. 304-337
6. Helwig, P. *Chart Parsing according to the slot and filler principle*, Processing of the 12th Int. Conf. On Computational Linguistics, Budapest, Hungary, 22-27 August 1988, Vol.1, 1988, pp. 242-244
7. Hudson, R *English Word Grammar*, Oxford UK, Basil Blackwell, 1990
8. McCord, M *Slot grammar: A system for simpler construction of practical natural language grammars*, in R. Studer (Ed.), Natural Language and Logic, Berlin Heidelberg Springer, 1990, pp.118-145
9. Kahane, Sylvain, Alexis Nasr, and Owen Rambow *Pseudo-projectivity: A polynomially parsable nonprojective dependency grammar.* In Proceedings of the 36th Annual Meeting of the Association for Computational Linguistics (ACL '98), Montreal, Canada, 1998
10. Mel'cuk, I.A., Pertsov, N.V. *Surface Syntax of English: A formal model within the Meaning-Text Framework*, Amsterdam/PA: John Benjamins, 1987
11. Mel'cuk, I.A. *Dependency Syntax: theory and practice*, State University of New York Press, Albany, 1988
12. Milward, D. *Dynamic Dependency Grammar*, Linguistics and Philosophy 17, December, 1994, pp. 561-606
13. Pollard, C. Sag, I. A. *Head-driven Phrase Structure grammar*, University of Chicago Press and Standford CSLI Publications, 1994
14. Shieber, Stuart M. *An Introduction to Unification Based Approaches to Grammar*, CLSII Lecture Notes Series, Number 4, Center for the study of Language and Information, Stanford University, 1986
15. Starosta, S *Lexicase revisited. Department of Linguistics*, University of Hawaii, 1992
16. Teich, Elke *Types of syntagmatic grammatical relations and their representation*, Papers of the Workshop on the Processing of Dependency-based Grammars (COLING-ACL'98), 1998, pp.39-48
17. Tesnière, L. *Éléments de syntaxe structurelle*, Paris, Klincksieck, 1959

# Towards a Development Methodology for Managing Linguistic Knowledge Bases

F. Sáenz and A. Vaquero
Departamento de Sistemas Informáticos y Programación, Universidad Complutense de Madrid, E-28040 Madrid, Spain

{fernan,vaquero}@sip.ucm.es

Abstract

We are on the way of defining a methodology aimed to create software tools supporting linguistic knowledge bases. One of our main concerns is to formally represent knowledge using a sound software engineering approach. In this setting, we first consider the linguistic concepts found in a multilingual dictionary, as vocabulary, meanings, semantic categories, semantic relationships, and (tree-shaped) taxonomy. Next, we start on ontologies, considering concepts as syntactic categories, orthography, phonology, syntactic features, lexical semantics and relations, and so on. We have represented in the conceptual levels these concepts, by using the well known entity-relationship model. In addition, we have applied the design cycle of databases in order to also fulfill the logical and physical models for representing the linguistic concepts at each development stage. In addition, we have developed both authoring and querying tools for both stages, and a migration procedure for interfacing them. Taking into account that the different existing linguistic knowledge bases have been built without following any formal methodology, our approach adds a way of integrating linguistic resources with a common structure. The resulting framework is useful for several applications, including multilingual information retrieval, document classification, and language translation, and also for their exploitation in education.

## 1. Introduction

Lack of standardisation is broadly felt as a very undesirable state into the community around ontologies, lexicons, and so on. For instance, standard terminology for a common reference ontology is a goal to be reached. But attention has not yet been paid on subjects about development methodologies for building the software tools supporting and handling those types of knowledge bases. We claim for this aspect of methodology as necessary in order to integrate the diverse available information systems of this kind now and in the future. A more or less automated incorporation of lexical and ontological databases into a common information system requires compatible software architectures and sound data management from the different databases to be integrated. With this vision in mind, paying attention to the software engineering aspects along the development of these kinds of systems from the beginning is mandatory.

In this paper, we present our ongoing work on developing sound conceptual models for terminological and ontological databases, with the aim of developing tools which can manage such lexical and semantic resources. There are many reasons for developing such tools. For instance, lack of the kind of dictionaries we propose (as will be introduced later) has been felt, as [2] states: "... we imagine, for some distant future, an online lexical resource, which we can refer to as a 'frame-based' dictionary, which will be adequate to our aims. In such a dictionary (housed on a workstation with multiple windowing capabilities), individual word senses, relationships among the senses of the polysemic words, and relationships between (senses of) semantically related words will be linked with the cognitive structures (or 'frames'), knowledge of which is presupposed by the concepts encoded by the words." In addition, it is well known the applications of ontological resources for different fields, as language translation, information retrieval, document summarisation, document classification, software localisation, language teaching, and so on.

Subjects about electronic dictionaries for diverse natural language processing applications have been extensively studied [12], as well as Lexical Databases [7], World Knowledge Bases [4], ontologies [6], and the like. But there are no references on how these information systems have been built, and generally, there is no registered information about how they have been developed and upgraded along their life. Moreover, tools for managing ontology-based information systems have been described [8], but there is neither formal support for their conceptual models nor a software engineering approach for the development. Our tools do enjoy from these two important issues. We have followed the classical relational database design (based on the conceptual, logical, and physical models) and software engineering techniques (based on UML).

The rest of the paper is organised as follows. Section 2 presents some concepts which has to be embodied in the lexical and ontological resources for their relevance in building different applications. The next three sections present the different conceptual models we present for several linguistic resources. For all of them, we have followed a classical relational database design cycle. First, from the conceptual model of each linguistic resource, we have developed the entity relationship model. Second, in the logical design stage, we have developed the relational model. Finally, in the physical design stage, we have developed the physical database schema. Section 3 presents the first conceptual model we develop to build a bilingual dictionary and that embodies some of the concepts listed in Section 2. Section 4 presents an extension of the first conceptual model in order to achieve a (dynamic) multilingual language. Section 5 develops a conceptual model for an ontology (we have selected MikroKosmos [6]). Section 6 sketches some tools we have developed for querying and building dictionaries, building ontologies and lexicons, and migrating information from our electronic dictionary to

MikroKosmos. Finally, Section 7 summarises our conclusions and points out some future work.

# 2. Concepts to be Attained

In this section, linguistic concepts incorporated in computing systems devoted to natural language processing are pointed out because of their relevance in the definition of the conceptual models.

## 2.1 Order, Classification, and Ontology

Typically, monolingual dictionaries show an alphabetical order that can be seen as a simple term classification: terms are classified in singletons by its lexicographic form. Other possible less naïve classifications are derivative (root-shape), grammatical, and semantic. Derivative classifications [5] are not common, and grammatical classifications are not intended for dictionaries. Finally, semantic classification groups terms by semantic categories (for instance, synonym and antonym dictionaries, or ideological dictionaries [1].) Semantic categories not also allow meaning classification, but the more meaningful taxonomy of meanings. Conventional lexical databases, such as WordNet [7], have term classification such as synonymy (grouped in the so called synsets.) Ontologies go beyond by playing the role of meaning taxonomy [9]. Our tools do support this important concept as will be explained along the paper.

Semantic categories are useless for term lookups since meanings will correspond, in general, to a set of (synonym) terms[1]. However, it has an important role on learning by both using and authoring dictionaries because each meaning of a given term (polysemy and/or homonymy) is precisely identified by its semantic category (categories from now on, for the sake of brevity), instead of the usual nonsense sequential number[2]. Therefore, semantic categories provide classification for meanings, and such classification can be arranged in a taxonomy. But this does not straightforwardly imply a term order since meanings are abstract ideas that cannot be expressed in general by one distinctive word[3]. It is commonly acknowledged that the best order for lookups is lexicographic (a derivative classification is a counterexample for this, but it still keeps a lexicographical order by repeating entries and adding links.) Figure 1 resumes the order for taxonomies in a hierarchy; it shows a taxonomy of categories along with the set of terms belonging to each category. From this point of view, there is a complete lexicographic order (provided categories are identified with terms or phrases.) A hierarchy is a natural structure for meaning classification. Each node in the hierarchy corresponds to a category. In principle, every category in the hierarchy can be used, no matter its

[1] Nevertheless, there are other kinds of term lookups as ideological dictionaries show.

[2] However, meaning identifications by numbers also show a coarse classification; e.g. Tech. for Technical.

[3] The question is: Which is the best word to represent a meaning? In general, there are several (synonym) words representing the same meaning.

hierarchy level. It must be noted that every category in the hierarchy contains at least the term which names the category, so that all categories are non-empty. On the other hand, the creation of new categories as intersection of several predefined ones should be avoided, in order to reach compactness.

```
Category 1 → {Terms of Category 1}
   ├──Category 1.1→ {Terms of Category 1.1}
   │      └──Category 1.1.1→ {Terms of Category 1.1.1}
   │         ...
   ├──Category 1.2→ {Terms of Category 1.2}
   │  ...
   └──Category 1.n→ {Terms of Category 1.n}
...
```

Figure 1. A Taxonomy

There are a number of advantages in classifying meanings as a taxonomy. First, meaning taxonomy is a useful facility for an electronic dictionary because meanings embody additional semantics which provides more information to the reader (more than that of sequential numbers noted above.) Second, the system may also gain a new dimension because it is possible to automatically generate specialised dictionaries under different categories (a sports dictionary may deal with soccer, tennis, or baseball dictionaries.) Third, it helps to develop a balanced dictionary by adding enough terms from different categories. Having the terms classified, it is easy to check out how many terms are under a given category. Fourth, it also helps to distribute the work between several authors by assigning categories to authors. A team of authors may develop a complete specialised dictionary by dividing the work by categories so that collaborative work is promoted for students.

## 2.2 Polysemy and Synonymy

In every language there exists the well known naming problem [3], which consists of two elements: one is polysemy (under the synchronic point of view, that is, embodying polysemy itself and homonymy), by which a term can have several meanings; and the other is synonymy, by which one meaning can be assigned to different terms, as can be observed in Figure 2. In this Figure, Term 1 and Term 2 are synonyms and have a shared meaning, as so for Term 2 and Term3, under another meaning. Moreover, Term 2 is polysemic since it has two possible meanings.

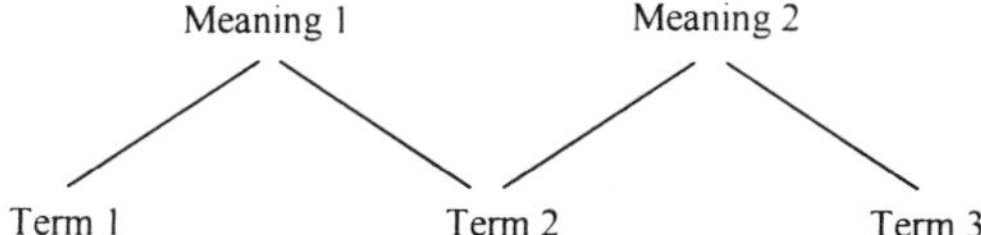


Figure 2. Polysemy and Synonymy

## 2.3 Relationships

### 2.3.1 Basic Relationships

Here we do some remarks about the relationships between categories, meanings and terms. On the one hand, a given term can belong to several categories under different meanings. On the other hand, a given term can belong to several categories under the same meaning. Figure 3 shows two categories (C1 and C2) which respectively contain the meanings {M11, M12, M} and {M, M21, M22}. Each meaning has one or more terms associated. The term T2 is associated to meanings M12 and M21, which respectively belong to categories C1 and C2. We also show the term T that is assigned to meaning M, which belongs to both categories C1 and C2. Polysemy is present in T2, and synonymy is also present in T3, and T4, as it can be seen. T1 is neither polysemic nor synonym. TC1 and TC2 are the terms used to denote categories C1 and C2, respectively.

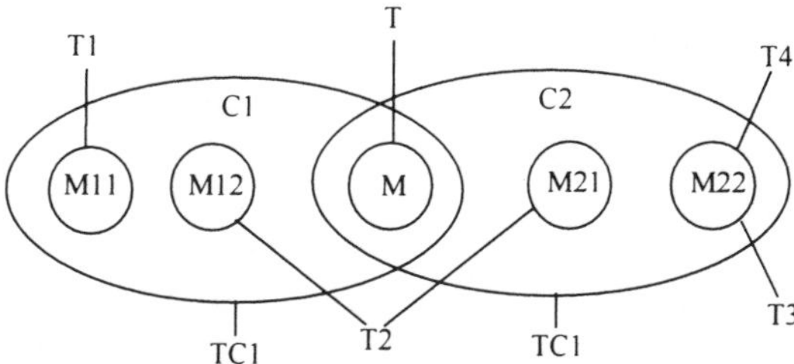


Figure 3. Relationships among categories, meanings and terms. Extensional definition

In this figure, the set of meanings {M11, M12, M} in C1 is the extensional definition of category C1. We must also note that a category has a meaning described by a definition. This figure does not embody this fact. In order to embody the meanings related to categories, we transform the scheme of Figure 3 to the one depicted in Figure 4. Now, C1 is the meaning of the category C1, and TC1 is the term assigned to such meaning, and the same applies to C2 and TC2. Then, we have one more meaning in each category. This meaning is the intensional definition of the category.

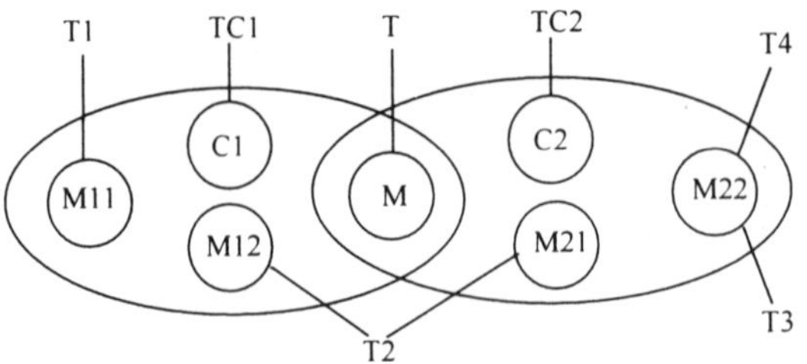


Figure 4. Relationships among categories, meanings and terms. Intensional definition

For a given language, we have a set of terms that holds the relationships with categories and meanings shown in Figure 4. If we now think of several languages, the same applies for each one. Then, relationships between terms from different languages come from considering jointly the involved schemes .

### 2.3.2 Other Lexical and Semantic Relationships

For all languages, knowledge in the discourse universe belongs to two types: conceptual and linguistic. Terms and sentences refer to concepts, but they have particular structural and morphological features for each language. Language mastery includes the ability to distinguish both knowledge types. In fact, language mastery traverses several stages until it is learned how to distinguish between concepts and the linguistic way of expressing them in a given language. It is needed to learn concepts and their relations, lexicon and linguistic properties of terms, compositionality defined by the syntactic structure and links between terms and concepts. These goals are relevant also for pedagogical interests.

Although ontology is not exactly the same as conceptual knowledge of discourse, there is no computer mean more adequate for representing it. All of the relations (meronimy, holonimy, hiperminia, hiponimia, and so on) represented in the more complete lexical databases as WordNet, are in ontology-based databases, as the MikroKosmos system, which is based in the ontology Ontos; but in these cases, relations are present in a level-structured way. In an ontology, concepts and their relations are represented, whereas each lexicon has the terms for each language and their linguistic properties, as well as their mappings with ontology concepts. The mapping between ontology and lexicons is the key for successfully coordinate all of the lexical and semantic relations.

## 3. Conceptual Model of the Terminological Database for a Bilingual Dictionary

Our work in developing the tools is based on a sound conceptual model for the terminological database (TDB) which shall eventually hold the terms, definitions, meanings, and semantic categories. Since it is intended to deal with two or more languages (bilingual or multilingual dictionaries), we need to represent instances of terms, textual definitions, and textual semantic categories for each language, but, as meanings are not language dependent, we shall use unique representations for them.

The entity-relationship model is used to describe the conceptual model we propose, shown in Figure 5. In this figure (following some recommendations in [10,11]), entity sets are represented with rectangles, attributes with ellipses, and relationship sets with diamonds connecting entity sets with undirected lines (many to many mapping cardinality). A one to many mapping cardinality from entity set A to entity set B is represented by an arc from B to A. (There is no such relationship set type in this first model.) Undirected lines also connect attributes to entity sets. Relationship set and entity set names label each diamond and box, respectively.

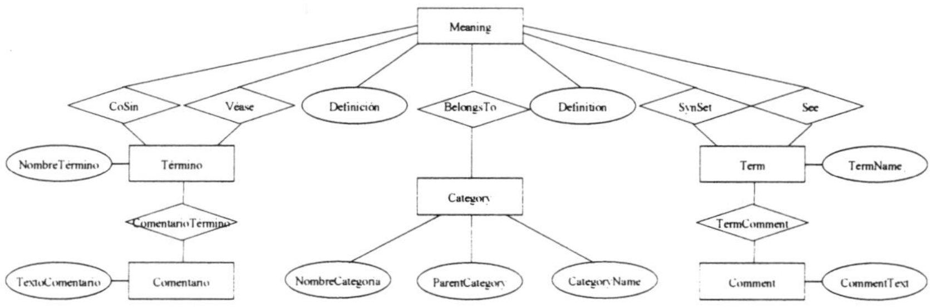


Figure 5. Entity-Relationship Model for an English-Spanish TDB

In this figure we show an instance of a bilingual terminological database for Spanish and English languages; further, its extension to support several languages is presented in Section 4. In the following, we firstly describe entity sets, then relationship sets, and, finally, attributes.

The entity set Meaning is the central entity set other entity sets rest on. In fact, this is the entity set which is language independent. The entity set Term represents all the English terms that compose the terminological database. The entity set Category denotes the category each meaning belongs to. The entity set Comment represents the comments about each term.

The relationship set SynSet between Meaning and Term denotes the English synonym set and it is many to many since a synonym set contains several terms, and a term may be contained in several synonym sets (obviously, with different meanings.) The relationship set See denotes the set of English terms related under a given meaning. This relationship which connects Meaning and Term is many to many because a meaning may refer to several English terms, and one term may be referenced by several meanings. The relationship set BelongsTo between Category and Meaning is many to many since many meanings are in a category, and a meaning could be in several categories (this situation is expected to be reduced to the minimum since the goal is to keep the classification as disjoint as possible). This relationship set embodies the fact that our classification is not lexical (there is not a direct relationship between Category and Term) but semantic (we relate meanings to categories, i.e., we categorise meanings.) The relationship set TermComment is many to many since a term may have several comments attached and a comment may refer to several terms.

The entity set Category has three attributes: CategoryName, NombreCategoría, and ParentCategory. The first two correspond to the textual name of the category in each considered language, English and Spanish, respectively. The last attribute, ParentCategory, represents the links in the taxonomy by relating a category with its parent. Since each entity Category has a monovalued attribute for parent, this means that we restrict taxonomies to trees. If we change this attribute by a multivalued attribute (or, alternatively, we connect the entity set Category with itself via a relationship set named ParentCategory), we allow a taxonomy graph instead of a tree. Meaning has two attributes: Definition and Definición, which correspond to the textual definition in the same considered languages. Term has one attribute: TermName, which denotes the textual term name. CommentText is an attribute which holds the textual comment for each term. The remaining entities and relationship sets (CoSin, Véase, Término, ComentarioTérmino y Comentario) are homologous to the ones in the other language (SynSet, See, Term, TermComment, and Comment.)

We have also developed (but not shown here for reasons of space) the logical and physical models for the development of our terminological database, which follow the design cycle of classical database design that ensures us a formal way of defining the data fundamentals the tools will adhere to.

# 4. Conceptual Model of the Terminological Database for a Multilingual Dictionary

We have developed a conceptual model the terminological database for a dynamic multilingual dictionary. With *dynamic* we refer to the user's ability for modifying the number of languages present in the dictionary without altering the database schema; in particular, the entity-relationship model. Figure 6 shows the model.

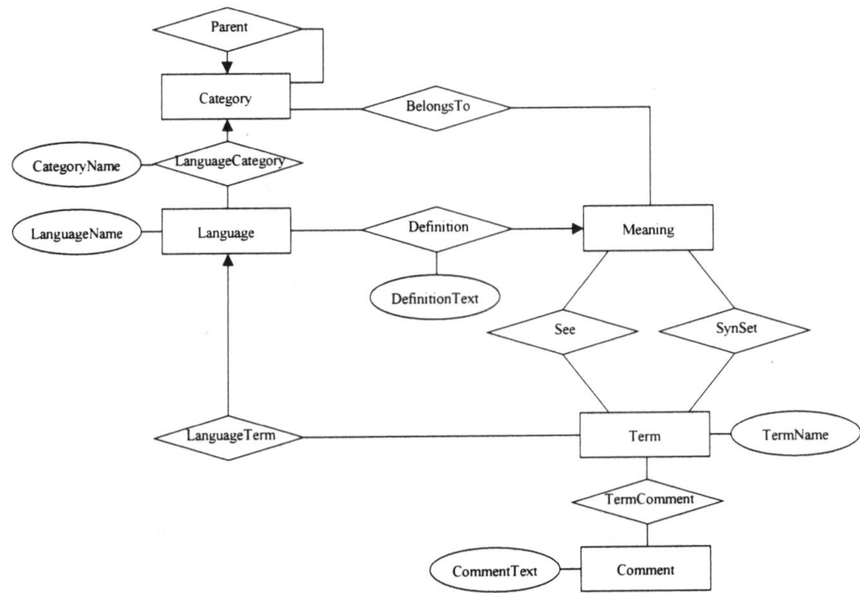

Figure 6. Entity-Relationship Model for a multilingual TDB

This model is more elaborated than the previous one in order to represent its dynamic feature.

A new entity is needed, Language, which denotes all the languages to be hold in the multilingual dictionary. The entity-relationship structure of meanings, terms, and comments is similar to the first conceptual model. However, the entity sets Term and Comment refer to all of the sets of terms and comments irrespective of the language. The key that indicates the language a term belongs to is the relationship set LanguageTerm.

On the one hand, by contrast, comments are linked directly to the terms by the relationship set TermComment. The comment itself is represented by the attribute CommentText of the entity set Comment.

On the other hand, the entity set Category is linked to a language via the relationship set LanguageCategory. In this case, we have to make explicit the language of a category since the category is independent from the language. Note that the attribute CategoryName is now linked with the relationship set LanguageCategory, that is, whereas the concept Category is independent from the language the text which describes the concept is not. Here, we have opted to use a relationship set Parent in order to avoid category hierarchies describing graphs (so, we have used a one to many mapping cardinality.) However, there is a lack of constraint information for describing trees in the conceptual model. For instance, we can represent forests with this model. Therefore, additional constraints are added in the conceptual stage as documentation (which has to be obeyed by the implementation).

Now, definitions are not attributes of the entity set Meaning; they are otherwise modelled with the attribute DefinitionText of the relationship set Definition, which link Meaning and Language (that is, a meaning has a definition in a given language.)

# 5. Conceptual Model of the Ontology for MikroKosmos

In order to be able of representing more detailed information about semantics and grammatical properties, we recourse to a database based on ontology. In this context, an ontology is a structured representation of world knowledge by means of symbols that represent the (language-independent) meanings, and possible relationships between them. The symbols are defined as concepts in the ontology, and also used to represent word meanings in lexicons.

Ontologies play an important role in NLP applications since they have an structure focused to the representation of knowledge about the world or a world domain. They hold symbols for meaning representation, organises these symbols in a tangled subsumption hierarchy, and interconnects these symbols using a rich system of semantic relations defined among the concepts. A concept is a primitive symbol for meaning representation with attributes and relationships with other concepts. An ontology is a network of such concepts.

We have selected [6] as an appropriate lexical database based on ontologies because of its structure. This structure is sufficient rich to support not only the conceptual and linguistic knowledge supported by the first tools previously described, but all the surplus required to improve the language mastery.

The ontology structure in [6] can be viewed as a directed graph with concepts as nodes. There are semantic relationships among nodes. The root concept is ALL (cfr. Figure 7) whose children are OBJECTS, EVENTS, and PROPERTIES.

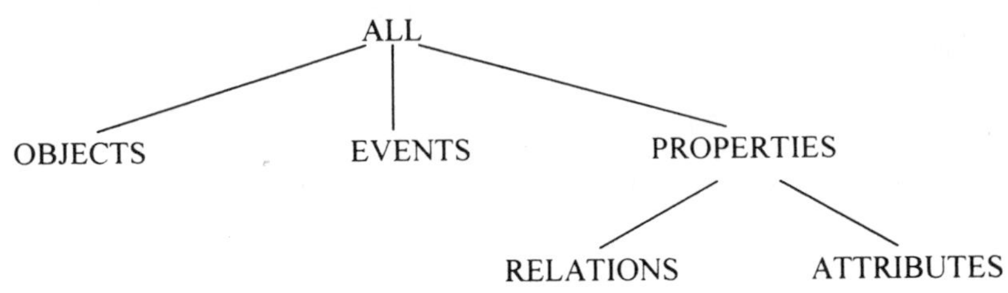


Figure 7. Ontology Hierarchy

One or more lexicons (for several languages) must be linked to the ontology in order to represent the language-dependent knowledge of the discourse. Lexicons are intended to hold terms and their lexical information. For instance, lexicons hold syntactic category, orthography (abbreviations and variants), phonology, morphological irregular forms or class information, syntactic features such as attributive, indication of sentence-level syntactic inter-dependencies (including subcategorization), lexical semantics, meaning representation, lexical relations (e.g., collocations), pragmatics hooks (e.g. for deictics, and stylistic factors), and annotations (user, lexicographer, and administrative information, such as modification audit trail, example sentences, definition in English, etc.) Through the lexicon, the semantic information can be located for a given term. Note that there is semantic information in both the ontology and the lexicon so that language-neutral meanings are stored in the former, and language specific information in the latter.

Figure 8 shows the entity-relationship model for the MikroKosmos ontology (ONTOLOGY), together with the model for the lexicon (LEXICON) and the connections between them (LINK). This figure represent one ontology which can be connected to many lexicons belonging to different languages.

The entity set Concept represents the concepts in the ontology (this entity set is close to Meaning in the former conceptual models). The entity set Relation represents the different relations which may be defined among concepts in the ontology. The entity set Attribute represents the different attributes which may be attached to concepts in order to describe them. These two last entity sets stands for "types of"; the instance relations are represented by the relationship set RelCon, and the instance attributes by the relationship set AtrCon. Finally, Term is the entity set representing terms belonging to a lexicon. In fact, this entity set represents the set of all of the lexicons. Each lexicon can be distinguished by the set of all the instance terms so that they have the same value for the attribute Language.

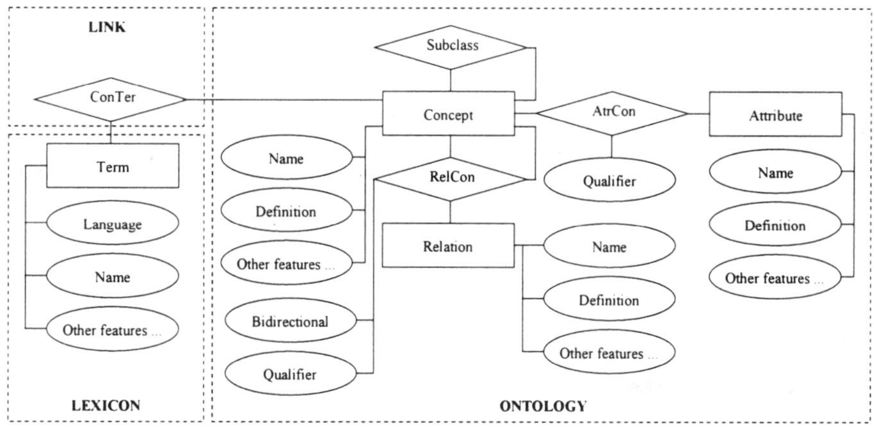


Figure 8. Entity-Relationship Model for the MikroKosmos Ontology

The relationship set Relation represents the link among two concepts by a relation. Each instance relation represents the link of one concept with another under a given relation type. Such relations are not bidirectional unless they are explicitly defined by the (boolean) attribute Bidirectional. The Qualifier attribute represents additional information which drills down the instance; for instance, by adding a value that further makes concrete the relation. The relationship set Subclass represents the relation "is a" in the sense of objet oriented programming. Here, graphs are allowed to represent object containment. The link among the ontology and the lexicon is defined by the entity relationship set ConTer. This set contains all the pairs <Term, Concept> which define the concept each term represents. Note that this has a many to many mapping cardinality (polysemy and synonimy). The mapping cardinalities of the remaining relationship sets should be clear.

# 6. Tools for the Linguistic Resources

We have developed several tools for the above linguistic resources, namely: a tool for querying dictionaries (query tool), a tool for creating dictionaries (author tool), a tool for creating ontologies (ontology tool), a tool for creating lexicons (lexicon tool), and a tool for migrating data from a dictionary to an ontology-based information system (migration tool).

The querying tool is a query interface which allows the user to easily recover the information about both English and Spanish terms as well as their relationships from the terminological database. This database holds the terms, categories, their attributes, and the relationships. The interface allows the user to navigate the semantic categories, also allowing to retrieve the relevant information of any term (definition, other related terms, translation, synonyms, ...). Figure 9 shows a snapshot of one screen of the interface.

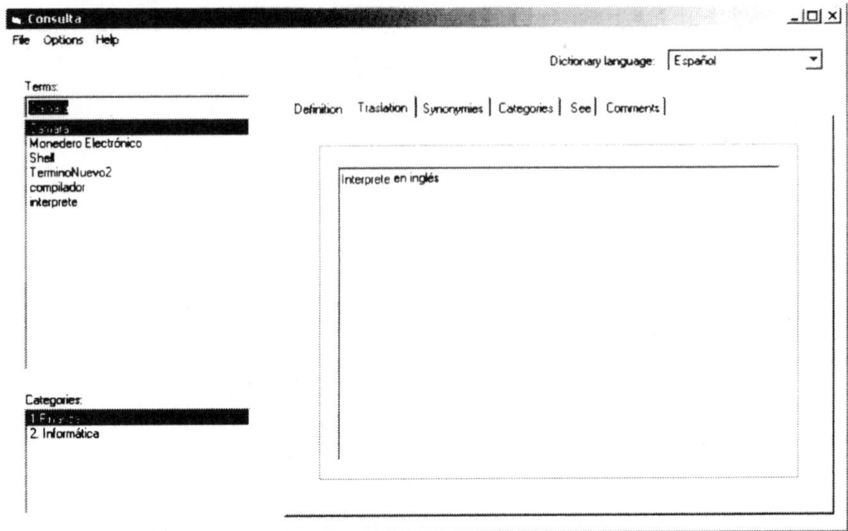


Figure 9. A Screen from the Querying Tool Interface

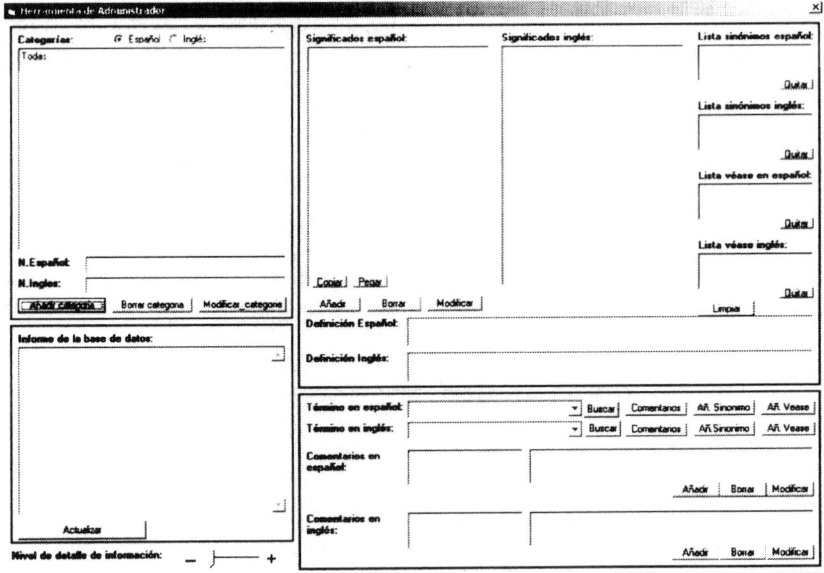


Figure 10. A Screen from the Author Tool Interface

The author tool allows the author to add new terms to the terminological database, and all the relevant information, such as its definition, semantic categories, meanings, synonym sets, and related terms. We have developed a Spanish user interface for this tool (easily rewritable for allowing to customise the use of any other language, as we have already done for the previous tool), and it consists mainly of one Author window. It has several areas for semantic category management, meaning management, synonyms and related terms management, and database consistency control. Figure 10 shows a snapshot of one screen of the interface.

The ontology tool allows the author to add new concepts to the ontology, define new relations and attributes, and all the features of each one. In addition, it also allows to define instance relations and instance attributes associated to the concepts in the ontology. Further development include a database consistency control as the previous tool. Figure 11 shows a snapshot of one screen of the interface.

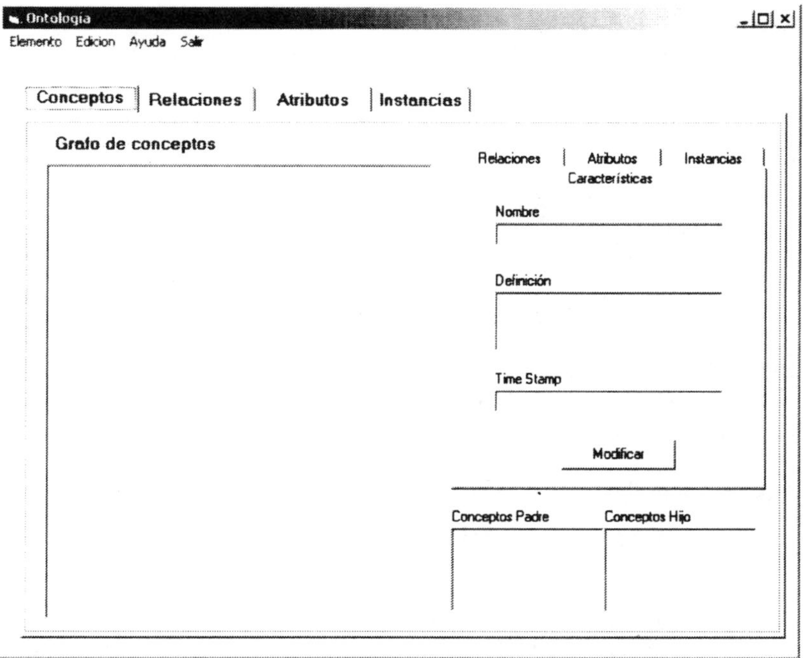


Figure 11. A Screen from the Ontology Tool Interface

The lexicon tool allows the author to add new terms as well as their features. It is in an early development stage and currently it is merged with the ontology tool.

Finally, the migration tool provides a way to interface the terminological database with the ontology and the lexicon. The migration is done with the supervision of an expert in the linguistic field selected. First, categories are migrated as concepts in the ontology, and the user is requested to map the category with an existing concept or a new one with the help of the existing concept graph. In addition, since categories represents relations between concepts, new instance relations are created for the meanings in categories. Terms from the terminological database are mapped to terms in the lexicon.

## 7. Conclusions and Future Work

We are in an very advanced step on the way to reach a sound and complete methodology to develop software systems for managing static linguistic knowledge bases. Based on this methodology we have built software tools for building and querying different kind of linguistic resources. Using these tools, information can migrate from one resource to another, thus permitting an easy integration among different knowledge bases. Naturally we must continue this work line taking into account more interesting conceptual and linguistic knowledge, augmenting the corresponding ontologies according to the adequate entity-relationship model, and adding the coherent target lexicons. The applications currently made embedding the conventional linguistic knowledge bases will take advantage using these stronger integrated ones, and applications will come to new domains. The domains of NLP applications will wide. Besides managing these tools for languages learning is very promising, the application to education is a way to explore in the next future.

## References


1. Casares, Ideological Spanish Dictionary.
2. C.J. Fillmore, and B.T. Atkins, "Toward a frame-based lexicon: The semantics of RISK and its neighbors", Lehrer and Kittay, pp. 75-102, 1992.
3. B. Katzenberg and P. Piela, "Work Language Analysis and the Naming Problem", Communications of the ACM, Vol. 36, No. 4, June 1993.
4. D.B. Lenat, and R.V. Guha, "Building Large Knowledge-Based Systems", Reading, Massachussets, Addison-Wesley, 1990.
5. María Moliner, Derivative Spanish Dictionary.
6. MikroKosmos, http://crl.nmsu.edu/Research/Projects/mikro/index.html
7. G. Miller, "WordNet: A Lexical Data Base for English", Communications of the ACM, Vol. 38, 11, 1995.
8. A. Moreno, and C. Pérez, "Reusing the Mikrokosmos Ontology for Concept-based Multilingual Terminology Databases", Proceedings of LREC2000, 2002.
9. S. Nirenburg, V. Raskin, and B. Onyshkevich, "Apologiae Ontologiae", Proceedings of the Sixth International Conference on Theoretical and Methodological Issues in Machine Translation, Center for Computational Linguistics, Catholic University, Leuven, Belgium, pp. 106-114, 1995.
10. R.S. Pressman, "Software Engineering. A Practitioner's Approach", McGraw-Hill, 1997.
11. A. Silberschatz, H.F. Korth, S. Sudarshan, "Data Base System Concepts", WCB/McGraw-Hill, 1996.
12. Y.A. Wilks, D.C. Fass, C.M. Guo, J.E. McDonald, T. Plate, and B.M.Slator, "Providing machine tractable dictionary tools". Machine Translation, 5, 1990, pp. 99-151.

# AUTHOR INDEX